RENEWALS 458-4574.

DATE DUE

GAYLORD			PRINTED IN U.S.A.

INTIMATE MUSIC

A HISTORY OF THE IDEA

OF

CHAMBER MUSIC

String Quartet Concert in a Monastery, with violinists and violist standing (1897). *Leipzig Illustrirten Zeitung* (September 8, 1898)

INTIMATE MUSIC

A HISTORY OF THE IDEA OF CHAMBER MUSIC

John Herschel Baron

Schawe Professor of Music
Tulane University

PENDRAGON PRESS
STUYVESANT, NY

PENDRAGON PRESS Musicological Series:

Aesthetics in Music

Annotated Reference Tools in Music

Bucina: The Historic Brass Society Series

The Complete Organ

The Croatian Musicological Society Series

Dance & Music

Dimension & Diversity: Studies in 20th-Century Music

The Festschrift Series

The Franz Liszt Studies Series

French Opera in the 17th and 18th Centuries

Harmonologia: Studies in Music Theory

Historical Harpsichord

Juilliard Performance Guides

Monographs in Musicology

Musical Life in 19th-Century France

The Complete Works of G. B. Pergolesi

Pergolesi Studies/Studi Pergolesiani

The Sociology of Music

Studies in Central European Music

Studies in Czech Music

Thematic Catalogues

Vox Musicae: The Voice, Vocal Pedagogy, and Song

In Honor of
Jerry and Harriet Dorf

Library of Congress Cataloging-in-Publication Data

Baron, John H.
    Intimate music : a history of the idea of chamber music / John Herschel Baron.
        p.   cm.
    Includes bibliographical references (p.   ) and index.
    ISBN 1-57647-018-0
    1. Chamber music--History and criticism.   I. Title.
ML1100.B36 1998
785'.009--dc21   98-14749
                                                                                CIP
                                                                                MN

Copyright 1998 Pendragon Press

TABLE OF CONTENTS

LIST OF ILLUSTRATIONS

INTRODUCTION

When I wrote my *Chamber Music: a Resource and Information Guide* (New York/London: Garland Publishing Co., 1987), I surveyed the literature about chamber music and discovered that there existed no overall book-length study of the history of the concept of instrumental chamber music that came anywhere close to being accurate and comprehensive. The reason for this was obvious. Until recently the spade work had not yet been done. During the past twenty years, however, most of this has been accomplished; excellent scholarly studies of specific chamber music genres, terms, styles, periods, composers, and nationalities, as well as supplementary studies on concert life and music in the home during different epochs in different cities and countries, have been written. Although much remains to be investigated, enough has now been published to make an overview possible. This history, then, is built upon those wonderful essays and draws heavily upon them; acknowledgments have been made in the footnotes.

The advantage of an overview is that different genres and composers and periods can be compared, situations for chamber music at different moments in history can be brought into a continuum, and all aspects of chamber music can be put into perspective. This advantage compensates for the fact that, in order to survey the field, many details had to be omitted or summarized in what to some might seem to be a perfunctory manner. However, scholars who have devoted their lives to a single aspect of chamber music and find that it gets only brief mention here should realize that, however brief, thorough investigation of that aspect was necessary before even that brief mention could be properly made within the book. My judgment on what is important is, of course, open to review, and therefore I do not consider this the definitive history of chamber music. It is merely one attempt to see the whole story and make some sense out of it.

As will be discussed in Chapter I, I have chosen the definition of chamber music as understood for the past century as the basis of this study, i.e., solistic instrumental ensemble music of a serious nature performed in intimate surroundings. Despite the fact that the expression "chamber music" has had various meanings since the middle 16th century, I will consider the kind of music subsumed by this recent definition and trace its ancestry back to the 16th century. In other words, this is not a history of the term "chamber music" but a history of the modern-day idea of chamber music.

The bibliography at the end draws heavily on the most important studies listed and discussed in my 1987 publication. Among the few important inadvertent omissions in that book should be mentioned Erich Reimer's "Kammermusik" (in *Handwörterbuch der musikalischen Terminologie*, ed. Fritz Recknow [Wiesbaden: Franz Steiner, 1971]), which is the basic study of the term "chamber music" and which has formed the basis of the discussion of that term in Chapter I. In addition, I have included important studies on chamber music that have appeared since 1986 (the termination date for items included in my previous book).

Except for Chapter I, which is largely devoted to defining the scope of this book, *A History of the Idea of Chamber Music* is chronologically organized at the most general level. Beyond that, national schools figure prominently, as well as genres and personalities. Throughout this book the composition of chamber music, the performance of chamber music, and the social, economic, political and aesthetic conditions for chamber music have been considered *per se* and as they interact. The emphasis in the chapter on the 18th century had to be placed primarily on genres since the most important aspect of the middle third of the 18th century was not nationalities or personalities but the formation of new, crucial genres which crossed national boundaries and personal repertories. The last chapter was the hardest to write, since the explosion in all areas of consideration for chamber music has been so great that it is impossible for anyone at this time to have the entire field under control. Here, more than anywhere else, I have had to be selective in choosing what I believe to be the most significant developments from an historic standpoint more than from an aesthetic one.

CHAPTER I

THE IDEA OF CHAMBER MUSIC

Chamber music is a term that has been used in English for two hundred years to denote solistic instrumental music for small ensemble.[1] In German it is *Kammermusik*, in French *la musique de la chambre*, in Italian *musica da camera* or *musica per camera*, and in modern Latin *musica cameralis*.

The term was first used in the middle 16th century to denote soft vocal ensemble music performed in a noble person's private palace, as distinct from full or loud vocal ensemble music performed in church. Nicola Vicentino, the first to mention the term (in his *L'Antica Musica* [Rome: 1555]), stated that chamber music (the Italian madrigal and French chanson) had subtleties of musical expression avoided in church music. But not all secular music was chamber music. Monteverdi's dance and theatrical music, for example, was secular but not chamber music. For most of the 17th century chamber music was sometimes understood (by Carlo Grossi, for example, in 1675 and 1681) as vocal ensemble music with or without instruments in the homes of nobility which served as background to dining or to conversation, while court music was the more formal musical entertainment in the same homes. By the end of the 17th century, however, all Europe accepted court and chamber music as essentially synonymous. This altered the original distinction; chamber music was any music performed at court, whether sacred or secular.

---

[1]Cf. Denis Arnold, "Chamber Music," in *The New Oxford Companion to Music* (Oxford/New York: Oxford University Press, 1983), and Don Michael Randel, "Chamber Music," in *The New Harvard Dictionary of Music*, rev. 2nd ed. (Cambridge: Harvard University Press, 1986), p.146. Most of the discussion of the term "chamber music" is based on Erich Reimer, "Kammermusik," in *Handwörterbuch der musikalischen Terminologie*, ed. Fritz Reckow (Wiesbaden: Franz Steiner, 1971).

Sébastien de Brossard, in his *Dictionnaire de musique* (Paris: 1703), returned to early ideas and contrasted chamber music with music for the church and theatrical music; it was now all secular vocal and instrumental music not associated with the theater. In Germany Johann Mattheson and Johann Scheibe copied Brossard but with further refinement of the term, whereby the chamber style of music was based on its function rather than on its location. Chamber music was the most serious kind of music because it concentrated on the music as music. Neither Scheibe nor Mattheson considered chamber music limited to music at court; it could be in the homes of the middle class as well. Sulzer, in his *Allgemeine Theorie der Schönen Künste* (1771), specifically regarded chamber music as music "for pleasure and for practice" by amateurs and dilettantes (Kenner und Liebhaber) whereby each player and each part has an ego-boosting importance not experienced in orchestral music. By the end of the 18th century C. F. Daniel Schubart (1784) regarded chamber music as primarily instrumental, either solistic or orchestral. Many concerts of chamber music obviously took place in aristocratic homes, but the original exclusivity of the court location was no longer relevant. By the beginning of the 19th century chamber music was generally recognized in Germany and England as private as opposed to public (concert) music, though the French (Castil-Blaze in 1820 and 1825) were slow to accept this. Only in the later 19th century was "chamber music" finally exclusively intimate, solistic, instrumental ensemble music.

Throughout the two earliest centuries, as will be seen in the following chapters, a steady stream of purely instrumental music was written which could be accepted as chamber music when, at the end of the 18th century, the music for the chamber became what has since been understood as chamber music. Thus, while a history of chamber music during the 19th and 20th centuries is well defined by the generally accepted idea of what chamber music is, a history of chamber music before 1800 is superimposing a later idea on earlier music. This is justified since much of what coalesced ca. 1800 was already present as early as the middle 16th century and because this early repertory has been revived in the 20th century within the modern idea of chamber music.

During the second half of the 18th century there evolved a type of music for small instrumental ensemble with only one player on a part. Such music had existed before in all four locations for music, though primarily in the chamber and church. Because the new music of the later 18th century was intimate, non-religious music and was best suited to the small chamber rather than to the church, the theater or the outdoors, it was called "chamber music." It was distinct from orchestral music because only one person played each part. A few well-defined genres of chamber music based on scoring developed during this time which became specifically associated with the term "chamber music": string quartet, trio and quintet, piano trio and quartet, piano-violin sonata, flute quartet, clarinet quintet, and a few others. These genres were defined exclusively by scoring. Once these genres became popular and firmly established in the minds of the audiences of the late 18th and early 19th centuries, all previous classifications of music were quickly forgotten. "Music for the chamber" was replaced by "chamber music" based on scoring of the music and not where the music was performed (location) or why it was performed (function); "chamber music" was performed publicly as well as privately, and by the middle and late 19th century almost all serious chamber music was performed as much in concert halls as in private chambers.

The term "chamber music" as understood in this book, however, implies different, specific genres of music based not only on scoring but on the specific function and location of the music as well. Some people, especially in the 19th and 20th centuries, have not seriously regarded the function or location of the music as of primary relevance. They latch onto a particular genre of music, defined primarily by its scoring, which remains the definitive chamber music for them despite inconsistencies in location and purpose. Thus for many central European musicians in the late 19th and early 20th century, chamber music meant serious string quartet music first and foremost; grudgingly, if at all, they allowed music for other string ensembles, rarely with piano; wind music had practically no place in their conception of chamber music. A string quartet performed in a large concert hall by professional musicians was chamber music, and a flute trio performed at home by amateurs was not chamber music (they called it, instead, "Hausmusik," which implied something inferior to chamber music). Thus, the genre "string quartet" was chamber music but the genre "woodwind quintet" was not. The average Western European and American music lover at the turn of the 21st century would greatly expand the realm of chamber music with not only music for string quartets but also for all other small ensembles of standard instruments, including very definitely woodwind groups, brass groups, and all sorts of mixtures of these instrumental types. A history of chamber music would, for these people, invariably entail a history of those score-based genres of currently-accepted species of "chamber music," i.e., a history of the music for string quartet, brass quintet, woodwind quintet, piano trio, and so forth. At this level, we focus on the evolution of one such genre from its first noticeable appearance until its last or present appearance; on the influences of one score-based genre upon another, or of many genres upon another, or of one genre upon others; and on the changing definitions or terminology for these score-based genres.

On a completely different plane is the concept of chamber music as a specific function or location of music, i.e., the intimate performance of music. At this level we are concerned with music performed privately by a small number of persons for their own enjoyment or for the enjoyment of a very small group of listeners. This approach is at cross purposes with the history of score-based genres, for a single genre of chamber music determined by scoring often changes its function. For example, the brass ensemble performing in church or in an outdoor public market place is not chamber music in the 17th century but becomes chamber music in the second half of the 20th century when modern-day brass ensembles play for their own enjoyment or for the enjoyment of a very small number of persons in an intimate setting. A Beethoven string quartet that is played by an orchestra of 100 players for an audience of thousands is no longer chamber music. On this plane there is no evolution of species but a jagged history of the continual antithesis of intimate, private music performance versus public, "showy" music performance.

The two—the scoring approach and the functional-location approach—are interconnected throughout the past four centuries when instrumental music in Europe attained the status of an art form on a par with vocal music. At any one time, particularly in the past two centuries, certain types of music are regarded as chamber music because then or at one time they were regarded as intimate, private music. The private nature of the music conditioned certain forms and styles and helped shape certain tastes, even if previously or later those very types became public. In many cases it is not the actual function or location of the music which is important but the impression of the function and location of the music in the eyes (ears) of the individual listener.

Certain guidelines must be established if we are to recognize "chamber music" when we hear or see it. On the one hand these guidelines must be firmly rooted in the concept of intimate music; on the other hand, they must take into account those types of music which the musically educated audience has regarded as chamber music over the centuries. While to some extent separate histories of the various genres based on scoring have been written, a history of the interaction of functions and locations with scoring has not. Thus here we will summarize the history of score-based genres in order then to deal with those genres as they are a product of the functions and locations of the music which gave them life.

The present study is of music that was or is *composed* as chamber music and music that is or was *performed* as chamber music. Any study that deals only with one or the other is incomplete. Willi Apel observed that there are numerous studies of the history of violin playing and none of the history of violin music.[2] On the other hand, there are many studies of the history of keyboard music and none of the history of keyboard playing. The differences between the two media and their repertories are the ground for the different approaches historians have had to take. A third situation exists with the history of chamber music. At all times in its history, the medium and the repertory are rapidly

[2]Willi Apel, *Die italienische Violinmusik im 17. Jahrhundert*, in *Beihefte zum Archiv für Musikwissenschaft*, Band 21 (Wiesbaden: Franz Steiner, 1983), pp. 1-2.

changing, and not only do medium and repertory continually interact, they also are continually in a state of flux reacting to the function and location of chamber music. It is the function and location
that ultimately define what at some time is chamber playing and
chamber music as opposed to any other kind of playing and music.

To distinguish between the performance and the music, it is
first necessary to define the concept "chamber music." There are
five basic ingredients that, taken together, constitute chamber music. 1) Chamber music is instrumental music. 2) Chamber music is
ensemble music, i.e., music for two or more performers. 3) Chamber music is solistic, i.e., no two players play the same music at the
same time. 4) The purpose of the music is to provide serious ensemble, not the virtuosic display of one member of the ensemble
(though the latter often intrudes in chamber music). 5) The core
feature of any chamber music is its overt or implied intimacy.
While these criteria can also be applied to various ethnic musics,
we limit our discussion in this book to the art chamber music of
Europe and its tributaries in North America. Each of these criteria
has exceptions, modifications, and sometimes built-in difficulties
which will require careful scrutiny, and indeed much of the discussion of "chamber music" of the earlier centuries involves those
works that in one or more ways do not follow the criteria yet are
commonly regarded as chamber music by at least one significant
present or past music authority.

1) Chamber Music Is Instrumental Music

Chamber music is instrumental music that involves voices only
in so far as they are treated as instruments. In the 17th and 18th
centuries there were many vocal works with or without instrumental accompaniment that were performed *da camera* (the so-
called "chamber cantatas"), and in the 19th and 20th centuries
Lieder and other art songs have been included as chamber music in
the writings of some critics. Home performance of chamber music
in the 19th and 20th centuries is often mingled with song. It is true
that these vocal works have a great affinity to exclusively instrumental chamber music in that they are intimate pieces of a serious

nature, but during the late 18th and 19th centuries intimate vocal music was concerned primarily with interpretation of a text while instrumental chamber music was not. It is a distinct kind of music from vocal "chamber music," and *our* history is concerned with this distinction. Only one exception will be made: for Schoenberg's Second String Quartet, where the voice comes in as an outside element in what is functionally a purely instrumental work.

Technically chamber music should include all instruments of intimate, instrumental ensemble art music of any culture (for example, the gongs of Balinese gamalan music and the saxophones of Afro-American jazz). Since we are dealing here only with a branch of chamber music that is European-originated art music of the past 400 years or so, we exclude ensembles composed exclusively of instruments not found there but do include individual non-European instruments that are mixed with standard European ones. This is not an arbitrary exclusion since European culture as a whole has recognized this and the chamber music of European art music is a distinct, cohesive entity. On the other hand we admit chamber music for percussion alone as well as percussion music with other instruments. In previous centuries this posed no problem since chamber music was dominated by standard bowed strings, a few woodwinds, the French horn, and several keyboard instruments; percussion did not intrude. But in the 20th century there have been changes which have challenged the traditional scoring. Besides the introduction of brass instruments, many kinds of percussion instruments have been introduced into chamber ensembles, and there are some compositions written for just percussion ensembles. The percussion ensemble by itself may include two to five percussionists playing non-doubling instruments, the setting is intimate and the music is serious; under these conditions the percussion ensemble is chamber music and, since many instruments in the percussion ensemble are of European origin, it is within the confines of the continuous European tradition.

Other ensembles are excluded here even though the instruments involved have legitimate claim to being part of some chamber music. For example, music for one or more pianos without any other instrument is excluded primarily because it is more fittingly an adjunct to the history of keyboard music. On the other hand, when the piano is with non-keyboard instruments and the music meets the other qualifications for chamber music, it is included. We are excluding music for pre-recorded tape by itself, but we are including chamber music that includes tape along with standard chamber instruments or with electronically reinforced instruments.

2) Chamber Music Is Ensemble Music

An important element in chamber music is the sharing of the experience among two or more players. Each player preserves his/her identity while contributing to the whole. Music for one performer alone lacks this element, and even if all the other ingredients are there for chamber music, it cannot be called chamber music. Thus a solo partita for violin alone by Bach or a Mozart piano sonata is not chamber music.

3) Chamber Music Is Solistic

An essential element of chamber music is the participation of individuals who, while blending with the whole, retain their own identity. The integrity of the individual would be lost if his/her part would be doubled by even just one other player; the music would immediately become orchestral. If only two or three players play the same part, the performance, while being orchestral, would not be as devastating to the individual as would be the case if fifteen or twenty musicians were performing the same part. The latter is the usual situation in major symphony orchestras; to distinguish the former from it we usually refer to the former as belonging to the idiom of chamber orchestra. Since this is a history of chamber music, not chamber orchestral music, the solistic performance of each part is a criterion for the music that is under consideration. In some chamber music of the 17th and 18th centuries it is impossible to ascertain if the original performance was for chamber ensemble (one player to a part) or chamber orchestral ensemble (two or more players to a part). This ambiguity will be discussed in the following chapters.

There are two exceptions to this rule of solistic performance: the basso continuo line in 17th- and 18th-century chamber music and isolated passages in unison or octaves in the course of a piece. Most chamber music of the two early centuries includes a bass line, and in most cases this bass line calls for the basso continuo. While the bass without continuo requires just one instrument on the part, the basso continuo itself implies two performers: a bowed string or wind bass instrument *and* an instrument which can realize (fill in) the harmonies. This latter instrument is often a keyboard instrument (harpsichord, organ or piano[3]) but can also be a plucked string instrument (harp, guitar, lute, theorbo). The result, however, does not mean that the basso continuo instruments lose their individualities. The bowed string or wind instrument that plays just the bass line is, by its sustaining power and its peculiar color, always audible, and the harmony instrument is, by its harmonic and contrapuntal additions to the bass line, also always audible. Therefore, although there is doubling of the bass line, the instruments remain solistic. Part of the history of chamber music is the changes in this basso part from an accompanimental support to a full-fledged partner.

Throughout the four centuries of chamber music there are isolated passages which find several or all the instruments playing in unison or octaves. This is an especially effective device in the music of classical and romantic composers, who like to vary the textures and styles of their movements and who therefore use unisons and octaves occasionally to contrast with strict counterpoint, homophony, concertato exchange of melody and accompaniment, and solo writing. If an entire piece is composed of this, the question of how appropriate the designation "chamber music" is to it may be raised, but such works are extremely rare.[4]

---

[3]But never the clavichord, which is too weak an instrument to be heard in an ensemble.

[4]A masterful use of paired octave parts comes in Haydn's String Quartet in D Minor, Opus 76, no. 2, third movement, where the two violins are in octaves in canon with the viola and cello in octaves. Haydn uses the octaves to contrast with the surrounding movements and with the trio. In any case, the individuality of each part is maintained because, in fact, no two instruments are playing the identical notes and each can be heard.

4) Chamber Music Is Serious

Composers, performers and audiences have regarded chamber music as one of the most "pure" forms of music. By "pure" is meant that the music stands on its own, as a musically logical happening, without the need of other considerations to give it its *raison d'être*. By contrast, music which has a program, music which achieves its *raison d'être* through arrangements of songs, and music which serves primarily to let a single musician show off is not regarded as serious music. It is regarded as weaker in formal design and is unimaginative in melody and rhythm. If a particular work meets all requirements for chamber music despite its program or borrowing of a song or catering to the virtuosity of a great artist, however, then it can be included as chamber music; such music has compelling musical form and imaginative melody and rhythm. Thus, for the most part, the program of the middle movement of Opus 132 of Beethoven does not detract from the greatness of its purely musical logic, and the borrowing of popular Russian folk songs in the Opus 59 quartets does not cheapen the supreme genius of their melodies and rhythms. While less successful, the seriousness of the quartets of Pleyel and Spohr is not weakened by the emphasis in some of them on the first violin. It is, however, necessary to exclude trifling character pieces of the 19th century, Cambini's arrangements of songs, and Kreisler- or Wieniawski-like encores, which despite their charm and usefulness are not pretentious enough to be regarded as chamber music. A few character pieces, by their artful construction and serious intentions, do merit consideration as chamber music; composers did not call them "sonatas" or "piano trios" but by some other designation because in the 19th century "sonatas" and "piano trios" had to be multi-movement works including sonata form. In the 20th century, as we shall see, the character piece often is more than a trifling composition; it is a major form of musical expression and therefore assumes a much more serious guise. As long as the music is logical *per se*, it can be taken seriously in the history of chamber music.

5) Chamber Music Is Intimate

Most devotees of chamber music find that the crucial element in chamber music is the intimacy of this kind of art.[5] Intimacy is obvious when two or three musicians play together in private quarters without any audience, but how is intimacy attained in a "chamber music" concert before an audience of 15,000 persons or before a video audience of millions? Obviously (as will be seen in the following chapters) the sociological position of chamber music as intimate music-making has changed radically during the past 400 years, for example, from the private performances in homes and palaces of the 17th and 18th centuries through the public performances of the 19th century concert hall and later through the "canned" performances of 20th-century radio, records, and videos.

Intimacy is a psychological perception; it suggests "smallness" and "closeness" on the part of performers and listeners. Smallness means that there are few people involved, both as performers and as listeners; ideally there are only a few performers who themselves constitute the only listeners. Smallness also means that the room in which the music is performed is just large enough for the sound to fully resonate and not any larger; the sound cannot disappear in empty space. Closeness suggests that the performers are physically as near to each other as possible; it also suggests that the performers are aesthetically of one mind and heart. Whatever audience there is must also be as close to the performers as possible.

While "smallness" and "closeness" are accepted as the essence of intimacy, each individual perceives "smallness" and "closeness" differently. In general we recognize a piano trio as small and a symphony orchestra as not small and therefore not intimate. But an ensemble of thirteen performers is more controversial; some perceive it as small while others perceive it as not small. Since pieces before the 20th century are rarely for this size an ensemble, recog-

[5]A survey of Czech audiences, reported in Rudolf Pecman, ed. *Colloquium Musica Cameralis Brno 1971*, in *Colloquia on the History and Theory of Music at the International Music Festival in Brno*, vol. 6 (Brno: Cesky Hudebni Fond, 1977), found that "intimacy" was the most often cited description of chamber music.

nition of its size as not small is often intermingled with prejudices against 20th-century music, especially—as is often the case with the most difficult new music—a conductor directs the piece. If one's concept of chamber music excludes winds and/or percussion, one probably will find the ensemble of thirteen performers including wind players and percussionists not small. If we separate such prejudice from the simple fact of size, then we are still dealing with a relative perception. At this point the perception (or, if you will, prejudice) of the particular historian enters in order to make a decision; I define smallness as including up to but not exceeding thirteen instruments, though I recognize that smallness generally refers to two to nine instruments.

Closeness has become the most widely disparate part of intimacy. While the performers have remained close to each other physically and aesthetically, the listeners have moved further and further away. In many cases this does not upset the perception of closeness by the listener as long as he/she can hear adequately. If the hall is large but not so large as to muffle the resonating sound, then the listener perceives closeness. If the listener is hearing the music on earphones or from powerful and balanced speakers, the listener perceives closeness. If, on the other hand, the listener perceives him/herself alienated from the sound by distance—the sound is too soft or the tone is unbalanced or there is interference or, simply, the players are barely visible or entirely invisible, then the listener does not perceive closeness and there is no intimacy. As we will see when we discuss outdoor performance of chamber music in the middle 20th century, the individual listener must come to his/her own conscious or unconscious decision as to smallness and closeness and on the basis of that decision accept or reject the feeling of intimacy.

In determining the relevancy of particular music to a study of chamber music, we must decide if the composer specifically intended the five basic criteria for this music, if he/she allowed the option of the five basic criteria, and/or if later interpreters of the music regarded it as constituting the five basic criteria. For example, in the study of canzonas, it seems that Italian composers usually composed these serious instrumental ensemble pieces for one person per part, but the location of the performances—in large, public churches—left an ambiguity as to the fifth criterion—was it intimate or not. Church canzonas for many parts, such as some by Giovanni Gabrieli, seem to be tied to performances in large buildings for large audiences and therefore too public to be intimate chamber music. On the other hand, an intimate (implied, at least) solistic performance nowadays by a brass ensemble in a chamber concert hall is chamber music. And there is also the ambiguity whether or not Gabrieli meant strictly solistic performance; an orchestral option existed then as now.

It is the purpose of this book, therefore, to study the genres of music from the late 16th century to the present that in one way or another can be considered chamber music. The performance situation at and about the time it was composed is crucial to an understanding of the music then and now. The present study is of music that was or is *composed* as chamber music and music that is or was *performed* as chamber music. It concentrates on the music itself, but since this music is to be defined by its performance, we must give a great deal of attention to performance situations and performers.

French consort of viol, gamba, lute and theorbo (ca. 1640, France). University of Leipzig, Instrument Museum, No. 85.

CHAPTER II

CHAMBER MUSIC BEFORE CORELLI

The first theorist to distinguish between chamber, church and folk music was Nicola Vicentino in his *L'Antica Musica Ridotta alla Moderna Prattica* (1555), but this distinction certainly existed before.[1] A part of life in renaissance Italy was the amateur musician singing and performing his or her own secular works, based on his or her own poetry or the poetry of close associates. The performances were for small audiences in the noble palaces, such as in that of Isabella d'Este (1474-1538) in Ferrara and Mantua and of Federico da Montefeltro (1422-1482) in Urbino. The instrumentalists, sometimes reaching the status of virtuosi, did not concentrate on the reproduction of older music but created their own new music. During the 16th century the chief instrumentalists were organists and lutenists. The lute was the preferred instrument of amateurs, but it was also cultivated by highly skilled professionals. These professionals composed much of the music for the amateurs from the aristocracy and the new, still small middle class, and it is the growth of this situation which led to some of the earliest surviving examples of chamber music during the second half of the century. Also important was the development of the viol and violin families at the beginning of the 16th century; the latter was used for dancing, but the former was used for polyphonic chamber music by mid-century.[2] The music of the chamber before the mid-16th century, however, was dominated by vocal music, especially the madrigal and chanson, and the performance by instruments alone

---

[1]Ludwig Finscher, *Die Musik des 15. und 16. Jahrhunderts*, in *Neue Handbuch der Musikgeschichte* (Laaber-Verlag, 1990), p. 123. Much of this paragraph is based on Finscher.

[2]Peter Holman, *Four and Twenty Fiddlers: the Violin at the English Court 1540-1690* (Oxford: Clarendon, 1993), pp. 15-19.

would have been primarily as substitution for voices. As we will see, when composers wrote ensemble music primarily for instrumental performance, not vocal, the history of chamber music begins.

During the second half of the 16th century, chamber music finally reached full status as a class of music. After many years when there was instrumental performance of vocal compositions (chamber performance but not composed chamber music), composers began to write new compositions for optional performance as chamber instrumental music or vocal music. Soon, however, the composer no longer gave the performers an option and wrote ensemble compositions specifically and solely for instrumental performance. Swiftly there developed several new genres of composition in which composers began to explore the potentialities of instrumental chamber music playing. It is from this point that the history of chamber music as opposed to chamber performance begins.

At the beginning of the 17th century, the Italian canzona and the English fantasia were the most important genres composed and played as chamber music. Then, during the course of the century these were replaced by the church and chamber sonata, which were largely developed in Italy. The three "countries" England, Italy and Germany played the most significant roles in the development of chamber music genres, while France—important for dance and orchestral music—was basically peripheral for chamber music.[3]

Essentially the new chamber music genres fall into two categories. There are one-movement pieces, usually sectionalized, such as canzonas, fantasias, variations, and most early church sonatas; and there are the multi-movement pieces, such as the dance suite, the English fantasia-suite, the Austro-German chamber suite, and some church sonatas (especially after 1650). In the multi-movement works, the individual movements often belong to the history of both the whole work and, separately, their particular genre (for example, fantasias can be considered as individual fantasias and as fantasias within the suite, allemands as allemands and as move-

---

[3]The French had a deep-seated distrust of instrumental music, which is discussed in Chapter IV.

ments in dance suites, etc.). To some extent the history of the separate movement is different from that of the whole work. Therefore, on the following pages, we will consider both dance music and suites; and we will treat fantasias both as fantasias and as elements in the fantasia-suite.

THE CANZONA

The most important chamber music in Italy at the end of the 16th century and beginning of the 17th was the ensemble canzona. Originally an optional instrumental performance of a vocal work, the canzona was then a keyboard transcription and later a keyboard adaptation of a polyphonic vocal work. After nearly half a century as a keyboard type, the instrumental ensemble canzona emerged in the 1570's as a distinct genre in its own right.[4] Yet the interaction of the keyboard and ensemble types continued well into the 17th century, not surprisingly since so many of the ensemble composers (Giovanni Gabrieli, Maschera, Merulo, Luzzaschi, Guami, and Frescobaldi) were famous professional organists.

Sometimes the canzona was a secular work since it appeared in vocal collections first of secular chansons and later also of madrigals.[5] As such it would have been performed for the same occasions as the chansons and madrigals: at parties, banquets, domestic entertainment, concerts, dramatic productions, and civic ceremonies and festivals. After 1620, as a secular piece, it usually appeared with dances. It was also used for didactic purposes, as indicated in the dedications. But from 1597 on, the canzona was much more frequently associated with specific Catholic liturgical functions. "Between 1597 and 1650, canzonas appeared in numerous collections alongside motets, Masses, and other sacred music."[6] Banchieri assigned the canzona to after the second Agnus Dei of the Mass, except on Maudy Thursday when it was to be played

---

[4]Leland Earl Bartholomew, *Alessandro Rauerij's Collection of* Canzoni per sonare *(Venice, 1608)* (Fort Hays: Kansas State College, 1965), pp. 196-201.

[5]*Ibid.*, pp. 205ff.

[6]Ibid., p. 238. Cf. Stephen Bonta, "The Church Sonatas of Legrenzi" (Harvard University Ph.D. dissertation, 1964), pp. 133-157, for an extensive discussion of the liturgical functions of 17th-century canzonas.

at the end of the Mass. Amante Franzoni (1613) placed the canzona during the reading of the Epistle; Valerio Bona (1614) put it
before each of the eight ordini at the litany of the Madonna in
Loreto; Michael Praetorius (1615-20) said it comes after any sacred vocal work; Carlo Milanuzzi (1622) had a canzona before or
after the Epistle, the Post Communion, and the Deo Gratias; and
both Giovanni Gabrieli[7] and Frescobaldi[8] wrote canzonas for Ves-
pers and the Mass, in the latter case for the Communion, the Post
Communion, and the Deo Gratias.

Since in most of these situations the canzona would have been
public music, i.e., music performed in large church buildings with
no apparent intimacy, there seems little ground for considering the
genre chamber music. However, the canzona represents that type
of music which, while not chamber in its origins, becomes chamber at a later time. In this case, the canzona becomes chamber
through its revival in the 20th century. This is possible because,
although it was public music in the 16th and 17th centuries, it does
often adhere to the other basic guidelines for chamber music: solo
performance of a few simultaneous lines of music, whose main
purpose is not showy glitter but the serious development of musical ideas. Furthermore, since we know that some instrumental ensemble music composed primarily for church use was also played
for private occasions in noble homes and may also have been
played for private enjoyment by the composer and his friends, it
seems reasonable to include the canzona as a viable genre of
chamber music in late 16th- and early 17th-century Italy.

The history of the instrumental ensemble canzona falls into
three periods based largely on scoring: 1572-1596, when the canzona was almost always for four instruments, its sections repeated,
nearly everything in duple meter; 1597-1620, when the canzona
was often scored for more than four instruments with some antiphonal writing, when sections rarely repeated immediately but
came back da capo, and when triple meter frequently appeared in-

---

[7]Eleanor Selfridge-Field, *Venetian Instrumental Music from Gabrieli to Vivaldi* (New
York: Praeger, 1975), p. 96.

[8]Stephen Bonta, "The Uses of the *Sonata da Chiesa*," in *Journal of the American Musicological Society*, xxii (1969), pp. 72-73. This is indicated in Frescobaldi's *Fiori Musicali*
(1635), a purely organ work.

ternally as contrast to duple meter else- where; and 1620-1645, when most canzonas were for fewer than four instruments, the basso continuo became more clearly defined, sections rarely recurred and were more clearly demarcated by metric, stylistic and tempo changes, and the scoring was for specific instruments. During the last period the terms "canzona" and "sonata" seem indistinguishable; "canzona" was the more conservative, old fashioned term, while "sonata" was the newer, more fashionable word. "Canzona style," on the other hand, by the second half of the century, referred to the typical polyphonic style of most sections of the first-period canzona (Banchieri, for example); a sonata or any other work is in "canzona style" when it is especially contrapuntal.

The history of the ensemble canzona probably begins with Nicola Vicentino's "Canzone da sonare" in his fifth book of madrigals (1572), which appeared in part books rather than in keyboard tablature. Since publication dates do not necessarily reflect dates of composition, some other early printed canzonas may have been written as early or earlier than Vicentino's. For example, Marc'Antonio Ingegneri's second book of madrigals in four voices (1579) contains two "Arie di canzon francese per sonare," and Andrea Gabrieli's ricercari published posthumously in 1586 and 1589 are in four part books. (As will be shown later, the term "ricercar" at this time probably did not refer to a style or form of music but to any imitative, instrumental work *newly composed*, not based on a vocal work, and therefore the term could be used for a *newly composed* "canzona.")

The first collection devoted entirely to instrumental ensemble canzonas is Florentio Maschera's *Libro primo de canzoni da sonare a quattro voci* (1582) in four partbooks. It contains twenty-one canzonas, each for four instruments. Although a few themes can be traced to specific vocal models, most seem newly composed without any vocal model. These canzonas show traits that became basic for the canzona for the next fifty years or more. All but two consist of a number of clearly delineated repeated sections (AABB . . .); two have no repeated sections. Most sections are in duple meter. Two have some thematic unity throughout. Nearly every canzona begins with the famous dactyl pattern long-short-short. Only number 5 begins homophonically; otherwise imitation predominates in a highly contrapuntal style, with only a few homophonic passages scattered about. There is not much difference between these canzonas and those in *Canzon di diversi per sonar con ogni sorte di stromenti a quatro, cinque, & sei voci, libro primo* (Venice: Giacomo Vincenti, 1588), except for the appearance of a few anonymous canzonas for more than four voices. The four-voice ones are by Claudio Merulo (1533-1604) and Gioseffo Guami (ca. 1530-40 - 1611), both important organists.

Perhaps the best of the early canzonas are those by Adriano Banchieri, which appeared primarily in two collections. The first, *Canzoni alla Francese* (Venice: 1596), contains ten canzonas by him and a single one by Guami, his teacher.[9] All are for four instruments, usually open with the dactyls, are preponderantly imitative, and are in duple meter. The form is expanded to include not only immediately repeated sections but also da capo sections. For example, canzona 1 has the form ABBA where B is the second half of A; canzona 2 has the form ABBA where B is similar to the countersubject of A; canzona 4 has the form ABAcoda where B is much longer than A and the coda is short; and canzona 5 has the form ABCABcoda where B is a rhythmic variation of A. Banchieri's skill in counterpoint is everywhere manifest. His second collection, *Fantasie overo canzoni francese per suonare nell'organo et altri stromenti musicali, à quatro voci* (Venice: 1603), which contains twenty canzonas for four voices, goes even further than the first one in the sophistication of his forms and counterpoint.[10] For example, canzona 1 has the form ABCBCA where B is derived from the middle of A and C is homophonic; canzona 7 is an unsectionalized single movement in which there is continual counterpoint utilizing two subjects, the second of which is derived from the second half of the first and the countersubject of the first; and canzona 10 has the form ABBCCDCE where B is derived from A, C is derived from B, and E is derived from both A and B. Fifteen of the twenty canzonas have dactylic openings,

---

[9]For an edition and discussion of this collection cf. Adriano Banchieri, *Canzoni alla Francese* (of 1596), ed. Leland Bartholomew, in Recent *Researches in the Music of the Renaissance*, vol. xx (Madison: A-R Editions, 1975).

[10]A complete transcription is in David T. Kelly, "The Instrumental Ensemble Fantasias of Adriano Banchieri" (Florida State University Education Ph.D., 1962).

while some of the others have dactyls opening internal sections. Canzona 11 is unusual in that it is entitled "In dialogo," which may refer to the fact that each half of the piece is immediately repeated an octave lower and that this antiphony suggests a dialogue between two groups of players.

The canzona, so far, was an intimate contrapuntal work that appeared in secular contexts (madrigal collections, for the entertainment of specific noblemen). Giovanni Gabrieli's *Sacrae symphoniae* (Venice: 1597), however, ushered in a new development of the canzona.[11] It contains fifteen sacred pieces for eight to fifteen instruments in polychoral settings. Rather than for the intimate courtier's apartments, these works were tailor made for the large San Marco Cathedral in Venice. The form is expanded, too. In six Gabrieli canzonas the opening returns at the end, sometimes with an added coda; in three others the opening section recurs at least twice and therefore resembles a rondo or ritornello; and in another five there are chains of non-repetitive sections. Sequences, wide skips, and runs suggest an advanced instrumental style. All fifteen are duple at the beginning and end, but nine canzonas include some contrasting triple meter in the middle. In a few cases Gabrieli mentioned specific instruments: cornets, trombones, members of the violin family, and organ. In his posthumous *Canzoni et Sonate* (Venice: 1615) Gabrieli continued in the same direction.[12] Although it is impossible to trace any consistent distinction between "canzona" and "sonata" during the first half of the 17th century, it is possible that Gabrieli had such a distinction in *his* mind applicable only to these works. "Canzonas" scored for fewer instruments (five to eight voices) in this collection are the more conservative works, while, with one exception, "sonatas" are the works for the largest number of parts (ten and twelve instruments). The exception, however, is his "Sonata con tre violini," which gives some intimation of things to come. At this point, however, the more modern trend seems to be larger ensembles; Lappi's *Canzoni da suonare a4, 5, 6, 7, 8, 9, 10, 11, 12, & 13, libro primo, con partitura* (Venice: 1616) and Giovanni Prioli's canzonas a6-12 in his

---

[11]Bartholomew, pp. 218-230.

[12]*Ibid.*, pp. 124ff.

two volumes entitled *Sacrorum Concentuum* (Venice: 1618-1619) are further evidence.

Perhaps as a reaction against this enlarged canzona there began to appear, occasionally from 1611 and increasingly after 1621, a new canzona with four or fewer instruments. Sometimes these works are sacred, like the second period ones, and sometimes they are secular, like the first period ones. They appear much more intimate in scoring—for fewer instruments—but the surroundings in which they were played were often public. While the canzona maintained its identity as a highly contrapuntal composition within the reduced format, it more and more began to be referred to as "sonata" and eventually, by mid-century, was all but subsumed by new definitions of the "sonata." The three composers Girolamo Frescobaldi, Biagio Marini, and Dario Castello each approached the canzona differently in this third period.

Frescobaldi's principal collection of ensemble canzonas appeared in three editions (two in 1628, one in 1635), each with some corrections, revisions, additior.s, and deletions.[13] In all, there are fifty different canzonas, with another twenty that are sufficiently revised versions as to merit separate count. They are scored for from one to four instruments with basso continuo. In general Frescobaldi strung together a series of sections that contrast in thematic content, tempo, rhythm, meter, and style. Now most canzonas have two sections in triple meter, several begin in triple meter, many tempo changes are clearly indicated with such terms as adagio and allegro, and note values differ from one section to another (for example, semi-minims and minims in one, breves and

---

[13]The complicated relationship among these editions is explained in Ernest C. Mead, "The Instrumental Ensemble Canzonas of Girolamo Frescobaldi" (Harvard University Ph.D. dissertation, 1983). Cf. also John M. Harper, "The Instrumental Canzonas of Girolamo Frescobaldi: a Comparative Edition and Introductory Study" (University of Birmingham Ph.D. dissertation, 1975); and Frederick Hammond, *Girolamo Frescobaldi: his Life and Times* (Cambridge: Harvard University Press, 1983), pp. 188-202. According to Mead, the first of these editions is that published by Robletti in Rome in 1628. It contains 35 canzonas, of which 9 are scored for four instruments with basso continuo and the remainder for from one instrument to three with continuo. The second edition was published by Grassi also in Rome in 1628. It contains 38 canzonas: three new ones and one replacing a Robletti canzona; eleven are now for four instruments with continuo, 27 for a lesser number of instruments. In 1635 Vincenti in Venice published a third edition with forty canzonas, of which thirty-five are altered versions of canzonas in the 1628 books and five are new (including a Ruggiero and a Romanesca).

semi-breves in another, fusae in a third). At least three allegro tempos seem to exist within a single canzona: a stately allegro at the opening when, usually, the dactyls are presented imitatively; a somewhat faster allegro at dramatic endings; and a slower one for internal, complicated contrapuntal sections There are also at least two adagio tempos: a slower one for sustained passages which often occur, briefly, between two faster sections; and a faster adagio for free rhapsodic sections, which occur frequently when a single instrument is alone with the basso continuo. Only in nine canzonas do sections recur, but in some of the other canzonas there is some evidence of thematic development from one section to another. (One Ruggiero and one Romanesca in the 1635 edition, by their very nature, belong to this variation type.) The continuo sometimes is a basso seguente, but much more often, especially in the canzonas for from one to three instruments above the continuo, the continuo has its own contrapuntal function. When one of the solo instruments is a basso, the continuo sometimes doubles it, but usually the two are independent or at least in heterophony. Melodic and harmonic sequences occur frequently, and the trend away from church modes to the major-minor system is apparent. The style in general is imitative, contrapuntal, but there are a few homophonic passages brought in for contrast. In most canzonas the dactylic opening clearly identifies the genre of the music, though in some cases the dactyls were saved for the openings of internal sections or in a few cases omitted altogether.

> The result of the [1635] revisions is one of consolidation in which the character, the "affetto," of each section is clarified. This is especially true in the addition of adagio sections that not only afford respite from the forward drive of other parts of the composition but also, through contrast of tempo and style, place in relief the character of the neighboring allegro movements. When these passages lead, or "modulate," from one allegro to another, they contribute cohesiveness to the overall design. . . . The simplification of the florid, rhapsodic passages, in conjunction with the absence of the direction, "come sta," perhaps indicates that the addition of ornaments, or "affetti,'" was at this later stage [1635] left up to the performer.[14]

---

[14]Mead, p. 121.

Frescobaldi worked for the Aldobrandini family in Rome until 1628 and presumably wrote these canzonas initially for them. He was involved in Cardinal Alessandro d'Este's academies once or twice a week from 1615 to 1628, and "his duties . . . included providing performers for the banquets at the Cardinal's villa in Frascati."[15] After a few years in Florence, he returned to Rome in 1634 to stay, both as organist of the Cappella Giulia in St. Peters and as musician to the private household of Cardinal Francesco Barberini, and it is possible the revisions and additions of the 1635 edition of ensemble canzonas were made for the cardinal. Francesco Barberini's household was deeply involved in music; there were players of viols listed in the household accounts, a set of six viols continually maintained, and music parts purchased in large quantity. There were frequent academies at the Casa Barberini and at the homes of other Romans and nearby gentlemen during which chamber music was performed; the viols' "special function was chamber concerts for the Barberini and for distinguished guests."[16] Although there is no direct evidence that Frescobaldi took part in any way in the Barberini chamber music sessions, it would be surprising if he did not given the coincidence of his own ensemble music and the situation at the cardinal's home.[17] Since the interest in academies and chamber music was by no means limited to the Barberini family, it is also possible, even likely, that a similar situation existed at the Aldobrandini home and that Frescobaldi's original editions of canzonas were stimulated by that situation.[18]

The fourteen surviving canzonas of Marini fall early in his career: two in Opus 1 (1617), two in Opus 2 (1618) and ten in Opus 8

---

[15]Hammond, *Life*, p. 62.

[16]Frederick Hammond, "Girolamo Frescobaldi and a Decade of Music in Casa Barberini: 1634-1643," in Friedrich Lippmann, ed., *Studien zur italienisch-deutschen Musikgeschichte XII*, in *Analecta Musicologica*, vol. xix (Köln: Arno Volk, 1979), pp. 94-124; and Hammond, *Life*, pp. 84-85.

[17]Hammond, "Casa Barberini," p. 107.

[18]There is more direct evidence for another composer. Domenico Mazzocchi's *Madrigali à Cinque voci* [Rome: 1638], dedicated to Francesco Barberini, contains a "Ruggiero à 5. per le Viole" and the madrigals themselves could have been played alternately on a set of viols. Cherubino Waesich, in his *Canzonia Cinque . . . da Sonarsi con le Viole da gamba* (Rome: 1632), may have written canzonas for the Barberini, though he did not become an official member of the household until a few years later.

(1626 or 1629).[19] After a gap of 29 years, when we are missing many of his works, Marini returned for one more instrumental collection in 1655, but now there are no more canzonas. The almost equal treatment that the sonata and canzona received in the earlier publications dispels any generalized distinction that he made between them, and in the last collection he simply gave up the term "canzona" in favor of "sonata." Yet his pieces entitled "canzona" do reflect the post-Gabrieli preference for few instruments, at the same time that they made an effort in Opus 8 to reconcile this preference with Gabrieli's big ensemble sound. The four early canzonas are for three instruments (in Opus 1 for 2 violins or cornets and bass, and for cornet or violin and 2 trombones with continuo); they are in numerous sections, with the second section in each in triple meter. Echo is used. The ten in Opus 8, however, are for four or six instruments, though in six of them there are many passages and occasionally whole sections for just two trebles and continuo. Sometimes the two florid treble instruments alternate with homophonic lower parts. All but the first canzona comprise a series of repeated sections, either immediately or after intervening sections, and many have triple meter sections. Fugal writing is more extensive in the opening sections of the canzonas in Opus 8 than in the earlier canzonas. No. 5 begins with dactyls in a strictly homophonic setting for four instruments with continuo; then the texture breaks up into pairs of instruments or solo instruments answering each other in short phrases. The virtuosic level is much greater than in Frescobaldi but not yet as difficult as in the canzonas of Castello, perhaps because so many of the parts are scored optionally for violin or cornet.

Castello's "Sonate" Book I (Venice: 1621) contains twelve pieces which, while maintaining strong ties to the earlier canzona, at the same time show some traits that bring them into the realm of the future sonata.[20] Thus while we can speak of sonata and canzona traits at this time, based on what the earlier canzona is and what the later sonata will be, these particular works are both sonata and can-

---

[19]Thomas D. Dunn, "The Instrumental Music of Biagio Marini" (Yale University Ph.D. dissertation, 1969).

[20]Richard Douglas Langley, "Sonate Concertante in Stilo Moderno by Dario Castello: a Transcription of Book I" (Washington University Ph.D. dissertation, 1974).

zona from a generic standpoint and in this regard the terms are therefore synonymous. All are in numerous sections (usually seven, eight or nine); in every canzona-sonata one section in the middle is in triple meter. No sections repeat. Ten of the twelve canzona-sonatas open with dactyls, and the other two have dactyls at the opening of the second section. All these characteristics are pertinent to the canzona, but other features are more characteristic of the new sonata. The scoring in eight of the pieces is for two treble instruments and basso continuo and, in the other four, for three treble instruments and basso continuo; in all cases the specific instrumentation is given. Since Castello knew well the specific instruments for which he was writing, the parts are much more idiomatically written with a degree of virtuosity not seen in any of the canzonas mentioned above. This virtuosity implies public performance, where the performers can show off their amazing skills to a bedazzled audience. The instrumental nature of all parts removes any lingering connection with vocal music so obvious in earlier canzonas. The dichotomy between solo(s) and basso continuo, which is to become a major characteristic of the Baroque sonata, is evident here.

The ensemble canzona continued in Austria, Germany and England longer than in Italy. In Germany and Austria, where Giovanni Gabrieli's influence was immense, many important composers such as Hassler,[21] Schein, Rosenmüller, Schmelzer, Biber, Muffat and Peurl made significant contributions to the canzona repertory. For much of the 17th century, Italian composers working in Austria (Giovanni Prioli, Francesco Stivori, Steffano Bernardi, Giovanni Valentini, Giovanni Battista Buonamente, and Antonio Bertali) provided most of the Austrian canzonas; these are often polychoral, with a rich mixture of strings and winds. Albert Biales assumes that these are orchestral, not chamber works, because in a few cases multiple parts survive and the instrumental resources available, especially at the imperial court in Vienna,

---

[21]For example, see the two polychoral canzonas by Hans Leo Hassler in *Sacri Concentus* (1601), ed. Joseph Auer, rev. C. Russell Crosby, Jr., in *Denkmäler der deutschen Tonkunst*, 1. Folge, vols. 24-25, pp. 195-214.

were immense.[22] While such an orchestral performance seems likely, nonetheless the scoring permits chamber performance as well and we cannot rule it out. The only native Austrian to compose canzonas before 1650 was Paul Peurl, but he was much more important for developing the variation suite than any canzona type.[23] By the 1670's, however, there were enough Austrians of ability to firmly establish an Austrian school of canzonas (which by this time were the same as sonatas): Schmelzer, Biber, Georg Muffat, and Ferdinand Tobias Richter, who could hold their own with their Italian contemporaries living in Austria: Alessandro Poglietti and Pietro Andrea Ziani. While their solo, duo and trio sonatas belong to the history of the sonata, their works for more than three instruments with continuo are the final stage in the history of the Austrian canzona. They show intense contrapuntal writing and a rich mixture of tonal colors, both of which distinguish them from any non-Austrian contemporary instrumental music during the last thirty years of the 17th century. Muffat has special significance because of his non-Austrian lineage and training (of English ancestry, raised in France, a student in Paris and Rome); he was able to blend the dances and graceful, elegant styles of Lully's Paris with the new violinistic forms of Corelli's Rome and the contrapuntal and colorful textures of his own Vienna to prepare Austria and Germany for the next generation of Fux, Bach and Handel (see chapter III).

In North Germany and Holland, however, the chamber canzona made little headway during the first half of the 17th century because of the preference for the suite as well as for orchestral ensemble music.[24] With few exceptions, the composers of ensemble instrumental music such as Vierdanck, Scheidemann, Selle, Schop and D. Becker wrote orchestral, not chamber music. After a few early chamber examples by Gregor Aichinger, there were some

[22]Albert Biales, "Sonatas and Canzonas for Larger Ensembles in Seventeenth-Century Austria" (UCLA Ph.D. dissertation, 1962), pp. 17 and 176ff.

[23]Biales, pp. 70-73.

[24]Marie-Elisabeth Brockhoff, "Studien zur Struktur der italienischen und deutschen Triosonate im 17. Jahrhundert" Innaugural dissertation, Westfälische Wilhelms-Universität zu Münster, 1944), pp. 55ff, 73ff.

more in the middle of the century by Vierdanck (1641), Hans Hake (1654), N. a Kempis (1644, 1647, and 1649), J.E. Kindermann (1653) and especially Matthias Weckmann, who wrote specifically for the Collegium Musicum in Hamburg which he founded in 1660 and which he directed until his death in 1674. The North German canzona tends to be sectional (the *Flickstruktur* derived from Giovanni Gabrieli[25]) and scored for wind instruments as much as or more than for string instruments. Even to the end of the 17th century, when the sonata began to be more important, the North Germans relatively rarely composed either sonatas or canzonas compared to the South Germans and Austrians, let alone Italians. An important exception was Buxtehude at the end of the century, who will be discussed in the next chapter.

In England as late as the end of the century

> Henry Purcell . . . included canzonas as movements within his sonatas and in instrumental pieces for his masques and operas. Invariably his canzonas are imitative and written in small note values; they are always introduced by a slower section. Ten of Purcell's twelve *Sonnata's of III parts* (1683) contain canzonas, as do eight of the posthumous *Ten sonatas in four parts* (1697).[26]

> If the word *Canzone* be added to a piece of instrumental music, it signifies much the same as Sonata. . . . If placed in any part of a Sonata, it signifies much the same as Allegro, and only denotes that the part to which it is prefixed is to play or sing in a brisk and lively manner.[27]

While there is some question as to the chamber music quality of much of the later 17th-century Austrian and German repertory of canzonas, there is no doubt, in the case of Purcell's canzonas, that we are still very much in the English tradition of chamber music.

---

[25]Cf. Brockhoff, p. 4: "Die Canzone wurde aus den unterschiedlichsten Sätzen zusammengebaut, aus vielen kleinen und grossen bunten Flicken ('Flickkanzonen')."

[26]Bartholomew, pp. 466-467.

[27]James Grassineau, *A Musical Dictionary* (London: J. Wilcox, 1740), p. 20, which is loosely based on Brossard, *Dictionnaire de Musique* (Paris: Chr. Ballard, 1703).

THE FANTASIA

The earliest fantasias in Italy—from the early 16th century—
were chordal pieces, but by the 1540's they were imitative. For all
practical purposes the fantasia was the same as the ricercar during
the mid-16th century but became much closer to the canzona by
the end of that century.[28] When Banchieri entitled his 1603 collection *Fantasie overo canzoni alla francese*, he made no distinction
between the fantasia and ensemble canzona. But when Frescobaldi
published his keyboard *Primo libro della fantasie a quattro* just
five years later, the fantasia was again a ricercar, not a canzona.
With Frescobaldi the history of the Italian fantasia came to an end.

It is rather in England that the ensemble fantasia had its most
important flowering. Isolated works, such as Philip Van Wilder's
"Fantasia con pause e senza pause," date from Henry VIII's reign
and give some witness to the fact that chamber music performance
(music in the privy chamber) existed during the first half of the
16th century.[29] But it was the chief genre of chamber music from
the middle of Queen Elizabeth's reign until the death of Henry
Purcell more than a century later. Although towards the end it gave
way to the latest Italian genres, it was essentially throughout this
period a specifically English phenomenon and one of the main
English contributions to chamber music before the 20th century.
The English fantasia differed from the Italian canzona in instrumentation (the English preferred soft instruments—recorder,
viol—and the Italians loud ones—trombone, cornet) and style (to a
much greater extent than the Italians, the English mixed popular
homophonic dances with a more severe imitative style within the
fantasia and then as separate movements following the fantasia in
the fantasia suites).

As Ernst Hermann Meyer has pointed out, after 1558 social
conditions presented themselves in England for the development of
chamber music. The individual middle class merchant needed musical recreation—the charm, sweetness, and magic of music—to
counter the increased strain and exhaustion of the new mercantile

[28]Bartholomew, pp. 94-112.

[29]Holman, *Four and Twenty Fiddlers*, pp. 72 and 76.

life. Thanks to Elizabeth's harsh policies of religious authority, the merchant turned away from religious expression and toward glorification of individual achievement. Music was the terratial fulfillment of music of the spheres—"a corrective influence on the [imperfect] nature of man," an important aid for man to achieve "a well-ordered society."[30] The first English chamber music came from Reformed Church musicians in the middle of the 16th century who, not being able to write motet-like pieces for church, did so for private performance. Two chamber music genres, in particular, developed out of this situation: the fantasia and the instrumental settings of *In nomine*.[31]

The history of the English ensemble fantasia falls into four periods. The first is when it emerged from the motet during the mid- to late-16th century. The second period, from 1600 to 1625, featured the fantasias of Thomas Lupo, Giovanni Coprario, Thomas Ravenscroft, Alfonso Ferrabosco, William Byrd, and especially Orlando Gibbons who introduced the Italian scoring of two trebles and bass. During this time the sections of the fantasia became more distinct, often with contrasting meters, and we see the rise of the fantasia-suite. The third period, 1625-1635, was dominated by the works of William Lawes (1602-1645). At this time the "whole" consort was preferred to the "broken" consort, which had been the norm before. During and after the Commonwealth there was a last flourishing of the fantasia, first by the elderly John Jenkins and Matthew Locke, then by John Blow and Henry Purcell.

Lupo (1587-1628) served the English court from 1591 until his death in 1628; during his last seven years he was designated "composer to the violins" as well as "composer to the lutes and voices."[32] He wrote fifteen ensemble fantasias for from three to six instruments, which are mostly imitative, contrapuntal works. In some cases there are overlapping sections demarcated by change of motives and sometimes rhythm and meter; in the larger scorings several of the instruments sometimes are grouped together homo-

---

[30]Ernst Hermann Meyer, *Early English Chamber Music* (New York: Da Capo, 1971; original title *English Chamber Music* [London: Lawrence and Wishart, 1946]), p. 80.

[31]*Ibid.*, pp. 88ff. See below for discussion of the *In nomines*.

[32]John M. Jennings, "The Fantasies of Thomas Lupo," in *Musicology*, iii. (1968-1969), p. 34.

phonically and as a single unit work contrapuntally against the other instruments. The six-voice fantasia in *Musica Britannica* stands out from the others not only in its homophonic opening but also in its unaccomplished counterpoint.[33]

Ferrabosco (ca. 1575-1628) wrote some forty fantasias.[34] They are imitative works with points of imitation throughout, and for the most part were written in a conjunct style that suggests vocal rather than string music. Sections are dovetailed and differ only slightly, especially when subsequent motives are derived from earlier ones. Ferrabosco used augmentation and rhythmic change in creating some monothematic fantasias. Only a few open with dactyls.

The exact dating of Byrd's (1543-1623) fantasias is impossible to establish.[35] One for four instruments and another for six were printed in 1611, and some scholars have suggested that the three three-instrument fantasias are mature works. In all, there are eleven fantasias: three for three instruments, four for four, one for five, and three for six; another four-voice fantasia survives in only one part. The three-voice ones are smoother with mostly stepwise motion, points of imitation, and dovetailing of sections; they evince the vocal motet origins of the fantasia. The four and five-voice ones, however, are much more idiomatically instrumental with jerkier rhythms, isolated phrases, faster passage work, and more and wider leaps. Only the six-voice fantasias are more substantial: longer with clearly demarcated sections, immediately repeated sections and some triple meter sections.

Orlando Gibbon's (1583-1625) fantasias were the culmination of the second period of the English ensemble fantasia.[36] He wrote six fantasias for two treble viols, nine for two trebles with a bass viol, seven for treble, bass and double bass viol, two for two trebles, bass and double bass viol, and nine for pairs of trebles, tenors

---

[33]Vol. ix, p. 127.

[34]John V. Cockshoot, "Ferrabosco, Alfonso (ii)," in *The New Grove Dictionary*, 6th ed. (1980), vol. vi, p. 484.

[35]These are collected in William Byrd, *Consort Music*, ed. Kenneth Elliott, in *The Collected Works of William Byrd*, vol. xvi (London: Stainer & Bell, 1971). See his comments on their chronology.

[36]Published in Orlando Gibbons, *Consort Music*, ed. John Harper, in *Musica Britannica*, vol. xlviii (London: Stainer & Bell, 1982).

William Lawes (1602-1645). Oxford University, Department of Music.

and bass viols. In none is there a basso continuo or accompanying instrument, though some later 17th-century manuscripts have added it. While the works for two, five and six viols are representative of the fantasia of the time, the sixteen three-voice and the three four-voice fantasias are the most innovative. All of this second group are sectional, with an increasing use of at least one triple meter section in most of them; some have two triple-meter sections. Most sections are clearly delineated by cadences, change of rhythm, and new motives, though in some, as in earlier fantasias, there is considerable dovetailing. While most still do not repeat sections, in some there is exact, immediate repetition of sections.[37] The three- and four-voice fantasias are twice as long as the fantasias with other scoring, and their motives are much more developed. Fantasia no. 24 is the longest with eleven sections, one of which repeats. In the four-voice fantasias and one three-voice one, Gibbons used tempo terms "Long," "Slow," "Away," and "Fast" to help demarcate sections. Dactyls occur occasionally at the opening of a section or piece, but they are by no means a characteristic as in the Italian canzona. In contrast to the sharp demarcation of sections in these fantasias, the six-voice ones blur the sections through dovetailing, no tempo designations, and no meter changes.

While Coprario and Ferrabosco had firmly established the fantasia as an idiomatic instrumental genre separate from its vocal motet origins, it was Coprario's pupil William Lawes who established the fantasia as one of the most vital genres in the history of chamber music.[38] Using the traditional fantasia structure, Lawes added his romantic ideas: longer themes, larger development, more varied and interesting rhythms, richer content and intense texture varying fugato, slow counterpoint, homophony, concertante and division. Among the 39 consort pieces for viols are sixteen extraordinary fantasias which demonstrate Lawes' emotional verve and originality. They resemble fugues and ricercari more than canzonas in that the imitation is tightly controlled with subtle devices of counterpoint especially in the opening section; they seem like

[37]E.g., in the four-voice fantasia no. 25, three of the five sections repeat immediately.

[38]Murray Lefkowitz, *William Lawes* (London: Routledge & Kegan Paul, 1960). See also Christopher D.S. Fields, "The English Consort Suite of the Seventeenth Century" (Oxford New College Ph.D. dissertation, 1970), pp. 103-129.

ensemble motets in that the sections (usually three) dovetail into each other with points of imitation. In addition there are two fantasias for five or six instruments among the sixty-six (mostly dance) works of the *Royall Consort*, five more fantasias as part of suites 26-30 of the harp consorts (for viol, bass viol, theorbo, and harp), the sixteen fantasias in the violin suites (for 1 or 2 violins, bass viol and organ), and the 2 fantasias in the suites for three lyra viols. In all cases Lawes' fantasias appear in connection with dances and are distinct from the dance movements in their imitative style and imposing size (see the discussion of fantasia-suites below). Although sections of triple meter are rare in these fantasias, they can be found in the middle of the fantasias in the second suite for three lyra viols and the eighth sonata for two violins, bass viol and organ. In the former the triple-meter section is homophonic, though Lawes exploited the chordal texture of the lyra viol throughout the entire collection. The triple-meter section of the sonata fantasia, however, is contrapuntal, since here Lawes treated even the organ not as accompaniment but as an integral part of the counterpoint with its own entries.

Of particular interest in Lawes' chamber music are the technically difficult divisions or variations for the viol and bass viol in the dance movements of the harp consorts; these and the fantasias in the "sonatas" for violin(s), bass viol and organ seem to have been written for professional or exceptionally talented amateur violists and violinists. That Lawes' chamber music remained in manuscript and was never printed in the 17th century was perhaps the result of its limited use by Lawes' own circle of gifted performers and of its not being intended for the many ordinary violists found throughout England at the time. Yet Lawes' music did circulate in manuscript copies and was popular itself or had an influence on the popular consort music of his successors (Jenkins, Locke, Purcell and others). This virtuosity in some works does raise the possibility, however, that the better performers were expected to add embellishments and variations to the written parts, though to do this without obscuring the fine contrapuntal lines of the fantasia as opposed to the blunt chords of the dances would have been beyond all but the best violists.

By far the most prolific composer of ensemble fantasias and one of the most original was John Jenkins (1592-1678).[39] With over 800 instrumental works to his credit spanning over half a century of creativity, it is not surprising that in his music we find a wide range of fantasia and fantasia-suite types as well as many other types of chamber music. Earlier in his career his preferred instruments were members of the viol family, for which he wrote mostly works for four, five or six parts; later, after the mid-17th century, the violin family became the choice instruments and the Italian duo- and trio-sonata influenced his preference for two- and three-part writing. The fantasias show a level of contrapuntal and harmonic development not seen elsewhere in England until Purcell and then not in the latter's fantasias. For example, Jenkins's first fantasia in six parts (two trebles, tenor, contratenor, two basses, and mostly seguente organ) is in five sections, the first of which (moderately fast) is immediately repeated; the second section (equally fast) has a motive rhythmically the same as that in the first section but with an inversion of two notes; the third section (slow) is the only mostly homophonic one; the fourth section (somewhat faster than the third) motivically grows out of the end of the third and is a rhythmically altered inversion of the counter motive of section 1; and the fifth section (moderato) motivically grows out of the motives of the first and fourth sections. At the same time, this fantasia, which is in C Minor, manages to traverse the keys of F and E♭ Major and G and F Minor and have passages such as that opening section 3: F-d-A-B♭-E♭-G-f-A♭-B♭. . . with only a few intervening appoggiaturas to soften the cross relations. The second six-part fantasia (92 measures) is in one, monothematic section where augmentation of the opening theme during the second half of the piece culminates in a massive, dramatic stretto among several statements of the augmentation and *its* augmentation. The Fancy No. 14 initially sounds quite conservative with its dactylic opening (that frequently reappears throughout the piece) and with its three dovetailed sections, but the clever, suggestive mixture of

---

[39]Andrew Ashbee, "The Four-Part Instrumental Compositions of John Jenkins" (University of London Ph.D. dissertation, 1966); Robert A. Warner, "The Fantasia in the Works of John Jenkins" (University of Michigan Ph.D. dissertation, 1951); Fields, pp. 129-191; and Ernst Hermann Meyer, *Early English Chamber Music from the Middle Ages to Purcell*, 2nd ed. (London: Lawrence and Wishart, 1982), pp. 243-258.

the rhythms and themes of the first two sections in the third section is of a subtlety not experienced in the fantasias of Jenkins's predecessors or contemporaries. Throughout all these huge, impressive fantasias, which are among his earlier works, Jenkins maintained an idiomatic viol writing of short, jerky, disjunct phrases which, however unvocal they are, always give an overall impression of smoothness.

In his later fantasia suites for two violins, two bass viols and organ, Jenkins tried to synthesize the new Italian sounds with his traditional English chamber music. Each of these eight works begins with a fantasia followed by an ayre or almain and a corant. The fantasia, which is much shorter than the earlier fantasias, falls into clearly demarcated sections that differ not only in motive but also in rhythm and meter (six of the eight now have a section in triple) and mode (no. 6 in F Major has a section in F Minor, and no. 7 in E Minor has a section in E Major). While there is some motivic relationship among sections, the amazing cohesiveness of the earlier fantasias is replaced in these suite fantasias by the need for contrast. And whereas the figurations in the earlier fantasias are idiomatic for the viol, the figurations now are much more virtuosic and characteristic of the violin. In general, these works now reflect more the Italian canzona of the 1620's (three of them begin with dactyls) than the earlier English fantasia.

At the same time that Jenkins was writing his fantasias, Matthew Locke (ca. 1622-1677) was producing a series of ensemble suites, most of which include fantasias.[40] Of the forty-two suites for strings, twenty-six contain at least one fantasia and some as many as four. He apparently began to write these suites about 1650, and while he continually wrote new ones, he felt obliged as time passed to reorganize and revise many of the earlier ones. Some of the fantasia suites are for two strings, others for three or four; in some cases, an optional continuo (either organ or theorbo) is indicated by a few figures over the bass viol part or by verbal instructions in an introduction, but in other cases there is no suggestion of any continuo and none needed. The duet fantasias are short, imitative movements without clearly defined sections, no triple meter, and

[40]Matthew Locke, *Chamber Music*, ed. Michael Tilmouth, in *Musica Britannica*, vols. xxxi-xxxii (London: Stainer & Bell, 1971-1972).

only a rare dactylic opening. The two suites for two bass viols each have four fantasias with a courante in the middle and a sarabande at the end. There are more and other dances in the other duets but with only one fantasia in each (except nos. 4 and 8 which have no fantasias). It is with the three- and four-voice suites in "The Flat Consort," "The Broken Consort I," and "Consort of Four Parts" that Locke fully developed his fantasias as well as the suites. In all these cases, the sections of the fantasias are clearly delineated by rests, cadences, change of motives, change of style, and in a few cases even by change of meter (triple added in what is otherwise exclusively duple). In the five trio suites of "The Flat Consort" there are two, sometimes three fantasias, each with a number of sections alternating slow (often homophonic) and fast (always contrapuntal, mostly imitative). The fantasias are now at least twice as long as the duet fantasias. The four-voice "Consort of Four Parts," built consistently like the suites of "The Broken Consort I," has the longest and most highly developed fantasias by Locke. The sections in some cases suggest separate movements. A final fantasia suite written in Oxford in 1665-1666 is the shortest; it consists of only two movements, a fantasia and a courante.

Purcell's fantasias,[41] which were written in or around 1680, are short, one-movement pieces scored for three, four or five viols without accompaniment and in from two to five sections. The sections are usually marked clearly by strong cadences, rhythmic changes, and new motives. There are no changes of meter and triple is never used. Only one of his thirteen fantasias opens with dactyls. There is a tendency, however, to alternate sections of slow and fast tempos, such as in Fantasia 9, where the scheme is slow-fast-slow-fast, suggesting the church sonatas written by Corelli at about the same time. Purcell, or at least his copyist, sometimes used such terms as "Brisk" and "Quick" on the one hand and "Drag" and "Slow" on the other to designate these tempos, though the notation itself often reveals them. Some of the slower sections begin homophonically, in contrast to the imitation always found at the beginning of fast sections. Perhaps the most intriguing fantasia by Purcell is that entitled Fantazia Upon One Note; the tenor viol 2

[41]Collected in Henry Purcell, *Fantazias and In Nomines*, ed. Thurston Dart (London: Novello, 1959).

has one repeated note (middle C) in long notes while the other instruments perform five sections alternating slow and fast, the latter highly imitative.

Purcell's fantasias were the end of more than a century of development of the genre, and while they are attractive works, their lack of innovation shows that it was now a finished development and that a great composer, such as Purcell, had to look elsewhere for the vehicle of his inspiration. That was the sonata, which was more suitable to the public concert, which with John Banister and Thomas Britton was established in London in 1672. Public concerts quickly became popular and demanded a more virtuosic rather than instrospective style of music. The English turned away from active participation in private music-making to passive listening to the public, virtuosic performance of others. Soon orchestral music became preferred to chamber music.[42]

The Italian ensemble canzona and the English ensemble fantasia have some things in common. They are, in the first place, the two most significant genres of chamber music in the early 17th century. Both tend to be mostly contrapuntal pieces divided into sections, predominantly when not exclusively in duple meter, opening with dactyls in many cases, with their origins in the polyphonic vocal motet or chanson of the 16th century. But the differences between the two repertories are more fundamental and stem largely from the different roles that these two genres filled in the different countries. In Italy, as we have seen, the canzona was primarily a public piece performed in church at specific liturgical moments or in the sumptuous homes of the great noble families for entertainment of visitors. Such public performance required, usually, loud instruments such as trombones and cornets, and it is altogether possible that when strings were used, they were doubled orchestrally. That there were private academies throughout Italy where intimate chamber music for strings existed and, at least in Rome, a number of noble families that supported more intimate chamber music does not mitigate the fact that during the first half of the 17th century—the period of the canzona—the primary functions of the canzona were public. The repertory survives almost

---

[42]Meyer, 2nd ed., pp. 235ff.

exclusively in printed editions of the time. In England, however, the ensemble fantasia was, from its outset, private chamber music performed by both professionals and amateurs for their own enjoyment, sometimes in the larger homes of nobility without audience but seemingly more often in the middle class or more humble apartments of the musicians themselves. Much of this repertory survives only in manuscripts and was not published in the 17th century. Most of the Italians were organists who wrote ensemble canzonas on the side; the English were string players who wrote ensemble fantasias for everyday use. The role of the fantasia seems not to have changed during the entire century of its pre-eminence. As a result, the English did not feel the need for more than six performers or for antiphonal choirs of instruments that characterize the Giovanni Gabrieli canzona, nor did they seek to dazzle audiences through virtuosic display that characterizes the Castello and Marini works. Instead the English concentrated on the subtle development of themes and harmonies and on idiomatic string ensemble sounds whether viol or violin. The English, furthermore, rarely have more than four sections, seldom employ a basso continuo (an optional basso seguente is much more typical), and triple meter sections are rare until the influence of the Italian sonata begins to overpower the traditional English sound during the Restoration of the monarchy. Ultimately, however, the canzona and fantasia do have in common their destiny: to be replaced by the Baroque church and chamber sonatas and to be forgotten until the second half of the 20th century.

RICERCARI, CAPRICCI, AND *IN NOMINES*

In addition to the canzona and fantasia, there are several other genres of chamber music which were common enough in the late 16th and early 17th centuries to merit attention here. Chief among these are the ricercar, the capricco, dances, and variations. The latter two in particular are significant both for longevity and for their interaction with the sonata and suite which came to the fore by the mid-17th century.

Although the ricercar was an important keyboard genre in 16th-century Italy and 17th-century Germany, it is of only minor importance in the history of chamber music.[43] Venice seems to have been a center for ricercari throughout this period, and they were probably performed in situations similar to the canzona and fantasia. The first ensemble ricercari were by Adrian Willaert in his *Musica nova* (Venice: 1540), which combine vocal compositional procedures with idiomatic (angular, rhythmically animated) instrumental writing. Jacques Buus follows with eighteen ricercari published in Venice in 1547 and 1549. They are longer than renaissance canzoni, consist entirely of points of imitation, and develop one or a few motives in a single section rather than introduce new motives in each section of a series of clearly delineated sections. Giuliano Tiburtino (Venice: 1549), Annibale Padovano (Venice: 1556), and Willaert (eight ensemble ricercari in *Fantasie et recerchari a tre voci, accomodate da cantare et sonare per ogni instrumento*, Venice: 1551) wrote ricercari which are similar to Buus's. Among Andrea Gabrieli's thirty-three ricercari (written ca. 1560-1570) are seven in four voices and one in eight voices (which introduced the polychoral antiphony of his vocal works and canzoni into the ricercar genre). These are canzoni in all but title; perhaps Gabrieli arrived at the term "ricercar" because in his time it meant a newly composed work without any borrowed material, whereas "canzona" implied an arrangement of a vocal work.[44] In the third quarter of the 16th century, then, all three genres of instrumental ensemble music—fantasia, ricercar and canzona—were equivalent or at least overlapped a great deal in their basic characteristics. By the end of the century, however, the fantasia remained the equivalent of the canzona but the ricercar had gone its own way. Or, more correctly, the ricercar had returned to the Buus type of structure and was intensified. Praetorius equated the terms "ricercar" and "fuga" in his *Syntagma musicum* (1615-19),[45] which is verified in the music itself. The 17th-century ricercar was a much more tightly knit contrapuntal composition that fully develops one or two short motives. While the ensemble ricercar disappeared by

[43]Bartholomew, pp. 94-106.

[44]Gustave Reese, *Music in the Renaissance*, rev. ed. (New York: W.W. Norton, 1959), p. 538.

[45]Alfred Mann, *The Study of Fugue* (New York: W.W. Norton, 1965), pp. 34-35.

1632, the keyboard variety continued for more than a century, culminating in the two ricercari in Bach's *The Musical Offering*. The ensemble capriccio first appeared during the second half of the 16th century in Vincenzo Ruffo's *Capricci in Musica a Tre Voci* (Milan: 1564). The exact meaning of the word "capriccio" is unclear here, as indeed throughout the 16th and 17th centuries. Ruffo's capriccio is a three-voice instrumental work paraphrasing a single voice of a pre-existing madrigal or dance song. It is contrapuntal and, at the beginning, imitative. There are no sections and no repetitions. Paolo Fonghetto's *Capricci, et Madrigali* (Verona: 1598) are two-voice instrumental works which follow in Ruffo's tradition. Another interpretation of the word "capriccio" comes from Ottavio Bariolla's *Capricci, overo canzoni à quattro* (Milan: 1594), where the word "capriccio" is considered the equivalent of the word "canzona." There are twenty capricci here, each for four instruments in careful counterpoint. While there is only one movement without repetition in each, the movement falls into two overlapping sections, each characterized by its own motives. These capricci are on the same, serious level as the canzoni by Banchieri. When Giovanni Cima published his *Concerti Ecclesuastici* in 1610, he included alongside vocal pieces six "sonatas," two of which are also called "Capricci" and are by his brother, Andrea Cima. One is for treble, bass and continuo, and the other is for two trebles, tenor, bass and continuo. Once again the term "capriccio" is equated with "canzona" by way of "sonata," and the type of canzona is that of Banchieri and Bariolla. It is in one long movement with continual points of imitation but no clear sectionalization. Apel suggests that the Cima brothers used the term "capriccio" as a conservative word with which everyone at the time would feel comfortable (by 1610 it was already an old term for a contrapuntal, instrumental work) and used the term "sonata" on the cover since it was the new, modish word likely to attract a more avant-garde audience.[46] A third treatment of the "capriccio" is as a dance-like movement in binary form. This is first found in Giovanni Piero Manenti's *Madrigali ariosi, con alcuni capricci sopra a cinque tempi della gagliarda* (Venice: 1586), where the four-voice capric-

---

[46] Apel, *Die italienische Violinmusik*, pp. 15-16.

cio has absorbed the form and style of the gagliarda. Although it was a relatively rare term, "capriccio" is found occasionally in important places in the 17th century. Most notably, Cazzati's *Varii, e Diversi Capricci*, Opus 50 (Bologna: 1669), is entirely devoted to capricci, each dedicated to a noble family and the whole collection dedicated to Anna Isabella Gonzaga. It is *"per camera e per chiesa."* The works are contrapuntal, but not as strictly so as in the canzona; Cazzati frequently used ornamental broken chords. Each is in binary form.

The instrumental arrangement by Taverner of his own vocal setting of the "in nomine" passages from the Sanctus of the Mass "Gloria tibi Trinitas" led to a whole series of chamber music pieces in the 16th and 17th centuries based on that particular cantus firmus. Among the important exemplars in the early 17th century are four- and five-voice instrumental settings by Byrd. In general, they resemble his fantasias, though with the use of the cantus firmus in long notes, usually in the alto line. Similar *in nomines* for four to six instruments are by Orlando Gibbons, John Ward, John Bull, Ferrabosco, and Thomas Weelkes.[47] In all cases the cantus firmus *in nomine* is presented in long notes in one instrument (mostly in the alto or tenor instrument) while the others play contrapuntally around it. Sometimes they paraphrase the cantus firmus, sometimes they seem to be a free fantasy around it. Usually there is no attempt at sectionalization—the cantus firmus is always given just once. In several cases, however, there are sections based on motivic or rhythmic changes, but triple meter is never introduced. Early in the century the English *in nomine* settings had some influence on the Germans as they developed chorale and other variation suites. After the middle of the 17th century, there were few *in nomines* written, the last by Purcell himself.

THE DANCES

The oldest genre of chamber music in Europe is dance music. Instruments as well as voices, hand clapping and foot stomping

---

[47]*Musica Britannica*, vol. ix.

have accompanied dance throughout the world for millennia, and of course, by the beginning of the 16th century in Europe, there was an already established repertory of instrumental ensemble dance music. During the second half of this century, however, as there arose other genres of instrumental ensemble music, the nature and function of the dance music underwent change affected by these other genres.[48] Some of the dance music was no longer limited to performance accompanying dance but was performed as chamber music: to be enjoyed by the performers and listened to by a limited, non-dancing audience. Much of this chamber dance music was performed side by side with canzonas, fantasias, and other genres of chamber music, and eventually, especially in the 17th century, dances merged with canzonas, fantasias, sinfonias, and sonatas to create new forms, styles and genres of chamber music. It is this evolution in the 17th century that must be traced in order to explain the origins of the sonata da camera, suite or partita.

Dance music at the end of the 16th and beginning of the 17th century consists of music for ballroom dance, music for theatrical dance (*ballet de cour* in France or its equivalents in other countries), and music for non-dance entertainment. While the third category is germane to the topic of chamber music, most of the music in this category came from the other two categories. Ballroom dance music must be simple, homophonic, rhythmically regular and specific, and in symmetrical, recurring phrases. Theatrical dance music is much the same, since anything else would be upsetting to the dancers, though some ornamentation and unusual phraseology and rhythms are suitable for special theatrical effects. Non-danced dance music, on the other hand, need not have any of these characteristics, and, indeed, the longer a dance type is used for chamber music, the more irregular the dance type will probably become. This fusion of dance music with art music becomes an important element in chamber music during its entire history.

The merging of dance music with art music seems to have happened in England first. It occurred in Anthony Holborne's collection *Pavans, Galliards, Almains and other Short Aeirs both Grave and Light in Five parts for Viols, Violins, or other Musicall Winde*

---

[48]Discussed in Bartholomew, *Rauerij*, pp. 169-195.

instruments (London: William Barley, 1599), which incorporates fantasia-like imitation, especially in the pavans.[49] Yet the dances retain their overall dance characteristics of homophonic style and binary (or related) form. As we trace the history of the fantasia-suite below, we will see further evidence of this merger in both England and Germany. In Italy, Rossi's dances remained true to their original ballroom purpose, but both Marini and especially Bononcini brought in imitation and other contrapuntal devices as they stretched the dances well beyond their original styles and shapes.

The dances that were used for chamber music were thought of, by the chamber music composer, in the same light as the original danced dances even though they may have undergone radical change as chamber pieces. Through this pre-Corelli period, the group dances (pavan, intrada, allemand, branle, balletto, and aria) were distinguished from couple dances (galliard, volta, sarabande, courante or corrente, and gigue). The former, often danced by the older, politically more established members of court as they formed lines or circles, tend to be sedate music of a slow or moderate tempo in duple (marching) meter. The latter, however, often danced by the younger members of court in couples without lines or circles, tend to be more frolicking music of a fast or moderately fast tempo, often in triple meter. This distinction among the dances was important for the formation of dance pairs, which are usually a group dance followed by a couple dance, and this continued as the dance pair expanded into the fantasia-suite and sonata da camera.

At the end of the 16th century, the pavan and galliard were the most common dances in the chamber music collections. As we move along in the 17th century, however, those two dances virtually disappeared to be replaced primarily by the allemand, sarabande, gigue, and courante (Italian corrente). These popular dances appeared frequently among all composers, while other, less popular dances are to be found here or there, occasionally treated as the preferred dance by one or another composer. Not too much need be said here about most of these dances, since they are discussed at

---

[49]Cf. Mueller, p. 42.

length in so many other books and articles.[50] "Balletto," however, must be briefly discussed here since it is not as well understood, yet it was, according to Richard Hudson, crucial for the development of the sonata da camera.[51] We will return to the dances, of course, at the end of this chapter when we deal with suites.

The instrumental ensemble "balletto" ran through three periods: the 16th century, 1598-1655, and after 1655. The first period finds the German tanz—not an ensemble but primarily a solo lute dance—copied extensively in foreign countries where it became an ensemble dance. In France, Belgium and The Netherlands it was often ensemble and was called "allemande," and in England, where it was termed "almain," it not only was an ensemble piece to accompany dancing but "was no doubt often played as purely independent chamber music."[52] The Italians, on the other hand, copied the German tanz as purely lute music (despite one keyboard and one ensemble collection) and named it "balletto tedesco."

Under the influence of the English, the Germans began in 1598 to write ensemble dances, and under the influence of the Italians (through the leadership of Hans Leo Hassler in 1601), they changed the name of the "tanz" to "balletto." This ushered in the second period of the "balletto" which was now subject to a great many changes and influences. The Italians developed a special sung balletto, whose chief composer—Giovanni Giacomo Gastoldi—published one collection for three voices and another for five. Both collections were extremely popular and extensively imitated. The three-voice collection led to a purely instrumental type of balletto for three instruments (two trebles and a bass) especially in the hands of Johann Hieronymus von Kapsberger (a German who spent his whole life in Italy) and Marini, whose influence among his contemporaries and successors was most decisive.

Among Biagio Marini's collections of chamber music, especially the earlier ones, there are more dances than sonatas, sin-

---

[50]For example, in Klenz, pp. 84-123; and by F. De Lauze, *Apologie de la Danse* (1623), trl. Joan Wildeblood (London: Frederick Muller, 1952).

[51]Richard Hudson, *The Allemande, the Balletto, and the Tanz*, 2 vols. (Cambridge: Cambridge University Press, 1986).

[52]Hudson, I, p. 118.

fonias or canzonas.[53] He was, like his older contemporary Salomone Rossi, a violinist who had many occasions on which to perform dance music for dancing as well as in chamber music situations. Of particular interest are his balletti, which in the Opus 3 collection refer simply to binary-form dances but which in the earlier collections are attempts to merge the dance with the prevailing larger, more imposing types (canzona, sinfonia) and in the later Opus 22 collection arrive at a new sonata da camera type. In Opus 1 and 2 Marini wrote his balletti as sectionalized pieces, with many more than the two or three sections normally found in actual dance music of the time. Phrases are irregular in length, which precludes any actual dancing to them, and he mixed duple-meter sections and triple-meter ones. In Opus 3, however, the balletti are individual dances on a par with the corrente; the duple balletto is followed by the triple corrente. Yet the phrase lengths are still irregular. It is in Opus 8 that Marini wrote simple binary-form balletti with symmetrical phrases, so that in some cases they are indistinguishable from other dances (such as the allemand).

Meanwhile, in France the "ballet" refers either to the whole "ballet de cour" or to a particular dance or scene of dances within a whole ballet de cour. Praetorius specifically defines the ballet scene as consisting of three dances: an entry dance, a main dance, and an exit dance.[54] This tripartite concept is then copied by the Italians Kapsberger (1615), Zanetti (1645), and Marini (1655); the previous two-section, one-movement balletto now became, in some of their examples, either a three-section dance or a suite of three dances. In Opus 22, Marini experimented with two of the four balletti contained therein. The first is a set of three variations on a simple balletto, followed by a corrente; the second is a five-movement "sonata da camera" (Entrada grave, Balletto allegro, Gagliarda, Corrente, and Retirata) which both suggests a typical scene from a danced ballet and was an important milestone in the development from the simple dance to the secular sonata of Corelli's time (see below). In the same year as Marini's last publi-

---

[53]Dunn, "Marini."

[54]Michael Praetorius, *Syntagma Musicum*, vol. 3, *Termini Musici*, 2nd ed. (1619), in *Documenta Musicologica*, *Erste Reihe*, vol. XV (Kassel: Bärenreiter, 1958), p. 19; quoted in Hudson, I, p. 233, footnote 13.

cation Salvador Grandini distinguished between the "balletto all'allemane" (conservative, binary, homophonic, represented by German composers and by Marini's Opus 8 as well), the "balletto francese" (the three-part, homophonic French ballet de cour scenes), and the "balletto all'italiana" (the merging of the French and German with Gastoldi's three-voice models into a new, contrapuntal, multi-part Italian type).[55]

After 1655 the principal development of the balletto is in Italy, where it was preferred as ensemble dance music to the allemande and other types of dances by all composers until Corelli in the 1690's. An important distinction was made in Italy in the 1660's between functional music meant to be danced to and pure music meant to be enjoyed for its own sake.

The expression *da camera* seems to be used in 1667 to distinguish purely chamber music from music for dancing, or *per ballare*. Bononcini published in this year his *sonate da camera, e da ballo*, with the implication that all the dances therein were either for listening or for dancing. Vitali in the same year, however, makes a distinction in his title *Balletti, Correnti all francese, gagliarde,' e Brando per ballare; Balletti, correnti, e sinfonie da camera*. The pieces in the book are entitled either *per ballare* or *per camera*.

The balletti per ballare are grouped in pairs with corrente, while the balletti da camera are all grouped together. The distinction seems to have disappeared after 1667, the last time "per ballare" was used, and the implication was now that "da camera" always referred to pure chamber music, not danced music.

The Renaissance balletto and allemanda are homophonic, were not separate from dancing, and were not pure art music except sometimes in England. Through much of the 17th century the German balletti retained the traditional form and were almost exclusively for dancing, and English ensemble balletti (as opposed to lute and keyboard balletti) also were almost exclusively for dancing. In Italy, however, the Baroque balletto and allemanda "participate fully in the style of the main Baroque art forms" and, with few exceptions, do not accompany dancing.[56] In Italy from 1656 to

[55]Hudson, I, pp. 167-168.
[56]Hudson, I, p. 212.

1700 the balletto and allemanda reach their zenith in an artistic sense.

> It was in the chamber works . . . particularly those of Legrenzi, Cazzati, and Vitali, that the constructive attitude of the Italian composers attained its complete fulfillment. This is where the Balletto and the Alemanda became superlatively unified through the counterpoint of rhythmic motives and through the sequences and cadences of a recently crystallized tonal system.[57]

The final step—the Corelli "sonata da camera"—will be discussed in chapter IV.

VARIATIONS

In 16th-century Italy, the concept of variations as a form was highly developed in lute and keyboard music before it made its initial appearance in ensemble music. Sometimes it was a set of variations of a theme, but more frequently it was a set of various melodies and rhythms over a repeated harmonic scheme. In the mid-16th century, ensemble variations over the *pass'emezzo* was common. It appeared, for example, in four-part settings, which could be played by strings, in Francesco Bendusi's *Opera Nova di Balli* (1553) where the variations over a harmonic pattern are few in number and each variation is short, and in Pierre Phalese's *Chorearum Molliorum Collectanea* (1583) where some of the variations are longer and there are more of them for each piece. Marini's "Pass'emezzo Concertante in Otto Parti" for two violins and bass (from Opus 8) is in ten parts [sic!] demarcated by change of rhythmic pattern, tempo, and/or style over the steady harmonic formula. Rather than following Marini, however, Carlo Farina (Dresden, 1628), Martino Pesenti (Venice, 1641), and Gasparo Zanetti (Milan, 1645) went in for much simpler *pass'emezzi* with fewer, shorter, simpler sections.

The first ensemble variations on the *romanesca,* one of the most popular harmonic schemes, did not appear in print until 1613 in Salomone Rossi's *Il Terzo Libro de Varii Sonate* for two trebles

---

[57]Hudson, I, p. 176.

(probably violins) and bass. Rather than clearly demarcating each new variation, Rossi overlapped the variations so that the piece as a whole is continuous. He did the same in his later "Sonata Decima sopra l'Aria della Romanesca",[58] as did Buonamente in three romanesca variations.[59] On the other hand, Marini's *romanesca* for solo violin and bass, published in his Opus 3 (1620), is divided into four distinct variations, followed by two dances—gagliarda and corrente—based also on the same *romanesca* pattern. The four variations differ in style or meter, especially the third and fourth, and of course the dances offer just as distinct contrast.

The word "sonata," as will be seen, could cover any instrumental ensemble piece, and, at this time in history, it was sometimes used for ground bass variations. Salomone Rossi labeled "sonata" his variations over a *romanesca* from the third book mentioned above, as well as another set of variations over a *ruggiero* in the same collection. The term "sonata" was also used for variations on a theme. Although variations on a bass or harmonic pattern remained common during the 17th century, variations on a theme became more popular than it had been earlier. Rossi, for example, wrote one such "sonata" in his third book (1613) "sopra l'aria Porto celato il mio nobil pensiero" and another five in his fourth book of sonatas (1622), all for two violins and bass. He wrote a symmetrical setting of the theme and then five or six variations of it, with the bass partaking in some ornamentation and eventually running in fast notes. Francesco Turini (1621) and Giovanni Battista Buonamente (1626) composed similar variations on popular tunes. Marini experimented further with the concept of variation. He used a theme rather than an harmonic pattern for his variations on "la Monica" (Opus 8); he did not present the set in the usual way, however, but brought back the opening of the theme intact and offered variations of other parts of the theme without presenting those variations in the order in which the original theme sections occurred. In his "Sonata sopra a voi ho vinto il cor" for two violins and chitarrone, he presented a tune and three variations in

---

[58] *Il Quarto Libro de varie Sonate* (Venice, 1622).

[59] "Sonata Ottava sopra la Romanesca," in *Il Quarto Libro de varie Sonate* (Venice, 1626); "Sonata Quinta detta la Barbera sopra l'Aria della Romanesca" and "Sonata Nona detta il Romanesco" in *Settimo Libro di Sonate* (Venice, 1637).

which the third variation stands out for its alternation of duple and triple meter between the two violins; the bass remains nearly unchanged for each variation. In his later "Sonata sopra Fuggi dolente cor" (Opus 22, 1655), Marini had altogether four sections in each of which the theme continually appears; rather than delineating each section as a separate variation of the complete theme, he developed the theme within each section through contrapuntal and rhythmic devices and harmonic change.[60]

In England the term "division" meant variation, and a piece called simply "divisions" was a set of variations. The most well-known examples of divisions came from the middle of the 17th century and were by Christopher Simpson (ca. 1605-1669).[61] A first-rate performer on the bass viol, Simpson published *The Division Viol* (1659), a treatise on how to perform divisions on that instrument. Divisions were performed over a ground, and he stated that grounds were of two sorts: a short bass melody of two or three strains that resembles the bass of a dance, or a long bass (thorough bass) that resembles the bass of a motet or madrigal. In his consort music Simpson himself wrote divisions only over the first, dance-like ground. He gave three ways to improvise divisions over a ground: by breaking the ground, by descanting upon the ground, or by mixing breaking and descanting; the last is the method he employed in his own chamber music divisions. By breaking the ground Simpson meant ornamenting the ground bass without obscuring it, and there were five ways to do this: 1) by varying the rhythm of a long note by dividing it into smaller notes without changing the pitch of the original unless jumping to its octave, 2) by weaving smaller notes around the notes of the ground bass while the original notes remain on the main beats, 3) by using passing notes to fill in leaps of a third or more in the original ground bass, 4) by arpeggiating between the original notes, or 5) by adding running passages to an original note of the ground bass with the first note the original note and the last a chord tone above or below it. By descanting upon a ground Simpson described a

---

[60]Uccellini also wrote a number of variations on popular Italian themes in his *Il terzo Libro delle Sonate* (1642) and Opus 4 (1645).

[61]Cf. Margaret Meredith, "Christopher Simpson and the Consort of Viols (University of Wales Ph.D. dissertation, 1969), especially pp. 38ff.

much freer improvisation in the treble instrument or instruments while the ground bass remains intact; it must remain above the bass at all times, and such errors as parallel fifths and octaves must also be avoided. Whatever instrument divides "should always be heard lowest," the other instruments playing "slow Notes and soft." Simpson gave these instructions for players who, he expected, would improvise their own divisions over a simply written dance, and indeed the tradition seems to have been primarily an improvised one since so few examples survive. Thus the importance of Simpson's instructions and examples are not only their didactic function for students of the viol but also their revelation to us more than three centuries later of a practice of chamber music that otherwise would be unknown to us. To understand the importance of division, i.e., improvised ornamentation in 17th-century chamber music, we must be aware of how popular Simpson's treatise was, how much it was praised by the best musicians of his time (e.g., John Jenkins writes a glowing forward), and how highly regarded Simpson himself was.

Simpson's own examples demonstrate his rules. His four divisions for treble and bass viol with continuo consist of a ground of several strains followed by a few variations. The first, for example, consists of four four-measure phrases, after which the whole is repeated twice, each time with extensive, free divisions in the upper part and very modest divisions in the continuo ground. In his "exercises" for two division viols, however, he had a simple dance in binary form, with divisions occurring for the repeat of each strain, followed by a series of variations of the whole (thus AA'BB' A"A'"B"B'" A""A""'B""B""' . . .).

Variations as a technique, as we shall see below, was an important element in the German suite. Variations as a form was also very important in Germany and Austria. A fascinating display of ground bass variations occurs in Johann Heinrich Schmelzer's *Sonatae Unarum Fidium, seu a Violino Solo* (Nürnberg: 1664). Among the six sonatas are four completely different treatments of ground bass variations. The first sonata is a long, one-movement work in five large sections; the opening and closing sections are in C meter and are the same but for a few notes. The second and fourth sections are in $\frac{12}{8}$ and $\frac{3}{2}$ meter respectively and again balance each other. The third section, however, is a set of eleven variations on a ground bass, and during the set there are three changes of meter. The second sonata is a collection of seventeen variations over a ground bass. Sometimes the meter changes, and two internal sections immediately repeat. The third sonata is a lengthy set of variations over a ground bass, but here the melodic phrases in the solo violin overlap the ground bass phrases so that the two rarely begin and end together. This effects a smooth flow and diminishes the danger of monotony from such a frequently repeated bass. The fourth sonata uses a short, four-note ground bass which goes through several meter changes. Suddenly, in the midst of the one long movement there occurs first a sarabande and then a gigue, both using the ground bass but imposing both their melodic dance rhythms and repeated sections. Both the third and the fourth sonatas look back to Marini's variations on the *romanesca* (see above).

THE SINFONIA

At the outset, the sinfonia had a specific function (as a short instrumental work in the midst of vocal music), but it had not found a specific style, form or scoring.[62] The earliest sinfonias appeared in Christoforo Malvezzi's *Intermedii et concerti* (1591), which contains three by Malvezzi for six instruments and another one for five instruments by Marenzio. These were followed by similar short, homophonic sinfonias by Monteverdi for five instruments (*Fifth Book of Madrigals*, 1605) and for five to seven instruments (*Orfeo*, 1607) and by Cesario Gussago for eight instruments (*Sonate a quattro, sei, et otto*, 1608).

Salomone Rossi, on the other hand, in all four of his collections (1607, 1608, 1613?, and 1622), wrote a second kind of sinfonia—chamber sinfonias independent of any larger, vocal work. The first three collections are for viols and bass (without continuo), while the last is for violins and bass (again without continuo). While Rossi was the first to write specifically for two treble and one bass instruments (one piece in 1607, all the sinfonias in 1608, and all

---

[62]Bartholomew, *Rauerij*, pp. 121-135.

the pieces in the other two collections), his "trio sonata" is not the same kind of "trio sonata" with basso continuo that is first met in Giovanni Paolo Cima's *Concerti Ecclesuastici* (1610) and that became standard during the rest of the century. Rossi's independent sinfonias are more substantial than the sinfonias that are part of large, multi-movement vocal works. Frequently he began imitatively usually with dactyls, and followed with a more involved counterpoint than his predecessors, though he stuck to the simple binary (AABB) or three-part (AABBCC) dance forms.

Viadana composed a third type of sinfonia in his *Sinfonie Musicalie a8* (Venice: 1610). These are a combination of the larger scorings found in the sinfonias of Malvezzi, Marenzio, Monteverdi and Gussago with the independent, substantial works found in Rossi. Viadana's sinfonias are polychoral canzonas similar to Giovanni Gabrieli's, with sections and repetitions of the sections. Another example of this massive canzona-like sinfonia can be found in Banchieri's *Eclesiastici Sinfoniae* (1607).

It was in the hands of Biagio Marini, however, that the sinfonia moved convincingly into a precise genre of music: duo or trio scoring, binary form, and a mixture of homophonic style with voice leading and occasional imitation. The eighteen sinfonias in Opus 1 (1617) and 2 (1618) are mostly for two treble instruments, bass and continuo; three are for one violin, bass and continuo. They are either balletto-like ("symmetrical, frequently articulated phrase structure") or canzona-like ("longer, less interrupted," with dactyl openings, though not as sophisticated counterpoint as actual canzonas). Many have triple-meter sections. In the five sinfonias of his next collection, Opus 8 (1626), Marini used only the trio scoring. He arrived at "binary form with a single meter used throughout, brevity in length, and a more concise, subdued melodic style than their predecessors."[63] The style is mostly homophonic, though some fugato passages occur in three of them. The only significant difference between these five and the next and last group of six, in Opus 22 (1655), is the scoring: two violins, viola, and Spanish guitar. Marini, furthermore, gave church tones for the Opus 22 sinfonias, in order to reconfirm their function as instrumental inter-

[63]Dunn, p. 135.

ludes in the midst of vocal works—in this particular case, their role as church pieces. While not all Italian composers of sinfonias at this time followed Marini (cf. Stafano Landi's opera *Il S. Alessio*, 1632; Buonamente's dance suites in *Quinto* and *Settimo Libri*, 1629 and 1637,[64] and Uccellini's *Sonate Sinfonie, et Correnti . . . Libro Secondo* [Venice: Alessandro Vincenti, 1639]), Marini's treatment of the sinfonia was the most significant historically as an important precursor of Corelli's sonatas.

THE PRE-CORELLI SONATA

The term "sonata" in the early 17th century meant a piece to be played on instruments, not sung, and it was usually used synonymously with canzona or sinfonia. Sometimes a "sonata" was used during a vocal piece, but as a purely instrumental introduction or interlude; and often during the 17th century a collection of vocal works could also have one or more sonatas within its covers. Initially the term sonata implied no particular form or style, though some theorists and individual composers directly stated or implied some formal and/or stylistic characteristics of the sonata which distinguished it from the canzona and/or sinfonia.[65] Chief among these characteristics of the sonata was the scoring for one, two, or three soloists accompanied by the basso continuo. The main reason for this seems to be retroactive, since by the late 17th century the sonata was best defined as an instrumental piece for one, two or three soloists with a continuo. During much of the early and even mid-17th century, however, such a scoring was also called canzona and, less frequently, sinfonia.

The evolution of the sonata before Corelli was in fact the gradual synthesis of all the above ensemble genres into a new genre defined by instrumentation and by style. Three dominant scorings for chamber works emerged—the so-called trio (three solo instruments, usually two trebles and a bass, and an accompanying con-

[64]Rosenmüller's use of "sinfonia" in 1667 refers to his five-voice German suites (see below).

[65]For example, Rossi's sonatas frequently are variations, while his sinfonias never are variations. Cf. Willi Apel, *Die italienische Violinmusik im 17. Jahrhundert*, in *Beihefte zum Archiv für Musikwissenschaft*, vol. xxi (Wiesbaden: Franz Steiner, 1983), pp. 12-14.

tinuo), duo (two solo instruments, either two trebles or treble and bass, with accompanying continuo), and solo settings (one solo instrument, usually treble, with an accompanying continuo).[66] These settings were the decisive factor that led to a new breed of virtuosic instrumentalists (corresponding to the rise of the virtuosic singer in the contemporary opera), who in turn demanded a new, idiomatically instrumental ensemble music way beyond the limitations imposed by the vocal origins of the imitative genres and by the simple, square, dance sources of the homophonic genres.

Apel[67] has listed the important Italian collections of violin sonatas defined by this scoring, chief among which are those published during the first half of the 17th century by Rossi, Cima, Farina, Fontana, Castello, Buonamente, Uccellini, and Marini. With Rossi and Cima the scoring of two treble instruments and bass (with or without continuo: the trio-sonata scoring) was established, and the scoring for one treble and bass was also new during the first two decades of the 17th century. These two scorings became essential for the later sonata idea. Also important was the treatment of the solo instruments, which began to dominate with technical and lyric passages idiomatic of the violin or whatever solo instrument was used. Rossi's sonatas, often variations of folk songs and associated with dances in his collections, seem intended for secular use, while Gian Paolo Cima's sonatas in *Concerti Ecclesiastici* (1610) were obviously for church use. Cima's *Concerti* "is the first collection which contains a varied selection of few-voiced instrumental pieces with b[asso] c[ontinuo]."[68] It contains sonatas and capricci for one to four solo instruments with continuo. In three sonatas for two soloists, one of the soloists is a bass instrument; the continuo is treated as a contrapuntal line separate from and equal to the bass and soprano instruments. The rich polyphonic texture including the continuo is a sign of the canzona

---

[66]Cf. Niels Martin Jensen, "Solo Sonata, Duo Sonata and Trio Sonata: Some Problems of Terminology and Genre in 17th-Century Italian Instrumental Music," in *Festskrift Jens Peter Larsen* (Copenhagen: Wilhelm Hansen Musik-Forlag, 1972).

[67]Willi Apel, "Studien über die frühe Violinmusik," in *Archiv für Musikwissenschaft*, xxx-xxxviii (1973-1981).

[68]Jensen, p. 85. The term "concerto" in the title here refers not to the sonatas but to vocal works in the collection.

background and in turn of the polyphonic chanson; it in no way suggests an instrumental transcription of monody as has been falsely propagated by Hugo Riemann and his followers.[69] There is no specific clue to whether or not Rossi's and Cima's pieces were originally performed as chamber music, i.e., in an intimate situation with one player per part, though it seems most likely that Rossi's, as secular music, would have been while Cima's, as public church music, would not initially have been. That the latter's music was published suggests that it was made available to others for chamber use.

The most important composer of chamber sonatas during the first half of the 17th century was, once again, Biagio Marini (ca. 1600-1665). In the San Marco orchestra in Venice as early as 1615, he was associated with the Venetian school even though he left for other Italian and German cities after only a few years and never served there again. Because of this physical separation from Venice,

> Marini is set apart from Venetian tradition by his inclination towards chamber features, such as dance movements and ostinato bass. The simple, symmetrical line of his style contrasts with the Venetian absorption in detail. Marini's interest in the solo *per se* also contrasts with the Venetian interest in *concertato* writing.[70]

With Marini's Opus 1 in 1617 there was now established the clear distinction between the solo scoring (treble + continuo) and the trio scoring (two trebles + bass + continuo), but these scorings are applicable to sinfonias, canzonas and other genres as well as sonatas. Of the three solo works, two are labeled sinfonia and one sonata; they differ in style and form among each other but as a group are simpler than the two trio sonatas in the same collection. The latter are florid, ornamental works much longer than the canzonas of 1617; both have brief homophonic sections with tremolos. Both are sectionalized and one has a recapitulation. Of the twenty sonatas in Marini's Opus 8, eleven are trio sonatas, four are solo sonatas, three are optionally either solo, unaccompanied or trio, and two have other settings. Some are sectional and some of these

---

[69]*Ibid.*, p. 76.

[70]Selfridge-Field, p. 129.

have sectional repetition; others are more unified without clear sections. In any case they show an affinity with the canzona in the frequent use of dactylic openings. Marini was conscious of the ranges and techniques of his instruments, with bigger leaps, faster notes and a thicker texture for the strings than for the winds. He experimented with numerous sonorities, including double and triple stops, scordatura, canonic echoes (in violins 2 and 3 of his "Sonata in ecco" played by "hidden" musicians) and organ obligato (in a canzona-like sonata for violin and organ with written-out right hand). His experiments extended to the optional use of solo bass parts and the alternative elimination of either treble or solo bass part in three works. All in all, Opus 8 evinces a wide range of possible treatments of the new trio sonata, from very simple to fairly complex in terms of style, form and instrumentation.

The four solo sonatas of Opus 8 were very important for establishing that genre. All four are sectionalized with at least one triple-meter section following a duple-meter one. The third sonata, with nine sections demarcated by change of style, has by far the most sections, while the second has only three sections. The fourth is particularly interesting in its indication of tempos "tardo" and "presto" to delineate sections and the use of double stops in an imitative fashion—the first such use of what is eventually to become a popular violinistic device in sonatas. The middle section of the second sonata also introduces another popular device: the use of scordatura to expedite double stops in thirds.

The principle composers of sonatas between Marini's Opus 8 (1626) and Opus 22 (1655) were Carlo Farina, Giovanni Battista Fontana, Dario Castello, Giovanni Battista Buonamente, Marco Uccellini, and Maurizio Cazzati.[71] Farina, who was Schütz's concertmaster in Dresden, published there five books of instrumental ensembles (1626-1628) including six trio and four solo sonatas. All are in three overall sections alternating duple and triple meter with many subsections, and the violin parts emphasize a rather inelegant technical display.

Fontana, who died in 1630, is remembered for six solo and six duo sonatas as well as six for three instruments with basso con-

[71]Dunn, "Marini," p. 184.

tinuo, all published in 1641. Not all of these sonatas are for violin; some of the solo instruments are in the bass clef. Fontana evinced a rhythmic flexibility not found in early Marini; two solo sonatas begin in triple meter, and there is much more frequent use of triple meter throughout. He is more careful than early Marini to delineate sections clearly with the use of full cadences, pauses, and/or final cadenzas. Overall the sonatas demonstrate three styles: canzona-like imitation, recitative, and aria.

Castello's sonatas of 1629 have been discussed above as transitional from canzona to sonata.

Buonamente's three collections of sonatas and light dance music for three solo instruments (1626, 1629, and 1637) have a basso continuo which is for optional use; the composer, in a letter dated September 19, 1627, stated that he had written the three solo parts of a sonata without continuo, that it could be performed without continuo, and that the continuo was added in order to give a greater sense of the harmony.[72] The sonatas in Buonamente's sixth book (1636) are also like canzonas but show a very conservative sectionalization without ever using triple meter. His scoring ranges from solo with continuo to six instruments with continuo. Since these sonatas are interspersed with canzonas for from three to six instruments, the tie to the canzona is reinforced.

The most important rival to Marini as composer of sonatas between 1626 and 1655 was Uccellini. While Marini's sonatas were written despite his one-time location in Venice, Uccellini worked in Modena where the sociological situation was congenial to chamber music. Initially he, too, seemed to be tied to the canzona tradition since many of his sonatas open with the customary dactyls, but once past the opening bars it is clear that the sonatas in his books II (1639), III (1642), and IV (1644) are both innovative and artistically wonderful. Although the sonatas are sectional, Uccellini's sonatas tended toward fewer and bigger sections than did Marini's sonatas. In some sonatas of Book III, Uccellini tied all the sections together with the same themes, and in Book IV, he tied them together with the same head motives. The eighteenth sonata of Book IV is a rondo. He used a variety of styles; one sonata of

[72]Jensen, p. 91.

Book II is completely fugal in only one section. Tempo markings abound, and he went so far as to introduce some sonatas with adagio sections. Most adagio sections are very brief, some just a single measure. Uccellini's most important contribution lies in his melodic style: "its use of broad, often wide ranging outlines, [gives] it a fine sense of sweep, without phrases always running together."[73] It was this which passed down to Corelli, rather than his innovations in form.

Whereas Marini's Venice was primarily a mercantile center and Uccellini's Modena an important court city, Cazzati's Bologna was a church fiefdom. Venetian music was grandiose and more secular than sacred. Modenese music was intimate and ceremonial whether written for the Este family at home or for the same family at church; the Modenese School was similar to the earlier school in Mantua (Rossi and for a short time Buonamente). Bologna's music was primarily public and religious but much more subdued than that in Venice, and Cazzati was required to write public church music to suit local tastes. There is a clear development in Cazzati's sonatas from the canzona-like Opus 2 and 8 to the virtuoso sonatas of Opus 35 and 55.[74] The earlier ones have a more equal vocal arrangement, and they are each in one long, sectionalized movement. The later sonatas, however, written not for the church but for the private Accademia filarmonica, are basically virtuosic and have separate movements (see below). Cazzati also belonged to the Accademia degli Eccitati, a literary society in Bergamo. Musical performances concluded each meeting, and while no descriptions exist, it seems likely that Cazzati and his pupil Legrenzi played chamber sonatas there. The meetings "were well attended by the public."[75] Cazzati's principal contribution to the sonata before Marini's Opus 22 (in his *Il secondo libro delle sonate a 1, 2, 3, & 4*, Opus 8 [1648] and *Suonate a Due Violini col suo Basso Continuo*, Opus 18 [1656]) was in the clear demarcation of sections

---

[73]Dunn, p. 198.

[74]John Suess, "The Ensemble Sonatas of Maurizio Cazzati," in Friedrich Lippmann, ed., *Studien zur italienisch-deutschen Musikgeschichte XII*, in *Analecta Musicologica*, vol. xix (Köln: Arno Volk, 1979), pp. 146-185, does not regard Opus 35 as important in the development of the sonata; rather, it is an important precursor of the trumpet concerto.

[75]Bonta, pp. 16-17.

within a lengthy one-movement sonata. He ended most sections with double bars and repeats[76] and gave contrasting slow and fast tempo characteristics to each section. Cazzati also carried on Uccellini's wide, simple melodic sweep, especially in slow opening homophonic sections and in faster, majestic arpeggiated openings.

The final collection of sonatas by Marini was his Opus 22 of 1655. It contains six sonatas, as well as six sinfonias, many dances, a passacaglia, and a dance suite. Four sonatas are for two violins and bass with continuo; one is for three violins with continuo and the last is for two violins, viola, bass and continuo. He followed Cazzati's strong delineation of sections by the use of double bars and repeats and usually added the term "parte" to the beginning of each new section. The first parte usually consists of two long subsections, and, in one case, the second subsection changes meter. There was now usually a limit of three large partes, and with the strong division of the first (or, in two cases, one of the subsequent) partes, there emerged a feeling of four distinct parts of the piece (the occasional intrusion of a very brief slow passage is ignored). In conjunction with the clear sectionalization of each sonata there is a rhythmic delineation as well. In two cases these four partes follow the pattern slow-fast-slow-fast, but in other works the pattern is slow-fast-fast-fast or fast-fast-slow-fast. Dactyls at the opening still occur, as in the second sonata; all sonatas but one open with a slow, homophonic section. But while Marini has changed his formal and rhythmic concepts in his new sonatas, his style of violin playing has not changed. Perhaps because these are trio or larger sonatas and not solo sonatas, Marini's melodic lines are not heavily ornamented with technical displays. Rather they are consistent with his earlier style with only slightly more leaps than before. This collection was his final synthesis of all his own earlier works with that which he valued most from his contemporaries.

Whether an ensemble sonata was played by soloists or by a chamber orchestra depended upon where it was performed. The cathedral in Modena, for example—where Uccellini founded a violin school in 1641 and which included among its leading musicians, besides Uccellini, G.M. Bononcini (1642-1678), Giuseppe

---

[76]Although Rossi had done this in his vols. 3 and 4, his pieces are much shorter.

Colombi (1635-1694), G.B. Vitali (ca. 1644-1692), T.A. Vitali (1663-1745), and G. Bononcini (1670-1747)—had in 1647 only one violinist, one violonist, one organist, as well as voices;[77] by 1690 only a second violinist had been added. Modena's cathedral was under the control of a single aristocratic family, the Este, and much of the musical establishment was at court, not at church. On the other hand, Bologna's cathedral had a much larger group of string players as well as trumpeters since Bologna, as a city controlled by the church and run by a group of lesser but wealthy families, did not have a court to dilute the manpower of musicians. Indeed, the absence of the much more esoteric court tastes among the churchgoers of Bologna was so detrimental to the Bolognese violinists that, to satisfy their artistic needs, they had to form accademias (most notably the Accademia filarmonica) where only the best professionals and amateurs were admitted as listeners as well as performers and composers. Thus, in Bologna's cathedral, orchestral performance was likely, particularly since there the trumpet concertos of Cazzati and Torelli blossomed as orchestral works. In the accademias, however, either chamber or chamber orchestral performance would have been possible.

After Marini, the development of the sonata da chiesa was in the hands of Corelli's immediate predecessors, chief among whom must be listed Cazzati (founder of the Bologna school), Bononcini (leader of the Modena school), and Legrenzi (a pupil of Cazzati and a representative of later Venetian chamber music).

Cazzati's earlier sonatas, as we have already seen, are one-movement works with clearly delineated sections. After his move to Bologna in 1657, however, he began to alter his style away from a traditional canzona-like sonata to a much more virtuosic, multi-movement sonata. The sonata "La Malvasia," of Opus 35 (1665), is in four movements and is scored for two violins, viola, violone,[78] and basso continuo of organ and either theorbo or contrabass. The

---

[77]William Klenz, *Giovanni Maria Bononcini of Modena: a Chapter in Baroque Instrumental Music* (Durham: Duke University Press, 1962), pp. 14, 19, 35.

[78]Bonta, pp. 183-196, discusses this instrumental designation at length. It refers either to a 6-string bass viol (transposes down) or a 4-string bass violin (non-transposing). It often is the same as "continuo." The "violoncello" etymologically suggests a smaller version of a violone.

first movement is a homophonic Grave; the second is a highly imitative Allegro; the third is another homophonic Grave; and the fourth is in three sections Vivace (partially homophonic, partially imitative) - Presto Presto (beginning imitatively, then strictly homophonic) - Grave (short, homophonic). The Presto Presto section is the only part of the sonata in triple meter. The sonata "La Casala" in the same collection is also in four movements but scored for two solo violins, solo violone, and continuo. The virtuosity in this sonata in all three solo instruments exceeds anything in Marini's works or for that matter in any sonata collection prior to it. There are wide leaps, fast runs, and arpeggiated passage work that forever after are known as violinistic music.[79]

G.M. Bononcini had a very important position among Corelli's immediate predecessors. A pupil of Uccellini in Modena and then, after Uccellini's death, leader of the Modenese school, he exerted great influence on his contemporaries there. In addition, he was a member of the Bolognese Accademia filarmonica (from ca. 1672 on) and had most of his music published in Bologna from 1669 on; thus beginning especially in the year 1669 he was an important influence on the Bolognese school as well. From ca. 1666 to 1670 Corelli was in Bologna and, in his final year there, joined the Accademia filarmonica; it seems likely that Corelli knew Bononcini's music if not him personally. But although he died young in 1678, Bononcini's influence extended well into the 18th century, at least in England, where his music was republished in the 1720's. It seems that Bononcini's patroness Laure d'Este, who was Mazarin's niece, was the mother of Maria Beatrice d'Este, who married James II of England. This daughter of the House of Este brought her Italian taste with her to England and made the music of her favorite Italian violinist (Bononcini) known to all around her, including the young Purcell.

Bononcini was a skilled contrapuntist, and therefore counterpoint played a major role in his thirty church sonatas. In his Opus 3, he stated that the mind as well as the ear must be stimulated in chamber music, and therefore he included here and elsewhere, even in chamber music dances, the canons and imitation that typify

---

[79] *Ibid.*, Musical Supplement, pp. 276-296.

his style.[80] The twelve duo sonatas of his Opus 6 (Venice, 1672) are the most consistent.[81] With only one exception, they are in four movements of which the first and last are highly developed fugal movements in duple meter, the second is either imitative or homophonic but always in triple meter, and the third is an expressive homophonic movement.[82] This idea of four movements, of which the third is the only slow and homophonic one, can be seen already in Marini's choice of sections for his 1655 collection and in Uccellini's sonatas. In only a few cases is there thematic unity between movements. In the Opus 1 collection for two violins and continuo, only four sonatas follow this scheme. The others vary in number of movements from three to five with various combinations of fugal duple- and triple-meter and homophonic movements. Only one of the five trio sonatas in Opus 9 follows the four-movement scheme of Opus 6. The others vary, but usually they begin with a slow, homophonic prelude, follow with a triple-meter movement, and end with a fast, fugal movement. The first sonata, for example, opens with a homophonic Adagio; follows with a triple-meter, imitative Allegro; moves on to another homophonic Adagio; and ends with a final imitative Allegro. This will eventually become a standard sonata da chiesa form. The second sonata of Opus 9, however, has two imitative Allegros, follows with an expansive Adagio, and concludes with another imitative Allegro. This pattern of movements (fast-fast-slow-fast) corresponds to that found in Marini's Opus 55.

Before coming to Venice, Giovanni Legrenzi (1626-1690) was organist in Bergamo (1645-1656) and Ferrara (1656-1665), where he composed most of his instrumental music. His whereabouts for the next few years are unknown, but ca. 1672 he was in Venice. Sometime during the next few years, Legrenzi, an ordained priest, was on the musical staff of the Ospedale dei Mendicanti in Venice, where girls were instructed in religious music. By the early 1670's its musical ensemble had six violins, an alto violin, a tenor or bass

---

[80]Klenz, p. 74. This problem in aesthetics between reason and sensuality in music will be discussed in Chapter V. Cf. Bellamy Hosler, *Changing Aesthetic Views of Instrumental Music in 18th-Century Germany* (Ann Arbor: UMI Research Press, 1981).

[81]Klenz, pp. 133-165, for a discussion of Bononcini's *sonatas da camera*.

[82]The exceptional sonata (no. 3) has an extra introductory homophonic movement.

violin, two violone, two theorbos, three cornetts, three trombones, a bassoon, a harp, and numerous keyboard instruments.[83] Obviously taken with the large instrumental forces available to him in the Ospidale, Legrenzi was not about to deal with a smaller group when he was appointed vice maestro at San Marco in 1681; from the moment of his appointment he started to enlarge the instrumental ensemble there. When Legrenzi was promoted to maestro di cappella of San Marco in 1685, his orchestra consisted of twenty-eight string instruments, two cornetts, three trombones and one bassoon, with frequent additions of trumpets and drums.[84] To them he joined, during the next four years, several additional instruments, including a permanent trumpet. Thus, the music which Legrenzi wrote for San Marco and probably also that for the Ospedale dei Mendicanti was orchestral. Sometime during the last three decades of the 17th century, there emerged an important distinction between *sonata da chiesa* and *sonata da camera* in Venice; the former was now an orchestral work, the latter a true chamber work.[85] In the smaller churches, however, where an orchestra was unaffordable, the *sonata da chiesa* would still be performed as chamber music. The chamber music that Legrenzi wrote, then, would seem to fall early in his career, when he worked in smaller churches in smaller cities and kept more intimate company with the musicians there than he was able to do when he worked in a larger church in a larger city. In Bergamo, he likely played chamber music with Cazzati at the Accademia degli Eccitati, to whose members he dedicated his Opus 4 sonatas, and he also tells us that other performances of his sonatas took place at "the accademies held by [Giovanni Carlo] Savorgnano, presumably at his residence."[86] But in Venice, Legrenzi also had private concerts in his home, at least in the 1680's, and while little is known about these private performances, it seems likely that here

---

[83] Selfridge-Field, p. 45; Bonta, p. 79.

[84] Selfridge-Field, p. 18; Bonta, pp. 79 and 100.

[85] Bonta, p. 208.

[86] Bonta, p. 18. In Ferrara, whither Legrenzi moved during the winter of 1656-1657, he belonged to sacred accademias and seemingly became increasingly involved with orchestral music. Cf. Bonta, pp. 28ff.

Legrenzi performed chamber music.[87] Since many sonatas of the last few decades of the 17th century are published as suitable for either *da chiesa* or *da camera* performance, it is possible that both *sonatas da chiesa* and *sonatas da camera* were performed as chamber music at Legrenzi's home.

Legrenzi wrote two volumes of instrumental ensemble music while still in Bergamo, his Opus 2 (1655, church sonatas) and Opus 4 (1656, both church sonatas and dances). These are scored for two violins and violone (or bassoon[88]) with continuo, and they reflect the influence of Marini. This is not music to be performed in the large churches such as San Marco but rather in smaller locales. The Opus 2 sonatas have the sequence of movements fast slow fast, while some of the sonatas in Opus 4 add an introductory slow movement. The next collection of sonatas, Opus 8 for two, three, five or six instruments with organ continuo, was written in Ferrara in 1663. Nearly all begin with a fast fugal movement and end with an adagio coda; most have one or two adagio-presto pairs, with all the fast movements fugal. The two sonatas for six instruments group the instruments into two choirs; in both cases the first choir consists of two violins and viola da brazzo, while the second choir of one sonata consists of two cornetts and bassoon and of the other sonata of two violas and violone. The strong feeling for counterpoint in the fast movements, the polychoral writing, the sectionalization of some movements, and the use of a final adagio coda all point to a residue of Venetian canzona style even at this late date. This continued in Opus 10, *La Cetra: Libro quarto di Sonate a due, tre, e quattro stromenti* (1673), when Legrenzi was already in Venice. Among these sonatas are three for two violins, viola, and cello with continuo, two for viol consort, and one for four violins with continuo. To the techniques and styles of Opus 8 he added echo. A fifth collection of church sonatas, Opus 17 for

---

[87]Selfridge-Field, p. 50; Bonta, pp. 112-113. Bonta, p. 90, also refers to a large number of soirees at the homes of the Venetian nobility, for which he wrote his cantatas and canzonettes Opus 12 (1676) and Opera 13-14 (1678) but apparently no sonatas or other instrumental chamber works.

[88]Bonta, p. 197, states that in the smaller sonatas Legrenzi never uses winds except as alternatives for strings, and therefore wind players should expect that these sonatas are never specifically idiomatic for winds.

trumpet and continuo, unfortunately is lost. Bonta suggests that the sonatas in the two early collections, which call for virtuosic violins, are "ideally suited to solo performance," while the sonatas for larger ensemble, which are "less brilliant," are "suited alike to orchestral or solo performance."[89] He also points out that Legrenzi reached a decisive point in the history of the forms of chamber music; he accomplished all the devices necessary for extended forms without applying those devices for those ends.[90]

THE EARLY SONATA NORTH OF THE ALPS

At this point in history Corelli published his first collection of church sonatas. They are a product of their time, a natural outgrowth of the church sonatas written by his predecessors and contemporaries, but imbued with a spirit that only the rare genius can give. They can be understood now from the standpoint of musical analysis, violinistic development, and their function as chamber music. We will look at them after we consider the development of the chamber sonata before Corelli in Germany and the chamber suite in England, Germany and Italy.

It was only natural that, as the popularity of Italian opera and other forms of music spread northward during the 17th century, wealthy Germans lured professional Italian musicians to their courts to perform this music. The Saxon court at Dresden, for example, was so successful at this that local German musicians soon complained about the large number of Italian instrumentalists there. Inevitably the Italians played the sonatas which they had played at home, and the German musicians, if they wanted to be noticed at these Italianized courts, had to follow the Italian lead. But not all Germans slavishly copied the foreigners; they began to develop their own indigenous sonatas.

Brief mention should be made of the sonatas of Johann Heinrich Schmelzer (ca. 1620-1680). From ca. 1643 until 1649 Schmelzer was an instrumentalist at St. Stephan's Cathedral in Vienna, and from 1649 until his death he served as court instrumentalist to

---

[89]Bonta, p. 210.

[90]The next chapters will consider this matter in much greater detail.

the Austrian emperor. In 1662 he published a collection of thirteen sonatas entitled *Sacro-Profanus Concentus Musicus Fidium Aliorumque Instrumentorum* (Nürnberg: 1662). He did not use the word "sonata," but they belong to this genre. They are ensemble works for instruments. Each piece is in one long movement subdivided into sections demarcated by tempo, meter, style, and figure. There are various scorings; the first sonata is for two trumpets, two violins, four violas (the fourth is in fact a bass) and continuo; the second sonata is polychoral, with the first choir consisting of a cornett and three trombones and the second of one violin, two violas, one bass viola, and continuo; most of the rest are only for four, five or six strings with continuo. The title itself demonstrates the ambiguity of purpose of these sonatas, and this is emphasized as well in the dedication. The sonatas serve both a sacred and secular function, and in either case they could certainly have been performed for the emperor as chamber music as well as orchestral music. Two years later Schmelzer published his *Sonatae Unarum Fidium, seu a Violino Solo* (Nürnberg: 1664). These six sonatas contain four ground bass sonatas (see above) and two others which in form resemble the *Concentus Musicus* sonatas. The latter are single-movement pieces in clearly delineated sections. One (no. 5) is in seven sections, one of which is immediately repeated. The other (no. 6) is in four sections of contrasting meter: $C - \frac{3}{2} - C - \frac{6}{4}$; the entire piece is contrapuntal, with imitation prevailing in the first section. What is interesting from the standpoint of the history of the "sonata" is the variety of styles and forms which Schmelzer included under that term in this collection. As has been observed above in the discussion of "variation," he included not only ground bass variations and sectionalized one-movement forms but even several dances (no. 4). In any case, Schmelzer's sonatas represent a fine development of chamber music at the Austrian court and firmly established a tradition for chamber music in Vienna, which will eventually blossom into the first and second Vienna Schools.

The principal contribution of Heinrich Biber to chamber music lies not in the *sonata da chiesa*, which we have been considering here, but in the chamber suite and, as a crucial immediate predecessor of Corelli, in the amalgamation of suite and *sonata da chi-*

esa concepts into the new *sonata da camera*. While Schmelzer represented the creation of the Viennese School of chamber music, Biber represented the creation of the Bohemian and provincial Austrian schools of chamber music. Schmelzer and Biber established the validity and importance of chamber music amid the ruling societies of Vienna, Bohemia and Salzburg, and even through social and political upheaval, chamber music has remained one of the most important musical phenomena of these societies.

THE PRE-CORELLI SUITE

In all countries of Europe collections containing dances appeared in both manuscript and print. Sometimes the dances are grouped by categories, i.e., all the allemands together, then all the courantes together, and so on; or danced pairs such as balletto - corrente are grouped together. In these practical collections the music was meant to accompany dancing, and as a result the dance music carefully follows the patterns associated with each particular dance choreography. On the other hand, there are other collections where a few different dances appear together, often with an introductory movement that is not a dance and sometimes with other non-dance movements as well. These suites were written not for dancing but for musical pleasure, and since no specific choreography was expected, the dances usually have irregular features. Such non-danced suites with both dances and non-dances seem to have originated in England and made their way in Germany and Austria before coming to Italy where, as we have seen above, they flourished from Marini on.

There were many suites, i.e., collections of dances, written by English composers during the 17th century, but the most important variety of English suite was that containing a fantasia as one of its movements alongside the dances.[91] The English Fantasia-Suite, devised first by Giovanni Coprario, consists of three movements: fantasia, alman, and corant or galliard. The useful term "fantazia-suite" or "fantasia-suite" was not used in the 17th century but coined by Helen Joy Sleeper in 1938. Other important composers

---

[91]Christopher D.S. Fields, "The English Consort Suite of the Seventeenth Century" (Oxford University Ph.D. dissertation, 1970).

include Lawes and Jenkins, and there are also a few examples by Christopher Simpson, Hingeston, John Birchensha, and Christopher Gibbons. Mathew Locke was the last important writer of fantasia-suites. All in all 133 suites of three or sometimes more movements survive. In addition there are over fifty pairs of fantasia and air or dance.

Coprario worked first for Edward Seymour, Earl of Hertford (ca. 1539-1621) and had there as pupils both Ferrabosco and William Lawes, with whom he certainly could have played his fantasia-suites. He was known at court from at least 1612, and could have been in the service of Charles I from as early as 1622 until his death in 1626. It is possible the king himself played these chamber works with Coprario, and it is certain the royal violinist, John Woodington, did so with the composer.[92]

Coprario wrote sixteen fantasia-suites for violin, bass viol and organ, and eight others for the same instruments with the addition of a second violin.[93] Occasionally the bass viol is independent of the organ, but in any case it remains simple. The organ was new in consort music at this time (ca. 1620) and became standard by 1640. It is not a continuo and the right hand is fully written out; in the fantasia movements the organ is often in counterpoint to the other instruments, while in the dances it is a series of chords. With Lawes the bass viol is freer, and he added divisions to all the viol parts.[94] The violin parts became technically more demanding, no doubt because he wrote for John Woodington and Davis Mell, two court violinists of considerable skill, and because he was aware of the new Italian violin virtuosi. Jenkins, who was the most prolific composer of fantasia-suites, substituted the corento for the galliard and added even more elaborate divisions to the viol (violin?) parts in the repeats of binary-form strains (thus, A + A' + B + B').[95] The

[92]Fields, pp. 48-50.

[93]Fields, "Consort Suite," pp. 46-102. Twenty-three suites by Coprario are in John Coprario, *Fantasia-Suites*, ed. Richard Charteris, in *Musica Britannica*, vol. xlvi (London: Stainer & Bell, 1910).

[94]Fields, "Consort Suite," pp. 103-129; and Lefkowitz, *Lawes*.

[95]Fields, "Consort Suite," pp. 129-190; Robert A. Warner, "The Fantasia in the Works of John Jenkins" (University of Michigan Ph.D. dissertation, 1951); and Andrew Ashbee, "The Four-Part Instrumental Compositions of John Jenkins" (University of [*continued*]

right hand of the organ often doubles the principle notes of the treble instrument or instruments, which are ornamented. Many fantasias open with the organ alone.

By the time of the Commonwealth the fantasia-suite was the basic type of English chamber music and remained so during the first years of the Restoration. Hingeston, who was Cromwell's composer, wrote many fantasia-suites for various combinations of viols or violins, bass viols, and organ.[96] In the mid-1660's Christopher Simpson added endless divisions and extended the dance by a number of repetitions (thus A + A' + B + B' + A" + A''' + B" + B''' + A'''' + A''''' + B'''' + B'''''). Simpson also added some spice to the history of English fantasia-suites by naming his collection of twelve "The Months"; beyond the titles for each month attached to each suite, however, there is no other programmatic element. Hingeston, pupil of Orlando Gibbons and teacher of Purcell, followed Coprario's type of fantasia-suite but allowed for the option of cornetts and sackbuts instead of violins; this scoring was unique in England for such pieces, though it was commonplace in Italy, and this fact perhaps reflects that they were to be played publicly as in Italy, not privately as elsewhere in England.[97] Christopher Gibbons wrote only ten fantasia-suites but they were extremely popular well into the 18th century.[98] His organ right hand is not written out, and, with his left hand almost identical to the bass viol part, the scoring takes a giant step toward the Italian continuo. This Gibbons also increased the difficulty of the violin part.

Matthew Locke wrote seven collections of consort music.[99] The first, *Little Consort* (1651; published by Playford in 1656), was written to teach boys how to play their instruments in consort, and

London Ph.D. dissertation, 1966). Holman, *Four and Twenty Fiddlers*, p. 280, points out that Jenkins was a close friend of the leading German virtuoso violinist Baltzar who first stormed England with his playing in 1655-1656.

[96]Fields, pp. 209-218.

[97]Emil W. Bock, "The String Fantasies of John Hingeston (ca.1610-1683)" (University of Iowa Ph.D. dissertation, 1956).

[98]Fields, "Consort Suites," pp. 232ff.

[99]Fields, "Consort Suites," pp. 247ff. Much of this music is in Matthew Locke, *Chamber Music*, ed. Michael Tilmouth, in *Musica Britannica*, vols. xxxi-xxxii (London: Stainer & Bell, 1971-1972).

the other collections were written for Locke's friends. Since Locke was "composer in the private musick" to Charles II after the Restoration and composer for the royal band of violinists, he should have had great influence on his contemporaries and immediate successors in England, but the fact is that foreign influences, at first from France and then from Italy, were about to drive out the English tradition of consort music and Locke's music with it. Locke was an innovator, however, and his music seems to have more importance for its impact on German suites. He was opposed to the extensive divisions of Simpson and others and promoted various new relationships among the movements. In several collections there are four-movement fantasia-suites (fantasia-corant-alman-sarabande or fantasia-corant-fantasia-saraband). The dances are invariably the courante and sarabande, with a jig in each of the first two suites. The six suites of "The Broken Consort I" are identical in the order and number of movements: fantasia - courante - ayre - sarabande, and the fantasias are as long and as sectionalized as in "The Flat Consort." No. 6 is unusual in that the courante has echoes (written-in "loud" and "soft") and the sarabande has written-out varied repeats. In some cases he placed the jig last and provided it with a slow coda that ends the entire suite; previously this was done only in final galliards. Fields has noted that Locke was concerned not only with the ordering of the dances within a suite to achieve maximum contrast but with the ordering of all the pieces within a collection to create tonal and scoring symmetry. Locke established the chamber suite for the Germans but brought the history of the English fantasia-suite to a virtual end.

The English influence on continental music at the end of the 16th century and until ca. 1660 has been well documented.[100] Particularly in Germany, though not there alone, English performers and the music of English composers were well known, and in the mid-17th century the mixture in Germany of traditional English ensemble music with new Italian Baroque styles brought about a peculiarly German chamber music.

---

[100]Paul E. Mueller, "The Influence and Activities of English Musicians on the Continent during the late Sixteenth and early Seventeenth Centuries" (Indiana University Ph.D. dissertation, 1954).

From the English *In Nomine* settings, late-16th-century continental composers had learned a type of theme and variations
structure. Through the popularity of English actor-musicians and
entertainers on the Continent during the end of the 16th and beginning of the 17th centuries, English dance tunes and styles were absorbed into the music of Germany, the Low Countries, and
Denmark in particular. The English "jig" or farce was so thoroughly enjoyed by the Continentals that the music for the jig (i.e.,
the jig dance) became everyone's favorite music. The dance suites
of the English composers Thomas Simpson (fl. 1610-1625) and
William Brade (1560-1630), both of whom spent most of their careers in Germany and Denmark, had decisive influence on the
leading composers of the early German chamber and orchestral
suite: Melchior Franck and Johann Schein. In particular, the collections of Brade published in Hamburg between 1607 and 1617,
seem to have given Schein models for his *Banchetto Musicale*
(1617). Brade wrote many suites pairing just pavan and galliard,
but in some suites in the 1609 *Newe ausserlesene Paduanen, Galliarden, Canzonen, Almand und Coranten* he added to that pair either an allemand or a courant.[101] This was the first time that three-
movement suites for ensemble were printed anywhere, but they
resemble the three-dance French ballet described by Praetorius in
1619 (see above). There is only a loose thematic connection between the head motives of the pavans and galliards and none between them and the allemands or courants in this 1609 volume, but
in Brade's 1614 collection, which has no three-movement suites,
the galliards often are variations of the preceding pavans; they are
more homophonic than the pavans, which often have imitation of
motives throughout. Schein combined the two three-dance suites
into a four-dance suite pavan + galliard + courant + allemand, and
then added to the allemand a final tripla that corresponds to English practice of adding a triple-meter dance to a duple (allemand)
dance. Brade also demonstrated to the Germans the mixture of the
canzona (his term for "fantasia") and dance (galliard) as a forerunner of the Coprario fantasia suite. Thomas Simpson also had an
introductory movement followed by dances. From both Brade and

---

[101]Calvin Raymond Huber, "Life and Music of William Brade" (University of North
Carolina Ph.D. dissertation, 1965).

Simpson the Germans learned to appreciate the amateur viol ensemble in preference to the ensemble of professional winds.[102] The variation suite involving more than just two movements, however, was not an English phenomenon but a German one, and Haussmann, Demantius and Hassler kept their German identity in this as well as in the overall style of intradas. Later, from the English fantasia suite, mid-17th-century continental composers learned a new multi-movement structure featuring a collection of dances preceded by a substantial prelude or fantasia. Reusner's *Delitiae Testudinis* (1667) for lute and Becker's *Musicalische Frülings-Früchte* (Hamburg, 1668) were the first published suite collections in Germany that have the order of movements allemand-courante-sarabande-gigue preceded by a pavan or a sonata. They come more than a decade after John Playford's publications of the same type of music in England, and there is every reason to believe that the Germans copied the English.

Heinrich Biber, in his *Sonatae, violino solo* (Nürnberg: 1681), was the first composer in Europe to use the term "sonata" in a publication to refer to a *whole* multi-movement work consisting of an introductory movement followed by some dances. Each sonata consists of a prelude-like movement followed by various combinations of dances, ground bass variations, and aria variations. The prelude movement is often a succession of written-out figurations in the solo violin over one unaltered chord in the continuo; in no. 3, this prelude falls into eight sections contrasting in figuration, tempo and sometimes also meter. Commonly the sonata ends with

---

[102]Kassel Mus.ms.72, written 1601-1603, with 86 dances a5 for trombones, cornetti, fiffero, and dolzano (a low, double-reed instrument), is the most significant source for English influence on German ensemble dance music c.1600 and demonstrates the predominance of wind ensembles at the time. Brade and Simpson, however, published viol ensemble dance music just a few years later. At first the Englishmen compromise with the German taste for winds. Christian Hildebrandt's *Erster Theil/Ausserlesener Paduanen und Galliarden* (Hamburg: 1607), which contains 31 pieces, 16 by Brade, is written "for use by all instruments, especially viols"; this optional scoring seems to be a gentle approach to changing German chamber music performance from winds to strings. Brade's *Newe ausserliche Paduanen* (Hamburg: 1609) gives no specific instrumentation, but his volumes of 1614 and 1617 give viols as the prefered instrument. Simpson's *Tafel Consort* (1621), on the other hand, is scored exclusively for two treble viols, one tenor viol, one bass viol, and basso continuo (the first time the Italian basso continuo occurs in German dance collections). Cf. Mueller, pp. 19, 37, 46 and 138, and Huber.

a movement that is similar in style and tempo to the opening movement. Only some of the dances and arias are in binary form. Usually, in each sonata, either one aria or one dance appears, often with doubles or variations. A few years prior to the *Sonatae*, Biber also completed a series of suites commonly referred to today as the "Mystery" or "Rosary" Sonatas but not entitled "sonatas" by Biber. The most famous features of this collection, again for violin solo and continuo, are the use of scordatura and the programmatic elements. In this collection most suites begin with a prelude of some sort, and sometimes (e.g., nos. 9 and 13) the prelude movement by itself is entitled "Sonata." This corresponds to the practice already established by Reusner and Becker. The sonata is sectionalized (in no. 13 there are four sections differing in meter and motives) but without any repetition of the sections. The dances (mostly allemands, sarabands, courants, gavottes, and gigues) are in binary form and often are followed by doubles or variations.

In his *Harmonia Artificiosa-Ariosa* (published posthumously in 1712) for two treble instruments and continuo, the suites followed the structure of the "Mystery Sonatas" but their style was now much simplified. Whereas the solo sonatas and suites were designed to show off the uncanny virtuosity of the violinist (Biber was arguably the best violinist of the 17th century), the duo sonatas seem much more inclined to develop the partnership of two equal artists that we expect in intimate chamber music. Biber, who was active at the Salzburg Cathedral from 1670 until his death in 1704, probably performed the sonatas at the end of services for the congregation; there is no record of Biber having toured as a concertizing virtuoso.[103] It seems contradictory that Biber's "Mystery Sonatas" were performed in church and are clearly religious program music, yet they consist mostly of dances (or purely secular types). On the other hand, another collection by Biber, published at the same time as the "Mystery Sonatas," is entitled *Sonatae, Tam Aris, quam Auli servientes* (Salzburg: 1676). Here the pieces are specifically termed "sonatas" and contain no dances or variations whatsoever, yet the title itself indicates that the works "serve both altar and chamber" (i.e., sacred and secular) functions. These seven

---

[103]Elias Dann, "Biber," in *The New Grove Dictionary*, 6th ed., vol. ii (1980), pp. 678-682.

sonatas, for various scorings up to eight instruments and continuo and sometimes adding trumpets to the strings, have barely definable movements; they are more like canzonas with numerous sections which differ in figuration, tempo, and meter. Sonata no. 5, despite the immediate repetition of each section, is more unified than the other sonatas.

While the Germans developed their ideas of suite under English influence, the Italians or more specifically Corelli learned this kind of piece from the Germans. As we have seen with the development of the "balletto" into the da camera suite from Marini to Cazzati, Legrenzi and Vitali, there were many Italian suites that pre-dated Corelli and some fusion of dance and art styles (see above). What seems to be missing until Corelli, however, was the use of an introductory prelude before the series of dances. This is perhaps what Legrenzi implied in his Opus 4 chamber sonatas (1656), each of which consists of only one sonata-like movement. As Selfridge-Field has suggested, the one movement may have been followed in performance by a group of dances from later in the same collection.[104] Marini's *Sonate, Symphonie, Canzoni* (1629) already paired balletti and correnti, and in his Opus 22 (1655) he had a "sonata da camera" in five movements (Entrada Grave, Balletto Allegro, Gagliarda, Corrente, and Retirata). When Rosenmüller arrived in Venice in 1658 to be a trombonist at San Marco, he had already published two instrumental collections in his native Germany.[105] Once in Venice, he continued to publish, including eleven sinfonias in 1667, most consisting of three introductory non-dance movements slow-fast-slow or slow-slow-fast, followed by dances (allemands, correntes, and sarabands). Despite this German example, Bononcini's suites of Opus 5 (1671) combine only dances, the allemand, corrente and sarabande, while his Opus 9 (1675) and Opus 12 (1678) suites combine the allemand and the aria, respectively, with the corrente. With Corelli the introductory prelude is firmly established in Italy, and in a few of his works (Opus 3, no. 12; Opus 4, nos. 6 and 10; and Opus 5, no. 1)

---

[104]Selfridge-Field, p. 166.
[105]*Ibid.*, p. 170.

he begins to approach the northern concept of an elaborate, multi-sectional introduction.

The chamber sonata and suite were firmly established during the second half of the 17th century as the principal genres of chamber music. They provided for the performer a variety of styles and techniques as well as aesthetic possibilities. The ambiguity of performance settings between the church and secular chamber gave the chamber musician room to experience a range in emotional utterances. But the rising standard of virtuosic possibilities on the instruments, especially the violin, raised an important new danger to the integrity of the chamber music idea. Chamber music requires a seriousness of purpose both in the composition and execution of the music, yet virtuosity for the sake of virtuosity became too tempting, particularly for some Italian masters of technique. As we will see, during the late 17th century and throughout the 18th, French intellectuals attacked the entire genre of sonatas for its espousal of virtuosity rather than seriousness (they used moralistic criteria in their judgment). The English wrestled with this problem as ever increasing numbers of virtuosi arrived in London from Italy to show off their skills. The Germans, caught between their love of the Italian sound and their respect for French thought, ultimately experienced a synthesis of the best of both aesthetics through the works of Haydn, Mozart and Beethoven. But that was a century away. What was needed in Europe by 1680 was the firm establishment of the chamber sonata and suite as serious art forms in the work of a master whom everyone could respect and emulate, and fortunately this happened first with Corelli, then with Bach and Handel.

SUMMARY OF CHAMBER MUSIC BEFORE CORELLI

Significant genres of chamber music existed before Corelli in 17th-century Europe. Some of these did not survive beyond the 1680's, such as the canzona, the fantasia, and the fantasia suite, but others continued to develop into the new Corellian age, such as the suite, the sonata, and the variation. While Italian musicians were extremely important, English and German musicians were equally so. Italian virtuosi, especially on the violin, set the standards upon which the violinist Corelli would build, and the English violists and keyboardists, some of whom were also formidable virtuosi, provided the first and some of the finest examples of intimate ensemble music. The Germans imported both Italian and English masters and soon synthesized the different foreign styles into their own, peculiarly German style, which would lead in the 18th century to Bach and Handel. The 17th-century musicians needed compositions in which to demonstrate their skills for the general public, the important patrons of the day, and their close circle of friends and colleagues; the types of chamber music they wrote served all three audiences. The types of pieces written for chamber music continually evolved; sometimes they even moved in and out of the intimate settings of chamber music as evinced by the ambiguous scoring in many cases between chamber (a setting for one instrument per part) and orchestral (a setting for two or more instruments per part). In Italy, where public performance was first firmly established, public chamber music was an accepted fact and allowed for virtuosic display and sometimes louder instruments. In England before 1672, when John Banister and Thomas Britton began public concerts, chamber music was a private affair, but thereafter, especially when Purcell wrote Italian sonatas, chamber music became as public an affair as in Italy, with all its consequences. Thus even in the 17th century, when chamber music was supposed to be distinct in function from concert music, the distinction became obscure when pieces composed as intimate chamber music were performed in non-intimate concert halls or churches. The dichotomy between public and private carries over from the early 17th century to today and serves as a chief problem in the characterization of chamber music on whatever level.

The existence of written and played chamber music throughout Europe in the century before Corelli's Opus 1 is well documented. With the English fantasia and fantasia-suite and the Italian solo, duo and trio sonatas there were prolific genres of written chamber music of the highest artistic level, and with the amateur and professional chamber groups in England, Germany, Holland and Italy chamber music performances flourished. While the idea of chamber music, i.e., solistic instrumental ensemble music of an intimate and serious character, frequently existed, there was also the creation of other genres of music that shared many attributes of true chamber music but lacked one or two basic ingredients. Some of these genres—especially the public church canzona and the Austrian and German orchestral suites—will later be played as chamber music as the concept of intimacy goes through changes.

CHAPTER III

CHAMBER MUSIC OF THE HIGH BAROQUE

Once the two basic genres of sonata were established as the nearly exclusive norms of chamber music (certainly by 1680), many chamber music composers concentrated on refinement of style and the expansion of instrumental technique. The norms of church and chamber sonata for one, two or three soloists with or without basso continuo were continually reapplied to works performed in private quarters or in small halls for a limited number of persons; the location of the performances earlier in the century had helped to establish the norms but were now no longer causing the creation of new norms. Within the established norms, however, some composers were able to arrive at original solutions, and with Corelli, Vivaldi, Handel and Bach chamber music composition reached a supreme level which it has been able to equal only a few times since. Eventually the distinction between church and chamber fell apart since both kinds of sonatas were performed in the same location and there was no longer the need for such a distinction.[1] In Italy the academy was firmly established by 1680, and it was in the academy during the next sixty years where chamber music had its primary location. There were different kinds of academies, such as those devoted exclusively to music (like the Accademia Filharmonica in Bologna) and those where music was only a side but

---

[1]In San Marco in Venice, for example, where church sonatas and before them canzonas had been so important during the 17th century, the practice of the solo violin accompanying the elevation of the eucaristic bread was abolished in 1692. The last two violinists to so perform were Francesco Donaducci and Antonio Fedeli. Principal violinists as leaders of the orchestra were still on the payroll, however, until the death of Antonio Nazzari in 1786. Cf. Francesco Caffi, *Storia della Musica Sacra nella già Cappella Ducale di S. Marco in Venezia (dal 1318 al 1797)*, ed. Elvidio Surian, in *Studi di Musica Veneta*, vol. 10 (Florence: Leo S. Olschki, 1987), p. 415.

regular feature (like the Accademia della Cavallerizza in Venice, devoted to equestrian matters, where a concert was held once a week,[2] and the Arcadian Academy in Rome, devoted primarily to literary matters, where musical performances often opened and closed the meetings). These academies were held in the private palaces of nobility and were attended by the local nobility, highly regarded local musicians, and foreign dignitaries. In some cases the nobility participated themselves in the performances, and in Venice the leading patrician families (e.g., Giustiniani, Cavalli, Contarini, Venieri, Mocanigli, Morosini, and Marcello) enthusiastically played chamber music at home with the best local artists.[3] The Italian academies were copied throughout Europe, though often under different conditions which led ultimately to different results. In Paris, Hamburg, and London the dissolution of the old distinction between church and chamber music is at least partly attributable to a new set of conditions imposed by another increasingly popular location for chamber music in the early 18th century: the public, rather than private hall.

ARCANGELO CORELLI

Corelli was active in Bologna from 1666 to at least 1670 (when, as we have noted in Chapter II, he was admitted to the Accademia Filharmonica there) and possibly to as late as 1675 when he was already established in Rome.[4] During these Bologna years he had ample opportunity to meet, play with, and study the compositions of Bologna's leading chamber music composers such as G.M. Bononcini. His studies with Leonardo Bruguoli and especially Giovanni Benvenuti enabled Corelli to perfect his violin technique and, more importantly, to develop a style of sonata com-

---

[2]Caffi, pp. 509-510. Cf. Michele Maylender, *Storia delle Accademis d'Italia*, 5 vols. (Bologna: L. Cappelli, 1930).

[3]Caffi, pp. 494 and 496.

[4]The biographical information on Corelli is derived from Michael Talbot, "Corelli," *The New Grove Dictionary of Music and Musicians* (London: Macmillan, 1975), vol. IV, pp. 768-774; Max Lütolf, *Arcangelo Corelli: historische-kritische Gesamtausgabe der musikalischen Werke*, vol. I (Laaber-Verlag, 1987), pp. 17-19; Jürg Stenzl, *Arcangelo Corelli: historisch-kritische Gesamtausgabe der musikalischen Werke*, vol. II (Laaber-Verlag, 1986), p. 15; and Marc Pincherle, *Corelli: his Life, his Work*, trl. Hubert E.M. Russell (New York: Norton, 1956).

position that was more musical than virtuosic.[5] His first published sonata, written probably while he was still in Bologna and printed in *Sonate a Violino e Violoncello de vari autori*, complied by Bruguoli (Bologna: ca. 1665-1680), shows him rigidly adhering to the slow-fast-slow-fast form of the "da chiesa" sonata and giving the "basso" accompaniment merely secondary importance. Yet Corelli did not make a virtuosic show piece out of the violin part; the line is simple and lyric. Most of the seven sonatas in this collection are virtuosic, but Corelli's and that by Carlo Mazzolini, also a student of Benvenuti, are much more concerned with musical expression. It is this seriousness of purpose which Corelli first expressed here and which dominated his later publications that set a standard for the future of chamber music.

From 1679 to 1689 Corelli was associated in Rome with the self-exiled Queen Christiana of Sweden, whose maestri di cappella at the time included Alessandro Scarlatti and Bernardo Pasquini. At her palazzo Riario and elsewhere she sponsored the most important private concerts in Rome, whose audience was the leading lay and religious leaders of the city and many foreign dignitaries. During the first years in her service Corelli was "a chamber musician and was busy composing sonatas for her first 'academy'." His reputation for sonatas was such that he received outside commissions as well, and, most importantly, began the publication in 1681 of his famous collections of sonatas (the first of which is dedicated to the Queen). From 1682 until his death in 1713 Corelli had at his side Matteo Fornari, his former pupil, who played second violin to Corelli's first. In 1684 the two violinists began regular playing at Cardinal Pamphili's academies held on Sundays at the Cardinal's Pallazzo al Corso. These academies, which featured operas and oratorios as well as chamber music, were a focal point of Roman musical life, and it was perhaps at these that Corelli's first set of chamber trios, published in 1685 as Opus 2 and dedicated to Pamphili, were first heard. The relationship with the Cardinal was so strong that from 1689 to 1690 Corelli actually lived in his home and there performed regularly with Fornari and the Spanish cellist Giovanni Lorenzo Lulier ("Giovannino del Violone"). In 1690,

---

[5]Cf. Adriano Cavicchi, "Corelli e il violinismo bologuese," in *Studi Corelliani*, ed. Cavicchi, Oscar Mischiati, and Pierluigi Petrobelli (Florence: Olschki, 1972), pp. 33-47.

Arcangelo Corelli (1653-1713). Oxford University, Department of Music.

after Pamphili's departure from Rome, Corelli, together with Fornari and Lulier, went to live in the palace of Cardinal Pietro Ottoboni, "whose academies were regularly held on Monday
evenings." In 1684 Corelli, along with Alessandro Scarlatti, joined
the Roman Congregazione dei Virtuosi di S. Cecilia, whose head
he became in 1700. In 1706 he joined Pasquini and A. Scarlatti in
the Arcadian Academy where under the name "Arcomelo Eriman-
teo" he frequently played. Here, too, he met Handel in 1707 and
played in Handel's oratorio "Il trionfo del tempo e del disinganno"
that May. But by now his technique was slipping (Handel found it
wanting), and he retired in 1708. That Corelli's many trio and solo
sonatas had a great impact on future generations of chamber musicians is obvious; but he was equally important as the teacher of the
next generation of chamber musicians (such as Carbonelli, Cas-
trucci, Fornari, Gasparini, Geminiani, and Somis in Italy, Anet in
France, Herrando in Spain, Störl in Germany, and Ravenscroft in
England; he may also have taught Bonporti, Locatelli, Mascitti,
and Mossi).

Corelli did not invent the sonata da chiesa or the sonata da
camera, nor was he the first to draw a distinction between the two.
All this had occurred well before Corelli's time. Corelli's first four
opus numbers, however, firmly codified the sonata norms for his
time and for the next generation. Corelli arrived on the scene just
as the two genres became distinct in everyone's mind so that he
could summarize in encyclopedic fashion all that each signified; at
the same time, in a musical language that is elegant in its modesty,
he transcended those genres and even blurred some of the distinction between them.[6] While the distinction between so-called "da
chiesa" sonatas and "da camera" sonatas is not clearly maintained
in Corelli's Opus V, these two types were at least the starting point
for his oeuvre and were perceived by his contemporaries and immediate heirs as the norms. More important to the future of chamber music than genre, however, was Corelli's style of chamber
playing, which while violinistic never succumbed to sheer brilliance and always gave full attention to lyricism. It was this new

---

[6]Ludwig Finscher, "Corelli und die 'Corellisierenden' Sonaten Telemanns," in *Studi
Corelliani*, pp. 75-76.

attainment of an ideal of beauty which set the standard for future chamber composers.

Opus I (1681) and III (1689) are each collections of twelve trio sonatas for two violins, a cello or arcileuto, with basso continuo for organ. The cello is not merely an accompaniment to the organ but a full partner with the two violins. Both collections were very popular; the first went through forty editions by the end of the 18th century and the second thirty-eight. Corelli did not use the designation "da chiesa" in any edition of these works until after 1700, no doubt because these sonatas were not intended for church performance but from the beginning for performance in the same secular settings as the "da camera" sonatas. In other words, by 1681 the designations "da chiesa" and "da camera" no longer specified just location of performance but also style and genre as well. The distinction between the two in terms of location goes back to the mid-16th century in vocal music, and both sonatas and canzonas for "da chiesa" and "da camera" were published in the 1630's and 1640's by Merula and Neri. By the time Marini used the terms in his 1655 volume, it was an accepted fact in Italian instrumental music that "da camera" meant dances, whether singly or in pairs, and "da chiesa" meant imitative, contrapuntal pieces in the canzona tradition. Corelli accepted this distinction without using the label "da chiesa," though he did specifically use the term "da camera" for the suites of Opera II and IV where both the genre "da camera" and the location "da camera" are still relevant. Apparently before 1700 the terms were used often enough to refer to locale as well as genre that Corelli avoided "da chiesa" to avoid misplacing the works, but after 1700 Corelli and/or his publishers inserted "da chiesa" on the title pages of his Opus I and III because by then the term unambiguously referred to the genre.

Five sonatas in Opus I and nine in Opus III are in the standardized "da chiesa" form slow-fast-slow-fast, but more than a third are not. Some of these are not in four movements (e.g., Opus I, No. 7 is in three and Opus III, No. 12 is in five), and in others where there are four movements, there are other arrangements of tempos (e.g., Opus I, No. 4 is fast-slow-fast-fast and Opus III, No. 10 is fast-fast-slow-fast). In some final fast movements there is a suggestion of a gigue (e.g., Opus I, No. 2 and Opus III, Nos. 6 and

7); the rhythm is a fast $\frac{3}{8}$, $\frac{6}{8}$ or $\frac{3}{4}$ and there may be binary form. This, of course, blurs the distinction between "da chiesa" and "da camera."

Corelli sometimes combined the idea of the multi-movement sonata, which had been developing for much of the 17th century, with the multi-sectional sonata movement, which had its origin in the multi-sectional canzona. While some movements combine just two contrasting sections within a single movement (e.g., Opus I, No. 9, movement 2, and Opus III, No. 5, movement 1), others are more complicated. Opus I, No. 9, movement 1 has three Allegro sections of which the theme of the third is the inversion of the theme of the first and the second has an Adagio subsection at the end. Opus I, No. 5, movement 3 has seven sections alternating slow and fast.

Multi-sectioned movements are not the only sign of the canzona origins of the church sonata. Every one of Corelli's twenty-four trio church sonatas has at least one highly contrapuntal, imitative movement. The fast movements are usually contrapuntal and some slow ones are as well. Another link to the canzona is the frequent use of a brief, slow ending to a fast movement, which we also encountered in later fantasias as well as canzonas.

The chamber sonatas of Opus IV (1694) are dedicated to Cardinal Ottoboni and written specifically for his academies (so stated on the title page), and it has been assumed that the Opus II chamber sonatas (1685), dedicated to Pamphili, were composed for his academies as well. The chamber sonatas differ from the church sonatas not only in form but also in scoring. While the church sonatas include both a cello or archlute and a continuo of organ, the chamber sonatas are written for either a cello *or* a harpsichord. Since we know that Corelli wrote for Fornari and Lulier to play with himself, the original performances of these sonatas were for string trio. It is only when the chamber sonatas were published in Northern Europe that Corelli's original intentions were thwarted to both cello *and* harpsichord.

Twenty-three of the pieces in the two da camera volumes are suites or collections of dances, while the last "sonata" of Opus II is a ciaccona. Nine sonatas in Opus II and all the sonatas in Opus IV open with a Prelude, an idea which Corelli probably got from Muffat and the Germans who, in turn, copied the English fantasia-suite. The preludes are in a slow tempo, usually in an open form (four are in binary form), and frequently in a contrapuntal style. Two preludes in Opus IV suggest canzona origins since they are tri-sectional (slow-fast-slow) with contrasting meters. The dances feature the allemanda in all the sonatas of Opus II and in some of Opus IV, correntes, a few sarabandas (sometimes Tempo di Sara-banda) and gavottas (sometimes Tempo di Gavotta), and the giga at the end of most of the sonatas. All the dances except two gavot-tas are in binary form. Although the dances are usually homo-phonic, Corelli often had the two violins imitating each other at the beginning of sections or during the course of passage work. The cello is extremely active, sometimes partakes in the imitation, and often has much more motion than the two violins; this is no doubt because Corelli was writing not only for himself and Fornari but also for Lulier.

Just as the church sonatas have some elements of dance (especially a giga-like movement at the end of some of them), so the "da camera" sonatas have some elements of "da chiesa." For example, the generous use of counterpoint and even imitation in some dance movements is the incorporation of a specifically church style within the dance. Also, the use of the Preludio, with its open form and imitative style, as well as some other slow, mod-estly contrapuntal, unnamed movements, are an intrusion of non-dance movements into the suite.

The twelve "solo" sonatas of Opus V, dedicated to the Elec-tress Sophie Charlotte of Brandenburg, are actually duet sonatas for solo violin and cello or harpsichord. The collection was divided by Corelli into two parts, of which the first is six "sonatas" and the second five suites and a setting of "La Folia." Despite this separa-tion of the two genres of sonata, the two types—da chiesa and da camera—merge to the point where there is, in several cases, no distinction at all between them. It is probably for this reason that Corelli this time avoided both terms altogether.

None of the first six "church" sonatas is in the "standard" four movements. All begin slow-fast and end fast. Four of them go slow-fast-fast-slow-fast and the other two slow-fast-slow-fast-fast. One movement—the first movement of No. 1—bears an especially strong resemblance to the old canzona; it is multi-sectional, with a recapitulation of each of the opening three sections varied tonally and, in the third case, extended. All the second movements also hark back to the canzona, in that all have a brief adagio section at the end. The final movements of Nos. 3, 4 and 5, on the other hand, are binary; while the first two suggest a dance, the third was actually called "giga: by Corelli. Only one other movement in the first six sonatas—the first in No. 5—is binary.

By contrast, nearly every movement of the suites (nos. 7-11) is in binary form, including three of the preludes that open each suite. What follows the preludios varies, and as a result there are some instances when the distinction between church and chamber fades. Nos. 7 and 8 are in four movements (in this regard alone more "da chiesa" than any of the actual "da chiesa" sonatas): preludio - corrente - sarabanda - giga, or preludio - allemanda - sarabanda - giga; and No. 10 is in five (in this regard alone more like the "da chiesa" sonatas of Opus 5 than any of the other suites): preludio - allemanda - sarabanda - gavotta - giga. Nos. 7 and 8, however, despite all the movements being in binary form, superficially resemble the overall structure of the normal "da chiesa" sonata more than any of the first six sonatas in Opus 5 in that their patterns of movements result in the typical slow-fast-slow-fast "da chiesa" pattern. But more significantly Nos. 9 (preludio - allegro - tempo di gavotta) and 11 (preludio - allegro - adagio - vivace - gavotta) each contain only one named dance and resemble sonata No. 5 (which has another binary movement besides the final giga). Both Nos. 9 and 11 also contain a fast second movement that, in canzona fashion, ends with an adagio coda, and since this occurs in all six sonatas of part 1 of Opus 5, these six and nos. 9 and 11 are ever more closely allied.

The final piece of Opus 5 is of another genre—variations over a ground bass—which we have seen in various guises in Chapter II. It is, without question, the most famous and influential ground bass variations ever written, surpassing even the Ciconnia of Opus 2. After Corelli published his Opus 2 and especially his Opus 5, there were many imitations, and not surprisingly a set of twelve chamber ensemble pieces (such as Vivaldi's Opus I) or even six (such as John Ravenscroft's Opus II) often had to include a single set of variations over La Folia or Ciconnia.

CHAMBER MUSIC IN CORELLI'S ORBIT

By the 1690's most of Corelli's contemporaries clearly distinguished "da camera" from "da chiesa" through the scoring.[7] Chamber sonatas were accompanied by harpsichord continuo and church sonatas by the organ. Most church sonatas published by Veracini, Bernardi, T.A. Vitali, Ruggieri and Caldara during this decade are in four movements with the tempo pattern slow-fast-slow-fast, though all of them also occasionally have other possibilities, especially three movements with the tempo pattern fast-slow-fast. This latter form was even preferred by Jacchini. It was the young Tomaso Albinoni (1671-1750; see below), however, who insisted, without exception, on the traditional slow-fast-slow-fast pattern in his *Suonate a trè, doi Violini, e Violoncello col Basso per l"Organo* (1694) and thereby firmly established this as "da chiesa" form. Although a small number of binary-form movements do appear in the twelve sonatas of this collection, Albinoni unambiguously set the parameters for what has been known ever since as the traditional church sonata.

There is somewhat more confusion about the da camera sonata. An extreme but revealing case, Veracini's Opus 2 is entitled *Sonate da camera a Violino Solo* (?1694) and is scored for violin with either harpsichord or violone. Except for the scoring option of harpsichord, there is nothing "da camera" about these works. There are no dances, though most of the final movements are binary, and there is typical da chiesa polyphony. Six of the ten sonatas are slow-fast-slow-fast and resemble Albinoni's church sonatas more than any chamber sonatas except, perhaps, Corelli's Opus V, No. 8. Showing that this collection was not unintentional, Veracini published his Opus 3 *Sonate da camera a due, Violino, e Violone, ò Arcileuto, col Basso per il Cimbalo* (1696) with all ten sonatas slow-fast-slow-fast and in all other regards like Albinoni's church

---

[7]Most of the following collections are described and discussed by Willi Apel, "Studien über die frühe Violinmusik 1691-1700," *Archiv für Musikwissenschaft*, xxxviii (1981), 110-141.

sonatas. Thus, for Veracini in the 1690's, the sole distinguishing factor between church and chamber sonata was the presence or potential presence of the organ or harpsichord.

The brilliant cellist Giuseppe Jacchini's Opus 2 *Sonate da camera a trè, e quattro stromenti, col Violoncello obligato* (1695), however, was not even "da camera" by scoring. There is no harpsichord or organ mentioned, and the pieces are a blend of some church and some chamber elements. Only three movements in the ten sonatas are dances (an aria and two correntes). The other fast movements are sometimes more homophonic, sometimes more fugal. Four sonatas have the movements in "da chiesa" slow-fast-slow-fast, while five are fast-slow-fast (the tenth sonata is slow-slow-fast). There is no distinction between the sonatas in this collection and those in his Opus I, which do not have the title "da camera" and do not have either organ or harpsichord. Since dance movements are so scarce in Opus I, it has automatically been included under church sonatas, and should we remove "da camera" from the title of Opus II, then Opus II could also be classified as "da chiesa." The only remaining possibility to explain Jacchini's use of "da camera" for this collection is that that was where he intended the pieces to be performed, rather than in church. Thus for him as well as for Veracini, location and only location was still the determining factor in how a chamber composition was classified. The gradual substitution of form and style over location to signify a particular genre, which is evident in Corelli's sonatas and in those of other contemporaries, is absent here.

Most others in the 1690's, however, recognized dance as the chief ingredient of "da camera" sonatas. Bartolomeo Bernardi, for example, had twelve suites in his *Sonate da camera a trè, due Violini, e Violoncello col Violone ò Cimbalo* (1692). Each one opens with a slow "Prelidio" and follows with a series of dances: "Alemanda" (fast, except for a largo example in No. 6) - Slow - Gavota, Giga or Sarabanda (always fast, except for a largo Corrente in No. 7). Thus, although in most sonatas the overall form is slow-fast-slow-fast, which resembles the traditional church sonata, the prevalence of dances as well as the use of the harpsichord define the "da camera" nature of the collection. Tomaso Antonio Vitali's Opus 3 *Sonate da camera a trè, due Violini, e Violone* (1695) also consists of suites, ten of which are three dances preceded in some cases by a preludio. Carlo Antonio Marini (b.1671) did not use the term "da camera" in his Opus 2 (1692) and Opus 5 (1700), but these are clearly in the "da camera" fold. Opus 2 *Ballettii Correnti, Gighe e Minuetti diverii a trè, due Violini, e Violoncello, ò spinetta* (which survives only in the second violin part) consists of nothing but dances, while Opus 5 *Suonate alla francese a trè* (only the first violin part survives) has an overture opening each of the twelve suites, followed by corrente, gig, gavotta or similar dances. The suites in Buoni's Opus 1 (1693) and Opus 3 (1693; composed ca. 1670), which begin with preludes, are further examples of the emphasis on dance in the "da camera" sonatas of this time.

Corelli's influence on Italian chamber music continued past the turn of the century especially with the solo sonatas of Opus 5. Corelli's pupils circulated far and wide, and it was in their hands that the immediate future of chamber music lay. They played Corelli's sonatas to an ever-broadening and appreciative audience, and they added their own new sonatas based on his. How this happened in Turin, Venice and foreign countries follows, but first let us consider the case of Alessandro Scarlatti, Corelli's lifelong associate.

Alessandro Scarlatti's interest in chamber music dates from late in his career, long after Corelli's death. He was first and foremost a composer of operas, cantatas, and vocal church music. There are, however, some unusual chamber works of his which, while not having as great an immediate impact as Corelli's, nonetheless are historically important. Apparently under the influence of the great flutist Johann Joachim Quantz, whom he met in 1724, Scarlatti wrote in Naples in 1725 (just before he died) a set of seven sonatas for flute, two violins, cello and continuo.[8] They are in four or five movements, one of which is a "fuga." The movements contrast in meter, tempo, and thematic material, and in the four sonatas in the minor some of the internal slow movements also contrast in tonality. One movement in Sonata No. 4 is in two

---

[8]In "Concerti di flauto, violini, violetta e basso," Naples, S. Pietro a Majella Conservatory, Music Library, ms. 38.3.13. Published in *Sette Sonate per Flauto, Archi, e Basso Continuo*, ed. Luciano Bettarini, in *Collezione Settecentesca Bettarini*, no. 1 (Milan: Casa Editrice Nazionalmusic, [1969]).

sections: "veloce" followed by "lento." Only two of the thirty-one movements are in binary form. The continuo takes full part in the counterpoint in most movements, but in some cases it also acts as an harmonic bass and even pedal point. In two adagio movements the bass drops out. The variety of texture within a single movement begins to point to the new transitional period that flourished during the middle half of the 18th century.

In addition to these flute sonatas and five others for from one to three flutes with or without violins and continuo[9], Scarlatti wrote four sonatas for two violins, viola and cello and three sonatas for cello and continuo. The former have been heralded as the earliest string quartets,[10] but they are only among several immediate precursors of the string quartet (see next chapter). The three violoncello sonatas are each in four movements slow - fast - slow - fast, with the fast movements shorter and in binary form. The third movement is in a related key and acts more as a transition between the two fast movements than as its own creature. The solo violoncello part dominates the texture while the continuo accompanies throughout. There is no imitation, but on the other hand the continuo, in its humble way, is in counterpoint to the soloist.

One of the last pupils of Corelli was Giovanni Battista Somis (1686-1763), who spent nearly his entire life in Turin. His first teacher was his father, a court violinist in Turin, and while still a child Somis was already admitted to the court orchestra. He studied with Corelli in Rome from 1703 to 1706 and possibly also with Vivaldi in Venice,[11] and in turn he was the teacher of Giardini, Guignon, Pugnani, Chabran and Leclair. The link from Corelli to mid-18th-century chamber music of the French school is largely

---

[9]In the Staatsbibliothek in Munich; see Grout, "Scarlatti," in *The New Grove Dictionary of Music and Musicians*, vol. XVI, p. 557. The sonata for three flutes and continuo in F Major, in Münster/W.: Episcopal Museum, Santini Collection, printed as *Quartettino*, ed. Waldemar Woehl (London/New York/Frankfurt: C. F. Peters, 1940), is far less interesting than the seven sonatas discussed here. It is in three movements adagio - allegro - minuet, of which the second and third are in binary form; there is little imitation or counterpoint and much writing in parallel thirds and sixths.

[10]Edward J. Dent, "The Earliest String Quartets," in *The Monthly Musical Record*, xxxiii (1903), 202-204.

[11]Boris Schwarz, "Somis," in *The New Grove Dictionary of Music and Musicians*, XVII, 476.

through Somis, though as we shall observe below, Corelli's pupils were already performing in Paris from the beginning of the century. Somis himself performed at the Concert Spirituel in 1733.

Somis's written chamber music—all da camera—consists of four volumes of *Sonate a violino e violoncello o cembalo* (Opus I, 1717; Opus II, 1723, Opus IV, 1726, and Opus VI, 1734), a set of trio sonatas *Trattenimenti per camera* for two violins and continuo (Opus V, 1733), and sonatas for violoncello and continuo.[12] Most of the sonatas are in three movements with the pattern Adagio - Allegro - Allegro. Opus I and II are virtually the same in form and overall structure, but while the first, dedicated to Maria Giovanna Battista, Duchess of Savoy, is written for an amateur violinist of average ability, the latter, dedicated to Vitorio Amedeo, King of Sicily, is written for a virtuoso of the first rank. Opus II includes many extensive passages of double stops, often in counterpoint, and the violinist is expected to possess a great deal of dexterity. It is likely that Somis composed his first set of sonatas for his pupils and perhaps for members of the Turin court whose abilities were somewhat proscribed, and that the second set was for his own use and for the use of his best students who would soon become famous virtuosi. The sonatas are all labeled "da camera," yet although each fast movement is a dance in binary form, rarely did Somis name the particular dance. In his sonatas for violoncello solo and violoncello accompaniment Somis maintained the same forms and overall structure even though now he omitted the term "da camera." We have already seen that Scarlatti's sonatas for violoncello and continuo are simple da camera works, though in four movements, and possibly these were in Somis's mind when he added to this particular repertory. In many of Somis's violoncello duet sonatas, however, the writing is not so simple; the two cellists perform equally difficult passages, often in parallel passages. Somis's interest in the cello was expressed not only in this set of duet sonatas and in the sonatas for cello without any accompaniment but also in the solo violin sonatas where the cello frequently demonstrates independence and virtuosity.

---

[12]Somis also composed a set of twelve sonatas for unaccompanied violoncello.

THE VENETIAN SONATA 1700-1740: VIVALDI AND ALBINONI

After 1700 and while Corelli's attention shifted to the concerto, the center of Italian chamber sonata composition moved back to the Venice of Antonio Vivaldi (1678-1741) and Tomaso Albinoni (1671-1751). Vivaldi and Albinoni, too, were mainly concerned with concertos during much of their careers and like Corelli had major roles in the development of the concerto. Both spent much of their lives, especially after 1710, with opera.[13] But during the first two decades of the 18th century both wrote dozens of sonatas which were published not only in Venice but also, in Vivaldi's case, in Amsterdam, Paris and London. They represent very well the state of the chamber sonata at this time in Italy, and even though they did not endure more than a few decades in the European repertoire, at the time they exerted almost as much influence as Corelli's in the spread of the Italian sonata throughout the rest of Europe.

Vivaldi was born into a family whose head, Giovanni Battista Vivaldi (ca. 1655-after 1729), originally a barber, joined the orchestra of San Marco Cathedral as a violinist when Antonio was 7 years old. Thus from childhood on, Antonio heard music at home—violin music, which would probably have been sonatas by his father's contemporaries. His father was his main childhood violin teacher, and the two probably played trio sonatas together. Although he was ordained a priest in 1703, Vivaldi could not exercise his priestly duties because of his severe asthmatic condition, which also forced him to continue to live in his father's house. Thus the possibility of his playing his own solo and trio sonatas at home with his father is considerable.

A few months following his ordination, Vivaldi began teaching violin at the famous Ospedale della Pietà, a boarding school for orphaned and abandoned girls where the principal study was music. As we saw in the previous chapter, Legrenzi worked there and helped enlarge the orchestra. Gasparini was the head musician from 1700, and other very impressive composers and performers

---

[13]For some idea of Vivaldi's operatic concerns, cf. Peter Ryom, "Les Catalogues de Bonlini et de Groppo," *Informazioni e Studi Vivaldiani*, vol II (1981), 3-30, and "Deux Catalogues d'Operas," III (1982), 13-44.

also taught there. Vivaldi was associated with the Ospedale della Pietà for more than thirty-five years, but his main periods of activity were 1703-1709, 1711-1718, and 1737-1740. In the large gap between 1718 and 1737 he was permitted to travel far and wide to perform as a violinist, to conduct his newest concertos, and to witness the performances of his many operas. That most of his chamber sonatas were published during the years that he was most active at the Ospedale strongly suggests that much of his instrumental music was written for performance there.

Despite the lack of discipline which the authorities of the Ospedale della Pietà exercised with the young women under their care and despite the girls' reputation for disreputable conduct throughout Venice, the level of virtuosity and musicianship learned by the girls was exceptional; the orchestra was deemed the best in Italy.[14] Although the accounts of the elaborate concerts at the Ospedale della Pietà concentrate on the vocal and orchestral works performed by the girls, it seems likely that Vivaldi composed many of his sonatas for performance at the Ospedale. Just as at his home, there were ample opportunities for the sonatas to be played by Vivaldi and his excellent students on the violoncello, violone and cembalo as well as violin. Perhaps they were played privately since they are not mentioned as part of the public concerts; the passion the girls had for music and their considerable skills would have made them ideal performers of such sonatas.

When Vivaldi became famous, he was asked to become part of the cappellas of various noblemen. For three years (ca. 1718-1722) Vivaldi served Prince Philipp of Hessen-Darmstadt, who was the governor of Mantua 1708-1709 and 1714-1735, and it was sometime while he was there that he probably wrote a collection of twelve sonatas for violin and harpsichord which remained in manuscript during Vivaldi's lifetime.[15] These sonatas were probably played by Vivaldi for the entertainment of his patron. When

---

[14]Marc Pincherle, *Vivaldi: Genius of the Baroque*, trl. Christopher Hatch (New York: Norton, 1957), pp. 18-27.

[15]Michael Talbot, "Vivaldi and a French Ambassador," in *Informazioni e Studi Vivaldiani*, vol. II (1981), 31-43. For the most up-to-date catalogue of Vivaldi's chamber works cf. Peter Ryom, *Répertoire des Oeuvres d'Antonio Vivaldi, les Compositions Instrumentales* (Copenhagen: Engstrom & Sodring, 1986), pp. 73-154.

Vivaldi was again in Venice later in the 1720's, he was frequently invited to perform and conduct music at the residence of the French ambassador to Venice, Jacques-Vincent Languet (1667-1734), and it was there that Vivaldi performed again his twelve Mantuan sonatas. At some point Languet obtained the collection and then gave it to Corelli's old patron, Cardinal Pietro Ottoboni. Thus the music circulated around and assuredly was played, possibly by gifted or enthusiastic amateurs, at different aristocratic homes in Italy during the 1720's, but since it was never published, it remained virtually unknown to the general public at the time.

Vivaldi's four published collections of sonatas, on the other hand, were widely disseminated. Opus I, a collection of twelve suites for two violins and either violone or harpsichord, was first published in Venice in 1705 and was soon republished in Amsterdam (before 1723 and in 1723) and later in Paris (1739). In 1709 he published his Opus II, a collection of twelve suites for violin and harpsichord dedicated to Frederick IV of Denmark and Norway who had visited Venice during the first few months of that year; it was reissued in Amsterdam (1712) and London (1721 and later). A second group of suites, Opus V, for two violins and basso continuo, this time containing only six works, was published in Amsterdam in 1716. Many years later, just before he left Venice for good and when his reputation was rapidly diminishing, Vivaldi published in Paris his last set of sonatas without opus number, a set of six violoncello sonatas with bass (1740; reprint 1748). In addition to the forty-eight sonatas accounted for so far in these four publications and in the Mantuan manuscript, there are another thirty-eight which survive in manuscript in individual archives in various places in Europe.

All the sonatas in the Mantuan manuscript and in Opera 1, 2 and 5 are suites (RV 63 in Opus I is a "La Folia" variations). All the suites begin with a prelude (in several cases not labeled "Preludio" but functioning as such), and many of them, like the church sonatas, are in four movements, usually in the pattern slow-fast-slow-fast. The dances are typical of the time: corrente, sarabanda, giga, allemanda, and gavotta. A number of suites in the printed editions are in the soon-to-be-popular three-movement form slow-fast-fast, but rarely are the same two dances used in the same order following the prelude. In a few cases the dance type is not given or there are alternatives like "siciliano" or "aria di giga" or "capriccio." The twelve cello sonatas and most of the remaining sonatas are da chiesa. In most cases they are in the typical four-movement pattern slow-fast-slow-fast. The pattern fast-slow-fast occurs in only nine sonatas—all trio sonatas and five involving wind instruments.

Vivaldi's style of violin playing was much more expansive than Corelli's. Besides the much greater use of double and triple stops, wide leaps, and trills, Vivaldi kept up a rhythmic drive, the so-called "motor rhythm" of the late Baroque, which was rare in Corelli. Breathtaking polyphony of two and three voices, startling leaps from the g-string to the e-string, Alberti figures in the violin, and complete control of all notes on all four strings in the first four positions were only natural from a violinist who was simultaneously writing these sonatas and developing the first great virtuosi violin concertos ever written. The carry over of the concerto's virtuoso style into the sonata is not unexpected; some of the movements of some sonatas reappear as concerto movements, and there is always the possibility that a sonata written for solo instruments was on some occasions played by two or more instruments on a part, and that some concertos written for orchestra were sometimes played by just soloists.

There is no evidence that Vivaldi studied with Corelli, but it is clear that the former was well acquainted with the latter's music. Since Vivaldi worked closely at the Ospedale della Pietà with Gasparini, he would have heard much about the Roman violinist from one of Corelli's most famous pupils. Vivaldi's Opus 1 and 2 were modeled on Corelli's Opus 5; some of the older violinist's motives were copied[16] and the idea of a set of variations on "La Folia" is here as well.

Although Albinoni and Vivaldi were contemporary violinists in the same city, there seems to have been little personal interaction between them. Their positions were different. Vivaldi, as we have seen, was a professional violinist and composer in the service of the Ospedali della Pietà and in various opera houses, while Albi-

---

[16]Cf. Pincherle, *Vivaldi*, pp. 71-72.

noni was a "violino dilettante veneto" (an amateur Venetian violinist) who held no important post. Albinoni did dedicate his first
collection of trio sonatas to Cardinal Ottoboni, who was Corelli's
patron and who owned a large collection of Vivaldi sonatas, but
there is no evidence that Albinoni and Vivaldi met at Ottoboni's
academies. Yet they certainly knew each other since during their
lifetimes their names were linked throughout Europe as the two
best violinists of their time, and in the area of concerto, where both
made substantial contributions, the two benefited from thorough
knowledge of each other's works. In 1716 Albinoni dedicated a
sonata to J.G. Pisendel, whom he met that year during a visit of
Friedrich August, Prince Elector of Savoy, to Venice. As early as
1709 "the foremost German violinist of his day" had performed an
Albinoni violin concerto in Leipzig.[17] But while in Venice, Pisendel actually studied not with Albinoni but with Vivaldi, and
upon his return to Dresden the following year Pisendel started the
Vivaldi craze there. As J.S. Bach showed, Albinoni's music, too,
was known and admired in Germany during the second and third
decades of the 18th century.

Of the seventy-nine solo da chiesa sonatas with bass accompaniment by Albinoni, all but two utilize the form slow-fast-slow-
fast. We have already noted his fixation on this form in his Opus 1
trio sonatas (1694). Albinoni seemed to think of the distinction
between da chiesa- and da camera-type pieces not in terms of location but in terms of the structure of the pieces since he dropped
both location terms in favor of the generic terms "sonata" and
"balletti" respectively and included both types of pieces in a single
collection (Opus 8). Since concertos were also performed in the
same homes and small halls as sonatas and balletti, he also published a collection (Opus 2) with both chamber works (one player
on a part) and concertos (several players on most parts).

The Opus 8 collection (ca. 1722) affords us a good opportunity
to compare Albinoni's sonatas with his balletti and to observe how
he differed from Vivaldi. This collection contains six sonatas for
two violins and basso continuo, each followed by a suite of three

[17]Pippa Drummond, "Pisendel," in *The New Grove Dictionary of Music and Musicians*,
vol. XIV, p. 775.

dances for the same scoring; as Albinoni stated, the dances are comic relief to the seriousness of the sonatas. And serious these sonatas are indeed! Each sonata contains two fast movements which are strict canons between the two violins at the unison and at varying time distances. Sometimes the continuo enters into the canon for at least several measures. C. David Harris points out Vitali's *Artificii musicali* (1689) as a model for Albinoni's canons, though the younger composer's inclusion of the continuo in some of the canons is a novelty in 1722.[18] The first sonata is in three movements fast-slow-fast while the remaining five are in the typical four movement slow-fast-slow-fast. The slow movements are lyrical and elegant and always simple; occasionally there is imitation between the instruments, though the first violin dominates. Albinoni wrote the second movement of the first (B♭ Major) sonata in the relative minor, and the second slow movement of each of the remaining sonatas is also in a related key (subdominant, relative minor, or relative major). The fast movements use typical violinistic passage work of the time, but are several levels less complicated than Vivaldi's passage work. No doubt owing to the complications of writing canons, Albinoni avoided multi-stopped notes, has few leaps over an octave, and stays almost exclusively in the first position. If Albinoni was in fact the equal of Vivaldi as a violinist, the compositions do not reflect this. And in the dances, where canon does not govern the style, Albinoni is equally simple. Each balletti (suite) begins with an allemanda, concludes with a sarabanda, and has either a gavotta or giga in between. All movements of a single suite are in the same key. There is some imitation and counterpoint, but mostly the first violin dominates and the others move along homophonically with it.

LATE-BAROQUE CHAMBER MUSIC IN FRANCE

The influence of the Corelli sonata spread beyond Italian borders. In Paris a number of fine violinists had introduced the music of Corelli by the beginning of the 18th century,[19] and the relative

[18]Albinoni, *Sonatas and Suites, Opus 8*, ed. C. David Harris, in *Recent Researches in the Music of the Baroque*, vols. LI-LII (Madison: A-R Editions, 1986), pp. vii-viii.

[19]Michel Brenet, *Les Concerts en France sous l'ancien Regime* (Paris: Fischbacher, 1900), p. 110.

neglect that was shown chamber music in France in comparison to the enthusiasm for it in Italy, England and Germany in the 17th century was now replaced by an avid interest in it. Paris and all France were teeming with amateur enthusiasts who gathered together to play chamber music as well as sing.[20] Aristocratic and bourgeois amateurs joined to make music with professionals from nearby opera or church orchestras. Until 1725 these gatherings were mostly private, or if public, on a small scale. The most famous in Paris were at court and at the private home of Antoine Crozat (1655-1738) on rue de Richelieu. As long as Louis XIV lived, there was music in the king's royal chamber; during the final few years of his reign, however, those concerts—of a very intimate nature—were given at the house of Mme de Maintenon by the leaders of the Royal Chapel: MM Duval, Philidor, Alarius, Dubois, and Couperin.[21] During the reign of Louis XV, however, who had no interest in music or any other art, the "Concerts de la Reine" became much more important. The queen had music performed in her Grand Cabinet every Monday and Saturday by her own musicians (who were, nonetheless, usually also members of the Royal Chamber), but her taste was for opera, not for chamber music. At Crozet's, however, chamber music began just as the scepter passed from Louis XIV to Louis XV. Here from 1715 to 1724, usually twice a week, several musicians gave concerts for Crozat who was Grand Trésorier de l'Ordre de Saint-Esprit.[22] These concerts were supplanted by the Concerts Italiens beginning in 1724 by Mme de Prie (1698-1726), a harpsichordist, at Crozat's home; upon her death these concerts moved to Le Louvre and then, later in 1726, to the Tuileries, where on every Thursday and Saturday sixty persons, each of whom paid 400 livres per year, had the privilege of participating. At Louis-Armand de Bourbon's home, a small circle of amateurs played regularly for their own enjoyment ("Concert des

---

[20]For a description of the academies outside Paris cf. Humphrey Burton, "Les Académies de musique en France au XVIIIe siècle," in *Revue de Musicologie*, vol. XXXVII (1955), 122-147.

[21]Pierre Daval, *La Musique en France au XVIIIe Siècle* (Paris: Payot, 1961), pp. 153-174. Cf. Wilfrid Mellers, *François Couperin and the French Classical Tradition*, new ed. (London: Faber and Faber, 1987), p. 213.

[22]Daval, pp. 114-115. On the Concerts Italiens and the other private concerts in Paris, cf. Daval, p. 115.

Mélophilètes"), while at fermier général Ferrand's violists Roland Marais and Antoine Forqueray and harpsichordist Daquin entertained. In the provinces these concerts were called "academies"; although imitations of the Italian accademias they differed from most of their models in that they were purely music-making groups, not study groups with music-playing as an adjunct. The popularity of such groups irritated the intelligentsia, which railed against the inadequacies of purely instrumental music. The philosophers and literary luminaries stressed the need for the arts to imitate nature, and since music was the art least capable of imitating anything, it was the least acceptable art form. It could be justified if it were set with text that depicted nature in some fashion; purely instrumental music was a very weak art since the most it could do was to back up the words in the title. Some French composers gave descriptive titles to their purely instrumental works, and Vivaldi's "Seasons" would have been an acceptable Italian importation. But most French enthusiasts for chamber music ignored their own intelligentsia and bathed in the beautiful sounds of the non-programmatic Italian sonata. The battle between an Italian and a French aesthetic in music had raged throughout the 17th century in France and would continue to do so throughout the 18th.

In 1725 the famous Concerts Spirituels opened in Paris under the direction of Anne-Danican Philidor (1681-1728) in the Salle des Suisses in the Tuileries. This was the first open, public, nonsubscription concert series in France. Originally planned as a series of both instrumental and vocal concerts to take place on religious holidays when the stages of Paris would be dark, it soon developed into the foremost concert series in Europe, terminating only with the Revolution in 1789. The Concerts Spirituels were not licensed to compete with the Royal Academy of Music, which was solely responsible for opera. No music could be sung in French, though this restriction was not fully observed as long as the vocal music did not suggest opera. Although it originally was predominantly a vocal music series, by 1728 instrumental music began to dominate, with a large percentage of Italian concertos, symphonies and sonatas. Here, before an audience of several hundred, the Parisian public first heard chamber music, and the problem which chamber music has faced in the 19th and 20th centuries—how to provide intimate music for a massive, non-participatory audience—has an important precursor here. The Concert Spirituel spread throughout France, with many other leading cities (Lyon, Bourdeux, Caen, Marseille) as well as villages keeping pace in their own fashion. In most of the provincial concerts and academies amateur members of any social class participated with the aid of local professionals, and an audience of non-participants from all social classes came to hear them.

At the same time as the Concert Spirituel another private concert series developed at the home of Alexandre-Jean-Joseph Le Riche de la Pouplinière (1693-1762), who first attended concerts at Crozat's home.[23] From 1731 to 1762 La Pouplinière hosted the finest orchestra in Paris under the leadership of Rameau, then Gossec and Johann Stamitz. A typical Sunday's musical activities included a grand concert with a grand audience at 5 pm followed by an after-supper "séance de musique plus intime" at 9 pm. There were other concerts during the week, especially on Saturdays, but it seems most likely that chamber music was the feature primarily of the "séances."

The three most important violinists in France during the first quarter of the 18th century were Jean-Jacques-Baptiste Anet, Jean Baptiste Senaillé, and Michele Mascitti. All three, under the influence of Corelli, performed and composed Italian sonatas in Paris and created a large audience for Italian chamber music which was severely attacked by French literati and philosophers. Anet, the son of a violinist who had studied with Lully and was in the King's Royal Chapel orchestra (24 violons du roi), was born in Paris in 1676 and ca. 1695-1696 studied with Corelli in Rome. In 1701 he made his debut at court playing sonatas ("Italian airs") with François Couperin on harpsichord and Antoine Forqueray (1671-1745) on viol. From 1701 into the 1730's he "appeared frequently in and around Paris—at court, at the homes of the nobility and after 1725 at the Concert Spirituel."[24] He spent the last two decades of his life in Lunéville, Lorraine, as a violinist to the exiled former king of Poland, and he died there in 1755. He composed two books

---

[23]Daval, pp. 115-122.

[24]Neal Zaslaw, "Anet," in *The New Grove Dictionary of Music and Musicians*, vol. I, p. 421.

of sonatas for violin with the accompaniment of continuo (Opus I, 1724) or bass (Opus 3, 1729) and four collections of chamber music for musette, flutes, oboes, violin, and vielle in various combinations. These latter pieces are in a French tradition of small tableaux each with a title just as in the ensemble works of Couperin (see below) and have nothing in common with the Italianate violin sonatas. Anet's importance was less as a composer than as the leading French virtuoso of his time who captivated audiences and sold them on the virtues of Italian chamber music with a tone described as "connected, sustained, mellow, impassioned, and conforming to the human voice, of which it is only the imitation and support."

Jean Baptiste Senaillé[25] (ca. 1688-1730), too, was a son of a member of the king's royal orchestra (24 violons) and himself a member of that prestigious ensemble from 1713 until his death. Possibly a pupil of Anet, he traveled to Italy ca. 1717 to 1719 where he learned first hand the music of the Italian concerto and sonata composers. In a posthumous critique *Le Mercur Galant* (August, 1738) found Senaillé not as good a violinist as Anet but a better composer, even better than Mascitti, though not so good as Corelli. Indeed, his sonatas are among the best written in the entire Baroque. They are more virtuosic than nearly all other French composers' works and were clearly intended for the professional and first-rate amateur.

Senaillé published five collections of sonatas for violin and bass, each with ten works or fifty sonatas altogether: 1710, 1712, 1716, 1721, and 1727. On the title pages it says that they are all scored for violin solo with basso continuo or simply basso accompaniment, but in fact two sonatas may substitute transverse flute for the violin (vol. I, no. 5 and vol. II, no. 1) and in all sonatas the violoncello is the equal of the violin in virtuosity. Usually the violoncello line simply doubles that of the continuo, but in a few cases the cello goes its own way (e.g., Vol. I, no. 1, movement 2; vol. II, no. 2, movement 4). It is quite rare when the bass line practically disappears and the solo violin is indeed "solo" (notably in vol. III, no. 10, movement 4). Although most of the movements in the col-

---

[25]On all his publications the name is Senallié.

lections are dance movements and the sonatas clearly are da camera, in the few cases when Senaillé specifically designated the instrument playing continuo it is always "organo" (vol. IV, no.4 movement 4 and no. 9 movement 4).

Most sonatas in the first four volumes are in four movements slow -fast - slow - fast (e.g., Adagio - Allemanda - Sarabanda - Giga, or Largo - Corrente - Aria - Allegro), while a few are fast - fast - slow - fast (vol. IV, no. 1) or in more than four movements (vol. II no. 3 is in 5 movements and no. 6 in is 6). In the fifth volume nearly every sonata has more than four. Clearly the model is Corelli, whose Opus 5 gives precursors of the forms in Senaillé's collections, though not the style. In addition in Senaillé's volume V, nine sonatas have an extra dance, which is a second aria or gavotta or minuetto paired with the first aria or gavotta or minuetto in a relative tonality; at the end of the second dance, the first is repeated as indicated by the term "al primo" or its equivalent. He had already experimented with this pairing twice in volume III and again twice in volume IV;[26] now in volume V it became standard procedure. Since most of these particular dances have an unusual form (AABACA - DDEDFD), it is difficult to determine how much of the first dance recurs after the second (a "fine" usually comes at the end of the first A). Corelli had already taken this kind of liberty with the form of the gavottas. Whatever was borrowed from Corelli, however, was only the starting point for Senaillé, who developed the overall forms of the chamber sonata and the individual movement's forms from volume I to volume V in the direction toward forms common later in the century. This is evident not only in the dance pairings of volume V but also in the expansion of binary form into sonata form (the last movement of the last sonata in volume V), greater concern for thematic and harmonic development, and the concern for tonal variety and melodic contrast.

Michele Mascitti, unlike the other two, was an Italian who emigrated to France. He brought with him the Italian style which he on a few occasions tried to link with native French chamber music. Born near Naples ca. 1664 and probably a pupil of Corelli

---

[26]Mascitti may have a similar double minuet in his Opus 6 (1722), no. 3.

ca. 1695-1699, Mascitti moved to Paris in 1704 as a mature artist and remained there with few interruptions until his death in 1760 at a very advanced age.[27] He was regarded by both the French and English as the equal of Corelli, Vivaldi, and Albinoni. A popular performer at the private chamber music concerts of the royal family during his earlier years in Paris, Mascitti seems at some point to have entered the service of the Crozat family (to whose members his last two published collections are dedicated in 1731 and 1738). He dedicated his Opus 1 to the Duc d'Orléans, his Opus 4 to the Elector of Bavaria (who was himself an active performer of chamber music), and his Opus 5 to the ubiquitous Cardinal Ottoboni, but he seems not to have actually been employed by any of these patrons. What is unusual with Mascitti is that he dedicated his Opus 2 (1706) to the public and three other collections have no dedications at all. All this could indicate that during much of his career (perhaps for as long as twenty years) Mascitti was able to be an independent violinist-composer who lived off his performances, his teaching, and the public sales of his sonatas.[28]

Mascitti wrote one hundred solo sonatas for violin with either violoncello or harpsichord, eleven trio sonatas for two violins with bass, a trio sonata for violin, viola da gamba, and continuo, and four concertos published in Paris in 1727. While the violin part is preeminent in the solo sonatas, the violoncello or viola da gamba sometimes reaches equality with the violin in the trio sonatas (especially in Opus 6, no. 15, where the continuo and viola da gamba or violoncello are independent of each other). In his Opus 1 (1704) Mascitti included three solo and three trio da chiesa sonatas (entitled "sonatas") and three solo and three trio da camera sonatas (entitled "sonatas da camera"). He was careful to distinguish between these two types also in his Opus 2 (1706) and Opus 3 (1707) collections, which together contain twenty-seven da camera sonatas. By Opus 4 (1711), however, he ceased to make a distinction and combined features of both types in individual sonatas. Thus, in

---

[27]The principal study of Mascitti's life and works is Robert Henry Dean, Jr., "The Music of Michele Mascitti (ca.1664-1760): a Neapolitan Violinist in Paris" (University of Iowa Ph.D. dissertation, 1970). Cf. also Michael Talbot, "Mascitti," in *The New Grove Dictionary of Music and Musicians*, vol.XI, p. 746.

[28]There is no indication that he was independently wealthy.

his first three works Mascitti followed the distinctions made in Corelli's first four works, and starting in *his* Opus 4 Mascitti followed Corelli in *his* Opus 5. In all his oeuvre (there are eight sonata volumes and one of concertos) the melodic writing in the violin part has some of the elegance and grace of Corelli without the violinistic virtuosity of Corelli's contemporaries and successors. In the sonatas nos. 4 and 5 of Opus 6 (1722) Mascitti attained an unadorned poignancy that even Corelli would have been hard pressed to equal. It is likely that Mascitti, who was still a new arrival in Paris when he composed his first several collections and was always conscious of being Italian in the French capital, was appealing to chauvinistic French taste, which was decidedly programmatic and not inclined to appreciate virtuosity for its own sake. The use of specific dance titles mixed with some pure movements, learned from Corelli, was conveniently suited to the French. It is possible, as Walter Kolneder has suggested,[29] that the simple violin technique and style of these pieces were the result of Mascitti's composing for his French pupils and patrons who were amateur violinists, but it seems just as likely that Mascitti followed Corelli's method of notating simply and improvising virtuosically as needed. The overall violin technique is no simpler than in Corelli's Opus 5.

Mascitti's compromise with French taste, which was basically anti-instrumental, occurred as the final piece of Opus V (1714), a collection of solo sonatas for violin and bass.[30] At the end of the sonatas is a "Divertissement" entitled "Psyche" in ten programmatic movements which suggest a ballet: Grand Air, Les Vents, Festes Galantes (Sarabanda), Badinage, Du Sommeil, L'Amour en Courroux - au Désespoir, Calme Amoureux, La Noce, Suite de la Noce, and Dernière Suite de la Noce. Since the only music that was of value was vocal because it is music in imitation of nature, chamber music was not popular among the leading intellectuals of France; but Italian chamber music had sufficient following among many music lovers that the intelligentsia found it necessary to continually attack it. To win some approval from that powerful group

---

[29]Michele Mascitti, *6 Sonate da camera für Violine und bezifferten Bass*, ed. Walter Kolneder, Heft 1 (Heidelberg: Willy Müller, 1963), p. [2].

[30]Modern edition by Frits Noske (Mainz: B. Schott's Söhne, [1959]).

as well as from the Italian music lovers, Mascitti included this bit of program music which, like Couperin's music, had some legitimacy. The movements are dance-like (seven are in binary form and several are actual ballroom dance types), yet there are imitations of nature (swooping of the wind in thirty-second notes in movement 2) and of passions (calm love in staccato notes in movement 6).

While François Couperin's fame as a chamber music composer has not survived the 18th century, in his own time he was the most influential chamber music personality at court and published some remarkable chamber compositions.[31] Born in Paris in 1668, he made his way early as an organist and church musician. In 1692 he surreptitiously composed four trio sonatas for two violins, bass (which is nearly identical to the continuo) and continuo in the Italian manner; he was "charmé de celles de signor Corelli" but was so unsure how Italian music would be received in Paris that he pretended the works were by an anonymous Italian and gave each of the sonatas descriptive titles: "La Steinquerque" (in honor of the victory at Steinkerque), "La Pucelle" (virgin), "La Visionnaire" (after a play by that name by Desmarets), and "L'Astrée." A few years later he added two more such sonatas: "La Sultane" and "La Superbe." That Couperin's fears of open hostility against any Italianism in his music were well founded is demonstrated in the bitter attack against him by Lecerf de la Viéville on that very ground. By 1726, however, there was no longer any need to hide a strong interest in Italian sonatas since by then their popularity in Paris was assured; therefore in that year Couperin published *Les Nations* which includes three of the four early trio sonatas (with new titles) plus a new sonata "L'Impériale," each with an accompanying suite that clearly demarcates the Italian da chiesa sonata from the French suite. Yet even in the supposedly "Italian" sonata Couperin was ever cognizant of his French heritage from Lully, who stood in equal stead with Corelli in Couperin's mind. Couperin gave French titles to each sonata and used French, not Italian terms for the names of dances, tempos, and dynamics. The sonatas contrast slow and fast movements or sections, but the divisions

---

[31]The following biographical and bibliographical information on Couperin is based on Mellers.

between movements or sections is in a continual state of flux. In "L'Espagnole," for instance, which is the new name of "La Visionnaire" in the printed edition, an opening slow movement ending on the dominant is followed by a movement that begins fast and ends slow. This is followed by another fast movement and then by a single measure entitled "Repose," followed by another fast section, another 1-measure "Repose," another fast movement, and an "Air tendre." Finally the da chiesa sonata concludes with a separate fast movement. While the principle of contrast is there, no Corelli model could have served Couperin in this piece. The overall impression is reminiscent of the pages of a Lully opera, where the distinction between récit and air is often equally blurred. The use of the air in the midst of the da chiesa sonata was a remnant of Lully in the midst of a confusion between the old sectionalized canzona and the new multi-movement sonata. By 1726, however, it was already commonplace throughout Europe to find da chiesa and da camera elements so intermingled that the terms were no longer relevant and rarely used. That Couperin then added a full-length suite to the "da chiesa" sonata was a different approach to this intermingling. He thought of the suite as French, and it was just an extension of the other suites that he wrote in his *Concerts Royaux* and *Les Goûts-Réünis*. All in all, then, Couperin was able to synthesize his heritage from Lully and Corelli into his own, clearly French chamber music, and among all the French composers of this period he is the only one not to completely succumb to the Italians.

In 1693 Couperin entered the service of the king as organist and the following year became harpsichord teacher of the royal children. So much did he impress Louis XIV that in 1696 the king ennobled Couperin. Certainly by the beginning of the 18th century, but perhaps also earlier, Couperin at the harpsichord was a main participant in the regular Sunday concerts before the king, though it was not until after Louis XIV's death that he was officially named director of these concerts. These Sunday concerts became increasingly important for Louis as he approached the end of his life, and he was fortunate in having not only Couperin but also Rebel on violin and Forqueray on viola da gamba. In addition the violinist Duval, the oboist Philidor, the violist Alarius, and the bassoonist Dubois took part. The music that Couperin wrote for these concerts does not survive in the original ensemble scoring but rather in harpsichord arrangements which the composer made in 1722 (*Concerts Royaux*, the last four compositions in his third book of harpsichord pieces) and in 1724 (ten suites entitled *Les Goûts-Réünis*). He made it quite clear that ensemble performance was expected wherever possible, though except for specific viol passages which Couperin retained and named in the harpsichord version, we can only guess at the exact makeup of the ensemble. On the surface these are typical dance suites, each of which is preceded by a prelude. But there is much more than that to them. Some dances have titles, such as "Les Graces" (courante françoise) or "La Noble Fierté" (sarabande). There are many airs, some with descriptive titles such as "Air tendre" and "Air de Diable." They are French dances (except when a dance is specifically called "italiene") mixed with non-dances of a peculiarly French nature, such as the "Muséte dans le Goût de Carillon" where repeated quarter notes on one pitch suggest the ringing of bells. Most of the preludes are called "Gravement" and one is "Majesteusement" which give a more picturesque indication of the nature of the movements than the word "Prelude" could give. There are numerous chaconnes and rondeaux. Two suites (nos. 8 and 9[32]) have special titles suggesting a more dramatic origin, if not in an actual ballet de cour at least in the style of the music for such a ballet. In the *Concerts Royaux* and *les Goûts-Réünis* several trends that we have noted in the sonatas of the violinists were repeated or carried further here. For example, the use of paired dances of the same kind with the first repeated after the second occurs in no. 9, and the alternation of dances in the home key and parallel major or minor is a more common occurrence. In no. 5, for instance, which consists of five movements, dances 1, 2 and 5 are in F Major and the others in F Minor. In no. 9, which has eight movements, dances 1 to 5 are in E Major, 6 and 7 in E Minor, and 8, which is a pair of minuets ("L'et Coetera ou Menuets") begins in E Minor, has

---

[32]These are the numbers given not in the original but in the modern edition, Fr. Couperin, *Musique de Chamber*, vols. I-II, ed. André Schaeffner, rev. Kenneth Gilbert and Davitt Moroney, in *Oeuvres Complètes*, section IV (Monaco: L'Oiseau-Lyre, 1980).

the second minuet in E Major, and repeats the first minuet back in E Minor.

In addition to these two collections of sonatas and suites and the three other sonatas of the 1690's which are not printed in the 1720's, Couperin also wrote two trio sonatas in honor of Corelli ("La Sultane") and Lully ("La Superbe") which were printed in 1724 and 1725. And the final works which he published in 1728 are two suites for two viols with continuo, which he probably wrote with Forqueray in mind. That he still wrote for the gamba when Italians were writing for the violoncello makes his works further distinguished from those of the Italians. Couperin was able to maintain his own, French style, and to write chamber music of the first order. Yet, despite his efforts, Italian chamber music had won over most French listeners and performers by the 1720's and it would take a new generation of French musicians to reestablish a French tradition.

After 1730 several new French chamber music composers appeared on the scene, especially the violinists Guignon and Leclair, and although Blavet got his start in Paris in 1723, his main contributions to chamber music (establishing woodwind chamber music on a foot with string) come after 1730. The only new arrival whose music can be said to continue the French tradition of the 1720's almost unabated after 1730 was Joseph Bodin de Boismortier (1689-1755). He was a facile, very popular composer who became so rich writing and publishing sonatas and other chamber works that he never needed a patron (practically unheard of before 1800). Nearly every chamber work (he published 101 opus numbers from 1724 to 1747) is for flutes, either alone or with keyboard and/or strings. There are sonatas and suites for one flute with bass or two flutes with or without bass. He was the first to write trios and quintets for flutes with or without the accompaniment of continuo. Boismortier was not a performer, so

> Most of [his music] was directed at small groups of amateur musicians with limited resources rather than at professional concert organizations, and many of his works are designated for flexible performing media; optional parts are often indicated.[33]

[33]Laurel Fay, "Boismoriter," in *The New Grove Dictionary of Music and Musicians*, II, p. 862.

In addition to sonatas Boismortier also wrote concertos for flutes without orchestra (Opus 15 [1727] for five flutes and Opus 38 [1732] for two flutes or other instruments), and there are numerous other varieties of chamber music including a few sets of violin sonatas accompanied by continuo (e.g., Opus 20 [1727] and 81 [ca. 1740; lost]) and "gentillesses" for musette, viols and other instruments. With few exceptions (mostly notably Opus 91 mentioned in the next chapter), all these works are in the styles, forms and character of traditional baroque music.

With the development of a more distinct French school after 1730, chamber music moved into new areas which are best discussed in the next chapter. While until now the chamber music of Corelli and other Italians was of paramount importance and a distinctly French style was secondary to it, during the middle third of the 18th century the French stopped simply aping the Italians and began new paths that eventually, by the 1780's, arrived at Classical Period chamber music. This half-century of transition finds Paris in the forefront.

ENGLISH CHAMBER MUSIC CA. 1690-1740

During the last quarter of the 17th century the focus of English chamber music shifted from a primarily private situation to a primarily public one. Chamber music continued to be popular in the homes of upper and middle class Englishmen throughout the country, and royal musicians continued to entertain the ruling class with ensemble music that often was chamber music. But beginning in 1672 with the opening of John Banister's public concerts in his home, chamber music increasingly became a public event. York Hall (ca. 1674-1734), the Vendu Room of Covent Garden (1691-1697), Stationers' Hall (ca. 1683-1718), Hickford's Room (early 18th century) and others, along with legitimate theaters provided public listening to the latest chamber music from England and the rest of Europe. The advent of public concerts meant that Englishmen could hear exciting virtuosi perform with a perfection of technique impossible with amateurs at home; nonetheless those very amateurs now took less interest in the traditional English chamber music types which were within their technical control and tried

hard to imitate the virtuosic chamber music they heard in the concert halls. In the eyes of many this resulted in a decline in public
musical taste, since the old English chamber music was a subtle
kind of music played on soft, delicate viols and recorders while the
new music played on the loud, vulgar violin (which had previously
been associated with street and dance musicians) was flamboyant
and blatant. The fantasias of Jenkins and Locke were replaced by
the new sonatas of Finger, Matteis father and son, Crofts, Corelli
and others, both foreign and domestic, and by countless arrangements for amateurs of popular songs and theater music.

   Henry Purcell, whose fantasias were the culmination of more
than a century of this genre, was the last exponent of the traditional
English style. Even in his sonatas, which pointed ahead to the new
phase of English chamber music, he was able to maintain a careful
balance between Italian and French ideas and his English heritage.
After his death, and even during the decade and a half before, his
fellow Englishmen succumbed to foreign styles. London was a
mecca for Italian musicians since the 16th century and became increasingly so after the turn of the 18th century. During the Restoration of the 1660's and 1670's French musicians began to arrive
in numbers, and by the beginning of the 18th century Germans
came as well. The particular national styles of these three foreign
lands, then, had a great impact on the chamber music of London
during the late 17th and early 18th centuries and completely replaced what during the first two thirds of the 17th century had been
one of the most viable chamber music traditions of Europe. By the
time Handel wrote his sonatas in London, the stage had been set
for the true genius to fully realize the potential of this new music.

   The French influence on English instrumental music was felt
especially in the 1670's with the orchestral overture and suite, but
except for the use of popular French dances, French music had little effect on English chamber music. Quite the contrary, while
chamber music composers in France before 1730 concentrated on
string chamber music, the French composers in England found a
more ready audience for recorder chamber music and thus wrote
more flute than string sonatas. French chamber composers working
in England before or during Handel's time include James Paisible,
Louis (Lewis) Mercy, D. Demoivre, and Charles Dieupart. Paisible

was active in London theater music ca. 1700, composed music for the Duchess of Mazarine's concerts in Chelsea, and was head of the king's band of music from 1714 to 1719. He composed primarily flute works, some of which were published in anthologies and others also in his *Six Sonatas of two Parts for Two Flutes, Opus 1* (published by Roger 1701-2 and by Walsh 1702) and his *Six Setts of Aires for two Flutes and a Bass consisting of Preludes allemands corants sarabands marches minuets gavotts and jiggs* (Walsh 1720). Mercy published two collections of recorder sonatas, the first, which is accompanied by a harpsichord or violoncello, in 1718 and the second sometime thereafter. In the introduction to the first volume Mercy defended the recorder; it is as agile as the violin, he said, and though it is soft, it is as good in consort. Little is known about Demoivre other than that he, too, wrote for the flute three collections of ayres (1701, 1704, and ca. 1707). Accompanied by a bass, the ayres include preludes, almands, sarabands, corants, minuets and jigs and are designed for dilettantes. Dieupart, harpsichordist and violinist, came to London ca. 1700 and died there ca. 1740. He worked with Haym at the York Hall concerts and also with Handel. Besides his famous harpsichord suites (which influenced Bach) he composed six easy sonatas for recorder and continuo published by Walsh in 1717 and dedicated to Lady Essex Finch.

German violinists had appeared in England as early as the mid-17th century with Thomas Baltzar of Lübeck. The English violinist William Young, who had published trio sonatas in Innsbruck in 1653 dedicated to the Archduke Karl Ferdinand, brought Austrian chamber music to London when he joined the private musicians to Charles II. At the end of the century, however, a greater number of Germans arrived who settled in England and became part of the English chamber music scene. Among these were Gottfried Finger, A. Kühnel, Gottfried Keller, J.E. Galliard, and J.C. Pepusch.[34] The 17th-century German preference for orchestral suites over chamber ones and for wind instruments was carried over to England by these men.

---

[34]Tilmouth, "Chamber Music in England" (Cambridge University Ph.D. dissertation, 1959), p. 313, discusses also Sigismund Cousser, James Kremberg, Kytch (the oboe player), and H. Thornowitz.

The Moravian Finger was a prolific composer of sonatas for various combinations of instruments. His five collections appeared between 1688 and 1702 and were designed for use in the Royal Chapel, where he served under James II. His *VI Sonatas or Solo's* (1690) were the first solo sonatas published in England; three are for violin and continuo and the other three for recorder and continuo. He also published a few collections of ayres, chaconnes, divisions and other da camera works for two or three violins, oboes or flutes. Kühnel's one collection of 1685 is interesting for its compromise between the older viola da gamba tradition and the newer violin one. Entitled *Several Sonata's Composed after the Italian Way*, it is scored for one or two bass viols with basso continuo. Keller's sonatas are for larger ensembles and may even be orchestral, especially in his three for trumpet, oboe or violins with double basses. Galliard's *VI Sonatas for a Flute and a Thorough Bass* was published in London in 1711 and is of minor musical value though typical of the time. Each sonata consists of a few short movements including a gigue. The most important of this group of second-rate chamber music composers, however, was Pepusch, whose works were very popular at the time. He came to England in 1719 to work as Handel's successor for the Duke of Chandos (James Brydges), whose orchestra also boasted the violinists Alexander Bitti and Nicolo Haym, the flutist Mercy and the oboist J.C. Kytch. Pepusch wrote serious trio sonatas, whose counterpoint is dignified and competent if not inspired, lighter solo flute and violin sonatas, and didactic duets for two violins (later arranged for two recorders). Pepusch seems to have written the serious works for the Duke and for other English noblemen, who by the first few decades of the 18th century were beginning to rival their Italian noble models in presenting private musicals in their homes.[35]

However interesting the French and German influence on English chamber music of this period may be, it is minuscule compared to that of Italian composers and particularly Corelli on it. Two important Englishmen working in Italy were John Ravenscroft and Robert Valentine. The former was actually a pupil of Corelli and published two collections for violin and continuo, the

[35]Tilmouth, "Chamber Music in England," Chapter II.

first (Opus 1) a set of church sonatas in direct imitation of Corelli's Opus 1 or 3 and the second (Opus 2) a set of five chamber sonatas (preludio plus several dances) and a chaconne. The former was printed in Italy and the latter in London in 1708, after the composer's death. Ravenscroft was a good professional violinist but not an inventive composer.

Robert Valentine in Rome was the most prolific of Englishmen working abroad. His first twelve opus numbers were church and chamber solo and trio sonatas for flutes or violins with continuo. He aped his model Corelli at nearly every turn, but without even as much skill as Ravenscroft, who was the better violinist.

From the turn of the century on, Corelli's influence was felt in England not only vicariously through Englishmen returning from abroad but also first hand through the direct experience with it by local chamber musicians in England itself. Within a very short time of its publication on the Continent, Corelli's music was available in England in large quantities through Italian prints or through copies printed and reprinted in Amsterdam and London for English consumption.[36] The development of cheaper printing methods ca. 1700 and the entrepreneurship of Walsh in London and Roger in Amsterdam made copies of music more readily available, and at that time Corelli was the most interesting composer whose works could be marketed profitably. The many amateur players could perform it easily, and all chamber music would now be judged in comparison to it. The sonatas of Cazzati, G.B. Vitali, and Vivaldi were also popular, but none achieved the lasting popularity of Corelli's.

But the Italian influence was even more solidified by the appearance of Italian virtuoso chamber music performers in London. Beginning with Nicolo Matteis, Sr., in the 1670's, London had resident Italian violin virtuosi who were trained in the new sonata school. Matteis Sr.'s compositions were almost exclusively da camera sonatas: four books of ayres for one violin and bass with an optional second violin. The composer worked with Purcell and had considerable influence on the latter's own sonatas. Nicola Cosimi and Nicola Francesco Haym, cellist and a pupil of Corelli, worked

---

[36]Tilmouth, "Chamber Music in England," Chapter V.

for various English patrons who were trying to emulate Cardinal Ottoboni. Cosimi worked in England for a short time for the Duke of Bedford and dedicated to him a collection of twelve violin sonatas in 1702 which are reminiscent of Corelli's Opus 5. Immediately thereafter Haym seems to have taken Cosimi's place as music master at the Duke of Bedford's. He dedicated his twelve Opus 1 sonatas (six da chiesa, six da camera, 1703) to the Duke, but the following year he found another patron in Richard Edgcumbe, to whom he dedicated his Opus 2 trio sonatas (1704; five for two violins and bass, four for two violins or two recorders and bass, two for violin, violoncello and bass, and a chaconne for two recorders and bass). Later Haym went into various theatrical enterprises and collaborated with Handel.

The Cremona born Gasparo Visconti (often referred to by the diminutive of his first name, Gasparini[37]) was a Corelli pupil who came to London in 1702 when he made his debut in the York Buildings. He served in the orchestra of the Theatre Royal and continued to give concerts in the intermissions of plays. Featured on his concert programs were the concertos of Albinoni, Corelli and Caldara and the sonatas of Corelli; indeed, he established the common practice of playing Corelli sonatas before a play, which was carried on in London long after his departure from the London scene in 1706.[38] In 1703 he dedicated his Opus 1 *Solos for a Violin with a thorough Bass for the Harpsichord or Bass Violin containing Preludes Allmands Sarabands &c* to the Duke of Devonshire. Tilmouth describes them as simpler than Cosimi's "and musically they are more effective." One of his sonatas, for recorder, violin and continuo (Walsh, 1706 and 1710) "may lay claim to have been the most popular chamber work of Queen Anne's reign."

Despite the contributions of these Italian violinists and composers to English chamber music, the Italian who made the biggest impact was Geminiani. Francesco Geminiani, who was a pupil of both Corelli and Alessandro Scarlatti in Rome during the first few

---

[37]Not to be confused with Corelli's other pupil Francesco Gasparini (1668-1727) who for a time was director of the Conservatorio della Pietà in Venice.

[38]Tilmouth, "Chamber Music in England," p. 308, and Charles Cudworth, "Visconti, Gasparo," in *MGG*, xiii (1966), cols. 1830-1831. Nothing is known about this Gasparini's later life.

years of the 18th century, published his first collection of sonatas for violin, violone and harpsichord, Opus 1, in 1716 in London. From 1714 on Geminiani lived in London and had a major impact on English chamber music. No other collection during the first few decades of the 18th century better displays the transition from the sonata and canzona styles and forms of Corelli to those of the pre-classical period discussed in the next chapter than Geminiani's Opus 1. Among the twelve sonatas in this collection are several multi-sectional movements (no. 1, movement 2 in 4 sections; and no. 3, movement 3 in 7 sections) and sonatas in the traditional da chiesa form of slow-fast-slow-fast (nos. 2, 4 and 5). Furthermore there are sonatas which blend da chiesa and da camera elements (e.g., nos. 7 and 10 in the slow-fast-slow-fast form have the fast movements in binary form and the last movements in giga-like $\frac{6}{8}$ and $\frac{12}{8}$ meters). All this we see from the 17th-century sonata and in Corelli. But pointing to a later sonata ideal Geminiani did not stay in one key for all four movements but had the second slow movement in a related key (usually the subdominant) or made it a tonally unstable movement. Also a more modern trait is Geminiani's use of three movements in several sonatas, usually fast-slow-fast (no. 6 is slow-slow-fast and no. 12 is slow-fast with a slow three-measure transition - fast). While only one movement (the final of no. 1) in the first six sonatas is in binary form, most movements in nos. 7-12 are in binary form. Perhaps Geminiani was thinking of dividing his collection along the lines of Corelli's Opus 5, though the similarity does not go very far. Binary form here is almost always asymmetrical and without any consistent tonal pattern other than beginning and ending the movement in the same key. In general Geminiani's harmony is rich and expressive with a preference for minor keys and minor chords. The final Allegro of no. 9, however, is extraordinary; way ahead of its time, it is as fine an example of sonata form as would be found later by the mid-18th century. Geminiani's violin technique was more demanding than Corelli's and Vivaldi's; at times he even wrote three-voice counterpoint for the violin alone, with the continuo adding a fourth voice (e.g., the Allegros in no. 2).

Surprisingly, Geminiani's later collections are not so encyclopedic as Opus 1 and also seem less adventuresome. Opus 5, a collection of 6 sonatas for violoncello and basso continuo published in London in 1747 (later adapted for violin and continuo), consists of four-movement sonatas all in the pattern slow-fast-slow-fast. Most fast movements are in binary form, but now this form is much more stylized in mid-18th-century fashion with rounded binary (no. 5, movement 4) and da capo binary (no. 3, movement 4 and no. 6, movement 4). The second movement Allegro moderato of no. 4 is in da capo aria form. There is no sonata form in any movement. The slow movements are much less stylized. The first three sonatas open with substantial slow movements that develop the opening melodic material; the latter three sonatas, however, open with short (4- to 6-measure) introductions to the following fast movement. In most cases the third movement is in another key (parallel minor, relative major, relative minor, submedient minor).

Native English chamber composers emulated their foreign visitors, especially the Italians, and at best they formed a very minor school of composition. "Many of [the English composers] applied themselves solely to instrumental chamber music as did their exemplar, Corelli. Corelli, however, in his day was formulating a style, whereas they were merely practicing one which was already formed."[39] Among the native composers were Daniel Purcell, William Crofts, William Topham, William Corbett, and James Sherard. Their works show little invention and much imitation of Corelli; Topham even went so far as to state on the title page of his *Six Sonatas*, Opus 3, that they are "in imitation of Corelli." Corbett, who had kept some identity in his earlier works, went to Italy in 1710 and came back without any; the "gavotta" of the tenth sonata in his Opus 4 (1713) flatly admits "Imitation of Corelli." Not only the sonatas for one or two violins but also the recorder sonatas copy the great Italian master. Perhaps the only original in this group was Sherard. He was professionally an apothecary, was a highly regarded amateur violinist and composer as well, and worked with both Haym at the Duke of Bedford's[40] and with Handel. His two collections of da chiesa sonatas (1701 and ca. 1711) demonstrate considerable skill at fugue-writing, and "the quick

---

[39]Tilmouth, "Chamber Music in England," p. 318.

[40]His Opus II is dedicated to the Duke of Bedford.

movements of these sonatas have a rhythmic intensity and drive which is often lacking in many of the professional imitations of Corelli."[41]

GEORG FRIEDRICH HANDEL

During his four years in Italy (1706-1710), Handel visited the homes of distinguished Italians in five cities: Rome, Venice, Florence, Naples and Sienna. There he frequently engaged in concerts where, sometimes, chamber sonatas were performed. We know that he performed often with other virtuosi at the Casa Colonna in Rome, for example, which was the scene of daily concerts throughout the year.[42] He also appeared as a foreign guest at meetings of the Accademia Arcadiana where, as mentioned above, he came into contact with Alessandro Scarlatti and Corelli. In Naples in 1708 he attended its branch of the Arcadian Academy as well as private concerts in the homes of the nobility. In all these academies and private concerts the principal music heard was vocal, but in most cases some purely instrumental music was also featured. Three solo sonatas and three trio sonatas composed by Handel between 1706 and 1710 were no doubt written for and performed on such occasions. They are scored differently: oboe and continuo (HWV 357), violin and continuo (HWV 358), transverse flute and continuo (HWV 378), two recorders and continuo (HWV 405), and two violins and continuo (HWV 391 and 392). All six seem to be da chiesa sonatas; three have the form fast-slow-fast and the other three the form slow-fast-slow-fast, in no cases with dances or binary form.

Of the remaining thirty sonatas which can be ascribed to Handel—if not definitely, at least with reasonable certainty, only one was not written while he lived in London. The trio sonata in G Minor (HWV 387) is the earliest dated piece by Handel[43] and, according to the composer's close friend Charles Jennens, it was written ca. 1700 while he still lived in Germany. It is scored for

---

[41]Tilmouth, "Chamber Music in England," p. 323.

[42]Richard A. Streatfeild, *Handel*, 2nd ed. (London: Methuen, 1910; reprint New York: Da Capo, 1964), pp. 32-33 and 339-40.

[43]*Händel-Handbuch*, vol. III (Kassel: Bärenreiter, 1986), pp. 171-172.

two violins and continuo and is in the common slow-fast-slow-fast da chiesa form. Several trio sonatas for two oboes and continuo, which have been attributed to Handel as a child in the 1690's, have not been authenticated. Handel was a pupil of Zachow when he would have written them, and they may have been intended as exercises. Whether the surviving examples are his or not, it seems that Handel later admitted to writing chamber sonatas for oboes in great number when he was very young.

The remaining sonatas were written in London throughout most of his lengthy sojourn there. During his lifetime three collections of sonatas were published. The two collections of trio sonatas Opus 2 (1732) and Opus 5 (1739) are quite different from one another. The former contains six sonatas (HWV 386-391) composed between 1700 (it includes the early German sonata) and 1718. It is possible that the five composed ca. 1718 were written for Matthew Dubourg (1703-1767) who had made his debut on the violin in London in 1714 at the age of 11 and later was associated with Handel both in London and in Dublin for the first performance of Messiah,[44] and for Geminani, who first played with Handel in London in 1715 and who was Dubourg's teacher.[45] All are da chiesa sonatas and five have the form slow-fast-slow-fast. No. 4 in F (HWV 389) also has that basic form, but with a fifth movement added that is binary and in $\frac{12}{8}$ meter. Handel used the same movement in his overture to *Athaliah* where it is entitled "gigue." The scorings vary; three are for two violins with continuo, a fourth sonata allows for the substitution of oboe or flute for the first violin and oboe for the second violin, and the other two sonatas are for flute, violin and continuo with the option of an oboe substituting for the flute in one and with the oboe or violin substituting for the flute and a flute for the violin in the other. The optional scorings may not have been Handel's idea but that of the publisher who foresaw greater sales with the increased options.

[44]Cf. Charles Burney, *A General History of Music*, ed. Frank Mercer (New York: Dover, 1957), vol. II, pp. 994 and 998. Burney recounts a performance in 1744 of a Corelli solo sonata with Dubourg on violin and Burney himself accompanying. For how Dubourg performed Corelli's sonatas, see David Boyden, "Corelli's Solo Violin Sonatas 'Grac'd' by Dubourg," in *Festskrift Jens Peter Larsen*, pp. 113-125.

[45]Streatfeild, p. 74.

The seven sonatas of Opus 5 (HWV 396-402) are all scored for two violins and, in each case, either continuo or cello. They are therefore in the tradition of Corelli's string trios Opus 2 and 4, which Handel could have heard played by Corelli and Fornari in Rome when the two met but which in any case Handel would have known very well by the 1730's. The fourth sonata, however, stands out for the optional addition of a viola part; if the viola is added to the string trio, the result is a string quartet (two violins, viola and cello) that at least in scoring is the same as the string quartet which emerges a decade and a half later. Unlike Opus 2, which are da chiesa sonatas with one dance movement tacked on, Opus 5 is a fusion of da chiesa and da camera movements. Two of them begin with the traditional da chiesa setup: slow-fast-slow-fast and then conclude with a gavotta or a gavotta and a menuet. Another has the five-movement form slow-fast-slow-slow-fast, to which is added a menuet and variation (or just a menuet[46]). The remaining sonatas consist primarily of dances but with at least one da chiesa movement in addition. The editors of the *Händel-Handbuch* suggest that Handel submitted a set of da chiesa sonatas to the publisher Walsh, who added dances to them to increase sales. In any case these seven sonatas were composed about twenty years later than those in Opus 2 and show a more standardized scoring (except for HWV 399) but more flexible forms. The most obvious new form to be included in the Opus 5 sonatas not found in any earlier trio or solo sonatas is the French overture, which begins HWV 400 and follows an introductory fast movement in HWV 399.[47] We have seen this already in Carlo Antonio Marini's Opus 5 suites (1700), which are specifically labeled "French," and in the fifteenth sonata of Mascitti's Opus 6 (1722), where it seems to be an accommodation of that composer's Italian background with his current Parisian environment. In Handel's case, he had already composed orchestral

---

[46]The autograph manuscript has the menuet and variations while the printed edition has just a menuet (not the same menuet as in the manuscript).

[47]It must be kept in mind that the French overture of 1730 consists of two movements of which the first is stern, homophonic with dotted rhythm, and repeated, the second is gay, imitative, and repeated. According to contemporary French records, the two movements are to be played at almost the same tempo, which is moderately fast. Cf. Hellmuth Christian Wolff, "Das Metronom des Louis-Lëon Pajot 1735," in *Festskrift Jens Peter Larsen* (Copenhagen: Wilhelm Hansen, 1972), pp. 208-210.

suites as well as some operas with French overtures, and the inclusion of the very popular French overture in a chamber sonata seems to have been as inevitable as J.S. Bach's inclusion of the same form in some of his keyboard suites.

The earliest publications of the solo sonatas, however, are more difficult to analyze and authenticate. At approximately the same time Roger in Amsterdam and Walsh in London published a set of twelve solo sonatas; the Roger is based on an earlier Walsh edition, and the surviving Walsh is a corrected edition of his earlier one. The 19th-century German scholar Chrysander combined both collections with a few other solo sonatas and published them together as Opus I (a designation that Handel's publishers never used). If we look just at the sonatas of Roger's and Walsh's prints, ten of the sonatas are the same, but there are two in the Roger that are not in the Walsh and two in the Walsh that are not in the Roger. In any case, the latest musicological research seems to find a total of fifteen authentic Handel solo sonatas, and some of the more famous ones from Chrysander's (and Roger-Walsh's) editions have been eliminated.

Most of the sonatas seem to have been composed ca. 1724-1725. Besides the three solo Italian sonatas, one dates back to 1710 and two others are later, 1727 and 1750. Most are da chiesa, but within the slow-fast-slow-fast scheme HWV 363 substitutes two dances for the final fast movement, HWV 365 inserts a tempo di gavotta between the second slow and final fast movements, and HWV 366 uses a bourrée anglaise for its final fast movement. HWV 367 has five da chiesa movements and two dances. The scoring varies; five are for violin and continuo (HWV 371 says harpsichord), eight are for flute or recorder and continuo (three of which say harpsichord), three are for oboe and continuo, and a few have optional alternate performance possibilities.

While all Baroque composers borrowed from earlier works by themselves or others, Handel seems to exceed all others in the number of times he borrowed from himself. This is true in and among the operas and oratorios, and it is particularly true in the sonatas. All the Opus 5 trio sonatas borrow from the Chandos Anthems, and many of them as well as others borrow from opera overtures. In turn many of the sonatas were adapted later as organ concertos. HWV 378, one of the early Italian sonatas, is surprising as the source for much of the greatest and grandest of all Handel sonatas, the late 1750 violin and continuo sonata in D Major. While Handel was free to borrow from himself, it was also commonplace in London during the years of popularity of his operas that others, presumably hack musicians, arranged arias and choruses from his operas and oratorios for various chamber music ensembles to be played by amateurs at home. This procedure is very important in the development of Hausmusik at the end of the 18th century and throughout the 19th and will be discussed in more detail later in this book, but it is interesting to note that it already was a part of the development of bourgeois chamber music in the early 18th century.

THE GERMAN SCHOOL OF SONATA CA. 1680-1740

In Germany as in the rest of Europe there were four distinct locations for chamber music at the end of the 17th and beginning of the 18th centuries.[48] Private chamber music in one's own home was not only a possibility but also, in some cases, a necessity. It was here that professional or amateur fathers (and mothers?) taught their sons (and daughters) instrumental and vocal skills and passed many family hours together making chamber music. A second location was the court chamber where an aristocrat ordered his paid musicians to perform chamber music. Enlightened noblemen would often join the professionals in making chamber music, which would be performed before a small, select group of friends of the host. A third situation was the public concerts such as those already described in Paris (especially the Concert Spirituel) and London. The free city Hamburg had its public concerts started by Telemann in 1721, at which professional artists employed by churches and various nearby courts would come together in the "Drill House" to play before a paying audience of persons from different social classes. The fourth possibility was the collegium musicum, a group of both professional and amateur performers, often students, from different social classes who met on a regular

---

[48]Cf. Hans Vogt, *Johann Sebastian Bach's Chamber Music: Background, Analyses, Individual Works*, trl. Kenn Johnson (Portland, OR: Amadeus Press, 1988), pp. 36-40.

basis (at least weekly) to play chamber music for the enjoyment of playing it. Such groups, found throughout Germany and Holland, were tightly organized and severe punishments were meted out to members who failed to appear at meetings thereby disrupting the ensemble. Again Telemann was important as the founder of such groups in Leipzig, Frankfurt am Main, and Hamburg, and all important German chamber musicians of the late 17th and early 18th centuries at some time in their careers were members of collegia musica. While these four locations are the most important, on rare occasions the church could also be the site of some chamber music, though the earlier Venetian use of liturgical chamber music had no chamber music counterpart at this time in Germany. On the other hand, the outdoor performance of brass ensemble music from the balconies of city buildings surrounding market places to entertain merchants and buyers on busy market days, such as in Leipzig and Lübeck, was a common location for a type of music which only later became chamber music.

In North Germany at the end of the 17th century the leading composers of chamber music were organists or theorists. The organist, who was beneath the cantor in the church hierarchy, in social status in the community, and in annual salary, was able to rise to the level of the cantor by usurping some of the role of the cantor when the latter was too busy to compose the more complicated vocal and instrumental music of the service.[49] In Lübeck the organist Franz Tunder had taken over the duties of the cantor quite early, and ever mindful of the upward thrust of his profession, he went one step further by creating the Abendspiel and concerts for market days. Matthias Weckmann did the same in Hamburg and Kuhnau in Leipzig with their collegia musica. By creating a new role for themselves within the community and outside the church, they established a newer, higher status for themselves in their communities.

---

[49]This has its roots in Dutch history; during the rise of Calvinism at the end of the 16th century, Dutch organists who were denied any creative freedom in the music of the service turned to public community concerts which were not bound by liturgy. As the most influential organist in Northern Europe at the time, Sweelinck's role in this inevitably influenced North German musicians as well. Cf. Christine Defant, *Kammermusik und Stylus phantasticus: Studien zu Dietrich Buxtehudes Triosonaten*, in *Europäische Hochschulschriften*, series 36, *Musikwissenschaft* vol. 14 (Frankfurt am Main: Peter Lang, 1985), p. 53.

Dietrich Buxtehude (1637-1707, at harpsichord), with chamber musicians. Museum für Hamburgische Geschichte.

The music for these concerts remained religious and not much different in structure from the fanciest liturgical music with voices and orchestra. When Dietrich Buxtehude took over the Lübeck Abendmusik in 1668 from the recently deceased Tunder, he at first continued the past tradition, but then, by the end of the century, he added purely instrumental chamber music. Other important North German organists and theorists also turned to the sonata at this time: Weckmann, Reincken, Theile, and D. Becker. This form of pure music, with neither words nor borrowed cantus firmus, was free to follow musical dictates and the composer's imagination. When Buxtehude published fourteen of these trio sonatas in two volumes in 1696, he went another step upward. Free of religious and functional ends, the music was now designed for the homes of any and every music lover throughout Europe. The publication's forward in Italian, not German, enabled Buxtehude's sonatas to enter households in the best of company (with Corelli, Albinoni and others) where the tones of North German organ music would have been unknown.

As an organist—indeed, probably the best organ player of his time—Buxtehude turned to the trio sonata in a way different from the South German sonata composer, who was a string player. The scoring of the fourteen sonatas suggests English, not Italian precedents: violin, viola da gamba, and cembalo, each treated as an equal partner. The forms of the sonatas suggest more the end of the canzona or fantasia tradition which would have been better known to an organist in 1696 than to a violinist; in each sonata there are numerous sections (rather than separate movements) distinguished by tempo, sometimes meter and key, and motives. The sections are contrapuntally conceived; a few are early fugues. In a few sections the viola da gamba drops out, and in some cases the cembalo is alone for a few measures. Only one section could be called an independent movement: the finale of Opus 2, no. 3 is a binary form gigue (the only dance and only binary-form section in the entire fourteen sonatas). In a number of sections improvisation was intended; the written-out notes with free rhythm are more typical of keyboard practice than ensemble and were the result of Buxtehude's organ orientation.

In South Germany and Austria the composers turning to sonatas in the 17th century were violinists: Schmelzer in Vienna and Biber in Salzburg. Whereas the North Germans were influenced by Sweelinck and the stern organ school of the North, the South Germans were heavily influenced by Italian music, especially the new schools of violin ensemble music. By the beginning of the 18th century the vitality of the Italian violin school began to make its way north, so that when Buxtehude died in 1707 the stage was set for the Italian take-over of all German sonata writing, culminating in the works of J.S. Bach.

The city of Leipzig was typical for major free German cities, yet it was also unique. When the Swedish armies evacuated the city in 1650, it began a steady growth economically and musically that soon brought it fame. Several attempts were made at establishing collegia musica during the early 17th century, but the most famous by Pezel (1672) and Kuhnau (1688) came after mid-century. The music played was orchestral suites as well as vocal music with instruments. Pezel, however, was also a city violinist and city wind player, and while nearly all his fellow city musicians were hack players without any creative ability, Pezel published a number of collections of music both for his collegium musicum and for his duties as city trumpeter (playing from the tower of the city hall on market days). While the music of the collegium musicum was orchestral, the tower music (one person per part, 4 or 5 parts) was chamber in all but location. At the beginning of the 18th century Telemann founded a rival collegium musicum to Kuhnau's (1704), and shortly thereafter one of Kuhnau's students, J.F. Fasch, founded yet another collegium musicum. During the next thirty years or so these new collegia flourished in Leipzig; they met once or twice a week in coffee houses and included, besides the orchestral suites and vocal works typical of the 17th century, some sonatas.

An important link between the Italian school of sonata and Bach's is the German violinist Johann Georg Pisendel (1682-1755). As the son of a cantor and a choirboy in Lutheran churches, Pisendel's background was similar to Bach's. But Pisendel early turned to the violin as his main instrument, and in 1704, as a member of the court orchestra in Ansbach, he studied this instrument with Torelli. In 1709 he was a student in Leipzig where he performed an Albinoni concerto with the collegium musicum founded by Telemann. In 1712 he moved to the court orchestra in nearby Dresden and remained there for the rest of his life; he was concertmaster from 1728. In 1717 he traveled with the Saxon Elector's son to Italy, and for a brief time that year was a pupil of Vivaldi. As stated above, both Vivaldi and Albinoni dedicated sonatas to him, and he was well acquainted with their latest works, which at the time were primarily sonatas and concertos. Upon his return to Dresden, Pisendel played a lot of Vivaldi and helped popularize the Venetian in Germany. Although Pisendel himself has left only a small amount of chamber music (two violin sonatas with bass), a few concertos and one sonata for violin unaccompanied, his enormous influence on Bach resulted directly in the latter's unaccompanied partitas and sonatas and probably also in his accompanied sonatas. For Bach Pisendel was the greatest German violinist and his friend since 1709 (they met in Weimar); Bach sent his eldest son Wilhelm Friedemann for violin instruction to Pisendel's pupil Graun in Dresden.

Gottfried Heinrich Stölzel (1690-1749), another contemporary of Bach, was more prolific as a composer of chamber music. He was active in the Leipzig collegium musicum founded by Telemann from 1707 to 1710 and no doubt knew Pisendel there. Wherever he moved (for example, Breslau in 1710 and Prague 1715-1717), he seems to have involved himself with the local collegium musicum and in chamber music. In 1719 he became a violinist in Saxe-Gotha and the next year Kapellmeister there, where he remained for the rest of his life. In 1713 he traveled to Venice where he met Francesco Gasparini, Alessandro Marcello, Pollarolo and Vivaldi, who must have strengthened his interest in chamber music as well as opera, oratorio and Catholic liturgical music. Stölzel's surviving chamber compositions include three quartets and twenty-three trio sonatas. His trio sonata in E Minor for flute, violin and bass shows the influence of Vivaldi and Albinoni.[50] The flute and violin are imitative throughout, and the bass is a mere harmonic accompaniment. The sonata is in three movements allegro-adagio-

---

[50]Stölzel, *Sonata a3 für Flöte (Violine, Oboe), Violine, Violoncell und Cembalo*, ed. Gotthold Frotscher, in *Collegium Musicum*, no. 72 (Leipzig: Breitkopf und Härtel, 1942).

vivace, with the second in the dominant minor. Only the third is in binary form; the second is the continual development of a motive in imitation between the two treble instruments, while the first is the development of two motives in a nascent but non-binary sonata form. The three-movement trio sonata for oboe and violin with harpsichord in C Minor is much the same, except the first movement is an Andante and the continuo is much more independent and active.[51] Much more unusual is the sonata quartet for corno di caccia, oboe, violin and bass—not for its three-movement structure, which resembles all the above trio sonatas but for its colorful scoring.[52] The horn (which is absent in movement 2) has its own idiomatic part while the oboe and violin play together around it and the continuo accompanies. The two trio sonatas in D and B♭ for two violins and continuo, however, are clear-cut old fashioned da chiesa sonatas slow - fast - slow - fast without any binary-form dances (the third movement of the B♭ sonata is a lengthy "Siciliana" but not otherwise different from da chiesa movements. The da chiesa or canzona background to these two sonatas is manifest as well in the frequent imitation, Stimmtausch, and echo, and in the simplicity of instrumental technique. The trio sonata in F Minor for two violins and continuo is also in the usual four movements, but here the key is substantially more difficult for the violins, yet offers room for greater expression. There is nothing remarkable about any of these works by Stölzel, and while both he and Pisendel established the chamber sonata in Germany, it is in the hands of the true genius of their generation that German chamber sonatas reach a worthy plain.

JOHANN SEBASTIAN BACH

There are four periods in his life when Bach was deeply involved with chamber music. As the scion of an important musical family and an important violinist and violist as well as keyboard player, J.S. Bach assuredly started hearing and playing sonatas at

---

[51]Dresden, Sächs. Landesbibliothek; ed. Günter Hausswald, in *Collegium Musicum*, no. 76 (Leipzig: Breitkopf & Härtel, 1950).

[52]Dresden, Sächs. Landesbibliothek, ed. Hausswald, in *Collegium Musicum*, no. 79 (Leipzig: Breitkopf & Härtel, 1952).

home while very young. This practice no doubt continued later on when Bach's children were at home learning various musical instruments. Then during his six years (1717-1723) as Kapellmeister to Prince Leopold von Anhalt-Köthen (1694-1728) he was responsible for both chamber and orchestral music at this small but impressive court. It is during this period when he probably wrote most of his chamber music. When Bach arrived in Köthen, he found excellent professionals, some of whom had just left the court orchestra in Berlin. The chamber musicians of the Köthen prince consisted of two violinists, an oboist, two flutists, a bassoonist, a cellist, and a gambist; Bach played viola and probably also harpsichord in ensembles, though C.P.E. Bach testifies to the fact that his father preferred to conduct ensembles from his violin or viola stand and not from the keyboard.[53] Thus there is a reasonable possibility that some chamber and orchestral music in Köthen was not played with keyboard continuo. As needed, especially for orchestral music, the prince himself—an accomplished violinist—as well as servants who were somewhat skilled on a string instrument would join in, and for very special occasions trumpeters, drummers and even horn players would be hired from the ranks of the nearby city musicians. The rehearsals often took place in Bach's own home, and the concerts occurred in a hall in the prince's Schloss of about one hundred seats before an unvarying audience of friends and family of the prince.

When Bach moved to Leipzig in 1723, he assumed directorship of the music at three churches, which would have kept him very busy. But from 1729 to 1738 he was also director of the Leipzig Collegium Musicum which Telemann started and was responsible for a good deal of both chamber and orchestral music playing. For occasions of the Collegium Musicum he probably wrote some additional chamber music and revised some of his earlier pieces. Then, in his last years, Bach had special occasions for which he wrote chamber music, such as "The Musical Offering" for Frederick the Great in Potsdam in 1747.

The chamber compositions of Bach represent on the one hand the culmination of all the developments of sonata writing that we

---

[53]Vogt, pp. 41-45.

have seen since 1680 in Italy, France, England, and Germany. On the other hand, by their emphasis on the keyboard partner in the chamber ensemble and by their advanced tonal organization they helped usher in the new age of transition which, in turn, culminated in the flowering of the Classical Period (see the next two chapters). Bach's chamber works include several early sonatas for violin and continuo (BWV 1020-1023),[54] three sonatas for flute and keyboard probably originating in Köthen (BWV 1030, 1034-1035), two trio sonatas probably from Köthen (BWV 1038-1039), three sonatas for viola da gamba and harpsichord (BWV 1027-1029), the six sonatas for violin and harpsichord from Köthen (BWV 1014-1019), and finally the trio sonata from "The Musical Offering" (BWV 1079). During the 1730's and 1740's Bach revised some of these works, in some cases changing the instrumentation, in others writing alternative movements. The three viola da gamba sonatas, for example, are probably all arrangements of earlier trio sonatas; BWV 1027 survives in both its original trio version for two flutes and continuo and in its da gamba arrangement where the viol plays the second flute part, the keyboard right hand plays the first flute part, and the keyboard left hand retains the continuo line. Bach now referred to the "cembalo obbligato" rather than to "continuo" or simply "basso," and it seems that when he accepted the keyboard as the equal partner of the violin, flute and/or viola da gamba, that he no longer had recourse to just a continuo in his chamber music.

It is difficult to generalize about Bach's sonatas since, unlike those by Corelli, Vivaldi, Handel and Couperin, no two sonatas are really alike. In general Bach wrote da chiesa sonatas; the only exception is BWV 1023. Bach was greatly influenced by Couperin,[55] but this influence affected Bach's keyboard suites and even the orchestral overtures and unaccompanied violin partitas rather than the ensemble chamber music. The transformation in the role of the continuo from an accompanying partner to a full partner is antici-

---

[54]There are some early chamber works attributed to Bach which are probably not by him; cf. Vogt, pp. 15-35, for a summary of questions of dating, authenticity, and sources. BWV 1020 and 1022 are questionable works. BWV 1031 and 1032 are flute sonatas which are doubtful and fragmentary respectively. Eppstein dates BWV 1030 (original G minor version), 1031, 1032, 1027, 1028, and 1029, and 1014-1019) from Köthen.

[55]Couperin and Bach met in Celle and corresponded.

pated in Couperin but comes to fulfillment in Bach, most of whose chamber music has either a full keyboard rather than continuo or a combination of left-hand continuo with a written-out right hand that is the equal of the solo instrument or instruments. Beyond an apparent hint of this new role for the keyboard, however, there is no apparent influence of Couperin's "Les Nations" on Bach's chamber sonatas. Rather in this area Bach seems to have been more influenced by the sonatas of Albinoni and Handel. The lingering popularity of the viola da gamba in Paris and London is also reflected in Bach's scoring for the instrument as a solo equal to the violin and keyboard.

Stylistically Bach was everywhere a contrapuntalist, even in those relatively few movements in binary form,[56] and when Bach put on a display of the intricacies of counterpoint, no one came close to being his equal. The two Allegro movements in BWV 1027 (= 1039), for example, are fugues employing inversion and stretto as only he could compose them, and the Andante of BWV 1015 is a strict canon between the violin and keyboard right hand at the unison and at one measure. Nearly every sonata is in four movements slow-fast-slow-fast, but there are a few exceptions (BWV 1019 is in five movements[57] with the middle movement for solo keyboard without violin, BWV 1029 is in three movements fast-slow-fast, and BWV 1030 is in four movements moderate-slow-fast-moderate [movements 2 and 4 in binary form]). The movements are usually separate, but in a few cases a slow movement ends on a dominant chord followed by the tonic at the opening of the next movement. Nearly all sonatas in the minor contain at least one movement in the major, and those in the major contain one movement in the minor. BWV 1019, however, in its most commonly accepted version, begins in G, movements 2 and 3 are in E Minor, movement 4 is in C Major, and the final movement returns to the tonic G. Besides the few movements in binary form, the principle of thematic evolution and harmonic modulation to dominant, subdominant and possibly several other keys determines the form of the movement. The early sonata BWV 1023 opens with

---

[56]Except in the first movements of BWV 1016 and 1023.

[57]There are three authentic versions of this sonata, two of which have five movements and the solo by the keyboard.

an unusual rhapsody in the violin for twenty-nine measures over an "e" pedal tone in the continuo, and BWV 1016 opens with a prelude that is homophonic and free.

While the Italians developed the new sonata that dominates chamber music playing and composition between ca. 1680 and ca. 1730, it was principally the non-Italians Handel in England, Couperin in France, and Bach in Germany who fully realized the artistic qualities of the sonata and wrote the most enduring examples. At the same time, their music had the seeds for change, which led to the development of chamber music from the Baroque sonata to the various Classical types of string quartet, piano and string trio, and others.

CHAPTER IV

18TH-CENTURY TRANSITION

During the mid-18th century, the forms, styles and instrumentation of chamber music underwent a radical change. Twenty years into the 18th century the duet and trio sonata, with its incumbent forms, styles and instrumentation, seemed to know no serious rival, but fifteen years before the end of the same century the sonata, considerably transformed, was seriously rivaled by the string quartet, the string and piano trio, and the string quintet. Whereas Corelli, Bach and Handel realized the full potential of the baroque sonata at the end of a century of development, Haydn, Mozart, and young Beethoven helped create the new types of chamber music which have dominated the chamber music repertory ever since. How the situation at the end of the century came to be is the focus of the following discussion.

Much of the chamber music from the 1730's to the 1770's was transitional in terms of the new genres that were coming into being and the evolution of old ones into new ones. There were many experiments, some of which were the result of new social situations, new aesthetic considerations, or simply changing fads. From an historical point of view almost all this music is important, but from a modern aesthetic standpoint much of it is inconsequential. Even in the 18th century some of the chamber music was *Unterhaltungsmusik* (background music to accompany conversation). Nonetheless, as we emphasize the historical aspects there are some works, for example the many quartets and quintets of Boccherini, which beyond their historical importance are well worth reviving. A few works which are important historically need no apology; they are masterworks belonging to the first rank of the total repertoire of chamber music (for example the violin and obligato harpsichord sonatas of Bach's and Haydn's early quartets).

An important consideration for this transition is the relationship among the instruments of the chamber ensemble. In the baroque sonata there were typically three basic relationships. Frequently there were one or two treble instruments which dominated, accompanied by a basso continuo. There were also other situations, such as the sonata for treble, bass, and continuo, where the bass instrument (a viola da gamba or violoncello in most cases) was independent of the continuo. The keyboard served primarily as a continuo accompaniment. A third situation found no continuo at all but rather a bass instrument (violoncello or string bass) providing support for if not equality with one or two upper instruments.

During the course of the 18th century we see a change in most of these relationships. Most significantly the keyboard continuo instrument as an accompanimental instrument was increasingly replaced by a harpsichord or piano which was the predominant or at least an equal partner in the ensemble. The baroque sonata had the solo violin or flute on top with the continuo accompanying; the pre-classical sonata had the keyboard central with the other instruments accompanying or *ad libitum*; the classical sonata had all participating instruments equal with a mixture of styles. The pre-classical is much easier to perform, which corresponds to the gradual diminishing of court chamber music and the rise of middle-class chamber music in the home; it also corresponds to an increase in numbers and importance of amateur and professional solo keyboardists.

The new simplicity in style of the pre-classic sonata may also have been the result of new aesthetic considerations apart from any sociological development. Whereas the baroque composer attained his greatest expression through the selection of poignant harmony and motor rhythm, the pre-classical composer attained his greatest expression through plain melody and broad rhythmic contrast. The forte-piano was also a product of this style change, since this new instrument is much more expressive than the harpsichord (the predominant continuo instrument) and many new ideas of the *Sturm und Drang* of the 1770's and 1780's are possible on the piano but not the harpsichord. Furthermore, the relationship of the violin to the keyboard changed once the more expressive piano replaced the harpsichord. The violin dominated the baroque continuo and doubled right hand melodies of pre-classical harpsichords because the violin can express emotions much more keenly than the harpsichord with its tiered dynamics and unsustained sound,[1] but since the piano not only has control over dynamics but can also express gradations of tone and sustain tones much longer than the harpsichord, the violin ceased to be necessary to the keyboard. For the pre-classical sonata the violin was *ad libitum*, and when the violin regained its importance in the classical sonata, the violin and piano were mature partners of equal stature.

In sonatas where the "upper" part (usually a treble instrument such as the violin, oboe or flute but in some cases a violoncello or bassoon) dominated with virtuosic display, the performances of such works were by gifted, mostly professional artists before an audience. On the other hand in sonatas where the keyboard part was completely written out and dominant and the other instrumental part is simple and often innocuous, either the keyboard was played by the talented patron or patroness with the others keeping their place in the background or the performance of the "upper" part was by amateurs of very limited ability with the assistance of their teachers, gifted students, and/or hired artists before no or very limited family audiences.[2] In actuality, the latter situation resulted in sonatas where the keyboard part was of principal interest and the "upper" part sometimes could even be omitted without harm to the work; indeed, publishers were known to have published easy violin and cello accompanimental parts unbeknownst to the composer in order to increase sales.[3] The former sonata is often referred to as the sonata for violin and continuo, which has been discussed at length in the previous chapter. The latter sonata is often referred to as the accompanied sonata with obligato keyboard.

---

[1] Cf. the references to William Jackson and Charles Avison on pp. 215-216 below.

[2] Hendrik Eduard Reeser, *De Klaviersonate met Vioolbegeleiding in het Parÿsche Muziekleven ten Tÿde van Mozart* (Rotterdam: W.L. and J. Brusse, 1939), pp. 18-19; and Zdenka Pilkova, "Die Violinsonaten der böhmischen Komponisten in den Jahren 1730-1770," in *Zur Entwicklung der instrumentalen Kammermusik in der 1. Hälfte des 18. Jahrhunderts* (Blankenburg/Harz: n.p., 1984), p. 53.

[3] C.P.E. Bach's thirteen sonatas (Wotquenne catalogue nos. 89-91) for piano were published in 1776 to 1777 without string parts, but because the public demanded accompanimental string parts, the publisher persuaded Bach to provide them.

THE ACCOMPANIED OBLIGATO KEYBOARD SONATA

Before the accompanied obligato keyboard sonata could exist it was necessary for composers to break away from the strong tradition of the baroque sonata. A variety of new relationships were tried out in the 1730's to 1760's, all of which contributed to the special obligato sonata of the 1760's to 1770's with violin accompaniment.[4] Unfortunately, terminology used during this period is ambiguous. Works were called sonatas, trios or simply *pièces* frequently without any apparent distinction among these titles. On the other hand when the terms *concertato, concertante, concerto, simphonie* or *simphonie concertante* were used, these titles implied a type of sonata wherein a few instruments shared more or less equally in histrionic motives; works with any one of these titles are distinct from those pieces without these words in the title. The Italians and Germans used "obligato" to mean a fully written-out keyboard part, but this did not dictate what relationship the violin or cello would have with the keyboard. The French did not use the term "obligato" for the keyboard and used the expression "sonatas for keyboard accompanied by violin" to cover a variety of relationships, from duets where both instruments are of equal importance to sonatas where the violin is trivial. The French did use *obligé* for the violin, especially in the 1780's, when that instrument was regaining its importance in the ensemble. To make terminology precise for this discussion, I will use "obligato keyboard" to refer to a fully written-out keyboard part, "duet" to refer to an equal relationship between violin and keyboard, "trio" to refer to a piece with three equivalent lines of music (which can include a duet between treble instrument and a fully written-out keyboard where each hand is monophonic), and "accompanied obligato keyboard" to refer to a fully written-out keyboard with a much less important violin (or flute) accompanying it.

The geographic centers for the cultivation of the accompanied obligato keyboard sonata and its immediate precursors were first and foremost Paris, but also Mannheim, London, and Vienna. Italian composers were important and Biagio Marini was apparently the first to write a sonata with a fully written-out keyboard, but al-

---

[4]The role of the cello will be discussed later.

most all Italians during the middle 18th century lived and published in the above-named foreign cities. The reason for the popularity of the sonata in those cities may be explained by the fact that each had active public instrumental concert series, important orchestras, and/or numerous publishers. A large audience there was tuned in to purely instrumental music at a time when aestheticians were debunking it in favor of vocal music, and many resident professional instrumental players were anxious to exploit their talents. In addition, the growing middle classes in Paris, London, and Vienna meant a growing clientele of amateur, home performers who would eagerly buy these sonatas and try to imitate in private what they heard publicly. German cities also experienced a growing middle class with a rising clientele for the accompanied obligato sonata, though Mannheim (and by the end of the 1770's its sister city Munich) stood apart; Mannheim was a court city where the nobility encouraged and attracted some of the best instrumentalists of the time. That many of these instrumentalists were Bohemian exiles is not surprising since in their native Bohemia the suppression of secular music by the Church led the best Czech musicians to seek elsewhere a more sympathetic climate in which to write and play secular music.[5]

The three most important precursors of the composers of the accompanied obligato keyboard sonata were J.S. Bach, Mondonville, and Rameau who because of their genius and influence on their younger contemporaries set the stage for this new kind of sonata.[6] Bach's influence is seen particularly on his son Carl Philipp Emanuel, Mondonville's was felt by all subsequent French violinists, whereas Rameau's influence spread to everyone in music in the 18th century.

---

[5]Pilkova, p. 54.

[6]Obligato keyboard with other instruments in Rameau and Bach began a new relationship among instruments (Jürgen Eppelsheim, "Funktionen des Tasteninstruments in J.S. Bachs Sonaten mit obligatem Cembalo," and Franciszek Wesolowski, "'Pièces de Clavecin en Concerts' von J. Ph. Rameau als Beispiel der französischen Kammermusik für Klavier mit Begleitung anderer Instrumente," in Günter Fleischhauer, Walther Siegmund-Schultze and Eitelfriedrich Thom, *Zur Entwicklung der instrumentalen Kammermusik in der 1. Hälfte des 18. Jahrhunderts*, in *Studien zur Aufführungspraxis und Interpretation von Instrumentalmusik des 18. Jahrhunderts: Konferenzbericht der xi. wissenschaftlichen Arbeitstagung Blankenburg/Harz, 17. Juni bis 19. Juni 1983*, vol. 22, [no publishing information], pp. 23-33, 50-52).

Paris

Although Mondonville's Opus 3 (ca. 1734) may be the earliest collection printed in Paris whose title states that the keyboard is accompanied by the violin,[7] this collection is, despite its title, not a collection of *accompanied* obligato keyboard sonatas.[8] The term "accompanied," which appears in the titles of numerous collections of sonatas in France and elsewhere especially during the 1740's and 1750's, referred at this time to the fact that the keyboard had attained full stature in the ensemble; both hands were written out, and a treble instrument (usually violin or flute[9]) plays along with this full keyboard. By the later 1750's, however, the "accompanied" sonata presumes that the keyboard was more important than the treble instrument, but this presumption was not the case in the "accompanied" keyboard sonatas of the 1730's to early 1750's. Mondonville was an important violin virtuoso who appeared frequently in public at the Concerts Spirituels and other places in France, and his first collection of sonatas (Opus 1) is fully in keeping with the baroque tradition of solo violin accompanied by figured continuo. Opus 3, despite its title, remained a collection of duets, not accompanied sonatas, since Mondonville, the virtuoso violinist, was not about to write innocuous violin accompaniments even if the keyboard had advanced beyond Opus 1 to a significant partner. In Opus 3 both keyboard and violin share equally in the counterpoint, thematic material, virtuosic display, as well as the accompaniment. The pieces themselves are typically baroque in all other aspects. The first begins with a French overture, continues

---

[7]Ronald R. Kidd, "The Emergence of Chamber Music with Obligato Keyboard in England," in *Acta Musicologica*, xliv (1972), 123.

[8]Mondonville's sonatas are beautifully reproduced in *Sonatas for the Violin*, ed. Edith Borroff, in *Masters of the Violin*, gen. ed. Gabriel Banat (New York: Johnson Reprint Co., 1982). Elizabeth Jacquet de la Guerre's *Pièces de Clavecin Qui peuvent se Jouer sur le Viollon* (Bibliothèque national music ms., dated June 13, 1707) survives only in a keyboard part and, as Thurston Dart points out in his edition of the sonatas (Monaco: Éditions de l'oiseau-lyre, 1965), "it is not clear from the text how [the violin] version was to be performed." It is the first time in France such an optional violin part to a keyboard work is mentioned. The two suites in the collection are in a typical Couperin-like keyboard style without the slightest suggestion of a violin-like line.

[9]Boismortier apparently wrote the first French sonatas for flute with a fully written-out harpsichord in his Opus 91 sonatas (ca. 1741-1742); cf. Laurel Fay, "Boismortier," in *The New Grove Dictionary of Music and Musicians*, II, p. 862.

with an aria in binary form, and concludes with a giga. The next four differ in the opening movement, which in these cases are binary-form allegros, and two of these sonatas substitute in the final movement an ordinary binary-form allegro for a giga. The sixth (last) sonata in the collection opens with a da capo "concerto" which only serves to emphasize the equality of the two instruments: the violin at times doubles the right hand of the keyboard (thus establishing a kind of concerto tutti), at others accompanies the keyboard, then takes over as pre-eminent instrument, and then again flows in equal counterpoint with the keyboard. It is significant that the term "concerto" was associated with this early pre-classical work since ultimately the concerto or "symphonie concertante" will have decisive influence on the development of the classical violin and piano sonata as well as on the classical string quartet.

While Mondonville's two collections Opus 1 and 3 were popular among violinists in France during the 1730's and 1740's, they did not lead to any immediate imitations.[10] His later *Pièces de Clavecin avec Voix ou Violon* (Opus 5, 1748) likewise seems not to have led to further exploitation of the medium, but these works come much closer in spirit to the accompanied obligato keyboard sonata than those in Opus 3. In his introduction Mondonville likened these pieces to those in Opus 3 in that the clavecin is not mere accompaniment but an equal member of the ensemble.[11] Here, however, the performers were given a certain flexibility in scoring depending on their particular circumstances. If there was a good singer around, the singer could accompany the harpsichord, but if

---

[10]Only in the 1740's do several collections appear: Michel Corrette's *Sonates pour le clavecin avec un accompagnement de violon . . . ces pièces se jouer sur le clavecin seul'* (Opus 25, 1742), Charles Clément's *Sonates en trio pour un clavecin et un violon* (1743), and Gabriel Guillemain's *Pièces de clavecin en sonates avec accompagnement de violon* (Opus 13, 1745). Rameau's collection of 1741 differs from Mondonville's in several important aspects (see below).

[11]Mondonville appears to be the first in France to raise the harpsichord to an equal partner in the ensemble. Charles Dieupart's *Six Suittes* (Amsterdam: 1701) exist in two versions published simultaneously but in separate volumes: one for flute or violin with continuo, the other for harpsichord alone. Since the latter is a harpsichord arrangement of the whole other version and not a duet or accompanied sonata (cf. David Fuller, "Dieupart, Charles," in *The New Grove Dictionary*, vol. V, p. 472, which refutes Boroff, p. 3), we are not dealing with the same situation as in Mondonville where the fully written-out harpsichord plays with the violin.

there was not a good singer available and there was a good violinist, then let the violinist accompany the harpsichord. If both were
available, then both (alternately) would accompany the harpsichord, and if neither were available, then let the clavecinist play
alone. The pieces were referred to as "concertos" in the Parisian
newspapers of the time; the term concerto was used here in the
older sense that refers to pieces combining voices and instruments.
Each of the six works is a Latin hymn with a purely instrumental
introduction, sometimes a ritornello for instruments, and a simple,
repetitive vocal movement with harpsichord accompaniment. The
violin can be omitted in the introduction and ritornelli, the voice
can be omitted and the violin replace it during the song, or the
harpsichord can play alone. Since only the harpsichord is indispensable and is always either dominant or equal to the other parts
(never subservient to them), it assumes the more important role of
the keyboard in the accompanied obligato keyboard sonata. Thus,
though hidden in the vocal concerto, the Opus 5 pieces placed the
keyboard in the same pre-eminence as in the accompanied obligato
sonata, but whatever the reason, Mondonville's Opus 3 and 5 were
not imitated and did not yet firmly establish the obligato sonata in
France.

Rameau, too, was important in establishing the possibility of
other options for the instruments than the traditional baroque one.
As in the case of Mondonville, Rameau did not write accompanied
obligato keyboard sonatas but explored a new balance among the
instruments that resulted in parity.[12] In his pioneering five *Pièces
de Clavecin en Concerts* (1741) scored for harpsichord with violin
or flute and viola da gamba or second violin, he was the first to
write two treble parts separate from the keyboard where the keyboard is neither more nor less important than the treble instruments.[13] All three instruments play a separate but equal role, which

---

[12]Rameau published *Cinq Pièces pour Clavecin Seul Extraites des Pièces de Clavecin en
Concerts* (Paris: 1741) which are solo harpsichord arrangements of earlier ensemble
works for harpsichord and two other instruments. The originals are chamber music
(discussed here), but the arrangements, as in the case of Dieupart (fn.11), are not.

[13]Christa Flamm, *Leopold Kozeluch: Biographie und stilkritische Untersuchung der
Sonaten für Klavier, Violine und Violoncello nebst einem Beitrag zur Entwicklungsgeschichte des Klaviertrios* (University of Vienna Ph.D. dissertation, 1968), pp. 93
and 108.

is the meaning of the word "concert." "Concert" also implies the contrast of tutti unison and accompanied solo that is characteristic of the baroque concerto. Thus the violin/flute and viola da gamba/second violin sometimes double the keyboard, either right or left hand, but they are also sometimes alone without the keyboard, with the keyboard as accompaniment, or in counterpoint with the keyboard. The harpsichord, in turn, is often contrapuntal (as for example at the opening of the fourth concert, "La Panto-mime," where the two hands of the harpsichord and the two other instruments are in four-part imitation, or during much of the opening of the fifth, "La Forqueray," a fugue, with the two hands of the keyboard sometimes acting as fugal voices, sometimes ac-companying the two other instruments with figured passages), but much of the keyboard writing is chordal with scalar figures. Dur-ing these figurations the other instruments play contrasting rhythms which heighten the effect of the harpsichord. All in all, the concerts were conceived for three interdependent instruments, none of which can be omitted. Each concert consists of a group of character pieces, usually in binary or rondeau form; titles of the pieces usually refer directly by name or indirectly by character to personages at court ("La Marais," "La Rameau," "L'Indiscrète," "L'Agaçante," "La Timide"). Since neither Mondonville nor Ra-meau wrote truly accompanied keyboard sonatas, it was left for Schobert to fully cultivate the accompanied obligato sonata in France a decade later.

In the years from 1750 to 1789, Paris was the center for the de-velopment of the pre-classical sonata. Often foreigners came to Paris and contributed to this development, but it was the special French ambience which enabled them to do so. Paris had its resi-dent orchestras and considerable public as well as private concert series. Paris had many music publishers and many resident com-posers and performers from all over Europe and America. What-ever happened in Paris was emulated everywhere else in Europe.

The reasons for the changing relationship among the instru-ments in these sonatas no doubt varied from case to case, but clearly the rise in importance of the keyboard in the compositions of the time evinces the new prominence of the keyboard among the patrons and amateur performers of keyboard instruments. In

France, where the violin and flute had been far more charismatic instruments during the 17th century, the appearance of virtuoso harpsichordists such as the Couperins and Rameau at the beginning of the 18th century sparked a vogue which carried through the rest of the century. Virtuoso harpsichordists now performed on an equal basis with virtuoso violinists and flutists, and noblemen and noblewomen began playing the harpsichord as well as violin in earnest. The new breed of solo-oriented clavecinists needed a new kind of music which featured them and perked their egos. Eventually composers, even violinist-composers, found it important for their careers to provide ever more prominent harpsichord parts, and the obligato and accompanied relationships emerged from this.

Before 1760 French composers were the principal ones to write "pièces de clavecin avec accompagnement de violon" in Paris. Besides those by Mondonville there were published collections by Simon, Damoreau, Legrand, and d'Herbain—all of which placed the violin and keyboard in an equivalent relationship. More important than establishing a new relationship between the instruments, these works (mostly sonatas) experimented with various forms and styles. Inherited from the French baroque were suites of three or more dances, usually with French character ascriptions. Damoreau, for example, opened his *Pièces* of 1754 with a rondeau entitled "La Sophie," and Legrand wrote "airs" with additional modifiers like "gaïment" and "gracieux sans lenteur" in his Opus 1 (ca. 1755). The dances are in binary form, and usually all the movements within a single suite are in the same tonality (perhaps moving from major to minor or minor to major). Simon's *Pièces* Opus I (ca. 1750) stand out, however, in their experimentation with the tonal relationship among movements. For example, the five movements of the third sonata are in G F c C and F, the three movements of the fifth in e g E, and the six movements of the sixth in G D d G d A. Such experimentation in tonal relationships was important in an era that was developing sonata and rondo forms that depend on tonal variety, and it ultimately made way for the rich harmony and tonal schemes of the entire 19th-century. By the 1770's until the 20th century most chamber music was written in these forms.

In the 1760's a group of immigrant Germans in Paris reshaped the sonatas for keyboard and violin into the accompanied obligato keyboard sonata: Schobert, Honauer, and Raupach. Suddenly the violin was reduced to mere accompaniment or doubling or even to triviality: it could accompany or be omitted *ad libitum*. This is understandable when we realize that these composers were keyboard players, whose stake in the perpetuation of violinistics did not exist. Of these, Johann Schobert (ca. 1720-1767) was the most important composer of the accompanied obligato keyboard sonatas. He firmly established the type as a legitimate genre of chamber music with his performances and many publications in Paris, and his influence particularly on Mozart ultimately determined much of the new chamber music of the late 18th century. All his works had been republished in London by 1775, and they remained in print until well into the 19th century. Since it was largely through Schobert that the obligato sonata developed into the classical piano trio and violin-piano sonata, we will defer discussion of his works until we deal with those genres.

Leontzi (Antoine) Honauer (ca. 1735- after 1790) published two collections (Opus 1, 1761; Opus 3, 1764) which firmly established the trivial nature of the violin. In the first he nonchalantly stated that the violin accompanies or does not accompany (as you will), while he entitled the second collection *Six Sonates pour le clavecin avec accompagnement de violon ad libitum*." Hermann Friedrich Raupach's *Six Sonates pour le clavecin avec accompagnement de violon, oeuvre I* (ca. 1765), on the other hand, does not blatantly allow an *ad libitum* violin, and actually the violin has some rhythmic counterpoint to the right hand of the keyboard and some quasi imitation. Yet here, too, the violin could be omitted and the keyboard could play entirely alone.

Although Schobert, Honauer, and Raupach are masters of the accompanied keyboard obligato sonata, their greater contribution lay in changing the nature of the forms and styles of the sonatas from baroque to classical. Almost all sonatas are in three movements fast-slow-fast, and almost all the fast movements and many of the slow ones are in a nascent sonata form. There is frequently an exposition of two distinct themes, the second in a contrasting key, and a rhythmic development section. What is weakest is the absence of a full recapitulation. The flow of the music is, likewise, pre-classical in that it often breaks the steady motion of the motor rhythm with rests and contrasting rhythm.

Once Schobert, Honauer and Raupach established the accompanied obligato keyboard sonata in Paris, Frenchmen were quick to imitate it. Especially French keyboardists such as A.L. Couperin, De Virbés, Lasceux, Séjan and Beauvarlet-Charpentier were eager to exploit this new relationship with the now emerging forté piano. Guillaume Lasceux (b. 1740) was one of the first to specifically call for the forté piano in his Opus 2 *Sonates pour le clavecin et le forte piano avec accompagnement de violon ad libitum* (1772),[14] but all five composers clearly were writing for this instrument. Gottfried Eckard and the piano maker Johann Andreas Stein came to Paris ca. 1740 to promote the new instrument, but although there was much interest in it at the time, it took another thirty years to catch on.[15] Nicolas Séjan (1745-1819) took advantage of the piano to write expansive melodies full of a pathos that anticipated Beethoven. The Alberti bass was typical for the piano left hand, and though it often became monotonous (especially in De Virbés' sonata of 1768), it could add a new dimension to the ensemble when used creatively (as in Jean Jacques Beauvarlet-Charpentier's Opus 2 [1773]). Five of Armand Louis Couperin's sonatas in his Opus 2 (1765) follow the typical fast-slow-fast scheme of movements, but the first sonata has a minuet between the slow and final fast movements thereby anticipating the standard order of movements of most classical symphonies, string quartets, and other genres, including some Beethoven violin-piano sonatas. Couperin's sonata-form movements have full recapitulations in the tonic, but the two theme groups of the exposition are not as clearly delineated as in Schobert, Honauer and Raupach. In addition to the emerging sonata form the composers of the 1760's and 1770's wrote rondos and, following the lead of Mondonville in his Opus 3, concertos ("symphonies concertantes"). The third sonata of Charpentier's Opus 4 (1775) is such a symphonie concertante with alternating tutti (violin doubles piano right hand) and soli (at different times the violin or the piano have solo, virtuosic passages). This sonata is

---

[14]Roesser's was the first in 1770; cf. below.

[15]Flamm, p. 99.

in two long movements, the first a sonata-form with an abbreviated recapitulation and the second a rondo-like "tempo di menuetto." As we will see with the string quartet, the concertant idea is first an emphasis on the participation of all instruments in solistic motivic passages and second the preponderance of two-movement structure with the first movement in sonata form. The concertant sonata, as in Charpentier's example, is consistent with the concertant quartet, but the orchestral concertant (sinfonia concertant), not the quartet concertant, was the model for the sonata. The tutti passages and some of the solo ones as well are much more homophonic than is typical of the French obligato accompanied sonata and was as much influenced by the concertos of Carl Stamitz, popular in Paris at the time, as the obligato sonatas of Schobert. Charpentier continued to write such sonatas, and sometime later in the 1770's published his Opus 8 *Trois sonates pour le clavecin dans le goût de la simphonie concertante, avec accompagnement de violon obligé.* The violin is still accompaniment, but now it is no longer trivial or dispensable; it must be there to create the concerto with the keyboard. Ultimately the merging of the obligato sonata and symphonie concertante brought in the French classical piano-violin sonata just as the merging of the Viennese divertimento quartet with the French symphonie concertante brought in the Viennese classical quartet.

Another group of German immigrants in Paris had an impact on the accompanied sonatas of the 1770's and 1780's. Although Valentin Roesser, Heinrich Joseph Rigel, Johann Friedrich Edelmann and Nikolaus Joseph Hüllmandel could not approach their forebears in originality, they were prolific and influential in their own day. Roesser was the first composer of accompanied keyboard obligato sonatas to specifically call for the forté piano in the title of his collection (Opus 10, 1770); these six sonatas were admittedly "tirées des ouvrages de J. Stamitz." Like Stamitz in his trios and symphonies, Roesser wrote two-movement sonatas (Andante - Menuet), but mindful of his Parisian audience he added character titles to most of the movements ("La Jeannette," "La Badine," "La Précieuse," "La Lutine," "L'Engageante" inspired by opèra comique ariettes). Rigel's five collections treat the violin as an *ad libitum* accompaniment and were greatly influenced by Schobert;

most of his sonatas are in three movements, but those of Opus 8 (1777) are in two. Opus 8 no. 4 was dedicated to Marie Antoinette, who was apparently taken with the music of Rigel.

Jean-Frédéric Edelmann (1749-1794) was an immensely popular composer and pianist in Paris during the reign of Louis XVI. He published eleven collections of accompanied obligato keyboard sonatas from 1773 to 1786, mostly in three movements fast-slow-fast. While most of his works are superficial, there are some in which he did experiment with form. The first sonata of Opus 2 (1774), for example, has the same coda for the first and third movements, and the third movement in "sonata" form has the exposition entirely in the tonic. Edelmann was so closely associated with the court that he eventually, like the royal family, had his head cut off.

Nikolaus Joseph Hüllmandel (1751-1823) wrote seven collections of accompanied obligato keyboard sonatas in Paris from 1776 to 1789. The earlier sonatas add nothing new in outward form to the genre but are attractive pieces. As a pupil of Carl Philip Emanuel Bach and eventually a resident of both Paris and London, Hüllmandel was an important link between the North German sonata composers and those in France and England. Furthermore, on his last visit to Paris (1778) Mozart took a particular liking to Hüllmandel's Opus 3 (1777) sonatas, where most of the movements are in sonata form and the violin displays some independence (for example, imitation of the right hand of the keyboard). A little later Hüllmandel wrote three more sonatas (Opus 6, 1782), of which the third places the violin in equal relationship to the piano as soloist, and he did the same thing in the third sonata of his Opus 8. In form, too, Hüllmandel took more care in Opus 6 and 8 than in Opus 3 or than is found in Schobert's sonatas to delineate the contrasting parts of the exposition and to make the recapitulation meaningful. "Het is de verdienste van Hüllmandel geweest, uit de Parijsche klaviersonate met vioolbegeleiding de 'moderne' vioolsonate gekristalliseerd te hebben, onafhankelijk van de meer of minder geslaagde pogingen, die elders ondernomen zijn."[16]

---

[16]Reeser, p. 128.

The last stage of the accompanied obligato keyboard sonatas in France occurred during the 1780's. As we have already noted with Hüllmandel's collections of this decade, there were already signs of the transition to the classical violin-piano sonata. Violinist-composers such as De Saint-Georges (1739-1799) and Marie Alexandre Guénin (1744-1835) inevitably favored the violin over the keyboard, and by re-emphasizing the violin (as was the case before 1750), the final stage of development to the classical violin-piano sonata was now prepared. The mulato Saint-Georges, a fascinating personality, was a professional soldier whose interest in the keyboard was at best perfunctory. Guénin, on the other hand a professional violinist and eventually (1817-1822) a member of a string quartet, took more care with the keyboard so that the two instruments were entirely equal. Isidore Bertheaume (ca. 1751-1802), who made his violin debut at the Concerts Spirituels at the age of 9, wrote baroque sonatas for one or two violins with continuo, violin duets, and violin concertos, but he also wrote shortly after 1780 two symphonies concertantes (Opus 6) which he then arranged (Opus 7) for violin and piano. With the equality of parts and with the concertante element now firmly in place, the classical violin-piano sonata was now ready to come forth.

London

Mondonville's and Rameau's sonatas and *concerts* were well known in London in the 1740's and 1750's. In 1751 or 1752 Felice Giardini, living in the English capital, published his Opus 3 sonatas, which demonstrate the transition from baroque continuo sonata to pre-classic obligato sonata. The sonatas have extensive passages where the violin dominates and the harpsichord is a typical figured continuo with the right hand to be realized. But the same sonatas have other extensive passages where the right hand of the harpsichord is fully written, the left hand provides accompaniment and the figures disappear, and the violin becomes trivial (reinforces the left hand). Occasionally there is one measure of one situation immediately followed by a single measure of the other, thus juxtaposing these two styles as forcefully as possible.[17] This "concer-

---

[17]Kidd, pp. 125-128.

tante" effect—opposing two different bodies of equivalent sound: the solo violin with continuo against the accompanied written-out keyboard—was just another manifestation of the effect of the popular baroque and pre-classical concertos on the sonata that we have already seen in France.

During the late 1750's other Englishmen experimented with the balance between violin and keyboard. Thomas Gladwin published eight "lessons" for organ (exact date unknown), three of which contain violin accompaniments that are mostly, but not entirely, subservient to the keyboard. Shortly afterward William Jackson published his set of sonatas for harpsichord and violin where once again the violin sometimes is pre-eminent, sometimes totally subservient to the keyboard. Jackson suggests that the keyboard could be played alone as "lessons," but interestingly advised the harpsichordist in such performances not to play one specified movement "as the Larghetto cannot have its proper effect unaccompanied."[18] The idea of strings accompanying the harpsichord, which was hesitatingly but convincingly introduced in Giardini's Opus 3, came into its own with Charles Avison's Opus 5 Sonatas for harpsichord with the accompaniment of two violins and cello. The violins and cello do no more than re-enforce the keyboard—there is none of the baroque continuo left—and all but the harpsichord are dispensable. In 1760 Avison printed another collection just like his Opus 5, and at the beginning stated that "The accompanying Violins which are intended to enforce the Expression of the Harpsichord, should also be kept *always* subservient to it; for thus an Effect results from the whole, as from the sound of one improved, or, if I may so call it, multiplied Instrument."[19]

Whereas Giardini wrote Italian sonatas in England, usually in two movements Allegro - Minuet, and continued a fascination with Italian music in general in England, the arrival of Franz Xavier Richter in London ca. 1759 also introduced the new German, especially Mannheim sonatas. Yet the sonatas he wrote were much like Giardini's Opus 5 in the relationship of the violin to the keyboard (what is different is the optional addition of a cello accompaniment

[18]Kidd, p. 131.
[19]Kidd, p.130.

to the sonatas not found in Giardini). Immediately thereafter there was a plethora of publications in England. Among these were sonatas by Christoph Wagenseil, Carl F. Abel, and John Christian Bach, as well as by lesser-known composers. During the early 1760's the trend was to follow Richter and Giardini with the concertante sonata, but by the late 1760's and beyond they generally followed Avison's accompanied obligato keyboard sonatas.

Germany

In Germany there were many developments parallel to those in France.[20] Before Mondonville experimented with the duet sonata with obligato keyboard, Germans were experimenting with this genre. Johann Pachelbel (1657-1706) wrote a *Sonata a Violino solo e Cembalo obligato* before the turn of the century, Christoph Förster (1693-1745) composed six such works ca. 1724-1725, and at about the same time J.S. Bach wrote a half dozen of his own for violin and harpsichord (BWV 1014-1019). Bach's differ from the typical baroque sonata in that both hands of the harpsichord are fully written out.[21] The harpsichord is not treated as a continuo but as an equal partner with the violin. The bass string instrument (in Bach's case the viola da gamba), which doubles the left hand of the keyboard, is superfluous ("col basso per viola da gamba accompagnato *se piace*"). There are three lines of music which share themes, counterpoint and accompaniment. In the one movement where Bach reduced the number of contrapuntal lines to two (third movement of the G Major Sonata), it is not the right hand that drops out but the violin, leaving a harpsichord solo. Bach, as harpsichord virtuoso, wanted a true duet between himself and the violinist, just as in the Fifth Brandenburg Concerto he did not want to be mere accompaniment to other solo instruments. In both cases he raised the harpsichord to parity with the other soloists through vir-

---

[20]Flamm, p. 98, oversimplifies when she states that the French cultivated the keyboard sonata with violin accompaniment, the Italians carried further the violin sonata with continuo, and the Germans developed the violin sonata with obligato keyboard accompaniment.

[21]Cf. Hans Eppstein, *Studien über J.S. Bachs Sonaten für ein Melodieinstrument und obligates Cembalo*, in *Acta Universitatis Upsaliensis, Studia Musicologica Upsaliensia, Nova Series 2* (Uppsala: Universität/ Stockholm: Almqvist u. Wiksells, 1966).

tuosic display and established the equality of both hands to each other and to the rest of the ensemble. His six sonatas are not *accompanied* obligato sonatas, as they have been frequently called, because the harpsichord does not dominate the violin; they are duets. But they are important to the history of the accompanied obligato keyboard sonata as an early manifestation of the break with the traditional baroque relationship among instruments.[22]

C.P.E. Bach's oeuvre gives in brief the story of the development from baroque continuo sonata to pre-classical accompanied obligato keyboard sonata. His early trio sonatas (W.143-149, 162) were mostly written during his student and apprentice years in the 1730's but published in Potsdam in 1747 where he was working for Frederick the Great. They are typical baroque sonatas in that the upper parts (for virtuosic flute and violin) completely dominate the figured continuo. Each is in three movements, the first and third of which are in binary form in the major key and the middle movement is a simple ritornello movement in the parallel minor key. There is no attempt to upset the traditional relationship, particularly since the flute part was written for either the King or his teacher, Johann Joachim Quantz, and the prudent young composer had enough manners to keep his own part modest.

But C.P.E. Bach knew his father's sonatas and the new role for the keyboard that J.S. Bach had demonstrated in that genre as well as in others. As soon as he felt secure at Frederick's court, he decided to proceed upon his father's footsteps. Once the traditional, somewhat hardened relationship among instruments could admit change, new possibilities were quickly tried out. By mid-century a number of composers had experimented with one of the two upper virtuoso parts of the trio sonata sometimes replaced by the right hand of the keyboard.[23] The most well-known example, perhaps, is

---

[22]The relationship between Bach's Trio Sonata BWV 1039 and gamba-harpsichord sonata BWV 1027, where the right hand of the harpsichord has taken over the flute part, is much the same as in Graun's pieces discussed below. The work is not an obligato sonata because the gamba remains as important as the keyboard. Cf. Hans Eppstein, and Alfred Dürr, "Zu Hans Eppsteins 'Studien über J.S. Bachs Sonaten für ein Melodieninstrument und obligates Cembalo,'" in *Die Musikforschung*, xxi (1968), pp. 332-340, and "Zu Hans Eppsteins Erwiderung," in *Die Musikforschung*, xxii (1969), p. 209.

[23]Cf. the Graun sonatas discussed below; also C.F. Rolle's arrangement of a trio sonata for violin and organ obligato (before 1751) and Johann Gottlieb Goldberg's (1727-1756) arrangement of two trios for obligato cembalo and violin.

Carl Philip Emanuel Bach's two trios (W.161) printed in 1751 with the title: *Zwey Trio, das erste für zwo Violinen und Bass, das zweyte für I. Qverflöte, I. Violine und Bass; bey welchen beyden aber die eine von den Oberstimmen auch auf dem Flügel gespielt werden kan.*[24] The "bass" is figured so that it is definitely played on the keyboard; there is no mention of a cello but one probably accompanied the keyboard as long as the latter served as a continuo (the *ad libitum* nature of the bass string instrument would have been inherited from his father's *se piace* viola da gamba mentioned above). In his forward C.P.E. Bach described the first sonata as a conversation between Sanquine and Melancholy who fight during the first movement and most of the second but who in the third (last) movement come to a pleasant conclusion in which both are transformed into better characters. Since the lower violin part is played with mute while the upper violin part is played senza sordino during the first and most of the second movements, the keyboardist is advised by Bach not to duplicate the muted violin in his right hand but rather the unmuted violin so the conversation effect is not lost. There is no need for such advice in the second sonata which does not have a program; the keyboard right hand can assume either the violin or the flute part. In both sonatas the three written-out lines (two treble parts and the continuo) are equal to each other, sharing themes, accompanimental patterns, and counterpoint, so that when the right hand assumes one of the upper parts the remaining top instrument is equal to both hands of the keyboard. The trio sonata is only somewhat altered when the right hand of the keyboard continuo takes over one of the two upper parts; the result is either a sonata for one upper part and a fully equal keyboard or for two upper parts, continuo keyboard, and cello. Such a new sonata allowed the transference of one of the virtuoso upper parts to the keyboard and thereby gave the keyboard a new importance beyond the accompanimental role of the traditional trio sonata. This situation is different from J.S. Bach's six sonatas discussed above, however, in that J.S. considers the keyboard equivalent to the violin at all times whereas C.P.E. allows for either the subservient role of accompaniment or the equal role of partner.

---

[24]Facsimile edition New York: Performers' Facsimiles, 1986.

If, as in J.S. Bach's six sonatas and C.P.E. Bach's trios, the keyboard is already equal to the upper parts, the resulting keyboard plus solo instrument sonata is equivalent to the late-18th-century piano plus violin sonata. However although this was the immediate result, the development of the *accompanied* obligato keyboard sonata in the 1760's and 1770's was a necessary pre-classical reaction to the basically baroque-oriented duet sonata, and the full classical duet sonata (as well as piano trio) as best represented by the later works of Mozart needed the obligato sonata as a stepping stone. Once the keyboard achieved equality with the solo instrument or instruments, the latter eventually lost its place to the keyboard and became accompanimental or trivial. Whatever instruments joined the keyboard—violin, flute, cello—they remained secondary or less to the clavier. This can be seen in C.P.E. Bach's thirteen late Trios published in London in 1776 and 1777. Now the keyboard was the solo instrument and the violin and cello accompanied. The Trio in C Major (W.90 no. 3) is typical. This is a striking, mature work by one of the great masters of the second half of the 18th century; the very elaborate first movement in C Major is in binary form, the second movement is in A Major and leads through A Minor without pause into the sonata-form third movement back in C Major. The harmonies are rich and exciting and were an inspiration especially to Beethoven. Yet the relationship of the parts remains pre-classical. Although the violin does have the main theme of the second movement once, although the violin and cello participate in fast-moving scales in the third movement, and although there are brief moments when the violin and cello fill in a beat of rest or inactivity in the keyboard, they are always treated as secondary to the keyboard and accompanimental.

Interestingly C.P.E. Bach was not happy with the genre of accompanied obligato keyboard sonatas. In a letter to Forkel he wrote ". . . allein noch habe ich wenig Lust dazu, ebensowenig als zu Claviersonaten mit einem begleitenden Instrument nach dem jetzigen Schlendrian."[25] But this was an aesthetic judgement, not an economic one, and in middle-class Hamburg Bach saw the eagerness with which the amateur pianist bought up moderately difficult

---

[25]Schmid, p. 149, quoted in Flamm, p. 112.

keyboard music with simple string accompaniment that would not rattle the keyboardist inexperienced in ensemble playing.

Like the French, C.P.E. Bach frequently used the term "concertato" in reference to the keyboard in these sonatas. But Bach was not the first German to blend the concerto and the sonata. Handel used "concertato" for the keyboard as early as 1705 for his sonatas for viola da gamba and keyboard. In the 1720's Johann Georg Linicke reversed the "concertato" instrument from keyboard to string instrument; he composed a *Concerto pour le Clavecin e Violino Concertato*, a three-movement piece (fast-slow-fast), which replaced the subservient baroque keyboard continuo with a full keyboard part that could compete on equal terms with the violin. The important concept in the term "concertato," however, was not whether one or the other instrument was designated "concertato" but the concerto-like interplay between the two instruments. This same idea was continued in mid-century by Christoph Schaffrath (1709-1763) who published *Sei Duetti a Cembalo Obligato e Violino o Flauto Traverso Concertato* (Opus 1, 1752), by Johann Georg Arnold in his *Deux Concerts pour le Clavessin avec le Violon* (ca. 1760), and by Georg Simon Löhlein (1725-1781), in his single *Sonata a Cembalo concertato e Violino o Flauto*. While these concerto sonatas were under the influence of Italian concertos, Georg Anton Kreusser's (1743-1810) *Sinfonie pour le clavecin avec l'Accompagnement d'un Violon* (Opus 6, 1771) and Ernst Eichner's (1740-1777) *Six Sonates pour le Clavecin ou Piano Forte avec accompagnement d'un Violon* (Opus 9, 1773) were under the influence of the Mannheim symphony with such devices as the Mannheim rocket (crescendos) and orchestral unison. C.P.E. Bach, too, used titles like "Sinfonia a Cembalo obligato è Violino." In both concerto- and symphony-sonatas, the concerto-like contrast between tutti and solo is maintained; in some cases the violin and keyboard share alternately the solo passages (Linicke, Schaffrath, Arnold), in others the keyboard has all the important solo material (Kreusser, C.P.E. Bach). As in the case of the French symphonie concertante sonata, the German concerto and symphony sonatas were attempts to incorporate some of the popular devices of contemporary concertos and symphonies into the sonata, such as the unison tutti passages contrasting with more solistic keyboard ones, which by the 1780's evolved into the classical violin-piano sonata.

Other German composers besides C.P.E. Bach demonstrated the development from trio sonata to accompanied obligato sonata.[26] Christoph Graupner's (1683-1760) three manuscript sonatas for violin with obligato harpsichord, for example, are further examples of the duet sonata; written ca. 1740 they are otherwise baroque in form and style. There is a large collection of sonatas by the brothers J.G. and C.H. Graun, presumably written in the 1750's and early 1760's, which exist in two formats: 1) as trio sonatas for flute and/or violin with continuo, and 2) as duet sonatas in which one of the flute and/or violin parts is rescored for the right hand of the keyboard.[27] In these cases, unlike C.P.E. Bach's W.161 trios, the two versions exist in separate manuscripts, and in a few of them the duet versions vary in some way from the original trio versions. For example, in several cases the right hand in the duet version does more than just duplicate what had been one of the treble parts in the trio version. The adapted right hand sometimes fills in what are rests in the trio part by doubling the remaining treble part, and at other times the right hand simplifies what had originally been a characteristically violinistic passage. In one case J.G. Graun transcribed the original trio for two violins and bass to the new duet for viola da gamba and cembalo; in two other cases the new duet version is transcribed for viola and cembalo. And finally there is an A-Major duet which has extensive changes from its trio version,[28] including a few which reduce the remaining solo treble to a secondary role while the two hands of the keyboard take over both original treble parts. In this case the original trio does not have three equal lines, as in C.P.E. Bach's W.161 sonatas; the bass here is purely accompanimental, typical of baroque trio sonatas. Therefore

---

[26]Cf. Walfred Wierichs, *Die Sonate für obligates Tasteninstrument und Violine bis zum Beginn der Hochklassik in Deutschland* (Kassel: Bärenreiter, 1981).

[27]David Sheldon, "The Transition from Trio to Cembalo-Obbligato Sonata in the Works of J.G. and C.H. Graun," in *The Journal of the American Musicological Society*, xxiv (1971), 395-413. Sheldon points out the seemingly apparant transcription of the trio versions to duet ones, but also allows for the transcription of duets into trios based on the case in C.P.E. Bach's works where the source of a duet version (W.83, 1745) predates the surviving source of a trio (W.151, 1747).

[28]Sheldon, Examples 4 and 5.

Graun[29] transformed a continuo sonata directly into an accompanied obligato sonata, at least for a few measures, accomplishing the realignment of parts necessary to go from the baroque to preclassic types—a transition for which C.P.E. Bach seemingly took one extra step.

Vienna

Probably the most important composer of the chamber sonata in Austria during this period of transition was Georg Christoph Wagenseil (1715-1777).[30] Wagenseil was born in baroque Vienna, studied under the great theorist Fux, and from 1739 until his death was court composer for the Austrian Emperor in Vienna. Early in his career he composed primarily religious music, but in the middle of the century he turned to opera where his reforms anticipated those of Gluck. He traveled to Italy several times, and his music was published extensively from the 1750's on in Paris and London. He was the teacher of, among others, the great Czech composer Dussek and J.B. Schenk, who later taught Beethoven. Both Mozart and Haydn knew Wagenseil's music well.

Half of Wagenseil's chamber music is trio sonatas for two violins and bass (presumably keyboard and cello).[31] Although within the baroque tradition of scoring, these forty "sonatas," "partittas," or "trios" consist of a more pre-classical style and form. Wagenseil's mind was sufficiently fertile that rarely do any two pieces resemble each other. Although two trio sonatas are in the baroque four-movement slow-fast-slow-fast order of movements, seven are in the three-movement fast-slow-fast and two in the slow-fast-minuet order. Some other sonatas have at least one minuet (with or without trio), and in tune with developments in the symphony and other genres of the 1760's and 1770's, Wagenseil also has four trio

[29]Here as in many of the sonatas and duets it is unclear which Graun brother is the composer.

[30]Biographical data on Wagenseil is from John Kucaba, "Wagenseil, Georg Christoph," in *The New Grove Dictionary*, XX, pp. 100-102.

[31]Bibliographical information on Wagenseil's chamber music is from Helga Scholz-Michelitsch, *Das Orchester- und Kammermusikwerk von Georg Christoph Wagenseil: Thematischer Katalog*, in Oesterreichische Akademie der Wissenschaften, *Tabulae Musicae Austriacae*, Band 6 (Vienna: Hermann Böhlaus Nachf., 1972). In many cases only the first movements of pieces are known which probably had three or more originally.

sonatas in the Classical fast-slow-minuet + trio-fast order. In most sonatas, whether or not the keyboard is obligato, there is at least one movement in sonata form, often a highly developed sonata form with two distinct themes in the exposition and modification of the themes in the recapitulation. His textures vary within single movements, often with imitation, unison passages, and accompanied melody.[32]

Wagenseil was also influenced by the new French and German experimentation in scoring. Even while retaining the continuo he used the viola or violetta with a violin in trio sonatas, wrote sonatas for one violin and continuo harpsichord, two violins and obligato cello with continuo and two violins with obligato cello without continuo, and composed a quintet for two violins, two violas and bass, a sextet for four violins, viola and cello without continuo, and a quartet for three cellos and continuo. Perhaps under the influence of the French and Germans during the 1750's and 1760's he wrote a "Divertimento" for obligato cello, *ad libitum* violin, and continuo, and a "Terzetto" for obligato keyboard and flute (i.e., a trio for flute, keyboard right hand, and keyboard left hand). By 1770 he was already writing for the obligato pianoforte with either one violin or one flute, or with one or two violins and bass, or with violin and viola. His trio sonata for two violins and continuo (M.459) was arranged for obligato harpsichord and violin by Wagenseil himself or by one of his contemporaries. Apart from adding to the variety of scoring already existing in Paris and elsewhere, Wagenseil wrote what seems to have been the first trio sonata for clarinet with violin and continuo.

---

[32]Wagenseil's *Sonata a Tre*, from his *Six Sonates en Trio pour deux Violons et Basse, Oeuvre premier* (Paris: Le Clerc, 1755), ed. Erich Schenk, in *Diletto Musicale*, no. 443 (Vienna/Munich: Doblinger, 1969) is typical. It is in four binary-form movements: allegro (B♭ Major) - allegro molto (G Minor) - menuet I (B♭ Major) and II (G Minor) - molto allegro (B♭ Major). The first movement is in an early sonata form, but without a well-defined second theme. All movements but the second are imitative, with the figured bass sometimes participating. In the final movement the bass rests eight times while the two violins continue. The violins are equal in importance to each other, while the bass is almost exclusively accompaniment. The scoring and the use of binary form are baroque, but incipient sonata form, the contrasting modes between movements and the unusual pattern of tempos reflect the groping transition from baroque to pre-classical.

Of significance are the terms that Wagenseil used for his chamber music. While many trios were simply called trio or sonata or partita, he frequently used the term "Trio Capricioso," which seems to have had no structural implications but does reflect a French affectation: the use of descriptive titles. Indeed, there are several trios and other chamber pieces with movements with Italian or French titles such as "Allegro la Confusione," "La Plaisanterie: Allegro assai," "Entrée" followed by "La Fantasie," and "La Negligente." The title "concerto" is used only once, for a sonata for violin and continuo; the three movements (in the order fast-minuet + trio-slow) do not resemble any concertos of the time. Of most importance is Wagenseil's use of the title "divertimento" for three unusual kinds of pieces: two octets for pairs of oboes, English horns, hunting horns, and bassoons, the one sonata for violin *ad libitum*, cello obligato and continuo harpsichord, and three sonatas for obligato keyboard, one or two violins, and bass. In wind music the term "divertimento" seems to have been interchangeable with "Parthia" (a common variant of the word "partita" in Austria at this time) since Wagenseil had an octet with that title which is much the same as one of the "Divertimento" octets: the same scoring and a large number of movements (eight and ten, including a minuet, a set of variations, and a number of alternating slow and fast movements). In string music with obligato keyboard Wagenseil used the term "Terzetto" for pieces scored for obligato keyboard with violin and viola, "Divertimento" for pieces scored for obligato keyboard with violin and bass, and "Sonata" for pieces scored for obligato keyboard and violin. Rather than a musical structure that determined the use of the title "divertimento," the term seems to have been used to refer to the function of the music: as background diversion.

*

Once the obligato sonata was recognized as commercially viable as well as aesthetically satisfactory by Schobert and others during the 1760's and 1770's, there were many composers who copied them. Some of them, like Hüllmandel and Edelmann in

Paris[33] and nearly all the English and Germans,[34] were minor figures, but C.P.E. Bach, Wagenseil, and especially Mozart gave the genre a central historical position. Mozart wrote obligato sonatas as a first step that would lead directly to the piano trio and the classical duet sonata.

There were probably several reasons why composers increasingly turned away from the baroque basso continuo and to the fully written-out obligato keyboard. Certainly the obligato setting was a very useful way to solve a sometimes embarrassing predicament for the court composer. The nobleman or noblewoman who had learned the violin or flute only modestly yet wished to perform publicly called the professional keyboard member of the court orchestra to accompany him or her; to more or less save the moment from utter disaster, the composer wrote a keyboard sonata with easy violin or flute accompaniment. The violinist or flutist played within his or her limits and sounded credible, while the keyboardist kept things interesting enough not to bore the audience. Another, just as practical reason would have been the growing shortage of good continuo players and the increased number of competent amateur keyboardists who were not trained in continuo realization.[35]

The principal results of the accompanied obligato sonata were the piano trio and the duet sonata of the Classical period. To a lesser extent the piano quartet and quintet were also products.

THE PIANO TRIO

If by the 1760's and 1770's the keyboard was now dominant and the violin was trivial, where did the violoncello stand that normally used to double the bass line of the continuo? In some cases, the cello is not mentioned and apparently was not used at all. In others it has the same trivial role as the violin, that is, it along with the

[33]On Edelmann and Hüllmandel see Reeser, pp. 112f and 120f; Rita Benton, "Nicolas Joseph Hüllmandel and French Instrumental Music in the Second Half of the 18th Century" (University of Iowa Ph.D. dissertation, 1961); and Georges Poullain, Comte de Saint-Foix, "Les Premiers Pianistes Parisiens," in *La Revue Musicale*, III, no. 10 (1922), 121-136, IV, no. 6 (1923), 193-205, V, no. 8 (1924), 187-191 and 192-198.

[34]Wierichs.

[35]Flamm, p. 92.

violin accompanies the obligato keyboard. Mostly it simply doubles the bass line of the keyboard. As the violin assumed more importance vis-a-vis the keyboard in obligato keyboard sonatas later
in the century, the role of the cello again changed. At the point
when the violin and cello established a more or less equal relationship with each other and with the keyboard, the classical piano trio
was created.[36]

Flamm has pointed out the important direct and indirect precursors of the piano trio.[37] She notes that Biago Marini published
his "Suonata per l'organo e Violino ò Cornetto," in 1626, which is
an early example of the duet sonata, and that J.S. Bach wrote his
"Sei Suonate à Cembalo certato e Violino solo" a century later "col
Basso per Viola da Gamba accompagnata, se piace," which already
allowed for the scoring of the piano trio. But she credits Rameau in
his "Concerts" with giving the violin and especially viola da
gamba increased importance; that the cello could replace the viola
da gamba is indicated by Rameau's inclusion of an alternate passage for the cello.

The development of this relationship culminating in the classical piano trio can be seen in the many keyboard trios written by
Mozart and Haydn over a thirty year span as well as in the works
of lesser composers. The lesser composer often copied the ideas of
the master, but sometimes the master could learn from his less-
gifted colleague. It has long been established that the German-
French composer Johann Schobert had a decisive impact on the
young Mozart not only in sonatas but also in concertos and other
instrumental types. Schobert, who was active as chamber musician
to the Prince de Conti in Paris from 1760 until his death in 1767,
published thirty-two sonatas in eleven collections. Two of the sonatas are for harpsichord alone, but the others are sonatas for harpsichord either with the accompaniment of one violin or one violin

---

[36]The classical piano trio came not from the baroque trio sonata but from the keyboard
sonata with obligato accompaniment of violin and cello. Cf. Flamm, pp. 77-137. See also
Nancy Dunn, "The Piano Trio from its Origins to Mozart's Death" (University of Oregon
DMA dissertation, 1975); Gaetano Cesari, "Origini del Trio con Pianoforte," in Franco
Abbiati, ed., *Scritti inediti* (Milan: Carisch S.A., 1937), pp. 183-198; and Albert Karsch,
"Untersuchungen zur Frühgeschichte des Klaviertrios in Deutschland" (University of
Köln Ph.D. dissertation, 1943).

[37]Flamm, pp. 77-134.

and cello or two violins and *ad libitum* cello or with the *ad libitum* addition of a violin or of a violin and cello. In other words, the harpsichord was the principal instrument, and the violin and cello were supplemental, often expendable adjuncts. These sonatas served as models for all subsequent accompanied obligato keyboard sonatas, even though they are not as striking as those by C.P.E. Bach mentioned above. The violin, completely in the first position, occasionally echoes the right hand of the piano, but otherwise it is subservient to the keyboard. In Opus 2 no. 1 the violin has tremolos and provides a backdrop over which the keyboard makes music. In Opus 16 no. 1 Schobert wavered between the old-fashioned continuo sonata and the new obligato sonata. During much of the sonata the cello doubles the left hand of the keyboard and, at the opening of the second half of the first movement, the right hand of the piano drops out and the left hand becomes a figured bass. The violin becomes momentarily more important than the keyboard and dares some independence. On the other hand, during most of the sonata the harpsichord is clearly dominant and the violin and cello, often in parallel thirds and sixths with each other, simply accompany. In Opus 16 no. 4 the keyboard never reverts to continuo and is always paramount, but Schobert did try to make the two accompanying instruments more interesting. The cello has some independence in the first movement, though quickly withdraws in subsequent movements, and the violin and keyboard right hand engage in some imitation during the Presto. While Schobert accepted the accompanied obligato keyboard sonata (perhaps to satisfy the needs of the amateur keyboard players in Paris), he clearly was not satisfied with the status quo and experimented within the limits imposed by the genre. No doubt it was his ingenuity within these limits which appealed to the young Mozart.

Many of Schobert's sonatas had already been published and most probably composed when the eight-year-old Mozart first visited Paris in early 1764. He quickly absorbed Schobert's works,[38]

---

[38] In a letter dated February 1-3, 1764 from Paris, Leopold Mozart writes "Schobert, Eckardt, Le Grand and Hochbrucker have all brought us their engraved sonatas and presented them to my children" (translated by Arthur Mendel and Nathan Broder in Alfred Einstein, *Mozart: his Character, his Work* [London/New York/Toronto: Oxford University Press, 1945], p. 114. Einstein points out Schobert's influence on Mozart's early sonatas.)

and in the next few months he composed his own collections of obligato sonatas. One collection is for keyboard accompanied by violin (K.6-9; see below). The other set (K.10-15) was printed the following year in two editions dedicated to the Queen of England. The two editions are nearly identical, but they differ in one crucial point.[39] The edition which Mozart kept permanently in his own possession is entitled *Six SONATES pour le CLAVECIN qui peuvent se jouer avec L'accompangnement de Violon ou Flaute Traversiere....* The edition which was presented to the Queen, however, is entitled *Six SONATES pour le CLAVECIN qui peuvent se jouer avec L'accompagnement de Violon ou Flaute Traversiere et d'un Violoncelle....* Both are authentic editions; that they both exist shows that the cello was expendable and that there was no appreciable difference between the obligato keyboard sonata accompanied by a violin alone and the sonata accompanied by both violin and cello.

The six sonatas K.10-15 can be played without either violin or cello or both. For the most part the cello doubles the left hand of the keyboard and the violin is only slightly more independent. Nonetheless, like Schobert, young Mozart sensed the need to explore the possibilities of the obligato sonata, particularly in the second group of three. In the second movement of K.13, for example, the violin and cello become more expressive in their counterpoint, and in both movements of K.15 the violin shows considerable independence. On the other hand, the keyboard never drops out in favor of the bowed strings, and the cello of K.15 remains tied to the keyboard left hand. The second minuet of K.14 ("Menuetto en Carillon") drops the cello altogether, but the violin adds a new color with a pizzicato accompaniment.

The gradual emancipation of the violin from the keyboard can be seen in the next work which Mozart wrote for keyboard, violin and cello: the Divertimento K.254 (1776). The keyboard remains on top, but the violin offers interesting counterpoint to the keyboard, especially its right hand, and fills in some short rests with pick-up notes. The violin never achieves the rank of soloist, however, which the keyboard does, and the cello is never independent.

---

[39]The Queen's copy also differs from the other in that the violin part is not printed but in Leopold Mozart's hand.

It is with the two trios of 1786, however, that Mozart finally granted the violin equality with the keyboard and freed the cello from its subservient role.[40] In the first movement of K.496 (G Major) the cello boasts its independence from the keyboard at times (e.g., mm.67-78) and is in dialogue with the left hand of the keyboard (mm.85-92). In the fourth variation of the third movement the cello is hauntingly independent. Between this piano trio and the next is a special trio scored for piano, clarinet and viola. Perhaps because Mozart himself played the viola and the famous Stadler played the clarinet in a private performance, Mozart wrote his first democratic piano trio in which all the parts are equal. In the first movement of K.498 (E♭ Major) the viola has distinct solo moments (mm.98-109), and in the Trio of the second movement Menuetto it stars. But in the third, Rondeau movement all three instruments reach parity. As if inspired by this turn of events, Mozart in his next piano trio K.502 (B♭ Major) allowed the violin numerous passages where it leads and the piano temporarily becomes accompaniment. Furthermore the cello now is completely independent and even has its own solo runs, though it is not allowed the virtuosity that the violin and piano have. In 1788 Mozart wrote his last three piano trios. While he kept the same basic relationship among the three instruments in the first of these K.542 (E Major), he took the final step toward equality in the second, K.548 (C Major). Here the cello is as much a solo as the violin and piano, especially in the second movement, and it shares fully in the counterpoint and supports as well the other two instruments. Equality, it must be pointed out, does not mean that all three instruments are entirely solistic throughout but rather that each has its legitimate independence at the same time that it must coordinate with the other two instruments. At times it must accompany and support, at other times dominate, and at still other moments join equally with the other instruments in counterpoint or in homophony. Thus from the accompanied obligato keyboard sonatas of 1764 through the divertimento of 1776 to the piano trios of 1786 and 1788 the genre *piano trio* evolved. This evolution was dependent on the scoring and

---

[40]C.P.E. Bach begins the emancipation of the cello with some passages in which the cello is as important as the keyboard, but essentially his late trios are keyboard sonatas with *ad libitum* violin and cello.

on the way this scoring was treated. Once the three instruments of keyboard, violin and cello were recognized as mandatory, the equality of the instruments had to be established in order for the genre to exist. This area of evolution (scoring) is not independent of the evolution of form and style, but it is the crucial matter separating the piano trio of the 1780's from other genres such as the string trio, the duet sonata, and the string quartet.

Haydn displayed a similar evolution in his piano trios, though most of his belong to the category of pre-classical sonata for piano with violin and cello accompaniment. They can be divided into three periods: the early trios (ca. 1755-1760), the middles ones (1780's-1790's), and the late ones probably written in England.[41] The early ones still have baroque rhythms and the pre-classical obligato keyboard relationship among instruments. The middle ones have more developed sonata form, more expansive melodies, a larger harmonic vocabulary, but not yet the full classical balance among the three instruments. For example, in 1785 Haydn published three piano trios of which two were originally composed as piano and violin sonatas by his pupil Ignaz Pleyel.[42] The two pieces have a fair balance between the two original instruments, with the violin and keyboard right hand alternating themes and participating in counterpoint. The left hand is supportive and accompanimental, and the added cello simply doubles the left hand. Here the piece has reached the point of equality between the piano right hand and violin but piano left hand and the cello have yet to achieve the independence and importance necessary for the mature piano trio genre. In the late trios, however, the keyboard is virtuosic while the other two instruments are independent and important partners to the whole fabric; the harmony is more expanded, there is more activity, and the three instruments offer more dynamic and orchestral effects. Haydn wrote the early and many of the middle trios to sat-

---

[41]Compare Georg Feder, "Haydn's Piano Trios and Piano Sonatas," trl. by Howard Serwer, in *Haydnfest: Music Festival: September 22-October 11, 1975: International Musicological Conference: October 4-11, 1975* (Washington, D.C.: Kennedy Center Program, 1975), pp. 18-23; H.C. Robbins Landon, *Die Klaviertrios von Joseph Haydn: Vorwort zur ersten kritischen Gesamtausgabe* (Munich/Vienna: Doblinger, 1970); and Lester Steinberg, "Sonata Form in the Keyboard Trios of Joseph Haydn" (New York University Ph.D. dissertation, 1976).

[42]Wolfgang Stockmeier, ed., Ignaz Pleyel (Joseph Haydn), *Trios für Klavier, Violine und Violoncello C-Dur und F-Dur* (Munich: G. Henle, 1976), p. 4.

isfy the appetite of the middle class and the publishers who catered to it; the vogue was for keyboard works with accompaniment of violin and cello, and the early ones, like the early quartets, are called "divertimenti." Only in the late ones did Haydn follow Mozart with the equality of roles of the three instruments, and since by this time Haydn was also writing mature sonata form movements instead of the simple binary form ones of the divertimenti, the late piano trios are his only fully classical ones. The classical late piano trios come more than a decade after the classical string quartets.

Other composers, especially in Germany and Austria, contributed to the repertory of pre-classical piano trios. To cite but one case, Telemann's Sonata in E is another example of a keyboard sonata with the accompaniment of a subservient violin and cello. But it was Mozart and to a lesser extent Haydn who were responsible for developing the sub-variety of pre-classical sonata for keyboard with the accompaniment of violin and cello into the full-fledged piano trio.

The early keyboard trios were probably written for the same situations as the obligato keyboard sonata, namely for professional keyboard players and amateur bowed string players or for headstrong keyboardists and meeker string players. That the trios became much more distinct and highly developed by the 1780's is due not only to the evolution of scorings, styles and forms but also to the change in social situation. By the 1780's in Vienna there were a great many good women amateur pianists in bourgeois homes who played trios with competent friends or members of their family, and for these groups Pleyel, Kozeluch, Vanhal and others wrote their pretty, easy, if sometimes too repetitive and superficial trios.[43] These were performed privately in the homes of the middle and upper classes for the enjoyment of the performers and their closest friends and family. Technique was limited, especially in the violin and cello parts, to suit the often limited abilities of the home performers. The truly great composers (Mozart and Haydn) wrote their trios, on the other hand, for their own use with

---

[43]Katalin Komlós, "The Viennese Keyboard Trio in the 1780s: Sociological Background and Contemporary Reception," in *Music and Letters*, lxviii (1987), 222-234.

other professionals so as to demonstrate to their peers the acme of trio playing and composition. Thus Mozart wrote his trios of 1786 and 1788 for sophisticated Viennese and Dresden audiences and Haydn wrote his late piano trios for London concert audiences in order to impress fellow musicians and leading patrons. The last two decades of the 18th century witnessed simultaneously the flourishing of both the amateur piano trio and the professional piano trio. Ultimately in the 19th century this dichotomy was between Hausmusik and public chamber music.

THE PIANO AND VIOLIN SONATA

Just as in the case of the piano trio, the classical duet sonata for piano and violin is the result of Mozart's transformation of the preclassical accompanied obligato keyboard sonata into the new genre.[44] As has already been shown, the eight-year-old Mozart learned the obligato keyboard sonata from Schobert and immediately upon visiting Schobert in Paris in 1764 published as his very first printed works the four obligato sonatas K.6-9. Each of these pieces is a keyboard sonata with accompaniment of violin, where the violin does not merely double the right hand but also fills in harmony and rhythmic pauses in the keyboard. Barely two years later, as he and his father were in The Hague returning from London to Salzburg, Mozart again wrote some accompanied obligato keyboard sonatas, this time a group of six (K.26-31). There is little difference between this group and the earlier one in the relationship of instruments, though the form has changed. In K.6-9 Mozart wrote three three-movement sonatas and one in four movements: Allegro - Andante or Adagio - Menuettos I and II (the first sonata ends with another Allegro). In K.26-31, on the other hand, five of the six are in two movements with a variety of tempo patterns: Slow - Fast, Fast - Fast, Slow - Menuetto or Moderato, Fast - Menuetto; the one three-movement sonata (K.26) is the Italianate Fast - Slow - Fast.

---

[44]Wilhelm Fischer, "Mozarts Weg von der begleiteten Klaviersonate zur Kammermusik mit Klavier," in *Mozart-Jahrbuch* (1956), pp. 16-34.

When Mozart returned to the keyboard sonata with violin in 1778, he no longer wrote simply to satisfy the needs of the amateurs who thrived on the obligato sonata but to show off his talents to the professionals and chief patrons of Paris and Mannheim where he was visiting. The seven sonatas written in this year (K.301-306 and 296) are no longer obligato sonatas but duets between the violin and piano where the two instruments share themes, accompaniment, and counterpoint. There is concertant-like answering back and forth, and even when the violin accompanies, it does so with a flare that adds rhythmic vitality to the piece (as in K.301, first movement, measures 52-56). The violin never attempts to dominate, and while there are occasionally some virtuosic passages in the piano, the keyboard recedes often enough to allow the violin its licks. Most effective within the context of duet are the unison passages and parallel thirds and sixths, which in the hands of lesser composers are usually trite sounds but which here are extraordinarily effective (hauntingly so in the E Minor Sonata). While the two-movement form is favored in five of the pieces (a form preferred also in the *quatuors concertants* to which these sonatas stylistically conform), the other two (K.306 and 296) are each in three movements. The last movement of K.306 is reminiscent of early 17th-century sonatas in that it is sectionalized by theme, tempo and meter. Typical of Mozart at this time, the weightier movements usually are first, with the lighter minuets or rondeaux last, though in K.305 Mozart ends with a theme and variation. Once these sonatas appeared, Mozart had established a level of violin-piano duet that he would further exploit in his next eight examples, which belong to the history of the classical chamber sonata.[45]

The pre-classical accompanied obligato keyboard sonata continued to be written after Mozart's creation of the classical sonata. The sonatas of Kozeluch are typical in that they continued to serve the function that the pre-classical accompanied obligato keyboard sonata fulfilled.

---

[45]Only in his last sonata, K.547 in F (Vienna, 1788) does Mozart revert to the style of the obligato sonata, but this piece was written for a special purpose: "eine kleine Klavier Sonate für Anfänger mit einer Violine." The type was not forgotten, but aesthetically Mozart had already passed it by.

THE PIANO QUARTET AND QUINTET

Keyboard quartets and quintets, like piano trios, evolved out of the accompanied obligato sonata during the 1750's to 1780's as well as out of the piano concerto. Neither piano quintets nor piano quartets were as popular as piano trios, string quintets, quartets, trios and duos and some of the wind combinations. Nonetheless at least the piano quartet by 1785 was a distinct and significant genre thanks to Mozart's two piano-quartet masterpieces of that year,[46] and the piano quintet, beginning with Antonio Soler in 1776 and Boccherini in 1797, from time to time over the next two centuries is significant through isolated masterpieces (Schumann, Brahms, Franck, Shostakovich).

In the years leading up to Mozart, however, there was already a clearly identifiable subspecies of the obligato sonata accompanied by two violins and cello[47] or by string quartet. A great many such sonatas or pre-classical piano quartets and quintets were published in London during the period from 1756 to 1790 by native Englishmen (Charles Avison [1709-1770], Thomas Ebdon [1738-1811], John Garth [ca. 1727-1810], Joseph Harris [1745-1814], William Jackson [1730-1803], Robert Wainwright [1748-1782]), Italian exiles in England (Felice Giardini [1716-1796], Tommaso Giordani [ca. 1730-1806], Pietro A. Guglielmi [1729-1804], Pasquale Ricci [1732-1817], Gabriel Piozzi [?-1809]), a German exile (Frederic Theodor Schumann [fl.1760-1780]), and a Frenchman of German origins (Schobert). In addition there were others writing and publishing sonata-piano quartets and quintets on the continent,

---

[46]Joseph Saam, "Zur Geschichte des Klavierquartetts bis in die Romantik," in *Sammlung musikwissenschaftler Abhandlungen*, no. 9 (Strassburg: Heitz, 1932) credits Schobert with the first piano quartet and states that it is descended from trio sonatas, chamber trios, chamber quartets, and piano concertos. Stanley Sadie, "British Chamber Music, 1720-1790" (University of Cambridge Ph.D. dissertation, 1958), finds pre-Mozart scorings for keyboard with the accompaniment of two violins and cello to be accompanied sonatas, not piano quartets, since the latter require parity among the instruments. Marion Stern, "Keyboard Quartets and Quintets Published in London, 1756-1775: a Contribution to the History of Chamber Music with Obbligato Keyboard" (University of Pennsylvania Ph.D. dissertation, 1979), p. 193, finds some earlier piano quartets by Harris and Italians living in London, while she emphasizes the role the sonatas for piano with three strings had in leading from the accompanied obligato keyboard sonata to the piano quartets of Mozart.

[47]Stern, p. 142, finds only this scoring in the English repertory.

especially in Germany (Holzbauer, Toeschi and Eichner in Mannheim) and Austria (Wagenseil in Vienna). Most of these sonatas are in three movements fast-slow-minuet or rondo; the others are in two movements. Many of the first movements are in binary form or early sonata form, while the final movements are often in either minuet-trio form, rondo form, or some variety of the two. The predilection for rondo finales came from England, which was then copied in Mannheim (Ernst Eichner) and the rest of Europe.[48] "This kind of music is not, indeed, calculated so much for public entertainment, as for private amusement. It is rather like a conversation among friends."[49] Jackson's sonatas "were composed and solely designed for a select Musical Party. . . ."[50]

The most popular composer of these sonatas in England was Garth, whose works were frequently republished not only in England but on the continent as well. Avison's 1756 collection of sonatas was the earliest specifically scored for the obligato keyboard-string trio instruments. He clearly stated that Rameau's *Pieces de clavecin* was his model, not the concerto, since the latter was boring with its ceaseless repetitions of the ritornello. The influence of the concerto on these pieces was almost negligible, but in a very few cases two concerto elements can be seen.[51] A few composers (Guglielmi, Harris, Piozzi, Giordani and Wainwright) in a few opening movements used the double statement of the exposition which was a feature also of the concerto first movement, and in several of these the opening measure or two resembles the opening gesture of concertos with three emphatic chords (on the tonic or tonic-dominant-tonic) followed by a steady eighth-note "drum" beat on the bottom.

The three *Sonates en Quatuor pour le clavecin avec accompagnement de deux violon et basse ad libitum* by Johann Schobert are good and well-known examples of the pre-classical obligato sonatas with the accompaniment of three strings. The title makes

---

[48]Stern, pp. 160-161.

[49]Charles Avison, preface to Opus 7 sonatas for harpsichord with accompaniment for two violins and a violoncello.

[50]Jackson, preface to *Eight Sonatas for the Harpsichord Accompanied with Two Violins, a Tenor and a Bass*, Op. 20 (London: Longman and Broderip, 1773).

[51]Stern, pp. 235-255.

clear the subservient relationship of the three bowed strings to the keyboard (the "basse" is assumed to be the cello[52]). Although various scholars of the past have called this the first piano quartet, it lacks the necessary parity among all instruments to qualify for that designation. There is not any difference in the relationship among instruments in *Six Sonates pour le clavecin dédiées a Madame de la Valette... Opera XIV... les parties d'accompagnements sont ad libitum*. What is different is the fully developed sonata form; whereas the recapitulations of the first themes of the earlier quartets are in the parallel minor of the tonic, the recapitulations of these later quartets are in the tonic as expected in sonata form. Thus while Schobert shows growth in his treatment of form (i.e., growth toward what historically is the next phase in the history of musical form[53]), there is no simultaneous growth in his conception of scoring. The treatment of form was left up to his own creativity, but the scoring was no doubt dependent upon the persons for whom he wrote the music: their tastes, their preferred scoring, and their own or their hired musicians' performance abilities.[54]

Schobert's sonata-piano quartets were published in London, and despite the appearance of occasional quartets and quintets on the continent, London was apparently the center of this new genre of chamber music. In Austria the only important pre-classical examples were Wagenseil's *Suites de Pièces* for piano, two violins and bass, which was apparently modeled on Rameau,[55] and his *Divertimento* of the same scoring which may have been as well. The former is in three movements fast-slow-tempo di menuetto. Despite the dearth of pre-classical examples, it was in Vienna that the classical piano quartet reached its first great manifestations and

---

[52]On the cello versus the bass as the "basse" instrument, see fn. 61.

[53]We might consider the earlier sonatas more interesting because of their unusual recapitulations, but the more Schobert conformed to the historically inevitable conception of sonata form during a time when that conception was forming, the more modern and the more historically important he is.

[54]Six years after Schobert's death Cambini arrived in Paris and quickly became the chief composer there of sinfonias concertants and quatuors concertants. His three piano quintets for piano and string quartet may be arrangements and his so-called piano quartets, which are arrangements, are actually scored for three instruments: piano, violin and cello (Dieter Lutz Trimpert, *Die Quatuors Concertants von Giuseppe Cambini*, in *Mainzer Studien zur Musikwissenschaft*, Band 1 [Tutzing: Hans Schneider, 1967], pp. 231-232).

[55]The French title strongly suggests this.

where during the late 19th century it reached its next peak (with Brahms).

An isolated collection of six piano quintets was composed in 1776 by Antonio Soler (1729-1783), Spanish pupil of Domenico Scarlatti.[56] They were written for the Infante Don Gabriel (brother of King Carlos V), who was an accomplished amateur musician. Soler lived as a monk in El Escorial and the Infante often visited him there in order to play chamber music. Typical of chamber music by Spaniards at this time, the music remained unpublished until modern times and therefore had no influence on the development of the keyboard quintet outside Spain.

In addition to the obvious link between the accompanied sonatas and the classical piano quartet and quintet is that between them and the pre-classic piano concerto. Some pieces scored for keyboard with several strings alternate tutti and solo passages just as in the concerto; during the tutti passages the keyboard is either a straight-forward basso continuo or a written-out continuo, while during the solo passages the keyboard plays independent, virtuosic passages of primary importance with the accompaniment of the strings.[57] Some piano concertos were published as late as the 1780's in optional scoring for piano solo and accompanying solo string quartet (Mozart) or piano solo and accompanying string trio (J.C. Bach). But while there are many similarities between concertos and the pre-classical piano quartet, there are also differences which are clear if these piano concertos with optional string quartet accompaniment are compared with those quartet-sonatas written just for solo performance. According to the theorists of the time, the tutti passages must come at the beginning and end of the movement as well as at the end of the exposition and start of the recapitulation,[58] but in the quartet-sonatas written just for solo performance, the tuttis are not presented in all the required places. In addition the virtuosity expected and found in the keyboard in con-

[56]Richard Xavier Sanchez, "Spanish Chamber Music of the Eighteenth Century" (Louisiana State University Ph.D. dissertation, 1975), p. 45.

[57]Michael Tilmouth, "Piano Quartet" and "Piano Quintet" in *The New Grove Dictionary of Music and Musicians*, 6th ed., pp. 714-715.

[58]Particularly in H.C. Koch, *Versuch einer Anleitung zur Composition* (Leipzig: 1782-1793); cf. Stern, p. 248.

certos is not a main feature of even the keyboard solo parts of the quartet and quintet.

Mozart's two great piano quartets, which are the models against which any classical piano quartet is to be judged, differ from the sonatas of his predecessors in several aspects. First, instead of two violins and cello the string section now consists of violin, viola and cello. Most significantly, all four instruments are equally important through the division of thematic material among all four and the continual contrast of textures of tutti, solo piano, and solo strings. This differs from the earlier sonatas where the strings either play tutti with the piano or accompany a piano solo. Mozart also omitted any double statement of the themes, which occurred sometimes in the sonata, and he introduced a new texture of keyboard figurations under strings playing important motives. These quartets, however, belong to the high classical period, as do the piano quintets of Boccherini (Opus 56 [1797] and 57 [1799]), which set the standard for that genre, and will be considered in the next chapter.

THE EARLY STRING QUARTET

While the Pre-classical composers established the new piano trio, violin-and-piano sonata, and piano quartet and quintet from the accompanied obligato keyboard sonata, the string quartet, trio, and quintet were generated by other types of music. Not considered a special genre of chamber music in 1750, the string quartet became within thirty years the preeminent genre of chamber music and the most seriously treated by the greatest masters of the time: Haydn and Mozart. In subsequent centuries many connoisseurs of chamber music equated chamber music with the string quartet and regarded all other forms of chamber music as inferior. Even though Beethoven himself wrote superior piano trios, violin-and-piano sonatas, and woodwind chamber music, it is his *string quartets* which often have been considered not only as the greatest pieces of chamber music ever composed but as the greatest works of Western musical art in toto.

The reason for this preeminence of the string quartet was not apparent before the 1780's when Haydn and Mozart began to write their masterpieces. The emergence of the string quartet during the 1760's can be traced along several lines of development according to the scoring, the textures, the forms, the styles, and the rhythm. It was the synthesis of all these lines, however, that led to the pre-classical string quartet of the 1760's and 1770's and then on to the great classical quartet masterpieces of Haydn, Mozart and Beethoven from the 1780's to the 1820's.

Obviously a necessity for a string quartet is the scoring peculiar to it: two violins, one viola, and one cello.[59] There are some examples of such scoring before the middle 18th century, most notably in Alessandro Scarlatti's sonatas,[60] and there are numerous examples of instrumental and vocal quartets prior to that time which hint at such a scoring but do not specifically call for two violins, one viola and one cello—let alone, for that matter, for strings or even instruments. If any instrumental piece of music has four lines of written music, there remains the flexible performance of the baroque period in which the bass line would probably have been played by a keyboard whose left hand doubled the cello and whose right hand was improvised, and in which any part could have been doubled thereby establishing a chamber orchestra situation. And indeed, through much of the 1760's, pre-classical works which seem to have been scored for two violins, one viola and one cello actually did not call for a cello but for a "bass," which could mean basso continuo or string bass or any bass-sounding instrument or instruments.

Most early works calling for the instruments of the modern string quartet are not part of the history of the string quartet per se because they lack the stylistic, formal and textural characteristics of the string quartet. Alessandro Scarlatti's four *Sonate a quattro*,

---

[59]The scoring of one violin, two violas, and bass (cello) occurs occasionally in the works of Cambini, Giardini, and Carl Stamitz, but for whatever reason these early experiments were not found satisfactory and the scoring remains unusual. Trimpert, p. 188, regards the scoring of minor importance since the first violin and flute are interchangeable in many early quartets. The question of orchestral or solo performance remains a thorny one for much four-part string music of the mid-18th century; cf. Roger Hickman, "The Nascent Viennese String Quartet," in *The Musical Quarterly*, lxvii (1981), 193-212.

[60]Marc Pincherle, "On the Origins of the String-Quartet," trl. M.D. Herter Norton, in *The Musical Quarterly*, xv (1929), 77-87, gives as precursors to Scarlatti, Benjamin Rogers (1653), Purcell, Florentio Maschera (1593), Adriano Banchieri (1603), Giovanni Gabrieli (1615), Gregorio Allegri (before 1650), etc.

on the other hand, have to be regarded as significant precursors even if they cannot be shown to have had a direct influence. The title pages of the manuscript copies state clearly the scoring: "Sonata prima [seconda, etc.] à Quattro: Due Violini, Violetta e Violoncello - Senza Cemb^o Del Sig^r Caval^{re} Aless^o Scarlatti." The sonority is that of the later string quartet, and the genius of the composer, the influence of Scarlatti on his younger contemporaries, and the popularity of these particular sonatas were significant enough to have potentially caused the composers of the 1750's and early 1760's to have turned to this particular scoring and to have created the pre-classical string quartet. Yet, even in Scarlatti's sonatas for string quartet, the pieces are not pre-classical but are much more part of the baroque trio sonata tradition than of later string quartet tradition. The forms, first of all, are baroque, not pre-classical; the four sonatas vary, but all begin with fugues and end with binary-form movements. The styles and textures of the movements differ as well. The D Minor Sonata, for example, opens with a fugue, follows with a simple, short slow movement, continues with a fast binary-form movement, and ends with a minuet. All four instruments are of equal importance in the first movement and share the themes; the texture, of course, is strictly contrapuntal. In the second movement, which is rich in harmonic motion and chromatic suspensions, the upper three instruments are equivalent to each other and contrapuntal while the cello provides a slow, sustained harmonic bass support. The third movement is essentially a melody in the first violin accompanied by the other three instruments chordally; one or another of the lower strings occasionally fills in a rest in the first violin. The fourth movement, finally, is a trio with the two violins playing in unison and the viola and cello either playing along in parallel thirds or sixths or adding slight counterpoint. Taken as a whole, the sonata demonstrates four distinct textures and styles, but each of the movements is consistent within itself. The pre-classical quartet struggles against this unity of style and texture *within a single movement*, and the achievement of the classical string quartet is the blending of all these styles and textures *within a continually evolving movement*. Likewise, each of the Scarlatti movements is homorhythmic, i.e., a single rhythmic drive or pattern governs a whole movement, whereas the pre-classic rhythm introduces gentle contrast and the classic rhythm juxtaposes this contrast with baroque rhythmic intensity to create a dramatic situation.

While Scarlatti showed the viability of the scoring for two violins, viola and cello, the composers of the late 1750's and early 1760's did not follow him but seem to have arrived at it on their own. Haydn, in his earliest quartets, wrote for two violins, viola and bass, and as James Webster has shown, it was not until the end of the 1760's that we can be fairly sure that Haydn meant a cello when he wrote "bass."[61] Yet the Boccherini, whose first quartets are scored for cello and not bass,[62] and Haydn string quartets of the 1750's and 1760's demonstrate those other characteristics of style, form and texture which Scarlatti missed. Certainly one of the most important traits of the classical string quartet and also of most preclassical ones as well was the appearance of "sonata form" in at least one movement (usually the first and most important movement). Sonata form developed out of rounded binary form during the middle of the 18th century. One of the earliest uses of the fully-developed form appeared in the first movement of the overture to Baldassare Galuppi's (1706-1785) opera *Il filosofo di campagna* (1754). The movement is in two large sections, each repeated; the first section contains two clearly contrasting themes and keys, and the second section contains a development followed by a complete recapitulation of the first section but without the tonal contrast. This new form was so successful and continued to be throughout the 19th century that theorists of the 19th and early 20th centuries could not conceive of a string quartet without at least one movement in this form. The form was born just shortly before the first string quartets were composed, so that, in the minds of many during the next century and a half, the form and the genre were inextricably linked. As the intensity of the Sturm und Drang and then Romanticism called for ever longer and more complicated forms, sonata form proved to be ideal for sustaining a single movement

---

[61]Webster discusses this question at length in his Ph.D. dissertation and in numerous articles, all of which he summarizes in "The Scoring of Haydn's Early String Quartets," in Jens Peter Larsen et al, *Haydn Studies: Proceedings of the International Haydn Conference Washington, D.C., 1975* (New York: W.W. Norton, 1981), pp. 235-238.

[62]Christian Speck, ed., Luigi Boccherini, *Quartett in c-Moll op. 2 Nr. 1 (G 159)* (Celle: Moeck Verlag, 1987), p. 4.

over a long period of time and providing some classical balance to the frenetic gestures of the new emotionalism.

While a specific instrumentation is a prerequisite for the string quartet, the treatment of the instruments varied. All string quartets of the pre-classical and classical periods clearly emphasized the first violin. Indeed, it was the struggle of the other three instruments to gain some sort of equality that marked the evolution from pre-classical to classical. The dominance of the first violin vis-à-vis the other three instruments was largely the result of the development during the 18th century of the Italian solo concerto, which was carried over into the *divertimento a quattro* and other early quartets. But the Italians also developed another type of concerto, called the *concertino a quattro*, which those Italians who went to France developed into a more flexible interrelationship among the four instruments.[63] In Italy the concerto often was reduced in sonority to the more intimate performance of a solo instrument on a part, and when there were four parts the concerto became the *concertino a quattro*. This intimacy allowed the four soloists to interact melodically in a way proscribed in an orchestral concerto. The cellist Boccherini, in his very first quartet written in Italy but revised and published in Paris (Opus 2 no. 1),[64] restated in measures 5-8 the opening four-measure first violin theme a third higher in the second violin while the first violin accompanies. He reinforced the equality of the instruments in the second theme by having the cello and violin enter in m.17 with the first part of the theme and the two inner instruments answer with the second part of the theme. This interplay among the instruments, rather than the unabated dominance of the first violin, became the root idea of the *quatuor concertant*. Cambini, three years younger than Boccherini and a friend and colleague before both left Italy, knew Boccherini's early quartets, and when Cambini arrived in Paris and began

---

[63]Trimpert, pp. 182-183; cf. Ludwig Finscher, *Studien zur Geschichte des Streichquartetts*, i: *Die Entstehung des klassischen Streichquartetts von den Vorformen zur Grundlegung durch Joseph Haydn*, in *Saarbrücker Studien zur Musikwissenschaft*, Band 3 (Kassel: Bärenreiter, 1974), pp. 56-58.

[64]Speck, p. 4, quotes the title page to the original print that labels these pieces "sinfonie" as well as "quartetti" in some copies; there is no question that these are meant as quartets and not orchestral pieces, but the confusion with sinfonie explains the appearance of the terms "solo" and especially "soli" throughout to indicate which instrument is at the moment the leading one.

to compose quartets, Boccherini's earliest ones were his immediate models. A violinist and violist, however, Cambini did not emphasize the cello but rather equally the second violin, viola and cello in interplay with the first violin. The first violin remains dominant and frequently shows off with virtuosic passages, but the lower instruments have their moments of glory, too. The influence of Boccherini and Cambini in Paris was so great that nearly all string quartets written there and a great many in London, Mannheim and elsewhere are *quatuors concertants*. This type of quartet flourished especially in Paris, London, and Mannheim because those cities had public concerts where musicians competed for public favor, while in Austria and Italy, where the musicians performed for private courts, there was no incentive for the second violin, viola and cello to show off even in chamber music. Thus for Haydn, most of whose career was in the private home of Prince Nicolaus Eszterházy, the lower strings were content to remain subservient, and Haydn could, for a long time, concentrate on quartets with the domination of the first violin.

Haydn's ten early "string quartets" are entitled "divertimenti" (Hob. 7, 8, 10 and 12) or "cassatio" or "nottorno" (Hob. 1, 2, 3, 4, 0, 6) for two violins, viola and bass. Probably written before 1760 and therefore before Haydn started his long relationship with Prince Nicolaus Eszterházy in the Hungarian countryside, they were typical music for diversion in Austria. The music is short and simple, with the first violin dominating, the bass providing a bland harmonic bass, and the inner instruments either doubling the violin or the bass or providing accompaniment. The viola, in particular, is there to fill out a sonority, not to participate in melody or counterpoint. Once in a while the second violin shares in the melodic material, as in the Adagio of No. 8, but the second violin never approaches the technical difficulty of the first violin, which in the cited example has double stops, high positions, and big leaps. The music is delightful and not profound and would serve admirably to accompany a meal or card playing at a noble home in Vienna or nearby. The quartets are each in five movements with two minuets (with trios) as movements 2 and 4, a slow movement as movement 3, and a fast binary-form movement in last place. The opening movement in the first nine quartets is a short sonata form; the repeated exposition has two short and distinct themes and keys, the development is short and does not move very far tonally, and the recapitulation is nearly exact (the development and recapitulation are repeated, too). In the tenth quartet, however, a brief adagio theme in binary form serves for four subsequent variations. Haydn occasionally used pizzicato and con sordino for coloristic effect.

The quartets of Opus 9 (ca. 1766-1770) demand only slightly more skill of the players, but the classical style was taking much stronger shape. The six quartets of this collection are still called "divertimenti" by Haydn and the lowest instrument is still "bass," but now there are only four movements which become the established classical order: fast - minuet + trio - slow - fast, and the movements are in general lengthier. Just as in the first ten quartets, there is one exception here (Opus 9, no. 5) in which an adagio theme is followed by four variations as the first movement. The decision to have four movements is important since except for Mozart and Haydn the composers of string quartets in the pre-classical period write either two or three movements.[65] The enormous success of Haydn's and Mozart's works drove out the prevailing preference for fewer movements along with the pre-classical style, and the standardization of the four-movement structure in the 1780's and 1790's shows the weight of these two geniuses in creating the classical style. In other respects the Opus 9 quartets are pre-classical. There is more sharing of themes between the two violins and on occasion the viola and bass participate in the motives, but at no time is there any doubt that the first violin is master of the group; especially in the opening movements of nos. 3 and 4 (G and E♭) the first violin performs as if in a solo concerto while the interplay of instruments that Boccherini had already written (the concertant idea) was not in evidence.

Although very little time elapsed between Opus 9 and 17, there was considerable change in Haydn's treatment of sonata form and therefore these six "divertimenti a quatro" moved much closer to the classical string quartet. The opening movement of the first quartet set the tone for the collection. Haydn assumed that everyone now (1771) knew what sonata form was supposed to do, and

[65]Trimpert, pp. 60-63.

therefore he started into games with the listener's expectations which he would also employ effectively in his symphonies and piano sonatas. After an opening theme in F Major and a brief modulation, the second theme enters surprisingly in D Minor and then corrects itself after a few measures to the expected C Major (dominant). No sooner has C Major presented itself, however, than Haydn switches to C Minor for a few measures before returning to the C Major key. After a development section that finds more keys to investigate, the quartet starts a recapitulation in C Major (instead of F Major) before arriving in F Major (with occasional jaunts in F Minor). The recapitulation is not exact but is further exploration of the themes of the exposition. Not only is sonata form more fully developed, but the key relationships of the movements are now in what became the norm in the classical quartet. The first and last movements are in F Major, the slow movement is in the subdominant B♭ Major, and the minuet starts in F Major but its trio is in the relative minor D. The cello assumes more motion in arpeggios and runs, though it is still subservient to the violins, and the viola has only a few token solo passages. In the third movements of these quartets the first violin attains a virtuosic level even greater than in the previous quartets.

Haydn's Opus 20 quartets (1772) were his last statement in the pre-classical string quartet genre. The profuse style and character influenced by the Sturm und Drang, which he suggested in Opus 17, came to fruition just a year later. He still refers to these pieces as "divertimenti a quattro," but now the "bass" was clearly replaced with the specific designation "violoncello" and the simple and slight character of most of the previous "divertimenti" was replaced with lengthy and complex forms and textures. One of the most important ingredients of the later, classical string quartet missing in the previous ones was counterpoint—not all the time, but a fair amount of it alternating with accompanied melody and unison textures. Haydn saw this deficiency in his earlier works, so in three of the six quartets of Opus 20 he wrote strict fugues for the final movements, a type of baroque music known for its intensity and profundity and against which the pre-classical composers had fought since the 1730's. He recognized the lack of counterpoint in the earlier "divertimenti," so he over-reacted with whole movements of nothing but counterpoint. Haydn was not yet ready to mix a contrapuntal passage with a more homophonic one and with strong concertante passages within the same movement; this would come a decade later in his Opus 33 quartets. With such a mixture and with acceptance of a rhythmic verve inherited from Mozart and the concertant idea from the Italians in Paris and Madrid, Haydn created the classical string quartet in Opus 33.

Although Mozart was still a child in 1770 and 1772 when he wrote his first four quartets (which he named "divertimenti"), his genius was already maturing and he was able to find his own way quite distinct from Haydn's. From the beginning (K.80) Mozart treated the four instruments with an equality not experienced in Haydn until the fugues of Opus 20. Mozart had visited Paris, Mannheim and London and heard the concertant quartet. Thus in his early quartets the second violin and viola have main themes and are technically as difficult as the first violin, while the cello is by no means limited to filling in the harmonic bass. With his first set of six quartets (K.155-160) Mozart was clear that the "basso" is the "violoncello."[66] All the quartets of this set are in three movements, a step back from the more modern four-movement form of K.80 (slow-fast-minuet + trio-fast) and from the two-movement form of the quatuor concertant. Every quartet opens with a sonata-form movement, though in K.155 the two sections are not repeated; most are fast, but K.159 opens with an Andante. Two quartets end with minuets (K.156 and 158) and one with a rondo (K.159). Nearly every movement is either in simple binary form or in sonata form.

The fluid counterpoint and sharing of motives of the earlier quartets were increased in the next set of quartets (K.168-173). While the accompanimental passages of the earlier quartets are often banal, in this set they already exude the spark of genius that is Mozart's. Whereas Mozart had various Italian, French and Mannheim models for his earlier works, Haydn's quartets, especially Opus 20, were the model for this collection. Now all the quartets are in the classical four-movement form which Haydn had

---

[66]Wolfgang Plath, ed., *Streichquartette*, vol. 1, in *Mozart Neue Gesamtausgabe* (1966), p. viii, points out that originally Mozart wrote "basso" and then added "violoncello" over the word.

standardized: fast - slow - minuet + trio - fast or fast - minuet + trio - slow - fast. Two quartets have fugues for the final movements (K.168 and 173) following the two fugues of Haydn's Opus 20. K.170 opens with a slow theme and four variations in the manner of Haydn's no. 10 and Opus 9 no. 5 quartets. But Mozart added his own touches, such as the use of a pseudo-fugue in the first movement of K.169 and of a slow introduction to the first movement of K.171. All in all, Mozart learned elements of form from Haydn but he showed the older master how to democratize the instruments.

Besides Haydn and Mozart, Georg Christoph Wagenseil also contributed a little to the development of the string quartet in Vienna. His two string quartets (nos. 446 and 449) are probably early; both are in three movements that suggest baroque forms (Simphonia Allegro-Andante-Allegro la Confusion and Poco Adagio-Presto Fuga-Tempo di Menuet respectively). More significant, however, are Wagenseil's six unpublished string quartets with the unusual scoring for three cellos and bass (1764).[67] Although the scoring would seem to exclude these from consideration, four of them are early examples of string chamber music with the four-movement form[68] which Haydn made standard for the string quartet and they predate the publication of Haydn's Opus 9 quartets by six years. In addition, Wagenseil had equal roles for all four instruments; within a single movement the texture alternates imitation, parallel thirds, unisons a2, a3, and a4, and accompanied melody—again much before Haydn's Opus 33 quartets. Wagenseil's celli-bass quartets are not of the same dimension as Mozart's and Haydn's, but since Haydn and Mozart were well acquainted with Wagenseil's music, there is at least a possibility that they knew these quartets and that Wagenseil's collection had some influence on their own string quartets with the customary scoring. To the extent that the Viennese string quartet eventually became the standard by which all others were judged gives Wagenseil a place in the history of the quartet.

---

[67]First printed in modern edition by Rudolf Scholz in *Diletto Musicale*, nos. 791-2, 559, and 794-6 (Vienna/Munich: Doblinger, 1978-1981).

[68]While all six are in four movements, the sixth quartet has the order Andante-Allegro-Andante-Tempo di Menuet (without trio) and the fourth has the order Comodo (not in binary form) -Allegro molto-Larghetto (not in binary form)-Tempo di Menuet (without trio).

While Haydn was leading the development of the string quartet in the Viennese orbit, Boccherini simultaneously was writing string quartets in Italy and Spain and publishing them in Paris. His first set of string quartets Opus 2[69] was written in 1761 or before while he was still in Italy but published in Paris only upon his triumphant arrival in that city as a cello virtuoso in 1767. His next five sets of quartets Opus 8 (1769), 9 (1772), 15 (1773), 22 (ca. 1776) and 24 (ca. 1778) were also published in Paris but written while Boccherini served the court of Spain in Madrid. The contrast with Haydn is considerable even though outwardly (e.g., the pairing of instruments) they seem to be much alike. Boccherini's earliest quartets are not in five movements, like Haydn's, and he stayed with the three-movement fast-slow-minuet or slow-minuet-fast order after Haydn had already gone to four movements.[70] Boccherini was continually experimenting with novel ideas of form even when he stayed within his three-movement norm. For example, quartet Opus 24 no. 4 has the movements allegro spirituoso - larghetto - minuet with trio—not an uncommon order with him. But what is amazing and terribly effective is the return of subsidiary four-beat themes from the first movement as a lengthy three-beat coda following the trio (the minuet is not repeated). Boccherini also wrote several series of "quartettini" or quartets in only two movements (Opus 15, 22, 26) which probably influenced Cambini to do the same but which Haydn never did. By the 1780's Boccherini had come to know Haydn's later quartets quite well[71] and thereupon wrote mostly quartets following the Austrian order of movements. Boccherini in 1769 treated all his instruments more equally than Mozart, not surprisingly since one

---

[69]There are two orderings of opus numbers for the works of Boccherini: the original, and those (used here) from Yves Gérard, *Thematic, Bibliographical and Critical Catalogue of the Works of Luigi Boccherini*, trl. Andreas Mayor (London: Oxford, 1969), with additions by Christian Speck, *Boccherinis Streichquartette. Studien zur Kompositionsweise und zur gattungsgeschichtlichen Stellung*, in *Studien zur Musik, Philosophische Facultät, Münchener Universitäts-Schriftum* (Munich: Wilhelm Fink, 1987). This latter is the most comprehensive study of the music and sources of Boccherini's chamber music.

[70]Only two of his first 18 quartets are in four movements, both in Opus 9 which was influenced by Boccherini's own four- movement quintets.

[71]Boccherini presumably played the earlier Haydn quartets with the Nardini-Manfredi-Cambini-Boccherini ensemble but there is some inconsistency in the report. Cf. Tripert, pp. 10-12.

would expect Boccherini the cellist to at least give his own instrument its fair share. Both viola and second violin, along with the other two instruments, have major themes. Although there is never any doubt that the first violinist was in charge, the introduction of the concertant quartet to Paris by Boccherini and then Cambini eventually had a major impact not only on the French but on the Austrians as well. Interestingly when Boccherini turned to the four-movement structure of Haydn's quartets in such works as his Opus 32 no. 6 (written in 1780), he also copied Haydn's preference before 1782 of allowing the first violin to dominate and ignored the even-handed counterpoint of his (Boccherini's) own earlier quartets.

Although a great many early composers of the string quartet were Italians, none except the obscure Cirri, Andreozzi, Bertoni, and Paisiello (obscure as an instrumental composer) wrote quartets and also remained in Italy. Besides Boccherini, Cambini was active in Paris, and in London there were Tommaso Giordani, Antonio Sacchini, Venanzio Rauzzini, and Felice de Giardini. Giovanni Giuseppe Cambini (1746-1825), one of the most prolific composers of string quartets in the 18th century, began to write his string quartets as soon as he moved to Paris ca. 1773. His first dozen quartets[72] (1773-1774), like Boccherini's earliest quartets, may have been composed in Italy before the composer reached Paris.[73] All told, Cambini published 144 string quartets[74] in Paris during the 1770's and 1780's which belong to the history of the pre-classical quartet; he also published six late ones (nos. 169-174,[75] 1804-1809), a string quartet arrangement of two sonatas by Boccherini, and a series of popular quatuors d'airs which belong more properly to the history of the classical quartet. There is no evidence that any of the quartets were written for performance at the Concerts Spirituels and Concerts des Amateurs, but it seems likely that they were

[72]To avoid confusion with conflicting opus numbers the quartets of Cambini are numbered consecutively according to Trimpert, whose definitive study of Cambini's chamber music is the source for the following discussion.

[73]Quartets nos. 7-12 have the optional scoring for flute in place of the first violin.

[74]Nos.66-71 are scored for one violin, two violas, and cello.

[75]Trimpert lists eighteen flute quartets (not to be confused with the optional flute-string quartets nos. 7-12) among the string quartets.

written in part "for small, private concerts in the homes of the nobility and rich middle class as a surrogate for orchestral music and
solo music accompanied by an orchestra."[76] Such quartets required
considerable skill by the first violinist (Cambini himself) and the
other performers. Most of Cambini's quartets, however, were
aimed at an amateur audience and were highly prized by that
group. Such amateurs could play reasonably well, though not with
the distinction of a publicly concertizing soloist. Cambini himself
wrote that "people who really love art should get together, study
quartets, and learn to perform them . . . often repeating the best
works of this genre in order to know all the nuances contained in
the work."[77] Outside Paris Cambini quartets were known in 18th-
century Sweden, Mannheim, Burgsteinfurt, Dresden, Vienna,
Modena, London, Philadelphia and New York; in a few cases they
may have been performed publicly, as reported in Mannheim by
Mozart and documented in Leipzig on October 30, 1783, Philadelphia on April 25, 1786, and New York on January 14, 1794, but in
most places the quartets were played privately.[78] The late quartets,
like Cambini's many string quintets (see below), were written for
private concerts at the home of Armand Séguier, of which Cambini
was in charge from 1794 on, while the arrangements of airs were
suitable for the amateur.

Most of Cambini's string quartets of the 1770's and 1780's
belong to the category of *quatuor concertante*, i.e., quartets with an
element of concerto. This type of quartet was not invented by
Cambini, but he popularized it in Paris at the time. The term
"concertante" means that there are episodes in which one or another of the instruments has concerto-like, solistic, virtuosic passages, and that during the course of a movement all four
instruments share motives and are more or less equal even though
the first violin continues to dominate. In a single *quatuor concer-*

---

[76]Trimpert, p. 210: "Einerseits stellten sie offensichtlich für die grosse Anzahl kleinerer
privater Konzertunternehmen in den Häusern des Adels und des reichen Bürgertums ein
Surrogat für die Orchestermusik und die orchesterbegleitete Solomusik dar."

[77]As quoted in Trimpert, p. 211: "Männer, die ihre Kunst aufrichtig lieben, sollten sich
zusammen tun und Quartetten studiren und ausführen lernen . . . die vorzüglichsten
Werke dieser Gattung oft wiederholen, alle Nüanzen des absichtigen Vortrags dadurch
kennen lernen."

[78]Trimpert, pp. 207-209.

tant there are passages when the first violin dominates accompanied by the other three instruments and other passages when the four instruments parry the motives back and forth. Each of the instruments often has virtuosic passages, while other passages have all four instruments in a rhythmically active tutti without special melodic interest. Whatever instrument is the solo (usually but not always the first violin), the other instruments accompany with sustaining notes or with repeated chords. Amateurs were possibly frightened by the term concertant because it suggested that the lower strings would have exposed and difficult passages, so Cambini wrote as the title of his Opus 22 *Six Quatuors Faciles et Concertantes* to ease their minds. Like many of his contemporaries but unlike Mozart and Haydn, Cambini favored a two-movement structure (usually fast-slower but also fast-faster and fast-fast) in 111 quartets. Only ten quartets are in four movements: four of the first dozen quartets and all of the late quartets (the first still under the influence of Boccherini and not Gossec and the latter clearly under the influence of Haydn and Mozart). All the remaining quartets are in three movements. The preference for two movements was no doubt determined by the taste of the audience at the concert series, at least as perceived by the directors of those series, who thought the audience would sit still for only two or at most three movements of a single piece. Whereas three or four movements were the norm in quartets that were not concertant, the two-movement form is clearly associated with the concertant quartet whether by Cambini or by his many imitators in Paris, London, and Mannheim. Cambini did not bring the two-movement form from Italy; he learned it in Paris from Gossec who had written a concertant trio as early as 1753[79] and who in turn may have learned it from the sonatas of Valentin Roesser. Haydn and Mozart, on the other hand, were writing for mostly private Viennese-oriented audiences and were not writing concertant quartets; therefore they followed initially the five or three but then the four-movement form inherited from the divertimento. Whatever the number of movements, the first movement was always the most pretentious and always in sonata form. That Cambini's reputation in Paris rested even more on the *sinfonia concertante* indicates that there

---

[79]Trimpert, pp. 191-193.

was a connection between the orchestral concertant and the chamber one.

It is not surprising that Italians living in Paris rather than native Frenchmen starred in string quartet writing and playing since French philosophers led an attack on purely instrumental music which threatened its aesthetic right to exist. Native Frenchmen were hesitant to write purely instrumental music and thereby risk attack by their country's intellectual leaders, and therefore they concentrated on operas, ballets and religious music, where the instrumental accompaniment and interludes were well written but within a vocal, textual context. When they did turn to purely instrumental music during the 18th century, they wrote mostly second-rate string quartets. There were numerous French examples of concertos for three violins and bass but these were orchestral. Gossec wrote quartets (Opus 14, 1770) for flute and string trio, and LeDuc wrote six quatuors for optional wind and/or string scoring including two violins, viola and cello in 1768. Names such as Davaux, D'Alayrac, Bullan, and J. Fodor l'Aîne are obscure, though each wrote quartets in the 1780's. The only significant exception to all this was François Joseph Gossec (1734-1829), a Belgian serving several noblemen in Paris, who wrote his first string quartets in 1759 and whose Opus 15 quartets (1772) in two movements anticipate and point the way for Cambini's quartets. Gossec's quartets are melodically and rhythmically simple and evince the rare influence of both French rationalism and opera buffa.[80]

In London there was a flurry of string quartet activity during the 1770's by a group of Italians who immigrated there. Giordani (ca. 1733-1806) published two collections in ca. 1773 and ca. 1775, Sacchini (1730-1786) a single collection in 1778, the castrato Rauzzini (1746-1810) two collections ca. 1777 and ca. 1778, and Giardini (1716-1796) various collections from 1776 to 1790. Yet it was the German Carl Friedrich Abel who was the leader in writing string quartets in quality as well as quantity. He published three collections: Opus 8 (1769), Opus 12 (1775) and Opus 15 (1780). He also published two quartets in a collection with Felice

---

[80]Trimpert, pp. 189-190.

de Giardini and Johann Christian Bach (1776) whose first violin part can be optionally performed by a flute. All of Abel's quartets are in three movements; the first is always a fast, sophisticated sonata form with varied recapitulation and motivic and tonal development, the second is always slow, usually in a related key, and never in binary form, and the third is often a tempo di menuetto but also occasionally a rondo or simply fast movement. Abel's conception of form is always interesting and unexpected; even minuets often do not conform to the expected binary form and in several cases only the first phrase of the minuet returns after the trio ("minore"). In the first two collections Opus 8 and 12 the first violin clearly dominates, but in some movements there is imitation among all four instruments. In the first two movements of Opus 8 no. 1, for example, the second violin and lower strings are almost without exception accompanimental (the second violin has the second theme once, just before the close of the first double bar); but in the tempo di menuetto each instrument enters in succession with the theme and all four instruments maintain both thematic and rhythmic independence. The six quartets of Opus 15 are different from the earlier ones. They are three-movement concertant quartets; at least two of the instruments in each quartet carry on alternately with extensive 16th-note runs while the other instruments accompany. In Opus 15 nos. 2 and 5 the cello has major concertant passages. Abel's quartets are among those that have been neglected since the 18th century that deserve restoration. His treatment of form, texture and rhythm clearly would have appealed to Mozart, who met Abel on his first trip to London in 1764 and who was influenced by the older man's symphonies.[81]

Carl Joseph Toeschi (1731-1788) led the way in Mannheim with his six quartets "il dialogo musicale" (1765), six quatuors dialogués Opus 5 (ca. 1766), six quartets of Opus 2 (1767), six further ones in Opus 9 (1770), and a few other quartets during the next few years. The concept "il dialogo" is important both for characterizing these quartets and for its implication for the future. By dialogue Toeschi meant that all four instruments are equal in much the way that Mozart democratizes the instruments. All four share fully in themes, counterpoint, accompaniment, and technical

[81]Einstein, p. 116.

difficulty. There are unison passages as well, which are borrowed from the Mannheim orchestra, in which all four instruments simultaneously submerge their individuality into the effect of the whole. The dialogue concept is one which Johann Friedrich Reichardt and Adorno pursue in their discussions of the social condition of the string quartet and chamber music in general and which we will discuss at length below.

The presence of Brunetti and Boccherini in Spain did not leave the Spanish unaffected by the new quartet. Manuel Canales (1747-1786), for example, who was a violinist in the Cathedral in Toledo, dedicated his six Opus 1 *cuartetos* to the Duke of Alba in 1774 and was designated "composer to the King of Spain" in his Opus 3 *cuartetos* published in London ca. 1780.[82] The poet Tomas de Iriarte (d.1791), an amateur violinist and violist who frequently hosted chamber music in his home, composed several string quartets now lost.

However widespread the writing of string quartets became elsewhere in the 1770's, Vienna and its neighborhood would prove to be the most important center for this genre of chamber music. The reason is that both Haydn and Mozart lived there. Mozart as a child toured Mannheim, Paris and London and thereby became acquainted with the string quartet as it was developing in those special cities. Haydn, too, was not provincial in his knowledge of the new music of his time, though as a servant-composer in the Hungarian countryside he had certain limitations imposed upon him. The interaction of these two geniuses, however, enabled the fledgling quartet to take a path different from the string quartet elsewhere.

THE STRING QUINTET

The string quintet was another popular genre of chamber music that developed after the middle of the 18th century in Italy and Austria. The Italian string quintet developed in the early 1760's as a variety of the concertant quartet, while the Austrian version developed at the same time as a variety of divertimento. They influ-

[82]Sanchez, p. 55.

enced each other during the 1760's, 1770's and 1780's as they evolved from a pre-classical type to a mature classical genre.

In Italy the earliest string quintets were by Francesco Zannetti (1763), Pasquale Ricci (ca. 1768), and Cambini, whose first quintets were probably written around 1770, three years before he arrived in Paris.[83] But outside Italy three Italian composers dominated the production of this genre: Cambini in Paris (114 quintets) and Boccherini (125) and Brunetti (66) in Madrid. All three wrote their quintets not because of aesthetic demands or some inevitable evolution but because the particular situation in which they were employed required that they do so. Brunetti came to Madrid in 1762 and from 1767 until his death in 1808 he worked for the kings of Spain. Beginning in 1771 he wrote string quintets for two violins, two violas and one cello because the king possessed a family of Stradivarius instruments of exactly that combination. Most are concertant quintets in four movements, but there are eighteen smaller ones in three movements. Brunetti was a violinist, but he was fair to the other four instruments and often wrote real five-voice counterpoint. This contrasts with Boccherini and Cambini, who often wrote for four instruments with another cello tacked on.

Boccherini came to Madrid in 1769 to work for Don Luis, brother of the king of Spain, and remained in that position until Luis died in 1785. Luis already had a string quartet ensemble in residence, and in order to work with it, the cellist Boccherini added a fifth part for himself.[84] Only in his last two collections of quintets (1801-1802), long after he had left Luis' Madrid, did Boccherini change the scoring to the then more popular Austrian ensemble of two violins, two violas and one cello.

While directing music at the home of the Parisian contractor Armand Séguier, Cambini regularly performed his own string quartets and quintets. Before he worked for Séguier, Cambini preferred the quartet over the quintet; there are 144 quartets during the 1770's and 1780's and only two quintets. After 1794, however, he

[83] Tilman Sieber, *Das klassische Streichquintett* (Bern/Munich: Francke Verlag, 1983), pp. 30-33.

[84] Louis Picquot, *Notice sur la Vie et les Ouvrages de Luigi Boccherini* (Paris: 1851), p. 29f, quoted in Sieber, p. 33.

wrote 114 quintets but only six quartets. Cambini was not thinking of the popular Parisian public when he wrote these late quintets but only of satisfying the special, highly developed taste of Séguier. His quintets are for two violins, viola and two cellos, like most of Boccherini's, with only one exception: the first quintet in Opus 23 (1781) for two violins, two violas, and cello following Brunetti and the Austrian model. Since they are influenced by the classical quintets of both Boccherini and Mozart, they are best discussed in the next chapter.

The string quintet, then, as developed by Italians, was an expansion of the string quartet. Since Boccherini and Cambini were both so prolific in quartets as well as in quintets, it seems inevitable that the two genres overlapped in styles, forms, and content. Boccherini wrote most quintets in four movements, just as he did in his quartets, and when he wrote two-movement quintets, he renamed them "quintettini" which corresponds to his two-movement "quartettini." Just as generalizations are difficult to make concerning the structure of the whole and individual movements of his quartets, so are they difficult concerning that of his quintets. But one generalization that can be made is that the two genres of string quartets and string quintets both exploited the Italian penchant for concertant. While Cambini began with a few quintets, almost all his quintets come after he had written 144 string quartets, so in compositional matters the quintets are more mature works. Whereas Cambini's quartets are mostly two or three-movement quatuors concertants, his quintets are mostly in three movements with the give-and-take among instruments that matured from the earlier concertant quartets. Part of this maturity came from his knowledge of the classical quintets of Mozart and the quartets of Mozart and Haydn, which he mingled with the Italian concertant style he brought from Italy to Paris thirty years before.

The North and Middle Germans did not favor the string quintet because they were bound to the baroque ideal of solo and trio with accompanied continuo and not even the string quartet made headway there. In Mannheim, however, the cello freed itself from any vestige of continuo, and once there were four concertant instruments, a fifth one was easily added. There were not many string quintets written in Mannheim in the 1760's to 1780's, but one figure of importance is Carlo Giuseppe Toeschi (1724-1788), who wrote five dialogue string quintets after 1766. In a dialogue quintet the two violins play together, the two violas or viola and first cello play together, and the bottom instrument accompanies. This contrasts with the Italian concertant where all five instruments alternately or in various groups participate in the main themes and motives.

In Austria the quintet was more popular than anywhere in Germany. In Vienna beginning in the 1760's the string divertimento developed into the string quintet. The designation "quintetto" meant scoring, not function or location, while the terms "divertimento," "notturno," "serenade," and "cassatio"—although also used frequently for works for five string instruments—meant function and location of the music, not scoring. Other terms that might be construed as generic—"sonata," "concertino," "partia," and "sinfonia"—did not designate specific scoring, location, function, contents or form.[85] Unlike most Italian quintets the Austrian was usually scored for two violins, two violas and cello. Joseph Haydn contributed to this genre with only a few very early divertimenti (one cassatio) each in five or six movements where the second viola and cello often are in parallel octaves. Michael Haydn's earliest quintets were similar to his brother's, though influenced by the later development of forms and styles of the early 1770's, whereas Wagenseil's three quintets are each in three movements and the instruments share the themes more. These three composers and such others as Franz Aumann, Leopold Gassmann, and Johann Baptist Vanhal wrote short, simple movements where all faster ones are in the tonic key, the slower ones are often in the dominant, and the trios of the minuets are in the parallel minor or dominant. Significantly Gassmann frequently favored the violas over the violins which then became accompanimental.

Mozart's one early string quintet is typical of the Austrian examples but also far superior to them. The stimulus for Mozart to write such a piece came from Michael Haydn.[86] In February 1773

[85]Sieber, p. 37.

[86]Ernst Hess, "Einzelbemerkungen," in *Streichquintette*, ed. Hess and Ernst Fritz Schmid, in Mozart, *Neue Ausgabe sämtlicher Werke*, Series VIII, Werkgruppe 19 (Kassel: Bärenreiter, 1967), p. viii.

Haydn composed his first string quintet in Salzburg, and when young Mozart returned to his native city a month later from an Italian trip, he learned his older colleague's piece and wrote his own string quintet (K.174) modelled on it. There are four movements: the first a substantial sonata form allegro moderato, the second a binary form adagio, the third a minuet with trio, and the last another sonata form fast movement. On December 1, 1773 Haydn finished his second string quintet, and immediately thereafter Mozart rewrote the final movement of his own quintet and replaced the trio of the minuet. K.174 differs from the five later Mozart string quintets (1787-1791) in the divertimento-like (i.e., orchestral or sinfonia concertante-like) character of the piece. The opening of the first movement sounds like a concerto first for violin 1 and then for viola 1 with the other instruments in typical concerto-like accompaniment. There is much dialogue or pairing of instruments in parallel thirds: violin 2 with viola 2, the two violins, the two violas; and there are also many unison passages even between violin 1 and viola 1 and among all five instruments (e.g., opening of the development). The basso (cello) barely escapes the role of continuo; the second theme clearly calls for a solo cello in a momentary passage highlighting that instrument. The second violin and viola, too, have little besides accompaniment. In the second movement, however, the second violin and viola have much more prominent concertant solos. While the first violin and viola dominate the minuet, the new trio is much longer than the old one in order to enable all five instruments more participation. This seems to be the message that Mozart learned from Michael Haydn's second quintet, for in the rewritten final movement the five instruments achieve a sort of parity that was a harbinger of what came in the mighty last five quintets. Nonetheless, even in this finale there is lots of unison and pairing between the violins and the violas.

After these early beginnings of the Austrian string quintet in the 1760's and early 1770's there was a pause before they again became popular. This pause may be attributed to the sudden popularity of the string quartets of Haydn, which by the early 1770's were eagerly consumed by performers and audiences alike throughout Europe.[87] Jumping on the bandwagon, other Austrian

[87]Sieber, p. 51.

composers poured out quartets and the quintet was lost for the time being. When Ignaz Pleyel, Franz Anton Hoffmeister (1754-1812) and Mozart returned to the string quintet in the late 1780's, the genre had a new life and, thanks to Mozart, achieved its greatest repertoire. By then the beauties of Boccherini's many quintets were known, and Pleyel, Hoffmeister and Mozart saw both a market and an aesthetic challenge in this genre. In addition to growth in the classical forms and styles, there was also a new relationship among the instruments in their later works. Whereas the earlier Austrian quintets pitted the two violins against the two violas with the cello accompanying, now the five instruments more equally participated as individuals and shared motives; even when paired, the violins and violas were more integrated with each other. The cello was no longer just a bass accompaniment but an equal partner in the melodic material. The classical string quintet had arrived.

Much less important than the string quintet is the string sextet. Occasionally the composer experimented with this enlarged ensemble, but clearly the idea of parity of instruments or concertant was strained too much by the number of instruments. It was dangerous enough to move a single motive around four or five instruments without boring the listener through endless repetition (a fate that even Beethoven suffered, for example, in his triple concerto when the necessity of giving each of the three soloists an equal hearing results in a redundancy that the audience does not need). Nonetheless a few composers did try string sextets, such as Wagenseil (for four violins, viola and cello). Rather the late-18th-century composer, when writing a sextet, chose instruments of contrasting timbre, such as different kinds of winds or a mixture of winds and strings (such as C. J. Toeschi's three sextets for flute, oboe, bassoon, violin, viola and bass of 1765).

THE STRING TRIO AND DUET

As we have seen in the previous chapter, the baroque sonata da camera often was a chamber work for two treble strings and a bowed string bass instrument without keyboard. This scoring, then, was firmly established by the middle of the 18th century when pre-

classical composers began to transform it into the "string trio."[88]
Actually the term "trio" designating a whole and separate piece of
music for an ensemble of three instruments (as opposed to three
lines of music as in the trio sonata which might be played by two
or four persons, or trios in the middle of larger works) is first used
in the second half of the 18th century in Philipp Valois de
Stoukarts' *Six Trio pour le Clavecin, Violin et Basse* (1767),[89] but
"string trio" does not become the title of a whole piece for three
bowed string instruments until late in the 19th century. Although
"trio" designating "three players" was firmly established by the
end of the 18th century, most of the 19th century referred to string
trios as "violin trios."[90] In the second half of the 18th century any
one of a variety of titles could appear meaning what we today cite
as "string trio." Haydn, for example, whose twenty-one string trios
seem to have been composed between 1752 and 1767, called only
one of them "trio" (no. 21) in his personal catalogue, while the
publishers called them "Divertimento a tre," "Notturno," "Cassatio," "Divertissment," and "Terzetto." The Italians and English
still called them "Trios" or "Sonatas" to link them to the baroque,
though there is nothing baroque about them. The French sometimes called string trios "Trietti" or "Conversazioni a tré" (Boccherini's Opus 2 and 7, both published in Paris).[91]

The scoring of the trio sonata and string trio are often the same,
but the two genres are distinct on stylistic grounds. The distinction
was best defined by the Germans who contrasted their trios with
those of the Italians. In the 1760's and 1770's the North Germans,
hanging on longer to Corelli's conception of the contrapuntal trio
sonata than many Italians, believed that all three instruments

---

[88]Hubert Unverricht, *Geschichte des Streichtrios* (Tutzing: Hans Schneider, 1969), p. 12,
warns that the string trio is not a forerunner of the string quartet, as has been purported in
much of the earlier literature.

[89]Unverricht, p. 26, who discusses in detail the various uses of the term in the 17th and
18th centuries. "Trio" designating a middle movement for three instruments occurs in
dance collections as early as 1695 (Unverricht, p. 27).

[90]Barry Brook, ed. *Streichtrios*, in *Joseph Haydn Werke*, Reihe XI, 1.Folge, Band 1
(Munich: Henle, 1986), "Vorwart"; and Unverricht, p. 38.

[91]Unverricht, pp. 36 and 31.

should take part in a more or less strict counterpoint.[92] They divided trios into four categories. 1) Da chiesa trios remained strict, while 2) da camera trios allowed a few virtuosic passages and figures. The Austrians and Italians of this time, on the other hand, were writing trios where 3) the upper two voices were concertant and accompanied by the bass (cello) (though in practice the bass shared some of the melodic material) or 4) the solo violin was accompanied by the other two strings. The North German theorists attacked the southerners for their misguided style of trio sonata, while the southerners created a new type of trio which we term "string trio." The distinction, therefore, between trio sonata and string trio at this time was a matter of the degree of polyphony and homophony there was in the piece. The more polyphonic it was and the less homophonic, the more closely it tied in with the traditional trio sonata. Composers of this type included Tartini, Tessarini, Locatelli, Lampugnani, Graun, Quantz, and others. The more homophonic and the less polyphonic the piece was, the more it tied in with the string trio, whose composers were Boccherini, Giardini, Cirri, Raimondi, Zannetti, both Haydns, Dittersdorf, Mislivecek, Toëschi, Gossec, Le Duc, Johann Stamitz, Wagenseil, Gassmann, and Abel.

The trios of Joseph Haydn can serve to demonstrate this new string trio. Haydn's eighteen surviving string trios are usually in three movements, and with only three exceptions all movements of all the trios are in binary form. Most string trios have a minuet, often with trio, which comes either second or third in the piece. There are two string trios with themes and variations, and those string trios are in only two movements. About half of the binary allegro movements are in sonata form; in some the form is barely recognizable, while in others the form is highly developed and sophisticated with varied recapitulation and lengthy development. The string trios with the least developed sonata form presumably were the earliest (nos. 1-4, 6), while those with the most advanced sonata form were the latest (e.g. no. 10). Whatever the age of the trios, the two violins share in the principal motives,

---

[92]This is best expressed in Johann Abraham Peter Schulz's "Trio," in Johann George Sulzer's *Allgemeiner Theorie der Schönen Künste* (Leipzig: 1771-1774), as summarized in Unverricht, pp. 97-99.

though the first remains dominant; the cello is not much more than accompaniment.

A contemporary of Haydn's reported that when Haydn presented six string trios ca. 1753, it was suggested to him that he add an instrument to make a quartet. It is possible that this sparked Haydn to write his first quartets, which came after his first trios, but there is very little in common between the early string trios (especially nos. 1-4, 6 but also all the others) and any quartets. The earliest string quartets are in five movements and then four movements, whereas all the string trios are in two or three movements. Furthermore in no early string quartets (before Opus 20) are the two violins as concertant-like as in the trios.

A special category of trios is the 126 or so baryton trios by Haydn.[93] During the years 1765 to 1774 Prince Nicolas Esterházy, for whom Haydn worked, played the strange string instrument called the baryton, which was held like a cello and had strings both above the fingerboard to be bowed by the right hand and below the neck to be plucked by the left hand. A few professional performers on the instrument at the time—Karl Franz, Anton Kraft, and Josef Weigl—inspired this enthusiastic dilettante to play the instrument, and he in turn commanded his servant Haydn to write ensemble pieces for it. Almost all are scored for baryton, viola and cello (bass); three are for violin instead of viola. All but a few are in three movements and have a minuet with trio, but the order of movements and tempi vary considerably. Most opening movements are in binary form but a few are themes with variations. In several cases the final movements are fugues. Number 97 is unusual in that it has seven movements of which two are minuets (with trios) and the last is a fugue. In addition to these trios Haydn also wrote other chamber music for the baryton including duets for two barytones and for baryton with cello. While all the baryton works by Haydn are typical in so far as they demonstrate how chamber music for aristocrats came to be, they are atypical in that almost no one else—and certainly not since—has written for such an instrument.

---

[93]Several survive only in part, and there are four unauthenticated trios which probably are by Haydn.

The style of string trios in France was different from that in Austria. Early in the 18th century French chamber music was already more homophonic than contrapuntal. Since the influence of the dance suite was greater on the baroque trio in France than in Germany or Italy, the French did not experience a conservative backlash at mid-century when the new types were promoted in chamber music. The third type of string trio according to the Germans, where the two upper instruments are concertant, was particularly enjoyed in Paris in the 1760's and 1770's; the term "dialogué" was used by the French in reference to this duet concertant style, and the term "concertant" was reserved for trios where all three instruments participated equally. To satisfy the needs of the growing number of amateur trio players, however, the "concertant" style was reduced in these "dialogues" from the complex, ornate baroque treatment of melody to simple, light pre-classical melody.

The string trio was one of the most popular types of chamber music in the second half of the 18th century. Many composers throughout Europe contributed to the formation of this genre. Among these there are various combinations of instruments. The most common is two violins and cello (or bass). Of Haydn's twenty-one string trios, for example, twenty are with this scoring; the exception, his no. 8 trio, is for violin, viola and cello. In Vienna Albrechtsberger wrote divertimenti for two violins and cello and others for violino picolo o primo, violino secondo e viola. In Paris during the 1770's and 1780's Cambini wrote twenty-four trios for two violins and cello, but he also composed at least thirty-four trios for violin, viola and cello and forty-two trios for two violins and viola (or optional viola or cello). Most of these are concertant trios similar to his quatuors concertants, but one set of six (date unknown) is *Trios d'Airs Choisis, Variés pour deux violons, Alto ou Violoncelle*.

The classical string trio emerged during the 1770's from the pre-classical prototypes but with important changes. Among these were the disappearance of the preferential treatment for the top instrument and of the last vestiges of figured bass, the full participation of the lowest instrument, and a number of other features discussed in the next chapter.

The history of the string duo differs considerably from that of the trio. While the trio, as well as quartet and quintet, were performed in front of audiences, even if small private ones, most duets seemingly belonged to the private quarters of the performers themselves and not to any public sphere. There were two principal reasons for such duets. For one, the string teachers of the 18th century found the duet a useful pedagogic tool to train young or at least uninitiated players in the elementary aspects of ensemble; the duet is still used today by string teachers to help the beginner with intonation, rhythm, and basic style. Although not advanced or difficult, such duets can be attractive and if serious are chamber music. For another, two string players of any ability found that getting together alone and informally to make music was an enjoyment unequaled in any other ensemble. It was less complicated than performing with two or more others, and it allowed for the meshing of homogeneous sounds of two string players that was not possible with a keyboard or wind. With performance in private the ensemble could not be influenced in any way by the pressures of a listening and criticizing audience. Since string player-composers knew their own ability and that of their comrades, difficult, even virtuosic duets could be written as well as extremely easy ones, and embarrassment was not a factor in such privacy.

The possible combinations for duets were all exploited. Preclassical duets are often for two violins, but there are many duets also for violin and viola, two violas, viola and cello, two cellos, and violin and cello. In Vienna alone between the years 1760 and 1810 Mazurowicz lists the composition, publication and performance of hundreds of duets for various combinations.[94] This excludes purely pedantic duets and string duets used for dancing. Many were called "concertant," which of course implies the equality of the two instruments as they exchange leading motives. Others were called grand duos, which implies a large and very serious format. Since most of this repertory came between 1780 and 1820 it will be discussed further in the next chapter.

---

[94]Ulrich Mazurowicz, *Das Streichduett in Wien von 1760 bis zum Tode Joseph Haydns*, in *Eichstätter Abhandlungen zur Musikwissenschaft*, Band 1 (Tutzing: Hans Schneider, 1982), pp. 211-366.

In Paris Cambini was almost as prolific in duets as he was in quartets and quintets. In the 1770's and 1780's he published well over forty-two duets for two violins (some duo concertant, some pedagogic works—"pour les commencants" or "d'une difficulté progressive"—and others "livre d'airs variés),[95] forty-two duets for violin and viola (including a set of "duo dialogués, opus 46, 1782),[96] a dozen for two violas[97] and some more for violin and cello.[98] Boccherini's duets for two violins were published in Paris in 1769 but, like his early string quartets, written in 1761 while he was still in Italy.[99] All are in three movements, usually fast-slow-minuet or tempo di minuetto. Only the first (G.56) varies this with grazioso-allegro-presto. In addition Boccherini wrote in his early Italian years a duo for two cellos in the same form allegro-largo-allegro. There remains one other duet by Boccherini—the "Notturno" for two violins (G.62)—which apparently was a later work influenced by Parisian program music and the classical four-movement form (see Chapter V).

In Vienna some duets written between 1760 and 1780 were in two movements and others in three or four. Vanhal, for example, wrote six two-movement duetti in 1779 and 1780 (Opus 28) which usually begin with an allegro moderato and end with a grazioso. That a two-movement duet might have been considered shorter than normal, however, is evinced by Sperger in 1770 with his twelve two-movement pieces that he labels "duettina." Most are two fast movements, and the rest include a minuet or slow movement or march instead of one of the fast movements. In contrast to these smaller duets are those by Bohdanowicz (1777) and Huber (1772). Bohdanowicz wrote six virtuosic duets, each with cadenzas between the penultimate and ultimate movements. Two duets are fast-slow-cadenza-fast, two are fast-slow-cadenza-theme and variations (one has a minuet theme), and one is moderato-slow-cadenza-fast rondo. The sixth duet, on the other hand (no. 3), is in four movements apart from the cadenza: fast-fast-slow-cadenza-

[95]Opus 2, 4, 16, 21, 28, and 52.
[96]The others are Opus 12, 14 and 18.
[97]Opus 13.
[98]Opus 35.
[99]Gérard, *Catalogue*, pp. 56-73.

fast, which points to the full symphonic and quartet form blooming at the time in Vienna and away from the Italian and French three- and two-movement forms. All the duets by Bohdanowicz pre- shadow the virtuosity of the concertant and grand duets of the end of the 18th and beginning of the 19th centuries. Huber's six duets are not as virtuosic, but their four-movement structure—based en- tirely on the symphony and string quartet (with sonata form first movements, a minuet and trio in second position, and so on)—lend a seriousness and breadth to the duet that places them in a different milieux from Sperger's duettinas and Vanhal's early duets.

Joseph Haydn's duets for violin accompanied by viola were probably composed by 1769.[100] In most early editions these were not considered duets but "Trois Sonates pour le Violon" (Offen- bach: J. André, 1799) with the viola on a lesser level than the vio- lin. When Bailleux published them (Paris: 1792), however, he called them "duo dialogués," but Haydn himself referred to them in his own catalogue in a way comparable to André's. Like Boc- cherini's duets and perhaps under his influence, all are in three movements "fast"-slow-tempo di minuetto (one "fast movement is actually an andante and another two moderato). Although Haydn stuck to the Italian structure in these works, his symphonies and string quartets which follow them within a year or two have a deci- sive impact on the larger duets which Bohdanowicz and Huber compose. And, as we shall see in the next chapter, when Michael Haydn wrote his four violin-viola duets in 1783, the torch was passed from the two Haydn brothers to Mozart.

WIND CHAMBER MUSIC IN THE 18TH CENTURY

Although the emphasis in this chapter has been upon chamber music for strings with or without keyboard, there was at the same time much chamber music involving winds. Throughout the ba- roque period the flute and oboe often substituted for violins in so- natas, and this practice continued through the pre-classical era. As we have already seen, the sonatas by the Graun brothers were written equally for violin or flute with either continuo or obligato

---

[100]Mazurowicz, pp. 34-36 and 284.

harpsichord. But in their own right the flute and oboe as well as other winds took part regularly in chamber music. Besides these instruments the bassoon, the horn (corno di caccia), the English horn, the basset horn and eventually the clarinet joined with each other and with the strings and keyboards. The variety of combinations of instruments was so great that it is difficult to generalize, though there are a few combinations that occurred often enough.

One of the most popular situations for the flute and oboe during the pre-classical period was in quartets. The similarity of the ranges of these two instruments to that of the violin (if the relatively little used g-string is omitted) suggested to composers at the time the same types of quartets that otherwise were being written for two violins, viola and cello. Cambini, for example, wrote eighteen quartets for flute, violin, viola and cello, an additional six for either flute or violin with a second violin, viola and cello, and one for either violin or oboe with second violin, viola and cello. Although he was an Italian, it was the Parisian setting which enabled Cambini to write these pieces. The wind quartet did not exist in Italy with its flowering schools of violinists, but in France with a long tradition of excellent flutists there were players available— both professional and amateur—and an audience for such pieces. Gossec's Opus 14 quartets (1770) and LeDuc's set (1768) have already been mentioned. Cambini's are very much like his string quartets: mostly concertant, usually in two movements, with the first in sonata form. The interplay of flute and violin in the concertant flute quartet is especially effective. The flute quartet was copied in Mannheim by Toeschi, Wendling, Eichner, and Vogler, in Austria by Michael Haydn, and in London by J.C. Bach, Abel, and Giardini (1772). While visiting Mannheim in 1777, Mozart wrote three of his flute quartets at the behest of Monsieur de Jean, a rich Dutch amateur, and on a trip to Paris in 1783 he wrote his last one.[101] The first three show the influence of Cambini's quatuors concertants (two are in two movements, the third in three, and the dominant flute allows the violin and viola some flourishes), while the last flute quartet, with its borrowed air from Paisiello, is modelled on Cambini's quatuors d'airs. Mozart's oboe quartet is similar to the quatuor concertant, though it was not written in either

---

[101]Einstein, *Mozart*, p. 178.

Paris or Mannheim but in Munich in 1781 for one of the great oboists of the day: Friedrich Ramm. It has concertant elements, including a cadenza, and it anticipates by two years much of the style of his mature classical string quartets. It stands out as the best among a series of oboe quartets by his contemporaries such as Cannabich. Sometimes other instruments took the place of the oboe or flute or first violin, such as the English horn in a quartet by Michael Haydn,[102] or the horn in quartets by Franz Aumann (*Cassation* "La Pastorella") and Anton Richter.[103]

The popularity of woodwind chamber music in Paris was not as great as that of string music, but there obviously were enough amateur performers to warrant the publication of many works calling for woodwinds in various combinations. Valentin Roesser, who worked variously in Vienna, Monaco, and Paris, found the sextet for pairs of clarinets, horns and bassoons particularly favored; he himself not only wrote a set of six original pieces and six arrangements for this combination but also published in Paris ca. 1779 *Essai d'instruction a l'usage de ceux qui composent pour la Clarinette et le Cor, avec des remarques sur l'harmonie et des exemples a 2 Clarinettes, 2 Cors et 2 Bassons*, which "shows that there was considerable interest in writing music for [such] ensembles."[104] Cambini, who was ever aware of public taste during the 1770's and 1780's, bears witness to this interest in woodwind music. Besides flute and oboe quartets Cambini used winds in many other settings. His three woodwind quintets (flute, oboe, clarinet, bassoon, and French horn) rank as among the most important early examples of the genre.[105] He wrote nineteen quintets for flute and string quartet (1777, 1784) and perhaps as many as a dozen for flute, violin, two violas, and bass (1782). He wrote twenty-four trios for flute, violin and bass (or cello), another six for flute, violin and viola, eighteen for two flutes and bass (or cello), five for oboe, violin and piano, and six for flute, oboe and bassoon. He also

---

[102]Modern edition in *Diletto Musicale,* no. 271.

[103]Modern edition in *Diletto Musicale,* nos. 593 and 679.

[104]Harry Jean Hedlund, "A Study of Certain Representative Compositions for Woodwind Ensembles, *CA*. 1695-1815" (State University of Iowa Ph.D. dissertation, 1959), p. 139.

[105]There are many quintets including winds: see Sieber, pp. 15ff, but a history of wind quintet music other than Reicha's has yet to be written. Cf. next chapter.

wrote a great many duets for flute and violin, flute and viola, two flutes, two clarinets, and clarinet and bassoon. Besides Cambini there were many others who wrote flute and clarinet duets in France during the 18th century.[106]

The introduction of the clarinet in the 1770's in Paris and Mannheim awakened interest in that instrument in chamber music there and in Vienna. We have already referred to Roesser's sextets including clarinet. Carl Stamitz (1745-1801) wrote some of the first clarinet quartets (for clarinet, violin, viola and bass) with his six examples of Opus 8 (published in 1773 in Paris) and followed it with another four in 1779 (Opus 19). Wagenseil called for the clarinet in his five *Suites des Pièces* for piano, two horns, two bassoons and two clarinets. But it was Mozart who, as in so many other genres, brought clarinet chamber music to perfection in his quintet for clarinet and string quartet K.581 (1789), dedicated to the great clarinetist Anton Stadler.

Other types of chamber music involving winds mixed with strings included oboe trios such as M. Haydn's *Divertimento* for oboe, viola and cello (violone) and horn trios such as those by M. Haydn for horn, viola and cello and by Carl Stamitz for horn, violin and cello. There were also horn quintets such as J. Sperger's *Cassation* for two horns, violin, viola and bass (cello) and sextets such as M. Haydn's for oboe, two horns, bassoon, viola and cello. The variety of such combinations was so great that it is impossible to list them all here, but it attests to the freedom which wind players felt during the second half of the 18th century to participate in chamber music or at least small ensemble music and the originality of their approaches to the sonority of the chamber ensemble.

While the combination of winds and strings dominated the activities of wind players in chamber ensembles in Paris and Mannheim and was also well known in Vienna, ensembles of just wind instruments without strings were especially common in Austria and parts of Germany during the second half of the 18th and early 19th

---

[106]Walter Jones, "The Unaccompanied Duet for Transverse Flutes by French Composers, *ca.*1708-1770" (University of Iowa Ph.D. dissertation, 1970), lists and discusses about 450 flute duets by thirty-two French composers, and David Randall, "The Clarinet Duet from *ca.*1715 to *ca.*1825" (University of Iowa DMA. dissertation, 1970), lists those for clarinets.

centuries. The size of the band varied usually from two to eight instruments. C.P.E. Bach wrote for bands of seven instruments (two flutes, two clarinets, two horns and one bassoon) and five instruments (two clarinets or oboes, two horns and bassoon). Roesser, whose sextets for pairs of clarinets, bassoons and horns have been cited above, may have learned this in Vienna before going to Paris. Or he may have learned it from Gossec, all of whose chamber music for winds alone is scored for two clarinets, two horns and two bassoons.[107] An interesting sextet by the Mannheimer Carlo Toeschi is "La Chasse Royale" for two clarinets, two horns and two bassoons.[108] It is a single movement work but with many sections set off by tempo and meter changes. Some of these sections are described programmatically by Toeschi as "ton pour la Guetta," "ton pour le chien," and "la vue." Prince Schwarzenberg had a sextet ensemble in his employ (two oboes, two French horns, and two bassoons) and Cardinal/Prince Batthyani had an octet ensemble in Pressburg (two clarinets added to Schwarzenberg's group). In 1782 Kaiser Joseph II ordered the creation of a band of eight winds like Batthyani's group for background music, and other nobility in Austria imitated him. Many composers including Mozart and Haydn wrote for these bands. The bands and their music were called "Harmonie" in the late 18th and early 19th centuries (when the number of players ranged from three to twelve). Much of its repertoire was arrangements of opera and ballet tunes (best known to us in the Supper Scene in Mozart's *Don Giovanni*). Since the actual performances of Harmonie mostly were as background music to conversation and dining or as outdoor garden music and since especially the arrangements were of a light, not serious nature, very little of this music can be regarded as chamber music of the time. But some of the music, especially that by Mozart written after he moved to Vienna in 1781, is indeed very serious chamber music; it is neither background music nor arrangements. And in many cases performances of this music—even the most blatantly

---

[107]Hedlung, p. 140: 6 *Pièces pour . . . le Prince de Condé, La Grande Chasse de Chantilli, Sinfonie à 6,* and an unnamed composition (all in undated manuscripts).

[108]Paris, Bibliothèque de l"Arsenal Ms.6784.83b; cf. Hedlund, p. 95. Cf. Gossec's *La Grande Chasse de Chantilli,* Hedlund, pp. 141-142.

outdoor and *Unterhaltungsmusik*—in the 20th century under very serious auspices ranks it today as chamber music.[109]

As we have seen, Wagenseil was one of the most important predecessors to Haydn and Mozart in Vienna in his string music, and he also was important for pre-classical wind music. Wagenseil's *Parthia in C* demonstrates once again the transition from baroque wind ensembles to classical ones. It is scored for two oboes, two English horns, two corni da caccia, and two bassoons, which Mozart later copied in his serenades (substituting or adding clarinets). It is in seven movements of which the first and fifth (both allegros) are the most substantial. As in other pre-classical pieces there is no equality in the parts. The first oboe dominates all movements, though the first English horn has considerable solo material in the fifth movement. The second oboe usually doubles the first oboe with thirds or sustains tones while the first oboe has passage work, and each of the other pairs of instruments also move along in thirds. There is a fine chordal sonority in seven of the eight instruments, which serve like an obligato keyboard to the solo oboe. An important sign that the piece is pre-classical is the fact that the first movement is in sonata form with two well defined themes and a clear recapitulation of both. On the other hand, the fifth movement is in a written-out da capo form so common in baroque wind ensembles. Movements 2, 3 and 4 are typical for either baroque or pre-classical music in that they are in simple binary form, with no. 4 (a menuet) followed by a "Variation" in binary form which returns for a da capo of the menuet. Movement 6, the only one in a contrasting key (C Minor), has a free form without repeats, and the final movement is a rondo. Wagenseil also wrote two *Divertimenti* (octets) with the same scoring as the *Parthia* and very much like it in other regards.

Mozart wrote two works specifically for a band such as that of the Kaiser (K.375 and 388). They are works at the threshold of the classical period and are the ripe culmination of his earlier band music. Mozart's purely wind chamber music began with the twelve pieces for two horns (K.487, 1768) and continued with larger works (which his father called "divertimenti"). Two written for a

[109]Frederick Niecks, "Music for Wind Instruments Alone," in *The Monthly Musical Record*, xlviii (1918), 122-124.

visit to Milan are scored for two oboes, two clarinets, two English horns, two French horns, and two bassoons (K.166 and 183, 1773), and five written for Salzburg are scored for two oboes, two French horns, and two bassoons (K.213, 240, 252, 253, and 270, 1775-1777). Although Einstein speculates that these divertimenti were written as background music for garden parties,[110] there is no evidence other than circumstantial that they were. Many divertimenti were background pieces, and Mozart's differ from them only in the potential for genius in each. They, and such divertimenti as the two "Lodron Serenades" (originally written as street marches to celebrate school graduation), may not have been chamber music when conceived, but today they are performed as chamber music. The two late wind serenades (K.375 and 388), on the other hand, were composed by Mozart for specific chamber music conditions. K.375, according to Mozart's own testimony, was written ostensibly to honor the sister-in-law of the court painter Herr von Hickel but actually to impress a potential patron Herr von Strack who was to be in the Hickel house when it was performed.[111] The occasion for his writing K.388, on the other hand, is unknown, but the resulting composition is one of the greatest masterpieces by Mozart, a serious, intense work in the full bloom of the classical style (see next chapter).

The composition of Harmonie (works for three to twelve wind instruments) continued through the end of the 18th and beginning of the 19th centuries.[112] Various titles were given to such works, such as divertimento, serenade, and parthie. Salieri, for example, wrote a "Picciola Serenata" for two oboes, two horns, and bassoon. Other composers included Schubert, Dittersdorf, Pleyel, Danzi, Gossec, Reicha, and Onslow. Most famous, however, was Beethoven in his Opus 71 Sextet for two clarinets, two horns, and two bassoons (written ca. 1796-1797).

Just as in the case of string duets, wind duets or duets for a mixture of a wind and string instrument served a different purpose from other types of chamber music. This was true in the baroque as

---

[110]Einstein, p. 202.

[111]Einstein, p. 204.

[112]Niecks, pp. 148-149, 170-171; and Daniel N. Leeson and David Whitwell, "Mozart's 'Spurious' Wind Octets," in *Music and Letters*, liii (1972), 377-399.

well. Mattheson tells us that he wrote his flute duets and trios for the true connoisseurs of music. By omitting the heavy accompaniment of continuo, the flute duets could avoid empty interludes of continuo music and concentrate on the melodic lines for educating a discriminating audience.[113] The duets are formally and stylistically baroque (usually slow-fast-slow-fast, with a chaconne, a French overture, allemandes, gigues, airs en Rondeau, etc.), in keeping with Mattheson's twelve flute-continuo sonatas, but the freeing of the treble instruments here from any keyboard support and the dependence of each one only on himself/herself and one other person links these works with the later duets of Pleyel, Viotti and others.

In Mannheim Carl Stamitz, who wrote many string duets, also wrote six duets for flute or violin on either part (1785) and a single duet for two flutes. Mozart had his horn duets (K.487, 1768) as well as his duet for bassoon and cello (K.292, 1775). Cambini wrote forty-two flute duets, two clarinet duets (one with bassoon and another with a second clarinet), and mixed duets of flute and violin or viola

CHANGING AESTHETICS OF CHAMBER MUSIC

The change from baroque and rococo to pre-classical was a change from complexity of rhetoric to simplicity of rhetoric and corresponded to ideas of simplicity by Jean Jacques Rousseau and Voltaire.

When C.P.E. Bach wrote a program to his Trio W.161 No. 1, he was trying to justify his writing of a purely instrumental piece. Non-vocal, non-programmatic instrumental music was regarded as the least important of all music, just as all music was regarded as the least important of all arts because of its inability to convey moral ideas clearly and directly. While vocal music at least could depend on the words to express important ideas and emotions, instrumental music was of use only in training instrumental performers; it was classified as pedagogical material and nothing more. To admit his trio to the realm of art and not pedagogy, Bach added not

---

[113]Mattheson, *Der vollkommene Kapellmeister* (1739), p. 350.

just any program but a distinctly moral one, in which two contrary temperaments learn to live together and to improve themselves by the other's example. Thus this particular trio was justified, but why did he not take similar pains with the second trio in the publication or with many of his other purely instrumental works? Perhaps he came to realize that purely instrumental music did not need such extramusical justification or that it did not change in any way the purely sensual enjoyment of the sounds. Clearly by the time he reached the late obligato sonatas of 1776-1777 his joy in the purely sensual sounds was at its fullest—a joy which he clearly evinced in his symphonies and concertos of the same time. The rich harmonies, unusual turns of phrases, unexpected keys, and playfully misdirected forms are so delightful to hear on their own account that their failure to deliver a precise moral message is irrelevant. The reason may also be practical, not aesthetic. By the 1770's chamber music was no longer played just for entertainment of an audience but for the enjoyment of the participants, i.e., the largely new bourgeois group of amateur players who were not interested in moral lessons from the music but in the pure pleasure of making harmony together.[114] Composer-keyboardists living in London, Vienna, Paris, Hamburg, and elsewhere in the 1770's found keyboard pupils more among the middle classes than among the nobility which previously had been their only pupils. Bach's sonatas for keyboard alone published at the same time were specifically directed to Kenner and Liebhaber, i.e., to the new, informed amateur players of the bourgeoisie. Yet the need for justification of chamber music for the aestheticians remained and perhaps explains the use, for example, of the concept of dialogue in reference to chamber music. Cambini's *Quatre Quatuor et deux quintetto dialogués et concertans* and several *dialogués et variés* in his *Quatuors d'Airs choisis,* Haydn's *Six Symphonies ou quatuors dialogués* (1764), and Desnose's *6 Quatuors dialogués d'un genre nouveau* (Opus 2, 1775) were but a few attempts to explain pure chamber music as conversations or dialogues—the give and take between at

---

[114]Cf. Avison's statement of purpose for his 1760 Opus 7 sonatas for harpsichord accompanied by two violins and cello (reproduced in Kidd, p. 130): "This kind of Music is not, indeed, calculated so much for public Entertainment, as for private Amusement. It is rather like a Conversation among Friends, when the Few are of one Mind and Propose their mutual Sentiments, only to give Variety, and enliven their select Company."

least two instruments with imitation and a continual exchange of the main material. This rationalization of irrational musical sounds is justified to a mind that must find a place in a literary scheme for non-literary material. Eventually Cambini and others turned to popular songs adapted for string quartet not only for the sake of their widespread appeal and thus salability but also because with a literary (libretto) connection the pieces had a place in the world of literary aesthetics. Yet Haydn and Mozart did not need such justification, and their classical works forged a new sense of place in the schemes of philosophy for purely instrumental musical art. While the idea of extramusical messages in the music remained a part of chamber music through the 19th century and into the 20th, the enjoyment of the music for its own sensuous sake was now acceptable.

CHAPTER V

CLASSICAL CHAMBER MUSIC: 1780-1827

The intensive development of new genres of chamber music during the middle of the 18th century culminated in the perfection of those genres during the years 1780 to 1827. Once Haydn and Mozart grew and interacted sufficiently in the 1770's to forge the classical style of chamber music of the 1780's starting with Haydn's Opus 33 and Mozart's Opus 10 string quartets, the new genres became fixed in the minds of performers, audiences and composers alike as the legitimate genres of chamber music. The composers of the classical period wrote monumental piano trios, piano quartets, violin and piano sonatas, various wind ensembles, and string quintets, trios and duets, but it was the string quartet which became the center of their highest efforts in chamber music. Beethoven took the classical string quartet of Haydn and Mozart and developed it at the beginning of the Romantic Age without changing its basic aesthetic.

Social conditions did change drastically during this period, between Mozart's late chamber music and Beethoven's late string quartets. The dichotomy between performance of chamber music by professional musicians before an audience and private performance of chamber music by amateurs at home was a reality already in the 1780's in Vienna and became an increasingly important factor by the turn of the century. Professionals still performed at the homes of nobility for limited audiences and more and more often in their own quarters or in those of middle class friends and devotes, but there were also active concert series in London, Paris and Vienna. By the late 18th century and early 19th chamber music was performed publicly in London, Vienna and other major cities of Europe in concerts in two "acts" (we would say "halves"). Each act consisted of some orchestral music, some vocal music, and a piece of chamber music (string quartet, quintet or trio, flute quartet or trio, violin and piano sonata, etc.). Concerts in which only chamber music was performed started early in the 19th century, and about the same time concerts in which only string quartets were performed started in Vienna and in other larger German cities.[1] Public concerts in London devoted solely to chamber music, for example, began with the founding of the Philharmonic Society there in 1813.[2] The audiences at these public concerts were respectful and listened intently to the music, a far cry from the noisy disregard of many aristocrats for their background chamber music. Yet some aristocrats did have respect for the music, as in the cases of the chamber music performed at the home of the Earl of Abingdon in London or at Prince Eszterházy's palace, where the earl and the prince themselves played along. At a private concert at Eszterháza in 1783 the dining was saved for after the concert, not during.[3]

The music of Wagenseil, C.P.E. Bach, Schobert and all the lesser talents of their generation was aimed primarily at the good amateur performer and the professional employed in private homes, whereas Mozart (after 1780), Haydn (after 1790) and Beethoven for their chamber music increasingly turned to the skilled public professional who had to make it on the concert stage. The result was that the late music of Mozart and Haydn and all the music of Beethoven became too difficult for all but the best amateur players, and when Beethoven set out on his Opus 59 quartets he no longer included any but the most virtuosic amateurs in his plans. Publishers wanted the prestige of publishing the great masterpieces of Haydn, Mozart and Beethoven, but their financial instincts led them to prize the easier music of these composers and a host of much less talented ones which could be sold to the vast majority of chamber musicians who were at most moderately talented ama-

---

[1] Hubert Unverricht, *Geschichte des Streichtrios*, in *Mainzer Studien zur Musikwissenschaft*, Band 2 (Tutzing: Hans Schneider, 1969), pp. 271-275.

[2] Stanley Sadie, "Concert Life in 18th-century England," in *Proceedings of the Royal Music Association*, lxxxv (1958-9), p. 17.

[3] Unverricht, p. 274. This order of playing and then dining becomes during the 19th and 20th centuries an entrenched custom in Central European middle class homes.

teurs. Chamber music, then, began to divide aesthetically and so-cially into two subspecies: public chamber music still called cham-ber music, and private chamber music called both chamber music and Hausmusik. The concept of Hausmusik was around from the beginning of chamber music (at least the mid-16th century), and through much of the first 200 years of chamber music there was overlap between public and private chamber music. The distinction between the two became necessary by the end of the 18th century, though it was only in the later 19th century that W.H. Riehl (1823-1897) first defined the terms as we now understand them.[4]

The "classical period" has been and can be described in several convincing ways. 1) Since the mature works of Haydn, Mozart and Beethoven are *classics*, the "classical period" has often been equated with the works of these three. 2) If the time frame 1781 to 1827 (when Haydn, Mozart and Beethoven wrote their *classics*) is the "classical period," then other composers from Dittersdorf and Cambini to Schubert, Viotti and Paganini must also be included. But after 1790 there was an emotional change in the music of many composers, particularly notable in Beethoven, and after 1800 subjectivity and asymmetry distinguished the music of that time from the music of the several preceding decades with its senti-mental objectivity and symmetry. Schubert and Mozart had little in common except as they both related to Beethoven. 3) There is also sometimes a stylistic distinction made between the "classical pe-riod" and the periods before and after; chamber music of the "classical period" had equality of instruments, motivic develop-ment, the full functioning of sonata and rondo forms, freedom to go from one texture to another within a single movement or phrase, periodization, contrasting rhythm, and a balance and order that is overtly smooth but subtly surprising. For the purposes of this study we will consider all three aspects: the classics of the three most important chamber music composers of the past 200 years (Haydn, Mozart and Beethoven), the time frame 1780-1827 (which will in-clude what other composers and performers of chamber music were doing at this time), and the stylistic traits of much of the mu-

---

[4]Erich Valentin, *Musica Domestica: von Geschichte und Wesen der Hausmusik* (Trossingen: Hohner, 1959), and Walter Salmen, "W.H. Riehls Gedanken zur Gesundung der Hausmusik," in *Hausmusik*, xvii (1953), 169-70, 172.

sic that set it apart from earlier and later chamber music. All three aspects will be considered within the following discussion of the various genres to which chamber music during this period belongs.

THE STRING QUARTET 1780-1827

By 1780 the string quartet was established as the most popular serious form of chamber music. In Paris Cambini was at the height of his vast production of quatuors concertants, and the Parisian publishers (as well as those in Amsterdam, London, Vienna and elsewhere) were mass producing quartet editions by composers from all over Europe. Boccherini, writing in Madrid, was known throughout Europe for his quartettini and quartets as well as his quintets, and although somewhat less famous, others like Giordani and Giardini in London made substantial contributions. Amateur quartet ensembles (ensembles whose performers were non-professional musicians) and quartet ensembles of professional musicians who met on an ad hoc basis flourished in every major European city and court.

Haydn

There were many composers and many influences which came together to produce the classical quartet, but, as everyone knows, one genius in particular—Joseph Haydn—put them all together and established a norm and an ideal against which all other quartets (by the 1780's) were to be judged. In his Opus 20 string quartets (1772), Haydn had grappled with several basic problems which the quartet presented to him. Haydn had come to the quartet from the five-movement divertimento, an altogether different direction from that taken by the Italians Boccherini and Cambini. The somewhat frivolous divertimento was by nature a light musical genre to which Haydn added a seriousness that was, by 1772, the very antithesis of the traditional divertimento. The sonata form first movement, as Haydn developed it, became a very weighty, pithy opening that immediately established the seriousness which Haydn wanted for the quartet, but the remaining movements retained much of the light-hearted divertimento flavor and by the end of the last movement none of that seriousness remained. In three of the

Opus 20 quartets, therefore, he sought to balance the mood more evenly by placing a fugue at the end; this very serious Baroque da chiesa type of music is the opposite of the dance and sweet, unpretentious cantabile movements, and its presence as a finale left no doubt as to the seriousness of the whole of these three Opus 20 quartets.

When Haydn returned to the string quartet after nearly a decade in his Opus 33 quartets (1781), much had changed. For one, the Viennese quartet was no longer struggling to be recognized as a serious chamber genre, thanks to the popularity of Haydn's Opus 9, 17 and especially 20 quartets. While the quartet norms of Cambini and Boccherini were two-or three-movement works with concertant elements, Haydn's four-movement pieces without concertant elements had gained wide acceptance. Perhaps because he felt a new surge of personal happiness through his successful romance with a mistress (Luigia Polzelli), Haydn wrote six jovial quartets rather than heavy, serious ones, and the new rapid pace of the quartets were influenced by the fast pace of comic opera with which Haydn had worked during the 1770's. There is a new burst of energy in these pieces, and while this energy applies primarily to the outer two movements, the inner two are affected as well, though to a lesser degree. Such enthusiasm apparently offended the Emperor, but even so stern a judge as C.P.E. Bach, upon hearing Opus 33 in Hamburg in 1783, "expressed his complete satisfaction about these works."[5] Haydn wrote these works for the public audiences of Europe, not for the provincial circle of Prince Eszterházy.

But beyond this, Opus 33 had the benefit of Haydn's new conception of sonata form as not just a binary piece whose exposition contains two contrasting themes.[6] During the 1770's Haydn developed the idea of motivic discourse whereby a potent theme would be dissected into its various components which would then be taken up in a conversational manner by all four instruments in various forms, styles, and combinations. The elements of the theme

[5]H.C. Robbins Landon, *Haydn: Chronicle and Works*, vol. II: *Haydn at Eszterháza 1766-1790* (Bloomington/London: Indiana University Press, 1978), pp. 456 and 582.

[6]Most of the data concerning the writing and premiering of Haydn's quartets, as well as much of the analysis of them is based on Landon, *Haydn: Chronicle and Works*. Concerning Opus 33 cf. II, pp. 447, 454-456, and 576-582.

could recur throughout the sonata form first movement and in subsequent movements as well (Opus 33, no. 6 has such thematic unity in all movements). This is not like a fugue; the voices are not equal and independent (a Baroque characteristic) but within each voice melody and accompaniment transform into each other.[7] Every detail functions within the whole work, whereas before Opus 33 some details never recurred or had no bearing on the movement as a whole. In Opus 20 counterpoint meant a whole fugue, while in all the quartets from Opus 33 on Haydn employed various techniques of counterpoint on an integrated basis: canon, fugato, simple, double and related counterpoint, contrary motion, inversion, pedal point, and strict and free imitation.[8]

In addition to motivic discourse and cyclic continuity among movements, Opus 33 differs from Opus 20 in the use of tonally and rhythmically ambiguous openings, which are a feature of some of his symphonies as well, and in the introduction during the middle of a movement of a "haunting tune" (an unforgettable motive that is not heard earlier) that then is repeated several times. What is new as well are Haydn's climaxes just after the start of the recapitulation, not before. Opus 33 differs also by changes in the inner movements. Although Haydn used the term "scherzo" or "scherzando" in place of menuetto (except in Opus 33, no. 1, which differs from the other five quartets in almost all regards), there is no musical distinction between these movements and the older minuets. Yet the mere fact that he used these terms was the result of his preoccupation with comic opera from 1776 on and his more light-hearted approach to quartet writing in general. On the other hand, the slow movements are no longer simply arioso but "often have a rhapsodic, yearning intensity and differ from those of Opus 20 in that Opus 33's are of a much denser texture, substituting massive, concentrated emotion."[9]

---

[7]Charles Rosen, *The Classical Style: Haydn, Mozart, and Beethoven* (New York: The Viking Press, 1971), pp. 111-142.

[8]Ekkehart Kroher, "Die Polyphonie in den Streichquartetten Wolfgang Amadeus Mozarts und Joseph Haydns," in *Wissenschaftliche Zeitschrift der Karl-Marx-Universität Leipzig*, v (1955-1956), 369-402.

[9]Landon, *Haydn: Chronicle and Works*, II, p. 579.

Haydn's Opus 33 quartets were probably first performed in Vienna on Tuesday, Christmas Day, 1781, before the Russian Grand Duke Paul (later Tsar Paul II) and his wife, the Princess of Württemberg, who was Haydn's piano pupil.[10] The work is dedicated to the Countess, whose assumed name for the holidays was Countess von Norden, and it was performed by Viennese and Eszterháza professionals: Luigi Tomasini, Franz Aspelmayr, Joseph Weigl, and Thaddäus Huber.[11] A few weeks before this premier Haydn offered the quartets to several "gentlemen amateurs and great connoisseurs and patrons of music"[12] as concertant quartets "written in a new and special way." There is nothing particularly concertant about these quartets, which in no way reflect the works of Cambini or the concertant works of Boccherini. Since Boccherini and Haydn exchanged letters at just this time and since Haydn was well aware of the need of publishers to provide pleasing music for the public in a way that Boccherini was so efficient in doing, the choice of the word "concertant" may have been to make the association with Boccherini's pleasing works rather than to offer technically correct "concertant" quartets. That the Opus 33 quartets were "new and special" has been recognized by musicologists and music lovers for a century, though the exact interpretation of what Haydn meant by those words has led to some disagreement. Following Sandberger some scholars cite Opus 33 as the first truly classical work (i.e., the first pieces to fully evince the classical style), while others, following Larsen, point out that symphonies by Haydn and works by other composers during the 1770's established the classical style. Whichever side is taken, the Opus 33 quartets and those that followed (Opus 42, 50, 54 and 55), even more than the Opus 20 quartets, firmly established Haydn's works as the models for all other quartet composers. As Rosen has stated:

> What Haydn had learned in ten years, what these new quartets show, is, above all, dramatic clarity. Expressive intensity had previously caused

---

[10]Landon, *Haydn: Chronicle and Works*, II, p. 456. An earlier performance may have taken place at Eszterháza on May 30th (*ibid.*, p. 447).

[11]Weigl and especially Tomasini were associated with Haydn from his earliest days in Eszterháza, premiered many of his compositions, and continued to perform them. Landon, *Haydn: Chronicle and Works*, II, pp. 80 and 82.

[12]Landon, *Haydn: Chronicle and Works*, II, p. 454.

Haydn's rhythm to clot, and rich, intricate phrases had been followed
all too often by a disappointingly loose cadence. With the *Scherzi* Quartets, he was able to construct a framework in which the intensity and
the significance of the material could expand and contract freely and
still be supported by the basic movement. They are, above all, lucid.[13]

Rosen notes a pattern in Haydn (and Beethoven) of simplifica-
tion to conquer a new problem and then reintroduction of contrapuntal complexities—"reconquer the past once the present had
been won." The

> sense that the movement, the development, and the dramatic course of a
> work all can be found latent in the material . . . [and that the music] is
> literally impelled from within—this sense was Haydn's greatest contri-
> bution to the history of music."[14]

The next quartet of Haydn's was the individual Opus 42 quartet, probably written for Spanish patrons ca. 1785. It may have
been part of a set of quartets, the rest of which are lost.[15] The piece
differs from the other quartets in its brevity (which was dictated by
the Spanish commission), in its order of movements (slow - allegretto minuet + trio -slow-fast), in its key scheme (D Minor - D
Major - B♭ Major - D Minor), and in the absence of a sonata-form
first movement. The first violinist is expected to play very high on
the e string, which was not yet required in the earlier quartets but
which recurred in the later ones. Could it be that with the arrival of
the new violinist Tost in Eszterháza in 1783 Haydn had a violinist
who enjoyed the high notes and that previously Tomasini was not
particularly adept at such notes?

Haydn's six Opus 50 (1787) quartets, not Opus 33, were the
first to present all classical style elements because while Opus 33
was an important breakthrough, it was with the later set that, in addition to the achievements of Opus 33, he first wrote unqualified
"Allegro" movements in $\frac{4}{4}$ meter (no. 5 is the only exception that
looks backward)—a rhythm learned from Mozart and applied in
both first and many fourth movements thereafter, that he treated all

[13]Rosen, p. 119.
[14]Rosen, p. 120.
[15]Landon, *Haydn: Chronicle and Works*, II, pp. 490, 588-589, and 624-625.

four instruments more equally in the manner of Opus 20 and, also as in Opus 20, that he recognized the need for a finale that balances the mood of the entire quartet.[16] Reconsideration of the relationship of the instruments came probably from acknowledgment of the dedicatee, Kaiser Friedrich Wilhelm II of Prussia, a cellist, patron of Boccherini, and dedicatee of three Mozart quartets as well. Although the cello is not as prominent as in the Mozart works (see below), Haydn felt obliged to open the set with a cello solo. Opus 50 no. 4 ends with a fugue just like the three quartets of Opus 20, but there is a difference between the fugue ending of this quartet and those in Opus 20. The intense passion of the *Sturm und Drang* which the Opus 20 fugues carried up to the last bar was left far behind in this fugue of fifteen years later. The new Haydn energy (fast pace) continued in Opus 50, as well as in the Opus 54 and 55 quartets.[17] The juxtaposition of unusual tonalities and the use of surprising modulations is even more astounding in Opus 50 than in Opus 42 or Opus 33. Most Haydn quartets have one movement in the dominant, subdominant or relative major, but nine, going back to Opus 9, no. 4, do not; instead, these make use of a key a minor or major third above or below the original tonic. In Opus 50 Haydn juxtaposed unusual keys *within* a movement even more so than earlier. The first movement of no. 1 in B♭, for example, emphasizes the relationship E♭ - D, which creates a rhythmic tension with the opening pedal on the tonic note B♭.[18] In the first five measures of the first movement of no. 2 in C, the introduction of C♯ and B♭ cause an harmonic instability that is quickly countered by a V to I cadence in the tonic (mm. 8-9), only to be further jolted by V of V to V by m. 13 in what turns out to be a false modulation to the dominant. Before the exposition ends we traverse C Minor, F Minor, and G Minor (all poignant keys in their own right and especially so in contrast to the "white" key of C). The tonic and dominant are clear and emphasized, but not before the listener journeys through moments of uncertain modulations and keys. The

---

[16]Orin Moe, "The Significance of Haydn's Opus 33," in J.P. Larsen, Howard Serwer and James Webster, *Haydn Studies: Proceedings of the International Haydn Conference Washington, D.C., 1975* (New York: W.W. Norton, 1981), pp. 445-450.

[17]Rosen, pp. 120, 139-142.

[18]Rosen, pp. 120-125.

development offers no respite; measures 107 to 150 continually modulate with chromaticisms (including diminished thirds, diminished sevenths, and augmented fifths quickly following each other), until we arrive at V of A Minor in m. 151. Haydn "explored . . . [tonal] resources that were not fully realized until a century after his death."[19]

Haydn dedicated his twelve quartets of Opus 54/55 (1789) and 64 (1790) to Johann Tost, who was a violinist at Eszterháza from 1783 to 1788 and whose colorful personality excited Haydn.[20] After he left Eszterháza, Tost went to France where he helped popularize Haydn's newest works, and then he settled in Vienna ca. 1799 where he continued to influence Haydn and others. It was his custom (and that of other patrons as well) to acquire exclusive rights to the newest chamber music for a period of three years, during which time any performance of the works would require Tost's presence; in turn, Tost traveled around Europe on business and used this exclusive music to attract the business of music lovers. Besides Haydn Mozart, Beethoven and Louis Spohr made such agreements with Tost.

Tost's arrangement with Haydn brought to a head a problem with his chamber music that would ultimately affect chamber music in general. Haydn wrote his early chamber music for private performance at Eszterháza, yet it was quite clear to him by the early 1770's that his quartets were being performed both privately and publicly throughout Europe. As his contacts with foreign publishers increased, Haydn became more conscious of the dichotomy between his "private music and his public face."[21] Public music demanded well-known conventions and an easy appeal that seemed in conflict with the demand of private music for subtle novelty and limited appeal. In his twelve Tost quartets, however, Haydn miraculously synthesized the two; his style including its novelties had become conventional, and the "limited" taste of Haydn's immediate circle proved to have broad appeal among connoisseurs

[19]Louise Cuyler, "Tonal Exploitation in the Later Quartets of Haydn," in H.C. Robbins Landon, ed. *Studies in Eighteenth-Century Music: a Tribute to Karl Geiringer on his Seventieth Birthday* (London: Georg Allen and Unwin, 1970), pp. 136-150.

[20]Landon, *Haydn: Chronicle and Works*, II, pp. 81-82.

[21]Landon, *Haydn: Chronicle and Works*, II, p. 347.

throughout Europe and America. The unreserved, joking nature of Opus 33 was replaced in the Tost Quartets by a controlled energy that matched popular enthusiasm with calculated balance. Public concerts in London's Hanover Square rooms in 1789 featured the Opus 54/55 quartets which met with full audience approval, and that "the mature power and variety of the six quartets of Opus 64, which followed a year [after Opus 55], were never surpassed by Haydn"[22] was soon recognized by musical audiences throughout Europe.

The twelve Tost Quartets differ from their predecessors in the emphasis on the high register of the first violin, in their formal breadth, in their driving modulations, and in their subtle use of silences. Opus 64 has an air of melancholy about it; Haydn wrote the set in the lonely summer of 1790 just before his faithful patron of many decades died. While Opus 54/55 have a tinge of staleness about them, this new emotion gave to Opus 64 an urgency which Haydn transformed into "six flawless masterpieces which . . . can be compared in unity of purpose, perfection of execution and profundity of spirit only with Opus 20."[23]

Haydn's London string quartets (Opus 71-74) were not in his old chamber style but meant for public audience in concert halls.[24] While Haydn recognized as early as Opus 50 that his quartets would be performed throughout Europe in both public and private quarters, he continued to write quartets for his own private concerts at Eszterháza, in the homes of Austrian nobility, or in the quarters of fellow musicians such as Mozart. But then he went to London in 1791. He was invited there by the German ex-patriot Johann Peter Salomon, an accomplished violinist who made his London debut in 1781. In 1783 he was involved with the running of a concert series in Hanover Square of professional musicians, the "Professional Concert," which tried unsuccessfully to bring Haydn to London throughout the 1780's. It is at their concerts that Haydn's Opus 54/55 quartets were first heard publicly in London. Haydn sent to the Professional Concert this set, which he dishon-

[22]Rosen, p. 140.

[23]Landon, *Haydn: Chronicle and Works*, II, p. 655.

[24]László Somfai, "Haydn's London String Quartets," in *Haydn Studies*, pp. 389-392.

estly claimed to be new and unknown at the time, and his relationship with the Professional Concert was tarnished. When Salomon finally succeeded in bringing Haydn to London after the death of Haydn's Prince Nicolaus Eszterházy, it was not for concerts at the Professional Concert, with which Salomon himself had severed ties, but at a new series which Salomon had organized at the same Hanover Square rooms. Haydn brought with him his new Opus 64 quartets, which were still written for private performance before Haydn knew he was coming to London. Immediately Salomon (first violinist) and three of his colleagues (Mountain, Hindmarsch and Menell) gave the London public premier of one of the Opus 64 quartets (February 24, 1791), and during the rest of this season and the next they premiered the rest of Opus 64.[25] From all accounts the Salomon ensemble was technically and musically superior to the Tomasini ensemble for which Haydn had written most of his previous quartets. When Salomon brought Haydn back to London several years later, Haydn honored him with a truly new set of six quartets later published in two groups of three as Opus 71 and 74. The Salomon Quartet premiered them in 1794.

The reviewer of the premier of one of the Opus 71/74 quartets wrote that Haydn's "new quartetto gave pleasure by its variety, gaiety, and the fascination of its melody and harmony through all its movements."[26] Haydn sought just this very pleasure in his audience; he had a paying public in mind when he wrote these quartets. The new quartets are brilliant, high-powered, intense and designed to show off the musical leadership of the first violinist (Salomon was apparently a much better violinist than Tomasini). They are not intimate, and the melodies are smooth, singable, easily recalled. The fact that five of the six quartets begin with slow introductions (and no other Haydn quartets do) reflects the influence of the symphony or overture on Haydn's thinking, since in orchestral music the slow introduction was a proven crowd-pleaser and orchestral music was the most successful public instrumental music of the day. The slow movements have a weight far beyond that for

---

[25]Mr. Damen replaced Mr. Mountain after the first concert.

[26]Landon, *Haydn: Chronicle and Works*, III (1976), p. 236; cf. pp. 455-482 for a fine essay on the London or Salomon Quartets, upon which our discussion is based.

slow movements in his earlier quartets since the simplicity of the slow movements made them readily accessible to the layperson.

After Haydn's final return to Vienna he wrote two more sets of quartets: Opus 76 (1797) and 77 (1799). A few years later he started yet one more quartet—Opus 103—a truly unique work which, however, he never completed. Opus 76 is dedicated to Count Joseph Erdödy, who had subscribed to the publication of Beethoven's Opus 1 piano trios and whose family became one of Beethoven's staunchest supporters. The presence of young Beethoven in Vienna by the mid-1790's was clearly felt by Haydn not only because Beethoven had come to study with Haydn but because the older man began to recognize the genius of the younger one. Beethoven's three piano trios Opus 1 were written in 1793-1794 and published in Vienna by Artaria in 1795 just as Haydn returned from London. They were played at the Palais Lobkowitz in private or semi-private concerts that also included much music by Haydn, and they are dedicated to Prince Lobkowitz, who also is the dedicatee of Haydn's Opus 77 quartets. Opus 76 was completed just two years after the publication of Beethoven's Opus 1 and several if not all of the six quartets were premiered at the Eszterházy castle in Eisenstadt before the crown prince of Austria on September 28, 1797.[27]

Even though these quartets were written, like those before Opus 71/74, for private performance, the forthright style of the public London quartets was continued in these. Instead of the "slow moving, intellectual, almost discursive style of even such a late work as Opus 64, No. 1 (1790)" we now find that "the tightness, economy and the explosive 'symphonic' style of the 'Salomon' Quartets are all elements that remain with Haydn's latest quartets."[28] Even though these are private quartets, Haydn knew now that every note he wrote would be public property within weeks. A complete master of the science of quartet-writing, Haydn concentrated on "tonal experiments which gave a new and—for the professional musician—immensely stimulating dimension to the art."[29]

---

[27]Landon, *Haydn: Chronicle and Works*, IV (1977), p. 260.

[28]Landon, *Haydn: Chronicle and Works*, IV, p. 284.

[29]Landon, *Haydn: Chronicle and Works*, IV, p. 285.

Especially effective are the slow movements, which take on a new, extraordinary dimension of melancholy, but, within the framework of the public Opus 71/74 quartets, he added subtle details that expanded upon his earlier writing. The intricate and compact weaving of the fifths of the opening movement of the second quartet and the clever canon in its minuet, for example, are musical technique at the most advanced level, yet the expressiveness and general feeling of the quartet also remain at the highest level; previously only J.S. Bach achieved such synthesis at such an exalted degree of inspiration, and probably only Beethoven, Brahms, Bartók and Shostakovich would be able to follow it. While the London quartets were written for a virtuoso quartet ensemble, the Opus 76 quartets were written for a virtuoso quartet ensemble of extraordinary interpretive skills.

Haydn, who had absorbed into his Opus 50 quartets a few of Mozart's ideas without sacrificing his own style, now absorbed into his Opus 76 quartets a few of Beethoven's ideas again without losing his own identity. Most obvious of these borrowed ideas is the acceleration of the minuet into the "scherzo". Although Haydn used the terms "scherzo" and "scherzando" in the Opus 33 quartets, the movements so designated remained minuets in character and tempo. Now, under the influence of Beethoven's fast scherzos, Haydn replaced the traditional minuet with the new fast movement (still called "menuetto" but with such tempo designations as presto and allegro).

But the situation with Opus 77 proved different; the Beethoven influence had a negative effect.[30] Haydn was commissioned by Prince Lobkowitz in 1799 to write a set of six quartets, and he proceeded to write two of them at once (now known as the complete Opus 77 consisting of only two quartets). At the same time, Prince Lobkowitz also commissioned Beethoven to write another set. Beethoven had refused to write quartets in Vienna out of deference to his former teacher, but now the two had become alienated. By the beginning of 1800 Beethoven had completed his six Opus 18 quartets, which were performed frequently in Vienna that year by the best musicians available (including Schuppanzigh as first violin

---

[30]The following discussion is based on Landon, *Haydn: Chronicle and Works*, IV, pp. 502-508.

and Anton Kraft, the younger, as cellist), and quite clearly Beethoven had scored a great triumph with the young musicians and patrons of Vienna. Haydn found that he had lost his audience, that the Viennese patrons were no longer interested in the subtleties of his composition which, in Opus 76 just two or three years before, had thrilled them. In the face of this Haydn did what he had done twenty years earlier when he confronted Mozart's concertos and operas: he stopped writing them since he felt he could no longer compete. Instead he turned almost exclusively to vocal music, where Beethoven was not able to compete. At first he adapted his style somewhat to Beethoven's, as in the Trio of Opus 77, no. 1, though in some cases it is hard to tell if Haydn copied Beethoven or Beethoven Haydn (neither would admit such weakness). When Haydn tried to write one more quartet for Opus 77 (a third in that set), he reached an extremely romantic notion of modulation and tonal juxtaposition that, in 1803, exceeded anything that Beethoven had done to that time. He completed only two movements (the two middle movements), which were published separately as the incomplete Opus 103.

By the beginning of the 19th century a whole new world of sound quickly replaced that of the classical 1780's. As Robbins Landon has pointed out,

> We have . . . reached a point in [Haydn's] music where many stylistic elements fuse with those of Beethoven at this period; and curiously enough, as both men continue, Mozartian elements are further and further left behind. We are only on the threshold of the nineteenth century, not even a decade after Mozart's death; yet [their music] could not possibly be confused with Mozart. A new musical language is being created before our very eyes; the vocabulary will soon be vastly extended, but the basic language is that of Haydn's late style.[31]

Beethoven picked up on Haydn's Opus 76 quartets, and where he came from can only be understood by studying Haydn's path from the early divertimento quartets to his late ones. Whereas Beethoven felt he was creating a new style, much of what he started out to do was built on the works of Haydn and Mozart. Despite Haydn's pessimism, his and Mozart's quartets continued to

---

[31]Landon, *Haydn: Chronicle and Works*, IV, p. 507.

be performed publicly and especially privately by amateurs at home throughout the 19th century and until the present, while Beethoven's were relegated primarily to the concert stage. Before we consider Beethoven further, though, Mozart's quartets must be reckoned with.

Mozart

Mozart's mature quartets were written after he moved to Vienna, had at his disposal top-level professional performers, and was in more frequent contact with Haydn and his works. While there was little direct influence of Mozart on Haydn and only slightly more of Haydn on Mozart, the two were driven out of deep respect for each other to write works that would be appreciated by the other. In Haydn's case, when he recognized the absolute superiority of Mozart in a genre, he stopped trying to compete with Mozart (in piano concertos and comic operas) and turned instead to those genres (symphony and quartet) where his individuality was well worthy of the other's respect.[32] Mozart, in turn, spoke with a different voice even if in the same genre as Haydn. Mozart's orchestration is more dense and concentrated, while Haydn's is lighter and more baroque or pre-classical. "Haydn was a master of irony, while Mozart is a master of ambivalence."[33] Mozart's tempos are faster, more demonic.

The purpose of analysis is to find the unity of a work in its diversity; "all great music is latently monothematic and, if in more than one movement, cyclic."[34] Yet such unity—though a basic factor in Haydn's classicism and Beethoven's romanticism—was not inherent in Mozart's style. Mozart, the writer of concertos and operas, found the homogeneity of Haydn quartets a problem for his own works; he preferred to juxtapose contrasting musical elements (essential in concertos and operas) in the quartets by abrupt rhythmic transformation, unusual tonal levels, and chromaticism versus

---

[32]Landon, *Haydn: Chronicle and Works*, II, p. 512.

[33]Landon, *Haydn: Chronicle and Works*, II, p. 513.

[34]Hans Keller, "The Chamber Music," in H.C. Robbins Landon and Donald Mitchell, *The Mozart Companion* (New York: Oxford University Press, 1956; reprint New York: W. W. Norton, 1969), pp. 90-137.

diatonicism.[35] Mozart's reaction to Haydn's Opus 33 was not to write motivically unified quartets (rare in Mozart's music) but quartets unified by an idea, such as in K.387 the antithesis between a standard diatonic interval of a third, fourth, fifth, sixth or octave and a chromatic line.[36] A dramatic intensity pervades all movements of all the last ten quartets, and each work is a unique reshaping of traditional forms, a unique choice and contrast of themes, and a demonic *Sturm und Drang* (chromaticism and minor keys).[37] The quartets written from 1782 to 1785 were the reconciliation of Mozart's Italian training and vocal instincts with Haydn's instrumental techniques and "German tone."[38] Mozart's study of counterpoint when he first moved to Vienna from 1781 to 1783 and his contact with the music of J.S. Bach led him to unify a piece through the use of a small amount of material, which first manifested itself in his string quartet K.387.[39] Mozart was first taken with the quartets of Italian composers, especially Boccherini, and he imitated them in his earliest quartets. Afterward, however, he regarded both Italian and French string quartets as too much concertant and so turned increasingly to Haydn. Yet the Italian cantabile element often recurs,[40] and in the Italian-like slow movements the structure evolves not out of some contrast necessary in sonata form but out of the one, simple cantilena theme. Each cantabile movement is therefore unique and untransferable; it de-

---

[35]Louis Cuyler, "Mozart's Six Quartets Dedicated to Haydn," in Gustave Reese and Rose Brandel, eds., *The Commonwealth of Music in Honor of Curt Sachs* (New York: The Free Press/London: Collier-Macmillan, 1965), pp. 293-299.

[36]Karl Grebe, "Das 'Urmotiv' bei Mozart: Strukturprinzipien im G-Dur-quartett KV 387," in *Acta Mozartiana*, vi (1959, 9-14.

[37]Walther Siegmund-Schultze, "Mozarts 'Haydn-Quartette,'" in Bence Szabolcsi and Dénes Bartha, eds., *Bericht über die internationale Konferenz zum Andenken Joseph Haydns (Budapest 1957)* (Budapest: Verlag der Ungarischen Akademie der Wissenschaften, 1961), pp. 137-146.

[38]Alexander Hyatt King, "Mozart's String Quartets," in *The Listener*, xxxiv (1945), p. 633.

[39]Isabell P. Emerson, "The Role of Counterpoint in the Formation of Mozart's Late Style" (Columbia University Ph.D. dissertation, 1977).

[40]Guido Salvetti, "Mozart e il Quartetto Italiano," in Friedrich Lippmann, ed., *Colloquium "Mozart und Italien" (Rom 1974)*, in *Analecta Musicologica*, xviii (Köln: Arno Volk, 1978), pp. 271-289.

pends on the particular melody for its structure.[41] Mozart's dissonant introduction to K.465 has baffled theorists who found no logic
in the juxtaposition of such a dissonant beginning to such a non-
dissonant remainder of the quartet. Yet from an extra-musical
standpoint it makes sense; it coincided with Mozart's initiation into
the Masonic Movement, where the introduction corresponds to the
trials of initiation and the rest of the quartet corresponds to the
light of revelation once the trials have been successfully completed.[42] The last three quartets, the so-called "Prussian" (along
with the opera *Così fan Tutte*), were products of a new period of
creativity of Mozart's after a lull during which he renewed himself.
Among other new traits is the prominence of the cello.[43] Mozart
wrote these quartets for Frederick Wilhelm II of Prussia, Boccherini's great patron and himself a cellist and the dedicatee of
Haydn's Opus 50.[44] While the six Haydn Quartets were written to
please Haydn and show the ultimate in taste and science, the last
three quartets were written to show the world the fullness of his
powers and genius. Mozart had just finished reorchestrating two
Handel works when he wrote the last two quartets, and especially
in the finale of the last one he successfully combined the two traits
of thematic unity and contrapuntal expertise which had been so difficult for him through most of his career. Just as in the finale of the
Jupiter Symphony, in his final quartet movement he pointed the
way for a new Mozart in style and depth of expression which he
did not live to complete but which Beethoven brought to fruition.

[41]Friedhelm Krummacher, "Kantabilität als Konstruktion: zum langsamen Satz aus Mozarts Streichquartett KV465," in Werner Breig, Reinhold Brinkmann and Elmar Budde, eds., *Analysen: Beiträge zu einer Problemgeschichte des Komponierens: Fest-schrift für Hans Heinrich Eggebrecht zum 65. Geburtstag*, in *Beihefte zum Archiv für Musikwissenschaft*, xxiii (Stuttgart: Franz Steiner Verlag Wiesbaden, 1984), pp. 217-233.

[42]Jacques Chailley, "Sur la Signification du Quatuor de Mozart K.465, dit 'Les Disso-nances,' et du 7ème Quatuor de Beethoven," in Bjorn Hjelmborg and Sorensen, eds., *Natalicia Musicologica Knud Jeppesen Septuagenario* (Copenhagen: Wilhelm Hansen, 1962), pp. 283-292.

[43]A. H. King, "Mozart's 'Prussian' Quartets in Relation to his Late Style," in *Music and Letters*, xxi (1940), 328-346.

[44]Georges de St. Foix, "Le Dernier Quatuor de Mozart," in *Studien zur Musikgeschichte: Festschrift für Guido Adler zum 75. Geburtstag* (Vienna/Leipzig: Universal-Edition, 1930), pp. 168-173.

Cambini and Boccherini

Haydn's and Mozart's late quartets essentially supplanted all other national types of string quartet. Both Cambini and Boccherini, when confronted with the later masterpieces of Haydn and Mozart, gave up their previous styles and started imitating the now universally admired styles of Haydn and Mozart. Idealistically some believe that, because Mozart has been unequaled in the sureness of his ear, some of his innovations came out so perfect that he left no room for real followers.[45] That did not stop some composers from trying, such as Cambini and Boccherini. Yet it is probably Haydn who had the greater immediate impact.

Cambini wrote some quartets for professionals for public performance and some quartets for amateurs at home. From the time he arrived in Paris he was active in public concerts (Concerts spirituels and Concerts des amateurs) but from 1794 on he directed private concerts for the Parisian contractor Armand Séguier where his own quartets, quintets, symphonies and other works were regularly performed.[46] His last six quartets date from this period and differ markedly from all those that preceded them. They are each in four movements modeled on Haydn's quartets.

Next to Haydn and Mozart, the late-18th-century valued Boccherini as an exponent of the classical string quartet. But while some of his quartets have many elements of classicism about them, the cello virtuoso Boccherini never seemed fully adjusted to the classical style and none of his quartets has ever reached the plateau of the classics. Boccherini's first set of quartets from 1761 were "more advanced" than Haydn's ten early quartet-divertimenti,[47] but whereas Haydn continued to grow and eventually arrived at the *classic* string quartet, Boccherini interrupted his development with the domination of the first violin (Opus 8, 9 and 15) and concentrated on the two-movement quartettini (Opus 15, 22 and 26). In all of these his style was not motivic development, which was be-

---

[45]Hans Keller, "Mozart—the Revolutionary Chamber Musician," in *The Musical Times*, cxxii (1981), 465-468.

[46]Dieter Lutz Trimpert, *Die Quatuors Concertants von Giuseppe Cambini*, in *Mainzer Studien zur Musikwissenschaft*, Band 1 (Tutzing: Hans Schneider, 1967), pp. 16-17.

[47]Cf. Chapter IV, p. 176.

coming a trade mark of Haydn's, but rather a succession of building blocks which sometimes did not inevitably lead from one set to
another.[48] When he returned to a pattern of instrumental equality in
Opus 22, he resumed the concertant style of Opus 2 rather than a
sharing of motives among all instruments. Boccherini clearly was
influenced by Haydn's quartets from 1776 on when he published
his first series in Vienna rather than in Paris (Opus 24), and with
few exceptions after that his quartets were in three, then four movements following Haydn. He even attempted some motivic development, but while sonata form became more sophisticated and the
forms in general more monumental, Boccherini did not feel at
home in Haydn's classicism. After the death of his Madrid patron
Don Luis, Boccherini moved to Germany where he worked for
King Friedrich Wilhelm II of Prussia, a cellist for whom he wrote
quartets in his old style of periodic, symmetrical building blocks
(Opus 39 [1787]). When this patron died in 1797, Boccherini became dependent upon the sales of his quartets through his publishers (primarily Pleyel in Paris) and so turned to the style of quartet
that the publishers felt had the best marketability. The last quartets
(Opus 58 [1799] and the one quartet of Opus 64 [1804]) are orchestral rather than chamber (lots of tremolos, drum-like repeated
notes in the bass, arpeggios, sequences), the first violin is brilliant
rather than a leading partner, the leading theme is not motivically
pregnant but dull, and the recapitulation is mechanically unchanged from the exposition. All this suggests public rather than
private performance since the vast public in general was then, as
well as from then on, much more interested in the large, bombastic,
ingenuous orchestra than the small, subtle quartet.

In addition to the quartets which Haydn, Mozart, Boccherini
and Cambini wrote especially for professional musicians, there
were also quartets composed specifically for amateurs. These
quartets, mostly written by the second-rate composers of the late
18th century, often were arrangements of popular opera airs which
the dilettante could enjoy at home on his or her instrument together
with three other performers. Probably the most successful composer of such pieces was Cambini, whose arrangements of airs
(quatuor d'airs) for string quartet were best sellers during the

[48]Speck, pp. 119-137.

1780's.[49] A single *quatuor d'airs* consists of an opening and closing variation movement and, in half the quartets, a slow middle
one. Each variation movement is an arrangement of an air followed
by four or more variations; the first violin dominates, but other instruments, especially the cello, can have a prominent part in a single variation. Cambini also arranged for string quartet two Boccherini sonatas specifically for the amateur ensemble. These arrangements of airs have parallels in other genres; both Haydn and
Beethoven arranged British folk airs, the latter for voice with piano
trio accompaniment, whereas Kozeluch wrote piano trios without
voice based on Scottish and Irish airs. But there was an aesthetic
difference which theorists of the 18th century quickly noted. The
popular opera air arrangement was regarded as an inferior kind of
music, whereas the folk song was so idealized by late 18th-century
composers and those at the beginning of the 19th as a gift of nature
that an arrangement of it was a work of high art. The former was
fit for Hausmusik, not the concert stage or the private concert,
while the latter was entirely acceptable in all quarters.

Beethoven

The events which led to Beethoven's first set of quartets have
been discussed above. Beethoven began composition of the D
Major quartet in 1798 and was still finishing some of the quartets
in 1800. The quartets were played at Prince Lichanowsky's palace
and then all over Vienna. The Prince thought so highly of Beethoven's first quartets that he presented the composer with four instruments (a Guarnerius violin and cello, an Amati violin, and a
Ruger viola) so that Beethoven could hear the quartets in his own
lodgings. During this time Beethoven became a pupil of Emanuel
Aloys Förster (1748-1823), whose quartets were also performed at
Prince Lichanowsky's. On Sunday noons and Thursday evenings
Förster regularly held private chamber music concerts in his own
home for the best professional and dilettante chamber musicians in
Vienna (among whom were regularly Beethoven, Zmeskall,
Schuppanzigh, Weiss, Linke, Heinrich Eppinger, Mayseder, J.N.
Hummel and occasionally distinguished foreigners), and it is here

---

[49]Listed in Trimpert, pp. 298-305, and discussed pp. 165-166.

that Beethoven claimed that for the first time he had "learned to write quartets properly."[50] What is of particular interest for the history of chamber music playing is that in Vienna by the 1790's private chamber music concerts were taking place not only in the homes of the aristocrats but also in the private quarters of composers, performers and middle class persons.

Following the pattern set by composers and publishers of the 18th century, Beethoven wrote six works as a set, which were meant to compliment each other and to belong to a single aesthetic plan. The Opus 18 quartets were originally published in 1801 in two sets of three, but they were commissioned as six and composed with that number in mind. When Beethoven returned to quartets with the Opus 59 set, he likewise composed a group of works that aesthetically are linked. The three quartets of Opus 59 are longer and much more complicated from formal and technical standpoints, and they share many stylistic features which separate them as a group from his earlier and later works. About 1804 Beethoven was asked by Andreas Kyrillovich Razumovsky (1752-1836), brother-in-law of Prince Lichanowky, to compose some quartets, which he completed in 1806. Razumovsky had served as Russian ambassador to the Austrian court since 1792 (except for 1799-1801) and had proven himself as a second violinist to be "one of the best connoisseurs and players of Haydn's quartets."[51] In honor of his benefactor Beethoven included a few Russian melodies in the quartets. Most of the reviews of the first performance by Schuppanzigh's quartet in February, 1807, were negative; Czerny, Beethoven's pupil, reported that the audience laughed,[52] but the quartets were published in 1808 and were soon performed in Russia and England, though there, too, to negative reviews. Beethoven's famous remark to a bad reviewer has often been quoted:

[50]Hans Josef Wedig, *Beethovens Streichquartett op. 18 Nr. 1 und seine erste Fassung*, in *Veröffentlichungen des Beethovenhauses in Bonn*, Band 2 (Bonn: Beethovenhaus, 1922), and Janet M. Levy, *Beethoven's Compositional Choices: the Two Versions of Opus 18, No. 1, First Movement*, in *Studies in the Criticism and Theory of Music*, ed. Leonard B. Meyer (Philadelphia: University of Pennsylvania Press, 1982) both discuss the meaning of Beethoven's remark. Landon, *Haydn: Chronicle and Works*, vol. IV, pp. 504-505, challenges Beethoven's debt to Förster as opposed to his debt to Haydn.

[51]Alexander W. Thayer, *Life of Beethoven*, rev. and ed. Elliot Forbes (Princeton: Princeton University Press, 1967), p. 401.

[52]Thayer, p. 409.

"Oh, [the quartets] are not for you, but for a later age!" Spohr found the quartets incomprehensible, and although he helped popularize Beethoven's Opus 18 throughout Europe, he could not do so well with this new set. By 1816, however, the quartets were better appreciated at least in Vienna, where in the palace of Count Deym the Schuppanzigh Quartet performed the third number to the "deafening applause of the crowded audience."[53]

Following the Opus 59 set, Beethoven wrote individual quartets (Opus 74 and 95), which stand alone in time and style from each other and from both the earlier and later quartets. This follows a tendency in general in the early 19th century to individualize a single work: to unify it within itself and to verify its uniqueness in the world of art as a whole. Opus 74 was written in 1809 for Prince Lobkowitz and published the next year, while Opus 95 was written in 1810 for Mr. Zmeskall and printed in 1816.

The late quartets of Beethoven (written in the 1820's), however, while they maintain to some extent their individuality, are not entirely independent. They differ in form and in opus number, but four of them (Opus 130, 131, 132, and 133) share a similar motivic idea and all five have much in common stylistically; they are also part of a larger unity encompassing many of Beethoven's last works, which share a single motivic idea and a style. In one way they have come full circle, from a closely knit set (Opus 18) to an integrated collection (Opus 127, 130, 131, 132, 133, and 135). On the other hand the changes in conception of form, style, technique, harmony, rhythm and programmatic content are monumental from Opus 18 through Opus 59 through the two independent quartets to the last quartets.

Opus 127 was begun in 1822, nearly finished in 1824, and premiered on Sunday, March 6, 1825, in the small Vereinsaal at the "roten Igel" at the request of the Russian Prince Galitzin, who wanted altogether three quartets (eventually Opus 127, 130, and 132). Beethoven at first promised Schuppanzigh the right to premier Opus 127, but Linke, cellist in Schuppanzigh's Quartet, had also received Beethoven's permission to premier the work at a special benefit concert for himself. To satisfy both Schuppanzigh and

[53]Thayer, p. 640.

Linke, Beethoven wrote another quartet, Opus 132, which he handed to Linke who gave its first public performance on Sunday, November 6, 1825 in the Music Society's room at the "rother Igel." These two premiers and the events surrounding them reflect the growing presence of chamber music concerts—public and private—in Vienna during the 1820's. Beethoven gave Schuppanzigh the finished parts of Opus 127 a mere two weeks before the March 6th premier, which was too short a time for the famous violinist, and as a result Schuppanzigh's underrehearsed first performance was a failure. Beethoven was furious, so he turned to another violinist, Joseph Böhm (1795-1876), for another, better performance. Böhm apparently was not as virtuosic a violinist as Schuppanzigh, but he was a great musician; he was professor of violin at the Vienna Conservatory and—extremely important for the future of Beethoven's late quartets and chamber music in general—was the violin teacher of Joseph Joachim, the dominant performer of string quartets during the second half of the 19th century. Böhm took over Schuppanzigh's Quartet (Holz, Weiss, and Linke) and a few days later tried out Opus 127 before a small audience; then on March 23, 1825, in front of a much larger audience at a benefit concert for himself he performed the quartet twice on the same program. Connoisseurs thrilled at Beethoven's first contribution to quartet writing in over a decade and a half and clamored for more performances; Joseph Mayseder with his own quartet ensemble played the quartet again in April and December in private homes. Meanwhile, on September 9, 1825, the Schuppanzigh Quartet premiered Opus 132 privately before an audience of fourteen persons at the hotel quarters of Mr. Adolph Schlesinger, the Parisian music dealer, who was visiting Vienna and had just bought the manuscript. The ensemble performed it twice in a row, and the following Sunday it was again performed privately for a larger audience, again in Schlesinger's hotel room. The first public performance, as was noted above, took placed on November 6, 1825, in a benefit concert for Linke.

Each of the late quartets has a unique history, and the stories of their genesis and first performance could up take half a volume.[54] What is evident in tracing the evolution of all of Beethoven's

[54]Cf. Thayer, p. 1131, for the basic data.

quartets is that the audience and performance situations for chamber music had changed from 1799 to 1825. Several factors accounted for this: the establishment of permanent professional string quartet ensembles, the French Revolution and the Industrial Revolution, the beginning of the emancipation of European Jewry (Jewish performers and patrons were beginning to affect the history of chamber music), the new aesthetic ideals of the Romantic Age, and the particular genius of Beethoven himself. It was not simply a case of either the genius shaping the age or the age shaping the genius; they interacted. Beethoven demanded more from his quartet players because the quartet players were better prepared to play more difficult music. Audiences expected and got the Romantic ideals of drama and subjectivism from the music of Beethoven because Beethoven was a product of the age that brought on those ideals—the age created by the French Revolution and Industrialization.[55]

The contributions of Beethoven's string quartets have been the topic of several monumental books.[56] Therefore it would be redundant to rehash all this material here. Rather, we need to summarize the main contributions and changes in string quartet writing effected by these quartets and how they affected the conceptualization of chamber music in the minds of performers and audience. Beethoven's quartets are important to the history of string quartet writing because they expanded the technique of ensemble music, they introduced new sounds and color effects, they changed the macro and micro forms of the quartet, they introduced subjective programs, and they changed the nature of the "individuality" of the independent work of art.

Already in Opus 18 Beethoven increased the ranges of the instruments and the technical demands upon all the players, and

---

[55]Beethoven's personal tragedy—his deafness and his struggle with his brothers, sister-in-law, and nephew—affected the rate of his composing but not his skill or inspiration.

[56]Among the most prominent are Joseph Kerman, *The Beethoven Quartets* (New York: Alfred A. Knopf, 1967); Joseph de Marliave, *Les Quatuors de Beethoven*, ed. Jean Escarra (Paris: Librairie Félix Alcan, 1925); Dan Gregory Mason, *The Quartets of Beethoven*, (New York: Oxford, 1947); and Philip Radcliffe, *Beethoven's String Quartets* (London: Hutchinson University Library, 1965). Special mention must be made of the beautiful history of the performances of the late Beethoven quartets in the 19th and early 20th century by Ivan Mahaim, *Beethoven* (Paris: Desclée De Brouwer, 1964).

these increased in Opus 59 and on to the late quartets. Haydn asked the first violin to soar to tremendous heights, but he did so on relatively few occasions. Beethoven, on the other hand, expected the first violinist to be entirely at home in the higher positions, so there is a larger per cent of high notes and a lot of passage work in those ethereal locations. For example in Opus 18, no. 2, first movement, the first violin scoots up the scale in sixteenth notes from a1 to a3 and a measure later from b1 to b3, followed several measures later by some broken chords equally high, followed by three measures of broken octaves in upward scales in sixteenth notes. Despite these frequent virtuosic passages Beethoven conceived of them within the framework of the string quartet and not the concerto; the only exception to this is the cadenza-like bridge for the first violin accompanied by the other three instruments between the Marcia and the last movement of Opus 132, which resembles the "concerto" cadenzas that Boccherini had used in his brilliant quartets. Here or in any of Beethoven's quartets, this is not material for a dilettante. But not only the first violinist must now be a virtuoso. Whereas there is considerable distance between the technical demands of the first violinist and second violinist in Haydn and Mozart, the second violinist in a Beethoven quartet has to be as polished as the first violinist. The same holds for the violist and cellist. For example the cello in Opus 18, no. 1, adagio movement, mm.96-101, plays an exposed solo that is high on the A string. For anyone but a top virtuoso these and many, many others in Opus 18 require so much attention that there is no room left for ensemble questions, yet all these passages are part of ensemble playing that requires close cooperation among all four players. Add to this some very difficult rhythmic situations, which involve either all four instruments together or various combinations of some against others, and the complexities of ensemble far outshine those in any quartet before Opus 18. Beethoven carried to an even greater extent the variety of styles that Haydn used, and the balancing of changing textures of the same motive (as in Opus 18, no. 1, movement 1, measures 1-47) requires a great deal of musical understanding. Nothing in Haydn's work before Opus 103 is so demanding of individual and ensemble technique as what is required in Opus 18. This all goes to show the great advance in playing technique that Schuppanzigh's Quartet was capable of, and no doubt this virtuosity so bedazzled the audience at Prince Lichnow-sky's and at later concerts that public performances of Beethoven would be much more in demand than public performances of the relatively mild Haydn and Mozart quartets. These latter, on the other hand, were still performable by good dilettantes and therefore became more solidly entrenched in Hausmusik circles. When Beethoven moved on to Opus 59, 74, 95 and then the late quartets, the technical problems so increased that even the venerable Schup-panzigh Quartet had to work very hard to master their difficulties (for example, as mentioned in connection with the premier of Opus 127). Yet there were other professionals—Böhm, Hellmesberger and Mayseder—who were helping to bring quartet playing to ever higher technical and musical levels.

Beethoven also introduced new sounds, some of which grew out of his expansion of the ensemble technique. Passages, such as the opening of the last movement of Opus 132, with its first violin - cello polyrhythm and second violin - viola chords, or like the be-ginning of the Adagio, ma non troppo of Opus 74, produce a thick-ness of sound that at this time was unique to Beethoven. Beethoven drew on the big sound of the lowest string of the cello for a dra-matic effect that, again, did not exist even in the cello-dominated music of Boccherini. The pizzicato of later in the same movement (which gave the name "harp" to Opus 74), the pizzicato accompa-niment in the cello at the opening of the Andante con moto to Opus 59, no. 3, and the brief pizzicato introductions to the main theme throughout the No. 5 Presto of Opus 131 were novel expansions of the color of the quartet sound. The sotto voce sections of the Molto Adagio movement of Opus 132, which if performed correctly re-semble the sound of a harmonium or poor church organ, are also new Beethoven tone colors.

Even more important to Beethoven than the expansion of tech-nique and the introduction of new sounds is the change in formal concept of the quartets. Beethoven's struggle with form dominated his composition from the 1790's until his death. Basically he in-herited the classical form of Haydn, which placed primary interest in the first movement in sonata form and often trivial interest in the other movements. The final movement could gain, under both Mozart and Haydn, if it were also in sonata form or at least considered as seriously as the first movement, and both these earlier composers experimented with shifting some weight to the last movement (Haydn in Opus 20 and Mozart in the Jupiter Symphony). Sonata form itself, as a binary form in the late 18th century, is a balanced, symmetrical form, with the exposition repeated exactly, and the development-recapitulation repeated exactly. The recapitulation, within the binary form, was itself a more or less complete repetition of the exposition. Such repetition could be charming and relaxing, but it could not produce the drama that Beethoven needed.

For Beethoven drama was more important than symmetry or balance, yet the forms he inherited and mostly chose to use were based on anti-dramatic symmetry. To enhance the dramatic nature of sonata form Beethoven, as is well known not only in quartets but also in sonatas, symphonies and other pieces, set about destroying the very essence of sonata form: its symmetry and balance. He expanded the development section and the coda, modified the recapitulation, heightened the tonal clashes of the bridge and closing sections, tried slow or chordal introductions which recur during the movement, but eventually even abandoned sonata form altogether in favor of theme and variations or simply continual variations (Opus 131 is the epitome of this rejection of sonata form). If sonata form was inadequate, Beethoven from the start found that the traditional balance of movements was even more inadequate. In the first five quartets of opus 18 he made his finales sonata form movements (one a rondo) as long and serious as his first movements, and in Opus 18, no 6 he introduced a very serious "malinconia" to the allegretto finale that recurs near the end and gives unprecedented seriousness to the whole quartet. Later Beethoven wrote fugues for the last movement (Opus 59, no. 3, and the earlier version of Opus 130, which later became Opus 133), numerous sonata forms with unusual twists (Opus 59, no. 1 uses a Russian melody as its primary theme and Opus 132 has two codas), and a free form that vaguely suggests sonata form (Opus 135). With increased emphasis on the final movement, Beethoven had achieved a somewhat dramatic move from the first movement to the last, but without the drama continuing in the movements between the outer two, the drama would still fall flat. Thus the inner movements are often heightened in intensity. Opus 95 pointed the way with a unity that begins at the opening of the first movement and continues until the very end of the last. The unity is actually a conflict between F Minor and D Major, two unrelated keys that are continually contrasted. The first movement in F (with momentary D Major interjections) is followed by a second movement ambiguously in D Minor and Major. Without break the second movement goes into the third, a scherzo like movement in F Minor whose trio is largely in D Major. The final movement begins with a very slow introduction that hones in on the somber nature of F Minor; the movement proper (Allegretto agitato) is solidly in F Minor, but it ends with an allegro coda in the one obvious key that has been avoided until now: F Major. F Major is a logical compromise between the bright key of D Major and the somber key of F Minor; it also relieves with a burst of joy the agony that had been building to it from the first measure of the first movement. The unity of a quartet, then, according to Beethoven, is not only following a traditional order of movements with a traditional order of tonalities, but an emotional and dramatic contour that rises from the opening of the quartet to the denouement near the end.

To separate one drama from another, each drama has its own, individual character, its own particular problem. As already pointed out, the early 19th century placed an increased artistic value on each individual work. A Beethoven symphony stood by itself;[57] it needed no other symphony to bolster its raison d'être (commissions came singly rather than in groups) and it need not be composed with or published with other works (though Beethoven did work on more than one composition at a time). Haydn composed six Paris symphonies, twelve London symphonies, while Beethoven created nine individual symphonies. But this independence of each work of art seems contradicted by four of Beethoven's last six string quartets (the *Grosse Fuga* is considered here a separate string quartet). They, as well as the late Bagatelles, the *Diabelli* Variations, and the Ninth Symphony, while premiered and printed separately and quite different in content, nonetheless are all unified by sharing the same four-note "Bach" motive (represented,

[57]This despite Beethoven's practice of working simultaneously on numerous pieces of the same and different genre.

for example, in Opus 132 by g♯ - a - f' - e).[58] Not much time separated Opus 132 (the earliest in the quartet group) from the last
movement of Opus 130 (the last movement Beethoven completed),
yet the four quartet pieces are considered separate works. What
Beethoven contributed here is the idea that a composer's whole
output during a period of time is a manifestation of a single, individual human character and that despite the outward differences
each particular work takes, the meaning of each piece is the same.[59]
Opus 130, 131, 132, and 133 have nothing in common outwardly;
they are, however, different expressions of the same melodic root
and same intellectual pattern. Clearly Beethoven's concept of unity
here flies in the face of the prevailing early romantic idea of individuality, and no composers of chamber music during the rest of
the 19th century understood what Beethoven was trying to do. The
most obvious successor to Beethoven in this was Bartók in the
20th century, who took up the same four notes and over a period of
more than three decades wrote six independent quartets which, like
these Beethoven four, express the unity of Bartók's character and
thought.

For many in the Romantic Era the unity of a work was not in
its musical structure but in its portrayal of an extra-musical idea.
Haydn and Mozart may have had some occasions to insert extra-
musical ideas into their quartets, but they did so privately; it took
150 years before a musicologist unraveled the programmatic reason for the slow, dissonant introduction of Mozart's K.465
"Dissonance" Quartet. But programs had been an essential part of
French chamber music since the 17th century, and the idea was not
unknown in solo sonatas and symphonies throughout the 18th
century. Thus when Beethoven refers to the Adagio of Opus 18,
no. 1 as depicting the burial scene of *Romeo and Juliet*, he was
following a long-standing French tradition, but by revealing this

---

[58]The "Bach" motive is defined by two pairs of notes of which each pair contains a half-
step interval; the interval separating the two pairs can vary. It receives its name from the
famous third subject in the last fugue of Bach in his *Kunst der Fuge*, which is a play on
his name (in German notation, the notes b (= b♭) - a c h (= b♮). Many composers in the
19th century, conscious of Bach's treatment of the motive, used it as a source for improvisation and composition. It is uncertain if Beethoven came upon it on his own or was
purposefully influenced by the association with Bach's name.

[59]This theory has been expressed best by J.W.N. Sullivan, *Beethoven: His Spiritual Development* (New York: Alfred A. Knopf, 1927).

program in an Austrian string quartet, he was breaking new ground. Although Beethoven did not overindulge in programs, he did on a few other occasions refer to them. We have already mentioned the "melancholy" of the final movement of Opus 18, no. 1. The use of folk tunes in the first and second Opus 59 quartets does not constitute program music, but in Opus 132 Beethoven gives his most important program.[60] On the score of the third movement he writes about his recent recovery from an illness (which was in early 1825) and his thanks to God for his recovery. The movement consists of two different ideas which alternate. At the beginning is Beethoven's somber religious mood, in the church mode which Beethoven calls "Lydian," where the strings play extremely slowly in sotto voce and imitate the sound of a country church organ; in contrast is the bright mood of rejoicing upon recovery from illness, in the major mode and in a sprightly tempo. Beethoven suffers a relapse, makes another recovery, and then settles into a simple religious mood once again to show his utter dependence upon God's will.

The rest of the 19th century was concerned with learning from Beethoven's string quartets. As they became the worshipped ideal, other composers imitated them and audiences justified their high tastes in music by their appreciation of Beethoven's quartets. That Beethoven allowed program music into chamber music opened up to the 19th century listener and theorist the same problem experienced then in orchestral music: does one listen to music as pure organization of sounds or as the representation of philosophical/artistic concepts? Whatever the meaning of the quartets, they were listened to much more than played by the vast majority of enthusiasts. While the quartets of Haydn and Mozart remained household quartets, the increasing number of professionals took upon themselves the arduous task of learning how to interpret at least the earlier quartets for concert hall performance. The late quartets did not become really popular until the 1920's, and Opus 133 is known to have been performed publicly between 1825 and

---

[60]This movement has been closely studied by Sieghard Brandenburg, "The Historical Background to the 'Heiliger Dankgesang' in Beethoven's A-Minor Quartet Op. 132," in Alan Tyson, ed., *Beethoven Studies*, vol. iii (Cambridge: Cambridge University Press, 1982), pp. 161-191.

1925 by only two professional quartet ensembles.[61] The domination of Haydn's, Mozart's and Beethoven's early quartets made it difficult for others to enter the repertoire, though there were some significant contributions and some popular successes before 1890, especially by Schubert, Schumann, Mendelssohn, Tchaikovsky and Brahms.

The String Quartet Ensemble

One of the most significant developments of the second half of the 18th century was the establishment of the first professional string quartet ensembles. The earliest known string quartet ensemble whose members were professional musicians is that of Nardini and Manfredi (violins), Cambini (viola), and Boccherini (cello).[62] In either 1763 or 1766 these four great Italians were together for a brief time and played, among other things, the early Haydn quartets and probably Cambini's and Boccherini's earliest exemplars. But although this was a string ensemble of professional performers, it was not a professional string quartet, i.e., a string quartet of professional musicians that performed on a regular basis. One of the two earliest known professional string quartets, then, seems to have been that of the Font family in the service of Don Luis in Madrid. It consisted of a father and his three sons, who performed on a regular basis for the concerts held in Don Luis' home.[63] Boccherini joined this quartet in 1769 as a second cellist, and it is presumably for this quintet ensemble that he wrote most of his quintets and quartets. Simultaneously with the Font Quartet there obviously was a quartet ensemble in residence at Eszterháza for whom Haydn wrote his quartets. The members of this quartet were mainly front desk court orchestral musicians, of whom the most prominent was the concertmaster Luigi Tomasini, who served in this capacity from 1761 until 1808 (with the exception of 1790 to

[61]Sidney Grew, "The 'Grosse Fuge': the Hundred Years of its History," in *Music and Letters*, xii (1931), 140-147.

[62]Christian Speck, ed., Luigi Boccherini, *Quartett in c-Moll op. 2 Nr. 1 (G 159)* (Celle: Moeck Verlag), 1987, p. 4; and Trimpert, pp. 10-12.

[63]Germaine de Rothschild, *Luigi Boccherini: His Life and Works*, trl. Andreas Mayor (London: 1965), pp. 37, 44 and 67.

1792).[64] The leader of the second violin section from 1781 to 1788 was Tost, who apparently had a more modern technique than Tomasini's and for whom Haydn wrote twelve quartets. Haydn's cellist from 1761 to 1769 was Joseph Weigl, who left Eszterháza to join the Court Orchestra in Vienna. While membership in the Eszterházy Quartet often changed during Haydn's nearly three decades in the service of Prince Nicolas, the continual presence of Tomasini as first violin renders this ensemble as the longest lived of the early professional string quartets. After the death of Nicolas his son disbanded the orchestra, Haydn left for Vienna and London, and Tomasini himself was let go for two years; the prominence of the Eszterháza Quartet could not be restored.

The professional quartet was still a rarity until the 1790's and in any case seems to have been primarily the private servants of nobility; alternative ensembles were often made of a mixture of professionals and wealthy patrons such as the famous group that met at Baron von Swieten's home in Vienna and of which Haydn and Mozart were occasionally members.

Louis Spohr's published string quartets demonstrate another aspect of the quartet ensemble in the early 19th century. In 1807 he wrote three quartets, the first two (Opus 4) in four movements with equal instrumentation and normal classical layout but the third (Opus 11) in three movements with the first violin entirely dominant. Opus 11 is entitled *quatuor brillant*, which is a term that emerged in the early 19th century to designate chamber music in which the top instrument not only dominates but is extraordinarily virtuosic. Spohr imitated "Rode's three quartets op. 11, the first of which, in E♭, Spohr had often played to the delight of audiences that did not relish Beethoven."[65] The young Spohr needed, sometimes, to show off his skill on his instrument, even when not playing publicly concerti with orchestras, and this virtuosity was appealing to a shallow but sizable audience. Spohr visited homes for private soiree concerts and requested that the host supply a string trio ensemble of local musicians who could sight read the

---

[64]Landon, *Haydn: Chronicle and Works*, II, p. 81.

[65]Clive Brown, *Louis Spohr: a Critical Biography* (Cambridge: Cambridge University Press, 1984), p. 43.

lower parts, while Spohr showed off his wares. In effect, these were violin concertos performed as string quartets.[66] Later Spohr's tastes improved, and when he instituted a series of chamber concerts during the winter season 1818-1819, the weekly events included classical quartets by Mozart, Haydn, Beethoven, Fesca, Onslow and himself.[67]

A different situation occurred in London during the 1790's. When Johann Peter Salomon (1745-1815) organized his concert series and included regular string quartet works as part of the extravaganza (see above), the ensemble that performed the quartets was Salomon's own. When the Salomon Quartet premiered an Opus 64 quartet by Haydn on February 24, 1791, the ensemble consisted of Salomon himself as first violin, Mr. Mountain as second violin, Mr. Hindmarsch as viola, and Mr. Menell as cello. During the next several years this ensemble, with the substitution of Mr. Damen for Mr. Mountain, was responsible for numerous premiers of Haydn quartets from Opus 64 and 71/74 and works by other contemporaries including Pleyel. What distinguished the Salomon Quartet from the Font and Eszterhása Quartets was that this group performed publicly at subscribed concerts and became a publicly recognized string quartet. Salomon, not some prince or wealthy merchant, determined where and when and what the ensemble would perform (though, of course, princes and wealthy merchants were courted as subscribers). When the London Philharmonic Society was founded in 1813 and Salomon became its first director and conductor (he led the first performance of the London Philharmonic Orchestra on March 8, 1813), independent chamber music concerts were established in conjunction with them. Giovanni Battista Viotti (1755-1824), the last great Italian violinist of the 18th century, whose *quatuors concertants* during the 1780's competed in Paris with Cambini's,[68] broke his retire-

---

[66]This is similar in practice to Mozart's performances of his early piano concertos with a string quartet instead of a full orchestra.

[67]Brown, p. 119.

[68]Viotti, famous for his duets and concertos, wrote twelve quatuors concertants (opus 1 and 3, ca. 1783-1785) and three more in 1817.

ment in London in the early 19th century to perform at these new chamber concerts.

Certainly there were string quartet ensembles in Paris by the time Cambini began to live and publish there, but since quartets were performed in private (the vast majority were performed by dilettantes in their own homes), there is no record of specific groups. Paris was a Mecca for great violinists, and Viotti established there by the 1780's a new school of French violinists. His most famous pupil was Pierre Rode (1774-1830), remembered today for his caprices and concertos, but at the turn of the 19th century he composed twelve *quatuors brillants*—string quartets which showed off the first violin. Since Cambini, Viotti and Rode wrote their quartets in Paris, it seems safe to assume that there were professional or at least good amateur quartet ensembles in Paris from ca. 1770 to ca. 1800.

In Vienna the first known professional quartet was organized at the apartments of Prince Lichnowsky and flourished from 1794 to the end of the century. Every Friday morning there was a quartet concert. The leader was Ignaz Schuppanzigh (1776-1830), the teenage violinist who was at first the champion of Haydn's quartets and later premiered most of Beethoven's quartets and other chamber music as well. Schuppanzigh's first quartet ensemble included the great cellist Anton Kraft (for whom Haydn wrote his cello concerto in D and the only adult in the group) or his young son Nikolaus (then 14), the second violinist Louis Sina (a pupil of Beethoven's "quartet teacher" Förster), and the youthful violist Franz Weiss (age 15). Although except for the Krafts none of these men were the most renowned virtuosi of their time and although there were occasions from 1794 to 1799 when someone substituted for the young Kraft (his father or Zmeskall) or Sina ("the master of the house when they were engaged for private performance"), the ensemble practiced and performed together as a unit under the eyes and ears of Haydn and Förster and achieved a level of ensemble playing unmatched anywhere before then.[69] All their performances, however, were in private salons, as indeed were performances by

[69]Thayer, p. 228.

other, less renowned amateur groups.[70] For example, in 1803 August von Kitzebue, while passing through Vienna, described frequent "amateur concerts at which unconstrained pleasure prevails. . . . The beginning is usually made with a quartet by Haydn or Mozart. . . ."[71]

In 1808, Prince Razumovsky called on Schuppanzigh to assemble the best musicians into his house quartet. Schuppanzigh was to be first violin, Weiss was brought in for viola, and the talented Joseph Linke played cello. The second violin part was left open, since Razumovsky himself could handle that part in many quartets; as needed, Joseph Mayseder was called on to replace the Prince. For several years (until the Prince's palace was destroyed by fire in 1815) the Razumovsky Quartet was the best in Europe, and Beethoven wrote his famous works for this ensemble. During the winter of 1815 to 1816 Schuppanzigh was responsible for public chamber music concerts in Vienna with Weiss and Linke, but by early 1816, the connection with Razumovsky terminated and the winter season at an end, the musicians scattered. Schuppanzigh went to St. Petersburg where (sometimes joined by Weiss, Linke and Mayseder) he introduced Beethoven's quartets to the Russians; Linke went primarily with the Erdödy family to Croatia. In 1825 Schuppanzigh reorganized his quartet in Vienna with Linke and Weiss and with a new second violinist Karl Holz (who worked closely with Beethoven). For the next five years, the last of Schuppanzigh's life, this quartet dominated the scene in Vienna with both public and private concerts. Occasionally there were substitutions, most notably that for the premier of Opus 127 when, as cited above, Joseph Böhm took Schuppanzigh's place. Schuppanzigh's quartet ensembles were not the first chronologically, but through long years of emphasis on quartet playing and through his association with Haydn, Beethoven, Förster and many lesser composers

---

[70]Mary Sue Morrow, *Concert Life in Haydn's Vienna: Aspects of a Developing Musical and Social Institution*, in *Sociology of Music No. 7* (Stuyvesant, NY: Pendragon Press, 1989). There were many private salon concerts where chamber music would be played by both dilettantes and professionals along with symphonies, concertos, solo keyboard pieces, and vocal music; chronicles some of these from 1761 to the early 1800's and shows that some were weekly events, others more frequent (even daily), still others regular but less frequent—during the winter season and not during the summer, when musicians would scatter to the country.

[71]*Freymüthige* no. 58 (April 12, 1803); cited in Thayer, p. 324.

he became the foremost interpreter of the principal works in the repertoire and established a standard of excellence not only in technical matters but in musical ones as well. Both Böhm and Mayseder followed Schuppanzigh in the organization of professional ensembles, and the former, as teacher to a number of the leading chamber musicians of the next two generations, passed Schuppanzigh's torch on to the future. The institution of professional quartet ensemble was now firmly in place.

Schubert

The most important remaining member of this great generation of string quartet composers is Franz Schubert (1797-1828), fifteen of whose nineteen known quartets survive intact.[72] Although he was born sixty-five years after Haydn and almost three decades after Beethoven, his early death just a year after Beethoven's places him within the period of this chapter. In many ways he belonged to the next, post-Beethoven generation, since his style was more that of Schumann and Mendelssohn than that of Haydn and Mozart. But in other regards he was very much a member of the group of classical string quartet composers—a prolific group that produced the masterpieces upon which string quartet writing ever since has been based.

Schubert, the lyricist, wrote melodies for his chamber music that are unequaled; they give his string quartets a unique character. Yet he was also influenced by the quartets of his three great predecessors. The influences of Haydn, Mozart and Beethoven, however, are felt more in the inner movements than in the outer ones.[73] Schubert's chamber music resolved the contrast between classical clarity of harmony, tonality and forms based on tonal direction and romantic ambiguity of harmony, tonality and forms based on thematic organization.[74] Schubert inherited the high level of violin technique demanded by Beethoven and realized by Viotti, Rode,

---

[72]Otto Erich Deutsch, "The Chronology of Schubert's String Quartets," in *Music and Letters*, xxiv (1943), 25-30.

[73]Hans-Martin Sachse, *Franz Schuberts Streichquartette* (Münster in Westfalen: Max Kramer, typescript, 1958).

[74]Martin Chusid, "The Chamber Music of Franz Schubert" (University of California Ph.D. dissertation, 1961).

Spohr, Böhm, Mayseder, and Hellmesberger,[75] and also cello technique from Romberg and Linke, including the high range of the instruments and trills. Schubert tended to orchestral string writing in his quartets.[76] He did not excel writing the big, heavy finales that Beethoven wrote but was much more successful at lighter finales;[77] he did not think in the big dramatic curves that dominated Beethoven's art. Dahlhaus warns that we must not assume that Schubert knew what motivated Beethoven in his quartets and therefore he should not be judged by Beethoven's standards. Instead, Schubert combined a basic idea of sonata form (two contrasting themes) with a basic idea of variation (later musical thoughts grow out of earlier ones), especially evident in the first movement of the G Major Quartet (D.887).[78] Entitled "Death and the Maiden," this is not a programmatic, cyclic tone poem that deals with death but a cyclic string quartet wherein purely structural elements recur from movement to movement and the spirit of the song affects all movements.[79] The first three movements of this quartet reach the "sublime" and the fourth movement serves as a contrasting "grotesqueness" which brings the listener back to earth; the continual contrast of "sublime" and "grotesque" throughout the quartet is the unifying factor in the piece.[80]

The large number of string quartets that were written in the period 1780 to 1828 include an amazing number of great master-

---

[75]Georg Hellmesberger, the elder (1800-1873), father of Joseph Hellmesberger (1828-1893) who founded the Hellmesberger Quartet in 1849.

[76]Edmund van der Straeten, "Schuberts Behandlung der Streichinstrumente mit besonderer Berücksichtigung der Kammermusik," in *Bericht über den internationalen Kongress für Schubertforschung Wien 25. bis 29. November 1928* (Augsburg: Dr. Benno Filser, 1929), pp. 131-140.

[77]Thomas A. Denny, "The Finale in the Instrumental Works of Schubert" (Eastman School of Music of the University of Rochester Ph.D. dissertation, 1982).

[78]Carl Dahlhaus, "Über Schuberts Sonatenform: der erste Satz des G-Dur Quartetts D.887," in *Musica*, xxxii (1978), pp. 125-130.

[79]Christoph Wolff, "Schubert's 'Der Tod und das Mädchen': Analytical and Explanatory Notes on the Song D531 and the Quartet D810," in Eva Badura-Skoda and Peter Branscombe, eds., *Schubert Studies: Problems of Style and Chronology* (Cambridge: Cambridge University Press, 1982), pp. 143-171.

[80]Harold Truscott, "Schubert's String Quartet in G Major," in *The Music Review*, xx (1959), 119-145, suggests this analysis and Judy Gillet, "The Problem of Schubert's G Major String Quartet (D.887)," in *The Music Review*, xxxv (1974), pp. 281-292 carries it out.

pieces. The previous epoch produced an ever-increasing number of quartets but with relatively few great works. The succeeding epoch, which will be discussed in the next chapter, witnessed a drastic decrease in the number of new and masterful string quartets. Only in the 20th century has the string quartet once again become a major genre with some examples already accepted as "classics." Nonetheless, the great period of string quartet writing is that from 1780 to 1828, when Haydn, Mozart, Beethoven and Schubert gave us those monumental works which have served as the core of the string quartet repertory ever since.

THE STRING QUINTET

Following the publication in 1781 of Haydn's Opus 33 string quartets, both Pleyel (Haydn's pupil) and Hoffmeister wrote and published their own string quartets clearly modeled on Opus 33. Appearing in 1782 and 1784 respectively, they combine the divertimento character with motivic development so important for Opus 33. Immediately afterwards (1786 and 1787 respectively) both composers published string quintets incorporating the new ideas of Opus 33.

> Not only the instruments but also the individual sections of a movement, even occasionally different movements are now interrelated in a variety of ways that gives the character to a composition and alters the previous quintet with its background-like, light nature.[81]

All instruments now exchange roles. The concertant solo idea becomes more obvious in the Austrian quintet than before and unites with motivic development, while the technique of "durchbrochenen Satz" (dividing the melody among the various instruments) is now more noticeable in the French quintet (Cambini). The principle of contrast—so important in classical music (contrasting themes, dynamics, tonalities, tempos, rhythms)—is also manifest in quintets but augmented by the contrast in groups of instruments.

---

[81]Tilman Sieber, *Das klassische Streichquintet* (Bern/Munich: Francke Verlag, 1983), p. 56. Much of the following discussion of the string quintet is based on Sieber.

Eight of Pleyel's sixteen string quintets were directly influenced by Haydn in that they are in four movements, but the other
eight are in three movements more typical of French quintets. All
sixteen stylistically still have much in common with Cambini's
quartets and early quintets. The first violin predominates and is
doubled by the second violin at the octave; the two violas and cello
are much less prominent except in development sections. But at the
same time all sixteen quintets also have all instruments participating with the principal motives. Pleyel never has more than four instruments dividing up a motive at a given time, but in a whole
movement at one time or another each of the five instruments does
have the motive.

Most of Hoffmeister's eighteen string quintets, on the other
hand, are in three movements (slow-fast-fast) with a few in two or
four. For the final movement he frequently used a theme and
variation movement or a set of strophic variations over a short
(eight-measure) repeated pattern, rondo, or a two-part movement
contrasting two tempos or meters. All five instruments take equal
part in motivic development and all five can appear doing so in a
single passage. Following Mozart rather than Haydn, Hoffmeister
used more tonal contrast and distant keys, more dynamic contrast,
more variety of styles within a passage or movement, as well as
more equality of instrumentation.

There were numerous composers of the new, classical string
quintets, some of whom, like Boccherini and Cambini, wrote
quintets before the 1780's but eventually altered their styles to conform with the new style. A list of these composers includes Brandl,
Förster, Pichl, the brothers Wranitzky, Krommer, Johann Friedrich
Peter,[82] as well as Pleyel and Hoffmeister, but the greatest of them
all is, of course, Mozart. Mozart's last four quintets were the result
of the development of the quintet through Hoffmeister and
Mozart's own special genius. Each of these late quintets is distinct
in style, theme structure and color. Each carries the weight to the
finale. They differ from his string quartets in their greater dimensions, which are evident already in the first two quintets. All six of
Mozart's quintets are of necessity of greater size through the length

---

[82] 1746-1813, whose 1789 collection of six string quintets may be the earliest examples of
chamber music composed in America (Sieber, p. 62).

of themes, through the use of counterthemes in all instruments, and through the enlargement of codas in the first and fourth movements. The violas and cello work with the themes, in addition to the two violins, which creates wonderful contrast with the violins but also causes the movements to last longer. While all this is present in the first two string quintets, Mozart expands on the clarity and the balance of these factors in the last four. All five instruments participate fully in numerous contrapuntal passages contrasting contrapuntal method, the number of voices, and the grouping of the voices (for example the first violin and viola in parallel sixths in stretto with the second violin and viola which are themselves in parallel sixths). These contrapuntal passages, in turn, are in contrast to various homophonic passages of three, four or five voices, to concertant passages where one instrument has elaborate figures which the other instruments accompany, or to passages of broken-up melodies (such as at the opening of K.515). Principal motives or just accompanimental ideas are transferred from one movement to the next, transformed in tempo or color but clear enough so that the unity of the whole composition is easily perceived (for example the main theme of the first movement of K.614 recurs transformed as second theme in that movement and as opening theme of the last movement[83]). Individual features mark each quintet, such as the slow introduction to the first movement of K.593 which recurs at the end of the movement as well,[84] or the lopsided rhythm and somber G-Minor tonality of the "menuetto" of K.516 which shatters the idea of a dance and produces, instead, a dynamic and intense drama that foreshadows Beethoven's Opus 95 string quartet in character and all of Beethoven's somber scherzi as well. Mozart worked within the overall classical Viennese forms for his late quintets and concentrated on elaborating and perfecting these forms rather than, as in Beethoven's case, altering them to suit a more urgent need (for drama). By adding a fifth voice and fully realizing the potentialities and consequences of this act within the context of the four-movement chamber string work, Mozart perfected the genre to a level where there was no

---

[83]Hans Mersmann, *Die Kammermusik des xvii. und xviii. Jahrhunderts bis zu Haydn und Mozart*, vol. I (Leipzig: Breitkopf und Härtel, 1933), p. 321.

[84]Sieber, p. 61, points out previous instances of this in Boccherini's quintets.

more room for others to grow. Growth had to come in other directions, such as that taken by Beethoven in his quartets and Schubert by a change of instruments in his "Trout" Quintet.

While Mozart's string quintets are the highest achievements of the genre, other less gifted composers at the time and shortly thereafter produced a huge quantity of quintets that satisfied a large appetite for such works among the dilettanti. The Italian composers Boccherini, Cambini, Brunetti and others wrote many quintets for their Spanish and French audiences before 1780 and continued to do so after 1780. The Austrians and Germans, on the other hand, were not so prolific, though they, too, found a ready group of performers and audiences. There is some variety in the scoring of the quintets. Boccherini, as we observed in the last chapter, wrote mostly quintets for two violins, viola and two cellos so that he could play along with the Font Quartet. After he left the court of Don Luis and encountered Mozart's masterpieces, however, he switched to the same scoring as Mozart's. Anton Wranitzky (1761-1819), on the other hand, although a pupil of Mozart, chose a unique scoring that distinguished his quintets from those of all others: he wrote for violin, two violas and two cellos. The majority of composers, however, followed Mozart's example.

Boccherini, the most prolific composer of the string quintet and next to Mozart and Schubert the best, concentrated most of his artistic talent on this genre. He combined various elements from different genres and styles into the quintet and whipped them together with his own special genius into his own brand of quintet. There are elements of Italian lyric melody, Spanish rhythm, French string writing, and German forms. To them he added his own taste for refined string colors, contrasting textures, and flowing melody. He often used slow introductions to movements, which are rare in German and Austrian quintets. The change of scoring in Opus 39 (1787) to two violins, viola, cello and bass shifts their respective roles.

> The upper four voices—particularly the first violin and the cello—carry all of the thematic activity. The double bass provides harmonic support and does not participate thematically in the music. Nevertheless, it is

treated as an independent voice, and its bass line—in many passages the only bass support—is indispensable to the ensemble.[85]

In his last twelve quintets, written during the 1790's and published in 1801-1802 (Opus 60 and 62), Boccherini followed Mozart's scoring, but the cello is rarely anything other than a bass line underscoring the harmony. The other four instruments do share the material. Boccherini used orchestral effects here, such as tremolos and double stops in the middle instruments.

Brunetti's quintets fall mostly in a pre-classical style and have been discussed in the previous chapter. Cambini's 110 late string quintets, written for Armand Séguier after 1794, are mostly in three movements and thereby reflect the French form of Cambini and others. They utilize motivic development and rich imitative counterpoint, however, which places them closer to the Austrian quintets than to Boccherini's. Cambini's blending of the Italian concertant style with the French form and Austrian method of motivic development gives his quintets their unique sound. Their huge number, in turn, reflects their popularity at the home of Mr. Séguier, but their origins in the private taste of one patron did not allow them to become influential in the chamber music market in general.

Austrian and German quintets were at first less influenced by the Italian-French concertant style than by their own divertimento and the newly developing classical styles of Mozart and Haydn. By the end of the 18th century, however, new ideas were about to change the quintet as they had the quartet. While many of the quintets at the turn of the century were in four movements, some composers reverted to the three-movement form (for example Carl Ditters von Dittersdorf [1739-1799] and Johann Brandl [1760-1837]) or more than four-movement divertimento (for example Anton Wranitzky in a few of his quintets). In general the quintet composers were, by the 1790's, masters of motivic development

---

[85]Ellen Amsterdam, "The String Quintets of Luigi Boccherini" (University of California Ph.D. dissertation, 1968), p. 70.

and modulation. Although he was certainly a master of these, Beethoven's only real quintet, Opus 29 (1800-1801), is not a good example of the quintet of the time. It is orchestrally conceived, like so many quintets ca. 1800, with tremolos, octave doublings, and separation of the middle and lowest voices; his other two quintets are arrangements (Opus 104 as a transcription of the piano trio Opus 1 no. 3 and Opus 4 as a transcription of the wind octet Opus 103).

Schubert was more successful than Beethoven in his one string quintet because his profuse melodic style, as opposed to Beethoven's style of motivic fragmentation, was more suited to the larger dimensions of the quintet. Schubert needed a synthesis between chamber and symphonic music which he seemingly suppressed in his quartets.[86] In the quartets, especially the late ones of the 1820's, there is a dichotomy between melody-group and rhythmic-group instruments. In the quintet in C, Opus 163 (D.956), which Schubert wrote at the very end of his short life, this dichotomy became a basic principle in all but the scherzo, and the larger format of the five-voice piece enabled the contrast of these sound groups more room to develop and interact. This contrast was carried out in D.956 as a psychological exploration by Schubert into the relationship of structure and scoring[87] and is quite distinct from the dramatic motivation of Beethoven's chamber music. Schubert has been criticized for the gangly forms of his late quartet and quintet movements, especially the last movements, because critics have looked for the compact development of tiny motives so characteristic of classical thinking, but Schubert's 1828 quintet was no longer classical; it is romantic in its gentle treatment of the long, flowing melody as it moves from one instrument to another.

The last important writer of classical string quintets was Franz Krommer (1759-1831), whose twenty-four examples were written from before 1797 to after 1816. His quintets are mostly in four movements, sometimes in five, with frequent reuse of materials from an earlier movement in a later one. Most slow movements are

---

[86]Anna Amalie Abert, "Rhythmus und Klang in Schuberts Streichquintett," in Heinrich Hüschen, ed., *Festschrift Karl Gustav Fellerer zum sechzigsten Geburtstag am 7. Juli 1962* (Regensburg: Gustav Bosse, 1962), pp. 1-11.

[87]Peter Gülke, "In What Respect a Quintet? On the Disposition of Instruments in the String Quintet D956," in Badura-Skoda and Branscombe, *Schubert Studies*, pp. 173-185.

variations over a repeated bass. His use of a variety of tonal areas in the course of a piece is reminiscent of his contemporary Beethoven. These quintets move away from Mozart's ideal of equality of instrumentation and toward a virtuosic, brilliant first violin, with the second violin and second viola almost totally limited to accompaniment. The brilliant quintet was cultivated not only by Krommer but also by Adalbert Gyrowetz (1763-1850) and Peter Haensel (1770-1831) in Austria and outside Austria by Ferdinand Ries (1784-1838), Franz Xaver Gebel (1787-1843), Friedrich Ernst Fesca (1789-1826), Louis Spohr, and others.

THE PIANO TRIO

The popularity of the sonata for keyboard accompanied by violin and cello increased during the last two decades of the 18th century and into the 19th. While Mozart changed the relationship of the instruments so that the violin and cello were as important as the keyboard—thus creating the piano trio as we understand it, nearly all other composers before 1800 retained the older relationship. Even Haydn did so, though he alone (apart from Mozart) regarded this sonata as an important medium for harmonic, tonal, and formal experimentation. The reason for such popularity of the accompanied sonata was primarily the fact of who was playing them. In London and Vienna amateurs—mostly women—learned the piano rather well, while amateur string players were not as good. This was a sexist phenomenon in bourgeois homes, since the violin, flute and cello were exclusively instruments for men and men were too busy at other affairs than music to learn these instruments well. So the keyboard continued to dominate.

The importance of the accompanied sonata in London and Vienna was owing to the peculiar situation of society in those cities. Both were large, important European capitals with a cosmopolitan population and a long tradition of instrumental music. But there were differences as well. London was a mercantile city whose royalty was not the primary patrons of music; the aristocracy and numerous upper middle class patrons lived in the city year round and were available for concerts the entire time. A sizable group of top professional musicians kept these concerts going, while the overwhelming majority of amateur musicians were mediocre. Vienna, on the other hand, was a city run by an autocratic monarch who controlled most of the public musical entertainments, and the aristocracy, which were the chief patrons of music, lived in the countryside and spent only part of the year in Vienna. Public concert life was then more attractive in London, and the bourgeois amateurs were adjuncts to the concert life; public concerts were much rarer in Vienna, and the chief music-making took place in aristocratic and bourgeois homes with professionals joining amateurs, who were often quite good.

When Haydn came to London in 1791, then, he found a different kind of audience from that in Vienna. The latter had a small but well-informed public chamber music audience, but "the [broad based] London musical public of the late eighteenth century was guided more by enthusiasm or a desire for social advancement than by knowledge and sophistication."[88] Not only the concert life flourished; there were fourteen publishing houses in London during the 1790's and there were many opportunities for a musician to make a living which became increasingly difficult elsewhere as wars spread throughout the continent. Thus London was filled with foreign composers and their music, and since the accomplished lady pianists of London were purchasing huge quantities of music for piano accompanied by their less accomplished husbands, fathers, sons and brothers, a large number of sonatas for piano with violin and cello accompaniment were published there.[89]

Besides Haydn, who wrote all but three of his late trios for London, there was Clementi, Cramer, Gyrowetz, Kozeluch, Pleyel, Dussek, and a host of others.[90] In a few of their trios the violin has some independence, but the cello is always subservient and the piano always dominates. The only exception to this and the only composer who seems to have been influenced by Mozart's bal-

[88]Howard Lee Irving, "The Piano Trio in London from 1791 to 1800" (Louisiana State University Ph.D. dissertation, 1980), p. 4.

[89]Gyrowetz (trl. Irving, p. 95) described the scene: "The girls are mostly musical and either well versed in the piano or in singing, and know how to spend their evenings very pleasantly in this way. The men, however, are slightly or not at all musical, but they love to listen to music."

[90]Irving, pp. 76ff., lists thirteen others whose trios were published in London in the 1790's.

ancing of the instruments was Johann Franz Xavier Sterkel (1750-1817) whose three Opus 30 sonatas have the cello and violin in concertant with the piano. Most of the accompanied sonatas were in three movements (usually fast [sonata]-slow-fast [rondo or sonata]), nearly all the others in two.[91] There was one programmatic trio, *Cape Saint Vincent/ a Grand Sonata/ for the Piano Forte/ with Accompaniments for a Violin and Violoncello/ Expressive of the Glorious Naval Victory Obtained over/ the Spanish Fleet on the 14th of Feb. 1797* (Opus 8) by Matthew Peter King (1773-1823). It commemorates a battle that took place near Cape St. Vincent off the southwest coast of Portugal and is in six movements: Introduction, Night, Daybreak, Action, Dismay of the Enemy, and Novale Finale; King provided a prose description of the events in each movement.[92]

During the 1780's there were a great many piano trios written by Viennese composers and most of these were dedicated to women since there were a great many fine women amateur pianists there then.[93] The growth of the bourgeoisie meant the growth of music for it. Most of the same composers whom we find publishing trios in London were also doing so in Vienna. Kozeluch was the most important piano teacher for the Viennese amateur and also one of the most important composers of piano trios there. Others in Vienna were Hoffmeister, Mozart and Vanhal, while those in the Viennese orbit but not in Vienna were Haydn, Clementi, Pleyel and Sterkel. The popular trios were praised in the periodicals of the time for their beauty and easy performance by amateurs, though some critics bucked the trend and found these works too superficial and repetitive. Haydn's late piano trios do not fit into this mold since they were written for the professional ensembles in London, and Mozart's trios, also for professional or at least highly talented performers, were written more for his own use than for a public of amateurs.

[91]Only one trio is in four movements: by John Lewis Hoberechts (ca. 1760-ca. 1820); cf. Irving, p. 108.

[92]This bears a striking resemblance to Johann Kuhnau's *Biblical Sonatas*.

[93]Katalin Komlós, "The Viennese Keyboard Trio in the 1780s: Sociological Background and Contemporary Reception," in *Music and Letters*, lxviii (1987), 222-234.

Haydn figured prominently in the development of the keyboard sonata accompanied by violin and cello alongside Schobert, Filtz, F.X. Richter and others. Nearly all of these sonatas were written for home performance, but especially Haydn in his London trios had in mind a public as well as private performance. The piano is brilliant and provides a richness of timbre that equals that of the orchestra. Yet it was Mozart who changed the nature of the accompanied piano sonata and created the piano trio for concert performance, a trio that combines piano brilliance, concertant among all three instruments, intimacy, and the grand manner.

The importance of the piano trio was not just in the intrinsic greatness of these works but also in the fact that the two greatest European composers of the second half of the 18th century and among the greatest of all time included piano trios prominently among their works. Most of their younger contemporaries, however, continued to write sonatas rather than trios well into the 19th century. Johann Nepomuk Hummel (1778-1837), for example, certainly was not one of the great composers of his age, though he was one of the first outstanding concert pianists. As a pupil of Mozart for two years, then of Albrechtsberger and Haydn, he was in an ideal position to know exactly what both Haydn and Mozart were striving for in their new piano trios. His virtuosity on the piano brought him into personal contact with Clementi in London, Baillot in Paris, Beethoven in Vienna, and nearly everyone else of importance in music during his lifetime, and, even though he remained a classicist, he was aware of all the new trends in music that Beethoven and other modernists were promoting. Much of his early chamber music, including three string quartets (before 1804), two string trios (1799 and 1801), and a clarinet quartet (clarinet, violin, viola, and cello, 1808), was written to impress potential patrons and conformed to the most popular types of the time, but after 1808 he wrote no more chamber music without piano. Even though most of his chamber music was published and Hummel tried to make the keyboard part easy for amateurs, it was seemingly written, nonetheless, for his own performances, not for other pianists to perform. When Hummel arrived in Paris in 1825, he scheduled four concerts, on three of which he performed his chamber compositions. For the April 22nd concert he announced his piano trio Opus 83, which had been written in 1819 for a previous tour of England. Whatever the reason, he elicited the help of Baillot on violin and Norblin on cello only a week or so before the concert, which would have been impossible, even for so talented a group of performers, had the piece not been written the way it was: for piano with the accompaniment of violin and cello.[94] Thus Hummel was combining the old, out-dated piano trio of the 1770's with the grand trio of his own day, a synthesis which Beethoven hinted at in his Opus 1 trios but which he rejected by the later ones.

Hummel wrote eight piano trios of which the first (originally entitled "sonata," not "trio," 1792) has an optional scoring of flute or violin, piano or harpsichord and cello[95]; the keyboard totally dominates it. Generally, in the seven mature trios scored for violin, cello and piano, the influence of Mozart on the strong melody line is evident, as well as the cantabile in the independent cello line.[96] All eight trios are in three movements fast-slow-fast. Beginning with the second trio (ca. 1803) Hummel strove to make the roles of the three instruments more equal, but the concert pianist could never completely surrender his leadership. The sixth trio Opus 83 (1819) is strikingly different from the others and shows much more of an influence of Beethoven. It is a brilliant trio with colorful piano. The themes, which in early trios resemble those of Mozart and Haydn, here are long and asymmetrical. The flamboyance of the piano writing led Hummel to striking modulations which correspond to late Beethoven, Berlioz, Chopin and other radicals. Then, having produced this wonderfully romantic trio, Hummel reversed himself in his last two trios: Opus 93 (1821) and 96 (ca. 1822). Much more controlled, he reduced the brilliancy of the piano and once again aimed to equate the roles of the three instruments.

Besides Hummel important trios were written by other contemporaries of his and Beethoven's.[97] Most prominent were Prince

---

[94]Joel Sachs, *Kapellmeister Hummel in England and France* (Detroit: Detroit Monographs in Musicology, 1977), pp. 22-23.

[95]He also wrote an "Adagio, Variations and Rondo" (opus 78, ca. 1818) for flute, cello and piano.

[96]Dieter Zimmerschied, "Die Kammermusik Johann Nepomuk Hummels" (Johannes Gutenberg University of Mainz Ph.D. dissertation, 1966), p. 245.

[97]Catherine Anne Horan, "A Survey of the Piano Trio from 1800 through 1860" (Northwestern University Ph.D. dissertation, 1983), pp. 191-282.

Louis Ferdinand (1772-1837), Ferdinand Ries (1784-1838), George Onslow (1784-1853), Henri Jérôme Bertini (1798-1876), Anton Reicha (1770-1836), Karl Gottlieb Reissiger (1798-1859), and Friedrich Wilhelm Michael Kalkbrenner (1785-1849). Their compositions, like Hummel's, were transitional: partly classical and partly early romantic. Prince Louis Ferdinand and Ries wrote their trios in three movements, whereas Onslow's and early Reicha's are in four. Reicha wrote two sonatas (Opus 47 and 54) where the piano dominates, and later he wrote grand trios (Opus 101 and others) where the instruments are equal. Reissiger wrote twenty-seven piano trios and from the first they are in four movements with all instruments balanced. Some of the trios are grand trios for public display, while most are salon pieces for private or limited public performance.

Beethoven turned to the piano trio early in his career and returned to it again during his mature years. In 1791 he composed his first one, which is in three movements fast (sonata form) - scherzo with trio - rondo and which remained unpublished in his lifetime. Beethoven did publish six piano trios, however, which are among his greatest chamber music.[98] The first set, Opus 1, consisting of three works, was written when Beethoven arrived in Vienna for the second time and was played at a soiree at Prince Lichnowsky's in 1793 before a select audience including Haydn. Haydn had some reservations and other musicians made suggestions, so during 1794 young Beethoven revised them. Beethoven, together with Schuppanzigh, Weiss, Kraft and others, continued to play them at the Prince's regular Friday morning concerts where they obviously had a fine reception. "After the concert, the musicians generally stayed to dine. Here there gathered, in addition, artists and savants without regard to social position."[99] Beethoven called them "grands trios" because they assumed the full, most serious forms of the classical era. All three are in four movements: fast in sonata form - very slow and lyrical - scherzo or minuet with trio - fast sonata form. The second has a slow introduction to the first movement and the third has a theme and variations for the second movement. The huge dimensions of these trios and the virtuosic nature of the

---

[98]The 1812 Brentano trio was not published and is not one of his major works; cf. below.
[99]Thayer, p. 171.

instruments separate them from the much shorter and easier late works of Haydn. The popularity of the pieces resulted in the arrangement of the third as a string quintet (Opus 104) in 1817, which was first performed at a musical entertainment of the Gesellschaft für Musikfreunde in Vienna the next year. Arrangements, rather than new compositions, for a particular ensemble were made when a piece was so popular that a different sized and composed ensemble had to play it. Beethoven frequently did this with his wind music where the right combination of performers was not available after the initial performance.

The two Opus 70 piano trios date from the same time as the Opus 69 cello-piano sonata and the Sixth Symphony (1808). Dedicated to the Countess Erdödy, at whose home Beethoven lived while he wrote them, they were premiered at a Christmas-time concert at her home with a small audience including the musical savant Johann Friedrich Reichardt, and became very popular during the next two decades.[100] The first trio, later called "The Ghost," is in three movements, of the which the second is unique in Beethoven literature with its extreme use of tremolo not as an orchestral filler but as a coloristic device. The second trio is in the conventional four movements but otherwise is not conventional. The first movement opens with a slow, sustained introduction in which the cello enters first, followed by the violin and lastly by the piano; the introduction returns at the end of the movement proper, which is an allegro ma non troppo sonata. The prominent descending scale at the opening returns as countermotives in the fourth movement.

In 1812 Beethoven returned to the piano trio with a short, one-movement composition dedicated to Maximiliane Brentano, whose parents' home Beethoven frequently visited for musical and social events. The girl was studying the piano, and later, when she became Madame Plittersdorf, he also dedicated his Opus 109 piano sonata to her. The movement is designed for a student, much like his Opus 49 "easy piano sonatas," and is one of the composer's rare works that can be designated as Hausmusik.

---

[100]For concerts in 1825 with the opus 70 trios performed by Schuppanzigh, cf. Thayer, pp. 962 and 969.

Beethoven's last piano trio, known as the "Archduke" (Opus 97), was written in a very short three weeks and premiered on Monday noon, April 11, 1814, at the Hotel zum römischen Kaiser. The concert had been arranged by Schuppanzigh as a benefit for a military charity, and Beethoven, who was becoming very deaf, agreed to play the piano part. Though it lacked the greatness of his earlier piano playing, still it had "many traces of the *grand* style of playing. . . ."[101] The trio was played again three weeks later at a morning concert given again by Schuppanzigh. The famous trio is again a grand trio in four movements, but with the scherzo second rather than third. All six published piano trios share a grand conception and were clearly intended by Beethoven for public performance even if most of the public performances took place in the quarters of noble persons.

The last great piano trios of the classical-early romantic era were the two late ones of Schubert coming just after Beethoven's death. Schubert wrote his E♭ trio (Opus 100) in November, 1827, and it was premiered on December 26th of that year at a concert of the Musikverein in Vienna with members of the Schuppanzigh Quartet and Karl Maria von Bocklet as pianist. The B♭ trio (Opus 99) probably was written after the E♭ trio and is a more concise composition.[102] Unlike his quintet and octet, Schubert here resorts to the standard form of the late classical instrumental work. There are four movements: allegro - andante - scherzo with trio - allegro. The first movements are in sonata form; the last movement of Opus 99 is a rondo. The tonal scheme of Opus 99 is B♭ - E♭ - B♭ + E♭ + B♭ - B♭ and that of Opus 100 is slightly more afield with E♭ - C - E♭ + A♭ + E♭ - E♭—all of which is typical of classical compositions though not what Beethoven would have done had he lived another year.

As he did in his 1819 piano quintet (see below), Schubert borrowed the melody of a song for his slow movement in Opus 100: a lost Swedish song. The borrowing of songs for chamber music was not a unique phenomenon of Schubert's, though his lofty treatment of such borrowed songs is unparalleled by any composer. We have

---

[101]Moscheles' account, cited in Thayer, p. 578.

[102]Schubert himself made changes in the fourth movement of Opus 100 in order to shorten it.

already seen that Cambini borrowed French airs for his *quartets d'airs* of the 1780's. Both Haydn and Beethoven made arrangements of English and Scottish songs for voice with the accompaniment of a piano trio. All these, then, prepare us for the piano trios of Kotzebue which are arrangements of Scottish and Irish airs and which were very popular at the turn of the century, and for the use of a borrowed song in Schubert's piano trio.

THE PIANO QUARTET AND QUINTET

Although the piano quartet and quintet were not as common as the other genres of the time, there were important examples and there were some unique situations in which they were performed. Later in the 19th century, when much of the chamber music was written by professional pianists, the piano quartet and piano quintet were as popular as the piano trio and string quartet.

The most famous piano quartets of the 18th century are the two by Mozart written in 1785 and 1786. Mozart was not writing for untalented amateurs or ignorant listeners but for technically and musically accomplished performers and informed persons—a fact that was resented by some at the time but also appreciated by others, such as a writer in a Viennese periodical in 1788.

> A little while ago a quartet of [Mozart] (for keyboard, violin, viola and cello) came out in print. It is very artistically arranged and demands the utmost precision from all four voices, but even with a successful performance, as it appears, [it] can delight only connoisseurs of music in a chamber [atmosphere]. The call, "Mozart has written a new, really special quartet, and this and that Princess and Countess have it and are playing it," gets around quickly, arouses curiosity and leads to the foolishness of producing this original composition in grand noisy concerts and therewith to be heard, *invita Minerva*, in splendor. Many other pieces can survive even a mediocre performance; but this product of Mozart can hardly be listened to when it falls into the hands of mediocre dilettantes and is carelessly performed. . . .[103]

---

[103] *Journal der Moden* (June, 1788), pp. 230-33, cited in Morrow, p. 18 (the original German in appendix). Morrow adds that this view downgrading dilettantism belongs to the 19th century and was not commonly held in the 18th century.

This is evidence of the beginning of a rift between chamber music for dilettantes and chamber music for professionals which will come to the fore in the music of Beethoven. The need for the great musician to express himself in realms not possible by the amateur was felt by Mozart and echoed by the anonymous critic and presaged the aesthetics of the 19th century whereby the musical genius was entitled by God to compose and play music that ordinary mortals could never hope to understand but must, nonetheless, worship as manifestations of the Divine Creator. In fact Mozart had been commissioned by Hoffmeister to write the quartet for publication in a series of volumes of the piano works of Haydn, Mozart, Vanhall and Hoffmeister himself, and since Hoffmeister was apparently primarily interested in sales and the Mozart volume lost money, Hoffmeister refused to publish any more piano quartets. The second of Mozart's piano quartets, published not by Hoffmeister but by Artaria, is somewhat easier to perform and may reflect Mozart's willingness to compromise a little to the abilities and tastes of the dilettantes.

Few followed Mozart in writing piano quartets until later in the 19th century. His pupil Hummel wrote two movements of such a quartet, probably just after 1819,[104] but this work which remained in manuscript at his death was probably unknown to anyone but the composer. Weber's piano quartet in B♭ (1809) was an unimportant youthful work. Prince Louis Ferdinand's two piano quartets were promising works which did not lead anywhere because of the composer's early death. Johann Baptist Cramer wrote two (Opus 28 [1803] and Opus 35 [before 1805]), Dussek one (1804), and Ferdinand Ries three (Opus 13, 17 [1810], and 129 [1826]).

The piano quintet (for piano and string quartet), like the piano quartet, was rare in the 18th century. Boccherini's two piano quintets Opus 56 and 57 came only at the very end (1797-1799). During the first few decades of the 19th century, on the other hand, the piano quintet was more popular and several important composers made important contributions to this genre. Spohr's first piano quintet (1820) was an arrangement of his quintet for piano and winds (flute, clarinet, horn and bassoon) of the same year; his sec-

[104]Zimmerschied, p. 156.

ond piano quintet (1845) was post-Schumann and belongs to the next chapter. Prince Louis Ferdinand wrote two piano quintets. Most of the early 19th-century piano quintets, however, have a slightly different scoring: piano, violin, viola, cello and bass. Dussek's piano quintet Opus 47 (1799) may be the first for this particular scoring, which was then followed by the three piano quintets of Hummel, the two of Johann Baptist Cramer (Opus 60 [before 1817] and Opus 69 [1823]), and one of Ferdinand Ries (Opus 74 [1818]). Hummel's first quintet, Opus 74, published ca. 1816, was an arrangement of his Septet Opus 74 for piano, flute, oboe, horn, viola, cello and bass. The second, Opus 87, published in 1822,[105] was a well-known composition by one of the leading piano virtuosi of the day, and it was performed by Hummel on his tours.[106] The third was another arrangement of a septet (Opus 114) published in 1829. All three piano quintets are in four movements in the classical patterns fast - minuet - slow - fast and fast - slow - minuet - fast.

Hummel's quintet Opus 74 was probably the model for the most important piano quintet of the epoch: Schubert's famous "Trout" Quintet (D.667). Written in 1819 for the amateur cellist Sylvester Paumgartner, Schubert's quintet was premiered in Paumgartner's home in Steyr. The "Trout" is scored for the same instruments as the Hummel (as well as the quintets of Dussek, Cramer and Ries). However, it is in five movements alternating fast and slow; the fourth movement is a set of variations on Schubert's song "Die Forelle" (D.550) which gave its name to the whole chamber work. The first, third and fifth movements are in A Major, the second in F Major and the fourth in D Major; in addition the trio of the third movement scherzo is in D Major. Thus the overall symmetry of fast - slow - fast - slow - fast is reinforced by the tonal symmetry A - F - A + D + A - D - A (an important pattern for Schubert which we will see again in his Octet). Such a classical concept of form is quite different from Beethoven's sense of dramatic form, and as a result Schubert has often been abused by critics for his failure to accept the Beethovenian concept which they have accepted as the only valid one by the early 19th century.

---

[105]The date "1802" on the manuscript is open to question. Cf. Zimmerschmied, pp. 17-18.
[106]Sachs, p. 21.

From Schubert's formal perspective, however, which was built not on Beethoven but on Mozart and Haydn, the logic of such pieces as the "Trout" Quintet is unassailable.

THE SONATA

Sonatas in the Baroque fashion continued to be written through much of the 18th century, and the accompanied keyboard obligato sonata and all its varieties continued to be performed well into the 19th century. Nonetheless, the status of the duo sonata was sinking considerably in proportion as that of the string quartet, string and piano trio, and duet were rising during the last two decades of the 18th century and the first two of the 19th. There were occasions when string or wind players and pianists needed sonatas for specific public or private concerts, but these were clearly minor occasions or the compositions were by inferior composers. There were, however, two very notable exceptions to all of this: Mozart and Beethoven. The greatness of these two inevitably would place their sonatas into prominence, but their sonatas are much more than perfunctory works. They are major contributions to chamber music aesthetically and historically, and they made it possible for the small but significant contribution of later 19th-century duo sonatas.

With the publication in 1778 of his six Opus 1 sonatas (K.301-306 = K.293a-293d, K.300c and K.300l) for harpsichord or pianoforte with the accompaniment of a violin, Mozart established the classical sonata for keyboard and string instrument. Written in Mannheim and Paris in 1778, these sonatas—despite the title—balance the two instruments as equal partners. Mozart's model for this was the six divertimentos *da camera* for harpsichord and violin written ca. 1777 by the Dresden composer and conductor Joseph Schuster (1748-1812), where for the first time after the domination of the keyboard in obligato sonatas the two instruments were restored to parity. To Schuster's idea Mozart added his genius, and the result were six masterpieces. Mozart followed the typical titles of the time, but in effect these sonatas have little in common with the accompanied sonatas by other composers; even the ambiguous designation of "harpsichord or fortepiano" was meaningless since these were clearly scored for piano.[107] Each Opus 1 sonata is distinct but they are all in two movements except for the last which is in three. Mozart experimented with combinations of movements; after a fast first movement in sonata form he tried another fast movement in ternary form, an andante grazioso rondo, a tempo di menuetto sonata, or a theme and variations (in one case using a tempo di menuetto theme). In K.303 the molto allegro first movement is introduced by an adagio. The three-movement K.306 is fast - slow - fast. The first and second movements are in sonata form and the third is a rondo whose rondo theme differs in tempo and meter from the intervening sections. The first movement is unusual in that its recapitulation reverses the order of themes. Thus while Mozart followed the idea of writing six similar pieces in one set, he actually produced six dissimilar works that belong together only because they treat the two instruments on an equal footing.

Mozart's Opus 2 *Six Sonates pour le Clavecin, ou Pianoforte avec l'Acompagnement d'une Violon* (Vienna: Artaria, 1781; K.376-380, 296 = K.374d-374f, 317d, 373a, 296) differ from the preceding in the overall forms and in their dimensions. All the sonatas here are in three movements except K.379, which instead has a very slow, lengthy introduction to the first movement which, if counted separately, would make a third movement. Four of the six were written in Vienna after Mozart moved there in 1781, and the group as a whole is more dramatic than the previous set. The development sections are more intense, visit more different tonalities, and make better use of the principal motives of the exposition. Apparently Mozart wrote some of the sonatas for the violin virtuoso Antonio Brunetti who was a member of the Archbishop of Salzburg's orchestra in the 1770's and 1780's.

Following the two sets of six sonatas each, Mozart began several sonatas for violin and piano without completing them (K.372 and 402-4). Then he wrote four isolated sonatas, which belong to his most mature years and which foreshadow the trend a decade or two later of individualizing pieces rather than lumping six or three together in sets. The first of these, K.454, was written in Vienna in 1784 for the Italian sensation Regine Strinasacchi (1761-1839) and

---

[107]As in so many other publications of the time, Mozart's publisher here—Sieber in Paris—tried to sell more copies by expanding the potential scoring.

was premiered by her on the violin and Mozart on the piano on April 29, 1784, in the Kärntnertortheater in Vienna. In three movements with a largo introduction, K.454 is even larger and more monumental than any of his previous chamber sonatas. A few orchestral effects (crescendos, tremolos) in both violin and piano are intermingled with fast scales, trills and multi-stops to give a brilliant effect to the whole. The next year Mozart wrote his K.481 sonata for the Fürsten von Fürstenberg in Donaueschingen, and in 1787 he composed K.526. Both are still entitled clavier sonatas with the accompaniment of a violin, even though Mozart had gone almost a decade since he abandoned the old accompanied sonata for the duet sonata. Both sonatas are in the three movement pattern established in 1781 as his norm, and both are grand sonatas though without the brilliant virtuosity and orchestral effects of K.454. The final movement of K.526 was written after Mozart learned of Abel's death in London on June 20, 1787, so he incorporated Abel's piano trio Opus 5, no. 5 in this movement. Mozart's last sonata, K.547, differs from the other three in that the first movement is the slow andante cantabile usually reserved for the middle; also different is the piano cadenza that occurs in this movement.

In general there is tighter control of motives in these three sonatas, though at no time is there as powerful a treatment of motives as in the string quartets. There is an affinity among the triadic themes of the three movements of K.481, and the scalar theme of the first movement of K.526 recurs at the opening of the final movement, while the more triadic theme of the second movement recurs in the third movement as a secondary theme. Nonetheless, the duo sonatas of Mozart are classical not in a Haydnesque sense of motivic development but in the equality of instruments, the variety of rhythms and styles within a single movement, and in the use of mature classical forms.

Beside Mozart's great duo sonatas stand those of Beethoven, who wrote ten for piano and violin, five for piano and cello, and one for horn and piano.[108] His first set of violin-piano sonatas (published as Opus 12, 1799) bore the same title as Mozart's: *Tre*

---

[108]Beethoven's sonata for viola and piano, opus 42, is an arrangement of his opus 8 serenade for string trio.

Sonate per il Clavicembalo o Forte-Piano con un violino and, just as in the earlier composer's case, the pieces themselves belie the correctness of the title. The keyboard is clearly piano oriented, and the violin shares importance with the keyboard. There is much in common between the Mozart and Beethoven works. The sonatas, dedicated to his teacher Salieri, are each in three movements fast - slow - fast, with the first movement in sonata form and the third a rondo. The second movement varies. Both instruments are more virtuosic than in Mozart's sonatas since the technical level of piano and violin playing both had increased in the ensuing decade, but they continue the pattern of equal participation that Mozart (and Schuster) established. Beethoven wrote these sonatas for his own use at private concerts together with Schuppanzigh, and together they premiered one of them on March 29, 1798, at a benefit for the singer Josefa Duschek.

The next five sonatas continued the tradition of misrepresentational titles. Opus 23 and 24, originally published separately but then in 1801 as *Deux Sonates pour le Piano Forte avec un Violon* (Vienna: Mollo), are dedicated to M. le Comte Maurice de Fries, one of Beethoven's important patrons and the dedicate also of the Opus 29 quintet and the Seventh Symphony. While Opus 23 retains the customary three-movement form, Opus 24 (the famous "Spring" sonata) is in four movements patterned after the Haydn-Mozart-early Beethoven four-movement string quartets and symphonies. Opus 23 is already considerably enlarged over the Opus 12 sonatas, and the addition of a scherzo between the slow and final rondo movements in Opus 24 makes this sonata of the same dimensions as Beethoven's most important works of the period. The length of melodic and accompanimental phrases, as is expected in new romantic works, far exceeds the length of such phrases in Opus 12 and Mozart's sonatas. Beethoven's dialogue between the piano and violin continues from the general exchange of melodies and accompaniments of Opus 12 to the hocket of the second movement of the a minor sonata (Opus 23) to the pizzicato hocket of the finale of Opus 24.

The three sonatas of Opus 30, dedicated to Tsar Alexander I of Russia in 1802, were written just before the depressed Beethoven entered the spa at Heiligenstadt. Aware of his incurable deafness and the resulting end of his career as a concert artist and his participation as a social human being, Beethoven worked out his future during the next month to be that of humanitarian composer dedicated to the works of God. The seriousness with which Beethoven approached life and music gave a depth of expression to his chamber music as well as to all his composition that has never been equaled and accounts for the unusually high esteem in which he has been held by the most sensitive persons in Western civilization ever since. The Opus 30 sonatas reflect this. The first sonata in A Major and the third in G Major are each in three movements and do not yet evince the crisis that was looming, but the middle sonata in C Minor in four movements is as profound as the third or fifth symphonies. The play of motives, the contrapuntal finesse, the juxtaposition of keys (the second melody of the first movement returns in the recapitulation to an eerie C Major which is shattered by a return to C Minor), lengthy codas, expansion of the piano color downwards, continued hocket in the scherzo, and the rhythmic drive are far beyond the limits of any earlier sonata. The other two sonatas have important things to say, too, especially the third which houses a middle movement in E♭ Major in considerable contrast to the surrounding movements in G Major. The monumentality of these sonatas individualizes them even though they were published as a group.

The last two sonatas of Beethoven stand apart even from those of Opus 30. Opus 47, the famous "Kreutzer" Sonata, was written in 1803 and originally dedicated to the mulatto violinist George A. Polgreen Bridgetower (1779-1860). Bridgetower, born in Dresden, was concertizing in Central Europe and reached Vienna in 1803. Beethoven met him at Prince Lichnowsky's and agreed to help him in his public debut concert, which took place on May 24th at the Artensaal. They played Opus 47 together, Beethoven reading from sketches of the first two movements while Bridgetower was given the completed violin part shortly before. While Beethoven thought his earlier duo sonatas suitable for the small salon; this sonata, on the contrary, was designed from the start for the concert hall. Finally recognizing the inaccurate titles of his earlier works, Beethoven took pains in his sketchbook and in the earliest edition to call this a "Sonata scritta in un stilo molto concertante quasi come d'un concerto."[109] By concertante Beethoven clearly meant that both instruments were equal and shared roles as soloist and accompanist as well as members of a duet. By "concerto" Beethoven meant that the virtuosic level expected of both artists was that of a touring virtuoso playing a concerto. Originally Beethoven used the word "brillante" after the word "stilo" which was just another way of saying that the technical level needed for this piece was that of the traveling virtuoso. It corresponds to the use of the term brilliant in the string trios (see below) and in Spohr's quartets. Bridgetower apparently played the work wonderfully, but before the violinist left Vienna, he and Beethoven quarreled over a girl and Beethoven struck out the dedication. He then dedicated it to Rudolph Kreutzer (1766-1831), whom he met in 1798, and who he thought would be quite capable of rendering justice to its difficulties. According to Berlioz, however, Kreutzer never played it.[110] It is full of multistops, fast passage works, cadenzas, 64th-notes, pizzicatos, trills, and rapid tempo changes during the first two movements, but the finale, written originally for one of the Opus 30 sonatas, is generally simpler though very rapid.

The last violin-piano sonata, Opus 96, was premiered on the evening of December 29, 1812, by the French violinist Pierre Rode and the accomplished dilettante pianist Archduke Rudolph at Prince Lobkowitz's home. They repeated it there on January 7, 1813. It was printed in 1816 in Vienna by S.A. Steiner as *Sonate für Piano-Forte und Violin*, which at last equates the two instruments in the title. It is a much more subdued work than Opus 47, but it is in four movements and has the maturity of tonal development that Beethoven had reached with the pivotal compositions at this time (including the F Minor String Quartet Opus 95 and the Archduke Piano Trio Opus 97). The Scherzo, for example, which is no longer in traditional binary form, begins in G Minor and flirts with E♭ Major; the Trio is in E♭ Major, after which the Scherzo returns, followed by a Coda in G Major.

The cello-piano sonatas are few in number but are among Beethoven's most successful works. He wrote the two Opus 5 so-

---

[109]Cf. Nottebohm, *Zwei Skizzenbücher von Beethoven aus den Jahren 1801 bis 1803*, ed. Paul Mies (Leipzig: 1924), p. 74.

[110]H. Berlioz, *Voyage Musical en Allemagne et Italie* (Paris: 1844), vol. I, p. 261.

natas in 1796 for Pierre Duport (1741-1808), first cellist of King Friedrich Wilhelm II of Prussia (whose interest in the cello has been noted above), and Beethoven and Duport played them at several concerts at the Court in Berlin at this time. Later that year or the beginning of the next Beethoven and his old Bonn friend Bernard Romberg played them in Vienna. In 1799 Beethoven met Domenico Dragonetti, possibly the greatest double bass player in history, and to Beethoven's astonishment Dragonetti performed on the bass the second sonata with the composer in the latter's home. Opus 5 was published as *Deux Grandes Sonates pour le Clavecin ou Piano-Forte avec un Violoncelle obligé* (Vienna: Artaria, 1797), and, as in the case of most of the violin-piano sonatas, the title is somewhat misleading. These sonatas, like the violin ones, are scored for piano and the inclusion of the harpsichord was purely the publisher's device to sell more copies. The role of the cello, however, is more precisely described than is that of the violin; a violoncelle obligé is much more equal with the piano than an accompanimental violin is. Perhaps Beethoven used different terms here because the cello is much more virtuosic in Opus 5 than the violin in Opus 12, 23, 24, and 30. Both Opus 5 sonatas begin with long, slow introductions followed *attaca* by a sonata-form allegro. The grand nature of the pieces is reflected in the very long development sections and codas. Both sonatas end with a fast rondo

In 1807-1808 Beethoven wrote another sonata Opus 69, dedicated to the gifted dilettante cellist and patron Ignaz Baron de Gleichenstein (1778-1828), and premiered in public on March 5, 1809 by the cellist Nikolaus Kraft and the dilettante pianist Baroness von Ertmann at the Akademie for Kraft's benefit concert. It was performed a few years later (1816) in the hall of Zum Römischen Kaiser in Vienna by Czerny and Linke on an all-Beethoven concert.[111] This sonata, coming after the "Kreutzer," leaves no doubt as to the equality of the cello and piano in the title of the first edition: *Grande Sonate pour Pianoforte et Violoncelle* (Leipzig: Breitkopf und Härtel, 1809). Perhaps the German publisher was more aware of what Beethoven had done to the instruments of the sonata than the Austrian publisher Artaria, whose second edition of the sonata later in 1809 reads *Sonata per il*

---

[111]Thayer, p. 641; there was one piece by Romberg on the program.

Clavicembalo con Violoncello. Opus 69 is the only cello sonata by Beethoven that could reasonably be considered in four movements; an opening sonata allegro is followed by a free scherzo which is then followed by an adagio cantabile that flows *attaca* into the allegro vivace finale (sonata form). The sonata is less blatantly virtuosic than the previous two, but it is still difficult. Beethoven's skill in motivic development is evident here.

The last two sonatas Opus 102 were written for Linke in the summer of 1815 after Razumovsky's palace was destroyed and just before he left for Croatia with Gräfin Marie von Erdödy. Beethoven's other publisher Simrock of Bonn and Cologne published them as *Deux Sonates pour le Pianoforté et Violoncell*. Now there is no doubt as to the scoring, and the publishers finally recognized the existence of this new duo sonata genre which Mozart and Beethoven had written before the turn of the century. The first Opus 102 sonata resembles a baroque sonata in its tempo scheme slow - fast -slow - fast, while the second sonata—allegro con brio - adagio con molto - allegro—ends with a fugue. Beethoven often turned to the baroque fugue in his late years (cf. the string quartet Opus 133 and the piano sonata Opus 110) as he groped toward a more dramatic conclusion of cyclic works.

Beside the sonatas of Mozart and Beethoven all other sonatas by their contemporaries pale in comparison. Ferdinand Ries' many sonatas are for piano with optional violin or the accompaniment of a violin. Hummel wrote six sonatas for violin and piano, four of which have optional scorings. The first (1792) is scored for violin or flute and piano or harpsichord; the fourth (ca. 1810) is scored for mandolin or violin and piano or harpsichord; and the fifth and sixth (ca. 1810-1814) are for violin or flute and piano. Clearly with such choices in the scoring the parts in these three sonatas are not idiomatically written; in the first and fifth the balance is weighted toward the piano (a similar situation to Hummel's first piano trio) while in the mandoline/violin sonata the mandoline/violin totally dominates the piano. On the other hand, the sixth flute/violin and piano sonata is Hummel's one truly concertizing sonata and shows in general more ingenuity than the other five. The other two violin-piano sonatas (ca. 1798) and the viola- and cello-piano sonatas (ca. 1798 and 1824) are no different from the first five violin sonatas; they are old fashioned, rather uninteresting pieces, and there is no concertant. Hummel thought in terms of classical patterns—like his piano trios all his sonatas are in three movements fast - slow - fast—and except in the piano parts never seemed to enjoy the fledgling romantic period. The solo instruments are with only one exception accompaniment to the piano in the fashion of the 1760's and 1770's (the dominance of the mandoline/violin in that sonata harks back even further to late baroque sonatas), though Hummel's piano writing reflects his contributions to the new early 19th-century advances in piano technique.

Among other composers of sonatas was Spohr, though they form a relatively small part of his output. Spohr's first wife was a fine harpist, and for her he wrote his first three sonatas for violin and harp (1805-1806). The two had intended to go on tour, performing the sonatas, but Dorette Spohr's pregnancy prevented this.[112] In fall, 1809, however, after the birth of their second child, the Spohr's set out on a concert tour performing the three previous sonatas, a new one, and various other pieces by Louis including his Opus 4 and 15 string quartets. They gave public concerts, for which tickets were sold, in Weimar, Leipzig, Dresden, Bautzen, Breslau, Golgau, Hamburg and Berlin. With large, public audiences in mind, Spohr wrote these sonatas as brilliant virtuoso pieces. Opus 114 differs from the others in that, instead of three movements fast (sonata) - slow - fast, it has two movements: an opening sonata followed by a potpourri of themes from Mozart's *Zauberflöte*, which was a concession to the public that especially enjoyed variations on well-known airs. Indeed, the genre of variations on a popular air (usually from an opera) for piano and string or wind instrument seriously rivaled and even replaced the duo sonata during the classical period even more than variations threatened the traditional string quartet and piano trio. They were written not only by Spohr and lesser composers but by Beethoven himself.

By 1815, then, the avant-garde duo sonata equated the two instruments which shared in themes, motives, secondary material, and accompaniment. The more virtuosic sonatas were called "grande" or "concertante" or "brillante" while the less technically

---

[112]Brown, p. 39.

demanding sonatas were without such rubrics. Mozart and Beethoven set the trends. While Ries and Hummel represented the conservative, old-fashioned sonata of unequal instruments, Schubert's violin-piano sonata (1817) entitled "Duo" equated the roles of the two instruments; they are equal partners, as are the "arpegione" and piano in the one sonata for that combination (1824). In his three sonatinas (1816) Schubert stated that they were "*für Pianoforte mit Begleitung der Violine*" yet they balance the two instruments in a Mozartian manner. They are easier, shorter, but just as beautiful as the *Duo*; two of the *Sonatinas* are in four movements just like the *Duo* (the other is in three). Although Weber's six early *Sonates Progressives* (1810, Opus 13) for violin and piano suggest an amateur performance, they are as difficult as any Mozart sonata and the early Beethoven ones and are attractive works with full participation of both instruments. Weber wrote them when he was desperate for money and figured that the title would appeal to a broad market, but they were not destined to make him anything. He submitted them to the Offenbach (Germany) publisher André who rejected them because

> they were far too good, and must be made more commonplace for sale. I [Weber] declared most positively that I could not write trash, and that I would not.[113]

Clearly the Mozart and Beethoven duo sonatas were of an aesthetic level that they have been held up as models ever since. They have remained in the repertory both of concertizing artists in public chamber music concerts and of dilettante performers in private chamber music or as Hausmusik. Others, such as Spohr, wrote sonatas during this time, and no doubt some of this music is worthy of revival, but the duo sonatas of Mozart and Beethoven remain the essential ones.

In addition to sonatas there were many works for piano and one solo instrument written during this time that belong to the category of chamber music. For example, there were many duos that are themes with variations (Weber's *Nine Variations on a Norwegian*

---

[113]Weber, in J. Palgrave Simpson, *Carl Maria von Weber: the Life of an Artist*, from the German of his son Baron Max Maria von Weber (London: Chapman and Hall, 1865), vol. I, p. 174.

Air for violin and piano [1808] and *Seven Variations on a Theme from Silvana* for clarinet and piano [1811], Hummel's variations for cello and piano [ca. 1810-1814], etc.) which are of a higher artistic level than the "trash" for Hausmusik consumption which Weber abhorred (see quotation above). Other duos have such titles as "Fantasy" (Schubert's for violin and piano D.934 [1827]), "Rondo" (Hummel's *Rondo Brillant* for violin an piano [1834], Schubert's *Rondo Brillant* for violin and piano D.895 [1826]), "Divertimento" (Weber's *Divertimento assai Facile* for guitar and piano [1816], Hummel's *Amusement in F* for violin and piano [1825]), and so on. When such music is in more than one movement, it resembles the sonata even if it lacks a movement in sonata form (particularly in rondos and variations). When it is in only one movement, however, then the fine line between "encore" or purely "virtuoso" function and chamber music becomes blurred, as discussed in Chapter I. The proliferation of "encore" and "virtuoso" pieces during the 19th century was so great that it is necessary to distinguish between them and the "character piece," which maintained the highest level of artistic integrity and thus was part of the history of chamber music. Once we move into the 20th century, when many sonatas were written in one movement and without sonata form, the distinction between popular pieces (encores and virtuoso works) and serious art works (sonatas and character pieces) is vital for the determination of the historic course of chamber music.

THE STRING TRIO[114]

The pre-classical string trio emerged as distinct from the trio sonata during the middle of the 18th century, and during the late part of that century and the first twenty-five years of the next, the string trio was a very popular genre of chamber music. By the 1770's there were changes in the string trio that led to several new types. Among these changes were that the top voice no longer dominates, there is no more figured bass, the scoring is completely solo (as distinct from the confusion surrounding the orchestral trio and optional orchestral and chamber performance), the scoring is

---

[114]This discussion of the string trio is a summary of Unverricht.

for specific instruments without optional substitutions, the melodic material is broken into motives with periodization, the melodic rhythm slows down, the first movement is regularly in sonata form, minuets virtually disappear except in South German trios, and the Italians establish a three-movement norm of allegro - andante - allegro (presto rondo).

Most trios published from the 1770's to the early 1800's are for two violins and cello, but the scoring for violin, viola and cello remained a viable option. The majority of Italians writing trios continued to live abroad, mostly in France and England, less so in Germany, Spain and Russia, and with their peregrinations the Italians spread their type of three-movement string trio throughout Europe. The South Germans, Austrians and Bohemians had their own version of the string trio in the 1770's and 1780's, and the French developed theirs, yet the Italian trio influenced them all and united them. In the 1790's and thereafter the structure and overall style of the string trio underwent further changes as chamber music in general turned to romanticism.

Four types of string trio develop during the period from the 1770's to the early 19th century: the grand trio, the concertant trio, the brilliant trio, and the Hausmusik-trio. The similarities and differences among these four are a microcosm of the new antitheses of musical aesthetics of the 19th century.

The grand string trio developed from the serenade and notturno of the 1760's and 1770's in South Germany and Austria. All serenade and notturno trios of this time have more than four movements. Basically they are written by minor composers such as Ivanschiz, Dorsch, Kirmayr, Holzbogen, Sperger, and Polz. But when Mozart wrote one in 1788—a very powerful example, the type was legitimatized and developed further. Mozart seems not to have had occasion to write a string trio until his late *Divertimento in E♭* (K.563). It resembles other divertimenti of the second half of the 18th century in its multi-movement structure: six movements, of which one is a minuet with one trio and another is a minuet with two trios. But two movements are in sonata form and another is a rondo, and whereas the movements of most pre-classical divertimenti are in the same key or perhaps one other, Mozart has continual contrast of tonic, dominant and subdominant keys.

This trio was unique, and young Beethoven immediately saw in it ideas for his own trios. Beethoven entitled his string trio Opus 3 *Gran Trio* (published in 1796), but the work is modelled on Mozart's: it is in six movements, and except for its grandiose, pathetic nature is as much a serenade as Mozart's K.563. The Gran Trio, a term Beethoven may have invented, is apparently used to distinguish it from the lighter serenade, which Beethoven himself wrote the same year as Opus 8 for violin, viola, and cello and as Opus 25 for flute, violin and viola. Opus 8 is in eleven short movements, some of which recur, and although the parts are virtuosic, nothing is so serious as in Opus 3. The opening movement, for example, is a simple march, not a profound sonata form. Opus 25 is in seven movements and opens with an "entrata," a small, gay dance-like piece with an eight-measure "trio" in the middle. Two years before, however, Beethoven had written what was much later published as the trio Opus 87 for two oboes and English horn which is a much weightier composition in four movements and deserves the title grand trio, and upon completing his Opus 3 trio Beethoven then wrote three more, published as Opus 9, which also fit the mold that the grand trio was establishing. The principal difference between the Opus 87 and Opus 9 trios on the one hand and the Opus 3 trio on the other is not seriousness of purpose (they all have that) but in the overall structure; Beethoven settles on the four-movement form of the symphony and string quartet for these trios and thereby raises them above the diversionary role of the serenade to the high art level of the symphony and quartet.

Immediately all the lesser composers in Vienna copied Beethoven, and soon afterwards composers throughout Europe. But unlike Beethoven's early examples, the others adopted the three-movement form advanced a generation before by the Italians—a few two- and four-movement exceptions aside. As for the serenades and notturni of others in the early 19th century, they differed from the grand trios in that they retain the multi-movement structure of the 18th-century examples and are not as ponderous as the grand trios.

The second type of trio was the French concertant trio, which since the 1780's shared with the concertant quartet a predilection for two movements and the exchange of themes among the three instruments. While the parity among the instruments suggests the ideal trio sonata as described by German theorists rather than the string trio (see last chapter), this parity did not come about through polyphony. Each instrument has a moment when it is the soloist and the others accompany. The moments are longer than in the dialogue trios. This type originated in France and remained popular there (Cambini was the most important and prolific composer but was surrounded by many others), while the grand trio is initially Austrian. It is the period 1780 to 1800 when most concertant trios were written, but examples occurred throughout the 19th century. The idea of concertant, however, influenced other types of trios as well as quartets, such as Mozart's K.563.

The concertant trio differs from the grand trio not only in the number of movements but also in the intent. The grand trio is pretentious, while the concertant trio is not. This is a distinction, however, that comes from Beethoven; the earlier serenade and notturno trios were as light as other divertimenti, and all these trios before Mozart were intended for professional or amateur performance as background music. The other two trio types—*brillant* and *Hausmusik*—are much more divergent in intent. The former is a vehicle for the virtuoso, while the latter is played by amateurs at home or is used by teachers to train their not-always-so-gifted students.

The brillant trio supplanted the concertant trio as the most popular string trio in France after the beginning of the 19th century. In the concertant trio one instrument at a time has virtuosic passages while the other two instruments accompany; in the brillante trio the first violinist always has the virtuosic passages and the other two always accompany. France's leading violinists took over the trio as a vehicle for their excessive technique, and no amateur violinist could keep up with these professionals. Rudolph Kreutzer was the first to use the term "brillant" in string music ca. 1800 with his *Trois Trios Brillans pour deux Violons et Basse*, and although his colleague Baillot also wrote such trios, he did not actually use the word. Baillot also followed Cambini (*Six Trios d'Airs choisis Variés* [1782]) in the publication of arrangements of airs with variations for string trio (e.g., *Deux Airs Variés pour le Violon avec Accompagnement de Second Violin et Basse* [Paris: ca. 1804]), but while Cambini's are each in two movements and, as cyclic and more equal in scoring, can therefore be considered as part of the string trio tradition, Baillot's are one-movement pieces in the nature of encore pieces (therefore not within the scope of what we consider chamber music). The brillant trio is generally in three movements with the first in sonata form (fast - slow - fast) while the concertant trio is generally in two movements, with the first either in binary or sonata form.

Although it was very popular in France where Kreutzer, Baillot and Rode triumphed on the violin, the Germans rejected this type of trio because they considered it empty display of virtuosity. Indeed the brillant trio resembles the three-movement violin concerto of the time more than the grand trio of Beethoven. But not only violinists in France wrote such trios; cellists such as the renowned Bernard Romberg (ca. 1800) wrote brillant trios for cello accompanied by other instruments (violin, viola, bass, another cello). A large number of wind composers also wrote brillant trios (see below). Some composers such as Robert Lindly ca. 1820 wrote brillant trios but avoided the term in order to try to appeal to the generally hostile Germans.

Clearly the brillant as well as the grand trio was too difficult for amateur performers. Already in the 18th century composers saw the need to write trios for amateurs and students who could not handle the more difficult trios. J. Vanhal, for example, as early as ca. 1785, wrote *Six Favorite Sonatas for two Violins and a Violoncello with a Thorough Bass for the Harpsichord Expressly Composed for the Use of his own Scholars*. Some of these trios were purely exercises, while others served both as exercises and home entertainment. They bore the titles *trios faciles, trios progressives, trios élémentaires.*

Many collections of trios appeared by 1820, but their function changed importantly during the first few decades of the 19th century. Originally the Hausmusik trios were written for their own sake or for the student's preparation in eventually playing the grand or brillant trio. Soon, however, the Hausmusik trios were thought of solely as a student's preparation for eventually playing string quartets. Once the string quartet reached its supreme position in the hierarchy of chamber music, as this clearly shows, all other types of chamber music were valued in-so-far as they related to the string quartet. Very suddenly in the 1820's the production of string trios—whether of the Hausmusik, grand or brillant types—nearly ceased. While Beethoven, Schubert, and the great French virtuosi of the early 19th century wrote string trios, after 1830 and for the rest of the 19th century few great composers turned to this genre and preferred, instead, the piano trio. Some felt at the time that string trios were unsuited to large concert halls and belonged, instead, to small salons where the smaller audience would be educated to understand them.[115] Trios that were written were by unknowns, even hacks, who continued to produce trite pedagogic works. While it was not able to survive aesthetically at this time, the string trio could look back to a 75-year history with not only historical importance but some very great compositions.

THE STRING DUO

As was shown in Chapter IV, the string duet differs from most other chamber music in its function. Since the 16th century duets were mostly performed in private by amateurs or by students with their teachers. The pedagogic purpose was the most important, and although there were some serious duets written, most were aesthetically trivial. After 1780 there is a flourishing of duet composition serving much the same function, but also with a difference.[116] Publishers, such as Hoffmeister and Pleyel, published many sets of duets in order to make money; they saw a substantial market in the amateur string players of Paris, London, Amsterdam, Vienna and elsewhere in Europe. Pleyel, the excellent pupil of Haydn, wrote many of his own duets for this market, and Hoffmeister, himself an amateur, did likewise.[117] Their duets were relatively simple, often graded. Other composers of duets, such as Adalbert Gyrowetz and Jan Kleczynski, were resident violinists at courts, in the homes of the wealthy, and in the thriving music centers of Europe. They earned their living by playing in various private and public orches-

---

[115]Trimpert, p. 276.

[116]Ulrich Mazurowicz, *Das Streichduett in Wien von 1760 bis zum Tode Joseph Haydns* (Tutzing: Hans Schneider, 1982), pp. 102-117.

[117]Hoffmeister moved his publishing firm from Vienna to Leipzig ca. 1800 and there teamed up with Ambrosius Kühnel. In 1814 the firm changed its name to C.F. Peters.

tras and by teaching. For their students they composed duets where the student as first violin would cover the lesson of the day and the teacher as second violin would provide accompaniment (that could exceed the first violin in difficulty). Franz Krommer wrote many duets in which he recognized that the two performers may not be of the same ability, but in his case he gives the first violin the edge; the second violin, however, is not accompaniment but, with less virtuosity, also partakes in the themes and motives. A third type of composer of duets was the traveling virtuoso violinist who composed brilliant duet sonatas where the first violin part had excessive virtuosity to show off the composer-violinist and where the second violin was almost unmitigated accompaniment. Giovanni Mane Jarnowick, for example, was a touring virtuoso whose duets seemed to be concertos for violin with the accompaniment of another string instrument. On only one occasion did he give equality to the two instruments: his *Duo Favorit* for violin and cello, where both instruments are concertant. The accompanying violinist might be the virtuoso's pupil, such as in the case when Spohr played second violin accompaniment to his teacher Franz Eck's virtuosic first violin part on a tour to St. Petersburg in 1802-1803; in this case and in others the second violinist was not second-rate but treated in a traditional teacher-pupil role. Despite these classifications, some violinists did not fit into it. Although Viotti was one of the greatest violinists at the turn of the century, he did not turn to the duet to display his virtuosity. Twice exiled (from revolutionary Paris and from anti-French London) Viotti in his anguish wrote his duets for himself, for artists and amateurs, as Hausmusik.

Just as in the case of the string trio, the string duet was very popular at the end of the 18th and beginning of the 19th century and then virtually disappeared as a serious type of composition. Like the string trio, the string duet became a purely pedagogic piece for composers after 1830, though many of the serious duets from before have continued to be practiced by violinists of all abilities right to the present day. The most prolific composers of string duets during its golden age were Antonio Bartolomeo Bruni (an Italian living in Paris, 147 published duets), Johann Baptist Vanhal (Viennese, seventy-four), Antonin Kammel (a Bohemian living in London, fifty-five), and Ignace Joseph Pleyel (an Austrian living in Paris, forty-nine). Others include Venzeslaus Pichl, an Austrian pupil of Nardini living in Italy (whose fugues for unaccompanied violin are also called "Duos" because there are two lines of music), and Alexander Pössinger, working in Vienna, whose twenty-one surviving duets are all pedagogic. French examples are mostly in two movements, Viennese examples mostly in three. Earlier and easier movements tend to be shorter and in simpler forms, while later and virtuosic movements tend to be longer and in complicated sonata and rondo forms. As in the case of string quartets, there is a tendency as we move into the 19th century to concentrate on the individual duet by making it more substantial in length and difficulty, as opposed to the earlier duet which is published in groups of six.

WIND CHAMBER MUSIC

Chamber music for only wind instruments or including winds flourished during the classical-early romantic period. The history of such music differs somewhat from that of the strings and keyboards, however, since wind players served somewhat different functions from those of the other musicians. Winds were traditionally employed for "outdoor concerts, occasional entertainments, and various festivities such as weddings, visits of high personages, and folk festivals."[118] Marches, divertimenti, Tafelmusik (dinner music) and Harmoniemusik were largely wind genres, not string ones. Mozart, Haydn and even Beethoven still conceived most of their wind music in these terms, though they and many of their contemporaries also enjoyed the combination of a single wind with strings (especially flute quartets). In most such cases the wind instrument was merely a substitute for a violin, though in the quintets for a wind instrument (clarinet) and string quartet the relationship between the wind and the strings was like that in a concerto. In a few cases composers of the time experimented with several winds together with several strings, which culminated in the septet Opus 20 of Beethoven. The combination of piano and winds is high-

---

[118]Ernst Bücken, *Anton Reicha: sein Leben und seine Kompositionen* (Munich: Wolf, 1912), p. 133; cited in Millard M. Laing, "Anton Reicha's Quintets for Flute, Oboe, Clarinet, Horn and Bassoon" (University of Michigan D.E. dissertation, 1952), p. 39.

lighted by two masterworks: Mozart's K.452 (oboe, clarinet, horn, bassoon and piano) and Beethoven's Opus 16.

The possibilities for experimentation with winds were limitless and composers took advantage not only of well-established ensembles but experimented with others as the need arose. Thus there flourished the duets, trios and quintets for winds alone, sonatas, quartets, quintets and on up to octets and nonets for winds and traditional strings, even combinations of winds with unusual strings such as harp and guitar, and various ensembles with piano. A list of such works not only would be endless but is not the purpose of this study. Rather, the general conditions under which such music was written and performed and major stylistic and formal innovations will help give us a better picture of the status of chamber music at the turn of the 19th century.

The duet for two flutes, two oboes, or two bassoons, which was used in the baroque period largely for pedantic purposes or for the private enjoyment of two amateur players, was continued in the late 18th and early 19th centuries. Techniques advanced as the instruments themselves developed (the transverse flute essentially displaced the recorder, new keys and materials were tried), but the types of pieces performed—mostly dance airs, played separately or in suites—continued as before. Also the horn duet, less common before 1780, made an occasional appearance afterwards (as in Mozart's K.487[119]). The clarinet duet, on the other hand, was new in the second half of the 18th century because it was a new instrument and only slowly became accepted by serious composers.

The earliest duets which include clarinets as one of several possible pairs of instruments which could perform them were published in Amsterdam ca. 1715 and were seemingly written for amateurs; only the upper part of the register was used.[120] The earliest duet collection specifically for clarinets is found in an anonymous clarinet method book from Paris in 1765. As in the earlier collection these are single movement dances, but whereas the two

---

[119]David M. Randall, "A Comprehensive Performance Project in Clarinet Literature with an Essay on the Clarinet Duet from *ca.* 1715 to *ca.* 1825 (University of Iowa D.M.A. dissertation, 1970), p. 80, briefly discusses the controversy over the scoring of these duets: for French horn or basset horn.

[120]Randall, pp. 11-15.

instruments are equal in the earlier work, the first clarinet domi-nates[121] in this one and the middle register is used more. Further collections, clearly written for teachers to play with their students or for amateurs, were written by the Englishman William Bates (*Eighteen Duettino's for two Guittars, two French Horns, or two Clarinettes*, London ca. 1768), by the Frenchman Jean Jacques Rousseau ("Airs à deux Clarinettes," ms. 1770), by the German Gaspard Procksch (eight *Recueil*[s] *contenant . . . airs en duo pour deux clarinettes ou deux cors de chasse*, Paris, after 1776), and by others. Increasingly at this time the duets were arrangements of opera pieces, as evinced particularly by Abraham's *Recueil d'ariettes choisés des meilleurs auteurs et de divers operas comiques* (Paris, 1778), or of marches, as in *The Clarinet Instructor* (London, ca. 1780). C.P.E. Bach may have been the first great composer to write a clarinet duet; it was probably written in the 1770's and is in two, binary-form movements: slow - fast.[122]

"After 1780, the number of published clarinet duets increased greatly."[123] Several clarinet virtuosi published vast numbers of duets, such as Michel Yost (1754-1786) who wrote perhaps as many as twenty collections,[124] and Jean-Xavier Lefèvre (1763-1829), pupil of Yost and first professor of clarinet at the Paris Conservatoire, who published ten collections. Yost's first set of six duets consists of six binary-form themes in C Major, each followed by a set of variations. Of the thirty-eight remaining duets, all but one are in two movements; the first movements are always allegro in sonata form, and thirty-five of the final movements are fast rondos (the other three are themes with variations). The middle movement of Opus 2, no. 6 (the only one in three movements) is a romance and is the only duet movement by Yost that is primarily lyrical, not virtuosic. In all Yost duets the two clarinets share fully all the material.

Lefèvre's earliest duets were probably written for himself and his teacher, Yost, and were dedicated to Yost who died at the time

---

[121]The second clarinet is technically just as difficult but the first has all the themes—appropriately enough for a didactic set where the teacher plays the second clarinet.

[122]Randall, p. 34.

[123]Randall, p. 40.

[124]Most were published posthumously and some may be duplications.

of publication (1786). Of his fifty-four duets, forty-two are in two movements and the others in three. All first movements are allegros in sonata form, forty-five last movements are rondos (five others are themes with variations, the four others various forms). The twelve three-movement duets have slow, lyrical middle movements, which show Lefèvre's greater interest in this style than Yost's; the themes, always in the first clarinet, are accompanied by the second clarinet, which frequently goes to the chalumeau register for Alberti bass and other accompanimental figures (the register was avoided by Yost). While Yost's duets are more musical and less banal, Lefèvre's duets have greater balance between lyricism and virtuosity.

Lefèvre, as professor at the Conservatoire from 1785 to 1825, had tremendous influence on clarinet players and music during his own time and for a generation or so afterward. While he was first clarinetist at the Concerts Spirituels from 1787 to 1791 and then at the Opera until 1817, his teaching was his preoccupation and, thus, the duets that he wrote served primarily for his pupils and their student recitals, not for public concerts. Among his pupils was the Finnish clarinetist Bernhard Crusell (1775-1838), who spent most of his career in Stockholm. His two collections of clarinet duets demonstrate a more virtuosic style of the early 19th century than do his teacher's. Joseph Pranzer, a pupil of Haydn, composed his *Trois Duo Concertans pour deux Clarinets* (Paris: Winnen, 1790) as serious, three-movement sonatas with a fine balance between the lyrical and the virtuosic. But these seem to have been the exception; most other clarinet duet collections were pedantic or specifically for Hausmusik, as in the arrangements of Haydn's string quartets (from Opus 9 and 33) published by Sieber ca. 1804, those of Mozart's piano and piano-violin sonatas published ca. 1799, and those of Ignaz Pleyel published over a period of years. Even the famous clarinetist Anton Stadler (for whom Mozart wrote his concerto and quintet) published his duets as *Six Duettinos Progressives* and the prolific Amand-Jean-François-Joseph Vanderhagen (1753-1822) dedicated his huge repertory of clarinet duets to students.

Beethoven, himself, wrote four wind duets, three for clarinet and bassoon and one for two flutes. The former were probably written in his youth in Bonn for dinner music at the court,[125] while the latter was written "for friend Degenharth by L.v. Beethoven August 23rd, 1792, midnight."[126] The clarinet and bassoon are equal in all three duets; the first two are in three movements fast sonata - slow - fast rondo, while the last is in two movements of which the second is a theme and variations.

Less numerous than the duets but still abundant were the wind trios of the late 18th and early 19th centuries. The popularity of the string trio during the last few years of the 18th century and the first few decades of the 19th was equaled by that of the wind trio. The principal difference, however, was that in the string trio two basic scorings predominated (two violins and cello or violin, viola and cello) whereas in the wind trio the variety of scorings was manifold. Trios for three flutes were perhaps the most popular (for example by Rozelli, Devienne, James Hook [1746-1827], Quantz, H. Brenner) and that scoring is found well after the string trio waned after 1830. The possibilities in scoring seem limitless; a few are trios for clarinet, horn and bassoon (Devienne); flute, clarinet and bassoon (Devienne); flute, clarinet and viola; flute, viola and horn; two clarinets and bassoon (Devienne); oboe or clarinet, viola and bassoon; clarinet, violin and viola; two clarinets and viola; two clarinets and horn; three basset horns or two clarinets and bassoon; flute and two horns; two oboes and English horn; two English horns and bassoon; oboe, viola and cello; oboe, horn and bassoon; flute, viola and horn; flute, horn and bass; flute, oboe and trumpet; two horns and bass trombone; two flutes and viola; flute, violin and viola; oboe, viola and cello; three horns; horn and two strings; two horns and bass; etc. Although there were grand trios and pedagogic trios for these scorings, the particular nature of the brillant trio—top instrument accompanied by the other two—set up the possibility of effective mixed scoring (different sonorities of winds and/or strings but not all flutes or all strings). François Devienne (1759-1803), on the other hand, wrote trios for two flutes and bassoon and two clarinets and bassoon where the contrast in sonority was much like that in the baroque trio sonata: two upper parts against the bass. Scorings for three flutes or for three of any in-

---

[125]Thayer, p. 124.

[126]Thayer, p. 122.

strument allowed for trios to be written where all three instruments shared equally in the material and were in counterpoint; this satisfied those demands by the Germans who were unhappy with the French concertant and brillant trios.

The woodwind quartet also occasionally appeared, though not as frequently as the duets and trios. Ernst Haeussler (1761-1837), for example, wrote six *Notturni pour 2 Cors et 2 Bassons* (Leipzig: ca. 1800), of which each is in two movements or sections adagio - fast; the scoring is the same in Johann Wilhelm Hertel's (1727-1789) "Sonata a 4" (undated manuscript), though here there are three movements slow - fast -minuet.[127]

A popular woodwind ensemble in England during the last third of the 18th century was the quintet for two clarinets, two horns, and one bassoon. In general it was considered military music and was in a light, divertimento style, and although it might sometimes have been performed outdoors as band pieces, it was also on occasion performed indoors as chamber music.[128] The most significant composer of this music in England was J.C. Bach, who published a collection of six sinfonias in 1782 (the year of his death) and also wrote four quintets published posthumously in ca. 1794. The sinfonias are each in four movements (fast - slow - minuet or march or grazioso - rondeau or cotillon) while the quintets are in three or two movements; the bassoon is purely accompanimental in the sinfonias whereas it is an equal contrapuntal partner in the quintets. Rockeman and Alters published a similar set of *Six Sonatas . . . as performed in the Militia* (ca. 1763-1776), of which three are in three movements (fast - slow - minuet or fast) and three are in four movements (fast - slow - minuet - fast); and there were other collections such as *Twenty-Four Military Pieces* (ca. 1780-1791) by Joseph Gehot which are single-movement pieces of a very light nature (often dances and marches).

In Germany the traditional quintet for two oboes, two horns and one bassoon (such as the manuscript suite by Telemann in

---

[127]Harry Jean Hedlund, "A Study of Certain Representative Compositions for Woodwind Ensembles, *CA*. 1695-1815" (State University of Iowa Ph.D. dissertation, 1959), pp. 69-70.

[128]Hedlund, p. 21.

eight movements[129]) remained popular through the end of the century and seemingly served the same function as in England. C.P.E. Bach, for example, wrote two marches (Wq.187, ca. 1775) for this ensemble, while the oboist Carlo Besozzi—an oboist in the Dresden orchestra—wrote twenty-four sonatas for two oboes, two horns and bassoon where the oboes dominate. Each of Besozzi's sonatas is in four movements (fast - slow - minuet - fast) but in none did he use sonata form.

The woodwind quintet for flute, oboe, clarinet, horn and bassoon, which has become the most important type of wind group in the 20th century, was only a minor kind of ensemble during the classical and romantic periods. At the beginning of the 19th century there was a short vogue for this combination, especially in Paris and in the works of Reicha. Anton Reicha (1770-1836), who knew Beethoven in Bonn and started his career in Paris 1799-1801, apparently wrote most of his chamber music while living in Vienna (1801-1808) and working with Haydn. When he returned to Paris in 1808, he published a lot of chamber music, but most of this was music composed previously in Vienna. His most important works written in Paris were his twenty-four wind quintets (flute, oboe, clarinet, horn and bassoon), which may be the finest examples of this kind of chamber music. They were written for Joseph Guillou (flute), August-Gustave Vogt (oboe), Jacques-Jules Bouffil (clarinet), Louis-François Dauprat (horn), and Antoine-Nicola Henry (bassoon)—five prominent wind players in Paris at the time, all graduates of the Conservatoire, members of the Opera orchestra and also individually and in smaller groups involved in other Parisian institutions such as the Conservatoire, the Opera comique, and the private Chapel of King Louis XVIII ca. 1808 - ca. 1830. The quintets were written between 1811 and 1818 and "were performed with singular success both at public concerts and private musicales; everyone wished to hear them, and they were the talk of all Paris."[130] The earliest performances were by students and faculty at the Conservatoire, where they continued to be performed into the 1840's when general interest in them had waned. All were published between 1817 and 1824 in France and Germany and thus

---

[129]Hedlund, p. 55.

[130]Reicha, *Autobiography*, in Laing, p. 323, English trl. pp. 65-66.

were available for professionals and amateurs throughout Europe.[131] Reicha had hoped that he had begun a new genre of chamber music that would grow after his death in the same way that the string quartet grew, but it was not until over 120 years that the vogue for woodwind quintets started again both with performing ensembles and composers.

Upon first hearing audiences were excited by the strength of the harmony and the inventiveness in the blending of the five disparate instruments. Reicha was modern in his own day with his "rich harmonization, his juxtaposition of sharply contrasted keys, . . . his original modulations . . . [and his] use of keys related by thirds."[132] He thought he invented the wind quintet, which was quite different from any other type of ensemble. The string quartet and quintet are based on the homogeneity of sound of the members of the ensemble; the piano trio and quartet contrast two different sonorities, each with a pair or more of homogeneous members (the piano has both hands). The woodwind quintet, on the other hand, pits five heterogeneous sonorities against each other, and the challenge is considerably greater as a result.

> The members of the quintet all have different powers of expression, and these powers vary with each successive degree within their ranges. Dynamically the quintet as a body is much more restricted than the string quartet, yet its massed effect can be much greater in power than that of the quartet. . . . It is chamber music in color . . . [B]alance, while possible, is difficult, and a true blend of the entire body is out of the question. Thus Reicha set a difficult problem for himself when he sought to resolve these difficulties.[133]

Reicha achieved a perfect balance among the instruments. Each player plays his/her own instrument idiomatically and with the assurance of a virtuoso, and each instrument retains its identity while blending with the others. "The tone of the horn acts as a cohesive agent."[134] The ideal of string quartet writing, wherein each player

---

[131]Laing, p. 70, refers to a performance in Lisbon in 1823.

[132]Laing, p. 33; cf. Rudolph Felber, "Reicha," in Cobbett, *Cyclopedic Survey of Chamber Music* (London: Oxford University Press, 1929), II, 285.

[133]Laing, pp. 43-44.

[134]Laing, p. 44.

shares in the thematic and accompanimental material (and which Reicha would have learned from his teacher, the aging Haydn), was carried over here into the woodwind quintet.

Beyond the modernity of sonority and harmony, however, each quintet is traditional and classical. Each quintet is in four movements of which the outer two are large and fast and the inner two a slow aria or theme and variation and a fast scherzo or minuet. All but one are fast - slow - scherzo or minuet - fast; the exception (no. 2) reverses the inner movements. The first movement is invariably in sonata form with three or more themes in each theme group; the profuse treatment of theme groups was attacked by Spohr and others as a sign of weak construction and helped lead to the failure of the quintets at repeated performances. Five scherzos stand out because Reicha replaced the normal trio with passacaglias, a sign of academic influences weighing down on the composer-turned-theorist. The finales are either rondos or in sonata form.

Reicha was a master of the classical style, which he learned first hand in Vienna from Haydn, and it was his special mission to transport this style to Paris and during the next decades teach it to younger generations of French composers. He taught both privately and at the Conservatoire, and among his pupils were Dancla, Liszt, Paër, Berlioz, Gounod, and Franck. He also published several treatises on different facets of composition. The woodwind quintets, written while he was teaching, reflect his classical instincts and his rational rather than emotive approach to composition. Since the new romantic age had the reverse priorities, Reicha's chamber music was doomed from the start, though his pupils and wind players made a valiant effort to champion his pieces for a while.

Reich was not the first to write for this combination of instruments. Nikolaus Schmitt (d.ca. 1802) wrote such a quintet, which may have been the earliest, but it is lost. Cambini wrote three *Quintetti concertans* (1797-1799) for the five instruments; "they are brief and very simple making extremely limited use of the possibilities of the instruments."[135] Franz Anton Rösler's (ca. 1750-

---

[135]Laing, p. 45; cf. Udo Sirker, *Die Entwicklung des Bläserquintetts in der ersten Hälfte des 19. Jahrhunderts* (Regensburg: Gustav Bosse, 1968), pp. 24-25.

1792) quintet for five different winds is earlier (written sometime ca. 1773-1789) but for English, not French horn. The nine quintets by Franz Danzi (1763-1826) were published ca. 1822 and probably were written at the same time as Reicha's. "The individual parts are much simpler than Reicha's, and repetitious accompanying figures support solo passages with little attempt at independence of parts."[136] Among Reicha's successors, few tried to write wind quintets and when they did, these were isolated pieces. Henry Brod (1801-1839) wrote two, Onslow wrote one (1852), and the obscure Germans Lindner, Lickl, and Benzon each wrote one; there are no others known until much later.

Combinations of six or more winds together were frequently regarded as *harmonie* music, whose origins we have discussed in the previous chapter. Peter von Winter (1754-1825), for example, wrote two "harmonie" ca. 1800. The first, a nonet for pairs of clarinets, oboes, horns and bassoons with an additional contrabassoon, is in four movements (fast - fast - minuet - fast); the first movement is a combination of a rondo and a theme with five variations (each variation features a different instrument and is followed by the rondo refrain), while movements two and four are also rondos. The other "harmonie" is a sextet for two clarinets, two horns, and two bassoons, also in four movements (fast - minuet - slow - fast). About the same time Hoffmeister wrote an octet "harmonie" (two oboes, two clarinets, two horns and two bassoons),[137] and two sextets: a "Parthia ex Es" (pairs of clarinets, horns and bassoons) and "Variazioni" (same ensemble).

While the Central Europeans cultivated this music in the 18th century, it was popular as well in France, England, The Netherlands and Belgium by the end of the 18th century and during much of the 19th. François Devienne (1759-1803), flute professor at the Conservatory in Paris and first bassoonist of the opera orchestra, wrote among many wind chamber works his twelve suites for from eight to twelve wind instruments, which were popular throughout the Continent and England. Joseph Küffner (1776-1856), beginning in 1811, turned out a massive amount of wind music for

---

[136]Laing, p. 46.

[137]Hedlung, pp. 122-124, suggests that the octet "Harmonie" by an otherwise unknown composer Weilland is actually by Hoffmeister himself.

amateurs, much of it for a large number of solo brass players, and this music was very popular especially in The Netherlands but also in Paris and London as well as in his native Germany.[138] Other composers of such wind music included Pleyel, Louis Emmanuel Jadin (1768-1853), Louis Javault (fl. 1800-1820), F.X. Wolf (fl. end of 18th century), and a host of other early-19th-century, mostly obscure composers.[139]

The greatest of all the composers of wind ensemble music for six or more instruments is Beethoven. While in Bonn, Beethoven often wrote music for the court harmonie band that performed at dinner.[140] Such works as the sextet March (two clarinets, two horns, two bassoons), the *Rondino* (two oboes, two clarinets, two horns and two bassoons) and the octet (called "parthia"[141] and later published as Opus 103; two oboes, two clarinets, two horns and two bassoons[142]) served such a function. The last was advanced for its time in that it is in the standard classical four-movement form; the first players of each pair are equal to each other and share leading motives, while the second players, equal to each other, are accompanimental. All his other larger wind music was also early, but written in Vienna, such as the sextet (published later as Opus 71; two clarinets, two horns, two bassoons) and the trio (1794, published as Opus 87; two oboes and English horn). Both are in the customary four movements; the sextet favors the first clarinet and first oboe while all three instruments are equal in the trio.

Ensembles of one or more winds with strings continued to be written during the classical-early romantic period. The flute quartet, immensely popular earlier in the 18th century and best represented by Mozart's examples, remained a major genre of chamber music (Ferdinand Ries, for example, wrote six such quartets).

---

[138]Frederick Niecks, "Music for Wind Instruments Alone," in *The Monthly Musical Record*, xlviii (1918), p. 124.

[139]Hedlund discusses a number of these and lists others; cf. pp. 125, 147.

[140]Sirker, p. 7.

[141]"Parthia" or "Partia" was apparently another term for "harmonie" (Hedlung, p. 6). There are numerous examples by older contemporaries of Beethoven such as Carl Stamitz (1745-1801), Wilhelm Friedrich Ernst Bach (1759-1845), Wagenseil, and Dittersdorf.

[142]Hummel's "Parthia" (October 27, 1803) was written for the same instruments.

Hummel still allowed for either flute or violin in several piano trios. Other combinations were also common, such as those found in the quintet for flute, oboe, violin, viola and cello of Pleyel (Opus 10) and in the quintet for flute, violin, two violas, and cello of Ries (Opus 107, 1820). The new clarinet began to assume a greater role in works with winds and strings, and once Mozart had written his clarinet quintet, many other composers tried their hand at it, too. Carl Maria von Weber's Clarinet Quintet in B♭ (1815) is one of several works he wrote for the clarinetists Carl and Heinrich Baermann.[143] Prince Louis Ferdinand wrote an octet for clarinet, two horns, two violins, two cellos and piano. Ries included clarinet in his larger chamber music: his sextet Opus 142 (for clarinet, horn, bassoon, bass, piano and either second piano or harp), his septet Opus 25 (1807, for clarinet, two horns, violin, cello, bass and piano), and octet Opus 128 (clarinet, horn, two bassoons, viola, cello, bass and piano). Hummel wrote a clarinet quartet (1808) in four movements, of which the second is unusual in that the parts are notated in different meters.[144] Hoffmeister, too, wrote a clarinet quartet.

In the early 19th century the combination of several winds with several strings was sufficiently popular to entice not only the Hausmusik composers and composers of minor importance but also Spohr, Hummel, Schubert, and Beethoven. Spohr's Nonet for violin, viola, cello, bass, flute, oboe, clarinet, horn and bassoon (1813) uses the same wind complement as Reicha's wind quintet (it pre-dates Reicha by several years) together with the string trio so common at the same time. The following year Spohr also wrote an octet for a much less popular combination of violin, two violas, cello, bass, clarinet and two horns (1814). Both the Octet and the Nonet were written for Tost for his private music parties and were given to him for three years of exclusive use (Tost's similar relationship to Haydn has been discussed above).

---

[143]Wolfgang Sandner, *Die Klarinette bei Carl Maria von Weber*, in *Neue musikgeschichtliche Forschung*, Band 7 (Wiesbaden: Breitkopf & Härtel, 1971).

[144]Zimmerschied, p. 59; the different meters seem like a student prank to confuse the players, since the music could just as well have been written in $\frac{6}{8}$ throughout.

Hummel wrote four major works for the combination of winds, strings and piano. The two quintets (*Sérénade en potpourri* and *Sérénade* no. 2 [both published ca. 1814-1815]) are scored for piano, violin, guitar, clarinet or flute, and bassoon or cello. The septets, on the other hand, have different scoring. The Septet Opus 74 was originally written for piano, flute, oboe, horn, viola, cello and bass and was revised as a piano quintet ca. 1816 (which possibly served as a model for Schubert's famous "Trout" quintet). The other septet, *Septett Militaire* in C Major, Opus 114, had the same fate; it was originally scored for piano, flute, clarinet, trumpet, violin, cello and bass but was revised as a piano quintet in 1829. The use of the trumpet was very rare in chamber music of this time,[145] though in military band music it was common. Thus Hummel was crossing generic boundaries and experimenting with a new sonority.

Schubert's Octet (D.803) was written in February, 1824, and was first performed privately probably that same year in the Vienna lodgings of Count Ferdinand Troyer, a clarinetist for whom Schubert wrote the piece. It received its first public performance by the Schuppanzigh Quartet and assisting artists at the Musikverein in Vienna on April 16, 1827. The Octet is scored for string quartet with bass, clarinet, horn and bassoon. It resembles the old Viennese divertimento in that it is in six movements, the third and fifth of which are minuets with trios. Schubert was once again, as in his "Trout" Quintet, concerned with classical symmetry rather than any dramatic form. The overall form is slow + fast - slow - fast - slow - fast - slow + fast, the balance of which is reinforced by tonal symmetry: F + F - B♭ - F + C + F - C - F + B♭ + F - f + F (the opening two F's correspond to the closing two F's, the third tonality B♭ corresponds to the third last tonality B♭, and the middle alternates regularly F and C).

Beethoven authored three principal works for winds and strings without piano. The oldest was his unremarkable three-movement sextet for two horns and string quartet written ca. 1794 (published much later as Opus 81b). The next work was the *Serenade* for flute, violin and viola (Opus 25) written ca. 1795. It is a relic of the

---

[145]I know of no other example.

old Austrian divertimento in style and form (it is in seven movements, of which the second is a minuet with two trios and the
fourth an andante theme with three variations and a coda). Beethoven wrote his septet (Opus 20), for violin, viola, cello, bass, clarinet, horn and bassoon—the most substantial of his works for
strings and winds—between 1799 and 1800. Like the *Serenade* it
is formally and stylistically a divertimento in six movements, but
the first, introduced by a slow section, is in a grande sonata form
and the finale is a massive rondo march whose mundane theme
clashes with Beethoven's high treatment of it. It was premiered at a
concert which Beethoven directed to benefit the royal Burgtheater
on April 2, 1800. The performers were Schuppanzigh, Schreiber,
Schindlecker, Bär (= Beer, famous clarinetist), Nickel, Matauschek
(bassoonist) and Dietzel.

Chamber music for winds (with or without strings) with piano
has already been mentioned. There were also sonatas for a wind
instrument (clarinet, flute, horn) and piano, where the wind instrument is more or less equal in importance to the piano. Weber's
Grand Duo Concertant for clarinet and piano (1815-1816) is an
example of the brilliant public sonata which is also concertant. On
the other hand, many more sonatas were written for private use and
parallel the situation with violin sonatas or trios.

Beethoven composed four works for winds with piano. Opus
38, which is an arrangement of the septet Opus 20, is scored for
piano, clarinet and cello and was done in 1802-1803 in honor of
Beethoven's physician Dr. Johann Schmidt. The Opus 11 trio, for
the same combination of instruments, is an original setting that was
possibly written for the clarinetist Beer ca. 1798. It is in three
movements of which the last is a set of variations on a tune borrowed from an opera by Joseph Weigl.[146] The third piece for a wind
instrument and piano is the horn sonata (Opus 17), composed for
the horn virtuoso Johann Wenzel Stich and premiered at a concert
by Stich and Beethoven in April, 1800. It was repeated at the royal
Redouten-Saal in Vienna on January 30, 1801 to aid war victims.[147]
The concert was a typical one of the time: each of the two acts be-

---

[146]Thayer, p. 214.
[147]Thayer, p. 270.

gan with a Haydn symphony conducted by Haydn, several vocal pieces, and, on each half, a piece involving horn. The sonata was on the first half. It is in three movements, fast sonata - slow - fast rondo, and the horn is on a completely equal footing with the piano.

Beethoven wrote his quintet for piano, oboe, clarinet, horn and bassoon (Opus 16) in 1796-1797 and it was premiered on April 6, 1797 at a public concert run by Schuppanzigh. Beethoven himself performed the piano part and surprised the wind players by inserting little improvised cadenzas which delighted the audience. He performed the quintet again in 1798 at a Widows and Orphans concert run by Salieri and once more in 1804 on an evening concert at which the "Eroica" Symphony was premiered; on the latter occasion he once again shocked his fellow musicians, including the renowned Munich oboist Friedrich Ramm, by improvising cadenzas.[148] The quintet is in three movements fast sonata - slow - fast rondo; the piano is virtuosic and dominates, but the wind instruments do share motives as well as accompaniment on an equal basis with each other.

In addition to the four works that Beethoven composed for winds and piano, he also arranged sixteen "national airs" for piano and either flute or violin (Opus 105 and 107). These were designed as Hausmusik, since Beethoven was paid handsomely by Thomson in Edinburgh and Preston in London for "variations in a style that is *familiar* and *easy* and a bit brilliant, so that the majority of our ladies may play them and relish them."[149] The pieces stand apart not only because they are designed as Hausmusik (Beethoven rewrote them to completely satisfy Thomson) but also because they are the only chamber music pieces for winds that Beethoven wrote in his maturest years (1818).

Other composers of chamber music for winds with piano include Hummel, whose Opus 74 septet has already been mentioned, and Spohr, who wrote his quintet for piano, flute, clarinet, horn and bassoon (Opus 52) in 1820. Hummel also wrote works for guitar with piano, strings and winds (his Serenades nos. 1 and 2, Opus 63 and 66, ca. 1814-1815) and another septet ("Septett mili-

---

[148]Thayer, pp. 197, 204, 350.
[149]Thayer, p. 716.

taire") including trumpet, piano, flue, clarinet, violin, cello and bass (1829).[150]

Chamber music for brass alone was rare since brass instruments were associated mostly with larger military bands. There were a few exceptions. Reicha wrote twenty-four trios for horns for his student Dauprat, who was one of the best hornists in Paris at the time and from whom Reicha learned a great deal about the technique of the instrument. Written ca. 1810, they served as preliminary studies for Reicha's woodwind quintets.[151] Beethoven's three *Equale* for trombone quartet were written in 1812 while he was visiting his brother in Linz. They were written to fulfill an old Linz tradition where they were used for funerals. One was eventually played at Beethoven's own funeral. Beethoven heard some equales played especially for him at a private home and thereupon sat down and wrote his own. The three pieces are very short, each with only one movement; the first has a little counterpoint but the other two are strictly homophonic.

18TH-CENTURY CHAMBER MUSIC AND THE DAWN OF THE 19TH CENTURY

The development of new forms and idioms for chamber music was parallel to the changing concepts of society and politics during the 18th century. From the 1730's to the 1790's Europe witnessed an intellectual assault on its established stratification of society and on its political order which culminated in the French Revolution. This aimed at the equality of all men regardless of wealth, religion, family background or nationality. Whether or not political or social equality was ever reached during this or the next century, the idea became a dominant one in the thought not only of philosophers but of the common man as well. Music was not unaffected by this process of democratization. In terms of style, the domination of a treble instrument over the subservient continuo accompaniment was replaced, by the end of the 18th century, by equal partners in string quartets, piano trios, string trios, and other forms of chamber

---

[150]The opus 114 septet was, like the opus 74 septet, arranged for piano quintet.

[151]Laing, p. 64-65.

music. Furthermore, by solistic performance of each part, the individual worth of each performer and his/her musical line was carefully nurtured. This democratization of chamber music so transformed composers' thinking about music that chamber music became for some of them and some of their audience the most important vehicle for musical art. Mozart honored Haydn in the finest way he could: by dedicating six string quartets (not symphonies or operas) to the older master. Beethoven's life-long dedication of his art to the betterment of mankind took its most famous form in the finale of the *Ninth Symphony*; this finale was originally the *Grosse Fuge*, for string quartet, which was replaced as the final movement of the *Ninth Symphony* when Beethoven realized that the general public would only understand his call for democracy through sung words rather than abstract fugal equality; trained chamber musicians, on the other hand, did not need the spelling out of this ideal in the famous choral movement to understand what Beethoven himself expressed in the *Grosse Fuge*.

Democratization of chamber music also went hand in hand with the change in the social location of chamber music. At the beginning of the 18th century chamber music was disappearing as a church phenomenon and was largely replaced by concert hall performance and performance in private palaces of the wealthy. The distinction between da camera and da chiesa was no longer relevant by the middle of the 18th century when new types of chamber music emerged that never had a place in the church. But lingering quietly, rarely chronicled, was the private performance of chamber music by amateur as well as professional musicians for their own enjoyment and that of a few close friends and family. This has been observed above in 16th- and 17th-century England and in Germany and Italy in the homes of some famous violinists. While the practice of public and aristocratic performance continued in the 18th century, seeds were sown for the expansion of private chamber music. To fully effect this, as Adorno has shown, a class of educated, musically trained persons was necessary that was unconcerned with class distinctions based on wealth or family background and which provided itself with sufficient leisure for introspection and chamber music. After a tedious day of strenuous public activity, a musician, physician, lawyer, politician, scientist,

teacher or businessman needed time to reflect on the purpose of
life and other non-competitive, intellectual things. This was often
best accomplished by meeting with a small number of other persons who were equally reflective, and the proper mood and setting
for such reflection would be established by playing chamber music
in the private home of one of them. Each member of the chamber
group was of equal importance and had an important contribution
to make. There was competition among the individuals, but not in
the dog-eat-dog variety of the outside capitalistic bourgeois world
where the competition was only the means to acquiring wealth and
power; in chamber music the competition itself (the means) was
enjoyed for its own sake. This democratization of chamber music
replaced an aristocratic chamber music dominated by a single class
and instrument; it was possible once the political and social ideal-
ism of the mid-18th century was accepted by a large enough group
of trained performers and the industrialization of Europe by the
end of the 18th and beginning of the 19th century afforded such
persons the time and conditions for reflection. The danger for
chamber music lay thereafter in the maintenance of some quality in
the playing, since the ability of an ever expanding number of
trained amateurs varied considerably and the new pieces of chamber music by Beethoven and others were too difficult for most. In
the early 19th century this led to the dichotomy between Hausmusik and chamber music. In the 18th century almost any piece of
public chamber music (performed in church or in the larger salons
of the rich) could also be played privately in the musicians' own
homes; there was basically no musical distinction between Hausmusik and chamber music other than the location of the particular
performance. In the 19th century, however, there was a difference;
Hausmusik was chamber music technically and spiritually easy
enough for the lay musician to play in his/her own social milieu.[152]

The change in the personalities who played chamber music
from professionals and aristocrats to average citizens and the
change in the location of performances had a profound effect as
well on the regard in which composers and professional performers

[152]Ludwig Finscher, "Hausmusik und Kammermusik," in *Musica*, xxii (1968), pp. 325-
329, and in Richard Baum and Wolfgang Rhem, eds., *Musik und Verlag: Karl Vötterle
zum 65. Geburtstag am 12. April 1968* (Kassel: Bärenreiter, 1968), pp. 67-76.

of chamber music were held. Aristocrats considered musicians servants, and composers as well as performers were treated as part of the necessary work force to maintain palaces and estates. The middle class chamber performer, however, looked to the professional performer and composer as the perfection of what they, the middle class, strove for but never could quite reach. By late in the 18th century even many aristocrats took this new view. It was not family status which singled out the professional, but a gift from God— a special talent. The new chamber music was increasingly special art, not the background material with which aristocrats usually treated it earlier in the 18th century and as which some still regarded it into the 19th century. Early in the 18th century composers wrote collections of six works, which in the case of inferior composers meant six barely distinguishable works which could be played as background music; this was hack work, handicraft, expected by aristocrats from menial musicians against which the true genius (in our terms) fought and for which he was often criticized by his patrons. By the end of the century composers turned increasingly to single compositions, not sets, since the individual work was now looked to as a potential masterwork by the genius composers. The middle class citizen and those who were part of the new age no longer denigrated the genius's individual and unique works of art but now raised them indeed to the status of masterworks by geniuses.

While this process of urbanization, industrialization, and democratization was occurring in some measure throughout Europe, nowhere did they lead to such cultivation of chamber music as in Central Europe toward the end of the 18th and beginning of the 19th century. There had been several centuries of Hausmusik in the average Central European household, but the emphasis was on vocal music and, by the 18th century, the quality of the music was not comparable to the music written for the theater, the palace or the church. What distinguishes the chamber music of the late 18th century from the Hausmusik of the past was not only the democratization of the players and the music but, because of that, the serious participation of the greatest composers Central Europe had at that time: Haydn, Mozart and Beethoven. While Bach, Vivaldi and Handel each made major contributions to chamber music, this kind of music was not central to their art; for Haydn, Mozart, and Beethoven, on the other hand, chamber music was not only a favored vehicle but, at times, the only vehicle for their art. Thus the development of chamber music takes on a new intensity and a new direction that is socially and aesthetically apart from its past. So intrinsically great is this new chamber music that writers about chamber music from the early 19th century to Ulrich, Adorno and other recent writers cannot conceive of chamber music in any other terms. Chamber music becomes for them exclusively the chamber music of Mozart, Haydn, Beethoven and their heirs (to Brahms and Schoenberg) not only because of the five basic elements of chamber music which we have settled upon but because of the formal and aesthetic criteria of these masters. Composers who did not compose string quartets for two violins, viola and cello or did not employ the scorings presumably preferred by these undisputed geniuses, who did not write sonata-form movements, who did not develop motives in the contrapuntal fashion so highly developed by the Viennese Classics: such composers did not write chamber music even if they, in their own right, were also great composers. Yet apart from these stylistic differences and the rigidification of the solistic, instrumental scoring (primarily string quartets) after 1780, the history of the genre "chamber music" is a continual one from the late 16th to the late 20th century. Particular forms, styles and scorings change during the entire 18th century, but the five fundamental elements of chamber music remain constant and can be seen to evolve. Thus the cleavage between the chamber music prior to the 1780's and from the 1780's on is founded on a too narrow, often self-defeating definition of chamber music.

CHAPTER VI

ROMANTIC CHAMBER MUSIC AFTER BEETHOVEN

The intense activity in chamber music that began in the later 17th century and culminated in the works of Haydn, Mozart and Beethoven was not able to sustain itself in the years immediately following Beethoven's death. There was a growing interest in Hausmusik, where the quality of new compositions was not of the same ilk as that produced before 1827. Weaker composers found a livelihood by supplying simple and amusing but shallow compositions for the masses. The major composers turned instead to opera, symphony, song, and solo piano music for their chief expression, and when a great romantic composer did write chamber music, it was usually as an aside. Both Mendelssohns and both Schumanns, the most important composers of chamber music of the next generation, did enjoy chamber music and wrote important works, but the percentage of their output that is chamber music is small in comparison with that of their predecessors. Not until Brahms, Dvořák, and Debussy made chamber music a central part of their work was the interest in chamber music among great composers thoroughly re-established.

The dichotomy between trivial chamber music for the home (Hausmusik) and great chamber music for the concert stage became ever stronger after Beethoven. Public concerts of chamber music performed by fine professional musicians in front of a relatively small but very devoted audience continued throughout the 19th century, and at times there was chamber music of high quality in private homes. The private concert in the home of nobility, however, ceased to be the center of the development of chamber music as a whole; rather what was new and important was occurring in the homes of the bourgeoisie and on the stage. What was most important for the repertory and history of chamber music, however, was not so much new developments in the principal centers of chamber music of the past (in Italy, France, England, and Germany) but in the dispersion of chamber music to a much wider area of Europe and the New World. European ethnic chamber music, which had some role in some cases before the 19th century, became crucial during the 19th century in such countries as Russia, Bohemia, Spain, Denmark, Norway, and even the United States. This ethnic chamber music involved new compositions with ethnocentric ideas, as well as the cultivation of standard European chamber compositions in the new ethnic surroundings.

HAUSMUSIK BEFORE 1920

During the first half of the 19th century a distinction was made as to the location of chamber music in much the same way that the Baroque distinguished its chamber music by location. Chamber music for public performance in larger halls retained the designation *chamber music* while music performed in "private quarters" was regarded as *Hausmusik* or *salon music*.[1] Although public chamber music often suggested to the composer the chance to show off the virtuosity of the players (*trios* or *quatuors brillants*) and private chamber music often suggested to the composer a much more intellectual treatment of form, harmony, and style, in fact any given piece of chamber music was played one day publicly and the next day privately. This is exactly parallel to the baroque distinction between *da camera* and *da chiesa*, which at first did not determine form or style but only location; later the physical location of the performance did come to bear on the form, style and performance practice of the chamber music; completing the cycle, eventually all types of chamber music were played in the same location.

The private music performances of chamber music were of a variety of situations that eventually led, by the middle 19th cen-

---

[1]Erich Valentin, *Musica Domestica: von Geschichte und Wesen der Hausmusik* (Trossingen: Hohner, 1959) distinguishes between Hausmusik (ensemble music) and salon music (primarily for the piano); he also distinguishes between *Dilettanten* (superficial, non-professional in standards) and *Liebhaber* (concerned with the essence of music and professional standards).

tury, to a variety of styles. Some "private" concerts were held in sizable rooms in a very wealthy middle class or aristocratic palace before a select audience, while other "private" concerts were held in the small living rooms of middle class homes before no audience at all. As long as an audience was present, the performers had to adhere to a degree of technical respectability that was irrelevant when a family of players performed for themselves with no outsiders admitted. As the number of small private concerts (without audience) increased, publishers and hack composers found an increasing buying public for *their* chamber music; since most of these performers were very modestly endowed with musical talent and had minimal musical training, the types of pieces they required had to be easy to perform and easy to understand. The relatively smaller number of large private concerts (with audience) required more dashing music that did not need to be easy to perform and which required more listening skills of the audience. Some of these large private concerts were serious affairs, following in the tradition of Lobkowitz's, Razumovsky's, and the Earl of Abingdon's concerts, where the audience was trained in music, had high expectations of the performers and the music itself, and listened intently to every note. Other large private concerts were basically tea parties where the musicians played background music to an inattentive and uninformed audience.[2] Where the background music of the 18th century, written by the professional composers in the employ of a nobleman (including even Mozart and Haydn), was of a high technical level even if light hearted and not as complicated as more serious genres of music, the background music of the 19th century, written by professional hack composers who had to make a living by selling such music, was increasingly of a low technical level as well as uncomplicated. Thus most of the performance situations for chamber music in the 19th century involved, at best, modestly competent performers and, more often, mediocre beginners. For them the publishing mills turned out an enormous amount of chamber music or Hausmusik.

---

[2] Robert Schumann, *Gesammelte Schriften über Musik und Musiker*, ed. M. Kreisig, 5th ed. (Leipzig: 1914), p. 180, drew this distinction between "aristocratic" salon music and "tea party" salon music; cited in Imogen Fellinger, "Die Begriffe *Salon* und *Salonmusik* in der Musikanschauung des 19. Jahrhunderts," in *Studien zur Trivialmusik des 19. Jahrhunderts*, ed. Carl Dahlhaus (Regensburg: Gustav Bosse, 1967), pp. 132-133.

Nearly every middle class home in 19th century Europe had a piano, which was the center of the musical life of the family. Both boys and girls studied the instrument as a part of becoming well-bred citizens in the new bourgeois society. As they achieved some meager proficiency they began to participate in family music-making, which might occupy an evening or any part of a Saturday or Sunday. In many cases each member of the family would take a turn playing his or her most recently learned piece; often, however, they would play together. Four-handed piano music was very popular. Besides the piano, members of the family played the flute and harp, and the bowed string instruments—no longer as central to musical life as they had been in the 18th century—were none-theless still popular. While the string quartet was respected as the highest level of chamber music, at home the piano trio was at least equally popular since it allowed the ubiquitous pianist an opportunity to participate. From 1830 to 1860 close to two hundred piano trios were written by great or important composers (Mendelssohn, Schumann, Berwald, Marschner), famous performers (Mayseder, Kalkbrenner, Hiller, Anton Rubinstein) and insignificant hacks (Reissiger, Kalliwoda, Litolff, Hopfe, Pixis).[3] The family also sang a great deal, and probably few family music-making sessions took place with only instrumental music.

Family music-making was not only a fine way to pass the time in a society that had not yet discovered the sports palace, the cinema, the phonograph, or the television; it was also a marvelous means for a family to be together as a family, with each member making a contribution to the harmony of the whole. Since strong families make a strong nation, a strong family music-making tradition was encouraged by society as a whole and by political leaders as well. The decline in the German social order after the Franco-Prussian War was attributed, in fact, to a decline in family music-making at the end of the 19th century.[4]

---

[3]Catherine Anne Horan, "A Survey of the Piano Trio from 1800 through 1860" (Northwestern University Ph.D. dissertation, 1983), lists these in volume 2. While most of the piano trios were grand trios which could be played in concert as well as at home, a great many were specifically entitled "leicht" or "facile" and were never intended for anything other than home use.

[4]The idea comes from W.H. Riehl; cf. Walter Salmen, "W.H. Riehls Gedanken zur Gesundung der Hausmusik, "in *Hausmusik*, xvii (1953), pp. 169-170.

The music composed for these gatherings originally was not different from public chamber music. Although Beethoven was not comfortable writing for these family salons, he did manage a few easy pieces. Some of his contemporaries—Hummel, Kotzebue, Pleyel, to name a few—wrote serious public chamber music with the full expectation that it would be played privately as well. While they explored interesting tonalities and were up with the latest concepts of form, they nonetheless kept the technical aspects of playing within reach of the modestly talented dilettante and the musicality of the pieces within their understanding. So also did the composers of purely piano music such as Moscheles and Czerny. Perhaps it is because these were compromising composers, who let passing and fickle popular taste dictate their own taste, that their music has passed into oblivion while the uncompromising Beethoven, who was determined to raise public taste to his own level, wrote music of lasting value.

As the century progressed the serious composer of art music found that the easy music for amateurs was also aesthetically unrewarding (as Weber stated; cf. chapter 5); the simple sentimental melodies and modest development of them in the course of a dilettante piece ran contrary to his/her goals of deep emotional melodies and intricate development of them. The ever-growing number of concert halls and concert opportunities for the virtuoso performer gave more and more people a chance to hear the best of public chamber music, and the great composer had more opportunities away from private homes to hear his/her own art music well performed. At the other end of the spectrum, composers interested in making safe money ignored the perils of the concert stage and turned to the home musician. Hierarchies of music were conceived by mid-century, which rated dance music at the bottom and salon music barely above it. This was catchy music that had lots of glitz but no substance. The average family musician could not tell the difference, except that salon music was pleasing and easy to play and art music incomprehensible and too difficult to play. During the second half of the 19th century the gulf between public chamber music and Hausmusik became not only one of location and style but also one of social distinction; the sensitive and informed romantic musician and music lover who at least listened to and enjoyed public chamber music (even if he/she could not perform it) considered him/herself intellectually, morally, and spiritually above the crass middle class boor who enjoyed and limited him/herself to Hausmusik (salon music).[5]

The actual chamber music performed in the home varied depending on ability, taste, and available instruments. In some homes the classics of Mozart, Haydn and eventually Mendelssohn were performed regularly. In others the music was arrangements of various sources. Some arrangements were of more difficult music simplified for home use; this enabled the family musician to enjoy playing the otherwise too difficult chamber music he/she might hear at a public concert. Other arrangements were made to accommodate different scorings; the common alternative scorings of flute or oboe or violin in 18th-century scores was extended in the 19th to include a much wider variety of possibilities (see below in our discussion of Schumann). Still other arrangements were of vocal pieces, particularly opera arias or choruses and popular folk songs. These were adapted to the modest voices of the family or to a substitute flute or violin (for a soprano), with the orchestral accompaniment arranged for piano with or without other home instruments. Finally during the second half of the 19th century there were arrangements of baroque music made palatable for 19th-century tastes.[6]

ART CHAMBER MUSIC 1825-1850

After the deaths of Beethoven and Schubert the quantity of great art chamber music fell off considerably. As we have seen above, a lot of chamber music was written, but it was intended for beginners or modestly trained amateurs in the home. Hack composers of Hausmusik and the publishers who encouraged them were clearly filling a market need, and almost none of them were interested in advancing the cause of the highest art of music. There

[5]Fellinger, pp. 135-137, traces the change in attitude toward salon music during the 19th century.

[6]Cf. Volker Freywald, *Violinsonaten der Generalbass-Epoche in Bearbeitungen des späten 19. Jahrhunderts*, in *Hamburger Beiträge zur Musikwissenschaft*, Band 10 (Hamburg: Karl Dieter Wagner, 1973).

were, however, three composers who during the first half of the 19th century fought to sustain the tradition passed down to them from Haydn, Mozart and Beethoven: Spohr, Mendelssohn, and Schumann.

Spohr

Spohr (1784-1859), as we saw in the last chapter, began his career early in the 19th century as a traveling virtuoso violinist and composer of concertos. Even though Vienna and London could boast string quartet ensembles of a more or less permanent nature, the quartet performances of Spohr represent the more typical situation during the first four decades of the 19th century. Spohr, it will be recalled, traveled from city to city where he requested from his hosts that a string trio be provided for his accompaniment when he performed not only *quatuors brillants* but even Beethoven string quartets.[7] At the age of 21 he became concertmaster in Gotha (1805-1813), and after brief tenures and tours in Vienna, Italy, Frankfurt, London, Paris and Dresden, he assumed the role of court music director in Kassel in December, 1821, where he remained (with the exception of intermittent tours) until his death. Within a very few weeks of coming to Kassel he had organized a quartet circle which continued to perform every winter season until 1857-1858. Concerts were held in various quarters, including in Spohr's own home and at the home of Otto von der Malsburg, "whose music room was the largest of those in which his quartet circle's meetings took place."[8] Even during one of the bleakest times financially and politically in Kassel, the season 1832-1833, when most concerts and operas had been suspended, there was still considerable chamber music in Kassel; although

> [Moritz] Hauptmann complained that the only opportunity to hear chamber music had been a series of quartet concerts mounted by Wiele and Hasemann [and] that "from the first they gave us an overdose of late Beethoven"[9]

[7]John Horton, *Mendelssohn Chamber Music* (Seattle: University of Washington Press, 1972), p. 6.

[8]Clive Brown, *Louis Spohr: a Critical Biography* (Cambridge: Cambridge University Press, 1984), p. 164; cf. also p. 170.

[9]Brown, p. 223.

it is remarkable enough that such concerts took place at all. There were always good performers available in Kassel in the opera orchestra, some of whom were Spohr's own pupils (like his brother Ferdinand), and they joined Spohr in the chamber music meetings. While Spohr himself led these concerts, he sometimes invited visiting artists to perform the first violin part, such as the young Ole Bull in January, 1839.

Spohr wrote chamber music throughout his life but especially after he settled in Kassel. Nineteen of his thirty-six string quartets were written after he assumed the post in Kassel, as were five of his seven string quintets, six of his fourteen violin duets, all five of his piano trios, his second piano quintet, his sextet, septet and all his double quartets (octets). His harp music falls early in his career since the wife (the first of two) for whom he wrote the music was sickly and finally died in 1834. Spohr wrote his chamber music for various occasions and artists, but he always had in mind highly skilled amateur performers or professionals like himself. Spohr made a point of insisting on the profession of music as worthy of the highest regard, and he strove always to write up to this profession rather than down to an amateurish crowd.

Spohr made major contributions to established genres of chamber music such as the string quartet, piano trio, string quintet, violin duet and piano and wind quintet. Beyond the successful continuation of styles and forms which he had inherited from Haydn, Mozart and Beethoven, Spohr added several new things to chamber music. He established the double quartet as a new genre, and strengthened the repertory of duo concertant with such large scale works as Opus 95, 96 and 112 (1836-1837). In the second of these duos he brought program music into chamber music far in excess of the tentative programs in Beethoven and more in keeping with the works of Kuhnau and King (see last chapter). As he wrote,

> In the first movement I endeavored to describe the love of travel, and in the second the journey itself, by introducing the postillion's horn calls customary in Saxony and the neighboring part of Prussia as the principal idea of the Scherzo, played by the violin on the G string in a horn-like manner, worked out with striking modulations on the piano, and then in the Trio I depicted a daydream such as one so willingly yet unconsciously surrenders to in the carriage! The subsequent Adagio represents a scene in the Catholic court chapel of Dresden, beginning with

an organ prelude on the piano alone; after this the violin plays the intonation of the priest at the altar, after which follow the responses of the
choristers in the same tones and modulations as they are given in
Catholic churches, including the one in Dresden. This is followed by an
aria for castrato, in which the violinist must imitate the tone and style
of that kind of singing. The last movement describes in a Rondo the
journey through Saxon Switzerland, endeavoring to recall in places the
grand beauties of nature and in other places the merry Bohemian music
which one hears echoing from almost every rocky glen; a task which in
such compressed limits could of course only imperfectly be realized.[10]

While early in his career Spohr favored the first violin, his later
chamber music reflects a much greater degree of parity among the
musicians. His late string sextet Opus 140 (1848), for example,
does not favor the first violin or any single instrument. It takes
considerable skill to perform any piece by Spohr, and any amateur
who undertakes one of his works must be well trained and take
great care in preparing the piece.

Mendelssohn

While Spohr as a young contemporary of Beethoven formed a
link between the chamber music of Beethoven's generation and the
chamber music of the post-Beethoven generation, Mendelssohn
(1809-1847) was one of the few great musicians of the post-
Beethoven generation to feel entirely at home in the performance
and composition of classical chamber music. Mendelssohn was
adulated by bourgeois society in Germany, England and America
of the 1830's to 1860's because he wrote music that was immediately appealing to the sentimental tastes of his time, that was musically comprehensible by modestly informed amateurs, and that was
playable by many well-trained dilettantes. But Mendelssohn was
also under attack by modernists who criticized his music as too
classical in form (he seemingly ignored the challenges of Beethoven) and on the other side by conservatives who objected to his
liberties with classical forms.[11] His chamber music was found to be

[10]Brown, p. 241 (spellings Americanized).

[11]For an extensive analytic review of the criticism of Mendelssohn's music and particularly his chamber music cf. Friedhelm Krummacher, *Mendelssohn - der Komponist: Studien zur Kammermusik für Streicher* (Munich: Wilhelm Fink Verlag, 1978), pp. 13-35,
484-495. Krummacher is careful to try to separate anti-semitic diatribes from valid aesthetic criticsm.

too orchestral by some writers of the late 19th and early 20th century, though it is no more so (except, perhaps, for the octet) than the chamber music of Schubert and Brahms. He has been criticized for allowing the piano to dominate when all he did was expand the piano techniques of his time, and at the same time he has been criticized by others for making the piano fully a part of the chamber music. The problem with Mendelssohn's chamber music is that changing aesthetics since the mid-19th century have resulted in changing attitudes towards it, but also individual taste is a factor. Aesthetics is affected by changing historical conditions, and history is affected by the taste of the historian. How one judges Mendelssohn's chamber music is affected by one's own personal bias or viewpoint and by one's knowledge of the aesthetics of Mendelssohn's own time. Generally it is viewed that

> So far as the history of chamber music in general is concerned, Mendelssohn is now recognized as the most significant figure between Schubert and Brahms. More specifically in the field of the string quartet, he may even be accounted the greatest master of the medium between Beethoven and Bartók.[12]

His quintets are the best between Mozart and Brahms, and his D Minor piano trio is the most popular of the middle third of the 19th century.

Mendelssohn's childhood surroundings were a model of the rich bourgeois home in which music was cultivated. While mostly Christians dominated this new class of patrons at the end of the 18th and early 19th century, some Jews had become wealthy enough and integrated enough in the general European culture to take prominent roles supporting chamber music. Felix's father had taken advantage of new freedoms offered to Jews in post-French Revolutionary Germany, outwardly converted to Christianity (though never fully accepted by anti-Semitic Germans as Christian), and became a rich banker, first in Hamburg and then in Berlin. Felix heard chamber music in his home all his young life, and since he showed precocious interest in classical music at a tender age, he was indulged with the finest that Berlin had to offer. Talented family members and good local professionals gathered in the

---

[12]Horton, p. 5.

Mendelssohn home every Sunday morning for rehearsals and concerts where the best of Haydn, Mozart and Beethoven was aired and where Felix could try out his newest compositions. Thus Mendelssohn was born and bred in a chamber music environment that was quite different from that of the opera and pianist composers of his time, and because of this he turned early in his career to chamber music (1824-1828) and continued to return to it (especially in 1838 and 1843-1847). Although Mendelssohn played both violin and viola, his main instrument was the piano. In this regard he was like most of his 19th-century colleagues, who wrote chamber music for piano with the accompaniment of strings. The title of the three piano quartets, his first published works, make this point very clear: "pour le Pianoforte avec Accompagnement de Violon, Alto et Violoncelle." Even so famous a virtuosic violinist as Heinrich Wilhelm Ernst (1814-1865), trained by the great chamber musicians Böhm and Mayseder, was asked to *"accompany"* Mendelssohn for a performance of his D Minor Trio at Ella's Musical Union in 1844—a piece where in fact the three instruments are more or less equal.

The chief influences on Mendelssohn were, of course, Haydn, Mozart and Beethoven. From Haydn he learned the art of motivic development, the varied recapitulation, the choice tonality, and the relationship of instruments. From Beethoven he learned, especially in his earliest chamber music (for example, Opus 12 and 13), the use of cyclic elements, and continuing throughout his career the intense brooding of Beethoven's Opus 95 (copied in Mendelssohn's Opus 80). When Mendelssohn was 16 he went to Paris where he met Baillot and heard the Baillot Quartet ensemble perform publicly early and middle Beethoven (the late quartets were still being written, though Baillot played them only privately when he did get hold of them). Especially significant for Mendelssohn was hearing Cherubini's string quartets, which had become by 1825 the most important French examples of the genre. He was impressed with the active state of chamber music in Paris, where besides Cherubini chamber music was being written by Hummel, Onslow ("prolific and popular dilettante composer of quartets and quintets"[13]), Baillot and Reicha and performed by Baillot, Ha-

[13]Horton, p. 29.

beneck, and Rudolph Kreutzer. Yet Mendelssohn saw that the French were primarily concerned with the *brillants* trios and quartets, and for him the Germanic approach of Spohr (in his serious quartets), Bach and Beethoven—with equal voices, tightly knit counterpoint, and integrated forms—seemed a higher path.

Among Mendelssohn's early group of chamber pieces (1820's) are violin-piano sonatas, string quartets, piano quartets, a string quintet (modeled on Mozart's viola quintets, his clarinet quintet, and the "Jupiter" Symphony), and two larger ensemble works: the sextet Opus 110 (violin, two violas, cello, bass and piano) and the octet Opus 20 (for two string quartets). This last work was unique at the time and still is the greatest work of its kind. Unlike Spohr's octets for two separate string quartets, Mendelssohn's is scored for eight continually interacting instruments. There are massive strettos or telescopic imitation with all the instruments taking part, especially in the Scherzo movement which became Mendelssohn's most famous kind of movement. These scherzos have mocking gestures similar to Goethe and Shakespeare's confrontation of the real and supranatural worlds. He wrote in the score: "This Octet must be played by all the instruments in symphonic orchestral style." With the larger format of eight instruments he was able to absorb not only all kinds of typical string quartet and quintet relationships but also symphonic devices like tremolo, unison and octave doubling, and extreme dynamics—a much greater extension of the symphonic style to chamber music than Schubert tried. So close does the Octet come to orchestral music at times that orchestral conductors during the 19th century led and even today lead their orchestras in it; Mendelssohn himself was prevailed upon to orchestrate the scherzo.

The Octet is unique, but the string quartet in A Minor, Opus 13, is more typical in its dependence on Beethoven. Written in 1827, the year of Beethoven's death, it owes a great deal to Beethoven's late A Minor Quartet (Opus 132) in its key, in its cyclic use of a three-note rhythm, in its advanced harmony, and in the recitative opening to the last movement. With a fugue it suggests Beethoven's Opus 133. It also resembles Beethoven's Opus 135 quartet in that the basic three-note motive comes from a short song, which Mendelssohn prefixed to the quartet and quotes in full at the end. The song poses the question: "Ist es wahr?" (Is it true?), which is similar to Beethoven's question in Opus 135: "Muss es sein?" (Must it be?). This beautiful quartet is the most extreme case of Mendelssohn's copying Beethoven, but it is only the first of a number of quartets by composers of the 19th and 20th centuries that use Beethoven's as their starting point. It was a very popular quartet, especially in Paris where Baillot made all his students at the Paris Conservatory learn it.

The string quintet was originally written in 1826 with a fast opening movement followed by a scherzo, a minuet and trio, and a final fast movement. Then Mendelssohn revised the work in 1832 by writing a new slow movement in memory of his violin teacher Eduard Rietz (to whom he had dedicated the Octet and who died very young); the slow movement comes second, the old scherzo is moved to third, and the minuet-trio is dropped. The resulting order of movements poses a problem, since there is little difference in character and tempo between the scherzo and the finale. As long as the third movement of the classical quartet was a true minuet, the form fast - slow - minuet - fast offered enough contrast between movements and allowed for a significant ending. The form fast - minuet - slow - fast offered an equally satisfactory contrast, which was a modification of the popular baroque pattern slow - fast - slow - fast and a continuation of the very old idea in chamber music of contrasting sections. With the change of form to delete the minuet and replace it with a scherzo, the romantic composer was faced with a dilemma. Beethoven had two solutions: either he made the last movement truly monumental or he placed the scherzo second and the slow movement third. Mendelssohn could have followed either Beethoven or the French (written only three movements ending with the scherzo). From this point on Mendelssohn chose the Beethoven solutions.

After a decade of strenuous activity as traveling pianist and conductor, Mendelssohn returned to the composition of chamber music in 1838. The Ferdinand David Quartet ensemble in Leipzig was emerging as one of the best in Germany, and Mendelssohn wrote three more string quartets for it (Opus 44).[14] Home chamber

[14]David was also the violinist for whom Mendelssohn wrote his famous E-Minor Violin Concerto.

music of the highest quality—not the prevailing Hausmusik variety—was always the ideal for Mendelssohn, whose brother Paul was a fine cellist. For his brother he wrote several cello pieces, including the first sonata in 1838. Actually Mendelssohn had written a sonata-like piece *Variations Concertantes* for Paul in 1829, but because it does not contain a sonata-form movement (it is a theme and variations), Felix could not entitle it "Sonata." The 1838 sonata was praised by Robert Schumann, who recognized the rare appearance of a piece for home chamber music ("family music") that maintains the highest artistic standards. But the crowning achievement of this second period of chamber music came the next year with Mendelssohn's great D Minor Piano Trio (Opus 49). Together with the piano trio that he wrote in 1845 during his last flash of chamber music, they are

> the only important works of their kind between [Beethoven and Schubert] and Brahms, although the piano trio was more intensively cultivated as an ensemble at that period than any other.[15]

Once again with the family ensemble in mind, Mendelssohn wrote a piece that is much easier to play than Beethoven's trios and that balances the three instruments so that none feels slighted.

After a few more strenuous years as conductor, Mendelssohn returned to chamber music in 1845 with the second piano trio mentioned above, his second viola quintet (requested by Ferdinand David, which though complete he may have abandoned as an inferior work[16]), and his last string quartet in F Minor (Opus 80), written at the end of his life while he was in mourning for his sister Fanny. Mendelssohn was a very public personality, who traveled around Europe and England performing and conducting and producing symphonies, oratorios and piano music. But when Mendelssohn turned inward, often out of grief for a lost friend or relative, he wrote chamber music. Chamber music was not commercial music, was not governed by the tastes of the more or less crude public; in chamber music Mendelssohn poured out his most

[15]Horton, pp. 52-53.

[16]Friedhelm Krummacher, "Mendelssohn's Late Chamber Music: Some Autograph Sources Recovered, "in *Mendelssohn and Schumann*, ed. Jon W. Finson and R. Larry Todd (Durham: Duke, 1984), pp. 76-80.

intimate thoughts and feelings, to be shared by his most intimate friends and relatives. The loftiest ideals of chamber music, then, were maintained by Mendelssohn in the post-Beethoven age when few others maintained it; much more trendy were operas and symphonies, the flaunting of personal emotions in front of vast audiences (Berlioz), or the public performance of chamber music. The schizophrenia between public chamber music as art and intimate Hausmusik as trivia was not an issue for Mendelssohn, who may indeed have been the last great exponent of classical chamber music.[17]

Schumann

Even more so than Mendelssohn, Robert Schumann (1810-1856) thought of the piano when he conceived chamber music. Except for his three string quartets, all his chamber music includes the piano. As a teenager Schumann participated in regular chamber music sessions as a pianist and listener.[18] Later as a student in Leipzig he wrote his first chamber music: the piano quartet originally listed as Opus 5 (1828-1829). In 1828 he founded a piano quartet ensemble there (it also played piano trios) which lasted one season, but when he left Leipzig for Heidelberg, these activities ceased. Instead Schumann was more active as a writer, music critic and editor. A phenomenon in the 19th century was the combination of literary writer and composer; such famous composers as Berlioz, Schumann, and Wagner wrote volumes of literature, and such famous writers as E.T.A. Hoffmann wrote chamber music and much other kind of music. The combination of a creative literary side with a creative musical side was not important in the artistic lives of Spohr and Mendelssohn, for whom program music is relatively insignificant. For Berlioz, Schumann and Wagner, on the

---

[17]Alfred Einstein's assessment of Mendelssohn as the last great classical composer rather than as a romantic composer (*Music in the Romantic Era* [New York: Norton, 1947], pp. 124-138) comes into focus in chamber music. His close association with most Haydn and Mozart in the area of chamber music—intimate music performed only before closest friends and family, easy enough to enable those friends and family to participate—is distinct from Beethoven and the romantic urge to professionalize the performance of chamber music and appeal to wide audiences.

[18]Hans Kohlhase, *Die Kammermusik Robert Schumanns* (Hamburg: Karl Dieter Wagner Musikalienhandlung, 1979), p. 9.

Clara Wieck Schumann (1819-1896). Private possession of author.

other hand, program music—the relationship of literature and music—was extremely important.

At certain periods of his life Schumann had little time for chamber music. During his first creative period as a composer before 1840, he wrote mostly piano music, no important chamber music, though it was on his mind (there are sketches and references to chamber music in his letters, but only the piano quartet in C Minor was worked out). Suddenly, with his marriage to Clara Wieck in 1840, he turned from piano music to song, concerto, symphony, and chamber music. In 1842 alone he wrote his three string quartets (Opus 41), his famous piano quintet (Opus 44), his piano quartet (Opus 47), and the *Phantasiestücke* for piano trio (Opus 88). During the ensuing nine years he added to them his three piano trios (Opus 63, 80, and 110) and the three violin-piano sonatas (Opus 105 and 121; on the third of 1853 see below). Like Mendelssohn Schumann turned to Haydn, Mozart and Beethoven as his models. The *Phantasiestücke*, however, was a new approach to serious chamber music. Schumann thought in terms of a series of character pieces, rather than the usual classical sonata cycle; the character pieces had served him well in his piano music, but this was a new idea for chamber music. In the hierarchy of music mentioned above, character pieces figure just above Hausmusik and dance music as the least worthy of art. He feared that he would mislead the public if he called the set a "Trio," so he substituted the term "Phantasiestücke." Despite its form and its availability to Hausmusik performers, Schumann's "Phantasiestücke" attains a position among the art works of the 19th century.

Unlike Mendelssohn Schumann also wrote chamber music for winds together with piano and/or strings. The pieces for horn and piano (Opus 70, for the horn player Schletterlau), clarinet and piano (Opus 73), oboe and piano (Opus 94), and clarinet, viola and piano (Opus 132) are not sonatas but, once again because of their character pieces, are given such titles as Adagio and Allegro (Opus 70, originally Romanze und Allegro), Phantasiestücke (Opus 73, originally Soiréestücke), and Märcherzählungen (Opus 132). In all cases the publisher allowed for the substitution of a violin for the wind instrument, sometimes also the cello, and the clarinet in the case of Opus 94. This substitution was probably not Schumann's idea, since when Simrock suggested that Schumann put "clarinet or oboe "on the title page of Opus 94, the composer protested vehemently; he meant oboe when he wrote oboe and did not consider it a clarinet piece. Simrock ignored him anyway.[19]

Schumann wrote the first two violin sonatas for Ferdinand David, but the third sonata was written for a special occasion. In 1853 Schumann contributed two movements to a violin-piano sonata which also had a movement by Brahms and another movement by Dietrich; it was dedicated to Joachim. Then Schumann took his two movements, wrote two more of his own, and dedicated it to Joachim as his third sonata. Clara and Brahms praised the work, but since Schumann was now mentally ill, they considered it a sign of his illness and suppressed the piece.[20] During his last years before being institutionalized Schumann had chamber music in his home. Clara and young Brahms performed with various other musicians the newest compositions of Schumann and other composers privately for their own enjoyment.

Germany

Spohr, Mendelssohn and Schumann shared at one time or another the musical life of Leipzig. Mendelssohn was called there in 1835 and was in charge of the Gewandhaus concerts until his death. He founded the Leipzig Conservatory in 1846. In 1836 he hired Ferdinand David as concertmaster, who also started regular evening string quartet concerts. Schumann lived in Leipzig from 1828 to 1844, and he, Mendelssohn and David were close associates. David was there, ready and willing, to play the quartets of his friends, and through his encouragement he was responsible for their creation and premiers. Spohr met Schumann in Leipzig in 1838; although he never lived in Leipzig, Spohr often traveled there over the years. Coming to the city in the summer of 1846, Spohr was mainly interested in meeting Wagner, who was there then. But while in Leipzig he attended, among other things,[21] the

---

[19]Kohlhase, p. 27.

[20]It was finally premiered publicly in 1935 and first printed in 1956.

[21]On one occasion during this visit the fifteen-year-old Joachim performed for Spohr one of Spohr's violin concertos with the Gewandhaus Orchestra.

private musical evenings at the homes of Moritz Hauptmann and Mendelssohn (Wagner was also there and recounted the events). He performed his new Opus 132 quartet at the Mendelssohn's on one evening, and on his final evening in Leipzig he and Mendelssohn joined other local musicians to play Spohr's first Trio (Opus 119) and third Double Quartet (Opus 87). Passing through again in May, 1849, he performed in Leipzig his Opus 141 quartet and his fourth double quartet.

Thus, as we can see from just the few instances mentioned above, in a city of about 30,000 inhabitants in the 1840's, chamber music of the highest level flourished in public concerts and in private homes.[22] Leipzig was an old music center and a prosperous commercial city, but it was not the center of an empire as were Vienna, Paris, Berlin, Hamburg, and London, each of which had ten times or more the population of Leipzig. Yet Leipzig, with its heavy concentration of composers, performers and intellectual elite, could sustain a type of music that today is thought to be the purview of a tiny elite. The intense interest in chamber music in Leipzig reflects as well the importance that chamber music assumed especially throughout central Europe at this time. This was not Hausmusik, which also was everywhere in Leipzig and Central Europe; this was serious chamber music performed both intimately and for a public audience.

Other German cities also experienced a chamber music boom during the second quarter of the 19th century. We have already described some of Spohr's activities in Kassel, which was not a free commercial city like Leipzig but the home of a petty prince who controlled his musicians (including poor Spohr) tightly. The prince was not particularly interested in chamber music, but the musicians and other residents were. In Breslau, Hannover, Munich, Berlin, Dresden, and Hamburg there were regular professional chamber music concerts by local musicians or traveling groups.

While each of these cities had resident musicians who performed chamber music regularly for the entertainment of certain local upper and middle class patrons, there also appeared for the

---

[22]William S. Newman, "Three Musical Intimates of Mendelssohn and Schumann in Leipzig: Hauptmann, Moscheles, and David," in *Mendelssohn and Schumann*, p. 89.

first time a professional string quartet that was not associated with a particular city but made its reputation by touring. The group was the first Müller Brothers Quartet (1830-1855).[23] Since this began a new trend which was only much later to become widespread, the Müller Brothers Quartet was the most important professional German chamber ensemble to emerge after 1825. The four brothers Karl (1797-1873), Georg (1808-1855), Gustav (1799-1855) and Theodor (1802-1875) were initially employed by the Duke of Brunswick, who greatly restricted their activities and treated them in the old way as servants. They practiced string quartets secretly, and in 1830 resigned their jobs in order to devote themselves exclusively to performing quartets. They began their new careers with a public performance in 1831 in Hamburg, and after a season in residence in Berlin (1832-1833), they became the principal German touring quartet, performing throughout Germany, France, Denmark, The Netherlands, and Russia. Their repertory was basically Haydn, Mozart, and Beethoven.

England

While local chamber music ensembles and composers flourished in Central Europe during the second quarter of the 19th century, in England the preference among connoisseurs was not for local performers or compositions but imported Germans and their music. In 1830 the English critic Edward Holmes noted

> there is a large body of amateurs, who, from one year's end to another, scarcely ever purchase an English piece. Weber's appearance in this country, the success of his operas, the favour of German instrumental music, the manner in which the quartetts, quintetts, etc., of Beethoven, Spohr etc., are performed in private parties show the progress of a taste for music of a high character.[24]

There was a proliferation of concert-giving organizations in London in the 1830's with the chamber music of Mendelssohn and

---

[23]Lynda Lloyd Rees, "Müller," in *The New Grove Dictionary of Music and Musicians*, vol. xii, p. 767. The Second Müller Brothers String Quartet was composed of the four sons of Karl Müller and flourished from 1855 to 1873; for a short time Leopold Auer played first violin in this quartet.

[24]Brown, p. 249.

Spohr alongside the music of the classics. During the 1830's and 1840's both modern composers spent considerable time in England. A spectacular tribute to Spohr was held on June 27, 1843, at the London home of Mr. Alsayer of *The Times*; a private music party for about fifty persons began at 2 p.m. with Act I (Double Quartets nos. 1 and 2, the quintet for piano and winds with Moscheles as pianist, and the Nonet), followed by dinner at 5 p.m., and concluding with Act II at 7 p.m. (string quintet, octet, and Double Quartet no. 3).[25] In 1847 Spohr also played the first violin in his Double Quartet no. 3 in a semi-private concert of the Beethoven Quartet Society[26] (a group consisting of mostly professional and keenly interested amateur chamber musicians), and in March of the next year Spohr's Piano Trio Opus 133 was performed at a soirée of Lindsay Slopes in London.

France

The Revolution brought an end to French hegemony in chamber music. Chamber music had been associated primarily with the royal family and with the aristocracy, and when they were executed or driven into exile, their musicians went with them. Several were killed, and some like Viotti went to England. Chamber music, which requires a considerable degree of musical sophistication on the part of listener as well as performer, was not the sort of music that the revolutionaries envisioned for the country. Instead marches, patriotic hymns, and rescue operas dominated the scene, and those talented composers who remained in France and who might in the *ancien régime* have written chamber music, found themselves compelled to avoid it. Much of the 19th century found the most musically sensitive Frenchmen trying to recover the lost French dominance in chamber music as a rebuttal to the unsubtle, unsophisticated popular music of the new middle classes.

Despite the prevalence of opera, symphony and other types of music in Paris in the 1820's and 1830's, there was also a devoted if small audience that regularly patronized public performance of

[25]Brown, p. 275.
[26]Brown, p. 302.

chamber music.[27] These concerts were sometimes public but more often in the private salons of the wealthy or upper middle classes, where the audience would include a small coterie of friends. Since French composers had necessarily turned away from chamber music at the end of the 18th and beginning of the 19th centuries, the new repertory of chamber music was basically German. At first the French public in general did not understand or care for German music, which included the works of Haydn, Mozart and Beethoven as well as Spohr, Mendelssohn, Schumann and others. On the other hand, a small group of professionals (Habeneck, Kreutzer, Baillot, Berlioz, Cherubini were the most famous) were quick to admire the instrumental music of these German composers and to try to popularize them among large numbers of Frenchmen. The social group most likely to be attracted by classical chamber music was the reinstated aristocracy that returned to Paris after the fall of Napoleon; this group had the musical education and sophistication to appreciate it and had a nostalgia for the music of the *ancien régime*. They and the new, social-climbing upper middle class opened rooms in their homes and their businesses to small chamber groups and a select group of listeners. Although this gave to concert chamber music the air of snobbery, it did keep alive chamber music beginning in 1814 and help foster it as it recovered some of its former glory by the end of the 19th century.

Just as in Vienna and London, there were several resident quartets in Paris by the 1830's. From February to April, 1830, the Bohrer Quartet[28] premiered the last quartets of Beethoven in Paris; in 1833 Théophile Tilmant founded another quartet,[29] in 1837 Delphin Alard yet another,[30] and in 1838 Charles Dancla one more.[31]

---

[27]Joël-Marie Fauquet, "La Musique de chambre à Paris dans les années 1830, "in Peter Bloom, ed., *La Musique à Paris dans les Années Mil Huit Cent Trentre*, in *La Vie Musicale en France au XIXe Siècle*, vol. IV (Stuyvesant, NY: Pendragon Press, 1987), pp. 299-326. She lists (pp. 312-321) subscribers to the concerts from 1823 to 1832.

[28]Anton Bohrer (1783-1852) was first violinist and leader; the others were Max Bohrer, cellist, Théophile Tilmant, second violinist, and Chrétien Urhan, violist.

[29]Tilmant (1799-1880), first violinist, was joined by Alexandre Tilmant, cellist, Camille Claudel, second violinist, and Chrétien Urhan, violist.

[30]Alard (1815-1888), violinist, was joined by Charles Dancla, second violin, Louis Croisilles, viola, Charles Lenepveu, second viola, and Alexandre Chevillard, cellist.

[31]Eugène Lecointe, second violin, Louis Croisilles, viola, and Arnaud Dancla, cello.

But the most important local group was that formed by Pierre Baillot, who from 1814 until his death in 1842 gave public concerts of quartets and quintets with a regular group of professional musicians. Between 125 and 250 persons attended each concert, among which were many amateur musicians and even some professionals (Habeneck, Kalkbrenner, Mendelssohn, Meyerbeer, Onslow, Szymanovska, Berlioz [once], Camille Pleyel, Chopin, Liszt, Hiller, Paganini [once], etc.).[32] At his series of chamber music concerts not only did Baillot's own group perform but also visiting ensembles such as the Müller and Franco-Mendès Quartets from abroad and the Bohrer, Dancla, and Tilmant Quartets from Paris. The concerts first took place in different small rooms such as the noisy showrooms of the piano maker Pape and the dirty Salle Chantereine (rue des Victoires), but then more satisfactorily in Baillot's own residence, in the showrooms of the piano maker Duport, in the studios of a rug maker Alerme, and in the private hotel of his friend, the financier Leroux.[33] None of these places was ideal, and Baillot continually fought for a better place to perform chamber music. Other ensembles preferred larger halls, and finally in 1839 the concert pianist Henri Herz built a chamber concert hall seating 400 which became a regular site of chamber music concerts.

Baillot favored the quartets and quintets of Mozart, Haydn and Boccherini, as well as of Cherubini (all his quartets were premiered by Baillot), Onslow and Mendelssohn. He tried to introduce Beethoven's late chamber music in concerts in 1829 but was threatened with the loss of his series if he persisted in such new music.[34] The chief supporting audience, it will be recalled, was people whose whole frame of reference was trying to hang on to the *ancien régime* and therefore whose tastes were exceedingly conservative. Instead he taught the Beethoven quartets to his many students and they, in turn, promulgated the Beethoven quartets a decade or two later. Baillot came to his performances without the exactness that Schuppanzigh was demanding in Vienna at the same time. He often changed programs seemingly on the spur of the

[32]Fauquet, p. 301.

[33]Fauquet, pp. 325-326.

[34]Fauquet, p. 304.

moment (though planned and rehearsed with his ensemble) and improvised at the concerts, especially his tempos, which made the ensemble shaky at best. His method of performance was to give an illusion of amateurishness which he felt important in any performance of chamber music. Berlioz and others railed against such looseness of performance practice, and Baillot's pupils and successors used the Schuppanzigh-like goals of tightness and perfection rather than Baillot's improvisatory ideas.

Cherubini

The chief composers of chamber music in Paris after the death of Cambini in 1825 were Cherubini and Onslow. Luigi Cherubini (1760-1842) settled in Paris in 1786, when Cambini was at his greatest popularity and when his friend, Viotti, was dazzling the French with his virtuosity. Cherubini, however, was not interested in purely instrumental music at this time and devoted himself to the composition of opera and sacred vocal music. He survived the Revolution because he was quick to change from a court composer to a composer of popular music. He was also an administrator of the Paris Conservatory from 1795 until 1842, the last twenty years of which he was head. In 1814, about the time that his pupil Baillot started his chamber music series, Cherubini surprisingly wrote his first string quartet. For whatever unknown reason, it remained unperformed until 1826. Then he wrote another one in 1829, which is a reworking of his only symphony, and from 1834 to 1837 he wrote four more. Of the six quartets, only the first three were published in Cherubini's lifetime; the other three were published after 1850. Upon completion of the sixth quartet, he also wrote a string quintet (1837), which was intended as the first of a series that was never completed. These seven works, then, are Cherubini's contribution to chamber music.

The quartets are a blend of Cherubini's inherited French and Italian tradition and his admiration for the Viennese tradition. From Cambini, Boccherini and Viotti's *quatuors concertants* and *brillants* he learned unusual technical demands on the performers, the lack of motivic development in some cases, eccentric harmonies, empty passage work, and a careless multiplicity of themes. From Haydn, Mozart and especially late Beethoven, however, he also learned the contradictory concepts of motivic development, cyclic forms, chromatic alteration of inner voices, and harmonic richness. If one views the quartets from the standpoint of French tradition, Cherubini was too restrained, too formalistic, too concerned with harmonic details. If, on the other hand, one views them from the standpoint of Viennese tradition, he was too free with melody and harmony, too demanding of his players, and not concise with his forms. But if Cherubini is taken on his own terms, the quartets are a personal expression of a composer who was in between the two styles and who sought a synthesis of their divergent approaches to chamber music.[35] Schumann, in reviewing a performance of the first quartet in 1838, found the work puzzling but also rewarding. Subsequent German audiences found the work intriguing, and by the second half of the century all six quartets were performed frequently. Each is in four movements fast - slow - scherzo - fast, with slow introductions to the first two first movements. Cyclic elements can be found in all six (e.g., the scherzo of no. 4 is related to the main themes of the first two movements, and midway through the last movement of no. 6 there are quotations of the first three movements).

Onslow

"The only French composer of [this] time to produce a substantial quantity of "chamber music was Georges Onslow (1784-1853).[36] Born in France of an English father, he studied piano in London under Hüllmandel, Dussek and Cramer but never distinguished himself on the keyboard. Returning to France ca. 1798, he joined an amateur chamber music group in Auvergne made up of close friends. He quickly learned the cello in order to play favorite Haydn, Mozart and Boccherini quartets and quintets with the group, and in 1806 he composed and published at his own expense his first compositions: three string quintets (Opus 1). Only two years later did he begin to study composition formally, with Anton Reicha who had just returned to Paris. For the next decade he

---

[35]Cf. Ludwig Finscher, "Cherubini's String Quartets" (Deutsche Grammaphon, Archiv 2723, 1976), booklet p. 3.

[36]Benedict Sarnaker, "Onslow," in *The New Grove Dictionary of Music and Musicians*, vol. xiii, p. 544.

wrote numerous student chamber works which were amateurish, but beginning in 1822 he began to pour out competent chamber music in great quantity and continued to do so until his death. By the late 1830's Breitkopf und Härtel in Leipzig was publishing large numbers of his quartets and quintets, which had become very popular throughout Europe. He wrote almost nothing else but chamber music and numbers among his works thirty-four string quintets, thirty-five string quartets, a nonet, a septet and a sextet for winds and strings, two piano quintets, ten piano trios, six works for violin and piano (four sonatas and two duos), and three sonatas for cello and piano.

Onslow wrote his chamber music during the summer for his friends in Auvergne; after hearing them performed in such a setting, he revised them as necessary and then, during the winter, took them to Paris for formal public performance and publication. As a result, the music, while written for public performance, was designed for modestly talented amateur groups. Emotionally they are cool and technically they are fairly simple. Until 1848 (Opus 69) the quintets are scored for two violins, viola, and either two cellos or one cello and one bass (Onslow had heard Dragonetti). After 1848 (Opus 70) Onslow turned exclusively to the Mozart setting of two violins, two violas, and cello. The year 1848 was also decisive for his string quartet writing; he wrote no more quartets after 1848. Instead he turned at this point to larger works, including the string quintets; his piano quintets for violin, viola, cello, bass and piano; his woodwind quintet (Opus 81); his nonet for flute, oboe, clarinet, horn, bassoon, violin, viola, cello and bass (Opus 77), which he also arranged as a sextet for flute, clarinet, horn, bassoon, bass, and piano; and a septet for flute, oboe, clarinet, horn, bassoon, bass and piano (Opus 79), which he also arranged for violin, viola, cello, bass and piano. The only other works written during his last five years are a symphony and a piano trio (Opus 83).

Every chamber piece that Onslow wrote (only one exception) from 1822 on is in four movements, following one of four patterns: fast - slow - minuet - fast, fast - minuet - slow - fast, fast - slow - scherzo - fast, and fast - scherzo - slow - fast.[37] The opening sonata

[37]Cf. Christiana Nobach, *Untersuchungen zu George Onslows Kammermusik* (Kassel: Bärenreiter, 1985), pp. 286-376.

movement is sometimes preceded by a slow introduction, and some slow movements are variations on a theme. Many movements have expressive rubrics ("Allegro impetuoso" in Quintet Opus 51, "Scherzo: il Cicalamento" in Quartet Opus 53, "Finale: Allegro animato "Le Coup de Vent" in the Piano Quintet Opus 76) which must have titillated his amateur friends, who were accustomed to the regularity of forms, style and technique of Onslow's chamber music. Indeed, Onslow's popularity with the very conservative chamber music audience was owing to his strict adherence to the classical Viennese forms, harmonies and style. Yet he was aware that Beethoven and younger romantics were writing program music, so he gave the outward appearance of being up-to-date by including a few programs. His Opus 38 string quintet is programmatic; its second movement is a "Menuetto: Presto "Dolore," its third an "Andante sostenuto Convalescenza," and its fourth a "Finale: Allegro Guarigione." Onslow was accidentally shot near one ear and lost his hearing on that side; the quintet portrays various phases of his injury and his recovery from it (the image of the third movement of Beethoven's Opus 132 quartet might have served as a model, though nothing else about Onslow's work suggests Beethoven's masterpiece[38]).

*

During the quarter century following Beethoven's death a major new phenomenon occurred in musical performance practice which was of little consequence before. This was the preservation and continual performance of music of the past to the exclusion, frequently, of contemporary music. In France this was the direct result of the Revolution and subsequent restoration of hyper-conservative upper classes; in Germany and Austria this was the result of the Napoleonic invasions and the bitter reaction of the same classes in those countries. They perceived the new as revolution and loss of their privileges, so they sought the old and the old stable order. When a 17th- or 18th-century musician played chamber music, he/she either performed his/her own compositions or those of the stars of their own time (Corelli was the only exception, though barely, whose music was continually performed long after

[38]The superficial influence of the "Lydian" movement of Beethoven's opus 132 is also to be seen in the "Adagio religioso" second movement of his string quartet opus 46, no. 3.

his death). The most popular chamber music composers during the quarter century 1825-1850, however, were Haydn, Mozart, and Boccherini, all of whom were popular in the *ancien régime* and none of whom were alive during the period under consideration. Gradually Beethoven's importance, long recognized by a small coterie of friends and colleagues, was understood by the general chamber music audience so that, a quarter century after his death, he reached a status equivalent to or even surpassing that of Haydn, Mozart and Boccherini. This interest in past music extended well beyond the area of chamber music when the rediscovery of J.S. Bach in the late 1820's, 1830's and 1840's became the hottest concern among music lovers. A few contemporary composers such as Spohr, Mendelssohn, and Onslow continued to write chamber music and hear it performed, since in general their styles were in keeping with those of Haydn, Mozart, Boccherini, and Beethoven and were readily appreciated by an ever more conservative audience. By mid-century, however, a progressive composer (and this included late Beethoven as well) could expect hostility from an uncomprehending and unappreciative audience (including also amateur and professional performers). Thus composers felt compelled not to write much chamber music but to venture into fields such as opera and symphony where the reliance on things past was not so burdensome.

ART CHAMBER MUSIC 1850-1897

By the middle of the 19th century chamber music institutions had taken hold in many places in Europe and the performance of great chamber music, both in the concert hall and in the home as one kind of Hausmusik, was an accepted part of the musical scene. The composition of chamber music, however, was mostly in the hands of composers whose main interests lay elsewhere. This was true especially in France, England, and Italy but also in Germany and Austria. By the 1870's, however, there was a renewed interest in chamber music by major composers, particularly in France and Austria.

France

In Paris after the death of Onslow serious chamber music was performed regularly in major concert series such as the Société Alard-Franchomme (also known as Société de Musique de Chambre), the Société des Derniers Quatuors de Beethoven, the Société des Quatuors de Mendelssohn, the Séances Populaires, and to a much lesser extent the Société Sainte-Cécile.[39] In addition there were still the matinée and soirée concerts in the salons of Paris, that is, in the private homes of the wealthy, the middle class, and the musicians themselves (Rossini, Kalkbrenner, Farrenc, Saint-Saëns, Chausson, etc.). Some of these were mere social gatherings where the music was politely or rudely listened to, while at others—such as the Gouffé Séances and the Lebouc Séances—the audience came enthusiastically to listen intently to the music.[40] The repertoire was the classics Haydn, Mozart, Boccherini and especially Beethoven. More recent composers included Mendelssohn, Onslow, and after the 1860's Robert Schumann. For about twenty years, until the 1870's, however, the contemporary French composers whose music was performed—Dancla,[41] Alard,[42] Farrenc,[43]

[39]Jeffrey Cooper, *The Rise of Instrumental Music and Concert Series in Paris 1828-1871* (Ann Arbor: University Microfilms International Research Press, 1983); and Joël-Marie Fauquet, *Les Sociétés de Musique de Chambre à Paris de la Restauration à 1870* (1986).

[40]Cooper, pp. 86-89.

[41]Charles Dancla (1817-1907) was associated with Habeneck's Société des Concerts du Conservatoire and was the leading violinist there from 1841 to 1863. Stimulated by Baillot he, his brothers and his sister organized their own quartet ca. 1839 and gave concerts in Paris. He did not tour, spent some years as a postal worker, and composed fourteen string quartets, four piano trios, six trios for three violins, violin duets, and various works for violin and piano, many based on opera airs and themes from famous symphonies.

[42]Jean-Delphin Alard (1815-1888), pupil of Habeneck and Fétis and teacher of Sarasate, was a superb chamber player with his own quartet. His only chamber compositions are a string quartet, a Grand Duo Concertant for violin and piano, and violin duets.

[43]Jeanne-Louise Farrenc (1804-1875), the most prominent woman composer of chamber music in mid-19th-century France, taught at the conservatory for many years. She wrote two piano quintets (piano, violin, viola, cello, and bass), four piano trios, two sonatas for piano and violin or cello, a string quartet, a nonetto for wind quintet, violin, viola, cello and bass, and a sextuor for wind quartet and piano. Cf. Bea Friedland, *Louise Farrenc, 1804-1875: Composer, Performer, Scholar*, in *STudies in Musicology*, no. 32 (Ann Arbor: UMI Research Press, 1980), pp. 119-153.

Blanc,[44] Lalo, Gouvy,[45] Mathias,[46] Castillon,[47] and Saint-Saëns—stood in the shadow of the German classics.

When Saint-Saëns stated in his *Harmonie et Mélodie* that there was no chamber music in Paris before 1871, he perhaps had his tongue in his cheek since not only was there an abundance of concerts of chamber music in Paris but he himself had already made numerous contributions as performer and composer.[48] Yet many historians took Saint-Saëns seriously, and only recently has research proven the overt falsity of his statement. But perhaps Saint-Saëns meant something else: that at that time no great new art works for chamber ensemble of a specifically French character were being composed in Paris. The Germans clearly dominated the scene. Despite this, several factors were preparing Saint-Saëns himself and his most distinguished French contemporaries for a rebirth of an idiosyncratic French manner in chamber music.[49] First there was the achievement of Berlioz, who, although he wrote no chamber music, established the aesthetic respectability of serious instrumental music among the French who in the 19th century preferred empty virtuosic display and opera to it. Then there was Chopin, the author of only one piece of chamber music (his cello-piano sonata), who through his unparalleled solo keyboard music

[44]Adolphe Blanc (1828-1885), violinist whose primary interest was playing chamber music, wrote string and piano trios, quartets, and quintets, a septet for strings and winds, four cello sonatas, and two trios for piano, cello and flute or clarinet.

[45]Théodore Gouvy (1819-1898), who was as popular in Germany as in Paris, composed five string quartets, five piano trios, a piano quintet, and various works for strings and winds.

[46]Georges Mathias (1826-1910), pupil of Halévy, Kalkbrenner and Chopin, wrote six piano trios.

[47]Alexis Castillon (1838-1873), pupil of Franck and a founder of the Société National de Musique, was the only member of Saint-Saëns' circle to devote himself almost exclusively to chamber music, but he died young as a result of the Franco-Prussian War. He composed two string quartets, two piano trios, a piano quartet and quintet, and a violin and piano sonata.

[48]Paul Landormy, "La Musique de Chambre en France de 1850 à 1871," in *Le Mercure Musical*, nos. 8-9 (1911), 37-50. Cf. Cooper, pp. 161-167, for commentary on the historian's underevaluation of French instrumental music of the 19th century. Cf. Serge Gut and Danièle Pistone, *La Musique de Chambre en France de 1870 à 1918* (Paris: Honoré Champion, 1978), for a summary view of chamber music in France in the 19th century, including lists of performing groups, programs, performing societies, and compositions.

[49]Max Favre, *Gabriel Fauré's Kammermusik* (Zurich: Kommissionsverlag von Max Niehans, 1949).

developed in the French ear a wonderful sense of color (harmonic, tonal, formal, melodic). Also César Franck in his great organ music reawakened a French interest in polyphony and counterpoint, traditionally French textures which had become contrary to the prevailing homophony and accompanied textures of the time. With the musical tools to create a purely French chamber music at hand, Saint-Saëns, Fauré, Franck, and Lalo created the institution to do so in the 1870's as a direct result of the political situation: at the outbreak of the Franco-Prussian War they founded the Société Nationale de Musique to promote *ars gallica*. Crowds of Frenchmen attended its concerts, though each had to have an invitation, which prevented the concerts of the Société from influencing the public at large. Only after 1918 were concerts of this sort made truly public.[50]

A quick glance over the programs of chamber music in 19th century France reveals the overwhelming predominance of German (and Austrian) music.[51] The chamber works of Haydn, Mozart, Beethoven, Mendelssohn, Spohr, and Schumann made up nearly the entire standard repertory in Paris—an even more overwhelming teutonic preponderance than in symphonic, operatic, keyboard, and religious music. The hostility between Germany and France was keenly felt in musical matters, and so it was incumbent upon France's greatest composers to show that they indeed could stand up to the giants of German chamber music. Talking about it was one thing; actually writing aesthetically satisfying music that was distinctly French was another. There was a lingering antagonism to instrumental ensemble music in official French quarters that was an impediment to a French instrumental style; chamber music was not taught to composers at the Paris Conservatory until the 20th century, and they were not expected to know anything about it.[52] Before they wrote new, French-sounding chamber music, they groped into the past (the glories of 17th- and 18th-century French music) and mastered what was best about the classics. Eventually

---

[50]Gut and Pistone, p. 62.

[51]Twenty-three percent of all instrumental music performed in Paris from 1828 to 1870 was by Beethoven alone and another 26% by Mozart, Mendelssohn, Haydn and Weber. Cf. Cooper, p. 108.

[52]Gut and Pistone, p. 65.

the path led through Chausson and Debussy to a new flourishing of French chamber music in the 20th century, and in the process they gave us some masterpieces.

César Franck (1822-1890), a pupil of Anton Reicha, wrote his four trios (1839-1842) early in his career before his style was fully matured, yet these works made him known to the important musicians of his time including Meyerbeer, Liszt, Donizetti, Halévy, Chopin, Thomas and Auber. Franck was a fine organist, however, and from 1858 he served as organist in Paris, where he was highly regarded, and composed mostly organ music. Fortunately he returned to chamber music much later with his piano quintet (1878-1879), the violin and piano sonata (1886), and the string quartet (1889)—all three major contributions to the repertory. Although these late works come after the chamber music of Saint-Saëns, Fauré and Lalo, they are the three works that firmly established the new era of French chamber music. They proved, and continue to prove, that chamber music could express as much as an orchestral piece.[53] Franck's late style was heavily influenced by Wagner's "juxtaposition of tonally unrelated chords by means of logical part movement."[54] He also devised on his own what is known as a "chord pair"—two immediate soundings of the same chord, the second slightly altered and stressed (especially noticeable in the sonata). Chord pairs influenced Debussy on his road to impressionism. Also Franck is famous for his development of the concept of cyclic unity in a multi-movement piece; he recognized that a piece could be cyclic by repeating parts of earlier movements in later ones or by being monothematic. With such unity in compositions Franck shied away from four-movement pieces (except in the sonata and quartet) and preferred the form fast - slow - fast. Thus Franck was loyal to the Viennese tradition of motivic development and the popular genres of sonata, trio, quartet, and quintet, but simultaneously he turned away from the traditionalists by incorporating new harmonic sounds of the modernists.

[53]Robert Jardillier, *La Musique de Chambre de César Franck: Étude et Analyse* (Paris: Mellottée, [1929]).

[54]John Trevitt, "Franck," in *The New Grove Dictionary of Music and Musicians*, vol. vi, p. 780.

Charles-Camille Saint-Saëns (1835-1921) wrote chamber music all his life, from the age of five to the age of eighty-six.[55] One of the great prodigies in musical history, he was brought up on Bach, Handel and Mozart, and by the age of ten could perform publicly by memory all the Beethoven piano sonatas. Like Franck Saint-Saëns was a brilliant organist and worked for La Madeleine as organist from 1857 to 1876; Liszt considered him the greatest living organist. During the 1850's and 1860's, however, he also played the music of Wagner and Schumann, which upset conservative opinion. Recognizing the need for an organization to perform only the newest French music, he and his friends, as mentioned above, founded the Société Nationale de Musique. But Saint-Saëns had a quirk in his personality that prevented him from becoming the principal composer of this new French style; he loved the classical and early romantic Germans and his own style clearly reflects this—"neat proportions, clarity, polished expression, elegant lines."[56] Perhaps he recognized that German-Austrian classicism, these very characteristics, owed a great deal to French taste of the 18th century. Intellectually he fostered French nationalism, and he edited for modern consumption the great French masterpieces of Lully, Charpentier and Rameau. But he could not separate himself enough from that tradition to create a new one.

As a fine pianist Saint-Saëns frequently performed chamber music. He was a frequent participant in the amateur chamber music society "La Trompette," where amateurs and professionals performed semi-privately for an invited audience the Viennese and modern German classics as well as a few new works by Frenchmen.[57] For "La Trompette" and for his Société National he wrote a lot of chamber music. Except for his two string quartets Opus 112 (1899) and 153 (1918), all his chamber music includes the piano. His piano quintet Opus 14 (1855) is his first serious piece of chamber music; it is cyclic and influenced by his discovery of the

[55]Elizabeth Remsberg Harkins, "The Chamber Music of Camille Saint-Saëns" (New York University Ph.D. dissertation, 1976).

[56]James Harding, "Saint-Saëns," in *The New Grove Dictionary of Music and Musicians*, vol. xvi, p. 402.

[57]Lucien Augé de Lassur, *La Trompette: un Demi-Siècle de Musique de Chambre* (Paris: Ch. Delagrave, 1911).

Édouard Lalo (1823-1892), violinist and violist, founding member of
the Armingaud Quartet. Private possession of author.

music of Schumann (whose piano quintet was *his* masterpiece). He wrote sonatas for violin and piano or cello and piano, two piano trios and two piano quartets. In addition he wrote a few works involving winds such as a *Caprice sur des Airs Danois et Russes* Opus 79 (1887), and the three late sonatas (1921) for piano with oboe (Opus 166), with clarinet (Opus 167) and with bassoon (Opus 168). The most important chamber work historically may be the septet for trumpet, string quartet, bass and piano Opus 65 (1881) which was an attempt to rediscover past French styles and which was a major forerunner of Busoni's neo-classicism. In this piece Saint-Saëns wrote an old-fashioned baroque suite, a collection of 17th-century character pieces "Préambule," "Minuet," "Intermède" and "Gavotte." This had proven in the past to be a clear indication of French taste, and it was on such roots that future French music had to build.

Édouard Lalo (1823-1892) was trained as a violinist and violist and for a short time studied with Habeneck at the Paris Conservatory. He was inclined toward chamber music as a performer, and was a founding member of the Armingaud-Jacquard Quartet in 1855, which specialized in the works of the German masters. He played viola, then later second violin, and remained with the ensemble even after it became a wind and string ensemble in 1872. He worked with the renowned flutist Paul Taffanel (1844-1908) as well as with the leader of the Armingaud ensemble, Jules Armingaud (1820-1900). While Lalo was sympathetic to the new French manner of the 1870's and showed it in his orchestral music and operas, most of his chamber music was written in the 1850's under strong German influence. He wrote a string quartet, three piano trios, a piano quintet, a violin and piano sonata and a cello and piano sonata; once again only the first of these pieces is without piano.

Gabriel-Urbain Fauré (1845-1924), a pupil of Saint-Saëns, started his career as an organist just as his teacher and Franck did. He wrote only ten major chamber music works, all for piano except his late string quartet (1923-1924), but only his sonata for violin and piano (Opus 13, 1875-1876) and his two piano quartets (Opus 15, 1876-1879, and Opus 45, ca. 1885-1886) were completed before the turn of the century. Fauré was much more at home in the salons than in the concert halls, and so he composed chamber music and songs for them. He was very popular in these private settings and was called on to perform as well as to present his new compositions. On February 3, 1892, for example, he played at two different matinée concerts: at 3 p.m. and at 5 p.m.[58] The piano quartets and sonata are classical in form (four movements fast sonata - slow - scherzo - fast sonata, or the two inner movements reversed) and do not yet show Fauré's mature style, which is evident in all the later chamber works.

Although a generation younger than the other Frenchmen discussed above, Ernest Chausson (1855-1899) died so early that he must be placed within their time frame. He was a rich man from the country, who maintained a salon in Paris where literati, artists and musicians mingled. He wrote only five chamber pieces, but they are important contributions to the new French style. The piano trio Opus 3 (1881) and the Concert for piano, violin and string quartet Opus 21 (1889-1891) show strong influence of Wagner and Franck. They are dark, heavy pieces, very dramatic, and they are cyclic. The chromatic harmonies are sometimes more Wagner, sometimes more Franck, while the melodies are similar to Massenet's, his teacher at the conservatory. In the early 1890's, however, Chausson consciously de-Wagnerized his music; to regain the clarity and precision of older French music he studied the works of Rameau and Couperin and replaced romantic German and Italian tempo designations with French terms from the 18th century. He also, like Debussy, became aware of new Russian sounds, which slowly began to enter into his music. His piano quartet Opus 30 (1897), incomplete string quartet Opus 35 (1897-1899), and his Pièce for cello and piano Opus 39 (1897) demonstrate a new-found French sound upon which he probably would have built had his life not been cut short at this time.

What Franck, Saint-Saëns, Lalo, Fauré, and Chausson had in common was their respect for classical chamber music and their effort to build a specifically French version of it. While some talented French composers immediately before them had composed chamber music, some a great deal of chamber music, these five

---

[58] Jean-Michel Nectoux, *Gabriel Fauré: his Life through his Letters*, trl. J.A. Underwood (London/New York: Marion Boyars, 1984), pp. 195-197.

major composers wrote chamber masterpieces. Their output is not large if compared with the classical composers, but with the individualization of each composition the weight of each of the chamber pieces in the totality of each composer's oeuvre is very heavy. Thus by the end of the 19th century France could once again boast its own school of chamber music composers and its own style of chamber music. This style involved a new sense of clarity and refinement of technique, a post-Wagnerian harmony that absorbed not only the extension of diatonic and chromatic harmony but also non-Western scales, and a continuity with both Viennese classics and French pictorial and dance music of earlier centuries. The works of Franck, Saint-Saëns, Lalo, Fauré, and Chausson led to it, but it was in the chamber music of Debussy and Ravel that it bore its first full fruits (see chapter VII).

Italy

While France (Paris) was able to recover its position as one of the leaders of chamber music performance and composition by the end of the 19th century, Italy was not able to do so. Dominant in the field during the 17th and 18th centuries, Italian musicians had gone abroad in such numbers to cultivate chamber music that little seemingly remained behind. Alfredo Untersteiner, writing in 1895, pointed to the lack of interest in chamber music in Italy because of a preoccupation with opera, and noted that only one Italian publisher, no longer in business, had published chamber music scores.[59] As in France and England, the greatness of Haydn, Mozart and Beethoven so overwhelmed local composers that few dared compete, and whatever Italian ensembles there were continued to perform the Austro-German classics to the exclusion of almost all else. There were, however, several notable exceptions.

Most of the chamber music of Italian composers of the late 17th century through 18th century was written by violinists or other string players for their own use. The last great Italian violinist of the 18th century, Viotti, carried on this tradition. And so did the first great Italian violinist of the 19th century: Nicolo Paganini

[59]Untersteiner, "Musica Istrumentale da Camera," in *Gazetta Musicale di Milano*, 1 (1895), 76-78.

(1782-1840). Until 1809 he held various positions at the courts of Italy, but from then on he was a free artist who relied on his concerts to make a living while residing in a given city. Paganini remained in Italy until 1823, mostly in the north, and there were a few instances when we know that he played chamber music. We know, for example, that in 1808, when the chamber orchestra of Princess Elisa Baciocchi (or Baccioci; Napoleon's sister) in Lucca was disbanded, Paganini and his brother, who were members of the orchestra, were retained as members of the personal string quartet of Prince Felix of Lucca.[60] From 1813 to 1814 Paganini resided in Milan where he frequently performed and from where he launched tours of nearby cities. While in Milan he joined the music society *Gli Orfei* and played chamber music with amateurs.[61] In 1819 in Naples he attacked with ease the difficult first violin part of a new quartet by a recent graduate of the conservatory, Giuseppe Danna.[62] When Paganini launched his international career in 1823, his public image of devilish virtuoso was everywhere heralded but there is scant reference to chamber music. His hundreds of concerts in Germany, France, England, Poland and elsewhere were causes for much scandal-ridden journalism and exorbitant adulation or debunking, but except for a few references to concertos and other works of virtuosic display, the actual programs he played—made up exclusively of his own compositions—were not mentioned; it seems unlikely, in any case, that he played chamber music in public. The only exceptions may have been in 1836-1837 when he traveled with the Italian guitar virtuoso Luigi Legnani (1790-1877) and would have performed together some of his duets for violin and guitar.[63] At the end of his life, however, when his public career was clearly over, chamber music was his major musical outlet. During the summer of 1838 and again in January, 1839, when his

[60]Geraldine de Courey, "Paganini," in *Die Musik in Geschichte und Gegenwart*, vol. x, col. 628.

[61]Alan Kendall, *Paganini: a Biography* (London: Chappell, 1982), p. 34.

[62]Kendall, p. 45; F.J. Fétis, *Biographical Notice of Nicolo Paganini with an Analysis of his Compositions and a Sketch of the History of the Violin*, 2nd ed. (London: Schott & Co., n.d. [reference is made to the current date 1851, which probably refers to the first French edition], p. 42.

[63]Wolfgang Boetticher, "Legnani," in *Die Musik in Geschichte und Gegenwart*, vol. viii, cols. 472-473.

illnesses overwhelmed him, he turned to the last quartets of Beethoven for solace.[64] In Spring, 1839,

> In retirement at the house of a friend, near the gate of the city, he still occupied himself with his art, and alternated between the Violin and the Guitar. One day he seemed to revive, and performed a quartett of Beethoven, his particular favourite, with the greatest energy.[65]

Although the instances when Paganini played chamber music are hard to document (since they were apparently private moments which he jealously guarded), Paganini as composer of chamber music can be more precisely discussed. Of the five collections of music published in his lifetime, four are chamber music: sonatas for violin and guitar (Opus 2 and 3, composed 1801-1806) and quartets for violin, viola, cello and guitar (Opus 4 and 5, composed 1806-1816). The presence of the guitar reflects Paganini's fame as a virtuosic guitarist as well as violinist, and these pieces remain the only classics of 19th-century guitar chamber music. Whereas the piano was ubiquitous in the chamber music of pianist-composers after 1830, the guitar was ubiquitous in the chamber music of the violinist-guitarist Paganini. In addition to the published music Paganini also wrote numerous other pieces for violin and guitar, such as the *Centone di Sonate* (eighteen sonatas, composed after 1828) which have remained in manuscript. In manuscript there are also his fifteen quartets for violin, viola, cello and guitar (only ten survive complete, composed 1818-1820), and the three regular string quartets (dedicated to the King of Sardinia). There are other duets and trios for strings.[66] Most of the music is virtuosic for the violin and fairly simple for the guitar and had nothing new to offer in terms of form, style or harmony. He wrote four *Nocturnes* for string quartet which are didactic rather than virtuosic, but these were the exception.[67] That he knew the late quartets of Beethoven is nowhere apparent in his compositions, which were more influenced by the sonatas and trios of Italian virtuoso composers of the

[64]Kendall, pp. 123 and 129.

[65]Fétis, p. 49.

[66]The only work for winds, outside the orchestrations, is the *Concertino* for bassoon, horn and orchestra, though Paganini might not be the composer of the entire piece.

[67]Manuscript in the Pierpont Morgan Library, New York.

18th century than by French or Austrian masters. Only the *Grand Sonata in A* for guitar with violin accompaniment (1804) seems in keeping with the grand trios and sonatas of other Europeans at the time.

Paganini's only authentic pupil, Ernesto Camillo Sivori (1815-1894), was not a composer of chamber music and was primarily famous in the second half of the 19th century as the greatest Italian virtuoso violinist. But in addition to his solo appearances Sivori was renowned as the leader of string quartet ensembles. As early as 1834 he performed string quartets in London, and in 1876 Verdi gave his only string quartet to Sivori's French ensemble (besides Sivori, Martin P.J. Marsick, P. Viardot, and J. Delsart) for the world premier. Sivori was the most prominent Italian string quartet player at the time.

Another Italian figure was Antonio Bazzini (1818-1897), who also had some encouragement from Paganini though he never was his student. The first half of his life was spent as a virtuoso, much of it in France and Belgium, and he lived in Paris from 1852 to 1864. When he returned to Italy in that latter year, however, he began to settle down and concentrate on composition, including an opera *Turandot* and various cantatas and orchestral works. He founded in Florence a Society for the Furtherance of German Music,[68] which clearly showed his dissatisfaction with the current state of Italian music and his preference for current German music. Thus it is not surprising that in his chamber music consisting of six string quartets and a quintet, he evinces influences of the Viennese classics.

While the violinist-composers made minor contributions to the performance and composition of Italian chamber music during the 19th century, opera composers also made a small contribution. Fernando Paër (1771-1839), for example, who was famous as an opera composer during Beethoven's life, published three grand sonatas for piano, violin and cello in 1811. When Gaetano Donizetti (1797-1848) went to study with Simon Mayr (1763-1845) in Bergamo, he found that his master was not only director of the Musi-

---

[68] A. Ehrlich (pseud. for Albert Payne), *Berühmte Geiger der Vergangenheit und Gegenwart* (Leipzig: A. H. Payne, 1893), p. 15.

cal Institute there but a violist in a local string quartet. Mayr was internationally famous, his operas were performed throughout Europe, and he was celebrated as well for his church compositions. Privately, however, chamber music was important for him; he had studied the keyboard sonatas of Schobert and Erard, and his German upbringing had no doubt included Hausmusik. When young Donizetti came to him as pupil—clearly his most gifted student, he obviously instilled in him a love for and appreciation of chamber music. Donizetti complied by writing eighteen string quartets.

Isolated but not to be ignored is the single string quartet of Verdi written after all his operas except *Otello* and *Falstaff*. It is the only piece of chamber music known by this master of the opera, yet it is a masterpiece that seemingly should follow years of concentration in the medium. As already mentioned, it was premiered by Sivori's quartet in 1876, and has survived as the single most important contribution to Italian chamber music in the 19th century.

Despite the isolated quartet of Verdi and the various other compositions and performances of chamber music mentioned above, Italy was not the center of this kind of music during the 19th century. It had lost out to the Germans and Austrians in particular by the end of the 18th century since so many Italian chamber musicians of the earlier epoch had left Italy for politically and economically better situations in the North. Opera flourished in Italy because it had direct appeal to the masses, particularly as a rallying point for the Risorgimento, but chamber music was too intimate and abstract. What had once been an Italian kind of music was by the middle of the 19th century thought of by Italians as a German-Austrian kind of music. For Bazzini the composition of chamber music was a contribution to German music, which was on a higher level than popular (and implied, trashy) Italian music.

England

The English, as noted above, preferred the chamber music of the Germans to their own, and with the importation of musicians, composers and their music from the Continent during the first half of the 19th century, a borrowed chamber music life existed. During the second half of the century there were, of course, many first-rate

English chamber musicians living in England, most in London, and apparently there was also a considerable amateur sub-society, but the string quartet that was most famous there then was the Joachim Quartet. True, the Joachim Quartet in England was not the Joachim Quartet of Berlin; only Joachim himself was common to both, and the other three members of his English quartet ensemble were Englishmen. Yet it took the foreign, German Joachim to lead the group to its spectacular success. Most Continental composers and performers of chamber music came to London to perform or at least witness, where the market was good and the people prosperous and interested in chamber music.

English contributions to chamber music in the 19th century were on the verge of being limited merely to patronage, but for the appearance of three gentlemen (all knighted) who began a movement toward the rebirth of English composition that would bear full fruition only in the next century, namely Sir Charles Hubert Parry (1848-1918), Sir Charles Stanford (1852-1924), and Sir Alexander Mackenzie (1847-1935).[69] All three set out to restore in England the highest level of performance, composition, criticism, and education of music in general and as a result also affected chamber music. Both Parry and Mackenzie were under strong German influence. Parry's chamber music, written during his early days, includes three string quartets, three piano trios, a piano quartet, a string quintet, a woodwind nonet, and various pieces for violin or cello and piano, while Mackenzie (who gave the Scottish premiers of Schumann's Piano Quartet and Piano Quintet in 1865) wrote a single string quartet, piano trio and piano quartet (1873-1875) and various pieces for piano with violin or cello. Stanford, on the other hand, was a much more formidable composer, and despite his personal friendship with Brahms, Joachim, Saint-Saëns and Von Bülow, he developed his own personal style built on a synthesis of the respected German styles and his love for his native Irish folklore. His eight string quartets, three piano trios, five sonatas for violin or cello and piano, two string quintets and various

---

[69]Stephen Banfield, "British Chamber Music at the Turn of the Century: Parry, Stanford, Mackenzie," in *the Musical Times*, cxv (1974), 211-213. Walter Parratt (1841-1924) was also important for raising musical standards in England, but his contributions were not specifically in chamber music.

other works reflect by their titles the current German dominance in England, but his character pieces (such as Irish Fantasies, Opus 54, for violin and piano [1894] and Six Irish Sketches for violin and piano [ca. 1917]) reveal a determination to be himself. However valuable the contributions of these three minor composers may or may not be to the overall repertory of chamber music, the new high standards that they set for themselves and their students (Stanford was the teacher of Vaughan Williams and many other dominant figures during the first half of the 20th century) would make a revival of great chamber music in England possible.

Germany and Austria

While new chamber music was struggling in England and France and had virtually ceased to be a factor in Italy, the performance of older chamber music at least continued in the second half of the 19th century in those countries and kept a small but select audience interested. In Germany and Austria, on the other hand, chamber music flourished. Central to this was the existence of outstanding chamber musicians, a willingness to admit new chamber music into the repertory, enough patrons to establish a viable economic base for chamber music, and a rapidly growing middle class that cultivated Hausmusik. Many German composers wrote chamber music, and the best of them all—Brahms—made chamber music a central part of his creation. There were, of course, German and Austrian ensembles capable of playing the most difficult chamber music to perfection. The quality professional string quartet ensemble, which had been established in Vienna with Schuppanzigh and in Paris with Baillot, continued in Vienna with the Hellmesberger Quartet and in Germany with the Joachim Quartet, and surrounding these quartet ensembles were performances not only of string quartets but also of other genres of chamber music.

Joseph Hellmesberger (1828-1893) founded his quartet ensemble in 1849 and maintained it until 1891.[70] The core of his repertory was not only Haydn, Mozart and Beethoven but also Schubert (whose quartets were being uncovered and premiered in the second

---

[70]Richard Evidon, "Hellmesberger," in *The New Grove Dictionary of Music and Musicians*, vol. viii, p. 463.

half of the century), Brahms, Bruckner and other contemporaries. When Brahms first moved to Vienna in 1862, he made his piano debut with members of the Hellmesberger Quartet in his own Piano Quartet Opus 26, and he continued this relationship for years (on December 2, 1886, for example, Brahms and Hellmesberger premiered the latter's A Major Violin-Piano Sonata). With lesser composers or those no longer living, Hellmesberger sometimes played abridged versions or interpolated movements from other pieces, but it is unlikely that he would have dared to do so with Brahms' music. After Joseph retired in 1891, the Quartet continued briefly with Joseph's son Joseph, Jr. (1855-1907) as leader; another son Ferdinand (1863-1940) was cellist from 1883.

With the establishment of the Berlin Hochschule für Musik in 1868, the Prussian capital became the true rival of Vienna in chamber music. The new director of the Hochschule was Joseph Joachim (1831-1907), probably the most important performer of chamber music in the second half of the 19th century. Joachim, who was, like Mendelssohn, a representative of the Jewish bourgeoisie that had since the end of the 18th century been intensely involved with the patronage, performance and composition of chamber music in Central Europe, studied chamber music performance with Joseph Böhm, and in 1843 he went to Leipzig to work with Mendelssohn. He performed the violin concerto under the supervision of the composer and Ferdinand David. The famous composer was taken with the child violinist, and the two frequently played duets together in private where Mendelssohn stressed not technique but the deepest musical expression of a piece. In 1851 Joachim instituted chamber music soirées in Liszt's Weimar, and the next year he moved to Hannover where he founded a string quartet. Here he first met Brahms and played the earliest chamber works which Brahms had written. In 1862 he started annual visits to London, where he organized a string quartet made up of local musicians. Then in 1868 he moved to Berlin and the following year established the Joachim Quartet, which lasted until his death. The Joachim Quartet performed primarily in Berlin, but it also traveled a great deal throughout Germany and Austria as well as to Paris, Budapest and Rome. Joachim's London ensemble remained a separate group until 1897, and only from 1900 to 1907 was the

Joachim String Quartet (ca. 1890, Germany). Private possession of author.

personnel entirely the same. While one can imagine that the quartet ensembles in which Spohr and especially Paganini had played in allowed the first violinist considerable freedom to show off, Joachim established once and for all the ideal of true string quartet ensemble: artistic and musical integrity above mechanical virtuosity.

Brahms

The towering figure in the composition of German-Austrian chamber music during the second half of the 19th century was Brahms (1833-1897). From the first version of his earliest piano trio of Opus 8 (1853-1854; revised 1889) to his last two sonatas for clarinet and piano Opus 120 (1894), Brahms considered chamber music on an equal footing with his Lieder, his choral music, his symphonies and his piano music. He wrote various chamber pieces before 1853 but later destroyed them when he found them less than perfect. Since he was a pianist and could not play the violin, he was timid in producing chamber music without piano, but by the early 1870's and with the assistance of Joachim he finally wrote his first string quartet and later two more and also two viola quintets. He stayed close to the traditional genres of chamber music and until late in his career ventured out only with his horn trio Opus 40 (1865). Then in 1891, a year after he told his publisher Simrock (now in Berlin) that he would write no more music, he met the great clarinetist Richard Mühlfeld and was so excited by the sound of this instrument that he quickly wrote his clarinet quintet Opus 115 (1891), the trio for clarinet, cello and piano Opus 114 (1891), and three years later the two sonatas for clarinet and piano Opus 120.

Brahms' chamber music has, like Beethoven's, been the subject of numerous books and articles and need only be summarized here. The pieces show a classical sense of motivic development and tight forms, a traditional harmony that builds on Beethoven, Schumann, and Chopin but not on Wagner, a thick color that exploits the full ranges of the instruments not for virtuosic ends but for purely expressive purposes, and a contrapuntal intricacy that is enhanced by frequent polyrhythm. The cyclic principles of monothematicism and repetition of melodies from one movement to another, so well established by Haydn and Beethoven and continued by Schumann and Mendelssohn, became a trademark of much of Brahms' chamber music. The C Minor String Quartet (1873), for example, utilizes especially the opening motive of the first violin in all the subsequent movements, and the second theme of the first movement returns in the second and fourth movements—always disguised, altered, developed, but nonetheless clearly audible.[71] The opening figure in the second violin and viola in the Opus 67 string quartet recurs in the viola at the opening of the third movement and forms a nucleus of a theme with variation in movement 4. The second sextet Opus 36 (1864-1865) is monothematic, based on the opening interval of a fifth, which in subsequent movements occurs in its inversion, a fourth. The opening turn-figure in the two violins in the clarinet quintet (1891) is the genesis for much of the rest of the composition. Brahms' approach to composition followed the concept of organic unity, which concerned Beethoven

---

[71]William G. Hill, "Brahms' Opus 51: a Diptych," in *The Music Review*, xiii (1952), pp. 110-124, analyzes the cyclic unity in these two quartets.

and other early 19th-century creative artists.[72] This extensive use of cyclic unity was imposed on standard classical sonata form, rondo, theme and variations, and scherzo form. Following Beethoven (such as in the Opus 69 cello-piano sonata) Brahms' scherzos alternate two distinct rhythmic and melodic sections but do not follow any internal binary form. But Brahms did not follow the radical innovations of the late Beethoven quartets and relied instead on easily recognizable classical forms.

Brahms exploited keys that were foreign to the classical composers but common to the romantics; he did so within a context that logically evolved from classical norms. For example in the opening sonata-form movement of the Opus 67 string quartet (1876) the opening key is B♭ Major, which modulates in a classical fashion through F Minor to the dominant F Major (m.58). The development, however is anything but classical; it quickly moves through D Minor and F Minor to the distant key F♯ Minor (m.127) before landing in G Minor and then on to a VII^7 or implied V^9 of the tonic B♭. His harmonic progressions are less dependent upon traditional 18th-century fifths and fourths and mix thirds and minor chords separated by a fourth or fifth (vi to iii) as in the first eight measures (and thereafter) of the same quartet movement.

Brahms' texture is very thick. This comes about because he frequently doubled melodic lines at the third and enriched the bottom lines with close doublings. The opening of the Poco Allegro finale of the second septet demonstrates this clearly and is typical even in sonatas with only two instruments (of which the keyboard fills in the thick texture). Here the two violins and first viola open with a close position triad in rapid sixteenth notes; in measure 7 the first cello has a solo doubled by the first violin on the G string at the sixth above, while the first viola and second cello on their open G-strings in close octaves surround the first violin and first cello (the other two instruments rest). This thickness is enhanced when

---

[72]For organic unity in Beethoven cf. John H. Baron, "August Wilhelm von Schlegel and Beethoven," in *Journal of Aesthetics and Art Criticism*, xxxi (1973), 531-537. For cyclic unity in Brahms cf. Werner Czesla, *Studien zum Finale in der Kammermusik von Johannes Brahms* (Bonn: Rheinische Friedrich-Wilhelms-Universität, 1968); in the opus 108 violin-piano sonata cf. Richard S. Fischer, "Brahms' Technique of Motivic Development in his Sonata in D Minor Opus 108 for Piano and Violin "(University of Arizona DMA dissertation, 1964).

pairs of instruments doubling at the third or sixth are in counterpoint to other pairs (mm.15-28). Brahms, who studied the contrapuntal masterpieces of the 16th century in great detail, loved to
weave contrapuntal lines throughout his works to offset otherwise
homophonic textures. His study of 16th-century choral works also
led Brahms to appreciate the rhythmic subtlety that this music
evinces and to incorporate some of it in his chamber music. He
frequently contrasted sections in different meter, such as in the
Adagio of the clarinet quintet, and he used meters such as $\frac{9}{8}$ and $\frac{3}{2}$
which were rare in the first half of the 19th century. Passages
moving in duple eighth-notes suddenly break into passages in triple eighth-notes, and eventually he combined duple and triple
notes simultaneously (e.g., Andantino, clarinet quintet, mm.64-69).
The complicated rhythmic counterpoint adds to the thickness of
Brahms' textures and to his idiosyncratic style.

In addition Brahms liked to incorporate Viennese and East
European (mostly Hungarian) folk songs and dances into many of
the otherwise classical sounds and rhythms.[73] The Viennese folk
song "Dort in den Weiden steht ein Haus" is used as the basis for
the adagio movement of his horn trio (it was written in memory of
his mother who had just died). The third and fourth movements of
his C Minor string quartet, on the other hand, resemble a Slavonic
and an East European dance respectively, the first and last movements of his second string quintet (Opus 111, 1890) contain suggestions of a waltz and czardas respectively, and the slow movement of his clarinet quintet contains an *alla zingarese*. In some
cases Brahms used his own songs for the basis of chamber music.
His "Regenlied" (Opus 59 no. 3), based on a poem by Klaus Groth,
is quoted extensively in the final movement of his first violin-piano
sonata, and the opening three notes of the song suggest the haunting opening of the first movement of the sonata as well. In addition
there are many song quotations in his second violin-piano sonata
Opus 100 (1886).

The significance of Brahms is not only that he made chamber
music a central part of his oeuvre throughout his life and that he

---

[73]Heinz Becker, "Das volkstümliche Idiom in Brahmses Kammermusik," in *Hamburger
Jahrbuch für Musikwissenschaft*, vol. vii, *Brahms und seine Zeit* (Hamburg: Laaber,
1984), pp. 87-99.

Johannes Brahms (1833-1897). Private possession of author.

contributed many masterpieces to the repertory, but also that he passed on to his younger contemporaries and future generations the recognition that chamber music is important. He demonstrated to them a way of writing chamber music that he learned and developed from his forebears. His respect for traditional forms, styles and harmonies, tempered with careful, logical, tasteful developments, and given in beautiful and inspired compositions, showed others that chamber music was indeed the most sophisticated kind of music that Europe had to offer and that there was still much chamber music that could be written.

Others in Germany and Austria

The Germans and Austrians of his own time at first tentatively followed Brahms in writing chamber music. In 1871 Bruckner (1824-1896), Brahms' most gifted contemporary in Austria, wrote his one major chamber music piece, his string quintet in F.[74] Bruckner did not overtly copy Brahms' quintets when he wrote his; indeed, it is possible Brahms copied Bruckner in this one instance.[75] But Bruckner must have been aware of the new chamber music that Brahms was writing in Vienna in the 1860's since this was the most important new chamber music in Vienna at the time, and the seriousness with which important patrons and performers took the Brahms works had to have had an effect on Bruckner's writing any chamber music at all.

Rather than his contemporaries, it was the younger generation that was most influenced by Brahms. Besides Dvořák (see below), younger Germans such as Mahler, Reger, Richard Strauss, Zemlinsky and Schoenberg wrote under the direct influence of Brahms. Zemlinsky and Schoenberg, who wrote a great deal of chamber music, will be discussed in the next chapter. Of the three others, only Reger was a prolific composer of this kind of music. Mahler

---

[74]The quintet in F was not performed publicly until 1885 by the Hellmesberger Quartet in Vienna. Bruckner also wrote an *Aequale* for three trombones in 1847 and began a string quartet in C Minor around the year 1861 which he did not complete.

[75]Hans Redlich, "Bruckner and Brahms Quintets in F," in *Music and Letters*, vol. xxxvi (1955), 253-258.

turned out only a piano quartet very early in his career,[76] and Strauss, who did write somewhat more chamber music, also did so as a very young man.[77]

Max Reger (1873-1916) was the son of an amateur oboist, clarinetist and bassist, and Hausmusik and chamber music were always a part of his life. He was a keyboardist—the most important German organist since Bach—and he learned the classical and romantic repertories largely through four-hand arrangements. Whether privately or publicly he was always performing chamber music. When he moved to Munich in 1901, he and the violinist Henri Marteau regularly gave concerts, and when he traveled to Russia in 1906, he and Ysaÿe performed Reger's own Opus 84 violin-piano sonata and Opus 93 suite. The importance of chamber music to Reger can best be judged by his compositions. Although primarily a composer of organ music and a contributor to nearly every genre of music except opera, Reger still had time to write nine violin sonatas (or suites), four cello sonatas, three clarinet sonatas, six string quartets, two piano trios, two piano quartets, two piano quintets, a clarinet quintet, a string sextet, and several other pieces. And he died young. Reger knew the music of Liszt and Wagner but was much more influenced by the other romantics: Beethoven, Schumann, Mendelssohn and especially Brahms.

> The strongest influences came from Brahms, in whose music Reger perceived "new, unsuspected spiritual impressions." As late as the Violin Sonata op. 139 and the Clarinet Quintet op. 146, echoes of a genuine reverence for Brahms bear witness to a close stylistic affinity.[78]

He kept to standard forms and genres, largely under the stern influence of his teacher Hugo Riemann, and he studied the music of the past. His Opus 93 "Suite im alten Stil" for violin and piano

---

[76]Klaus Hinrich Stahmer, "Drei Klavierquartette aus den Jahren 1875/76: Brahms, Mahler und Dvořák im Vergleich, in *Brahms und seine Zeit*, pp. 113-123.

[77]Franz Dubitzky, "Richard Strauss's Kammermusik," in *Die Musik*, vol. xiii.3 (1914), 283-296. Strauss' string quartet was a student work following Beethoven and Meyerbeer, and his piano quartet, his sonatas for piano with violin or cello, and his Serenade for thirteen wind instruments were early, interesting works showing his growth from post-Wagnerian harmony into his own peculiar style.

[78]Helmut Wirth, "Reger," in *The New Grove Dictionary of Music and Musicians*, vol. xv, p. 678.

(resembling baroque suites) and Opus 141 "Serenade" for flute, violin and viola (similar to serenades of the 1770's) are testimony to this study. Reger's chamber music has not received the international recognition that it probably deserves, but in Germany and Austria it has always had a following both among performers and audience.

The only remaining German figure of importance in the late 19th century was Ferruccio Busoni. Chamber music was not an important part of his work, but some of it was popular at the time and continues to be performed today. Busoni (1866-1924) was Italian by birth and through his father's side, but his mother's family was German and he spent nearly all his life away from his native country. His importance in helping to establish the neo-classic style and at the same time in preparing for atonalism had no bearing on his chamber music, which fell during the first half of his life. He wrote two string quartets (ca. 1880-1881 and 1889), two violin-piano sonatas (1890 and 1898) and a few miscellaneous compositions for piano with violin, cello, clarinet or flute. While he was not entirely at home in the area of chamber music composition (though the sonatas are good enough to continue to be performed), he felt compelled as an aspiring German composer to enter the field of chamber music where it was expected that a solid craftsman would show his skills.

CHAMBER MUSIC OF THE 19TH CENTURY FROM OTHER COUNTRIES

During the second half of the 19th century there was an increase in important composition of chamber music in areas of the world where there had not been much until now. Heretofore our focus has been on the creation of major works of chamber music in the traditional centers of Italy, France, Germany and England. The performance of chamber music occurred in many places outside these countries, but the most significant music played there was imported from or heavily influenced by that written in the four cited lands. In the second half of the 19th century, however, only Germany maintained a fully healthy chamber music tradition, and France fostered at least the performance of chamber music and eventually renewed its interest in composition as well. English composers were not major writers of chamber music, though the performance of chamber music remained important and there were some composers of local significance by the end of the century (Parry, Stanford and Mackenzie). Italy, however, lost its importance for the mainstream development of chamber music. Instead, the performance and composition of chamber music spread either to areas where there had never been much locally composed chamber music, such as in Scandinavia and America, or to areas where chamber music finally came into its own, as in Russia and Bohemia. While the emergence of chamber activities in Scandinavia, Spain, The Netherlands and other areas was important for the history of chamber music in those places, the development of a strong chamber music tradition in Russia, Bohemia and America is of importance for the history of chamber music in general. We will concentrate on those three countries and treat the other areas with less detail.

Russia

As we have seen above and in previous chapters, the performance of Italian, German and French chamber music in Russia occurred frequently in the 18th and early 19th century. Russian noblemen in the 18th century, following the lead of the tsars, aped foreign literature, architecture, music and even languages while deprecating or at least ignoring native Russian attempts at those things. One spoke French or German at the court, not Russian. Therefore it is not surprising that many Russian nobles' homes were filled with Western and Central European music. The works of the Mannheimers, Pugnani, C.P.E. Bach, Giardini, Abel, Vanhal, among others were very popular, and as the century drew to a close and the new one began, the chamber music of Haydn, Mozart and Beethoven became as important in Russia as in the rest of Europe.[79] Many rich Russians traveled abroad and listened to chamber music in Vienna or Paris (e.g., the future Tsar Paul II and

[79]Gerald Seaman, "Amateur Music-Making in Russia," in *Music and Letters*, vol. xlvii (1966), pp. 249-259.

his wife heard Haydn in Vienna on Christmas Day, 1781[80], the Russian ambassador Razumovsky became a benefactor of both Haydn and Beethoven, and Prince Galitzin was a special patron of Beethoven); there they discovered the music of the three Viennese masters and decided to bring it north upon their return to their homeland. The popularity of Austrian chamber music in Russia was a fact not to be ignored by Beethoven, who dedicated his Opus 30 violin-piano sonatas to Tsar Alexander I. In the major cities foreign musicians were brought in to entertain the royal court and other major noblemen, and even the great Schuppanzigh ensemble performed Beethoven and other Viennese works in St. Petersburg in 1816 and for a few years thereafter. Chamber music clubs were organized for the regular private or semi-private performance of chamber music, and occasionally public concerts were held.[81] Poets and artists performed chamber music or had good amateurs or professionals perform chamber music in their own homes. Even as great a musician as Liszt was paid by two Russian noblemen to play chamber music with them.[82] Landowners had their chamber music performed by serfs whom they had trained in the art by sending them to Italy as youngsters.

Russian chamber music composed by Russian composers appeared in the 18th century, though the Russian elite generally regarded it disparagingly. Ivan Khandoshkin's (1747-1804) trio sonatas are among the first chamber works by a Russian printed in Russia. His musically weaker variations on Russian songs and arias for violin and piano were favorites of Catherine the Great. Others ventured into string quartet writing, such as Ivan Ivanovich Vorobëv (1776-1838), Ferdinand Titz (1742-1810), Dimitri Stepanovich Bortnyansky (1751-1825), and Alexander Nikolayevich Aliabev (1787-1851);[83] all were influenced by foreign

---

[80]Cf. above, p. 318.

[81]Anne Mischakoff, *Khandoshkin and the Beginning of Russian String Music* (Ann Arbor: UMI Research Press, 1983).

[82] Richard Taruskin, *Defining Russia Musically: Historical and Hermeneutical Essays* (Princeton: Princeton University Press, 1997), p. xiii.

[83]Gerald Seaman, "The First Russian Chamber Music," in *The Music Review*, vol. xxvi (1965), 326-337; and Carol Greene, "The String Quartets of Alexander Alexandrovich Aliabev," in *The Music Review*, vol. xxxiii (1972), 323-329.

chamber music but also incorporated Russian folk tunes and/or bourgeois parlor romances.

But the beginning of a truly national Russian school of chamber music was the work of Mikhail Ivanovich Glinka (1804-1857), whose operas and symphonic poems ushered in Russian national music in general. Glinka heard chamber music from his childhood in the private homes of the artists and poets of his social circle, and his enthusiasm for this kind of music led him to write several chamber works early in his career: a septet for oboe, bassoon, horn, two violins, cello and bass (1824), a sextet for string quartet, bass and piano (1832), two string quartets (1824 and 1830), a *Trio Pathétique* for clarinet, bassoon and piano (1826-1827), a viola-piano sonata (1825-1828), a serenade on themes from Bellini's *Sonnambula* for string quartet, bass and piano (1832), and another serenade on themes from Donizetti's *Anna Bolena* for viola, cello, bassoon, horn and either piano or harp (1832). In and of themselves these works would not have secured Glinka a major place in the history of Russian chamber music, but because Glinka's other works, especially the operas, gained him the respect of those Russians of the 19th century who would fashion a great Russian national tradition, they are of historical importance. There was a new air in Russia beginning in the late 1820's with the coronation of the new Tsar Nicolas I, a despot of the worst sort but a believer in Russian nationalism. Glinka, though not a conservatory-trained composer, was an intelligent genius well-versed in Western European music as well as at home in the parlor music of the upper crust of Russian society; thus he experimented with melodic, harmonic, rhythmic and coloristic elements from the Russian bourgeois music which he instinctively knew and put them in a classical Western and Central European music setting. The resulting blend, most noticeable in his second and last opera *Ruslan and Lyudmilla* (1842), produced a new kind of sound that would make Russian composers of the rest of the century different from their counterparts in the West and would ultimately lead to some of the most successful new sounds of the 20th century.

During the second half of the 19th century Russian music blossomed so spectacularly that by the beginning of the 20th century Russian composers and performers had come to dominate the entire field of Western art music. A dichotomy developed during the third quarter of the century between followers of Glinka (the nationalists) and those who continued to prefer Western art music (the internationalists). Since the nationalists equated pure music, especially chamber music, with German national music, they basically steered away from it. This group included the so-called "Mighty Five": Balakirev, Cui, Mussorgsky, Borodin and Rimsky-Korsakov. The first three either avoided any kind of chamber music or treated it as a minor type of music,[84] but Borodin and Rimsky-Korsakov, who were much more inclined to compromise and respect Germanic music while retaining Russian sounds, did write some chamber music of lasting aesthetic value.

Borodin (1833-1887) taught himself the cello as a youth in order to take part in chamber music, and for this youthful ensemble he wrote a trio for two violins and cello and a trio for flute, cello and piano. While he was in medical school (1850-1856) he founded a chamber music group, which met at the apartments of the amateur cellist Gavrushkevich and played, among other things, Boccherini and Onslow cello quintets. They also played the works of Franz Xaver Gebel, a German living in Moscow. When Borodin graduated from medical school, he traveled to Germany where he came under the strong influence of the music of Mendelssohn; at this time he wrote a string sextet (1860) and a piano quintet (1862), both evincing the sounds of Mendelssohn. Back in Russia and working as a full-time chemist and professor of medicine, Borodin wrote his two famous string quartets (the first inspired by Beethoven's Opus 130 quartet), a cello quintet, a piano trio in D Minor (the Mendelssohn influence remained strong), and a trio based on a Russian folk song. Like his musical hero Glinka, Borodin blended the forms and styles of the Viennese and German classics and romantics with Russian colors, scales and rhythms. Unlike the other nationalistic composers, Borodin made chamber music central in his repertory. Borodin gave special prominence to the cello, util-

---

[84]Balakirev (1837-1910) actually composed a septet (1852) which is lost, a *quatuor original russe* (1854-1856) which is unfinished, and an octet for winds, strings and piano (1855-1856) which survives only in fragments; they are all juvenilia. Cui (1835-1918) wrote three string quartets (1890, 1907 and 1913) after the reconciliation of the nationalists and internationalists, a sonata for violin and piano (ca. 1860-1870), and miniatures for small ensembles.

ized the pentatonic scale, and wrote long, gangly romantic melodies comparable to those of Berlioz.

The most prolific Russian nationalist composer of this generation of composers was Rimsky-Korsakov (1844-1908). Earlier in his life and under the domination of Balakirev and Mussorgky he wrote purely nationalistic music and avoided German types—even in his symphonies, which despite the title are in their programs and sounds largely Russian. When he was appointed a professor at the St. Petersburg Conservatory, the main institution of the internationalists, however, Rimsky-Korsakov began to take a good look at Germanic types and especially chamber music. Soon he composed his first string quartet Opus 12 (1875), a quintet for flute, clarinet, horn, bassoon and piano (1876), a string sextet (1876), a string quintet on Russian themes (1878-1879), Four Variations on a Chorale for string quartet (1885), two movements of a quartet written jointly with Glazunov and Lyadov (1886-1887), and the piano trio and second string quartet (both 1897). To abet this sudden interest in chamber music, Rimsky-Korsakov joined the musical circle of Mitrofan Petrovich Belyayev, an amateur violist who placed his enormous fortune at the disposal of the newer Russian composers. Every Friday evening chamber music was played at his home by the leading amateurs and professionals in St. Petersburg. Rimsky-Korsakov and his pupils Glazunov and Lyadov, the pianist Felix Mikhaylovich Blumenfeld (1863-1931, the teacher of Horowitz), the young radical Scriabin, and others learned here the quartets of the Austrian and German masters and the newest chamber music which they themselves had written. For a few years Rimsky-Korsakov was inspector of naval bands and took advantage of this position to travel around Russia, to learn the various band instruments played throughout Russia, and to start to write his book on orchestration. As a result some of his later chamber pieces vary from the traditional scoring; he wrote his *Notturno* for four horns (ca. 1888), two duets for horn (1893-1894), and the *Canzonetta* and *Tarantella* for two clarinets (finished 1894).

By 1880 the old antagonism between nationalism and internationalism had given way to a rapprochement between Western and Russian musical elements. If one were to write a piece of chamber music in the traditional genres, then there was no denying the great models of the Westerners; at the same time there was now an authentically Russian sound, which no Russian could deny to his chamber composition without sacrificing personal integrity. The composer who best brought about this synthesis was not Borodin or Rimsky-Korsakov but Tchaikovsky. Tchaikovsky's (1840-1893) output of chamber music was not large, but what is there is very good. His three string quartets (1871, 1874, and 1877) stand with Borodin's as the best that 19th-century Russia produced, his piano trio (1881-1882) is the best of this popular genre written in Russia at the time, and his two *Souvenirs* (1878 for violin and piano and 1890 for string sextet—"Souvenir de Florence") have been standard repertory pieces for a century. Perhaps the best example of how Tchaikovsky blended the Germanic string quartet sound with Russian features comes in the second movement of the first string quartet. The basic sonority is Germanic and overtly the harmony is also traditional, but the melody—the very famous "Andante Cantabile"—is a borrowed Russian folk tune that quickly alternates measures of duple and triple meter (such rhythmic devices come from the study of Russian folk music which the Russians began during the 19th century).

Rimsky-Korsakov as teacher had two extraordinarily famous students: Glazunov and Stravinsky.[85] Alexander Konstantinovich Glazunov (1865-1936) was regarded at the turn of the century as Russia's most talented composer. That his reputation has fallen considerably since then is the result of the appearance shortly after that time of Scriabin, Prokofiev, Rachmoninof, Stravinsky and Shostakovich—all of whom were more original composers—and Glazunov's own predilection to write safe, uninspired music. He wrote a lot of it, and in many ways set the pattern for subsequent Russian composers to write extensively for chamber ensemble. Five of his seven so-called string quartets were written before the turn of the century and several of his other pieces for string quartets as well. Influenced by Rimsky-Korsakov's interest in wind instruments, he wrote frequently for winds, including his horn and piano "Rêverie" Opus 24 (1890), his brass quartet "In modo Religioso" Opus 38 (1892), and his saxophone quartet Opus 109

---

[85]See Chapter VII for more on Stravinsky.

Peter Ilyich Tchaikovsky (1840-1893).

(1932). This last work, however, is the result of 20th-century happenings that are quite distinct from early influences.

Thus by the end of the 19th century what was happening in Russian chamber music was no longer of purely parochial interest. A number of composers (especially Borodin and Tchaikovsky) had written chamber music that was becoming increasingly popular throughout Europe and America, and this music has elements which are distinctly Russian. In addition to the new varieties of rhythm, tone color, scale, and harmony, there was also added a thick, passionate melodic style that appealed less to the head than to the heart. This emotional appeal of the music became its most widely known feature, but when there was a reaction against such emotionalism in the 20th century, the other, more permanent features of the new Russian style remained.

Bohemia

Under the influence of Russian nationalism but also as a result of a centuries-long tradition of chamber music, Bohemia experienced a boom in chamber music in the 19th century and produced several great composers. As pointed out before, Bohemian composers had made important contributions to chamber music in the 18th century, but they had to go into exile in order to do so. Václav Tomásek (1774-1850) bucked the trend by remaining in Prague, and although he was himself not a nationalist, he recognized the importance to the future of Czech nationalist music of young Czech composers remaining in their homeland. Mostly self-taught, he was a private teacher and tutor and, while he composed within the Viennese classical tradition, he refused to associate himself with the German conservatory and opera in Prague. His greatest contribution lay in piano music, where he was the "father of the short character-piece that became an integral part of the Romantic keyboard tradition."[86] He wrote three string quartets (1792-1793), a trio for piano, violin and viola (1800), and a piano quartet (Opus 22, ca. 1805). Bedrich Smetana (1824-1884) was more truly the father of Bohemian national art music, especially in his orchestral

[86]Adrienne Simpson, "Tomásek," in *The New Grove Dictionary of Music and Musicians*, vol. xix, p. 34.

tone poems and in his operas. He left his country village at age 14 and went to Prague to study academic subjects, but instead he enjoyed music and wrote string quartets for his friends. Intermittently he played and wrote chamber music from that point until the end of his life. In 1847 he took part in chamber concerts in Prague, and when his favorite daughter died of scarlet fever in 1855, he mourned for her by writing his extraordinarily poignant G Minor piano trio (his first chamber masterpiece). The next year he moved to Göteborg, Sweden, where he remained for five years as director of a music school; he organized chamber concerts there with Josef Czapek (violinist) and August Meissner (cellist). By 1876 it was clear that Smetana was losing his hearing, so he wrote his most famous quartet "From My Life," which is a highly programmatic account of his life. Smetana describes each movement in detail; in the second, for example, he

> recalls the lively years of my youth among the country people and in the drawing rooms of aristocratic society . . . being known everywhere as a passionate dancer myself.

while in the third he

> recalls the blissful emotion of my first love for a girl who later became my devoted wife. Struggle against unfavorable circumstances and the final achievement of my aim.

The fourth movement reaches the fateful moment of deafness and his "submission to an irrevocable fate." The first movement is in sonata form, though the first theme of the exposition does not recur until the last movement. In his last quartet (written 1882-1883) he was again autobiographical; reconciled to deafness, he now was fighting insanity. In this quartet he abandoned the traditional forms which he had employed in his earlier quartet and trio, but it retains a touch of nationalism with its middle "polka" movement.

However important Tomések and Smetana were to the history of Bohemian national music, their contributions to chamber music remain largely provincial and few in number. The case was quite different with their heir, Antonín Dvořák (1841-1904), whose vast output in chamber music forms a central part of his oeuvre and a

major part of the international repertory of chamber music. Dvořák
started his career as a distinguished violist and only tentatively
wrote music, including some chamber music. By ca. 1872 his
chamber works were being performed at semi-private free musical
evenings and matinees in Prague. The year 1874 was the turning
point for Dvořák; he won the Austrian State Stipendium for composition, judged by Johann Herbeck, Eduard Hanslick (a former
pupil of Tomásek), and Brahms. He won again in 1876 and 1877,
and by 1878 with Brahms' help his music was published by Simrock and achieved immediate worldwide popularity. Major professional quartets like the Joachim and Bargheer were premiering his
music in Berlin and Hamburg, and Hellmesberger commissioned a
new quartet (Opus 61). When Brahms, Simrock and others belit-
tled Prague and its provincialism and encouraged Dvořák to move
to a major center like Vienna or Berlin, Dvořák's patriotism and
anti-German sentiments were fiercely aroused and he staunchly
remained in his native country. He befriended Tchaikovsky in Prague in 1888 and himself went to Russia in 1890. Just before he
sailed for America in 1892, he, his violinist friend Ferdinand
Lachner, and his cellist friend Hanus Wihan (for whom he would
later write the famous cello concerto) toured Bohemia and Moravia
playing, among other works, his *Dumky Trio*. The years in America were filled with new works and experiences; he continued to
write chamber music including his "American" Quartet, which the
Kneisel Quartet premiered in Boston in 1893.

Dvořák's chamber music basically fits into the standard mold
of the century. He was heavily influenced by Schubert and Schumann,[87] and he wrote in the standard forms of his Germanic predecessors.[88] He wrote fourteen string quartets, six piano trios, three
string quintets, two piano quintets and two piano quartets, three
violin-piano sonatas, a cello-piano sonata, and a string sextet. His
works including winds are his clarinet quintet [1865] and his octet
for two violins, viola, bass, clarinet, bassoon, horn and piano
[1873]. But within this group are movements that are Bohemian

---

[87]David Beveridge, "Dvořák's Piano Quintet, Op. 81: the Schumann Connection, in
Chamber Music Quarterly (Spring, 1984), pp. 2-10.
[88]Otakar Sourek, *The Chamber Music of Antonín Dvořák,* abr. trl. of *Dvorakovy Skladby
Komorni: Charakteristika a Rozbory* by Roberta Samsour (Prague: Artis, 19[56], repr.
Westport: Greenwood Press, 1978).

dances and folk songs (e.g., the slow movement of the piano quintet Opus 81 is a "Dumka"), and there are also character pieces with distinctly nationalistic sounds (e.g., the string trio "Drobnosti" [1881], the piano trio "Dumky" [1890-1891], the violin-piano "Slavonic Dance [1891], and the cello-piano "Slavonic Dance [1891]). Dvořák used pentatonic melodies and accompaniments in his "American Quartet, which has led some to consider it a conscious effort to bring the music of the American Indian into his European art music,[89] but Dvořák used pentatonic scales before coming to America and was inspired to do so from the pentatonic Slavonic folk music which was central to his entire output and from his knowledge of the pentatonic music coming from the new Russian art music.[90]

The importance of Dvořák's chamber music, beyond its internationally approved aesthetic value, is that it provided for the Czech people a major, non-Germanic local repertory that would justify the furtherance of chamber music composition and performance during the 20th century when anti-German sentiment would run high. For the Czechs, chamber music was not a Germanic art but an international European one that transcends national borders; it is the possession of musically highly sensitive people wherever they happen to live. In Dvořák's chamber music they saw a local version of this international music that despite its parochial origins appeals to chamber music enthusiasts worldwide, and they could take pride in this local contribution. Thanks to Dvořák Prague became during the second half of the 19th century one of the capitals of European chamber music. The Czech people in the 20th century have enthusiastically adopted chamber music as central to their lives, as reflected in the huge number of professional ensembles during the new century. How popular chamber music was in the 1930's is seen in the large collection of chamber musical instruments confiscated from Bohemian Jewish chamber

---

[89]For example, Henry Edward Krehbiel, *Antonin Dvořák's Quartet in F Major, Op. 96* (New York: H.A. Rost, 1894).

[90]David Beveridge, "Sophisticated Primitivism: the Significance of Pentatonicism in Dvořák's American Quartet," in *Current Musicology*, no. 24 (1977), 25-36; and Hans Kull von Niederlenz, *Dvořák's Kammermusik*, in *Berner Veröffentlichungen zur Musikforschung*, Heft 15 (Bern: Paul Haupt, 1948).

players (amateurs and professionals) by the Nazis before they ex-
terminated them and which now are in the Jewish National Museum in Prague.

Scandinavia

There were several important musicians in 19th-century Scandinavia who cultivated chamber music in their native countries and
whose music is occasionally performed elsewhere. The violinist
Niels Gade (1817-1890) felt very strongly about his Danish heritage early in his career, but after struggling at home for recognition, he left for Leipzig in 1843 to work under Mendelssohn, who
showed genuine appreciation for his music. The influence of
Mendelssohn, Schumann and this generation of romantics worked
very strongly on Gade, who later returned to Denmark with much
less nationalism in his music than heretofore. Although primarily a
composer of symphonies and choral music, Gade wrote two string
quartets, two string quintets, a string sextet and a string octet (this
last clearly under the influence of Mendelssohn), three violin-piano
sonatas, and a few other pieces of chamber music, among which
are the nationalistic *Folkedanse* (Opus 62, 1888) and the *Volk-
stänze im nordischen Charakter* (1886) for violin and piano. Copenhagen had several chamber music societies by the late 1860's,[91]
and thanks to Gade's international prestige at the time, these societies created a deep-seeded interest in chamber music in Denmark that has lasted to the present day. Carl Nielsen (1865-1931),
Denmark's most important composer at the turn of the century,
was brought up as a chamber music player and wrote numerous
chamber works including string quartets, violin-piano sonatas, and
the famous wind quintet Opus 43 (1922).

What Gade did for Denmark, Ole Bull (1810-1880) did for
Norway. Bull was precocious as a violinist and at age eight was
already playing chamber music weekly in his home. Within a few
years he was an internationally recognized violin virtuoso who
some said was better than Paganini. Unlike Gade, however, Bull

---

[91]Kammermusikforeningen, *Kammermusik i Hundrede ar: 1868 - 5. December - 1968*
(Copenhagen: Nyt Nordisk Forlag, 1968); and Lars Borge Fabricus, *Traek af Dansk Musiklivs Historie m.m. Omkring etatsraad Jacob Christian Fabricus' Erindringer* (Copenhagen: Nyt Nordisk Forlag Arnold Busck, 1975).

never stopped promoting his Norwegian nationalism, as composer, performer and political activist. He proudly displayed Norwegian folk melodies and even promoted folk instruments. For example, in Paris in 1833 he played his *Souvenirs de Norvège* using Norwegian slätter and folksongs arranged for Hardanger fiddle with string quartet, bass and flute. Bull traveled around Europe and not only played concertos and recitals with virtuosic compositions but also occasionally played authentic chamber music. In London in 1840, for example, he performed the Beethoven *Kreutzer* Sonata with Liszt at a Philharmonic Society concert, and on January 20, 1841, he took part in a chamber music concert with Mendelssohn and David in Leipzig. Bull traveled to America as well as Europe, where his reputation soared, and while he did much to strengthen Norwegian nationalism in music, he himself did not compose any chamber music. That was left for two Norwegians who were greatly influenced by Bull.

Johan Svendsen (1840-1911), the lesser known of the two, was a violinist who as a youngster studied at great length the Mozart and Beethoven sonatas. In 1859 he met Bull, but his teacher was another, Carl Arnold, and by 1863 he was studying in Leipzig. As a young man in Germany he then wrote the three chamber works which became his major contributions to the field: the string quartet Opus 1 (1865), his octet Opus 3 (1865-1866), and his string quintet Opus 5 (1867). The first two were premiered at the Leipzig Conservatory with great success, and when he went to Paris in 1868, the string quartet and quintet became popular at musical soirées. He and Saint-Saëns performed together a Grieg violin-piano sonata. Later that year he was in Weimar where his octet was performed, and in 1877 Sarasate performed all his chamber music in London. Svendsen's later life was taken up as conductor, partially in Norway and partially in Copenhagen. The three chamber works are not very original, but he is the first Norwegian to write serious chamber music which was played internationally.

Svendsen's great contemporary, Edvard Grieg (1843-1907), on the other hand, wrote some important chamber music that has continued to be performed. There is not much: three violin-piano sonatas, one cello-piano sonata, one complete string quartet, an incomplete and a lost string quartet, and a piano quintet. As long as his melodic, harmonic and rhythmic invention were at their best, he was able to overcome the antithesis between the traditional classical forms in which he felt these pieces should be written and the miniature, characteristic pieces with which he felt most at home. It was in the latter that he succeeded in portraying Norwegian folk life, and he risked becoming academic when he went to the bigger forms. Grieg's first two violin-piano sonatas succeed because they are melodic and do not let the form dominate the content, but his quartet is not as successful. It would take Bartók, a generation later, to show how folk music and traditional forms could synthesize into masterful chamber music.

While Norwegian composers were the most important in Scandinavia, Swedes were also involved in chamber music from at least the 18th century. Swedish composers such as Anders Wesström (ca. 1720-1781) and Joseph Martin (1756-1792) wrote quartets at the same time as Mozart and Haydn, and during the 19th century a variety of chamber genres were added to by composers from Sweden.[92] Swedish musicians formed ensembles in their homes and in clubs, the most famous of which was the Mazerska Kvartettsällskapet which was founded in 1849. The members of the club performed chamber music on a regular basis, and only occasionally did outside artists join in (e.g., Leopold Auer in the 1860's).

Finland's most famous composer, Jean Sibelius (1865-1957), actually wrote all his important chamber works in the 20th century. He composed numerous works for violin and piano in 1915 and 1929, and his string quartet in D Minor (1909) is appropriately entitled "Voces Intimae."

Other European Countries

Other countries in Europe also had their chamber music in the 19th century. In Switzerland, for example, there was a tradition of Hausmusik going back at least to the middle ages when psalm singing was a regular part of everyone's life at home and at

---

[92]Bo Wallner, *Den Svenska Sträkkvartetten: Del I: Klassicism och Romantik*, in *Kungl. Musikaliska Akademiens Skriftserie*, no. 24 (Stockholm: Kungl. Musikaliska Akademien, 1979); and Gereon Brodin, "Svensk Kammarmusikbibliografi," in *Ur Nutidens Musikliv*, v (1924), pp. 24-31, 66-68, 94-102, and 120-123.

school.[93] In the 17th century student groups organized Collegia Musica before the Germans did, and some of these developed into concert societies. In the 18th century professionals were admitted into the concert societies, and instrumental music eventually replaced nearly all the vocal music. In the 19th century musical life was democratized among males, so that every male participated in or attended public concerts, music societies, public music schools, and middle-class Hausmusik.[94] The market in Switzerland for new Hausmusik grew rapidly, and with it the repertory of available music expanded considerably. Every now and then a woman would be admitted, especially if she sang well or had an international reputation (such as Clara Schumann). But Switzerland did not produce a significant composer of chamber music until the 20th century.

Spain also had an old tradition of chamber music, and this continued during the second half of the 18th century. As noted in previous chapters, Boccherini and Brunetti were part of a very important chamber music scene in Madrid, but there were also Spanish composers such as Manual Canales, José Herrando, Francisco Manalt, Juan Oliver y Astorga, Juan Pla, José Pla, Manual Pla, Antonio Soler, Antonio Ximenez, and Nicolas Ximenez.[95] They wrote duet and trio sonatas, duets for treble instruments, and string quartets modeled on the Viennese classics of the time; there are no Spanish folk idioms to be found. In the 19th century the Conservatory in Madrid became the focal point for concerts of string quartets, and though the vast majority of the Spanish people were too downtrodden to be aware of chamber music, a small coterie of wealthy and educated Spaniards continued the traditions of the 18th century.[96]

[93]Martin Staehelin, "Basels Musikleben im 18. Jahrhundert," in *Die Ernte: Schweizerisches Jahrbuch*, xliv (1963), 116-141.

[94]Hans Peter Schanzlin, *Basels private Musikpflege im 19. Jahrhundert*, in *Basler Neujahrsblatt*, no. 139 (Basel: Helbing & Lichtenhaln, 1961).

[95]Richard X. Sanchez, "Spanish Chamber Music of the Eighteenth Century" (Louisiana State University Ph.D. dissertation, 1975).

[96]José de Castro y Serrano, *Los Cuartetos del Conservatorio: Breves Consideraciones sobre la Música Clássica* (Madrid: Centro General de Administración, 1866).

String quartet (1872) with Wilma Neruda (1838?-1911). University of Southampton.

There were Polish composers of chamber music from at least the early 18th century,[97] and by the end of the 19th century Warsaw had distinguished ensembles such as the Trio Wirtuozów Polskich and the Quartet Smyczkowy Stanislava Barcewicza.[98] In The Netherlands and Hungary, both of which figured importantly in the development of chamber music prior to the 19th century, chamber music institutions were developing and seeds were being sown for even more significant developments in the 20th century.

America

Chamber music was brought to America by European settlers who regarded it as part of the Old World civilization which they wished to retain in the New World. In what is today Canada, chamber music did not have an easy time because of the rigors of the lifestyle, but there were amateurs who sought each other out and who made efforts to organize concerts.[99] It is only in the 20th century that a successful chamber music scene fully developed.

In what is now the United States the situation developed earlier. In the 17th century the early Bostonians had chamber music instruments, which have survived until today, and it is possible that the existence of these instruments in 17th-century New England means that chamber music was performed by these pioneers.[100] By the late 18th century America already could boast several American-born composers of chamber music and concerts of chamber music (forty-six concerts of string quartets between 1786 and 1800 were recorded in seven East Coast cities[101]). The earliest known

---

[97]Antoni Poszowski, "Polnische Instrumentale Kammermusik in der ersten Hälfte des 18. Jahrhunderts," in *Musikzentren in der ersten Hälfte des 18. Jahrhunderts*, ed. Eitelfriedrich Thom (Magdeburg: Rat des Bezirkes, 1979), pp. 15-23.

[98]Andrzej Spóz, ed., *Kultura Muzyczna Warszawy Drugiej Polowy xix Wieku* (Warsaw: Pánstwowe Wydawnicturo Naukowe, 1980).

[99]J.S. Loudon, "Reminiscences of Chamber Music in Toronto during the Past Forty Years," in *Canadian Journal of Music*, i (1914), pp. 52-53.

[100]Roger Paul Phelps, "The History and Practice of Chamber music in the United States from Easliest times up to 1875" (University of Iowa Ph.D. dissertation, 1951).

[101]Anne Schaffner, "The Modern String Quartet in America before 1800," in *The Music Review*, vol. xl (1979), pp. 165-167.

American-born composer of chamber music was John Antes (1740-1811), who apparently wrote six string quartets and who published three string trios in London ca. 1790 which he had written in Egypt.[102] The oldest surviving pieces of chamber music actually composed in America are the six string quintets (Salem, NC: 1789) by Johann Friedrich Peter. Antes belonged to the American Moravian community, which had brought its German musical heritage to Georgia in the 1730's and then to Pennsylvania and the Carolinas.[103] Before the end of the 18th century the string quartets of Haydn and the trios of Mozart were being performed by the Moravians in Bethlehem, Pennsylvania. The Moravians also developed wind ensemble music, some of which apparently is chamber music. They wrote marches, chorales, and dances for these ensembles, which were called Collegia Musica (virtuosic woodwind ensembles). The chief composer of this group was David Moritz Michael (1751-1827), who came to America in 1795 and remained for twenty years. He wrote fourteen *Parthien* and two other suites for woodwind sextet (mostly two clarinets, two horns and two bassoons).[104] The first chamber music published in America was easy arrangements of popular and patriotic songs and of classical European music for three instruments in Samuel Holyoke's manual *The Instrumental Assistant* (Exeter, NH: 1800); these pieces and those that followed in companion volumes during the next decade were aimed at "social orchestras "(local instrumental clubs).

In the century from 1750 to 1850 Philadelphia's musical life grew rapidly, and with it the performance of chamber music. In this regard Philadelphia was like Boston, New York, Baltimore, New Orleans and several other American cities. We know from the accounts of distinguished American leaders that they played cham-

---

[102]In a letter to Benjamin Franklin Antes says that he is sending Franklin a copy of his six quartets, but the whereabouts of the music today is unknown. Cf. K. Marie Stolba, "Evidence for Quartets by John Antes, American-born Moravian Composer," in *Journal of the American Musicological Society*, vol. xxxiii (1980), pp. 565-574.

[103]Harry Hobart Hall, "The Moravian Wind Ensemble: Distinctive Chapter in America's Music" (George Peabody College Ph.D. dissertation, 1967).

[104]Karl Kroeger, "Michael," in *The New Grove Dictionary of American Music*, vol. iii, p. 223.

ber music.[105] In the 1770's, for example, the Governor of Pennsylvania, John Penn, played violin in a regular chamber group which also included the important early American composer Francis Hopkinson; their repertory was the music of Corelli, Handel and Johann Stamitz. Philadelphia had its foreign-born immigrant composers who composed chamber music: Jean Gehot (1756 - ca. 1820), who played under Salomon in the Haydn concerts of 1791 and who came to Philadelphia the next year where his string quartets were performed; John Christopher Moller (1755-1803), who came to the United States ca. 1785 after having published six string quartets in London; and Benjamin Carr (1768-1831), whose *Progressive Sonatinas* for piano with ad libitum violin or flute was published in Baltimore in 1812.[106] Later Philadelphia also had its native composers Charles Hommann and William Henry Fry. Hommann (ca. 1800 - after 1862), who spent most of his life in Philadelphia, wrote three string quartets and one string quintet. Fry (1813-1864), influenced by the Italian operas of Bellini and Donizetti and German symphonies, seemingly wrote at least eleven string quartets (only two survive complete: nos. 10 and 11).

Besides the major cities, frontier communities also had their chamber music. In Aurora, Oregon, for example, a town founded in 1856 by the religious leader William Keil, chamber music formed with religious music a basic part of the lives of its citizens.[107] While amateur chamber music making was occurring from New York, Washington, and Philadelphia to Cincinnati and Mt. Airy (North Carolina)[108] to Aurora (Oregon), professional musi-

---

[105]Thomas Jefferson and Patrick Henry played duets together, and Jefferson owned a collection of chamber instruments with which he often played chamber music.

[106]Myrl Duncan Hermann, "Chamber Music by Philadelphia Composers 1750-1850 "(Bryn Mawr College Ph.D. dissertation, 1977). Benjamin Franklin, who is listed by Hermann as a composer of chamber music in Philadelphia, was probably not the composer of the quartet for open strings and scordatura; cf. Hubert Unverricht, "Haydn and Franklin: the Quartet with Open Strings and Scordatura, "in Jens Peter Larsen, Howard Serwer, and James Webster, *Haydn Studies* (New York: Norton, 1981), pp. 147-154.

[107]Deborah M. Olsen, "Music in an American Frontier Communal Society, "in *Brass Bulletin*, no. 33 (1981), pp. 49-58, no. 34 (1981), pp. 13-22, and no. 36 (1981), pp. 64-77.

[108]Burnet Corwin Tuthill, "Fifty Years of Chamber Music in the United States 1876-1926," in *The Musical Courier*, xcix (August 17, 1929), 8, (August 24), 15, 20, (August 31), 10.

Piano quintet rehearsal in the home (ca. 1890, U.S.A.).
Private possession, New Orleans.

cians gathered to make chamber music for themselves or for audiences. Orchestral musicians in New Orleans, Boston, New York
and other cities played chamber music with their students and with
each other and with local pianists, organists and harpists. The Harvard Musical Association, for example, a group of students led by
the critic John Sullivan Dwight, had six concerts of chamber music
a year from 1844 to 1849. Professional chamber music ensembles
started with the Mendelssohn Quintet Club of Boston (1849-1898),
the Theodor Eisfeld series in New York (1851f.), the Mason-
Thomas Quintet of New York (1855-1868), the Briggs House concerts in Chicago (1860f.), and the Kneisel Quartet of Boston
(1885-1917).[109]

With the dispersion of chamber musicians throughout the
United States, composers of chamber music toward the end of the
19th century began to seek an American idiom within a decidedly

[109]Tuthill.

European kind of music. Many string quartets[110] and violin-piano sonatas[111] were written in America during the 19th century. One of the most important composers of chamber music was George Chadwick (1854-1931), who was trained in Germany in the 1870's and settled in Boston in 1881 where he remained for the rest of his life. He wrote five string quartets, which the Kneisel Quartet frequently played; they and his piano quartet (1887) are carefully written and attempt to show American traits—especially in the opening of the Fourth String Quartet (1896) with its Anglo-American psalmody rhythm (also heard in Dvořák's "American" Quartet). But while George Chadwick and others began to search for specifically American sounds, they still wrote essentially with a European voice. Dvořák's presence in Iowa and New York and his conscious attempt to be American heightened the discussion. Would the American sound come from the music of the American Indians or American Blacks or New England church hymns or Appalachian folk songs? Only later, in the mid-20th century, did a consensus develop that recognized the American contribution to chamber music as a synthesis of all these aspects and others as well (see the next chapter).

The rise of chamber music composition and performance in America changed the focus of this history not only from an Italian-French-German-Austrian-English development but also from a European one into an intercontinental one. By the end of the 19th century chamber music, though still conceived by most as a Germanic type of music, was already approaching that breakthrough which would lead in the 20th century to a revolutionary situation. Abetted by technological, largely electronic discoveries, the new ethnological approach to chamber music would in the course of a few decades alter the tastes, customs and expectations of chamber

---

[110]Thomas Warburton, "Historical Perspective of the String Quartet in the United States," in *American Music Teacher*, xxi (January 1972), no. 3, pp. 20-22, 37; and Nancy Page Smith, "The American String Quartet, 1850-1918" (University of North Carolina M.A. thesis, 1949).

[111]James A. Starr, "A Critical Evaluation of Performance Style in Selected Violin Works of Nineteenth Century American Composers" (University of Illinois D.M.A. dissertation, 1978) discusses seven violin-piano sonatas written by American composers in the 19th century, chief of whom is Horace Wadham Nicholl.

music enthusiasts. Russian, Hungarian, Bohemian, Scandinavian, American, and Latin American sounds coupled with the phonograph and radio would usher in a century without any equal before it. Audiences would drastically expand and change character, but through it all the five basic criteria for chamber music—however embattled—have survived.

CHAPTER VII

CHAMBER MUSIC IN THE 20TH CENTURY

During the first two decades of the 20th century chamber music began to undergo radical changes that increased in scope and intensity as the century progressed. The changes first were matters of style, form, rhythm, color and harmony in the compositions themselves, but gradually all other aspects of chamber music were affected. Social and economic changes in Central Europe, then in the rest of Europe and around the world, led to new conditions for both the public and private performance of chamber music and Hausmusik. Technological innovations such as radio, phonograph, cinema, television, video and the home computer have increasingly altered the relationship of the composers to the performers, the performers to the listeners, and the lovers of chamber music to their means for enjoying it. The most important of the five criteria for chamber music—intimacy—has undergone readjustment and, after many shocks, remains the essential basis upon which the future of chamber music will assuredly rest.

As a result of these social, economic, political, and technological changes, most composers have responded—not always directly or immediately but ultimately—with innovative means of achieving the basic goals of chamber music: intimacy through solistic instrumental ensemble works. New instruments not imagined before the advent of the new technologies have opened up new colors and compositional styles, and political conditions have often forced the hitherto iconoclastic composer to engage in his or her environment. But all this is not entirely new to the 20th century; much of it has been true throughout the over-four-hundred-year history of chamber music. What is new are the specific needs and conditions of the turbulent world of the 20th century and the intensity with which, as never before, the European culture which fostered chamber music has been upset through devastating wars, massive changes in political systems, and head-on clashes with the many different cultures of the rest of the world. As James McCalla has pointed out, nearly all important innovations in 20th-century classical music as a whole were first achieved in chamber music, and the most important new feature of modern and post-modern classical music is the centrality of chamber music to our musical culture.[1]

TRADITIONAL GENRES OF CHAMBER MUSIC IN THE 20TH CENTURY

Throughout the 20th century the inherited genres of chamber music have been cultivated, but in nearly all cases there have been changes in compositional procedures. Some of these changes have come about through expansion of ethnic ideas first suggested in the 19th century; others have come about through what has been conceived as the "logical evolution" of musical structure. The expression "logical evolution" is apparently a contradiction in terms; "evolution" is normally a natural phenomenon while "logical" is a human concoction. But in fact evolution in music is not a natural phenomenon, no matter how "scientific" some music theorists would have it; any evolution in music is a man-made evolution, not a divine one, and the logic of rational people is governed by all the foibles that mankind is capable of. It is propagandistic egotism of a composer to regard his/her music as evolving *naturally* from the classics of the previous generation; it is a cover to disguise what is a personal, individual reinterpretation of traditional compositional methods—a logical system that applies to a man-made set of conditions. However valid and/or exciting it is, it is one among many such systems.

---

[1]James McCalla, *Twentieth-Century Chamber Music* (New York: Schirmer Books, 1996). McCalla's definition of chamber music is more inclusive than mine; he includes works for two pianos, solo works, and vocal works, which border on the purely instrumental ensemble music that I accept but which I have chosen to exclude for practical reasons discussed in Chapter 1. He stresses the literary and dramatic nature of modern chamber music, which inevitably allows for program music and theatrics which I exclude by definition. Despite this, his work is by far the best study of 20th-century chamber music.

Debussy and Ravel

At the end of the 19th and beginning of the 20th century Debussy (1862-1918) and Ravel (1875-1937) wrote a small amount of traditional chamber music, i.e., string quartets, sonatas for piano with violin or cello, a piano trio, string and other duets. Each of their quartets (Debussy's G Major Quartet, 1893; Ravel's F Major Quartet, 1903) is in four movements contrasting in tempo. Both are mainly tonal quartets with some pentatonicism, and sonata form exists but without the traditional contrast of tonic and dominant. Debussy's occasional use of the pentatonic scale and even the whole-tone scale necessarily upsets a system of harmony that has been in place since the beginning of the history of chamber music and upon which the traditional forms are based; neither scale allows the leading-tone-to-tonic or dominant-to-tonic cadence that establishes keys and sections in traditional music. The result is a new importance for the tri-tone as a consonant interval[2] or the creation of new patterns of intervals as the basis for harmonic and tonal structure.[3] Debussy learned these seemingly exotic scales from the Russians; Glinka used them in his opera *Ruslan and Lyudmilla* (1842) as a source for harmony as well as melody, Mussorgsky used them throughout his compositions (1860's-1870's), and Debussy as a student heard them during his several summers in Russia and as he was formulating his *impressionistic* sounds in Paris with the performance of Russian music in the French capital in the 1890's. For the Russians the new sounds meant the birth of national Russian art music, i.e., the development of a classical art style whose unique sounds evolve from the pentatonic and whole-tone folk music of the Russian peoples with special emphasis on tritones, the French sixth chord, and the octatonic scale. Stravin-

---

[2] Judith S. Allen, "Tonal Allusion and Illusion: Debussy's Sonata for Flute, Viola and Harp," in *Cahiers Debussy, Nouvelle Série*, no. 7 (1983), pp. 38-48.

[3] Robert Moevs, "Intervallic Procedures in Debussy: Serenade from the Sonata for Cello and Piano, 1915," in *Perspectives of New Music*, vol. viii, no. 1 (1969), pp. 82-101, shows how Debussy divides the scale into two groups of two half-steps and a single group of a whole step, with a minor third interval between the first and second group and the second and third group (A♭-A-B♭ C♯-D-E♭ G♭-A♭) and then builds a movement upon this pattern.

Claude Debussy (1862-1918). Archives Photographiques, Paris.

sky's *Three Pieces for String Quartet* (1914) are perhaps the ripest fruit of this new Russian sound in chamber music.[4] For Debussy the incorporation of this Russian harmonic system opened a path to free French art music from nearly a century of domination by Germans (Haydn-Mozart-Beethoven to Wagner and Brahms). By accepting a harmonic system that shattered the fundamental principles of Germanic harmony and form, yet retained just enough of the outward appearances of traditional music to merit "logical evolution" from the past, Debussy opened up new possibilities for further development of form and harmony that were denied Germans like Schoenberg who, in turn, evolved their new music logically from the Germanic tradition. Debussy's Russian-based harmony needed a French twist, which came in the coloration and rhythm of his music. The Sonata for Flute, Viola and Harp (1915) has a color that no one had exploited before, and this follows after Ravel in his Introduction and Allegro for Flute, Clarinet, Harp and String Quartet (1905) pursued his own unique color. The flute-harp combination gave them both an "impressionistic sound" that came to be associated specifically with French music because these two masters used it. The rhythmic fluidity of Debussy Ravel carried even further, especially under the influence of Afro- or Latin-American blues (in the second movement of his violin-piano sonata), jazz, tango and other 20th-century dances. The fuzzy impressionistic colors and the rhythm which often defies strict metrical beats (the outlines are, as in Renoir's paintings, irrelevant) are seen more in the miniature works, such as Debussy's *Syrinx* for flute alone (1912) and *Petite Piéce* for clarinet and piano (1910) or in Ravel's *Tzigane* for violin and piano (1924), yet they also appear in the quartets, sonatas, trio and other chamber works.

The special problem of impressionistic music is that the impressionist ideal—to capture the character of conditions, the atmosphere of a movement—is impossible in music where the sound disappears immediately; to overcome this Ravel (following Debussy) does not use har-

---

[4]Richard Taruskin, *Defining Russia Musically: Historical and Hermeneutical Essays* (Princeton: Princeton University Press, 1997), pp. 412-414 and 416-424 analyzes this quartet from the standpoint of these Russian sounds.

monic motion and thematic development but dwells on the isolated sound—as close as music can come to the impressionism in visual arts. [Unlike Debussy, Ravel also] uses masks to disguise deeper feelings, and belongs to the movement of French dandyism—opposition to the vulgarization of art—and looks to the past with aristocratic reserve (a type of neo-classicism).[5]

Once the pattern of evolution formulated by Debussy and Ravel had become known, other composers of the time set out to make their own systems of evolution. During the first half of the 20th century several major systems came into being which affected the traditional genres of chamber music. Bartók, for one, evolved a new system of consonance and dissonance and a new sense of rhythm from the folk music of Hungary, Rumania and other peoples of that region; at the same time he pursued the concept of motivic development that Beethoven had worked with in his last quartets. Schoenberg, on the other hand, evolved his system of atonality—the dodecaphonic system—from the increasingly chromatic harmony of German composers of the late 19th and early 20th centuries, while remaining firmly rooted in the rhythm and forms of his Austro-Germanic heritage. Hindemith and Stravinsky, reacting against the extreme chromaticism of Schoenberg and Bartók and the over-charged romanticism of the Mahlerian late 19th and early 20th century, helped evolve (in a Hegelian sense) the neo-classic system. Chamber music, which had been a sidelight for most post-Beethoven composers of the 19th century, became in the first half of the 20th century the main vehicle for the expression of these new systems. Hundreds of composers throughout Europe and the Americas grappled with these three basic systems and the towering works of Bartók, Schoenberg, Hindemith and Stravinsky; many showed their own individual versions of the three basic systems and wrote their own masterpieces.

---

[5]Jürgen Braun, *Die Thematik in den Kammermusikwerken von Maurice Ravel*, in *Kölner Beiträge zur Musikforschung*, Band 33 (Regensburg: Gustave Bosse, 1966), as summarized in John H. Baron, *Chamber Music: a Research and Information Guide* (New York/London: Garland Publshing, 1987), p. 352.

Bartók

Bartók (1881-1945) was born in what is today Rumania but was then Hungary, and he spent his entire life researching the music of the people of his region of Europe. It is not surprising, therefore, that much of this music made its way into his art music. His mature chamber compositions include six string quartets, two violin-piano sonatas, two rhapsodies for violin and piano, another rhapsody for cello and piano, a piano quintet, the forty-four duos for two violins, and *Contrasts* for violin, clarinet and piano. By standards of the classical period Bartók did not write much chamber music, but in terms of the importance which he himself gave to his chamber works and the immense influence which they have exerted on the chamber music of the 20th century he ranks with Corelli, Haydn, Mozart, Beethoven and Brahms. While he accepted the classical ideal of chamber music, he was also the heir to

Béla Bartók (1881-1945). From photograph by Kellner Jeno in Agatha Fassett, *Béla Bartók* (New York: Dover, 1970).

the harmonic and melodic developments in France, Russia and elsewhere at the end of the 19th century, to the evolving concepts of form in light of Beethoven's late string quartets, Wagner and folk music, and to the changing styles about him in the music of Schoenberg and the neo-classicists. Although he came from a strong folk tradition, Bartók was not nationalistic but internationalistic since he did not limit himself to one folk music tradition.

Bartók's six quartets, which were written over a span covering most of his creative life, are the core of his chamber music. With the late quartets of Beethoven as his model, Bartók returned to the quartet again and again with new strategies for developing simple melodic patterns into major musical designs. Sometimes he used the same four-note "Bach" motivic idea that Beethoven used. Just as Beethoven used his four-note motive in many of his compositions during his last years and just as they serve as a unifying factor through much of his creative effort at that time, so Bartók used the four-note motive as the unifying factor whenever he turned to the string quartet—even if other motivic, harmonic, and rhythmic ideas are more important to him in specific quartets. Beethoven broke with the classical tradition in several of the quartets in terms of form and style, and also Bartók broke with that tradition as still exploited by Brahms and Dvořák. Beethoven and Bartók encompass the same tradition and tampered with that tradition as the music dictated; Bartók's reasons for doing so were the same as Beethoven's. Beethoven knew he was living at the height of bourgeois humanism and that the world was going to change for the better; Bartók, on the other hand, saw himself increasingly swept up in the destruction of bourgeois humanism as known in Central Europe.[6] In his earlier works, including the first four string quartets (1908, 1917, 1927 and 1928) he drew on the strength of the new nationalists in Bohemia, Russia and France to forge a new Hungarian nationalism that gave hope where the Austrians and Germans had squashed it. By the fifth string quartet (1934), however, Bartók sensed that the new world of nationalist states would be

---

[6]W. Siegmund-Schultze, "Tradition und Neueretum in Bartóks Streichquartetten," in *Studia Musicologica*, vol. iii (1962), pp. 317-328.

swallowed up by the Germans, and when he wrote his last quartet (1939-1940), this had already happened. The world was in shambles, evil had triumphed. Yet, once again, Bartók drew inspiration from Beethoven who had turned to his compositions to spread the message of hope to mankind after the liberating days of the French revolution and the new cry for brotherhood and freedom were replaced by the canons of reaction through the Congress of Vienna. Bartók's last two quartets proclaim the sanctity of life, progress, and the victory of humanity despite the anti-humanistic dangers of the time. Despite the tragedy and melancholy, an inner spirit radiates the indomitable spirit of man—a classical ideal. But while Beethoven became more complex in his late works, Bartók became more straight-forward so as to communicate directly with the vast audience.

Bartók never conceived these quartets for private performance but rather for large, public concerts.[7] He began sketches for the first quartet in 1907, worked on it in earnest in 1908, and completed it in January, 1909. The Waldbauer-Kerpely Quartet gave its premier on an all-Bartók concert at the Royal Concert Hall in Budapest on March 19, 1910. A few critics approved, but most found the piece disappointing (too modern or, for the nationalists, not Hungarian enough). Bartók so appreciated the enthusiasm of the ensemble that premiered this quartet, however, that he dedicated his second quartet to the Waldbauer-Kerpely group, which premiered the new quartet on March 3, 1918. The third quartet was completed in 1927 and submitted to the Philadelphia Musical Fund Society's composition contest, where it won first place (along with Casella's *Serenata* Opus 46). Universal Edition wanted to publish the work immediately, but Bartók would not allow it to appear until he had heard it performed. Several ensembles vied for that privilege, which was obtained finally by the Waldbauer-Kerpely Quartet for its concert in Wigmore Hall, London, on February 19, 1929. On February 21st it was performed again, this time in Frankfurt by the Vienna Quartet (Rudolf Kolisch and Felix Khuner, vio-

---

[7]János Kárpáti, *Bartók's String Quartets*, trl. Fred Macnicol (Budapest: Franklin Printing House, 1975), pp. 173-176, 185-186, 197-199, 209-210, 226-227, 244-246.

linists, Jenö Lehner, violist, and Benar Heifetz, cellist). Before the third quartet was premiered, however, Bartók had already completed the fourth, which was first heard on another all-Bartók concert (by the Waldbauer Quartet) on March 20, 1929, and repeated in October that year in Berlin and Vienna by the Pro Arte Quartet. The fifth quartet was commissioned by the Elizabeth Sprague Coolidge Foundation and completed in one month in 1934; it was premiered by the Vienna Quartet (under Kolisch) in Washington on April 8, 1935, on a program which also featured Beethoven's Opus 130 and Berg's *Lyric Suite*. The first Hungarian performance, on February 18, 1936, was by the new Hungarian Quartet, successor to the Waldbauer. Bartók began his last quartet in Switzerland in 1939 and completed it just as his world collapsed. His mother died, the war broke out, Zoltán Székely of the Hungarian Quartet reneged on his commission of the piece, and Bartók made the fateful decision to emigrate from Europe to America. The quartet was rededicated to the Kolisch Quartet,[8] which gave the first performance in New York on January 20, 1941.

The six quartets have been thoroughly discussed elsewhere so that here we need only summarize their main contributions.[9] In terms of form, Bartók constructed two of his quartets in a symmetrical fashion known as a palindrome. In the fourth quartet, for example, there are five movements; the first and fifth movements are fast and have some of the same motives, the second and fourth are very fast scherzo-like movements using contrasting colors (the second is *con sordino*, the fourth is pizzicato) and the middle movement is slow.[10] The palindrome form extends as well to the quartets as a whole since the first and sixth quartets, the second

---

[8]Rudolph Kolisch (1896-1978), through his leadership of the Vienna Quartet, then the Kolisch Quartet, and finally the Pro Arte Quartet, was perhaps, along with Hindemith, the most important chamber performer of the 20th century. He encouraged all the important composers of his time to write new chamber music, which he then performed repeatedly and eventually recorded. Because he played the violin left-handed (he bowed with the left arm), he sat on the right facing the second violinist; thus both violins were tilted toward the audience and this created a balance in concert halls that is unknown in other quartets.

[9]The most important is Kárpáti.

[10]Siegmund-Schultze.

and fifth and the third and fourth form pairs whose members are related in character. This kind of form, though not common in the classical period, does have its precursors in the five-movement divertimenti quartets of Haydn and in Schubert's "Trout" quintet and octet.

Since Bartók drew melodically from Hungarian and Rumanian folk music, he followed the Russians and developed harmonic and tonal systems based on the melodies. These harmonies were not used as textural devices but as important functions of the total structures. Since the relationship of dominant to tonic does not function here, other intervals become more essential, such as the major and minor second; a dissonant in classical and romantic harmony, the second now becomes the basic consonant and the third—the basic consonant in previous centuries—is the new dissonance.

The rhythms of Bartók's quartets are startling to the classically-trained musician but second-nature to the folk musician. An occasional $\frac{6}{4}$ and $\frac{5}{4}$ in the midst of $\frac{4}{4}$ in the first movement of the Fifth Quartet poses no problem, but when Bartók uses measures of $\frac{8}{4}$ subdivided 3 + 2 + 3 and also imposes $\frac{6}{8}$ on measures of $\frac{4}{4}$ scattered differently in the different instruments (mm.147ff), it becomes trickier. The second movement (scherzo) forsakes a classical $\frac{9}{8}$ meter and instead has $\frac{4+2+3}{8}$, "alla bulgarese" followed by a trio in $\frac{3+2+2+3}{8}$ instead of $\frac{10}{8}$.

Besides drawing on folk melodies, harmonies and rhythms, Bartók also imitated Hungarian folk instruments. A hurdy-gurdy drone, for example, is imitated in the second movement of the Sixth Quartet (mm.11-13) and the strumming on a folk guitar is imitated in many movements of the quartets (e.g., later in the same movement). Bartók also indicated clearly in the music the nature of the pizzicato: a snap pizzicato, a fingernail pizzicato, or a regular pizzicato. Subtle use of harmonics, glissandi, sordino, trills, quadruple stops, repeated down bows at the frog, repeated grace-note ornaments, and dynamics all play into each other and cause a striking palate of sound.

Schoenberg and Disciples

While Bartók drew on Hungarian and Rumanian folk music to give inspiration to a decadent Austro-German chamber music tradition, Schoenberg took that tradition to its "logical" conclusion. Schoenberg (1874-1951) was born into a relatively unmusical family, but with his Prague and Viennese childhood he could not escape studying the violin and playing chamber music at an early age. As a youngster he played Pleyel and Viotti duets, and in his early twenties he formed an amateur chamber group where he learned the classical repertory and for which he wrote his earlier chamber compositions. This strong rearing in traditional chamber music led Schoenberg to concentrate much of his later creative efforts in evolving a new system of harmony and form in the chamber music genres. Like Bartók's quartets Schoenberg's emanate over a long period of time, from the early quartet of 1897 (which he wrote under the supervision of his only real teacher, Alexander Zemlinsky [1871-1942]) to the Fourth Quartet of 1936 (which he wrote three years after his arrival in America). In addition he wrote a string sextet "Verklärte Nacht" (1899), several larger pieces for a mixture of winds and strings and sometimes piano, a wind quintet (1923-1924), a string trio (1946), and a few other pieces.

Brought up in traditional chamber music, Schoenberg accepted traditional forms, but these are based on classical conceptions of tonality. As long as he adhered to that traditional tonality in his 1897 and 1905 quartets and *Verklärte Nacht* sextet, Schoenberg could follow the model of Brahms, the dominant musical personality in Vienna during his youth.[11] But following Brahms did not necessarily mean imitating him; rather, he conceived the idea of writing single-movement chamber pieces as a contraction of numerous traditional movements. Thus, even though the Opus 7 quartet in D Minor is in only one movement, the movement is ac-

[11]Michael G. Musgrave, "Schoenberg and Brahms: a Study of Schoenberg's Response to Brahms's Music as Revealed in his Didactic Writings and Selected Early Writings" (University of London Ph.D. dissertation, 1980). Schoenberg was also influenced by Dvořák until Zemlinsky turned him away from that; cf. Reinhard Gerlach, "War Schönberg von Dvořák beeinflusst?: zu Arnold Schönbergs Streichquartett D-Dur," in *Neue Zeitschrift für Musik*, vol. cxxxiii (1972), 122-127.

tually in three parts, of which the first consists of a sonata exposition with fugato between the two themes and incorporating a scherzo with trio as well, the second corresponds to a development section, and the third to a recapitulation with a rondo finale.[12] He did the same thing in *Verklärte Nacht*, which consists of one long movement subdivided into two large sections separated by an interlude and framed by a prelude and postlude.[13] Once he conceived the "logical evolution" of German chromaticism into atonality and devised the dodecaphonic system, however, he was confronted with a formal dilemma. Since tonalities no longer exist, how do you write in a sonata form whose exposition is based on the contrast of two tonalities? Schoenberg, whose high regard for Brahms and the classics never waned and who regarded himself as a part of their tradition, needed to write in these old forms at least for some time after he came up with dodecaphonism. The Wind Quintet is in the traditional four movements, with the first in sonata form and the last in rondo form. The Suite Opus 29 (for three different size clarinets, piano and string trio, 1925-1926) abandons classical forms but only for the baroque suite form (also in four movements). In order to retain these forms he had to make some compromises either with his atonalism or with the traditional forms. For one, Schoenberg himself did not always avoid tonality (the Fourth Quartet sounds at times in D Minor[14]), but also he found that he could substitute for two contrasting tonalities two contrasting transformations of the row or two contrasting rhythms or two contrasting textures. The recapitulations cannot reflect changes in tonalities but must reflect a different transposition of the row. In the four-movement third quartet (the first atonal quartet in history) he stuck strictly to the clear forms of a classical string quartet. The first movement is the most important and in sonata form, the fourth

---

[12]Kurt Schindler, *Arnold Schönberg's Quartet in D Minor Op. 7: an Introductory Note* (New York: G. Schirmer, 1914).

[13]Wilhelm Pfannkuch, "Zu Thematik und Form in Schönbergs Streichsextett," in Anna Amalie Abert and W. Pfannkuch, eds., *Festschrift Friedrich Blume zum 70. Geburtstag* (Kassel: Bärenreiter, 1963), pp. 258-271.

[14]Oliver W. Neighbour, "A Talk on Schoenberg for Composers' Concourse," in *The Score*, no. 16 (June 1956), 19-28.

is next in importance but lighter, and the inner movements are even less weighty but contrasting.[15] In the second movement he explored the dual concepts of variation as a traditional form and continual variation as a basic procedure of dodecaphonism, but he was unable to establish a consistent relationship between these two varieties of the same basic idea.[16] The fourth string quartet is just as classical in its four-movement structure: fast sonata - scherzo in triple meter (for the first half) - slow - fast. The different rhythm associated with each form of the row creates a unity, and this rhythm-row unity then contrasts with other rhythm-row unities as a substitute for the traditional tonal contrasts.[17] In the late trio Opus 45 (1946), written just after the composer recovered from a near fatal heart attack and therefore a very intense work, Schoenberg reverted to the kind of form he employed in his tonal *Verklärte Nacht* and Opus 7 quartet. The trio is in one movement with three parts and two episodes in between; part 1 and episode 1 constitute the exposition, part 2 and episode 2 the development, and part 3 a condensed recapitulation.

Schoenberg, who was one of the great thinkers about music in the early 20th century, attracted numerous disciples who were themselves gifted composers. His teacher, Alexander Zemlinsky, never followed him and remained closer to Brahms and Wagner in his chamber music (four string quartets, a trio in D Minor for clarinet, cello and piano, a violin-piano suite). Alban Berg and Anton Webern, however, were followers of Schoenberg who were able to build their own styles on the master's system.

Alban Berg (1885-1935) was the romantic serialist. His *Lyric Suite* for string quartet, his most famous chamber composition, is a serial work which has a structural and aesthetic affinity with Beethoven's late quartets, Mahler's *Das Lied von der Erde*, and Zem-

---

[15]Norbert Dietrich, *Arnold Schönbergs Drittes Streichquartett op. 30: seine Form und sein Verhältnis zur Geschichte der Gattung*, in *Beiträge zur Musikforschung*, Band 12 (Munich/Salzburg: Emil Katzbichler, 1983).

[16]Glenn L. Glasow, "Variation as Formal Design and Twelve-tone Procedure in the *Third String Quartet* by Arnold Schoenberg" (University of Illinois DMA dissertation, 1967).

[17]Neighbour.

linsky's *Lyric Symphony*.[18] It also has direct quotations from Wagner. It mixes these romantic influences with the highly mathematical system of rows; it is built from an initial row that utilizes all intervals from a minor second to a major seventh (written as a diminished octave; first violin, measures 2-4). It is also program music, though of a private variety. Although married, Berg was in love secretly with Hanna Werfel (sister of Franz), and he wrote out for her a secret program with poems indicating the significance to their love of certain elements of form and meter.[19] The piece also has numerical symbolism. The quartet is largely structured on the number 23; it is the number of letters in Zemlinsky's name plus the letters "a" and "b" (for Alban Berg; the quartet is dedicated to Zemlinsky), and all the metronome markings and the number of measures in all movements (except the second) are 23 or multiples of 23.[20] The early string quartet, though not serial, is much like the *Lyric Suite* and also like the quartets of Debussy and early Schoenberg. Berg was looking backward in both pieces, though Opus 3 was written to express a "type of dramatic conflict associated with classicism," while "in the Lyric Suite, Berg was preoccupied with the expression of romantic lyricism."[21] Following Schoenberg's lead in experimentation with the traditional forms in new guises, Opus 3 is in two movements, the second acting as a development of the first.[22] The clarinet pieces represent Berg as a miniaturist who was rebelling against the "symphony of thousands" syndrome.

Anton Webern (1883-1945) wrote his serial chamber music as the result of his intensive study of music of the past. He was a mu-

---

[18]Hans Redlich, *Alban Berg: the Man and his Music* (New York: Abelard-Schuman, 1957), pp. 137-154.

[19]George Perle, "The Secret Programme of the Lyric Suite," in *The Musical Times*, vol. cxviii (1977), pp. 629-632, 709-713, and 809-813.

[20]Reginald S. Brindle, "The Symbolism in Berg's Lyric Suite," in *The Score*, no. 21 (October 1957), pp. 60-63.

[21]Shirley M. Blankenship, "Berg Lines: Opus 3, Lyrische Suite" (University of Illinois DMA dissertation, 1977).

[22]Redlich, pp. 49-58.

sicologist, who published scholarly editions of 18th-century music, and he was so well acquainted with contrapuntal techniques that he employed them extensively in his serialism. Canonic writing was especially important.[23] "The five pieces [Opus 5] are an interrelated 'set of pieces' based on five symmetrical tetrachords, their subsets, and related embedding supersets."[24] Opus 5, however, is not a dodecaphonic work. There are four symmetrical chords in this movement (for example, a minor sixth on either side of the tritone E$\flat$ - A).[25] The string trio Opus 20 uses traditional classical rondo and sonata forms, even though Webern used a row and its variations.[26] Webern's youthful piano quintet is tonal and a one-movement sonata form work, which like early Schoenberg and Berg owes a great deal to Brahms.[27]

The Neo-Classicists: Stravinsky, Milhaud, and Hindemith

While Bartók evolved his system out of folk music and the masterpieces of late 19th-century Russia, Bohemia and France, and Schoenberg evolved his system out of German late romanticism, the neo-classicists *reacted against* the emotionalism and extravagance of turn-of-the-century music of all kinds. Bartók and Schoenberg regarded their styles as continuations of the music of the immediate past, whereas Stravinsky (for much of his career), Hindemith and others of their school rejected most of that music as tasteless. Erik Satie debunked the pomposity of late-romantic composers, which he equated largely with Germanic music, and helped create a new spirit, which

[23]Colin Mason, "Webern's Later Chamber Music," in *Music and Letters*, vol. xxxviii (1957), pp. 232-237.

[24]John D. Vander Weg, "Symmetrical Pitch- and Equivalence-Class Set Structure in Anton Webern's Opus 5" (University of Michigan Ph.D. dissertation, 1983).

[25]Bruce Archibald, "Some Thoughts on Symmetry in Early Webern: Op. 5, no. 2," in *Perspectives of New Music*, vol. x, no. 2 (1972), pp. 159-163.

[26]Erwin Stein, "Anton Webern," in *Neue Musikzeitung*, vol. xlix (1928), pp. 517-519.

[27]Dika Newlin, "Anton von Webern: Quintet for String Quartet and Piano," in *Notes*, vol. x (1953), pp. 674-675.

teaches us to aim at an emotive simplicity and a firmness of utterance enabling sonorities and rhythms to assert themselves clearly, unequivocal in design and accent, and contrived in a spirit of humility and renunciation.[28]

The leaders of the neo-classicists included not only Satie, Stravinsky and Hindemith but also Ravel and Busoni. In seeking the new, pure spirit in music they looked both inwardly for styles and systems that fit their cooler natures and outwardly to the 18th century when, they believed, music was a cool, rational art and craft based on Greek ideas of symmetry and balance. Since the 18th century produced so much chamber music, it was inevitable that neo-classicists turned to chamber music for much of their expression.

Igor Feodorovitch Stravinsky (1882-1971), the greatest of the neo-classicist composers, actually is an exception: he wrote most of his chamber music either just prior to his adopting that style (ca. 1920) or just after his leaving neo-classicism for atonalism (ca. 1951). The brilliance of the Flonzaley Quartet attracted Stravinsky's attention to chamber music briefly; he heard it premier his three pieces for string quartet in Paris in 1915 with its Scriabin-like harmony, and with that sound in mind he then wrote the *Concertino* for the same ensemble in 1920. Stravinsky was not thinking like other 20th-century string quartet composers who emphasized the intimacy and special color of the quartet within a framework of the Germanic sonata form; he treated the Three Pieces, instead, as idiosyncratic Russian poems, and when he orchestrated them he gave names to the Three Pieces: Dance, Eccentric, and Canticle.[29] The octet (written between 1919 and 1923[30]) was Stravinsky's first major neo-classic chamber work. It was premiered in the Paris Théâtre de l'Opèra as part of a Koussevitsky series concert and was therefore at the center of French musical life and discussion

---

[28]Satie, in *Les Feuilles Libres* (March 1923), trl. in Rollo Hugh Myers, *Erik Satie* (London: Dennis Dobson, 1948), p. 130.

[29]Klaus Stahmer, "Der Klassik näher als dem Klassizismus: die Streichquartettkompositionen von Stravinsky," in *Hindemith-Jahrbuch*, xii (1983), 104-115.

[30]Robert Craft, "The Chronology of the *Octet*," in *Perspectives of New Music*, xxii (1983-1984), 451-463.

Flonzaley Quartet (1904-1929). Private possession of author.

from the beginning; its influence on European composers was strong and immediate. The five-movement *Duo Concertante* for violin and piano was premiered in 1932 at the Berlin Funkhaus by the composer and the violinist Samuel Dushkin. It is another neo-classic chamber work that recalls a popular title of the late 18th century and signifies the equality of the two instruments. The *Septet* for clarinet, horn, bassoon, piano, violin, viola and cello (1953), on the other hand, is a transitional work between the neo-classicism of his past thirty years and the dodecophonism that occupied him during his last two decades. The first movement is untitled, but following early 18th-century norms movement 2 is a passacaglia and movement 3 is a gigue. Yet despite this token of neo-classicism, the piece is built on fractional tone rows (movement 1 uses a 5-note tone row and movements 2 and 3 use 8-note rows, not 12-note ones) and utilizes three special techniques: unison or octaves between instruments proceeding in different rhythms, breaking up of melodies among instruments of different families, and dynamics glossed over so all the instruments sound on the same dynamic level.[31] The piece achieves unity through the use of the row,[32] and tone color is very important.

During his late years Stravinsky often wrote very short pieces in honor or memory of someone close or famous. The *Double Canon for String Quartet* (1959) was composed in memory of the artist Raoul Dufy and was premiered in Town Hall, New York, on December 20, 1959; it lasts barely a minute and a half. Just three months earlier Stravinsky's *Epitaphium für das Grabmal des Prinzen Max Egon zu Fürstenberg* for flute, clarinet and harp was first performed at the Donaueschingen Festival; it, too, lasts but a minuet and a half. For the opening of what is now Avery Fischer Hall, Lincoln Center, in New York, on April 19, 1964, he composed a *Fanfare for a New Theatre* for two trumpets that lasts only half a minute. Whether any of these pieces or the *Lied ohne Namen* (1918) for two bassoons which lasts a minute are long enough to be regarded as serious chamber music is not as vital a question as it was for 19th-century theorists who depended upon multi-movement pieces and sonata form; given the length of many chamber compositions of the 16th and 17th centuries and the occasions for which they were written, these works function as chamber music within the context of a comprehensive history of chamber music.

Darius Milhaud's (1892-1974) approach to neo-classicism came from a different direction. Born in southern France, he felt special kinship with the great painters of his region and identified with their struggles. Cézanne, to whom he dedicated his first string quartet (1914), was the greatest of them in his childhood, and like Cézanne Milhaud needed to "integrate impressionistic concepts of light and coloured shadow with cleaner-cut and more substantial formal designs."[33] Thus while his content was late impressionistic

---

[31]Hans Ludwig Schilling, "Zur Instrumentation in Igor Stravinskys Spätwerk aufgezeigt an seinem 'Septett 1953," in *Archiv für Musikwissenschaft*, xiii (1956), 181-196.

[32]Hilmar Schatz, "Igor Stravinsky: Septett," in *Melos*, vol. xxv (1958), 60-63.

[33]Christopher Palmer, "Milhaud," in *The New Grove Dictionary of Music and Musicians*, vol. xii, p. 307.

or partly expressionist, his forms were neo-classic. A gentle perfume is set in three-movement sonatas fast - slow - fast, in canons, fugues (the final movement of the string trio [1947] is "Jeu fugué"), contrepoints, and divertissements.

Milhaud was among the most prolific composers of chamber music of the 20th century. He wrote eighteen string quartets, thirteen sonatas for various instruments, three string quintets, a string sextet and septet, a piano trio, quartet and quintet, several works for woodwind quintet, several duos, and various other chamber works. All told he published over 400 compositions from operas and symphonies to songs and piano pieces. As a result much of his music is repetitive, and even if it is always well crafted, it often lacks inspiration. Nonetheless, there is a wealth of pleasing chamber material that has kept Milhaud's music on the programs of leading performers of the 20th century.

Milhaud started as a violinist and therefore had string chamber music close to his heart from childhood. In 1915 he found polytonality, which became his harmonic language. Since he traveled extensively and was intellectually attracted to everything, many influences came to bear on his music. He lived in Brazil from 1916 to 1918, with the result that Brazilian ethnic music crops up at various times (e.g., the *Danses de Jacaremirim* [1945] for violin and piano). He discovered jazz, rag and blues, first in London in 1920 and then on his first American tour in 1922. In the 1930's he wrote scores for amateurs and children, for movies and plays, and after 1940, when he fled Europe for America, he became integrated in all aspects of American music. He taught at Mills College in California for many years and also at the Aspen Summer Music Festival in Colorado. Through all this, however, he remained nostalgically loyal to his native Provençal and its pastoral life (especially noticeable in the first string quartet, *Le Printemps* [1914] for violin and piano, and *Pastorale* [1935] for oboe, clarinet and bassoon).

Milhaud wrote his chamber music for various occasions and under various conditions. Some of his string quartets were written to honor various persons, such as Cézanne (no. 1), Schoenberg (no. 5), Poulenc (no. 6), the Quatuor Pro Arte (no. 7), and Fauré (no.

12); following Stravinsky's models Milhaud wrote a short string quartet *Hommage à Igor Stravinsky* (1971) upon the Russian's death. The second violin-piano sonata (1917) is dedicated to the writer André Gide, and the sonatina for flute and piano (1922) is dedicated to the flutist Louis Fleury and pianist Jean Wiéner who premiered the work in Paris in 1923. Milhaud was often commissioned, such as by Elizabeth Sprague Coolidge (string quartets nos. 8, 9 and 10) and by the violist G. Prévost (two sonatas for viola and piano and the *Four Visages* [1943] all premiered in Madison, Wisconsin,[34] in 1944). He systematically wrote his piano quintet, three string quintets (each for a different scoring), the sextet and septet, the piano quartet and trio between 1952 and 1968, experimenting once with each genre. Aware of the greatness of performers of wind instruments and the dearth of good chamber music for winds in the early 20th century, he composed sonatas and sonatinas for piano with flute (1922), clarinet (1927) and oboe (1954), the *Duo Concertante* for clarinet and piano (1956), *Les Rêves de Jacob* (1949) for oboe, violin, viola, cello and bass, two woodwind quintets (*La Cheminée du Roi René* [1939] and the *Divertissement* [1958]), a *Concert de Chambre* (1961) for woodwind quintet, string quintet and piano, and two pieces for trio of oboe, clarinet and bassoon (*Pastorale* [1935] and *Suite d'après Corrette* [1937]). His most famous experiment, perhaps, is the octet for two string quartets, which can be played as two separate quartets (nos. 14 and 15) or as the octet; it was premiered by the Budapest and Paganini Quartets at Mills College on August 10, 1949. While most of these pieces were written for public performance, the *Duo* for two violins (1945) was actually premiered privately by Yehudi Menuhin and Roman Totenberg at the homes of Menuhin (first two movements) and the composer (last movement).

Perhaps the most dedicated chamber musician in the first half of the 20th century was Paul Hindemith (1895-1963) who was not only one of the great composers of the time but also one of the most important performers of chamber music. He began his career

---

[34]The dedication explains how Milhaud could combine such disparate visages: California, Wisconsin, Brussels and Paris.

as a second violinist in the Adolf Rebner Quartet in Frankfurt in 1915 and remained in that ensemble until 1921, except for a time when he was in the German army (1917-1918) and had his own string quartet. In 1919 he switched to viola. When his second string quartet Opus 16 was to have its premier at the Donaueschingen Festival in August, 1921, the scheduled ensemble refused to perform it, so Hindemith organized a new ensemble (the Amar Quartet[35]) which not only performed it but was for the next eight years a major European quartet. From 1929 to 1934, while teaching composition at the Hochschule für Musik in Berlin, Hindemith played viola in a string trio with Emanuel Feuermann, cellist, and with, at first, Josef Wolfsthal, then Szymon Goldberg as violinist. In the 1920's he also began to play the viola d'amore and became a champion of early music performance. When Hindemith came to America in 1940, he was primarily active as a composer and teacher at Yale University and essentially his days as a performer of chamber music were over, yet he organized a chamber group at Yale and he continued to write chamber music. Because of his professional involvement with the performance of chamber music throughout his life, his compositions for his own ensembles and those of his students in Berlin and New Haven were composed as much for the furtherance of chamber music as for the advancement of the art of composition.

Hindemith began his career as a composer of chamber music. The first public performance of his works at the Verein für Theater- und Musikkultur in Frankfurt on June 2, 1919, included his piano quintet Opus 7 (lost), two sonatas, and his first string quartet. By the time of the Donaueschingen Festival just two years later, Hindemith was recognized as the most important German composer of the new generation, and he reached this fame primarily on the worth of his chamber music compositions. "When most composers made their reputation with orchestral works and full-length operas, Hindemith made his largely with chamber music."[36] After

---

[35]Licco Amar and Walter Kaspar, violins, Paul Hindemith viola, and Rudolf Hindemith at first the cellist, then Maurits Frank.

[36]Ian Kemp, "Hindemith," in *The New Grove Dictionary of Music and Musicians*, vol. viii, p. 577.

several years of experimentation in different manners of expression and with different contents, Hindemith recognized in 1922 that his personal style was a tonal, neo-Baroque style that stressed lyrical beauty and harmonic clarity unmuddied by expressionism, impressionism, and romanticism. His models were the Stravinsky that emerged at the end of the First World War and the new French composers, particularly Milhaud. As a composer he broke completely with the nationalists in Germany and the atonalists in Vienna (though as a performer he championed any worthwhile contemporary music); his traumatic experience of playing the Frenchman Debussy's string quartet while he was wearing the uniform of a German soldier at war with France and, while performing it, learning of Debussy's death, made Hindemith into an internationalist philosophically, politically, and aesthetically. In his wind quintet *Kleine Kammermusik* (1922) and after the first movement of his third string quartet (Opus 22, 1922) he rejected the expressionism with which he had been toying, particularly in his short operas, and turned to the familiar Hindemith style of his clarinet quintet (1923) and the following works.

Hindemith's neo-classicism was based not only on a reaction to the overblown romanticism of the age of Wagner and Mahler but also on his interest in the practical side of chamber music. As a performer he recognized the need to communicate to amateur audiences, and while he based his harmonic system on quartal harmonies rather than tertial ones, he spoke in a language that was not so far removed from the common language of the bourgeoisie that the serious composer would be misunderstood. At first baroque, then after 1933 classical forms and conventional genres are obvious in the music. He wrote six string quartets (1919, 1921, 1922, 1923, 1943, and 1945), two string trios (1924 and 1933), four violin-piano sonatas (1918, 1918, 1935, and 1939), four viola-piano sonatas (1919, 1919, 1922, and 1939), three cello-piano sonatas (1919, 1942, and 1948) and several other traditional types. But Hindemith also wrote for the amateur performer—he called it *Gebrauchsmusik* but it is also Hausmusik or school music; he provided duet sonatas for piano and most common wind instruments: piano and flute (1936), bassoon (1938), oboe (1938), horn (1939),

trumpet (1939), clarinet (1939), English horn (1941), trombone
(1941), tuba (1955) and either horn or saxophone (1943). He also
wrote for various combinations of wind and/or string instruments
which provide interesting, though easy material for the moderately
advanced student, such as the *Konzertstück* for two alto saxophones (1933), *Zwei kanonische Duette* for two violins (1929),
duet for viola and cello (1934), nine pieces for clarinet and bass
(1927), *Ludus Minor* for clarinet and cello (1944), *Echo* for flute
and piano (1942), sonata for bass and piano (1949), pieces for bassoon and cello (1941), sonata for piano and viola d'amore (1922),
quartet for clarinet, piano, violin and cello, sonata for four horns
(1952), trio for piano, viola and either heckelphone or tenor saxophone (1928), and the trio for three guitars (1930). At the same
time that Bartók was writing his graded violin duets, Hindemith
also wrote *Vierzehn leichte Stücke* for two violins (1931), followed
in 1938 by his *Drei leichte Stücke* for cello and piano, but while
Bartók was international by exploiting very nationalistic elements
of a few cultures in his works, Hindemith tried to be international
and baroque without any nationalistic elements. He did write arrangements of folksongs for clarinet and string quartet in 1936, but
they had no affect on his other compositions, just as his cello-piano
variations on the English folksong "Frog he went a-courting"
(1941) had no affect on his American compositions. His return to
the music of the 18th century was more emphatic than Stravinsky's; Stravinsky, following Satie, was after a certain purity which
was basically a reaction against the 19th century, but Hindemith
turned to the 18th century to find what he believed to be an international, non-Germanic language. That the French had turned to
the 18th century to find a specifically French musical language was
not of concern to Hindemith, whose embrace of neo-classicism
was more altruistic than that of either Stravinsky or Satie. Hindemith's performances on the viola d'amore, an 18th-century instrument completely obsolete by 1922, is further evidence of his
dive into the 18th century, and it had much to do with the successful revival of early music performance later in the century (see
below).

Other Nationalists: Janáček, Bloch, Villa-Lobos, Prokofiev and Shostakovich

A number of composers followed Bartók, the Czechs and the Russians in utilizing specific, ethnic characteristics in their chamber music. What these ethnic characteristics are varies depending on the culture from which the composer came and the composer's own unique interpretation and appreciation of that culture. For example, the Czech Leos Janáček (1854-1928), who is actually older than Bartók, wrote his most important chamber works after Bartók had started to make his chamber music known. Both his string quartets (1923 and 1928) are Moravian in rhythmic and melodic inflection (his so-called "speech melody"[37]). Moravian dance rhythms and the timbres of native instruments appear in the third violin-piano sonata (1913-1921) and in the wind sextet *Mláda* (1924), and ethnic scales and tunes are ubiquitous.[38] Half way around the world the Brazilian Heitor Villa-Lobos (1887-1959), a contemporary of Bartók, created a specifically Brazilian string quartet.[39] His seventeen quartets fall into four groups (nos. 1-4 [1915-1917], 5 [1931], 6 [1938], and 7-17 [1942-1957]) and span his creative life. All the quartets have ethnic properties, but chiefly from no. 5 on; he avoided classical forms, was frequently atonal, and followed Beethoven's Opus 131 with continual variations.[40] His other chamber music, which includes duets, trios, and various other combinations up to nonets, is similar to the quartets, though not as consistently pursued as the quartet genre.[41] The Swiss Jew Ernest Bloch (1880-1956), too, turned to his Jewish heritage for the materials and inspiration for his chamber music. Besides his

---

[37]Milan R. Kaderavek, "Stylistic Aspects of the Late Chamber Music of Leos Janáček: an Analytic Study" (University of Illinois D.M.A. dissertation, 1970).

[38]Luigi Pestalozza, "Leos Janáček," in *L'Approdo Musicale*, vol. 3 (April-June 1960), 3-74, section 17, "Musica da camera," pp. 59-62.

[39]Virginia Farmer, "An Analytical Study of the Seventeen String Quartets of Heitor Villa-Lobos" (University of Illinois D.M.A. dissertation, 1973).

[40]Arnaldo Estrella, *Os Quartetos de Cordas de Villa-Lobos* (Rio de Janeiro: Museu Villa-Lobos, 1970).

[41]Eurico Nogueira França, *A Evolução de Villa-Lobos na Música da Câmera* (Rio de Janeiro: Museu Villa-Lobos, 1976).

numerous works for violin and piano with Jewish subjects (e.g., *Baal Shem Suite*, *Abodah*), there are ethnic traits in his string quartets (1916, 1946, 1951, 1953, and 1956).[42] He also drew on non-Jewish cultures, such as the music of Bali in his Quintet and quartet "Tongataboo."

By the death of Tchaikovsky in 1893 Russian music had reached international importance and much of the future of European music would be determined by the new generation of Russian composers led by Scriabin, Stravinsky, Prokofiev, and Shostakovich. Alexander Nikolaievich Scriabin (1872-1915) was extremely important for the development of 20th-century piano music, harmony and mysticism in music, but his only contribution to chamber music was a single movement for string quartet (variations on a Russian folksong, 1899) which he wrote with other Russian composers (Rimsky-Korsakov, Glazunov, Blumenfeld and others). Stravinsky's contributions to chamber music have already been cited.

The remaining two composers, Prokofiev and Shostakovich, were tonal composers who juxtaposed contemporary European idioms with conservative forms and styles demanded by the Soviet government. Both were chastised by their country's leaders for coming close to the "formalistic" experiments in pure music which dominated the music of Schoenberg, Webern, and Stravinsky, and both survived by adapting their avant-garde tendencies to the heroic and folksong preferences of Stalin and his bureaucracy. Sergey Sergeyevich Prokofiev (1891-1953) wrote several pieces of chamber music which have become standard repertory items. He worked on his flute-piano sonata Opus 94 (1943; arranged in 1944 as a violin-piano sonata Opus 94a) and his violin-piano sonata Opus 80 (1938-1946) while he was in protective exile (1941-1943) with other Soviet artists. Although he enjoyed the easy access to and stimulus from colleagues (David Oistrakh specifically requested the violin arrangement of Opus 94), he also brooded at the

---

[42]Yenoin Ephraim Guibbory, "Thematic Treatment in the String Quartets of Ernest Bloch" (University of West Virginia Ph.D. dissertation, 1970), and William Jones, "Ernest Bloch's Five String Quartets," in *The Music Review*, vol. xxviii (1967), 112-121.

disastrous war which the nazis had brought to Russia and Europe; both sonatas have to be interpreted with both moods. Both follow the baroque pattern of slow - fast - slow - fast and include dynamic rhythms normally associated with the composer's dance music (the final movement of Opus 80 alternates irregularly measures of $\frac{5}{8}$, $\frac{7}{8}$, and $\frac{8}{8}$ that suggest some of the Eastern European folk rhythms which Tchaikovsky and Mussorgsky had already employed and which Bartók also drew upon). Prokofiev also wrote sonatas for two violins alone (1932) and for cello and piano (1949).[43]

The two string quartets are more distinct from each other than are the two violin-piano sonatas from each other. Both are in three movements, but whereas the first quartet has movements fast - slow + fast - slow, the second has the simpler pattern fast - slow - fast. The first quartet was commissioned by the Elizabeth Sprague Coolidge Foundation in 1930 while Prokofiev was making a tour of America and was premiered at the Library of Congress in Washington in 1931. There is nothing Russian about the quartet. It is in the key of B Minor, which is not complementary to the strings (for example, when and how to use the sonorous open C strings of the viola and cello became a challenge to him). Prokofiev claimed that the opening movement was modeled on the Beethoven quartets which he was continually studying, and the movement is in sonata form. But he regarded the Andante finale as the most significant movement. The other quartet was written in November, 1941, when he was exiled to Nalchik, capital of the Kabardino Socialist Republic, and it is as nationalistic as the first quartet is not. He was told by a government official there to write a quartet using Kabardinian themes, which he proceeded to do. The first movement in sonata form contrasts two folksongs, the second movement is a transformation of a ledzhinka (islambey, source for Balakirev's famous piano tone poem), and the Getigezhev Ogorbi (joyful mountain dance) is the basis for the third movement in sonata-rondo form. While he was writing the piece, the nazis approached Nalchik and Prokofiev moved further east; the government official who had ordered the piece was killed, but Prokofiev continued

[43]The sonata for two violins in unison is by definition not chamber music.

work on it. It was premiered on April 7, 1942, in Moscow by the Beethoven Quartet and received its first American performance on a radio broadcast by the NBC Quartet on June 24, 1945.[44] In addition to sonatas and quartets, Prokofiev also wrote a quintet for oboe, clarinet, violin, viola and bass (1924), the *Overture on Hebrew Themes* for clarinet, string quartet and piano (1919), *Humoresque Scherzo* for four bassoons (1915), *Ballade* for cello and piano (1912), and *Five Melodies* for violin and piano (1925). The *Overture* was written in New York for Jewish friends and professional musicians who had recently emigrated from revolution-torn Russia and was an attempt to capture the sound of Jewish klezmer music. *Five Melodies* was based on five songs which Prokofiev had set earlier (Opus 35).

While Prokofiev spent many years in Western Europe and America and was acquainted first hand with the newest music of the major composers of his time, Dmitri Dmitrievich Shostakovich (1906-1975) spent his entire life in the Soviet Union.[45] The center of his creative output from 1944 until his death was his symphonies and his string quartets; he wrote an isolated quartet in 1935 and fourteen quartets from 1944 until 1974. By their very nature the symphonies, which were spread out more evenly throughout his creative years, were his public music and the quartets his private music. The symphonies reflect the changing tide of Soviet control of the arts, and as the attacks on formalism of the Stalinist era receded during the reign of Krushchev and then in the post-Krushchev era, Shostakovich gradually let the public in on his true artistic and political thoughts through his symphonies, especially the anti-government statements in the 13th and 14th. Programs abound in the symphonies, most notably in the "Leningrad Symphony," and even in the more introspective public works the composer aimed to reach a popular audience directly, quickly, and without much subtlety. The quartets, on the other hand, are more personal from the very beginning and reflect little of Soviet artistic

---

[44]Members of the quartet were Mischa Mischakoff, Daniel Guilet, Carlton Cooley, and Benar Heifetz.

[45]He made several short trips abroad and visited America only for a few weeks in 1959.

regulations; they are formalistic in that here Shostakovich is concerned primarily with musical expression and not with extra-musical messages that would please the commissars. That there are sometimes little private messages, however, is evident in the monothematic eighth string quartet (1960) based on the notes D - E♭ - C - B (which in German spelling is DSCH, for *Dmitri Sch*ostakovich), but the composer used these notes and their similarity to the four-note pattern of the late Beethoven quartets in a purely musical, non-programmatic way.[46] He referred to the quartet as "autobiographical," because he identified himself with a song which "it quotes . . . known to all Russians: 'Exhausted by the hardships of prison.'"[47] The fourth string quartet, too, was one of the composer's private expressions against anti-Semitism, but however potent his feelings in the piece, this never interfered with the structure of the work. Shostakovich was concerned with cyclic structure, as in the masterful seventh quartet (1960) and the one-movement thirteenth (1970), and his interest in Schoenberg's atonality and dodecaphonic method and Webern's pointillism and melodic and spatial effects, which Stalin stifled in the 1930's, returns in the last four quartets (1968-1974).[48] Whatever formalistic elements he investigated, he digested it and presented it in his quartets in his own simple style, which is crafted perfectly. The quartets are not bombastic and extrovertive; they are gentle, subtle, and introspective.

Besides the quartets, which rank among the greatest of the 20th century, Shostakovich wrote two piano trios (1923, 1944), a piano quintet (1940), two pieces for string octet (1924-1925), and three

---

[46]Yury Keldysh, "An Autobiographical Quartet," in *Sovyetskaya Muzyka* (1961), trl. Alan Lumsden, in *The Musical Times*, cii (1961), 226-228, errs when he reads into the quartet "Shostakovich's way of meditating on the fate of humanity in the modern world" and criticizes the rather mechanical repetitions of melodic fragments; it is the latter with which Shostakovich builds a musically sound composition and the former is irrelevant to it.

[47]*Testimony: the Memoirs of Dmitri Shostakovich, as related to and edited by Solomon Volkov*, trl. Antonina W. Bouis (New York: Harper and Row, 1979), p. 156.

[48]Laurel Fay, "The Last Quartets of Dmitri Shostakovich: a Stylistic Investigation" (Cornell University Ph.D. dissertation, 1978); and Hans Keller, "Shostakovich's Twelfth Quartet," in *Tempo*, no. 94 (Fall, 1970), 6-15.

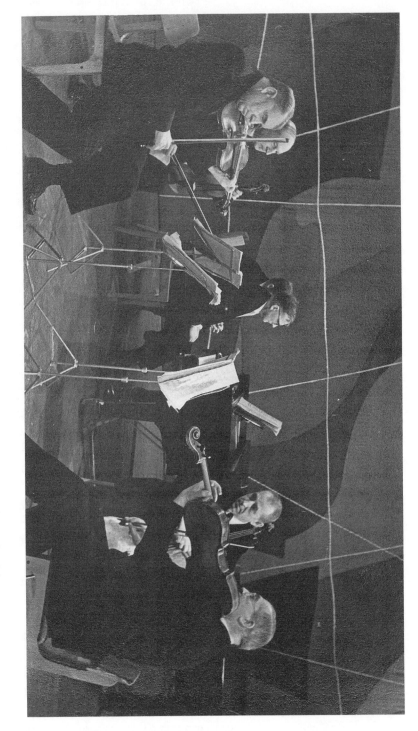

Dmitri Shostakovich with the Borodin String Quartet. Photograph courtesy I. Shostakovich, Moscow.

sonatas for piano and cello (1934), violin (1968), and viola (1975). For whatever unknown reason and despite mastery over all orchestral instruments in his symphonies, he never wrote any chamber music involving winds.

English Chamber Music: Britten

The English revival of chamber music began with the continued performances of chamber music during the 19th century and the renewed interest in the composition of chamber music at the end of that century which we noted in the previous chapter. The most important English composer during the first several decades of the 20th century, Ralph Vaughan Williams (1872-1958), was primarily a composer of symphonic music and songs and only incidentally wrote chamber music. His first string quartet (1908-1909, revised 1921) is full of folk music and is the result of the composer's study of the music of the English peoples; it was not a successful work. Much better received was his second string quartet in A Minor (1942-1944) and his violin-piano sonata in the same key (1954). William Walton (1902-1983), whose few chamber compositions came between the earliest of Vaughan Williams's and the latest of Britten's, were mostly derivative works. The first string quartet (1919-1922), which was highly praised by Alban Berg, was withdrawn by the composer because, as he later stated, it is "full of undigested Bartók and Schoenberg."

By the time Benjamin Britten (1913-1976) began to compose chamber music (the early string quartet [1931] and the oboe quartet [1932]), England had regained much of its stature as a center for this kind of music. What was wanting was the supreme master composer whose compositions would not only be English in flavor but international in dimensions. This Britten provided. A devoted listener to chamber music and himself a fine chamber pianist and violist,[49] he wrote chamber music for specific performers whose

---

[49]Peter Poole, "Benjamin Britten String Quartets Nos. 2 & 3," liner notes for CRD Records, Ltd. no. 1095 (1981): "Britten's first teacher of composition, Frank Bridge (1879-1941) was an excellent viola player and in his student days they would often enjoy an evening of quartets together."

personalities figure in the music, such as the great oboist Leon Goossens in the oboe quartet, the renowned violist William Primrose in the *Lachrymae* (1950) for viola and piano, and famed cellist Mstislav Leopoldovich Rostropovich in the cello-piano sonata (1961).[50] His most famous chamber music is his three mature string quartets (1941, 1945, and 1976) and the cello-piano sonata. Bartók was his chief foreign influence, especially in the second string quartet and the sonata,[51] but he also drew on earlier English masters of chamber music, notably in the second quartet which was written in tribute to Purcell. Premiered at London's Wigmore Hall on November 21, 1945, Britten commemorated the 250th anniversary of Purcell's death by writing a baroque-like "chacony" in the third movement; it consists of twenty-one presentations of a nine-bar chaconne phrase grouped into four sections: nos. 1-6 = harmonic variations, nos. 7-12 = rhythmic variations, nos. 13-18 = a new countertheme in the second violin, and nos. 19-21 = formal variations (each section is separated by a solo cadenza in the cello, viola and first violin respectively). The quartet was written in shocked reaction to the sights of war-torn continental Europe which Britten witnessed first hand in 1945.

The third quartet was written shortly after the completion of his last opera *Death in Venice* (1973) and combines somber reflection on the death theme of the opera with a parody on classical and baroque forms. Britten was now ill with heart disease, and as it turns out he died just two weeks before the Amadeus Quartet gave the premier. It has five movements, of which the first—"Duets"— explores all six possible duet scorings of the four instruments while remaining in sonata form. The second movement—"Ostinato"—is the iteration of a four-note pattern of leaping sevenths, while the third movement is an eerie, high-pitched first violin solo over arpeggios which outline the notes A♭ - F - A (the fatalistic "Muss es sein" theme of Beethoven's Opus 135 quartet). In the fourth

---

[50]Donald Mitchell, "The Chamber Music: an Introduction," in Christopher Palmer, ed., *The Britten Companion* (London/Boston: Faber and Faber, 1984), pp. 369-374.

[51]David Brown, "Stimulus and Form in Britten's Work," in *Music and Letters*, xxxix (July 1958), 218-226; and Hugh Wood, "Britten's Latest Scores," in *The Musical Times*, ciii (1962), 164-165.

movement—Burlesque with trio—Britten pays tribute to Shosta-kovich, who had just died and whom he regarded as the only other master of the string quartet of their time; the trio calls for unusual effects of *col legno* and playing behind the bridge in the second violin and viola. The fifth and last movement—"Recitative and Passacaglia" 'La Serenissima'—refers to the serene city Venice and brings in various themes from the opera. It also recalls forms of music so common in Purcell's England. Without being so obvi-ous as Vaughan Williams but yet also drawing on the great past of English music, Britten achieved a synthesis with the neo-classicists, Bartók, Shostakovich and his own perception of cham-ber music.

England, and especially London, has been a center for the per-formance of chamber music throughout the 20th century. All im-portant ensembles who seek world recognition perform regularly there. Because so many outstanding chamber musicians and their ensembles have been resident in that country, audiences and stu-dents have come to expect the highest standards in chamber per-formance, and the fulfillment of such high standards, in turn, generates a respect for and love of chamber music among a large group of people. Just in the realm of the string quartet, the presence of the Amadeus Quartet as the leader among many other such groups enabled and inspired Britten and other resident composers to write their best works for string quartet. Since the demise of the Amadeus Quartet, there have appeared numerous young groups—the Arditti, Brodsky and Balanescu Quartets, among others—who will continue the chamber music milieu of England into the next century.

American Chamber Music in the 20th Century

Whereas Czechs, Russians, Hungarians, Brazilians and Euro-pean Jews have found clearly defined characteristics in their ethnic musical heritages, American composers have been groping for a common American musical heritage that seemed until well into the 20th century to be elusive. America was not, even in the pre-colonial days of just Indians, a cohesive, unified, unique culture; the diversity of heritages, traditions, tastes, and possibilities was overwhelming to anyone who was trying to pigeon-hole American musical culture. Rather it was necessary for an individual American composer to find his/her own particular brand of American musical culture with which he/she could feel comfortable and then build new art music on that perceived and felt culture. Since many composers writing in America before the 20th century felt more intimately tied to European musical traditions than to any American culture, they wrote in a European style and eschewed any ethnicity in their music. This trend continued with most composers who entered the 20th century, such as Amy Beach (1867-1944), Walter Piston (1894-1976), and Roger Sessions (1896-1985).

Several Americans, however, felt differently and actively sought to build their chamber music on an American as well as European footing. One of the important pioneers in finding an American expression was Edward MacDowell, but he wrote no chamber music. The towering figure for this in chamber music was Ives. Charles Ives (1874-1954), the son of a Connecticut bandmaster, concentrated his compositional energies on smaller combinations (songs, choral music, keyboard music, and chamber music) because, as a musical radical who was professionally involved in the insurance industry and not in music, he had little opportunity to have larger works like operas and symphonies performed and he had little spare time to devote to composing them.[52] His chamber music was written from his earliest days as a composer (1896, while he was still a student at Yale University) until near the end of his creative life (1919), which occurred before his fiftieth year. He often chose established genres, such as the violin-piano sonata, the string quartet, the piano trio, and the clarinet trio, or at least in most cases the scoring was conventional (*Decoration Day* [1912] for violin and piano; *Halloween* [1906], *Largo risoluto* nos. 1 and 3 [1906] and *In re con moto et al* [1913] for piano quintet). What he did with these traditional genres and scorings, however, was not so conventional.

---

[52]Ives did compose four symphonies and other orchestral music, but these form only a small part of his total output.

Ives consciously or unconsciously wrote his music with American sounds, and these set his pieces apart from those of his predecessors. Like other early American composers, he gave titles to many of the pieces which suggest programs that are entirely American in their associations, such as in the three movements of the second violin-piano sonata (1907-1910): "Autumn," "In the Barn," and "The Revival." But while other Americans wrote American titles to German or French or Italian music, Ives captured a sound, too, that is entirely American. The real American essence in his music comes, even in his earliest compositions, from his need to quote familiar American music for its rhythms, its melodies, and its color. "In the Barn," for example, has American country dance fiddling, and in most chamber works there are direct or indirect quotations of American hymn tunes.

Ives's earliest surviving chamber music is his first string quartet "From the Salvation Army" (1896), and it immediately demonstrates the originality of the composer even though it is not yet a mature work. It is in the conventional four movements, but "conventional" only in that two violinists, a violist and a cellist play four movements. It opens with an organ fugue entitled "Chorale," which is then followed by "Prelude," "Offertory," and "Postlude" (terms which easily suggest a religious service such as that which would be performed by the Salvation Army). There are frequent quotations from hymns. The second quartet (1907-1911) was Ives's reaction to hearing a quartet concert by the Kneisel Quartet. He decided that the four members of the quartet needed independence and freedom so that each could act his own part. The result is that the four voices often sound unrelated to each other, and each reaches extremes of expression.

> One hears virtually every kind of melody, harmony, rhythm, phrase structure, plan of dynamics, scoring, and writing for the instruments. . . . The wildly varied materials succeed each other abruptly, sometimes violently; sometimes they literally co-exist. Alongside the most radical sort of jagged, wide-spanned, rhythmically disparate, chromatic melody is melody of the simplest stepwise diatonicism. Triadic harmony alternates with fourth- and fifth-chords, chromatic aggregates, and tone clusters. Canons without any harmonic underpinnings follow passages anchored to static harmonic-rhythmic ostinatos.

"Athematic" writing is set side-by-side against passages quoting pre-existent melodies in almost cinematic collage.[53]

In the Scherzo "Holding Your Own" (1903-1914) for string quartet from *A Set of Three Short Pieces* Ives pursues this independence of parts in the form of an exercise; each instrument is required to play alternately in a different rhythm much like a mensuration canon of the late 14th century, which frees the performer from the rigid rhythms of traditional 18th- and 19th-century music. To the untrained ear this sounds chaotic and it was necessary for Ives to find formal cohesion in the quartet. The first two movements seem related to each other by the common C Major key, and there is a whole tone scale that subtly weaves through all four movements. The four violin-piano sonatas, too, are traditional only in the scoring and the number of movements; the seeming disorganization, however, is only surface sound. As Hitchcock has pointed out:

> composed between 1902 and 1916, all are in three movements; each has a finale and at least one other movement based on hymn tunes; and all are direct and accessible in expressive content and without showy display or merely "idiomatic" writing. . . .[54]

Despite its three-movement form, the first sonata (1902-1908) actually is similar in form to the baroque four-movement structure; the first movement starts slow, then proceeds fast, and the next two movements are slow and fast again. The third sonata (1914), on the other hand, is unlike traditional classical or baroque structure in its order of movements: slow - fast - slow. Ives showed the first sonata to a member of Seidl's quartet, who then called Ives mad. He then simplified the violin part somewhat for the third sonata, and in his fourth sonata "Children's Day at the Camp Meeting" (1914-1916) he made the violin part easy so that his nephew, Moss White Ives, could play it. The piano trio (1904-1911) is in three movements, of which the first demonstrates Ives's layer technique. A

---

[53]H. Wiley Hitchcock, *Ives: a Survey of the Music* (Brooklyn: Institute for Studies in American Music, Monographs no. 19, 1977), p. 62.

[54]Hitchcock, p. 57.

duet for cello and piano is followed by a duet for violin and piano, which is followed in turn by a combination of the two duets. The second movement is a "Scherzo," which is the Italian word for "joke" and which Ives treated accordingly (he gave the title "Tsiaj" to it, which stands for "This scherzo is a joke"); it consists of a medley of numerous popular, patriotic, and student songs.

Ives's music was basically unknown to most American composers until well after he stopped writing music. Amy Beach, for example, wrote as if Ives (her contemporary) never composed. Her chamber music, including a violin-piano sonata (1896), a piano trio (1938), a string quartet (1929), a piano quintet (1907), a woodwind quintet (1942) and a few other pieces, is more influenced by Brahms than anything else, though the string quartet is slightly more dissonant. Piston, who certainly knew Ives's music by the 1950's if not before, wrote his five string quartets (1933-1962), two piano trios (1935, 1966), string sextet (1964), flute quintet (1942), piano quartet (1949), violin-piano sonata (1939), "Sonatina for Violin and Harpsichord" (1945), oboe-piano suite (1931) and much besides in a neo-classical style influenced by the French and by Stravinsky. Ruth Crawford Seeger (1901-1953), too, was under the sway of modern European masters (Scriabin, later Berg and Bartók) in her earlier chamber music such as the violin-piano sonata (1926) and the string quartet (1931), but later, under the influence of her husband and her children, she arranged American folk and children songs and incorporated them into her last works including the wind quintet (1952). Aaron Copland (1900-1990), on the other hand, who made his popular reputation on his American works (ballets, "A Lincoln Portrait," movie music), did not utilize that style in his more ponderous chamber music (the piano quartet [1950], one of his most serious works, is dodecaphonic); he did put some of his Jewish heritage into his piano trio "Vitebsk" (1929), however.

While these important American composers of the 20th century and many others like them have developed their styles along European lines and have rarely shown specific American traits, Elliott Carter (b. 1908) derived much of his chamber music style directly from his mentor Ives. Although he dabbled in a neo-classic style

from the 1930's until ca. 1945 strongly under the impelling influence of Stravinsky, Hindemith, and Piston (his last neo-classic
chamber piece is the woodwind quintet [1948]), he began to forge
his own style in the late 1940's beginning with his four-movement
cello-piano sonata (1948) and in the *Eight Etudes and a Fantasy*
for woodwind quartet (1949-1950). The sonata emphasizes

> the differences between [the] two protagonists. Although this contrast
> is still subsidiary to the character forms of the two inner movements . . .
> the opposition of melodic content, tone, articulation, and pace between
> the two instruments during large stretches of the outer movements is so
> great as almost to create the impression that the players are simultane-
> ously improvising independently. The "almost" is crucial, as the work
> adumbrated Carter's abiding aesthetic quest for a "focused freedom"
> and several of his most far-reaching coordinating techniques for the
> first time. Instead of relying on a received harmonic vocabulary, he
> permeated and "framed" his progressions by a recurrent chromatic ag-
> gregate of interlocking 3rds (the second movement is his last piece to
> bear a key signature), while by superimposing opposing rhythms—for
> instance, triplets on quintuplets—and shifting the basic pulse from one
> to another, he hit on the device later known as "metric modulation," a
> means of gearing continually fluctuating speeds in precise notation.[55]

It is in the three string quartets, however, that Carter achieved
his most popular success as a uniquely American composer of
chamber music.

> The monumental String Quartet no. 1 (1950-51) superimposes inde-
> pendent melodies in polymetric relationships as complex as 3 against 7
> against 15 against 21; and the pitch materials of its entire 40 minutes
> relate not to tonality but to a tetrachord, E-F-G#-A#, from which every
> interval may be obtained by permutation. Even more impressive, how-
> ever, is the work's grandly unified sweep through four movements. . . .

> With the String Quartet no. 2 (1959) Carter achieved at last an
> "auditory scenario for the players to act out with their instruments" that
> is virtually independent of received formal procedures. Each instrument
> is assigned a different "vocabulary" of characteristic intervals, rhythms,
> and expressive gestures, the parts evolving not in terms of constant
> themes against varied backgrounds, but rather in terms of constant

[55]Bayan Northcott, "Carter," in *The New Grove Dictionary of American Music*, vol. I, p.
366.

fields of possibilities realized in continually varied foreground shapes—as it were, the same tones of voice uttering ever new sentences. The conversational metaphor, which Carter doubtless derived from the precedent of Ives's Second Quartet, also accounts for the continuous nine-section form which is the direct result of the various controversies, dominations, and agreements among the four players.[56]

The rhythmic freedom and independence which Ives (the Yankee individualist) demanded from his string quartet players is carried even further by Carter in these two quartets and in the next (1971), which is

> a continuous interplay between two duos, of which the first (violin 1 and cello) plays *quasi rubato* throughout against the *giusto sempre* of the second (violin 2 and viola). The first duo is allotted four complete movements to play against the six of the second, but all ten are segmented and shuffled in such a way that each is sooner or later heard in combination with each of the others.[57]

Within the traditional genre of string quartet Carter, following Ives's lead, created a whole new type of composition, which, in turn, bears little resemblance to European string quartets of the first half of the century. Carter carried on much the same treatment in his other chamber music, such as the violin-piano duo (1973-1974), and extended it as well to works in new and revived genres.

The freedom in treatment of traditional chamber music genres came naturally to Americans who felt only partly obliged to follow European models. The creation of an American music depended upon new ideas which the Europeans excluded. When Europeans began to over-organize music (in the minds of many Americans with the dodecaphonism of Schoenberg, Webern and the post-Webern composers of the 1950's and 1960's), some Americans sought the opposite by under-organized music. John Cage (b. 1912) symbolized this radically in his chance music which included little from Europe and much from ordinary American sound experiences. In addition, as Americans discovered their own native

[56]Northcott, p. 367.
[57]Northcott, p. 369.

musics and the music of other non-Europeans during the 1960's and 1970's, most European musical preferences were discarded in favor of new sounds (not all, of course, ultimately successful). Despite all these new sounds, new styles, and new forms, many American composers of the 1980's remained faithful to the outer aspects of chamber music. Perhaps the most important is Terry Riley (b. 1935), who has worked intimately with the Kronos Quartet since 1978 and has produced with the performers three works for string quartet: *Sunrise of the Planetary Dream Collector* (1981), *Cadenza on the Night Plain* (1984), and *Salome Dances for Peace* (1986). The 1986 piece lasts two hours and

> mingles Asian modes, static drones, Arabic melodic arabesques and nontempered tunings—with dissonant Bartókian counterpoint, bluesy inflections, jazzy syncopations and Minimalist repetition. . . . According to the composer, such multi-cultural evocations arise in an entirely natural way.[58]

Riley was a major figure in the establishment of minimalism in the late 1960's but differed from other minimalists (mainly Philip Glass and Steve Reich) because he favored improvisation to writing music down on paper. He found in 1978, when he and the Kronos Quartet were fellow faculty at Mills College in California, that he liked the chamber music medium, but he was not sure how to reconcile his improvisational style with the need of the players for precise written music. As he stated,

> At first I tried to make improvisation charts, but that wasn't the way to work with the Kronos; they preferred to have everything written out— at least all the notes.[59]

So Riley worked with the quartet members.

> When I write a score for them, its an unedited score. I put in just a minimal amount of dynamics and phrasing marks. It's essentially a score like Vivaldi would have done. So when we go to rehearsal, we spend a lot of time trying out different ideas in order to shape the mu-

---

[58]K. Robert Schwarz, "A New Look at a Major Minimalist," in *The New York Times* (Sunday, May 6, 1990), Section H, p. 24.

[59]Riley, in Schwarz.

sic, to form it. At the end of the process, it makes the performers actually *own* the music. That to me is the best way for composers and musicians to interact.

Recently two English ensembles—the Brodsky Quartet and the Balanescu Quartet—have responded to the experiments of Riley and the Kronos Quartet by mingling minimalist ostinatos with rock and folk music.[60] Whatever the stylistic differences among all these composers of traditional genres of chamber music, they had in common the further development of a highly regarded medium through new colors, new forms, new rhythms, new melodies and new harmonies (atonal, neo-classic diatonic, polytonal or ethnic). Some were influenced by contact with other cultures, by a "logical" outgrowth of the chromaticism of the late 19th century, by structural intricacies of motivic development from Beethoven to Brahms (continual development rather than sonata or rondo form), and by a new awareness of early European music (isorhythm, modality, etc.). Most chamber music, which was hard enough to play in Beethoven's works, was now in the 20th century impossible except for the very best virtuosic ensembles. Aware of this, Bartók, Hindemith and others provided chamber music as well for the student and the amateur. This is not exactly the old Hausmusik of the 19th century, since the quality of the new music remained high despite the function of the music; it was not the "kitsch" that most Hausmusik of the 19th century has been called. In America and much of Europe the onslaught of modern technology has seriously curtailed Hausmusik, for better or for worse, and even in the Soviet Union and Eastern Europe, where Hausmusik was at its strongest before the Second World War, the social and political climate has hindered the music that once flourished in the homes of the bourgeoisie.[61]

---

[60] Allan Kozinn, "Rebels Marching to their Own Tunes," *The New York Times*, August 21, 1994, *Arts and Leisure*, pp. 24-25.

[61] Manfred Vetter, *Kammermusik in der DDR* (Frankfurt a/M: Peter Lang, 1996), pp. 14, 179, 232, points out that Hausmusik virtually disappeared in East Germany during the Communist rule not only because of competition with modern technology (radio, TV, recordings) and pop music but also because of the style of architecture for apartments, in which there was neither space nor soundproofing enough for ensembles.

The urgency with which composers of the first half of the 20th century turned to chamber music can be explained as a combination of three factors. The first is the strength of the legacy which Bartók, Schoenberg and others felt they inherited from the 19th century, especially from Beethoven. By the end of the 19th century the chamber music of Beethoven was worshipped as the ultimate divine message—a tonal, mystical message that transcended the messages of poetry and the other arts that were limited by their precise means of communication. Music was unspecific and therefore closer to the limitless expanse of God. Especially the quartets and piano trios and eventually the late quartets of Beethoven were regarded as the ultimate in musical expression where the contents dictated the forms and were not confined by the exigencies of the symmetrical, traditional forms. By the beginning of the 20th century there were numerous performing groups of great skill and musicality whose interpretations of the Beethoven quartets were regarded by the elite musical community of the Western World as the highest of musical art. No two interpretations were the same, which showed that the music itself was divine and each interpretation—each prophetic insight—was but an imperfect performance of what only God could render perfect. Late in their lives the octogenarians Toscanini and Stravinsky, to name but two of the most highly regarded musicians of the 20th century, spent their last days on Earth listening primarily to the late Beethoven quartets.

The second factor why composers of the first half of the 20th century turned to chamber music is the milieu of their youth. Although the composition of chamber music floundered in the last two-thirds of the 19th century, the interest in it remained keen in bourgeois Europe and America and the number of performers—both amateur and professional—actually increased. The composer born toward the end of the 19th century and beginning of the 20th in Europe, especially Central and Eastern Europe, experienced this boom in chamber music at home. Parents, siblings, neighbors, and friends were role models since so many of them actively performed chamber music and made the topic of interpretation of chamber music the center of household discussions. Chamber music was a part of the surroundings, part of the furniture, and it would be hard to escape its lure with such peer pressure. Opera and symphony were more spectacular, but neither was home music except in chamber music arrangements. Only the song and keyboard repertories could compete, and both were regarded as chamber music (actually Hausmusik) by many at the time. But song required persons with tolerable voices, who were rarer than adequate instrumentalists, and the majority of pieces for voice and piano was parlor music of a lower level of sophistication than chamber music. A composer needed to make his/her way in symphony and opera, song and keyboard music for international fame and fortune, but to satisfy one's own soul and earn the respect of one's professional equals, the composer had to write chamber music.

The third factor was economic. Time and time again, as the resources for opera and symphony dried up during war, depressions and other political, social and natural catastrophes, the composer found the small ensemble as the only one ready and eager for new music. Instead of hiring ninety performers for a new symphony, only three, four or five might suffice for a new chamber work. During the Depression in America in the 1930's, the Federal Music Project emanating from Washington, D.C., paid classical musicians to perform wherever they could find an audience, and in Denver, for example, from 1935 to 1941

> The String Quartet was reported to be the most popular of the performing ensembles. It appeared in schools, libraries, churches, art galleries, colleges, clubs and hospitals.[62]

Inspired by their legacy, nurtured by their surroundings, and encouraged by pragmatic assessments of their economic situations, composers of the first half of the 20th century produced chamber music in such quantity and quality that their era rivals that of the late 17th century and late 18th century.

[62] Marie Kroeger, "the Federal Music Project in Denver 1935-1941, in *American Music Research Center Journal*, III (1993), p. 52.

NEW GENRES OF 20TH-CENTURY CHAMBER MUSIC

Besides the traditional genres of chamber music (string quartet, piano trio, violin-piano sonata, etc.), which they inherited from the second half of the 19th century and altered by changes in tone color, form, harmony, rhythm and style, the composers of the 20th century have rediscovered genres that were lately ignored. The forgotten genres were uncovered first by the early musicologists, who showed them to the active composers, or they were called for by performers whose needs were best served by the older genres. The interest in performing music of the past, which began at the turn of the 19th century with the persistence of the works of Mozart and Haydn in the chamber music repertory long after they were written, continued throughout the 19th century with increasing depth. The uncovering of lost masterpieces by J.S. Bach in the 1830's and 1840's intensified this historical consciousness of performers, audiences and composers, and even Wagner—the arch modernist of the second half of the 19th century—made editions of the works of older masters such as Palestrina. With Brahms the student of older music and composer of new music merged in perfect union; as participant in many of the complete editions of famous composers of the past and as collector of extremely important and rare manuscripts and editions of early music, he had first-hand knowledge of the styles, forms and contents of those repertories and applied that knowledge to his symphonies, choral works, and chamber music. In the first half of the 20th century this continued with the neo-classicists, who specifically sought out music of the past upon which to base their new works, and also with the serialist Webern, who in fact was a trained musicologist as well as brilliant composer. With the growing popularity of early music performance groups and increased interest in performance practice of older music in the second half of the 20th century, nearly every young composer took the music of past centuries for granted as part of his/her style. Even as radical a composer as Alfred Shnitke (b. 1934), whose chamber music during the 1970's and 1980's had come to be among the most original and musically worthwhile, wrote a "Suite in the Old Style" in five movements: pastorale, ballet, minuet, fugue, and pantomime, of which almost all is early 18th-century harmony and melodic patterns. The most significant lesson which history-minded composers learned from the past was flexibility—the need to express themselves without being confined to rigid formulas. This opened up new ways of expressing accepted genres of chamber music; it also opened up new (or forgotten) genres.

The most pressing need to find new genres of chamber music came from wind players, especially brass. During the 19th century almost no new chamber music including brass (except, of course, the French horn) was written. Brass instruments were generally considered band instruments for outdoor performance and were popular in Europe and America as such. During the century they gradually became more important in symphonic music, providing not only a firm harmonic backdrop which the ever-larger halls required but also melodic and contrapuntal passages in contrast to the strings. Berlioz greatly expanded upon Beethoven's use of the brass, and during the second half of the century Wagner, Brahms, Tchaikovsky, Rimsky-Korsakov, Richard Strauss and Mahler made their era the great period of brass instruments. But except for the horn, which was used in various chamber ensembles throughout the romantic period, the brass was simply not regarded as suitable for chamber music. The brass players at the beginning of the 20th century, however, looked upon this differently. They discovered the brass canzonas and sonatas of Banchieri and the two Gabrielis and started a revival of late-16th-century and early-17th-century brass ensemble music. By doing so they transformed this music, much of which was originally designed for public church use and not for "chamber" use; they put this music into the intimate chamber hall and even into private homes. The effect was not only to revive a forgotten but great literature but also to stimulate contemporary composers to write new chamber music for these instruments. They succeeded right from the start, and during the 20th century brass instruments have played a large role in the new chamber music of this era. A few examples which show the diversity of the scorings are Ives's "Chromâtimelôdtune" for piano and brass quartet; Richard Rodney Bennett's *Jazz Calendar* (1963-

1964) for flute, three saxophones, horn, two trumpets, trombone, tuba, percussion, piano and string bass; Hans Werner Henze's *Fragmente aus einer Show* (1971) for horn, two trumpets, trombone, and tuba, and Carter's Brass Quintet (1974) and Fantasy about Purcell's "Fantasia Upon One Note" (1974) for two trumpets, horn, and two trombones.

The same kind of revival occurred with woodwind players, only this revival began in France in the late 19th century with the founding of the Société de Musique de Chambre pour Instruments à Vent in 1879 by Paul Taffanel.[63] The woodwinds had always remained important in chamber music, but certain genres, especially the woodwind quintet as popularized early in the 19th century by Reicha, were picked up by eager young woodwind players who, through increased opportunities for concertizing, needed to expand their repertory with concert music (as opposed to the large amount of woodwind music written for Hausmusik). Besides reviving Reicha, the woodwind quintet needed new music, which 20th-century composers have provided (Nielsen [1922], Hindemith [1922], Schoenberg [1923-1924], Milhaud [1939] and [1958], Beach [1942], Carter [1948], Irving Fine [1949] and [1958], Hans Werner Henze [1952], Seeger [1952], Piston [1956], Mario Davidovsky [1956], Elisabeth Lutyens [1960], Donald Martino [1964], Stockhausen [*Adieu*, 1966], Richard Rodney Bennett [1967-1968], among others). But the woodwind and brass revival was not just for those instruments; it also signaled the revival of chamber music which freely used different types of instruments such as was found in the later-18th-century divertimenti and the baroque suite (so-called "broken consorts"). While many 18th-century suites and divertimenti were not written for chamber performance, they were revived as chamber music.

Since the end of the 18th century, genres of chamber music were defined by scoring (string quartet, piano trio, flute duet); taken for granted in all chamber music of the time was the multi-movement structure with at least one major movement in sonata

---

[63]Serge Gut and Danièle Pistone, *La Musique de Chambre en France de 1870 à 1918* (Paris: Honoré Champion, 1978), p. 23.

form. Works were deemed chamber (the highest category in which many musicians could rank music) if they fit one of the genres of chamber music; if they did not, they were deemed inferior. With new interest in older types of chamber music, however, which were not based exclusively on scoring, the whole idea of genres came under attack—not theoretically by writers about music but by composers who began to ignore traditional genres. When a Corelli solo sonata for violin and continuo was performed in the early 20th century, it was performed as if it were a violin-piano sonata even though there was no sonata-form movement, and when historically conscious performers of the second half of the 20th century performed it, it was regarded as either a church or chamber sonata even if it was performed on a concert stage or on a recording. It became irrelevant if a Mozart, Brahms or Bartók violin-piano sonata belongs to the same genre as Corelli's violin-continuo sonata; the important thing is that all these works can be played as serious, intimate chamber music. While the major genres (string quartet, woodwind quintet, duo sonata, piano trio) were retained in the 20th century because they were especially esteemed, a myriad of scorings and forms appeared in settings that were chamber by any other definition (our five principal elements) and therefore genre through scoring or any other criterion became a largely meaningless consideration. Chamber music is chamber music.

With the opening up of new forms, the single-movement character piece not in sonata form and the multi-movement piece without any sonata form were re-evaluated. In most cases there was a clear distinction between a serious character piece and one that was not serious (a virtuosic display work or a shallow one for students or amateurs). The serious work was now accepted as legitimate chamber music if it met all other criteria for chamber music. In the 20th century many composers chose to write serious character pieces which have titles other than "sonata" or "quartet" or "piano trio," such as Honegger's *Rapsodie* [1917] for two flutes, clarinet and piano, Milhaud's *Pastorale* (1935) for oboe, clarinet and bassoon and *Hommage à Igor Stravinsky* (1971) for string quartet, Poulenc's *Elégie* (1957) for horn and piano, Mario Davidovsky's *Junctures* (1966) for flute, clarinet and violin, Witold Lutoslawski's *Preludia Taneczne* (1954) for clarinet and piano and *Epitaph* (1979) for oboe and piano, Aram Khatchaturian's *Tanz* (1926) for violin and piano, Shnitke's *Hymn No. 1* (1974) for cello, harp and timpani, and so on. They also wrote suites or other collections of character pieces none of whose movements are in sonata form, such as Milhaud's *La Cheminée du Roi René* (1939) for wind quintet and *Quatre Visages* (1943) for viola and piano; Shnitke's *Suite in the Old Style*[64] (1975) for violin and piano or harpsichord; Krzysztof Penderecki's *3 Miniatury* (1959) for violin and piano; Poulenc's *Suite Française* (1935) for two oboes, two bassoons, two trumpets, three trombones, percussion and harpsichord; and many others.

As the possible scorings expanded rapidly during the 20th century, the composer could choose to use traditional chamber instruments in new ways or to bring in instruments that had not been employed in chamber music before. The first option led to such innovations as prepared pianos, flutter-tongued flutes, and violin glissandos, harmonics, col legno, playing on the "wrong" side of the bridge, and others.[65] The second option was much broader since many "instruments" had been systematically excluded before the 20th century. We have already discussed the re-introduction of brass instruments in 20th-century chamber music through the revival of 16th- and 17th-century brass ensembles. When Schoenberg used the human voice in part of his Second String Quartet, he was not creating a new scoring per se but a new scoring in the realm of the purely instrumental string quartet; 18th-century chamber cantatas were similar in setting, but these works (thousands in number) were primarily vocal, not instrumental. The addition of percussion did not occur before the 20th century in chamber music and has become commonplace in the second half of the century. Pioneering in this as in so much else, Ives's chamber music includes "From the Steeples and the Mountains" (1901-1902) for trumpet, trombone and four sets of bells, and "All the Way Around

[64]The printed edition has "suite" but the record has "sonata."

[65]Many of these devices were not entirely new in the 20th century but their use in chamber music and the extent to which they were used is new.

and Back" (1906) for clarinet, bugle, violin, piano four-hands, and bells. Another pioneer in this was Edgar Varèse (1883-1965), whose *Intégrales* [1924-1925] combines eleven wind instruments with various instruments played by four percussionists and whose *Hyperprism* [1922-1923] combines flute, clarinet, three horns, two trumpets and two trombones with numerous noise instruments and a siren played by seven percussion players. Indeed, whole chamber compositions were written for just percussion instruments (the most famous is Varèse's *Ionisation* [1929-1931] for thirteen percussion instruments[66]). In the second half of the 20th century the mixture of percussion and more traditional chamber instruments is common. Luigi Nono (b. 1924), for example, wrote his *Polifonica-Monodia-Ritmica* (1951) for flute, clarinet, bass clarinet, saxophone, horn, piano and percussion, and Karlheinz Stockhausen (b. 1928) wrote his *Für Dr. K* (1969) for flute, clarinet, violin, cello, piano, vibraphone and tubular bells. Ives's disciple Elliott Carter combined glockenspiel with vibraphone and three trumpets in his *Birthday Fanfare* [1978]. Terry Riley combined a string quartet with "singers, keyboards, winds, bass, percussion and a variety of ethnic instruments" for a May 11, 1990 "impromptu version" of his *In C*.[67]

The most radical innovation in scoring, however, is the inclusion of electronics, which is often the amplification of traditional instruments which are then manipulated by an engineer (e.g., George Crumb's *Black Angels* [1970] for "electric string quartet"[68] and *Vox Balaenae* [1971] for electric flute, electric piano and electric cello). On other occasions composers prepare electronically generated tapes to accompany live musicians (e.g., Varèse's *Deserts* [?1950-1954] for 14 winds, piano, five percussionists, and two-track tape; Stockhausen's *Kontackte* [1959-1960] for piano,

---

[66]A few others are Berio's *Sequenza VIII* (1975), Henze's *Prison Song* (1971), and Boulez *Marges* (1962-1964).

[67]Schwarz, pp. 21 and 24.

[68]Crumb also calls for an array of special violin effects like harmonics and sul ponticello which through amplification have a unique sound; for whispering near the instrument which is then picked up by the amplification; and for both "traditional" percussive instruments such as gong and maraca and "non-traditional" percussive instruments such as two metal thimbles and seven crystal glasses.

percussion, and four-track tape, and *Solo* [1965-1966] for melody instrument and tape; Mario Davidovsky's *Synchronisms* [1962-1974] for flute and tape [no. 1], flute, clarinet, violin, cello and tape [no. 2], cello and tape [no. 3], percussion and tape [no. 5], piano and tape [no. 6], and wind quintet and tape [no. 8]; Luciano Berio's *Differences* [1969] for flute, clarinet, harp, viola, cello and tape; and Alfred Shnitke's *Prelude in Memory of Shostakovich* [1975] for live violin and pre-recorded violin).

The future of chamber music will no doubt see the continuation of both the most successful genres of the past (especially string quartets, piano trios, and duets of all kinds) and the innovations in scoring, styles, and forms that have characterized 20th-century chamber music. In addition, there will probably be more integration of traditional chamber music with non-Western or ethnic chamber musics such as American jazz and rock,[69] Asian gamelan and gagaku, African percussion ensembles, and so on. This integration, already underway, will no doubt cause turmoil in many traditional chamber music circles and will challenge the "accepted" conceptions of what constitutes serious art music as opposed to popular music.

THE PERFORMANCE

As in the previous century, chamber music in the 20th century is found in the home, in the concert hall, and in the conservatory. In addition chamber music is performed outdoors in small and large settings (which taxes the term "chamber" to its fullest), and, as we will see below, in radio and television studios. Chamber music in the home had become mostly Hausmusik by the end of the 19th century and remained very important in Europe and America until the Second World War, after which the increasing invasion of radio and recording reduced its scope considerably. In addition to Hausmusik, however, the tradition of home concerts with distin-

---

[69]McCalla, p. 252, points to the music of Lee Hyla, whose "background . . . in rock and roll, jazz, and original improvisation" allows him to integrate these musics into his serious chamber music.

guished local professionals continued, mostly in Central and Eastern Europe. Interestingly the Jewish refuges from Germany who settled in Palestine and Israel during the 1930's transplanted their German chamber music habits to their new country and have maintained them rigidly even though in their native Germany such home concerts have practically ceased to exist.[70] At the same time that home concerts dwindled in Europe and America, the number of professional concerts of chamber music increased many times over due in some measure to the greater ease of travel for such groups from city to city and continent to continent. Also important for the increase in chamber concerts has been the spiraling costs of orchestral concerts and the astronomical fees demanded by famous soloists, which have priced both out of the range of most audiences; chamber groups, which tend to be more dedicated to the music and less to money than virtuosi, are much more modest in their fees and therefore are more available to the wider listening public.

In the 19th century the conservatory became a central location not only for the instruction of chamber music but also for the performance of chamber music. The faculty of conservatories gave concerts in various combinations of instruments, which were open to students and the community at large. This has continued in the 20th century. In the early years of the century the Quatuor Pro Arte was established by young students at the Brussels Conservatory. By the middle of the century the Juilliard String Quartet, made up of faculty of one of America's most prestigious conservatories, had emerged as one of the premier quartets in the world; its student quartets (such as the Cleveland Quartet, Tokyo Quartet) have become its equals later in the 20th century. The California Institute for the Arts, which is an experimental school not just for music but for all the performing arts, has as its faculty quartet the Sequoia String Quartet. All these ensembles look back to the Joachim String Quartet which operated out of the Hochschule für Musik in Berlin during the second half of the 19th century.

[70]Philip V. Bohlman, *"The Land Where Two Streams Flow"*: *Music in the German-Jewish Community of Israel* (Chicago/Urbana: University of Illinois Press, 1989).

In America the university has become a center for the cultivation of chamber music. Composers, performers, and audiences have gathered there for concerts, chamber festivals, and for instruction in chamber music. The university in Europe had also been a site for the private performance of chamber music in past centuries; academics (teachers and students alike) had often assembled in their dormitory rooms for a few hours of private chamber music. But American universities have gone further than this. While in Europe the instruction of the performance and composition of music has traditionally been outside the university (in academies, Hochschüle, conservatories or privately), in America, besides conservatories, music schools within universities have flourished alongside other traditional academic programs. Thus not only was there the appreciative private academic interest in chamber music, there also was a considerable body of music students who needed chamber music as part of their music curriculum. The academics stimulated musicians more toward chamber music than toward virtuosic performance because chamber music was more to the taste of the intellectuals, while the musicians set standards of excellence in performance that raised the quality of chamber music in universities.

In 1940 the University of Wisconsin in Madison took the novel step of appointing the famous Pro Arte String Quartet as quartet-in-residence. Just after its arrival in Madison, however, its leader Alphonse Onnou (1893-1940) died, and after four years Rudolph Kolisch took over as first violinist and remained with the quartet in Madison until 1967. Since 1947 the quartet has been officially the University of Wisconsin faculty quartet; the members of the quartet have been responsible for teaching their instruments and coaching student ensembles, and the quartet has been expected to perform regularly on campus as well as on its regular tours. Other professional chamber music ensembles quickly followed suit, such as the Budapest Quartet and later the Cleveland Quartet at the State University of New York in Buffalo, the Fine Arts Quartet and the New York Woodwind Quintet at the University of Wisconsin in Milwaukee, the Concord Quartet at Dartmouth College, the Vermeer Quartet at Northern Illinois State University, and the Kronos

Quartet at the State University of New York at Geneseo, then Mills College, and most recently at the University of Southern California. In addition already-established faculty at universities began to form chamber groups, particularly woodwind quintets, brass quartets, and ad hoc combinations, and many universities have had chamber groups loosely affiliated with the schools (members drawn from local professionals, such as symphony players, private teachers, commercial musicians) who would be enlisted for particular concerts (such as the University of Illinois Chamber Players, the *Spectri Sonori* players at Tulane University, and the Brandeis University Chamber Players). University concerts of chamber music by top-flight resident ensembles draws in audiences from the local community and in many cases provides the only live concerts of chamber music in the area.

Besides performers and audiences the university also gathered in composers of chamber music. Practically every composer of chamber music living in America in the 20th century has been associated with universities as teacher and/or composer-in-residence. Those who have not have been, for the most part, teachers at conservatories. Some, such as Piston, Hindemith, Sessions, Crumb, and Babbitt, spent their entire professional lives in America as professors of music at a university, while others, such as Carter, Bloch, Harris, George Rochberg (b. 1918), Ralph Shapey (b. 1921), Donald Martino (b. 1931), John Harbison (b. 1938), Joan Tower (b. 1938), Bernard Rands (b. 1934), Paul Chihara (b. 1938), John Adams (b. 1947), Christopher Rouse (b. 1949), and Riley have served part of their American careers at universities. Only a few, such as Stravinsky, Copland, Libby Larsen (b. 1950) and Ellen Zwilich (b. 1939) have limited their appearances at universities to occasional lectures and short symposia or colloquia. Since the early 1950's hundreds of composers teach regularly at American universities and colleges. Because of the presence of chamber music performers at the schools and the built-in audiences of students and intellectuals for chamber music, the bulk of the music composed by these resident composers is chamber music. The music usually is experimental or avant garde (note the discussion of Terry Riley's three quartets above) and is too difficult mu-

sically and technically for amateur student and lay faculty performers, so the new university chamber music is performed by professionals for a small audience. In addition to students and faculty,
this audience also includes a small coterie of townspeople who live
near the campus.

A new milieu for chamber music in the 20th century is the outdoor concert, often associated with festivals. Most chamber concerts at famous summer festivals (Tanglewood, Ravinia, Marlboro,
Aspen, Salzburg) do take place indoors in smaller halls attached to
the festival since the festival organizers recognize that the balance
and intimacy so essential to good chamber performance are virtually impossible in true outdoor settings. But sometimes the appearance of several world-famous virtuosi has tempted promoters to go
outdoors where 15,000 persons, spread out over lawns, can bring
in financial returns far greater than the few hundred that would
crowd into an acoustically satisfactory chamber hall. When Isaac
Stern, Eugene Istomin and Leonard Rose played piano trios, thousands flocked to hear these superb artists. But was it intimate?
Outwardly the answer would seem to be "no" since intimacy is
normally conceived as something very small—in this case a very
small group of people. But intimacy is a psychological condition,
and if an individual feels privately an intimate connection with an
event or an art work, then there is intimacy governed by those conditions no matter what else happens. Not all 15,000 persons at the
Stern-Istomin-Rose concerts assuredly felt an intimate connection
with their performance, but some probably did. But cannot a listener at a symphony or choral concert or an opera feel equally such
intimacy? The answer is yes, but the Stern-Istomin-Rose event had
several other ingredients. First, the repertoire which they played
belonged to a (at that time) 150-year tradition of what audiences
had come to know as "chamber music." The piano trio had been
cultivated in very intimate surroundings from the late 18th to the
early 20th centuries, and so the music itself exuded intimacy. Then
the three musicians themselves suggested intimacy: three individuals giving of themselves so as to make a unity while retaining their
individualities. If the piano trio was an unknown quantity to that
mid-20th-century audience and if the audience could not see the

performers (both of which probably were the case for many persons in that audience), then a sense of chamber music intimacy probably did not happen. To them this may have been billed as a chamber music concert but they did not get what they paid for. However, a small group in that audience, which knew the piano trio repertory and watched the performers, could hurdle the difficult surroundings (14,999 other coughing, shuffling persons and the wide open air) and psychologically place themselves in an intimate situation with Stern-Istomin-Rose and the music.

The change in the conditions for listening to and playing chamber music has paralleled the changing role of women in the 20th century. Women took active part in all aspects of chamber music before the 20th century, but usually there were restrictions on them. We have seen that girls and women in Venice formed the finest string orchestra in Europe under Vivaldi's direction and probably were the performers of most of his sonatas, and we have noted that women pianists played a crucial role in the development of keyboard chamber music during the second half of the 18th century. Despite this, in the 19th century women were often considered "out-of-place" if they played certain instruments. Wilhelm Heinrich von Riehl, writing in 1853, found it objectionable that women played the piano; they should play the violin.[71] In Norway in the 19th century women were barred altogether from performing chamber music,[72] and in Basel, Switzerland, men allowed women to participate in their chamber music only when they were so distinguished that they could not avoid it (as in the case of the visiting Clara Schumann).[73] In the face of such prejudice women persisted anyway in playing chamber music publicly as well as privately. In 1887 the Austrian violinist Marie Soldat (1863-1955), a pupil of Joachim in Berlin, formed in Berlin a professional quartet with

[71]Riehl, "Viotti und das Geigenduett," in *Musikalische Charakterköpfe: ein kunstgeschichtliches Skizzenbuch*, Band 2 (1st ed. 1853; 7th ed. Stuttgard: J. G. Cottasche Buchhandlung, 1899), pp. 179-182.

[72]Bjarne Kortsen, *Modern Norwegian Chamber Music* (Haugesund: n. publ., 1965; 2nd ed. 1969).

[73]Hans Peter Schanzlin, *Basels private Musikpflege im 19. Jahrhundert*, in *Basler Neujahrsblatt*, no. 139 (Basel: Helbing & Lichtenhaln, 1961).

Ahn Piano Trio: Lucia, Angella, and Maria Ann (1997).
Photo by Arthur Elgort

lady colleagues, and when she married and settled in Vienna two years later, she founded a new quartet (with Elsa von Plank, Natalie Bauer-Lechner, and Leontine Gärtner). In the first quarter of the 20th century women were involved in several important professional chamber ensembles in The United States, such as the Olive Mead Quartet organized in 1904 (with Elizabeth Houghton [later Vera Fonaroff], Gladys North and Lillian Littlehales) and the Marianne Kneisel Quartet, and by the middle of the century women were appearing with men in many ensembles. Madeline Foley became the cellist of the Schneider Quartet and a regular performer with male musicians in New York, Boston, and Marlboro. Eudice Shapiro led the American Art Quartet and her recordings prove her to have been one of the finest chamber musicians this country has ever produced. As the century drew to a close, women played every conceivable chamber music instrument, including brass and percussion, cello and string bass, which until quite late were considered "not lady-like."

Women had also been important as composers, though they were not given ample opportunity to be professional until the 20th century. Both Fanny Mendelssohn and Clara Schumann were fine composers of chamber music, but they were neglected in favor of their more famous male relatives (brother Felix Mendelssohn and husband Robert Schumann). But the appearance of the determined Mrs. Beach laid to rest the most dogged male chauvinist assertion that women cannot compose chamber music. By the middle of the 20th century a number of women composers of chamber music had established themselves in America and Europe and by the end of the 20th century there are as many if not more women composers than men in the field of chamber music.

The change in the status of women in chamber music is not solely the result of a more liberal attitude among men but of the necessities of the new society which came to both Western Europe and America after the Second World War. Whereas women were confined to very time-consuming domestic duties and denied access to the commercial work force before then, the invention of countless time-saving devices for the home and the necessity for women to become wage-earners to supplement the husband's income have led many women out of the home and into professional musical careers. Very talented women who were capable of professional careers in chamber music now have the time and need to do so. Whereas in the past such a woman would have had to limit her chamber music to the home, now she can play for the world; concomitant with that is the disappearance of home chamber music which during much of the first half of the 20th century was supported by if not performed by women. Both husband and wife, caught in the economic squeeze in the Western world and in the professions that demand total dedication, find that there is no more leisure for music at home. The few hours a week that a family is together in leisure is now consumed by home video or running. The emancipation of the woman was a necessity, but the elimination of Hausmusik should not have been a necessary result of that.

THE TECHNOLOGICAL CHANGES OF THE 20TH CENTURY

However revolutionary the composition of new chamber music has become in the 20th century and the changes in location of live chamber music performance are, they are relatively minor when compared to the technological means by which all music can now be heard. Through amplification, radio transmission and recording, the way most people listen to music has changed radically from the 19th and previous centuries to the 20th century and beyond.

Chamber music, by definition, is intimate music, that is, music performed in intimate surroundings and enjoyed in intimate surroundings. If the room in which the music is performed is small, the sounds carry adequately for the few persons who are playing and/or listening to the music. As the room becomes bigger to accommodate more listeners, means must be found to amplify the sound so that the intimate character of the music is not lost. Amplification was developed within the instruments themselves during the 17th and 18th centuries; the viol and early violin gave way to the later and louder violin, the harpsichord and the early piano were replaced by the later and louder piano, and so on. But during the later 19th century, as halls became extremely large, amplification through adjustment of the architecture of the hall became necessary. Basic concepts in how sound bounces or does not bounce off flat or curved or irregular surfaces made of soft or hard wood or cement or artificial materials became essential to the building of any successful concert hall at the end of the 19th and throughout the 20th century.

For intimate music in very large halls and outdoors, when the acoustic properties of the facility were inadequate, modern technology provided the loud speaker comprising a microphone, an amplifier, and speakers. With the arrival of this equipment, which slowly crept in in the 1930's and which has dominated the performance of popular forms of music from the 1960's on, various problems were created which were nonexistent before. The placement and number of the microphones in chamber music, first of all, are crucial. If the microphone is too near an instrument, a lot of surface noise (keys clicking, bows scratching) is picked up that even in a small, intimate hall would be overlooked; if it is too near the performer, ugly sounds of breathing, creaking of furniture and shuffling of music on the stand risk drowning out the actual music. If only one microphone is used (as was the case in the early days of amplification), the balance among the instruments is at jeopardy; modern solutions have been to place a microphone above each performer, but just where above each performer has a great effect on what tone that the instrument exudes is picked up. This brings in the problems of the next stage, the amplification box itself. Here an engineer, who often as not is completely uneducated in music, sits in control of just how loud each instrument is and how they are to balance. The performers themselves no longer have control of this most crucial element in the intimate playing together of chamber music. The third stage, the speakers, are just as problematic; where they are placed will affect how the audience in the end will receive the sounds. But if a listener happens to be close to the speaker, he/she may lose all sense of intimacy because the sound coming out is too loud, whereas another listener at the furthermost point from any speaker may hear nothing at all. If one is satisfied, the other is sure to lose. If two or more speakers are placed in the hall or around the outdoor area, delays from one speaker to another

may cause echo or other distortion and the same problem of location for the individual listener exists.

The result of electronic amplification of live performances of
chamber music, then, is usually disastrous and, though still occasionally experienced at the end of the 20th century, is not tried as
much as it was earlier in the century. The big outdoor festivals (in
America Ravinia, Tanglewood, Aspen and others) usually reserve
their symphonic and choral presentations for outdoors and bring
the chamber performances into smaller enclosed or partially enclosed halls where non-electronic means for amplification have
generally more success at conveying the intimacy of the music.

The problems of amplification of live concerts to the audience
at hand remain problems for the other, more important technological innovations of the 20th century: radio and recording. When a
concert of chamber music is broadcast or recorded, there remain
the number and placement of microphones, the engineer who balances the sounds, and the placement of the speakers vis-à-vis the
listener. The differences are that the listener now controls the location of the speakers and shares control of tone and loudness with
the engineer. The listener to radio and recordings can eliminate
many of the problems of the speakers which affected the listener in
the concert hall, and with the development of stereo, quadriphon-
ics, and lasers the listener can simulate fairly well a live, intimate
performance of chamber music. Frequently the engineers mixing
the sounds (balancing the sounds coming in from the different microphones) have more knowledge of the music they are control-
ling, though whatever their skills and knowledge they and not the
performers still have virtual control over the balance and tone of
the broadcast or recording. During the earlier years of radio and
recording the quality of equipment and the knowledge of engineers
and listeners were so primitive that this way of listening to chamber music was no threat to being at a live performance. As wax
cylinders, Edison discs, other acoustic discs, 78's, LPs, wire and
reel-to-reel tapes, and cassettes have given way to CD's with laser
production, the quality of performance on radio and especially on
recordings has improved to the point where the listener can hear
balance and intimacy better through this technology than in almost

any concert hall. Even in the late 20th century, however, only the best equipment in perfect working order makes it possible to listen to chamber music without hums, hisses, scratches.

With the technological advances have come questions of aesthetics and sociological changes in music. These changes have often resulted in accusations that technology has destroyed chamber music and that technological advance is in inverse proportion to musical worth. The ferocity of these attacks only underscores how fundamental these changes are, and only time will tell if humankind will benefit from them.

Whatever their handicaps, radio broadcasts of live chamber music concerts by superior artists have made it possible for a large number of persons to hear a concert which could not take place in a hall large enough to accommodate such numbers. It makes the music accessible to persons who are house- or bedridden, too poor to afford tickets to concerts, too busy, or in locales where there are no performances of chamber music of top quality. It brings the live performance away from the public concert hall into the intimate surroundings of a private home or automobile. The "canned" recording of chamber music goes two steps further. Instead of limiting one's listening to chamber music to the whim of a radio schedule, recorded chamber music can be enjoyed at any time and in any situation. Furthermore, the listener can choose the piece to be heard. Both radio and cassette recording together make it possible to transport chamber music into any location, including anywhere in one's private quarters, cars, airplanes, ships, camping, subways, at work, at play, jogging. Sociologically the modern chamber music fanatic is usually not an amateur performer or regular concert-goer but a listener on electronic equipment. While the number of persons playing Hausmusik in Europe and America has steadily dwindled during the 20th century, the number of persons listening to radio and recorded chamber music has grown. Although it is impossible to measure whether more persons at the end of the 20th century are listening to chamber music than played it a century ago (proportional to the overall population), the professional chamber music performer clearly values radio and recording contracts as highly as live concert contracts.

Through these changes in how chamber music is appreciated by its public, chamber music has made some gains and had some losses. Alongside the increased availability of live chamber music concerts to the public is the expansion of the repertory in recorded chamber music. One no longer has to wait days or weeks or months to hear a top ensemble play; that ensemble's recordings of the standard repertory are now available, as are the recordings of the same repertory by other great and not so great ensembles from today and from earlier in the century. Furthermore, as the standard repertory is repeated over and over again at ever more frequent intervals, professional quartets and listeners require more variety. That variety has come in expanding the repertory to lesser known pieces of the past all the way back to the 16th century, by established composers and forgotten composers. It has also come through new compositions of chamber music which are better appreciated once the preceding repertories are mastered.

On the other hand, recorded music has made the interpretation of chamber music a stereotyped, uninteresting subject. As long as the audience is dependent upon live performance, it accepts and eagerly anticipates the novel interpretation that comes with each live event. Interpretation depends on the intelligence, knowledge, experience, temperament, skills and taste of the individual performers and how these interact in a given situation. No two performances are alike because no two performers or ensembles are alike and even the same performers are continually changing as individuals and in their interrelations within the group. There is growth, there is decay, there is always change. But in a canned performance, nothing ever changes. Our attention is focused away from the interpretation and over and over again to the musical composition as interpreted on a single occasion by one dead ensemble. We hear and understand the composition from only one standpoint (though as listeners we, too, are continually changing and we have the option to continually buy new discs). If the chosen interpretation is good, we can listen to it numerous times, but the danger is shutting the audience off from all the infinite number of other interpretations. In this regard recording is inferior to live chamber music.

The excessive listening to radio and recorded chamber music has also occurred at a time when few persons have the leisure to play chamber music at home or with friends. 20th-century people are increasingly busy with making a living, tending to the home and family, exercising, and participating in positive social activities. But human beings have not changed their needs, and the need that chamber music or Hausmusik filled in the past is still there. In the past chamber music allowed a family to be together to share in the musical ensemble and also to allow each member to refresh (calm) him/herself. Chamber music fanatics who only listen to chamber music satisfy the need to refresh themselves, but by doing so alone they do not share their skills and feelings with their closest family and circle of friends. Passive listening to music has isolated people from each other and shut them off from communicating with others the beauty that music can give. Since the passive listener depends on the professional performers to satisfy him/her and has reneged on his/her own possible contribution, the professional chamber musician in turn has made a business out of chamber music and commercialized it. Commercial musicians are interested in furthering passive listening because it will increase their income, and the danger lies in the loss of musical integrity among them. Fortunately this has not yet happened universally; there are still professional ensembles more interested in music than money and there are still chamber musicians who make chamber music at home in intimate circles.

Radio and recorded chamber music, while concentrating on the sounds of the music, have missed an important element in the live experience of chamber music, namely the visual. When one plays chamber music, one is continually aware of the other performer(s) not only by listening to the other part(s) but also by watching the other player(s). When one is in the audience of a chamber concert, one *watches* the performers visually interact with each other. Perhaps the most dynamic quartet of the 20th century was the Budapest Quartet, whose recordings are excellent; but anyone who heard the group play live will remember as much the important facial and body gestures of Alexander Schneider, who as second violinist made the ensemble always alive. Movies at first offered

Budapest String Quartet with Milton Katims, violist, in
recording studio (ca. 1950). Sony Classical.

the visual aspect of chamber music which is missing in radio and
recording, but movies transported the audience from the concert
hall to the theater—the movie house with popcorn, and the quality
of sound was never very good.

Television, arriving commercially in the immediate post-
Second World War years, provided a better source of visual chamber music since it, like radio and recording, came into the intimate
surroundings of the home. As camera technique improved and
public broadcasting and cable art channels developed, the possibility of enjoying the concert of chamber music increased, but there
were still limitations. There was no choice in what chamber music
one heard and saw, one could not pick the time for the performance, and the sound was of poor quality. The arrival of home
video in the early 1980's gave the listener and viewer the choice of
what chamber music one hears and sees, though the repertory of
chamber performances on commercially available video tape is

very small. The limitations of audio recording are the same with video: the listener is dependent on others to perform and there is no variety in the performance once it is canned. While video tape has little quality of sound, the recent perfection of laser disc video equipment makes possible acoustically desirable performances, which can be viewed and heard in the most intimate recesses of one's private dwelling.

The home computer has the potential for one person to play a whole chamber composition, but when only a single person performs without ensemble, there is no chamber music. It is like the organ of Bach's time; a new type of keyboard still does not replace the special aspect of a small group of performers struggling to make music together. For the composer who composes a whole "chamber piece" on computer for performance on computer, the same contradiction exists; there cannot be one-person chamber music.

Fraught with dangers to the whole concept of chamber music, the exciting technological developments of the 20th century can be used carefully to nurture this kind of music. It gives us all an easy way to become familiar with the sounds of a vast repertory of chamber music from over four hundred years and to hear that repertory performed by top professionals. Some different interpretations can be compared without surrendering the right of each performer to interpret his/her own way. It can set standards for students and amateurs to assist learning individual pieces and styles of chamber music. What it cannot do is replace the living performance, whether privately or publicly, by professionals or amateurs.

FINAL ASSESSMENT

The development of chamber music from the mid-16th century to the present is continuous and on-going. Throughout this period there is a body of music which shares common elements that include, besides the visible notes on the manuscript or printed pages, common performance situations. The intimate performance of this music is one of its primary (some would say *the* primary) characteristics. Some music was not written as chamber music, that is, was written for church or outdoor performance which is anything but intimate, but over the years it has become chamber music because more modern performance is intimate. It can become intimate and chamber music later because from the start it shares other characteristics with music originally intended as chamber music: it is instrumental, it is ensemble, it is solo for each part, and it is serious art music.

The forms of chamber music over four centuries have continually changed, yet some basic characteristics emerge. The dualism of unity and contrast, which are the concern of all forms of Western art music, has an especially important role in the development of the forms of chamber music since, basically unaffected by programs, texts and ulterior motives, the composer of chamber music has had to rely on musical forms alone to justify the piece as art music. Whether the piece is in one, sectionalized movement or in numerous separate movements, the same need for unity and contrast is there. The contrast was important to relieve monotony, to allow for variety in rhythm, key, instrumentation, melody, and to effect a longer composition. Once contrast was there, unity had to be restored lest the work fall apart. Sometimes unity came through repetition of some elements (e.g., ostinato or ground bass) within each section or movement but more often it was repetition of the peculiarities of some element heard earlier after an absence of that element's original character.

Many different instruments have participated in chamber music over the centuries, and the relationships among these instruments within a piece has changed. Yet there, too, common areas of relationship have appeared time and again in the overall repertory of chamber music. When two or more melody instruments play together, they are either of equal importance or not so. If they are equal, their style is usually homophonic or contrapuntal or a mixture of both; if they are unequal, one part has melodies and the other part has accompaniment. Every so often composers mix all these styles together within a movement, so that while only one style happens at a given moment, all or several styles occur at different moments of the piece. When the dominant melody and accompaniment exchange parts in the course of a movement, there is an equality of parts in toto but at any given moment only one part dominates; in the late 18th century this was called "concatenate." In the history of chamber music all these styles vie; at times "progress" is perceived as one replacing another, though usually we find that at any given moment in history, through a cross-section of all the chamber music of that moment, most if not all these styles coexist.

Throughout its history chamber music has satisfied a need among people to make intimate music together. Chamber music has provided a means for sharing—blending one's part with the whole and at the same time retaining a worthwhile identity—and that was an essential part of the democratization of Europe. It became the hope of suppressed peoples and the ideal in middle class bourgeois society. Many of the greatest composers the Western World has had to offer have developed their own styles, forms and colors of chamber music, but they did so within a medium accepted for its ability to grow, change and adapt while retaining the five elements essential to it. The sharing was intimate—it was an exchange with one to four others or perhaps up to twelve or thirteen. The basic criteria for chamber music were not arbitrarily chosen but came about through urgent need in 16th-century England, shortly thereafter in Italy, France and Germany, and eventually through most of the Western World.

Intimacy was stretched at various times to include not only performers but audiences as well. The locale influenced the intimacy; private quarters or small palace salons lent themselves to intimate and congenial music. Through adaptation churches, outdoor settings, small concert salons, large concert halls, and in the late 20th century massive video machines expanded audiences for a single event. When intimacy was not actually there, the illusion of intimacy replaced it. Just as opera is a grand illusion that accepts singing, stylized characters, and theatrical conventions, so chamber music accepts the fact of a million persons listening to and watching on video a performance by three or four players as intimate. The appearance of the other four elements of chamber music together with accepted conventions of listening to this music and the forms and shapes it takes gives the illusion of intimacy. Each member of the audience perceives him/herself as a spy into the intimate sharing of a few chamber musicians.

Taste is an evasive phenomenon that defies generalizations and analytical patterns. A taste for chamber music is elusive because it is a personal way of listening to music that some people have and others do not. It can be taught and cultivated but not defined. The way individuals listen to chamber music varies with personal taste and experience and musical education. For many the new technological media for listening to chamber music are not an impediment for enjoying chamber music and for feeling much what audiences in the 19th century or dilettante performers in the 17th and 18th century felt. For others the new media for chamber music is destructive of the very purpose of chamber music: a small group of congenial persons joining together in private surroundings to make music of a lofty nature; recordings and even concerts turn active participation into passive absorption. Fortunately today we have the best of all possible worlds since all means of enjoying chamber music are available. Furthermore, as never before, the repertories of chamber music from the 16th century to the present are available for hearing and for performing.

Despite the revolutionary changes through which chamber music has gone in the 20th century, the need of human beings for this kind of music is as urgent now as it was in 16th-century England, 17th- and 18th-century Italy, Germany, Austria, France, and England, and 19th-century Europe as a whole. Almost anyone in the world today can turn on a radio or cassette player at any time and hear music of any variety, and for those for whom the passive listening to great music does not replace the thrilling excitement of taking part in the playing of even dull, let alone great music, there are international chamber music societies with members eager to meet new players and make music together. Chamber music makes us all good team players, at the same time that it stresses the individuality of each player and the need of the group for the individual. Such a fulfilling experience was recognized by the small group of Englishmen in the middle of the 16th century who began this history and has been enjoyed, even if not always consciously, by the thousands of chamber musicians—amateurs and professionals—who have come since. Nineteenth-century middle-class citizens found chamber music an excellent therapy against the trying daily battles for survival in the new industrial society; 20th-century victims of political repression have found chamber music an enormous outlet for free thought and individual expression.[74]

In the present era of computers, corporate take-overs, and individual alienation, chamber music provides humankind with a unique chance to rediscover beauty through renewed emphasis on individual achievement and intimate relations. As an individual in a chamber music ensemble a single performer has intrinsic worth no matter how well or how poorly he/she plays, and through partnership with one or a few other performers, the individual feels the warmth of association with others without being overwhelmed by those others. The result is not something material, measured by statistics or money or power or social standing; rather the result is aesthetic: the beautiful in music that lifts the spirits of all who play or listen. Chamber music provides hope and a raison d'être to people whose purpose for existing has otherwise been blotted out by modern life, and it provides each person with the means for defiantly declaring his/her right to be him/herself. The presentation of chamber music by the world's great virtuosi and ensembles sets standards and goals of perfection, but only through the intimate sharing of musical parts in a small room is the full experience of chamber music possible.

---

[74]Vetter, *Kammermusik in der DDR*, p. 188, cogently presents the particular importance of chamber music for a suppressed East Germany during Communist rule and for modern-day humankind elsewhere.

BIBLIOGRAPHY

For an annotated bibliography of writings about chamber music, see John H. Baron, *Chamber Music*, in the following bibliography.

Abert, Anna Amalie. "Rhythmus und Klang in Schuberts Streichquintett," in Heinrich Hüschen, ed., Festschrift Karl Gustav Fellerer zum sechzigsten Geburtstag am 7. Juli 1962. Regensburg: Gustav Bosse, 1962, pp. 1-11.

Albinoni, *Sonatas and Suites, Opus 8*, ed. C. David Harris, in *Recent Researches in the Music of the Baroque*, vols. LI-LII. Madison: A-R Editions, 1986.

Allen, Judith S. "Tonal Allusion and Illusion: Debussy's Sonata for Flute, Viola and Harp," in *Cahiers Debussy, Nouvelle Série*, no. 7 (1983), pp. 38-48.

Amsterdam, Ellen. "The String Quintets of Luigi Boccherini." University of California Ph.D. dissertation, 1968.

Apel, Willi. "Studien über die frühe Violinmusik," in *Archiv für Musikwissenschaft*, XXX-XXXVIII (1973-1981).

Apel, Willi. *Die italienische Violinmusik im 17. Jahrhundert*, in *Beihefte zum Archiv für Musikwissenschaft*, vol. XXI. Wiesbaden: Franz Steiner, 1983.

Archibald, Bruce. "Some Thoughts on Symmetry in Early Webern: Op. 5, no. 2," in *Perspectives of New Music*, vol. X, no. 2 (1972), pp. 159-163.

Arnold, Denis. "Chamber Music," in *The New Oxford Companion to Music*. Oxford/New York: Oxford University Press, 1983.

Ashbee, Andrew. "The Four-Part Instrumental Compositions of John Jenkins." University of London Ph.D. dissertation, 1966.

Banchieri, Adriano. *Canzoni alla Francese*. 1596. Ed. Leland Bartholomew, in *Recent Researches in the Music of the Renaissance*, vol. XX. Madison: A-R Editions, 1975.

Banfield, Stephen. "British Chamber Music at the Turn of the Century: Parry, Stanford, Mackenzie," in the *Musical Times*, CXV (1974), 211-213.

Baron, John H. "August Wilhelm von Schlegel and Beethoven," in *Journal of Aesthetics and Art Criticism*, XXXI (1973), 531-537.

Baron, John H. *Chamber Music: a Research and Information Guide.* New York/London: Garland Publshing, 1987.

Bartholomew, Leland Earl. *Alessandro Rauerij's Collection of Canzoni per sonare (Venice, 1608).* Fort Hays: Kansas State College, 1965.

Becker, Heinz. "Das volkstümliche Idiom in Brahmses Kammermusik," in *Hamburger Jahrbuch für Musikwissenschaft*, vol. VII, *Brahms und seine Zeit*. Hamburg: Laaber, 1984, pp. 87-99.

Benton, Rita. "Nicolas Joseph Hüllmandel and French Instrumental Music in the Second Half of the 18th Century." University of Iowa Ph.D. dissertation, 1961.

Berlioz, Hector. *Voyage Musical en Allemagne et Italie.* Paris: 1844.

Beveridge, David. "Dvořák's Piano Quintet, Op. 81: the Schumann Connection," in *Chamber Music Quarterly* (Spring, 1984), pp. 2-10.

Beveridge, David. "Sophisticated Primitivism: the Significance of Pentatonicism in Dvořák's American Quartet," in *Current Musicology*, no. 24 (1977), 25-36.

Biales, Albert. "Sonatas and Canzonas for Larger Ensembles in Seventeenth-Century Austria." University of California in Los Angeles Ph.D. dissertation, 1962.

Blankenship, Shirley M. "Berg Lines: Opus 3, Lyrische Suite." University of Illinois DMA dissertation, 1977.

Bock, Emil W. "The String Fantasies of John Hingeston (ca. 1610-1683)." University of Iowa Ph.D. dissertation, 1956.

Boetticher, Wolfgang. "Legnani," in *Die Musik in Geschichte und Gegenwart*, vol. VIII, cols. 472-473.

Bohlman, Philip V. *"The Land Where Two Streams Flow": Music in the German-Jewish Community of Israel.* Chicago/Urbana: University of Illinois Press, 1989.

Bonta, Stephen. "The Church Sonatas of Legrenzi." Harvard University Ph.D. dissertation, 1964.

Bonta, Stephen. "The Uses of the Sonata da Chiesa," in *Journal of the American Musicological Society*, XXII (1969), pp. 72-73.

Boyden, David. "Corelli's Solo Violin Sonatas 'Grac'd' by Dubourg," in *Festskrift Jens Peter Larsen*. Copenhagen: Wilhelm Hansen Musik-Forlag, 1972, pp. 113-125.

Brade, William. *Newe ausserliche Paduanen*. Hamburg: 1609.

Brandenburg, Sieghard. "The Historical Background to the 'Heiliger Dankgesang' in Beethoven's A-Minor Quartet Op. 132," in Alan Tyson, ed., *Beethoven Studies*, vol. III. Cambridge: Cambridge University Press, 1982, pp. 161-191.

Braun, Jürgen. *Die Thematik in den Kammermusikwerken von Maurice Ravel*, in *Kölner Beiträge zur Musikforschung*, Band 33. Regensburg: Gustave Bosse, 1966.

Brenet, Michel. *Les Concerts en France sous l'ancien Regime*. Paris: Fischbacher, 1900.

Brindle, Reginald S. "The Symbolism in Berg's Lyric Suite," in *The Score*, no. 21 (October 1957), pp. 60-63.

Brockhoff, Marie-Elisabeth. "Studien zur Struktur der italienischen und deutschen Triosonate im 17. Jahrhundert." Innaugural dissertation, Westfälische Wilhelms-Universität zu Münster, 1944.

Brodin, Gereon. "Svensk Kammarmusikbibliografi," in *Ur Nutidens Musikliv*, V (1924), pp. 24-31, 66-68, 94-102, and 120-123.

Brook, Barry, ed. *Streichtrios*, in *Joseph Haydn Werke*, Reihe XI, 1.Folge, Band 1. Munich: Henle, 1986.

Brossard, Sebastian de. *Dictionnaire de Musique*. Paris: Chr. Ballard, 1703.

Brown, Clive. *Louis Spohr: a Critical Biography*. Cambridge: Cambridge University Press, 1984.

Brown, David. "Stimulus and Form in Britten's Work," in *Music and Letters*, XXXIX (July 1958), pp. 218-226.

Bücken, Ernst. *Anton Reicha: sein Leben und seine Kompositionen*. Munich: Wolf, 1912.

Buonamente, Giovanni Battista. *Il Quarto Libro de varie Sonate*. Venice, 1626.

Buonamente, Giovanni Battista. *Settimo Libro di Sonate*. Venice, 1637.

Burney, Charles. *A General History of Music,* ed. Frank Mercer. New York: Dover, 1957.

Burton, Humphrey. "Les Académies de musique en France au XVIIIe siècle," in *Revue de Musicologie*, vol. XXXVII (1955), pp. 122-147.

Byrd, William. *Consort Music*, ed. Kenneth Elliott, in *The Collected Works of William Byrd,* vol. XVI. London: Stainer & Bell, 1971.

Caffi, Francesco. *Storia della Musica Sacra nella già Cappella Ducale di S. Marco in Venezia (dal 1318 al 1797),* ed. Elvidio Surian, in *Studi di Musica Veneta,* vol. X. Florence: Leo S. Olschki, 1987.

Castro y Serrano, José de. *Los Cuartetos del Conservatorio: Breves Consideracions sobre la Mùsica Clássica*. Madrid: Centro General de Administracion, 1866.

Cavicchi, Adriano. "Corelli e il violinismo bologuese," in *Studi Corelliani,* ed. Cavicchi, Oscar Mischiati, and Pierluigi Petrobelli. Florence: Olschki, 1972, pp. 33-47.

Cesari, Gaetano. "Origini del Trio con Pianoforte," in Franco Abbiati, ed., *Scritti inediti*. Milan: Carisch S.A., 1937, pp. 183-198.

Chailley, Jacques. "Sur la Signification du Quatuor de Mozart K.465, dit 'Les Dissonances,' et du 7ème Quatuor de Beethoven," in Bjorn Hjelmborg and Sorensen, eds., *Natalicia Musicologica Knud Jeppesen Septuagenario*. Copenhagen: Wilhelm Hansen, 1962, pp. 283-292.

Chusid, Martin. "The Chamber Music of Franz Schubert." University of California Ph.D. dissertation, 1961.

Clément, Charles. *Sonates en trio pour un clavecin et un violon.* 1743.

Cobbett, *Cyclopedic Survey of Chamber Music*. London: Oxford University Press, 1929.

Cockshoot, John V. "Ferrabosco, Alfonso (ii)," in *The New Grove Dictionary*, 6th ed. (1980), vol. VI, p. 484.

Cooper, Jeffrey. *The Rise of Instrumental Music and Concert Series in Paris 1828-1871*. Ann Arbor: University Microfilms International Research Press, 1983.

Coprario, John. *Fantasia-Suites,* ed. Richard Charteris, in *Musica Britannica,* vol. XLVI. London: Stainer & Bell, 1910.

Corrette, Michel. *Sonates pour le clavecin avec un accompagnement de violon . . . ces pièces se jouer sur le clavecin seul'.* Opus 25. 1742.

Couperin, Fr. *Musique de Chambre,* vols. I-II, ed. André Schaeffner, rev. Kenneth Gilbert and Davitt Moroney, in *Oeuvres Complètes,* section IV. Monaco: L'Oiseau-Lyre, 1980.

Courey, Geraldine de. "Paganini," in *Die Musik in Geschichte und Gegenwart,* vol. X, col. 628.

Craft, Robert. "The Chronology of the Octet," in *Perspectives of New Music,* XXII (1983-1984), pp. 451-463.

Cudworth, Charles. "Visconti, Gasparo," in *Die Musik in Geschichte und Gegenwart,* XIII (1966), cols. 1830-1831.

Cuyler, Louis. "Mozart's Six Quartets Dedicated to Haydn," in Gustave Reese and Rose Brandel, eds., *The Commonwealth of Music in Honor of Curt Sachs.* New York: The Free Press/London: Collier-Macmillan, 1965, pp. 293-299.

Cuyler, Louise. "Tonal Exploitation in the Later Quartets of Haydn," in H.C. Robbins Landon, ed. *Studies in Eighteenth-Century Music: a Tribute to Karl Geiringer on his Seventieth Birthday.* London: Georg Allen and Unwin, 1970, pp. 136-150.

Czesla, Werner. *Studien zum Finale in der Kammermusik von Johannes Brahms.* Bonn: Rheinische Friedrich-Wilhelms-Universität, 1968.

Dahlhaus, Carl. "Über Schuberts Sonatenform: der erste Satz des G-Dur Quartetts D.887," in *Musica,* XXXII (1978), pp. 125-130.

Dann, Elias. "Biber," in *The New Grove Dictionary of Music and Musicians,* 6th ed., vol. II (1980).

Daval, Pierre. *La Musique en France au XVIIIe Siècle.* Paris: Payot, 1961, pp. 153-174.

De Lauze, F. *Apologie de la Danse (1623),* trl. Joan Wildeblood. London: Frederick Muller, 1952.

Dean, Robert Henry, Jr. "The Music of Michele Mascitti (ca. 1664-1760): a Neapolitan Violinist in Paris." University of Iowa Ph.D. dissertation, 1970.

Defant, Christine. *Kammermusik und Stylus phantasticus: Studien zu Dietrich Buxtehudes Triosonaten,* in *Europäische Hochschulschriften,* series 36, Musikwissenschaft vol. 14. Frankfurt am Main: Peter Lang, 1985.

Denny, Thomas A. "The Finale in the Instrumental Works of Schubert." Eastman School of Music of the University of Rochester Ph.D. dissertation, 1982.

Dent, Edward J. "The Earliest String Quartets," in *The Monthly Musical Record,* XXXIII (1903), pp. 202-204.

Deutsch, Otto Erich. "The Chronology of Schubert's String Quartets," in *Music and Letters,* XXIV (1943), pp. 25-30.

Dietrich, Norbert. *Arnold Schönbergs Drittes Streichquartett op. 30: seine Form und sein Verhältnis zur Geschichte der Gattung,* in *Beiträge zur Musikforschung,* Band 12. Munich/Salzburg: Emil Katzbichler, 1983.

Dieupart, Charles. *Six Suittes.* Amsterdam: 1701.

Drummond, Pippa. "Pisendel," in *The New Grove Dictionary of Music and Musicians,* 6th ed., vol. XIV, p. 775.

Dubitzky, Franz. "Richard Strauss' Kammermusik," in *Die Musik,* vol. XIII.3 (1914), 283-296.

Dunn, Nancy. "The Piano Trio from its Origins to Mozart's Death." University of Oregon DMA dissertation, 1975.

Dunn, Thomas D. "The Instrumental Music of Biagio Marini." Yale University Ph.D. dissertation, 1969.

Dürr, Alfred. "Zu Hans Eppsteins 'Studien über J.S. Bachs Sonaten für ein Melodieninstrument und obligates Cembalo,'" in *Die Musikforschung,* XXI (1968), pp. 332-340.

Dürr, Alfred. "Zu Hans Eppsteins Erwiderung," in *Die Musikforschung,* XXII (1969), p. 209.

Ehrlich, A. (pseud. for Albert Payne). *Berühmte Geiger der Vergangenheit und Gegenwart.* Leipzig: A. H. Payne, 1893.

Einstein, Alfred. *Mozart: His Character, His Work.* London/New York/Toronto: Oxford University Press, 1945.

Einstein, Alfred. *Music in the Romantic Era.* New York: Norton, 1947.

Ellis, Katherine. *Music Criticism in 19th Century France*. Cambridge: Cambridge University Press, 1995.

Emerson, Isabell P. "The Role of Counterpoint in the Formation of Mozart's Late Style." Columbia University Ph.D. dissertation, 1977.

Eppelsheim, Jürgen. "Funktionen des Tasteninstruments in J.S. Bachs Sonaten mit obligatem Cembalo," in Günter Fleischhauer, Walther Siegmund-Schultze and Eitelfriedrich Thom, *Zur Entwicklung der instrumentalen Kammermusik in der 1. Hälfte des 18. Jahrhunderts*, in *Studien zur Aufführungspraxis und Interpretation von Instrumentalmusik des 18. Jahrhunderts: Konferenzbericht der xi. wissenschaftlichen Arbeitstagung Blankenburg/Harz, 17. Juni bis 19. Juni 1983*, vol. 22, [no publishing information], pp. 23-33.

Eppstein, Hans. *Studien über J.S. Bachs Sonaten für ein Melodieinstrument und obligates Cembalo*, in *Acta Universitatis Upsaliensis, Studia Musicologica Upsaliensia*, Nova Series 2. Uppsala: Universität/ Stockholm: Almqvist u. Wiksells, 1966.

Estrella, Arnaldo. *Os Quartetos de Cordas de Villa-Lobos*. Rio de Janeiro: Museu Villa-Lobos, 1970.

Evidon, Richard. "Hellmesberger," in *The New Grove Dictionary of Music and Musicians*, 6th ed., vol. VIII, p. 463.

Fabricus, Lars Borge. *Traek af Dansk Musiklivs Historie m.m. Omkring etatsraad Jacob Christian Fabricus' Erindringer*. Copenhagen: Nyt Nordisk Forlag Arnold Busck, 1975.

Farmer, Virginia. "An Analytical Study of the Seventeen String Quartets of Heitor Villa-Lobos." University of Illinois D.M.A. dissertation, 1973.

Fauquet, Joël-Marie. "La Musique de chambre à Paris dans les années 1830," in Peter Bloom, ed., *La Musique à Paris dans les Années Mil Huit Cent Trentre*, in *La Vie Musicale en France au XIXe Siècle*, vol. IV. Stuyvesant, NY: Pendragon Press, 1987, pp. 299-326.

Fauquet, Joël-Marie. *Les Sociétés de Musique de Chambre à Paris de la Restauration à 1870*. 1986.

Favre, Max. *Gabriel Fauré's Kammermusik*. Zurich: Kommissionsverlag von Max Niehans, 1949.

Fay, Laurel. "Boismoriter," in *The New Grove Dictionary of Music and Musicians*, 6th ed., vol. II, p. 862.

Fay, Laurel. "The Last Quartets of Dmitri Shostakovich: a Stylistic Investigation." Cornell University Ph.D. dissertation, 1978.

Feder, Georg. "Haydn's Piano Trios and Piano Sonatas," trl. by Howard Serwer, in *Haydnfest: Music Festival: September 22-October 11, 1975: International Musicological Conference: October 4-11, 1975.* Washington, D.C.: Kennedy Center Program, 1975, pp. 18-23.

Fellinger, Imogen. "Die Begriffe Salon und Salonmusik in der Musikanschauung des 19. Jahrhunderts," in *Studien zur Trivialmusik des 19. Jahrhunderts*, ed. Carl Dahlhaus. Regensburg: Gustav Bosse, 1967.

Fétis, F.J. *Biographical Notice of Nicolo Paganini with an Analysis of his Compositions and a Sketch of the History of the Violin*, 2nd ed. London: Schott & Co., n.d.

Fields, Christopher D.S. "The English Consort Suite of the Seventeenth Century." Oxford New College Ph.D. dissertation, 1970.

Finscher, Ludwig. "Cherubini's String Quartets." Deutsche Grammaphon, Archiv 2723, 1976, booklet p. 3.

Finscher, Ludwig. "Corelli und die 'Corellisierenden' Sonaten Telemanns," in *Studi Corelliani*, ed. Adriano Cavicchi, Oscar Mischiati, and Pierluigi Petrobelli. Florence: Olschki, 1972, pp. 75-76.

Finscher, Ludwig. "Hausmusik und Kammermusik," in *Musica*, XXII (1968), pp. 325-329, and in Richard Baum and Wolfgang Rhem, eds., *Musik und Verlag: Karl Vötterle zum 65. Geburtstag am 12. April 1968*. Kassel: Bärenreiter, 1968, pp. 67-76.

Finscher, Ludwig. *Die Musik des 15. und 16. Jahrhunderts*, in *Neue Handbuch der Musikgeschichte*. Laaber-Verlag, 1990.

Finscher, Ludwig. *Studien zur Geschichte des Streichquartetts, I: Die Entstehung des klassischen Streichquartetts von den Vorformen zur Grundlegung durch Joseph Haydn*, in *Saarbrücker Studien zur Musikwissenschaft*, Band 3. Kassel: Bärenreiter, 1974.

Fischer, Richard S. "Brahms' Technique of Motivic Development in his Sonata in D Minor Opus 108 for Piano and Violin." University of Arizona DMA dissertation, 1964.

Fischer, Wilhelm. "Mozarts Weg von der begleiteten Klaviersonate zur Kammermusik mit Klavier," in *Mozart-Jahrbuch* (1956), pp. 16-34.

Flamm, Christa. *Leopold Kozeluch: Biographie und stilkritische Untersuchung der Sonaten für Klavier, Violine und Violoncello nebst einem Beitrag zur Entwicklungsgeschichte des Klaviertrios.* University of Vienna Ph.D. dissertation, 1968.

Frescobaldi, Girolamo. *Fiori Musicali.* 1635.

Freywald, Volker. *Violinsonaten der Generalbass-Epoche in Bearbeitungen des späten 19. Jahrhunderts,* in *Hamburger Beiträge zur Musikwissenschaft,* Band X. Hamburg: Karl Dieter Wagner, 1973.

Friedland, Bea. *Louise Farrenc, 1804-1875: Composer, Performer, Scholar,* in *Studies in Musicology,* no. 32. Ann Arbor: UMI Research Press, 1980.

Fuller, David. "Dieupart, Charles," in *The New Grove Dictionary of Music and Musicians,* 6th ed., vol. V, p. 472.

Gérard, Yves. *Thematic, Bibliographical and Critical Catalogue of the Works of Luigi Boccherini,* trl. Andreas Mayor. London: Oxford, 1969.

Gerlach, Reinhard. "War Schönberg von Dvořák beeinflusst?: zu Arnold Schönbergs Streichquartett D-Dur," in *Neue Zeitschrift für Musik,* vol. CXXXIII (1972), pp. 122-127.

Gibbons, Orlando. *Consort Music,* ed. John Harper, in *Musica Britannica,* vol. XLVIII. London: Stainer & Bell, 1982.

Gillet, Judy. "The Problem of Schubert's G Major String Quartet (D.887)," in *The Music Review,* XXXV (1974), pp. 281-292.

Glasow, Glenn L. "Variation as Formal Design and Twelve-tone Procedure in the Third String Quartet by Arnold Schoenberg." University of Illinois DMA dissertation, 1967.

Grassineau, James. *A Musical Dictionary.* London: J. Wilcox, 1740.

Grebe, Karl. "Das 'Urmotiv' bei Mozart: Strukturprinzipien im G-Dur-quartett KV 387," in *Acta Mozartiana,* vol. VI (1959), pp. 9-14.

Greene, Carol. "The String Quartets of Alexander Alexandrovich Aliabev," in *The Music Review,* vol. XXXIII (1972), pp. 323-329.

Grew, Sidney. "The 'Grosse Fuge': the Hundred Years of its History," in *Music and Letters,* XII (1931), pp. 140-147.

Grout, Donald J. "Scarlatti," in *The New Grove Dictionary of Music and Musicians,* 6th ed., vol. XVI, p. 557.

Guibbory, Yenoin Ephraim. "Thematic Treatment in the String Quartets of Ernest Bloch." University of West Virginia Ph.D. dissertation, 1970.

Guillemain, Gabriel. *Pièces de clavecin en sonates avec accompagnement de violon.* Opus 13. 1745.

Gülke, Peter. "In What Respect a Quintet? On the Disposition of Instruments in the String Quintet D956," in Badura-Skoda and Branscombe, *Schubert Studies: Problems of Style and Chronology.* Cambridge: Cambridge University Press, 1982, pp. 173-185.

Gut, Serge, and Danièle Pistone, *La Musique de Chambre en France de 1870 à 1918.* Paris: Honoré Champion, 1978.

Hall, Harry Hobart. "The Moravian Wind Ensemble: Distinctive Chapter in America's Music." George Peabody College Ph.D. dissertation, 1967.

Hammond, Frederick. "Girolamo Frescobaldi and a Decade of Music in Casa Barberini: 1634-1643," in Friedrich Lippmann, ed., *Studien zur italienisch-deutschen Musikgeschichte XII,* in *Analecta Musicologica,* vol. XIX. Köln: Arno Volk, 1979, pp. 94-124.

Hammond, Frederick. *Girolamo Fescobaldi: his Life and Times.* Cambridge: Harvard University Press, 1983.

Händel-Handbuch, vol. III. Kassel: Bärenreiter, 1986, pp. 171-172.

Harding, James. "Saint-Saëns," in *The New Grove Dictionary of Music and Musicians,* 6th ed., vol. XVI, p. 402.

Harkins, Elizabeth Remsberg. "The Chamber Music of Camille Saint-Saëns." New York University Ph.D. dissertation, 1976.

Harper, John M. "The Instrumental Canzonas of Girolamo Frescobaldi: a Comparative Edition and Introductory Study." University of Birmingham Ph.D. dissertation, 1975.

Hassler, Hans Leo. *Sacri Concentus (1601),* ed. Joseph Auer, rev. C. Russell Crosby, Jr., in *Denkmäler der deutschen Tonkunst,* 1. Folge, vols. 24-25, pp. 195-214.

Hedlund, Harry Jean. "A Study of Certain Representative Compositions for Woodwind Ensembles, CA. 1695-1815." State University of Iowa Ph.D. dissertation, 1959.

Hermann, Myrl Duncan. "Chamber Music by Philadelphia Composers 1750-1850." Bryn Mawr College Ph.D. dissertation, 1977.

Hess, Ernst. "Einzelbemerkungen," in *Streichquintette*, ed. Hess and Ernst Fritz Schmid, in Mozart, *Neue Ausgabe sämtlicher Werke*, Series VIII, Werkgruppe 19. Kassel: Bärenreiter, 1967.

Hickman, Roger. "The Nascent Viennese String Quartet," in *The Musical Quarterly*, LXVII (1981), pp. 193-212.

Hildebrandt, Christian. *Erster Theil/Ausserlesener Paduanen und Galliarden*. Hamburg: 1607.

Hill, William G. "Brahms' Opus 51: a Diptych," in *The Music Review*, XIII (1952), pp. 110-124.

Hitchcock, H. Wiley. *Ives: a Survey of the Music*. Brooklyn: Institute for Studies in American Music, Monographs no. 19, 1977.

Horan, Catherine Anne. "A Survey of the Piano Trio from 1800 through 1860." Northwestern University Ph.D. dissertation, 1983.

Horton, John. *Mendelssohn Chamber Music*. Seattle: University of Washington Press, 1972.

Hosler, Bellamy. *Changing Aesthetic Views of Instrumental Music in 18th-Century Germany*. Ann Arbor: UMI Research Press, 1981.

Huber, Calvin Raymond. "Life and Music of William Brade." University of North Carolina Ph.D. dissertation, 1965.

Hudson, Richard. *The Allemande, the Balletto, and the Tanz*, 2 vols. Cambridge: Cambridge University Press, 1986.

Irving, Howard Lee. "The Piano Trio in London from 1791 to 1800." Louisiana State University Ph.D. dissertation, 1980.

Jackson, William. *Eight Sonatas for the Harpsichord Accompanied with Two Violins, a Tenor and a Bass*, Op. 20. London: Longman and Broderip, 1773.

Jacquet de la Guerre, Elizabeth. *Pieces de Clavecin Qui peuvent se Jouer sur le Viollon* (Bibliothèque national music ms., dated June 13, 1707) survives only in a keyboard part, ed. Thurston Dart. Monaco: Éditions de l'oiseau-lyre, 1965.

Jardillier, Robert. *La Musique de Chambre de César Franck: Étude et Analyse*. Paris: Mellottée, [1929].

Jennings, John M. "The Fantasies of Thomas Lupo," in *Musicology*, vol. III, (1968-1969), p. 34.

Jensen, Niels Martin. "Solo Sonata, Duo Sonata and Trio Sonata: Some Problems of Terminology and Genre in 17th-Century Italian Instrumental Music," in *Festskrift Jens Peter Larsen*. Copenhagen: Wilhelm Hansen Musik-Forlag, 1972.

Jones, Walter. "The Unaccompanied Duet for Transverse Flutes by French Composers, ca. 1708-1770." University of Iowa Ph.D. dissertation, 1970.

Jones, William. "Ernest Bloch's Five String Quartets," in *The Music Review*, vol. XXVIII (1967), pp. 112-121.

Kaderavek, Milan R. "Stylistic Aspects of the Late Chamber Music of Leos Janáček: an Analytic Study." University of Illinois D.M.A. dissertation, 1970.

Kammermusikforeningen, *Kammermusik i Hundrede ar: 1868 - 5. December - 1968*. Copenhagen: Nyt Nordisk Forlag, 1968.

Kárpáti, János. *Bartók's String Quartets*, trl. Fred Macnicol. Budapest: Franklin Printing House, 1975.

Karsch, Albert. "Untersuchungen zur Frühgeschichte des Klaviertrios in Deutschland." University of Köln Ph.D. dissertation, 1943.

Keldysh, Yury. "An Autobiographical Quartet," in *Sovyetskaya Muzyka* (1961), trl. Alan Lumsden, in *The Musical Times*, CII (1961), pp. 226-228.

Keller, Hans. "Mozart—the Revolutionary Chamber Musician," in *The Musical Times*, CXXII (1981), pp. 465-468.

Keller, Hans. "Shostakovich's Twelfth Quartet," in *Tempo*, no. 94 (Fall, 1970), pp. 6-15.

Keller, Hans. "The Chamber Music," in H.C. Robbins Landon and Donald Mitchell, *The Mozart Companion*. New York: Oxford University Press, 1956; reprint New York: W. W. Norton, 1969, pp. 90-137.

Kelly, David T. "The Instrumental Ensemble Fantasias of Adriano Banchieri." Florida State University Education Ph.D. dissertation, 1962.

Kemp, Ian. "Hindemith," in *The New Grove Dictionary of Music and Musicians*, 6th ed., vol. VIII, p. 577.

Kendall, Alan. *Paganini: a Biography*. London: Chappell, 1982.

Kerman, Joseph. *The Beethoven Quartets*. New York: Alfred A. Knopf, 1967.

Kidd, Ronald R. "The Emergence of Chamber Music with Obligato Keyboard in England," in *Acta Musicologica*, XLIV (1972), p. 123.

King, A. H. "Mozart's 'Prussian' Quartets in Relation to his Late Style," in *Music and Letters*, vol. XXI (1940), pp. 328-346.

King, Alexander Hyatt. "Mozart's String Quartets," in *The Listener*, vol. XXXIV (1945), p. 633.

Klenz, William. *Giovanni Maria Bononcini of Modena: a Chapter in Baroque Instrumental Music*. Durham: Duke University Press, 1962.

Koch, H.C. *Versuch einer Anleitung zur Composition*. Leipzig: 1782-1793.

Kohlhase, Hans. *Die Kammermusik Robert Schumanns*. Hamburg: Karl Dieter Wagner Musikalienhandlung, 1979.

Komlós, Katalin. "The Viennese Keyboard Trio in the 1780s: Sociological Background and Contemporary Reception," in *Music and Letters*, vol. LXVIII (1987), pp. 222-234.

Kortsen, Bjarne. *Modern Norwegian Chamber Music*. Haugesund: n. publ., 1965; 2nd ed. 1969.

Krehbiel, Henry Edward. *Antonin Dvořák's Quartet in F Major, Op. 96*. New York: H.A. Rost, 1894.

Kroeger, Karl. "Michael," in *The New Grove Dictionary of American Music*, 6th ed., vol. III, p. 223.

Kroher, Ekkehart. "Die Polyphonie in den Streichquartetten Wolfgang Amadeus Mozarts und Joseph Haydns," in *Wissenschaftliche Zeitschrift der Karl-Marx-Universität Leipzig*, vol. V (1955-1956), pp. 369-402.

Krummacher, Friedhelm. "Kantabilität als Konstruktion: zum langsamen Satz aus Mozarts Streichquartett KV465," in Werner Breig, Reinhold Brinkmann and Elmar Budde, eds., *Analysen: Beiträge zu einer Problemgeschichte des Komponierens: Festschrift für Hans Heinrich Eggebrecht zum 65. Geburtstag*, in *Beihefte zum Archiv für Musikwissenschaft*, XXIII. Stuttgart: Franz Steiner Verlag Wiesbaden, 1984, pp. 217-233.

Krummacher, Friedhelm. "Mendelssohn's Late Chamber Music: Some Autograph Sources Recovered," in *Mendelssohn and Schumann*, ed. Jon W. Finson and R. Larry Todd. Durham: Duke, 1984, pp. 76-80.

Krummacher, Friedhelm. *Mendelssohn—der Komponist: Studien zur Kammermusik für Streicher*. Munich: Wilhelm Fink Verlag, 1978.

Kucaba, John. "Wagenseil, Georg Christoph," in *The New Grove Dictionary of Music and Musicians*, 6th ed., vol. XX, pp. 100-102.

Kull von Niederlenz, Hans. *Dvořák's Kammermusik*, in *Berner Veröffentlichungen zur Musikforschung*, Heft 15. Bern: Paul Haupt, 1948.

Laing, M. "Anton Reicha's Quintets for Flute, Oboe, Clarinet, Horn and Bassoon." University of Michigan D.E. dissertation, 1952.

Landon, H.C. Robbins. *Die Klaviertrios von Joseph Haydn: Vorwort zur ersten kritischen Gesamtausgabe*. Munich/Vienna: Doblinger, 1970.

Landon, H.C. Robbins. *Haydn: Chronicle and Works*, vols. II and IV. Bloomington/London: Indiana University Press, 1977-1978.

Landormy, Paul. "La Musique de Chambre en France de 1850 à 1871," in *Le Mercure Musical*, nos. 8-9 (1911), pp. 37-50.

Langley, Richard Douglas. "Sonate Concertante in Stilo Moderno by Dario Castello: a Transcription of Book I." Washington University Ph.D. dissertation, 1974.

Lassur, Lucien Augé de. *La Trompette: un Demi-Siècle de Musique de Chambre*. Paris: Ch. Delagrave, 1911.

Leeson, Daniel N., and David Whitwell, "Mozart's 'Spurious' Wind Octets," in *Music and Letters*, vol. LIII (1972), pp. 377-399.

Lefkowitz, Murray. *William Lawes*. London: Routledge & Kegan Paul, 1960.

Levy, Janet M. *Beethoven's Compositional Choices: the Two Versions of Opus 18, No. 1, First Movement*, in *Studies in the Criticism and Theory of Music*, ed. Leonard B. Meyer. Philadelphia: University of Pennsylvania Press, 1982.

Locke, Matthew. *Chamber Music*, ed. Michael Tilmouth, in *Musica Britannica*, vols. XXXI-XXXII. London: Stainer & Bell, 1971-1972.

Loudon, J.S. "Reminiscences of Chamber Music in Toronto during the Past Forty Years," in *Canadian Journal of Music*, vol. I (1914), pp. 52-53.

Lütolf, Max. *Arcangelo Corelli: historische-kritische Gesamtausgabe der musikalischen Werke*, vol. I. Laaber-Verlag, 1987.

Mahaim, Ivan. *Beethoven*. Paris: Desclée De Brouwer, 1964.

Mann, Alfred. *The Study of Fugue*. New York: W.W. Norton, 1965.

Marliave, Joseph de. *Les Quatuors de Beethoven*, ed. Jean Escarra. Paris: Librairie Félix Alcan, 1925.

Mascitti, Michele. *6 Sonate da camera für Violine und bezifferten Bass*, ed. Walter Kolneder, Heft 1. Heidelberg: Willy Müller, 1963.

Mascitti, Michele. *Opus V*. 1714. Modern edition by Frits Noske. Mainz: B. Schott's Söhne, [1959].

Mason, Colin. "Webern's Later Chamber Music," in *Music and Letters*, vol. XXXVIII (1957), pp. 232-237.

Mason, Daniel Gregory. *The Quartets of Beethoven*. New York: Oxford, 1947.

Mattheson, *Der vollkommene Kapellmeister*. 1739.

Maylender, Michele. *Storia delle Accademis d'Italia*, 5 vols. Bologna: L. Cappelli, 1930.

Mazurowicz, Ulrich. *Das Streichduett in Wien von 1760 bis zum Tode Joseph Haydns*, in *Eichstätter Abhandlungen zur Musikwissenschaft*, Band 1. Tutzing: Hans Schneider, 1982, pp. 211-366.

Mazzocchi, Domenico. *Madrigali à Cinque voci.* Rome: 1638.

McCalla, James. *Twentieth-Century Chamber Music*. New York: Schirmer Books, 1996.

Mead, Ernest C. "The Instrumental Ensemble Canzonas of Girolamo Frescobaldi." Harvard University Ph.D. dissertation, 1983.

Mellers, Wilfrid. *François Couperin and the French Classical Tradition*, new ed. London: Faber and Faber, 1987.

Meredith, Margaret. "Christopher Simpson and the Consort of Viols. University of Wales Ph.D. dissertation, 1969.

Mersmann, Hans. *Die Kammermusik des xvii. und xviii. Jahrhunderts bis zu Haydn und Mozart,* vol. I. Leipzig: Breitkopf und Härtel, 1933.

Meyer, Ernst Hermann. *Early English Chamber Music from the Middle Ages to Purcell,* 2nd ed. London: Lawrence and Wishart, 1982. Original title *English Chamber Music*. London: Lawrence and Wishart, 1946. Reprint of first ed., *Early English Chamber Music*. New York: Da Capo, 1971.

Mischakoff, Anne. *Khandoshkin and the Beginning of Russian String Music*. Ann Arbor: UMI Research Press, 1983.

Mitchell, Donald. "The Chamber Music: an Introduction," in Christopher Palmer, ed., *The Britten Companion*. London/Boston: Faber and Faber, 1984, pp. 369-374.

Moe, Orin. "The Significance of Haydn's Opus 33," in J.P. Larsen, Howard Serwer and James Webster, *Haydn Studies: Proceedings of the International Haydn Conference Washington, D.C., 1975*. New York: W.W. Norton, 1981, pp. 445-450.

Moevs, Robert. "Intervallic Procedures in Debussy: Serenade from the Sonata for Cello and Piano, 1915," in *Perspectives of New Music*, vol. VIIIi, no. 1 (1969), pp. 82-101.

Mondonville, Jean-Joseph Cassanéa de. *Sonatas for the Violin*, ed. Edith Borroff, in *Masters of the Violin*, gen. ed. Gabriel Banat. New York: Johnson Reprint Co., 1982.

Morrow, Mary Sue. *Concert Life in Haydn's Vienna: Aspects of a Developing Musical and Social Institution*, in *Sociology of Music* No. 7. Stuyvesant, NY: Pendragon Press, 1989.

Mueller, Paul E. "The Influence and Activities of English Musicians on the Continent during the late Sixteenth and early Seventeenth Centuries." Indiana University Ph.D. dissertation, 1954.

Musgrave, Michael G. "Schoenberg and Brahms: a Study of Schoenberg's Response to Brahms's Music as Revealed in his Didactic Writings and Selected Early Writings." University of London Ph.D. dissertation, 1980.

Myers, Rollo Hugh. *Erik Satie*. London: Dennis Dobson, 1948.

Nectoux, Jean-Michel. *Gabriel Fauré: his Life through his Letters*, trl. J.A. Underwood. London/New York: Marion Boyars, 1984.

Neighbour, Oliver W. "A Talk on Schoenberg for Composers' Concourse," in *The Score*, no. 16 (June 1956), pp. 19-28.

Newlin, Dika. "Anton von Webern: Quintet for String Quartet and Piano," in *Notes*, vol. X (1953), pp. 674-675.

Newman, William S. "Three Musical Intimates of Mendelssohn and Schumann in Leipzig: Hauptmann, Moscheles, and David," in *Mendelssohn and Schumann*, ed. Jon W. Finson and R. Larry Todd. Durham: Duke, 1984.

Niecks, Frederick. "Music for Wind Instruments Alone," in *The Monthly Musical Record*, vol. XLVIII (1918), pp. 122-124.

Nobach, Christiana. *Untersuchungen zu George Onslows Kammermusik.* Kassel: Bärenreiter, 1985.

Nogueira França, Eurico. *A Evoluçâo de Villa-Lobos na Música da Câmera.* Rio de Janeiro: Museu Villa-Lobos, 1976.

Northcott, Bayan. "Carter," in *The New Grove Dictionary of American Music,* 6th ed., vol. I, p. 366.

Nottebohm, Martin Gustav. *Zwei Skizzenbücher von Beethoven aus den Jahren 1801 bis 1803,* ed. Paul Mies. Leipzig: 1924.

Olsen, Deborah M. "Music in an American Frontier Communal Society," in *Brass Bulletin,* no. 33 (1981), pp. 49-58, no. 34 (1981), pp. 13-22, and no. 36 (1981), pp. 64-77.

Palmer, Christopher. "Milhaud," in *The New Grove Dictionary of Music and Musicians,* 6th ed., vol. XII, p. 307.

Payne, Albert. See A. Ehrlich.

Pecman, Rudolf, ed. *Colloquium Musica Cameralis Brno 1971,* in *Colloquia on the History and Theory of Music at the International Music Festival in Brno,* vol. 6. Brno: Cesky Hudebni Fond, 1977.

Perle, George. "The Secret Programme of the Lyric Suite," in *The Musical Times,* vol. CXVIII (1977), pp. 629-632, 709-713, and 809-813.

Pestalozza, Luigi. "Leos Janáček," in *L'Approdo Musicale,* vol. 3 (April-June 1960), 3-74, section 17, "Musica da camera," pp. 59-62.

Pfannkuch, Wilhelm. "Zu Thematik und Form in Schönbergs Streichsextett," in Anna Amalie Abert and W. Pfannkuch, eds., *Festschrift Friedrich Blume zum 70. Geburtstag.* Kassel: Bärenreiter, 1963, pp. 258-271.

Phelps, Roger Paul. "The History and Practice of Chamber music in the United States from Easliest times up to 1875." University of Iowa Ph.D. dissertation, 1951.

Picquot, Louis. *Notice sur la Vie et les Ouvrages de Luigi Boccherini.* Paris: 1851.

Pilkova, Zdenka. "Die Violinsonaten der böhmischen Komponisten in den Jahren 1730-1770," in *Zur Entwicklung der instrumentalen Kammermusik in der 1. Hälfte des 18. Jahrhunderts.* Blankenburg/Harz: n.p., 1984.

Pincherle, Marc. "On the Origins of the String-Quartet," trl. M.D. Herter Norton, in *The Musical Quarterly,* vol. XV (1929), pp. 77-87.

Pincherle, Marc. *Corelli: his Life, his Work*, trl. Hubert E.M. Russell. New York: Norton, 1956.

Pincherle, Marc. *Vivaldi: Genius of the Baroque*, trl. Christopher Hatch. New York: Norton, 1957.

Plath, Wolfgang, ed. *Streichquartette*, vol. l, in *Mozart Neue Gesamtausgabe* (1966).

Poole, Peter. "Benjamin Britten String Quartets Nos. 2 & 3," liner notes for CRD Records, Ltd. no. 1095 (1981).

Poszowski, Antoni. "Polnische Instrumentale Kammermusik in der ersten Hälfte des 18. Jahrhunderts," in *Musikzentren in der ersten Hälfte des 18. Jahrhunderts*, ed. Eitelfriedrich Thom. Magdeburg: Rat des Bezirkes, 1979, pp. 15-23.

Poullain, Georges. Comte de Saint-Foix, "Les Premiers Pianistes Parisiens," in *La Revue Musicale*, vol. III, no. 10 (1922), pp. 121-136, vol. IV, no. 6 (1923), pp. 193-205, vol. V, no. 8 (1924), pp. 187-191 and 192-198.

Praetorius, Michael. *Syntagma Musicum*, vol. 3, Termini Musici, 2nd ed. (1619), in *Documenta Musicologica*, Erste Reihe, vol. XV. Kassel: Bärenreiter, 1958.

Purcell, Henry. *Fantazias and In Nomines*, ed. Thurston Dart. London: Novello, 1959.

Radcliffe, Philip. *Beethoven's String Quartets*. London: Hutchinson University Library, 1965.

Rameau, Jean-Philippe. *Cinq Pièces pour Clavecin Seul Extraites des Pièces de Clavecin en Concerts*. Paris: 1741.

Randall, David M. "A Comprehensive Performance Project in Clarinet Literature with an Essay on the Clarinet Duet from ca. 1715 to ca. 1825." University of Iowa D.M.A. dissertation, 1970.

Randel, Don Michael. "Chamber Music," in *The New Harvard Dictionary of Music*, rev. 2nd ed. Cambridge: Harvard University Press, 1986, p. 146.

Ratner, Leonard G. *The Beethoven String Quartets: Compositional Strategies and Rhetoric*. Stanford (CA): Stanford Bookstore, 1995.

Redlich, Hans. "Bruckner and Brahms Quintets in F," in *Music and Letters*, vol. XXXVI (1955), pp. 253-258.

Redlich, Hans. *Alban Berg: the Man and his Music.* New York: Abelard-Schuman, 1957.

Rees, Lynda Lloyd. "Müller," in *The New Grove Dictionary of Music and Musicians,* 6th ed., vol. XII, p. 767.

Reese, Gustave. *Music in the Renaissance,* rev. ed. New York: W.W. Norton, 1959.

Reeser, Hendrik Eduard. *De Klaviersonate met Vioolbegeleiding in het Parÿsche Muziekleven ten Tÿde van Mozart.* Rotterdam: W.L. and J. Brusse, 1939.

Reimer, Erich. "Kammermusik," in *Handwörterbuch der musikalischen Terminologie,* ed. Fritz Reckow. Wiesbaden: Franz Steiner, 1971.

Riehl, W.H. "Viotti und das Geigenduett," in *Musikalische Charakterköpfe: ein kunstgeschichtliches Skizzenbuch,* Band 2. 1st ed. 1853; 7th ed. Stuttgard: J. G. Cotta-sche Buchhandlung, 1899.

Rosen, Charles. *The Classical Style: Haydn, Mozart, and Beethoven.* New York: The Viking Press, 1971.

Rossi, Salomono. *Il Quarto Libro de varie Sonate.* Venice, 1622.

Rothschild, Germaine de. *Luigi Boccherini: His Life and Works,* trl. Andreas Mayor. London: 1965.

Ryom, Peter. "Les Catalogues de Bonlini et de Groppo," *Informazioni e Studi Vivaldiani,* vol. II (1981), pp. 3-30, and "Deux Catalogues d'Operas," vol. III (1982), pp. 13-44.

Ryom, Peter. *Répertoire des Oeuvres d'Antonio Vivaldi, les Compositions Instrumentales.* Copenhagen: Engstrom & Sodring, 1986, pp. 73-154.

Saam, Joseph. "Zur Geschichte des Klavierquartetts bis in die Romantik," in *Sammlung musikwissenschaftler Abhandlungen,* no. 9. Strassburg: Heitz, 1932.

Sachs, Joel. *Kapellmeister Hummel in England and France.* Detroit: Detroit Monographs in Musicology, 1977.

Sachse, Hans-Martin. *Franz Schuberts Streichquartette.* Münster in Westfalen: Max Kramer, typescript, 1958.

Sadie, Stanley. "British Chamber Music, 1720-1790." University of Cambridge Ph.D. dissertation, 1958.

Salmen, Walter. "W.H. Riehls Gedanken zur Gesundung der Hausmusik," in *Hausmusik*, vol. XVII (1953), pp. 169-70, 172.

Salvetti, Guido. "Mozart e il Quartetto Italiano," in Friedrich Lippmann, ed., *Colloquium "Mozart und Italien"* (Rom 1974), in *Analecta Musicologica*, vol. XVIII. Köln: Arno Volk, 1978, pp. 271-289.

Sanchez, Richard Xavier. "Spanish Chamber Music of the Eighteenth Century." Louisiana State University Ph.D. dissertation, 1975.

Sandner, Wolfgang. *Die Klarinette bei Carl Maria von Weber*, in *Neue musikgeschichtliche Forschung*, Band 7. Wiesbaden: Breitkopf & Härtel, 1971.

Sarnaker, Benedict. "Onslow," in *The New Grove Dictionary of Music and Musicians*, 6th ed., vol. XIII, p. 544.

Scarlatti, Alessandro. "Concerti di flauto, violini, violetta e basso," Naples, S. Pietro a Majella Conservatory, Music Library, ms. 38.3.13. Published in *Sette Sonate per Flauto, Archi, e Basso Continuo*, ed. Luciano Bettarini, in *Collezione Settecentesca Bettarini*, no. 1. Milan: Casa Editrice Nazionalmusic, [1969].

Scarlatti, Alessandro. Sonata for three flutes and continuo in F Major, in Münster/W.: Episcopal Museum, Santini Collection, printed as *Quartettino*, ed. Waldemar Woehl. London/New York/Frankfurt: C. F. Peters, 1940.

Schaffner, Anne. "The Modern String Quartet in America before 1800," in *The Music Review*, vol. XL (1979), pp. 165-167.

Schanzlin, Hans Peter. *Basels private Musikpflege im 19. Jahrhundert*, in *Basler Neujahrsblatt*, no. 139. Basel: Helbing & Lichtenhaln, 1961.

Schatz, Hilmar. "Igor Stravinsky: Septett," in *Melos*, vol. XXV (1958), pp. 60-63.

Schilling, Hans Ludwig. "Zur Instrumentation in Igor Stravinskys Spätwerk aufgezeigt an seinem 'Septett 1953," in *Archiv für Musikwissenschaft*, vol. XIII (1956), pp. 181-196.

Schindler, Kurt. *Arnold Schönberg's Quartet in D Minor Op. 7: an Introductory Note*. New York: G. Schirmer, 1914.

Scholz-Michelitsch, Helga. *Das Orchester- und Kammermusikwerk von Georg Christoph Wagenseil: Thematischer Katalog*, in *Oesterreichische Akademie der Wissenschaften, Tabulae Musicae Austriacae*, Band 6. Vienna: Hermann Böhlaus Nachf., 1972.

Schulz, Johann Abraham Peter. "Trio," in Johann George Sulzer's *Allgemeiner Theorie der Schönen Künste*. Leipzig: 1771-1774.

Schumann, Robert. *Gesammelte Schriften über Musik und Musiker*, ed. M. Kreisig, 5th ed. Leipzig: 1914.

Schwarz, Boris. "Somis," in *The New Grove Dictionary of Music and Musicians*, 6th ed., vol. XVII, p. 476.

Schwarz, K. Robert. "A New Look at a Major Minimalist," in *The New York Times* (Sunday, May 6, 1990), Section H, p. 24.

Seaman, Gerald. "Amateur Music-Making in Russia," in *Music and Letters*, vol. XLVII (1966), pp. 249-259.

Seaman, Gerald. "The First Russian Chamber Music," in *The Music Review*, vol. XXVI (1965), pp. 326-337.

Selfridge-Field, Eleanor. *Venetian Instrumental Music from Gabrieli to Vivaldi*. New York: Praeger, 1975.

Sheldon, David. "The Transition from Trio to Cembalo-Obbligato Sonata in the Works of J.G. and C.H. Graun," in *The Journal of the American Musicological Society*, XXIV (1971), pp. 395-413.

Shostakovich, Dmitri. *Testimony: the Memoirs of Dmitri Shostakovich, as related to and edited by Solomon Volkov*, trl. Antonina W. Bouis. New York: Harper and Row, 1979.

Sieber, Tilman. *Das klassische Streichquintet*. Bern/Munich: Francke Verlag, 1983.

Siegmund-Schultze, Walther. "Tradition und Neueretum in Bartóks Streichquartetten," in *Studia Musicologica*, vol. III (1962), pp. 317-328.

Siegmund-Schultze, Walther. "Mozarts 'Haydn-Quartette,'" in Bence Szabolcsi and Dénes Bartha, eds., *Bericht über die internationale Konferenz zum Andenken Joseph Haydns (Budapest 1957)*. Budapest: Verlag der Ungarischen Akademie der Wissenschaften, 1961, pp. 137-146.

Simpson, Adrienne. "Tomásek," in *The New Grove Dictionary of Music and Musicians*, 6th ed., vol. XIX, p. 34.

Simpson, Christopher. *Tafel Consort*. 1621.

Simpson, J. Palgrave. *Carl Maria von Weber: the Life of an Artist, from the German of his son Baron Max Maria von Weber*. London: Chapman and Hall, 1865.

Sirker, Udo. *Die Entwicklung des Bläserquintetts in der ersten Hälfte des 19. Jahrhunderts*. Regensburg: Gustav Bosse, 1968.

Smallman, Basil. *The Piano Quartet and Quintet: Style, Structure, and Scoring*. Oxford: Clarendon Press, 1994.

Smallman, Basil. *The Piano Trio: Its History, Technique, and Repertoire*. Oxford: Oxford University Press, 1989.

Smith, Nancy Page. "The American String Quartet, 1850-1918." University of North Carolina M.A. thesis, 1949.

Somfai, Lászlo. "Haydn's London String Quartets," in *Haydn Studies: Proceedings of the International Haydn Conference Washington, D.C., 1975*. New York: W.W. Norton, 1981, pp. 389-392.

Sourek, Otakar. *The Chamber Music of Antonín Dvořák*, abr. trl. of *Dvorakovy Skladby Komornì: Charakteristìka a Rozbory* by Roberta Samsour. Prague: Artis, 19[56], repr. Westport: Greenwood Press, 1978.

Speck, Christian, ed. *Luigi Boccherini, Quartett in c-Moll op. 2 Nr. 1* (G 159). Celle: Moeck Verlag, 1987.

Speck, Christian. *Boccherinis Streichquartette. Studien zur Kompositionsweise und zur gattungsgeschichtlichen Stellung*, in *Studien zur Musik, Philosophische Facultät, Münchener Universitäts-Schriftum*. Munich: Wilhelm Fink, 1987.

Spóz, Andrzej, ed. *Kultura Muzyczna Warszawy Drugiej Polowy xix Wieku*. Warsaw: Pánstwowe Wydawnicturo Naukowe, 1980.

St. Foix, Georges de. "Le Dernier Quatuor de Mozart," in *Studien zur Musikgeschichte: Festschrift für Guido Adler zum 75. Geburtstag*. Vienna/Leipzig: Universal-Edition, 1930, pp. 168-173.

Staehelin, Martin. "Basels Musikleben im 18. Jahrhundert," in *Die Ernte: Schweizerisches Jahrbuch*, vol. XLIV (1963), pp. 116-141.

Stahmer, Klaus Hinrich. "Drei Klavierquartette aus den Jahren 1875/76: Brahms, Mahler und Dvořák im Vergleich," in *Brahms und seine Zeit*. Hamburg: Laaber, 1984, pp. 113-123.

Stahmer, Klaus. "Der Klassik näher als dem Klassizismus: die Streichquartettkompositionen von Stravinsky," in *Hindemith-Jahrbuch*, vol. XII (1983), pp. 104-115.

Starr, James A. "A Critical Evaluation of Performance Style in Selected Violin Works of Nineteenth Century American Composers." University of Illinois D.M.A. dissertation, 1978.

Stein, Erwin. "Anton Webern," in *Neue Musikzeitung*, vol. XLIX (1928), pp. 517-519.

Steinberg, Lester. "Sonata Form in the Keyboard Trios of Joseph Haydn." New York University Ph.D. dissertation, 1976.

Stenzl, Jürg. *Arcangelo Corelli: historisch-kritische Gesamtausgabe der musikalischen Werke*, vol. II. Laaber-Verlag, 1986.

Stern, Marion. "Keyboard Quartets and Quintets Published in London, 1756-1775: a Contribution to the History of Chamber Music with Obbligato Keyboard." University of Pennsylvania Ph.D. dissertation, 1979.

Stockmeier, Wolfgang, ed. *Ignaz Pleyel (Joseph Haydn), Trios für Klavier, Violine und Violoncello C-Dur und F-Dur*. Munich: G. Henle, 1976.

Stolba, K. Marie. "Evidence for Quartets by John Antes, American-born Moravian Composer," in *Journal of the American Musicological Society*, vol. XXXIII (1980), pp. 565-574.

Stölzel, *Sonata a3 für Flöte (Violine, Oboe), Violine, Violoncell und Cembalo*, ed. Gotthold Frotscher, in *Collegium Musicum*, no. 72. Leipzig: Breitkopf und Härtel, 1942.

Stölzel. *Trio Sonata in C Minor, for Oboe, Violin and Harpsichord*. Dresden, Sächs. Landesbibliothek; ed. Günter Hausswald, in *Collegium Musicum*, no. 76. Leipzig: Breitkopf & Härtel, 1950.

Straeten, Edmund van der. "Schuberts Behandlung der Streichinstrumente mit besonderer Berücksichtigung der Kammermusik," in *Bericht über den internationalen Kongress für Schubertforschung Wien 25. bis 29. November 1928*. Augsburg: Dr. Benno Filser, 1929, pp. 131-140.

Streatfeild, Richard A. *Handel*, 2nd ed. London: Methuen, 1910; reprint New York: Da Capo, 1964.

Suess, John. "The Ensemble Sonatas of Maurizio Cazzati," in Friedrich Lippmann, ed., *Studien zur italienisch-deutschen Musikgeschichte XII*, in *Analecta Musicologica*, vol. XIX. Köln: Arno Volk, 1979, pp. 146-185.

Sullivan, J.W.N. *Beethoven: His Spiritual Development.* New York: Alfred A. Knopf, 1927.

Talbot, Michael. "Corelli," in *The New Grove Dictionary of Music and Musicians,* 6th ed., vol. IV, pp. 768-774.

Talbot, Michael. "Mascitti," in *The New Grove Dictionary of Music and Musicians,* 6th ed., vol.XI, p. 746.

Talbot, Michael. "Vivaldi and a French Ambassador," in *Informazioni e Studi Vivaldiani,* vol. II (1981), 31-43.

Taruskin, Richard. *Defining Russa Musically: Historical and Hermeneutical Essays.* Princeton: Princeton University Press, 1997.

Thayer, Alexander W. *Life of Beethoven,* rev. and ed. Elliot Forbes. Princeton: Princeton University Press, 1967.

Tilmouth, Michael. "Chamber Music in England." Cambridge University Ph.D. dissertation, 1959.

Tilmouth, Michael. "Piano Quartet" and "Piano Quintet" in *The New Grove Dictionary of Music and Musicians,* 6th ed., pp. 714-715.

Trevitt, John. "Franck," in *The New Grove Dictionary of Music and Musicians,* 6th ed., vol. VI, p. 780.

Trimpert, Dieter Lutz. *Die Quatuors Concertants von Giuseppe Cambini,* in *Mainzer Studien zur Musikwissenschaft,* Band 1. Tutzing: Hans Schneider, 1967.

Truscott, Harold. "Schubert's String Quartet in G Major," in *The Music Review,* vol. XX (1959), pp. 119-145.

Tuthill, Burnet Corwin. "Fifty Years of Chamber Music in the United States 1876-1926," in *The Musical Courier,* vol. XCIX (August 17, 1929), 8, (August 24), 15, 20, (August 31), 10.

Uccellini, Marco. *Il terzo Libro delle Sonate.* 1642.

Uccellini, Marco. Opus 4. 1645.

Untersteiner. "Musica Istrumentale da Camera," in *Gazetta Musicale di Milano,* no. 1 (1895), pp. 76-78.

Unverricht, Hubert. "Haydn and Franklin: the Quartet with Open Strings and Scordatura," in Jens Peter Larsen, Howard Serwer, and James Webster, *Haydn Studies.* New York: Norton, 1981, pp. 147-154.

Unverricht, Hubert. *Geschichte des Streichtrios.* Tutzing: Hans Schneider, 1969.

Valentin, Erich. *Musica Domestica: von Geschichte und Wesen der Hausmusik*. Trossingen: Hohner, 1959.

Vander Weg, John D. "Symmetrical Pitch- and Equivalence-Class Set Structure in Anton Webern's Opus 5." University of Michigan Ph.D. dissertation, 1983.

Vetter, Manfred. *Kammermusik in der DDR*. Frankfurt a/M: Peter Lang, 1996.

Vogt, Hans. *Johann Sebastian Bach's Chamber Music: Background, Analyses, Individual Works*, trl. Kenn Johnson. Portland, OR: Amadeus Press, 1988, pp. 36-40.

Waesich, Cherubino. *Canzonia Cinque . . . da Sonarsi con le Viole da gamba*. Rome: 1632.

Wagenseil, *Six Sonates en Trio pour deux Violons et Basse, Oeuvre premier*. Paris: Le Clerc, 1755. Ed. Erich Schenk, in *Diletto Musicale*, no. 443. Vienna/Munich: Doblinger, 1969.

Wagenseil. *Six unpublished string quartets*, ed. Rudolf Scholz in *Diletto Musicale*, nos. 791-2, 559, and 794-6. Vienna/Munich: Doblinger, 1978-1981.

Wallner, Bo. *Den Svenska Sträkkvartetten: Del I: Klassicism och Romantik*, in *Kungl. Musikaliska Akademiens Skriftserie*, no. 24. Stockholm: Kungl. Musikaliska Akademien, 1979.

Warburton, Thomas. "Historical Perspective of the String Quartet in the United States," in *American Music Teacher*, vol. XXI (January 1972), no. 3, pp. 20-22, 37.

Warner, Robert A. "The Fantasia in the Works of John Jenkins." University of Michigan Ph.D. dissertation, 1951.

Webster, James. "The Scoring of Haydn's Early String Quartets," in Jens Peter Larsen et al, *Haydn Studies: Proceedings of the International Haydn Conference Washington, D.C., 1975*. New York: W.W. Norton, 1981, pp. 235-238.

Wedig, Hans Josef. *Beethovens Streichquartett op. 18 Nr. 1 und seine erste Fassung*, in *Veröffentlichungen des Beethovenhauses in Bonn*, Band 2. Bonn: Beethovenhaus, 1922.

Wesolowski, Franciszek. "'Pièces de Clavecin en Concerts' von J. Ph. Rameau als Beispiel der französischen Kammermusik für Klavier mit Begleitung anderer Instrumente," in Günter Fleischhauer, Walther Siegmund-Schultze and Eitelfriedrich Thom, *Zur Entwicklung der instrumentalen Kammermusik in der 1. Hälfte des 18. Jahrhunderts*, in *Studien zur Aufführungspraxis und Interpretation von Instrumentalmusik des 18. Jahrhunderts: Konferenzbericht der xi. wissenschaftlichen Arbeitstagung Blankenburg/Harz, 17. Juni bis 19. Juni 1983*, vol. 22, [no publishing information], pp. 50-52.

Wierichs, Walfred. *Die Sonate für obligates Tasteninstrument und Violine bis zum Beginn der Hochklassik in Deutschland*. Kassel: Bärenreiter, 1981.

Wirth, Helmut. "Reger," in *The New Grove Dictionary of Music and Musicians*, 6th ed., vol. XV, p. 678.

Wolff, Christoph. "Schubert's 'Der Tod und das Mädchen': Analytical and Explanatory Notes on the Song D531 and the Quartet D810," in Eva Badura-Skoda and Peter Branscombe, eds., *Schubert Studies: Problems of Style and Chronology*. Cambridge: Cambridge University Press, 1982, pp. 143-171.

Wolff, Hellmuth Christian. "Das Metronom des Louis-Lëon Pajot 1735," in *Festskrift Jens Peter Larsen*. Copenhagen: Wilhelm Hansen, 1972, pp. 208-210.

Wood, Hugh. "Britten's Latest Scores," in *The Musical Times*, vol. CIII (1962), pp. 164-165.

Zaslaw, Neal. "Anet," in *The New Grove Dictionary of Music and Musicians*, 6th ed., vol. I, p. 421.

Zimmerschied, Dieter. "Die Kammermusik Johann Nepomuk Hummels." Johannes Gutenberg University of Mainz Ph.D. dissertation, 1966.

INDEX

471